GW00363261

Kevin McDermott
Simon Coury
Ellen O'Reilly
Consultant reviewer:
Patrick Murray

Discovery

Leaving Certificate Poetry Anthology for Higher and Ordinary Level 2022

Edco

The Educational Company of Ireland

First published 2020

The Educational Company of Ireland
Ballymount Road
Walkinstown
Dublin 12

www.edco.ie

A member of the Smurfit Kappa Group plc
© Kevin McDermott, Simon Coury, Ellen O'Reilly, 2020

ISBN 978-1-84536-914-9

Editor: Jane Rogers
Layout: Graftrónaic
Cover: Slick Fish
Cover Photography: Adobe Stock

The paper used in this book comes from Managed Forests in Northern Europe. For every tree felled, at least one new tree is planted

Audio CD

1. 'The Fish' by Elizabeth Bishop
2. 'The Prodigal' by Elizabeth Bishop
3. 'Filling Station' by Elizabeth Bishop
4. 'I Felt a Funeral, in my Brain' by Emily Dickinson
5. 'I Heard a Fly buzz – when I died' by Emily Dickinson
6. 'On First Looking into Chapman's Homer' by John Keats
7. 'La Belle Dame Sans Merci' by John Keats
8. 'Ode to a Nightingale' by John Keats
9. 'To Autumn' by John Keats
10. 'Begin' by Brendan Kennelly
11. 'Bread' by Brendan Kennelly
12. 'I See You Dancing, Father' by Brendan Kennelly
13. 'Saint Brigid's Prayer' by Brendan Kennelly
14. 'Baby-Movements II, *"Trailing Clouds"*' by D. H. Lawrence
15. 'Humming-Bird' by D. H. Lawrence
16. 'Snake' by D. H. Lawrence
17. 'Bavarian Gentians' by D. H. Lawrence
18. 'Aunt Jennifer's Tigers' by Adrienne Rich
19. 'The Uncle Speaks in the Drawing Room' by Adrienne Rich
20. 'She Dwelt among the Untrodden ways' by William Wordsworth
21. 'Composed upon Westminster Bridge' by William Wordsworth
22. 'It is a beauteous evening, calm and free' by William Wordsworth
23. from '*The Prelude*: Skating' by William Wordsworth
24. from '*The Prelude*: The Stolen Boat' by William Wordsworth
25. 'The Lake Isle of Innisfree' by W. B. Yeats
26. 'The Wild Swans at Coole' by W. B. Yeats
27. 'An Irish Airman Foresees his Death' by W. B. Yeats
28. 'Sailing to Byzantium' by W. B. Yeats
29. 'Self-Portrait in the Dark (with Cigarette)' by Colette Bryce
30. 'Shrines' by Moya Cannon
31. 'Driving to the Hospital' by Kate Clanchy
32. 'Valentine' by Carol Ann Duffy
33. 'If Love Was Jazz' by Linda France
34. 'Frogs' by Randolph Healy
35. 'The Cadillac in the Attic' by Andrew Hudgins
36. 'Hawk Roosting' by Ted Hughes
37. 'An Arrival (North Wales, 1897)' by Denise Levertov
38. 'The Russian Doll' by Paula Meehan
39. 'Interlude' by Caitríona O'Reilly
40. 'My Father, Long Dead' by Eileen Sheehan
41. 'Zoo Morning' by Penelope Shuttle
42. 'Oranges' by Gary Soto
43. 'Traveling through the Dark' by William Stafford
44. 'This is Just to Say' by William Carlos Williams

The following permissions and acknowledgements refer to the audio materials included on the compact disc accompanying printed copies of this book: 'The Fish', 'The Prodigal' and 'Filling Station' by Elizabeth Bishop courtesy of Farrar, Straus and Giroux. 'Begin', 'Bread', 'I See You Dancing, Father' and 'Saint Brigid's Prayer' by Brendan Kennelly courtesy of Bloodaxe Books. 'Aunt Jennifer's Tigers' and 'The Uncle Speaks in the Drawing Room' by Adrienne Rich courtesy of the author's Estate. 'Self-Portrait in the Dark (with Cigarette)' by Colette Bryce courtesy of Macmillan Publishers Ltd. 'Shrines' by Moya Cannon courtesy of Carcanet Press. 'Driving to the Hospital' by Kate Clanchy courtesy of Rogers, Coleridge & White Ltd. 'Valentine' by Carol Ann Duffy courtesy of Rogers, Coleridge & White Ltd. 'If Love Was Jazz' by Linda France courtesy of the poet. 'Frogs' by Randolph Healy courtesy of the poet. 'The Cadillac in the Attic' by Andrew Hudgins courtesy of the poet. 'Hawk Roosting' by Ted Hughes courtesy of Faber & Faber Ltd. 'An Arrival (North Wales, 1897)' by Denise Levertov courtesy of New Directions Publishing Corp. 'The Russian Doll' by Paula Meehan courtesy of the author and Dedalus Press. 'Interlude' by Caitriona O'Reilly courtesy of Bloodaxe Books. 'My Father, Long Dead' by Eileen Sheehan courtesy of the poet. 'Zoo Morning' by Penelope Shuttle courtesy of the poet and David Higham Associates. 'Oranges' by Gary Soto courtesy of Chronicle Books LLC. 'Traveling through the Dark' by William Stafford courtesy of The Permissions Company LLC on behalf of Graywolf Press. 'This is Just to Say' by William Carlos Williams courtesy of Carcanet Press.

For more information on copyright see page 1.

Foreword

This anthology, which includes all the poems prescribed for the Higher and Ordinary Level English Leaving Certificate Examinations of 2022, has been prepared by experienced teachers of English. Each of the contributors has been able to concentrate on a limited number of the prescribed poets and their work, thus facilitating a high standard of research and presentation.

Guidelines are given which set each poem in context. In addition, each poem is accompanied by a glossary and appropriate explorations, designed to allow the student to find his/her authentic response to the material.

Relevant biographical details are provided for each poet. A list of examination-style questions is provided for each prescribed poet at Higher Level along with a snapshot of the poet's work and a sample examination-style essay to aid revision. A snapshot is provided for all Ordinary Level poems.

Guidelines are included for students on approaching the Unseen Poetry section of the course. There is also advice on approaching the prescribed question in the examination. Students will find the glossary of poetic terms a valuable resource in reading and responding to poetry.

The poetry course for Leaving Certificate English demands a personal and active engagement from the student reader. We hope that this anthology makes that engagement possible and encourages students to explore the wider world of poetry for themselves.

Teachers can access the Discovery for Leaving Certificate Higher and Ordinary Level e-book by registering on www.edcolearning.ie.

Contents

Ordinary Level poems

Discovery Student CD

Listening to poetry

Discovery is accompanied by a student CD that includes 44 poetry tracks. Each track is read with expression and feeling, which brings the poems on the page to life.

A selection of these poems has been read by the poets, which gives an even greater insight into our understanding of the poems.

The poetry tracks are also available through the *Discovery* interactive e-book on **www.edcolearning.ie**. Click on the 🔊 beside relevant poems throughout the book to hear poems being read aloud.

Track listing

ACKNOWLEDGEMENTS

'The poems in this book have been reproduced with the kind permission of the publishers, agents, authors or their estates as follows:

'The Fish', 'The Bight', 'At the Fishhouses', 'The Prodigal', 'Questions of Travel', 'The Armadillo', 'Sestina', 'First Death in Nova Scotia', 'Filling Station', 'In the Waiting Room' (complete poems) from *Poems* by Elizabeth Bishop. © 2011 by The Alice H Methfessel Trust. Publisher's Note and compilation © Farrar, Straus and Giroux. Used by permission of Farrar, Straus and Giroux.

'Begin', 'Bread', 'Dear Autumn Girl', 'Poem from a Three Year Old', 'Oliver to His Brother', 'I See You Dancing, Father', 'A Cry for Art O'Leary', 'Things I Might Do', 'A Great Day', 'Fragments', 'The soul's loneliness' and 'Saint Brigid's Prayer' by Brendan Kennelly from *Familiar Strangers, New & Selected Poems 1960-2004*, Bloodaxe Books. Reprinted by permission of the publisher.

'Aunt Jennifer's Tigers', 'The Uncle Speaks in the Drawing Room', 'Storm Warnings', 'Living in Sin', 'The Roofwalker', 'Our Whole Life', 'Trying to Talk with a Man', 'Diving Into the Wreck', 'From a Survivor', 'Power' by Adrienne Rich from Collected Poems: 1950–2012. Copyright © 2016, 2013 by the Adrienne Rich Literary trust. Copyright © 2011, 2007, 2004, 2001, 1999, 1995, 1991, 1989, 1986, 1984, 1981, 1967, 1963, 1962, 1975, 1973, 1971, 1969, 1966 by W. W. Norton & Company, Inc. Used by permission of W. W. Norton & Company, Inc.

'Self-Portrait in the Dark (with Cigarette)' by Colette Bryce © Colette Bryce, 2008, reproduced with the permission of Macmillan Publishers Ltd.

'Shrines' by Moya Cannon from *Keats Lives* (2015), with the permission of Carcanet Press.

'Driving to the Hospital' by Kate Clanchy from *Newborn*. Published by Picador, 2004. © Carol Ann Duffy. Reproduced by permission of the author c/o Rogers, Coleridge & White Ltd, 20 Powis Mews, London W111JN.

'Valentine' from *Mean Time* by Carol Ann Duffy. Published by Anvil Press Poetry, 1993. Copyright © Carol Ann Duffy. Reproduced by permission of the author c/o Rogers, Coleridge & White Ltd, 20 Powis Mews, London W11 1JN.

'If Love Was Jazz' by Linda France from *Red* (1992), Bloodaxe. Reprinted with permission of the poet.

'Frogs' by Randolph Healy from *Green 532: Selected Poems 1983–2000* (2002), Salt Publishing. Reprinted with the kind permission of the poet.

'The Cadillac in the Attic' by Andrew Hudgins from *Ecstatic in the Poison* (2003), Overlook Press. Reprinted with the permission of the poet.

'Hawk Roosting' by Ted Hughes from *Collected Poems* (2005), with the permission of Faber & Faber Ltd.

'An Arrival (North Wales, 1897)' by Denise Levertov from *Candles in Babylon*, © 1982 Denise Levertov. Reprinted by permission of New Directions Publishing Corp.

'The Russian Doll' by Paula Meehan used with the kind permission of the author and Dedalus Press

'Interlude' by Caitriona O'Reilly from *The Nowhere Birds* (Bloodaxe Books, 2001), reprinted by permission of the publisher.

'My Father, Long Dead' by Eileen Sheehan. Reprinted with permission of the poet.

'Zoo Morning' by Penelope Shuttle from *Unsent: New and Selected Poems*, published by Bloodaxe Books. Reproduced with kind permission of the poet and David Higham Associates.

'Oranges' by Gary Soto from *New and Selected Poems* © 1995, used with permission of Chronicle Books LLC, San Francisco. Visit www.chroniclebooks.com.

'Traveling through the Dark' by William Stafford from Ask Me: 100 Essential Poems. Copyright © 1998 by the Estate of William Stafford. Used with the permission of The Permissions Company, LLC on behalf of Kim Stafford.

'This is Just to Say' by William Carlos Williams from *Collected Poems Volume 1* (2000), with the permission of Carcanet Press.

'Blessing' by Imtiaz Dharker from *Postcards from God* (1997), Bloodaxe Books. By permission of the publisher.

'The Envoy' by Jane Hirshfield from *Each Happiness Ringed by Lions: Selected Poems* (2006), Bloodaxe Books. By permission of the publisher.

'Darling' by Jackie Kay from *Darling: New & Selected Poems* (2007), Bloodaxe Books. By permission of the publisher.

'Saint Francis and the Sow' from *Mortal Acts, Mortal Words* by Galway Kinnell. Copyright © 1980, and renewed 2008 by Galway Kinnell. Reprinted with permission of Houghton Mifflin Harcourt Publishing Company. All rights reserved.

For A Five-Year-Old by Fleur Adcock from *Poems 1960-2000* (Bloodaxe Books, 2000). Reprinted by permission of the publisher.

While every care has been taken to trace and acknowledge copyright, the publishers tender their apologies for any accidental infringement where copyright has proved untraceable. They would be pleased to come to a suitable arrangement with the rightful owner in each case.

The photographs in this book come from the following sources: Topfoto pp2, 113, 245, 370, 431, 454, 474, 508, 513, 538, 567, 587; Shutterstock pp3, 10, 21, 26, 31, 36, 44, 45, 46, 50, 56, 73, 76, 80, 87, 92, 96, 100, 101, 119, 125, 126, 132, 156, 161, 168, 182, 187, 195, 201, 205, 214, 220, 221, 225, 230, 234, 238, 246, 251, 255, 260, 264, 270, 276, 281, 285, 288, 295, 311, 317, 320, 325, 327, 330, 334, 344, 356, 358, 361, 363, 380, 384, 388, 392, 397, 404, 405, 407, 414, 423, 435, 440, 443, 448, 458, 462, 468, 478, 479, 482, 483, 491, 501, 511, 519, 529, 535, 540, 546, 552, 559, 564, 569, 576, 583, 589; Alamy pp4, 154, 176, 298, 432; Getty pp62, 307, 480, 544; Keats House, City of London p145; Phyllis Christopher p497; Carcanet Press p504; Courtesy of Andrew Hudgins p532; Stephanie Joy p550; Bloodaxe Books p556; courtesy of Carolyn Soto p573; Special Collections, Lewis & Clark, Oregon p580.

Elizabeth Bishop

1911–1979

Biography

Early life

Elizabeth Bishop was born in Massachusetts USA on 8 February 1911. While still an infant, her father, William, a construction firm executive, died of a condition which affects the kidneys. Her mother, Gertrude, suffered a complete breakdown following her husband's death and was committed to an asylum in 1916, where she remained until she died in 1934. During this whole time Bishop never visited her mother or saw her again. Poems like 'First Death in Nova Scotia' and 'Filling Station' reflect the lack of a mother – the 'someone [who] loves us all' – in the poet's life.

Nova Scotia, where Bishop lived until she was six.

Bishop was taken to Great Village in Nova Scotia where she had a very happy time with her mother's parents. It seems to have been a simple existence but one where she was cared for, especially by her grandmother; this close relationship is at the heart of the poem 'Sestina'. Bishop was six when her paternal grandparents took her back to Massachusetts to live in a much stricter and more formal home. This enforced move from Nova Scotia affected her deeply and she later commented that it felt like a kidnapping. 'In the Waiting Room' was written about this time and features her paternal aunt, whom Bishop seems to have had little regard for. She then went to live in Boston with her maternal aunt, who introduced her to the work of many poets, including Alfred Lord Tennyson, Robert Browning and Elizabeth Barrett Browning. Here she attended boarding school where she wrote for the school magazine, and then Vassar College, from which she graduated in 1934. She often missed school due to illness.

Before becoming a full-time poet Bishop considered becoming a composer or a doctor. She rejected music as a career because she was terrified of performing in front of an audience. She painted and travelled around Europe and Africa for a time. Her love of painting and eye for colour and detail are major features of her poetic style, and the musicality and use of sound in her poems reflect her talent for music.

Being orphaned at an early age and moved around between various relatives affected Bishop hugely; she drank heavily at times and suffered from skin conditions like eczema. Poems like 'The Prodigal', 'Sestina' and 'First Death in Nova Scotia' reflect these events.

Gerard Manley Hopkins

The poet Gerard Manley Hopkins influenced Bishop's work. When she was twenty-one, she published an essay entitled 'Notes on timing in the poetry of Gerard Manley Hopkins'. Her biographer, Brett C. Millier, says this essay 'contains the seeds of all her later thinking on rhythm in poetry'.

Adult life and love

Bishop was a lesbian. She lived in New York with her classmate Louise Crane, a lover of jazz music, which led the pair to know the legendary singer Billie Holiday, for whom Bishop wrote 'Songs for a Coloured Singer'. Also at that time Bishop met Maria Carlota Costallat de Macedo Soares (or 'Lota' as Elizabeth would call her), who would later become the love of her life. Crane also encouraged Bishop's love of fishing and introduced her to the delights of Key West in Florida, where the pair bought a house in 1938. 'The Fish' is set here, and the sea is a central image in much of Bishop's work.

Her first published poems featured in a 1935 anthology called *Trial Balances*, a collection compiled by her great mentor and friend, the modernist poet Marianne Moore. Her first complete collection was *North & South*, published in 1946 to rave reviews. The renowned critic Randall Jarrell said at the time, 'Her work is unusually personal and honest in its wit, perception and sensitivity'.

Bishop's friend Robert Lowell.

Her close friend, the poet Robert Lowell, convinced her to accept a Poet Laureate position in the Library of Congress in 1949, a very prestigious job but one she was very nervous about. Lowell was a very successful poet and a huge influence on Bishop. He was seen by many as a voice to represent the nation. In an essay on Bishop, Jonathan Ellis writes, 'she was never the most read or respected at the time. Allen Ginsberg's *Howl* (1956) and Sylvia Plath's *Ariel* (1965) both sold more copies than any of her collections, while Robert Lowell's *Life Studies* (1959) continues to take the critical plaudits as the key work of poetry for most post-World War II readers.'

Ellis contends that Bishop had as much influence on Lowell's poetry as he did on hers. Certainly, Bishop is a much more well-known poet these days than Lowell. They wrote many letters over the years of their friendship – in fact Bishop was a prolific letter-writer, and several thousand letters survive. The book *One Art* features over 500 of these, selected and edited by Robert Giroux.

In November of 1951 Bishop won a scholarship of $2,500 and decided to travel to South America – a fateful decision, as she met Lota there again and the two became lovers. Bishop made her home in Brazil with Lota, so that a planned two-week holiday lasted fifteen years. Their relationship was a close and loving one. Bishop dedicated her poetry collection *Questions of Travel* to Lota and wrote to Lowell saying, 'I am extremely happy for the first time in my life'. She published *A Cold Spring* in 1955 and won the Pulitzer Prize for Literature the following year.

Later life and death

Elizabeth and Lota became celebrities in Rio de Janeiro, where Lota was very political, and both did a lot of charity work to regenerate parts of Rio and better the lives of children there. For example, they built a complex called Flamingo Park (Aterro do Flamengo) with many amenities for the local children. The park was designed by Lota, who was an architect, and the famous landscape artist Roberto Burle Marx; it was completed in 1965 and is still used extensively today, for example for cycling and athletics events in the 2016 Olympic and Paralympic games.

In 1966 Bishop was invited to be writer-in-residence at the University of Washington. Lota was in Brazil and ill at this time. She came to visit Bishop on 16 September 1967, clearly very unwell (with arteriosclerosis). In the early morning she took a bottle of valium, a drug used to treat anxiety, and slipped into a coma. Lota died on 25 September. Following this Bishop found herself excluded by many of their mutual friends and Lota's family, who blamed the poet for Lota's suicide. Bishop suffered from depression and sought help in psychoanalysis with Dr Ruth Foster, which led to poetry which explored her troubled childhood more openly. She writes about her grief over Lota's death and earlier losses in the poem 'One Art':

> 'I lost my mother's watch. And look! my last, or
> next-to-last, of three loved houses went.
> The art of losing isn't hard to master ...
>
> – Even losing you (the joking voice, a gesture
> I love) I shan't have lied. It's evident
> the art of losing's not too hard to master
> though it may look like (*Write* it!) like disaster.'

Working with Dr Foster 'on the origins of her depression and alcoholism' led Bishop to feel that she would have to live with the after-effects of losing her mother always, and be affected by this loss in ever-changing ways. The poetry that came out of that time attempts to put a shape on these tragic events and help Bishop cope and deal with her past. 'Sestina' is a good example of this. It is interesting that though the loss of her mother hovers in the background of many of her poems, 'First Death in Nova Scotia' is the only one on our course where her mother is overtly mentioned.

In 1969 Bishop published her *Complete Poems* and won the National Book Award for poetry. Her last book, *Geography III* in 1976, was received to great acclaim. 'In the Waiting Room' is from this short collection of only ten poems.

Bishop died of a cerebral aneurysm on Saturday 6 October 1979.

Social and Cultural Context

Spending part of her childhood in Nova Scotia added a dimension to Bishop's life, and **landscape and childhood experiences within a family** were central to her work. Her education in Massachusetts is a factor she shared with other famous poets like Dickinson, Plath, Emerson and Frost. All are poets who used the natural world extensively to convey themes in their work.

A movement called 'Imagism' – where **a central image is key to the theme of the poem** – influenced Bishop greatly, but she didn't align herself to any particular literary movement.

Despite being gay and a very successful and influential woman in her time, she refused to have her work included in women-only

The Confessional Poets

Bishop is considered by many critics to be one of the 'Confessional Poets'.

This refers to poets (including also Sylvia Plath) who place the 'I' at the centre of their poems and often use personas or speakers while the poems deal with private experiences from the life of the poet which are generally negative ones. Plath and Lowell are good examples of this. According to Jonathan Ellis, 'Robert Lowell was godfather to the Confessional Poets.'

anthologies, which showed how forward-thinking she was in terms of equality and moving beyond gender. To be openly gay at this time in a very conservative America was very brave. Without fuss or flourish, Bishop flouted the convention of the very domestic, demure type of woman that US culture and society demanded of her gender – just by simply being herself.

Themes

Travel

Bishop adored travel and wrote about the flora and fauna of places she visited. She was ahead of her time in questioning the ethics of travel and **criticising the harm we sometimes do to the natural world** as we move through it. 'Questions of Travel', 'The Armadillo' and 'Filling Station' are poems which feature this theme.

Nature

Nature itself plays not only a major role in Bishop's imagery, but is also a central theme. 'The Fish', 'The Bight', 'At the Fishhouses' and 'The Armadillo' all focus heavily on aspects of the natural world. Bishop has a very original style when describing nature in her poetry, often using **unusual and striking similes** and **metaphors** which **add vibrancy and interest to her work**, for example comparing fish scales to sequins, hay bales to clouds, or sparks of flaming ash to 'rose-flecks'. Her fascination with nature and her deep love for it permeate her poems, and even in the urban grot of 'Filling Station' she finds time to notice and describe embroidered daisies and a 'hirsute begonia' plant.

Loss, struggle and survival

This is a side of Bishop's poetry that connects her to the 'Confessional Poets'. In 'The Fish' she admires the struggles the fish has survived, while in 'The Prodigal' the main character's resolve to lift his life from its denigrating circumstances is the focus of the poem. In her later poems she explores her experience of being orphaned and her unsettled childhood. Her tone in these poems is often conversational and can almost seem flippant, but the **underlying themes and experiences are often profound**, as in 'Filling Station' and 'First Death in Nova Scotia'.

'At the Fishhouses', 'Questions of Travel', 'Sestina', 'First Death in Nova Scotia', 'Filling Station' and 'In the Waiting Room' are all concerned with Bishop's troubled childhood and her **search for a home**. Bishop returns again and again to childhood experiences in these poignant poems but without a trace of self-pity. There is a **melancholy mix** of nostalgia, loss and pain, combined with an almost **mischievous sense of fun** that is reminiscent of the poetry of Emily Dickinson – 'Why should I be my aunt, / or me, or anyone?' ('In the Waiting Room').

Timeline

1911	Born 8 February in Massachusetts; father dies
1916	Mother hospitalised due to mental illness; Elizabeth taken to Nova Scotia to live with maternal grandparents
1917	Taken to live with paternal grandparents and later her aunt Maud in Massachusetts
1930-34	Attends Vassar College, New York
1934	Death of mother
1935	First poem published in an anthology called *Trial Balances*
1938	Moves to Key West in Florida
1942	Meets Lota for the first time through mutual friend Louise Crane
1946	Publishes *North and South*, her first poetry collection; wins Houghton Mifflin Poetry Award
1949	Appointed consultant in poetry (Poet Laureate) at Library of Congress
1951	Wins scholarship which allows her to travel to South America; settles down there with Lota
1955	Publishes second poetry collection, *A Cold Spring*, winning the Pulitzer Prize for Poetry in 1956
1964	Awarded fellowship of the Academy of American Poets
1965	*Questions of Travel* published, her third collection of poetry
1967	25 September, Lota kills herself while visiting Elizabeth in the USA; Bishop moves to San Francisco for a year
1970	Appointed poet-in-residence at Harvard University in Boston
1976	Publishes her final poetry collection, *Geography III*, consisting of ten poems
1977	Close friends and mentors Marianne Moore and Robert Lowell die
1979	Dies in Boston on 6 October
1983	*Complete Poems* published

The Fish

I caught a tremendous fish
and held him beside the boat
half out of water, with my hook
fast in a corner of his mouth.
He didn't fight.   5
He hadn't fought at all.
He hung a grunting weight,
battered and venerable
and homely. Here and there
his brown skin hung in strips   10
like ancient wallpaper,
and its pattern of darker brown
was like wallpaper:
shapes like full-blown roses
stained and lost through age.   15
He was speckled with barnacles,
fine rosettes of lime,
and infested
with tiny white sea-lice,
and underneath two or three   20
rags of green weed hung down.
While his gills were breathing in
the terrible oxygen
– the frightening gills,
fresh and crisp with blood,   25
that can cut so badly –
I thought of the coarse white flesh
packed in like feathers,
the big bones and the little bones,
the dramatic reds and blacks   30
of his shiny entrails,
and the pink swim-bladder
like a big peony.
I looked into his eyes
which were far larger than mine   35
but shallower, and yellowed,
the irises backed and packed
with tarnished tinfoil
seen through the lenses
of old scratched isinglass.   40
They shifted a little, but not
to return my stare.
– It was more like the tipping

of an object toward the light.
I admired his sullen face,   45
the mechanism of his jaw,
and then I saw
that from his lower lip
– if you could call it a lip –
grim, wet, and weaponlike,   50
hung five old pieces of fish-line,
or four and a wire leader
with the swivel still attached,
with all their five big hooks
grown firmly in his mouth.   55
A green line, frayed at the end
where he broke it, two heavier lines,
and a fine black thread
still crimped from the strain and snap
when it broke and he got away.   60
Like medals with their ribbons
frayed and wavering,
a five-haired beard of wisdom
trailing from his aching jaw.
I stared and stared   65
and victory filled up
the little rented boat,
from the pool of bilge
where oil had spread a rainbow
around the rusted engine   70
to the bailer rusted orange,
the sun-cracked thwarts,
the oarlocks on their strings,
the gunnels – until everything
was rainbow, rainbow, rainbow!   75
And I let the fish go.

Glossary

8	*venerable*: deserving respect
9	*homely*: ordinary, plain looking
16	*barnacles*: tiny shellfish that cling to rocks, boats and larger fish, etc.
31	*entrails*: intestines
33	*peony*: a large rose-like flower
40	*isinglass*: a yellowish glass-like substance; the word was originally applied to a gelatine extracted from the swim bladder of certain fish, but is also used for sheets of mica, a semi-transparent mineral
52	*wire leader*: the short piece of wire that links the hook to the fishing line
53	*swivel*: a connecting moveable part that sits between the line and the leader on a fishing line
59	*crimped*: curled from being stretched then broken
68	*bilge*: dirty water that collects in the bottom of the boat
71	*bailer*: metal bucket to scoop the bilge from the boat
72	*thwarts*: the benches for the rower to sit on
73	*oarlocks*: holders for the oars on each side of the boat
74	*gunnels*: top parts of the sides of the boat

Guidelines

'The Fish' is a poem from Bishop's time in Florida where fishing was a favourite pastime. She had caught a Caribbean jewfish. From her first poetry collection *North & South*, it is Bishop's most well-known poem and she came to refer to it as 'That damn fish' due to the number of requests she received for its publication. The poem traces how the speaker's admiration for the fish grows as she examines it more and more closely.

Commentary

Lines 1–21

Our narrator has caught a huge and impressive fish ('tremendous') and is surprised that it puts up no struggle, but just hangs there on the end of her rod. This makes sense later on when we discover the fish has been caught many times before and may not have any fight left. In a **trio of adjectives**, something she often uses, Bishop describes the fish as 'battered and venerable / and homely'. It has suffered, deserves respect and is ordinary looking.

In a quirky simile she compares its tattered skin to peeling wallpaper decorated with roses. It is covered in barnacles and riddled with lice. Strands of seaweed hang from him. This fish has clearly been through a lot. **Bishop is often fascinated with things most people might find uninteresting or ugly.**

Lines 22–33

The narrator notes the sharp blood-red gills and the fish's panic at not being able to breathe. Her **imagination comes into play** as she visualises its insides and compares its 'pink swim-bladder' to a peony – another floral image.

Lines 34–44

Bishop begins to empathise with the fish while at the same time realising the fish does not react to her in the same way. She notices its eyes are different from hers; larger, shallower and yellowed, but they do not return her gaze; rather they just seem to follow the light. She is careful not to personify the fish here.

Lines 45–64

Now she ascribes **human qualities** to him – 'his sullen face'. She notices five hooks embedded in his mouth, indicating that he has escaped capture at least five times before this. She compares these to medals a soldier might win or the beard of a wise old man. The lines are 'crimped from the strain and snap', showing the strength and determination the fish once had. This **contrasts** greatly with the lack of struggle in the fish when Bishop catches it.

Lines 65–76

Noticing these hooks, together with everything else Bishop has observed about the fish, leads her to an epiphany – a moment where she suddenly understands something important. She experiences **a feeling of marvel and wonder, expressed as colour filling up the rusty, cracked boat like a rainbow**. This fish deserves another chance – like her, he is a survivor and has been through difficult and testing times: 'And I let the fish go.'

Themes

Surviving difficulty is a major theme here. The fish has clearly been through many battles and survived, but these hardships have taken their toll. The fish has no resistance left in him, 'He hadn't fought at all'; but despite his lack of struggle Bishop feels that 'victory filled up / the little rented boat'. She is full of **admiration** for the fish; he reminds her of a war hero decorated with medals hanging from his uniform on ribbons. This adds a sense of **honour** to the fish's achievements. Bishop has a **moment of epiphany** at the end of the poem — 'rainbow, rainbow, rainbow!' She suddenly realises that she is like the fish, and deserving of another chance in life.

Loneliness is apparent here also. Bishop seems to be fishing alone and the fish itself is a **solitary figure**. She once wrote to her good friend the poet Robert Lowell, 'When you write my epitaph you must say I was the loneliest person who ever lived' (1948). The poem **reflects her struggle with illness, alcoholism and anxiety**, and the trials of her childhood. Upon starting a new job in the Library of Congress in 1947 she said, 'I have never felt so nervous, like a fish out of water.'

Imagery

Similes, metaphors and **personification** are all used very effectively by Bishop. Her imagery is also **strikingly original** and **highly imaginative,** for example comparing the skin of the fish to old rose-patterned wallpaper and the barnacles to rosettes, as well as the bladder of the fish to a peony. There is great detail in her description of the fish; she even goes so far as to imagine the intestines and flesh inside the creature: 'coarse white flesh', 'the big bones and the little bones', 'reds and blacks'. Bishop is clearly no stranger to angling and boating and uses **specialised language** – wire leader, swivel, bilge, bailer, gunnels – that lends a real **authenticity** to her account. The boat too is as battered and damaged as the fish; it is 'rusted' and 'cracked'. Bishop seems to appreciate these qualities and values these **signs of resilience and determination.**

Language and form

Alliteration, assonance and sibilance are among the main sound effects Bishop uses. These speed or slow the poem depending on Bishop's level of **concentration or excitement.**

Repetition also conveys excitement: 'rainbow, rainbow, rainbow!' **Trios of adjectives** are a feature of Bishop's style and she uses them to great effect here; 'battered and venerable / and homely' is an example of this. This creates an effect of balance and detail, and is often used in persuasive writing such as advertising and political speeches.

You will also notice some rhyming though there is no formal rhyming scheme. These sound effects help to strike a balance between the speaker sounding poetic and conversational.

The poem is written as one long **narrative**; the narrator is too captivated by the fish to pause for stanzas. The poem moves **from observation to imagination**: Bishop first describes the outer appearance of the fish but then uses her imagination to wonder what his insides might look like. In a real sense this is **what poets do:**

they observe and describe the world, but also **connect it, on a deeper level, to their imagination and their personal experiences.** As well as what we know and can see, there are things we cannot know for sure, and we use our imagination to think about these things, a concept Bishop explores further in 'At the Fishhouses'.

Exam-Style Questions

Understanding the poem

1	How can you tell that the fish does not put up a struggle when caught?
2	'Battered and venerable / and homely.' What is the poet's meaning in this trio of adjectives? What other trios can you find in the poem? List them.
3	What simile is used to describe the skin of the fish? Do you think this is an effective simile?
4	What else do we learn about the appearance of the fish?
5	In lines 45–64 the poet notices the lines and hooks hanging from the jaw of the fish. Describe them. What two things does the poet compare them to?
6	'Victory filled up / the little rented boat'. What victory, do you think, is the poet talking about?

Thinking about the poem

1	In your opinion, why does the poet release the fish in the end? Was it the right decision? Why? Discuss in pairs or groups.
2	Choose two of your favourite images from the poem and explain why you chose them.
3	Read Bishop's biography. How might the fish reflect her own life experiences?

Imagining

1	Write Bishop's diary entry **or** a letter to a friend recounting her experience of fishing that day.
2	'Rainbow, rainbow, rainbow!' Write a short story with this title, in which the main character realises something about life through an encounter with nature.

SNAPSHOT

- A fable
- Highly descriptive
- Speaker learns a lesson
- Poet admires the fish more and more as she looks at it
- Poet has an epiphany – the fish deserves to be set free
- Based on a real event
- Link to 'The Prodigal' – use of animals as a central symbol

Before you read

What would your thoughts and ideas be if you decided to write a poem on your birthday? Where would your setting be and why?

The Bight

On my birthday

At low tide like this how sheer the water is.
White, crumbling ribs of marl protrude and glare
and the boats are dry, the pilings dry as matches.
Absorbing, rather than being absorbed,
the water in the bight doesn't wet anything,   5
the color of the gas flame turned as low as possible.
One can smell it turning to gas; if one were Baudelaire
one could probably hear it turning to marimba music.
The little ocher dredge at work off the end of the dock
already plays the dry perfectly off-beat claves.   10
The birds are outsize. Pelicans crash
into this peculiar gas unnecessarily hard,
it seems to me, like pickaxes,
rarely coming up with anything to show for it,
and going off with humorous elbowings.   15
Black-and-white man-of-war birds soar
on impalpable drafts
and open their tails like scissors on the curves
or tense them like wishbones, till they tremble.
The frowsy sponge boats keep coming in   20
with the obliging air of retrievers,
bristling with jackstraw gaffs and hooks
and decorated with bobbles of sponges.
There is a fence of chicken wire along the dock
where, glinting like little plowshares,   25
the blue-gray shark tails are hung up to dry
for the Chinese-restaurant trade.
Some of the little white boats are still piled up
against each other, or lie on their sides, stove in,
and not yet salvaged, if they ever will be, from the last bad storm,   30
like torn-open, unanswered letters.
The bight is littered with old correspondences.
Click. Click. Goes the dredge,
and brings up a dripping jawful of marl.
All the untidy activity continues,   35
awful but cheerful.

Glossary

Title	*Bight* = a wide shallow bay
1	*sheer*: smooth
2	*marl*: soil below water
3	*pilings*: timber posts driven into the ground (e.g. for a fence)
7	*Baudelaire*: French poet (1821–1867); used symbolism extensively
8	*marimba*: a large wooden xylophone-like instrument with an echoing and lively sound
9	*ocher*: pale yellowish-brown colour
9	*dredge*: machine which lifts mud away
10	*claves*: wooden tubes struck against each other as a musical instrument; marimba and claves are both South American instruments used in Latin and jazz music
16	*man-of-war birds*: large tropical seabirds
17	*impalpable*: unable to be felt by touch
17	*drafts*: light air currents
20	*frowsy*: messy and smelly
21	*retrievers*: hunting dogs, a friendly and loyal breed
22	*jackstraw gaffs*: gaffs are hooks to land large fish; they are long and would be stored on a boat pointing upwards; they remind the poet of the thin sticks of wood used in the children's game 'spillikins'
25	*plowshares*: blades of a plough
29	*stove in*: smashed
32	*correspondences*: letters; also associations, connections in the mind between things

Guidelines

From the collection *A Cold Spring* (1955), this poem is set in Garrison Bight in Florida, where Bishop lived with Louise Crane. The poem describes the small messy harbour there with keenly observed detail and unusual metaphors, both common features of Bishop's work. As the mud in the harbour is dredged the **things the poet observes lead her thoughts inwards** to her own life. She wrote to her friend Robert Lowell that the harbour was 'always in a mess … reminds me of my little desk'. This move from **the exterior world to interior thoughts and memories** is often found in her poetry. What a poet observes of the world often **'dredges up' associations and memories** like the action the dredge performs at the harbour.

Commentary

This poem reflects Bishop's love of Florida, South America and jazz music.

Surveying the busy, messy, storm-damaged harbour, Bishop **compares it to her own situation**: she has been through personal storms and survived, perhaps even thrived in the messy chaos of her working life. Despite the ugliness of the scene, the poet takes a positive feeling away from the experience about the harbour and herself: 'All the untidy activity continues, / awful but cheerful.' This quote was, at Bishop's request, carved on her gravestone as her epitaph.

Baudelaire and synaesthesia

Baudelaire used symbolism to link the physical and spiritual worlds and often found unusual comparisons. Bishop imagines him not merely seeing and smelling the gas but hearing it as marimba music also, for Baudelaire experienced synaesthesia, where one sense triggers a response in another, for example hearing music and experiencing it as colours.

The subtitle 'On my birthday' may reflect the idea that the poet sees this as a special time to **reflect on her past and present**, though she admitted to Lowell in a letter that it was not actually her birthday at all.

Lines 1–15

The tide is out and through the thin layer of water remaining, the poet marvels at how she can see the thick ribbed soil beneath. Despite the seaside setting, everything is dry – the boats, the pilings. It's as if the water is turning to gas in **texture, colour and smell**. The water strangely doesn't dampen anything but rather evaporates as it comes into contact with things. **Sound is evoked** in the regular beat of the dredge, the crashing pelicans (like cymbals) and the suggestion of marimba. There is a veritable orchestra of sound at play here. The energetic efforts of the pelicans seem futile, 'rarely coming up with anything to show for it', yet their 'humorous elbowings' suggest **a spirit of play and fun**. This theme will develop with relation to Bishop's own view of work at the end of the poem. Despite the music, bustle and fun, there is a **creeping tension also**. Danger is alluded to in lines such as 'the gas flame', 'dry as matches' and 'crash / … unnecessarily hard, / … like pickaxes'; this haphazard way of life is not without its risks.

Lines 16–36

Another mechanical simile is used to depict the huge man-of-war birds which open their tails 'like scissors' as they fly on the air currents. Their 'trembling' sustains the underlying atmosphere of tension established in stanza 1. The harbour becomes very busy; 'frowsy sponge boats' come in like retriever dogs that seem eager to please, as if they are playing a game of fetch. Even the fishing gear seems playful, reminding the poet of toys: 'jackstraw gaffs', 'bobbles of sponges'. It is clearly a working harbour, with its wire fence and shark tails drying out to be used in 'the Chinese-restaurant trade'. She surveys the damage storms have wreaked on the 'little white boats … / … stove in.' These remind her of the papers on her desk and as she is thinking this the musicality returns: 'Click. Click. Goes the dredge, / and brings up a dripping jawful of marl', just as her mind has dredged up the image of her correspondence lying unanswered on her desk. Her final thought though seems a cheerful one: she is happy to be productive in this chaotic untidy way of working.

Themes

Often out of chaos comes creativity and productivity – a poem has been created out of the seemingly random group of sounds and images recorded. Perhaps allowing this messiness in how she works and thinks, Bishop can **open her mind to unusual connections and ideas**. This **originality** is part of her style as a poet and gives her a **freedom**. However, there may be dangers in working this way too, as some of the images suggest.

There is an air of **celebration** hinted at in the subtitle ('On my birthday'), but at the same time a suggestion that we should **take stock** of our life and our work. **Exploring and observing** the bight so keenly corresponds to the introspective exploring and observing that the poet is conducting into herself. **Bringing outer observations and experiences to her imagination** and **allowing them to 'correspond' with her inscape** and her life is at the heart of how Bishop's poetry generally works.

Imagery

The overall effect of the imagery is **ugly yet lively**. **Images from nature** – the water, the birds – go **hand in hand with man-made and mechanical objects** like the dredger and the boats. The idea that the marl beneath the water has ribs not only suggests the shaping influence of the tides but also **personifies** the seabed. **Metaphors and similes abound**: the birds are like tools, 'scissors' and 'pickaxes', the smashed white boats remind the poet of her 'torn-open, unanswered letters'. **Colour and sound collide** and a poem filled with energy and vigour results which, like the often fruitless diving of the pelicans, is fun nonetheless.

Language and form

The language used by the poet accentuates energy and vigour. There is strength here, and plenty of **lively sound**: 'Pelicans crash / into this peculiar gas … /… like pickaxes'; the 'p', 'c' and 'ck' sounds are harsh and hard like the action being described. The many **hard consonants** reflect the energy and industry of the scene.

More gentle sound effects abound too, like the **long vowels** and sibilance in the lines, 'bird̲s ̲soar / on impalpable dra̲ft̲s / and **o**pen their t**ai**l̲s like ̲sci̲s̲so̲r̲s on the c**u**r̲ve̲s' and 'fr**ow**̲sy ̲sponge b**oa**t̲s'. These lines provide a gentler, sweeter contrast to the harsher sounds in the poem, and together the sound effects have a musical quality to echo the many musical references in the poem.

The poem is written in one continuous list of observations and associations, adding to the statement at the end of the poem that life and work can be 'untidy'.

Questions

1	Write, or draw and label, a description of the scene described by Bishop, including as many of the details she gives us as possible.
2	What senses are evoked in her description of The Bight? Discuss.
3	List and comment on the sounds and sound effects the poet uses.
4	What atmosphere is created by the combinations of sounds and images in the poem?
5	Choose a simile or metaphor which particularly appealed to you; comment on its effect and give a reason for your choice.
6	How is the poet's desk like the damaged boats in the second stanza? Is this a negative comparison?
7	How does the poem move from the exterior world to the poet's interior thoughts? Trace and comment on this in the poem.
8	'Bishop combines a very realistic view of the world around us with highly original and amusing imagery.' Discuss in relation to this poem.
9	What do you learn about the speaker from reading this poem? Try to find three or four adjectives to describe her and back up these ideas with reference to the poem. You may choose from the following list if you wish: optimistic, imaginative, observant, humorous, critical.
10	'The final line changes the poem from something possibly negative to an optimistic vision of life.' Do you agree? Explain.
11	Suggest images and music that you would combine to create an audio-visual accompaniment to a performed reading of this poem.
12	In groups or pairs, choose a character from one of your Paper II texts and suggest a place that would have a special meaning for that person. Describe the place and suggest the memories and thoughts it might evoke for that character.

Before you read

What work might go on at fishhouses? What setting do you think you would find fishhouses in?

At the Fishhouses

Although it is a cold evening,
down by one of the fishhouses
an old man sits netting,
his net, in the gloaming almost invisible,
a dark purple-brown,   5
and his shuttle worn and polished.
The air smells so strong of codfish
it makes one's nose run and one's eyes water.
The five fishhouses have steeply peaked roofs
and narrow, cleated gangplanks slant up   10
to storerooms in the gables
for the wheelbarrows to be pushed up and down on.
All is silver: the heavy surface of the sea,
swelling slowly as if considering spilling over,
is opaque, but the silver of the benches,   15
the lobster pots, and masts, scattered
among the wild jagged rocks,
is of an apparent translucence
like the small old buildings with an emerald moss
growing on their shoreward walls.   20
The big fish tubs are completely lined
with layers of beautiful herring scales
and the wheelbarrows are similarly plastered
with creamy iridescent coats of mail,
with small iridescent flies crawling on them.   25
Up on the little slope behind the houses,
set in the sparse bright sprinkle of grass,
is an ancient wooden capstan,
cracked, with two long bleached handles
and some melancholy stains, like dried blood,   30
where the ironwork has rusted.
The old man accepts a Lucky Strike.
He was a friend of my grandfather.
We talk of the decline in the population
and of codfish and herring   35
while he waits for a herring boat to come in.
There are sequins on his vest and on his thumb.
He has scraped the scales, the principal beauty,
from unnumbered fish with that black old knife,
the blade of which is almost worn away.   40

Down at the water's edge, at the place
where they haul up the boats, up the long ramp
descending into the water, thin silver
tree trunks are laid horizontally
across the gray stones, down and down   45
at intervals of four or five feet.

Cold dark deep and absolutely clear,
element bearable to no mortal,
to fish and to seals . . . One seal particularly
I have seen here evening after evening.   50
He was curious about me. He was interested in music;
like me a believer in total immersion,
so I used to sing to him Baptist hymns.
I also sang 'A Mighty Fortress Is Our God.'
He stood up in the water and regarded me   55
steadily, moving his head a little.
Then he would disappear, then suddenly emerge
almost in the same spot, with a sort of shrug
as if it were against his better judgment.
Cold dark deep and absolutely clear,   60
the clear gray icy water . . . Back, behind us,
the dignified tall firs begin.
Bluish, associating with their shadows,
a million Christmas trees stand
waiting for Christmas. The water seems suspended   65
above the rounded gray and blue-gray stones.
I have seen it over and over, the same sea, the same,
slightly, indifferently swinging above the stones,
icily free above the stones,
above the stones and then the world.   70
If you should dip your hand in,
your wrist would ache immediately,
your bones would begin to ache and your hand would burn
as if the water were a transmutation of fire
that feeds on stones and burns with a dark gray flame.   75
If you tasted it, it would first taste bitter,
then briny, then surely burn your tongue.
It is like what we imagine knowledge to be:
dark, salt, clear, moving, utterly free,
drawn from the cold hard mouth   80
of the world, derived from the rocky breasts
forever, flowing and drawn, and since
our knowledge is historical, flowing, and flown.

Glossary

3	*netting*: mending fishing nets	
4	*gloaming*: dusk; twilight	
6	*shuttle*: a tool used to repair fishing nets	
10	*cleated*: with anti-slip pieces of wood nailed on	
11	*gables*: ends of a building just under the roof	
15	*opaque*: almost transparent but not quite	
18	*translucence*: transparent enough to see light shining through	
24	*iridescent*: shiny and rainbow coloured	
24	*coats of mail*: armour made of knitted metal worn by medieval knights	
28	*capstan*: machine used to wind up rope	
32	*Lucky Strike*: an American brand of cigarette	
52	*total immersion*: a form of baptism practised by some Christians	
74	*transmutation*: changing from one shape to another	
77	*briny*: salty like sea water	

Guidelines

This poem is from the collection *A Cold Spring* (1955).

As we have come to expect, **Bishop begins with concrete and meticulous description** (of the place, a seal and the sea) and then, prompted by the associations these descriptions produce, **turns her examination inward to explore a more abstract question – what is knowledge?**

She has returned to Nova Scotia **for the first time since her mother's death** in 1934. Some **painful memories** and a deep sense of **loss and alienation** are evident here. The **transformative power of the imagination** is central to this poem.

Commentary

Lines 1–12

The poet sees an old man in the cold dusk mending his nets with a shuttle. Already an air of magic and mystery is introduced: he is 'almost invisible'. The place reeks of fish; there are five fishhouses here and the poet describes them. The image of the planks against the side walls for 'wheelbarrows to be pushed up and down on' echoes the rhythmic movement of the fisherman's shuttle. **Many of our senses**, including smell and sound, **are engaged already**.

Lines 13–25

The poet builds **mystical nuances** into the factual and detailed account of this very ordinary place: 'All is silver'. The detritus of harbour life abounds; the 'lobster pots, and masts' seem translucent. Other workaday objects undergo a similar transformation and become extraordinary: 'big fish tubs' are 'lined / with … beautiful herring scales'; wheelbarrows also covered in scales are iridescent like 'coats of mail', and even the flies glitter with a rainbow of colour. This **recounting** of the ordinary, even ugly, **everyday world being transformed by the poet's imagination** is typical of Bishop.

Lines 26–40

The narrator notices the broken old capstan; it has fallen out of use and seems wounded, with 'stains, like dried blood'. **Human contact** is made through a shared cigarette. The fisherman is an old family friend (possibly a painful association for the poet given her childhood experiences of loss in this place). They discuss the dwindling fish stocks and many details suggest that this man's way of life is under threat, just like the 'black old knife, / the blade of which is almost worn away.' He too is plastered with fish scales – 'sequins'; he has almost become a fish himself. 'Sequins' is a typically humorous choice of image for an old fisherman; **Bishop often injects wry humour into even her saddest poems**.

Lines 41–46

This short stanza **links** the longer sections of the poem effectively – **the ramp** Bishop describes where the boats are dragged down to the water **symbolises the downward path the poet is about to take into her thoughts and imagination, dragging the reader with her**. This area is silver with scales – the whole world of the poem is taking on this shining quality as we are led into **an imaginative experience**. The poet uses **light, colour and depth** to **draw us in**, and our vision is guided simultaneously 'up the long ramp' and down – 'descending into the water'.

Lines 47–66

Plunging with her mind's eye into the sea, Bishop **meditates** upon how she can never truly enter and be a part of its icy chill, for it is an 'element bearable to no mortal' and will not tolerate her presence. She can only imagine how it might feel. Similarly **how can one ever fully enter knowledge or know anything with total certainty? Like the sea, knowledge is fluid and ever-changing**.

A seal appears and seems to know the poet; another gentle touch of humour is present here as she sings him a Baptist hymn. He watches from afar but engages no further; it seems the exchange is rather one-sided compared to the earlier chat with the fisherman. The water is too cold for Bishop to be 'baptised' here. In **another religious image** she notes the 'dignified tall' Christmas trees back on the land awaiting their seasonal felling.

Lines 67–77

Despite her familiarity with this stretch of sea – 'I have seen it over and over' – she cannot complete her knowledge of it. The water is so chill that it burns like fire: 'If you should dip your hand in, / your wrist would ache immediately, / … your hand would burn'. With a detached brutality, the sea rebuffs her quest to know more.

Lines 78–83

Bishop imagines the water's briny taste and **ponders the concept of knowledge**. She fancies that we imagine knowledge would taste and appear like this sea water: 'dark, salt, clear, moving, utterly free'. Knowledge is **not fixed or constant or something humans can control and define**, it is 'flowing, and flown'. It is also 'historical', i.e. **shaped by the lived reality of each person**: Bishop derived her own knowledge 'from the cold hard mouth / of the world, … the rocky breasts' of **childhood pain** and the **absence of a mother**. Perhaps this knowledge is hard for the poet to bear; **nature is personified as cold and unknowable**, **indifferent** to the suffering and history of the humans who inhabit it and who, like the old fisherman, use it to sustain them.

Themes

Nature, knowledge, change and the **transformative power of the imagination** are all strong themes here. Although we know the world in many ways, we can never know anything completely. Obviously Bishop's own past is a huge theme also; returning to Nova Scotia was bound to produce many **conflicting emotions** for her. From letters written at the time it seems she was quite depressed during this visit, but though she based much of the poem on her actual visit, other parts came to her in a dream.

Sea as symbol

This poem is a natural progression from 'The Bight' and 'The Fish'. All three use the sea as an important symbol to convey themes of survival and loss. The changing nature of the human world is contrasted with the seeming permanence of an indifferent elemental world exemplified by 'the wild jagged rocks' and 'the dignified tall firs [that] … stand / waiting'.

Imagery

Factual description combines with dreamlike mysticism to link the themes and imagery of this poem. Bishop typically uses a **multisensory** approach to bring the scene **vividly to life** for the reader: 'The air smells so strong of codfish / it makes one's nose run and one's eyes water.' **Detail is key** for Bishop, from the brand of cigarette to how many feet lie between the tree trunks on the ramp. Details are conveyed with a **cinematic quality** to communicate an **impression** of the 'real world'. **Bishop uses more abstract imagery to make the leap into the imaginative, creative world**: 'an apparent translucence', 'water seems suspended' and 'transmutation of fire' are examples of this.

Language and form

In the first section of the poem Bishop's language is straightforward and almost conversational: 'although it is a cold evening'; but as the poem progresses, the language becomes, like her imagery, more abstract: 'our knowledge is historical, flowing, and flown.'

She uses many **sound effects** in the poem including **softening sibilance**, for example, 'All is silver: the heavy surface of the sea / swelling slowly as if considering spilling over'. The imagery and language combine here to effect **lines of great beauty and impact**. Repetition, **assonance** and alliteration also feature, 'forever, flowing, and 'flowing, and flown' bringing the poem to a wistful conclusion.

Often the poet speaks directly to the reader: 'If you should dip your hand in', creating an **immediacy and engagement**. Long assonant sounds give that background an **air of mystery and yearning**: 'the cold hard mouth / of the world'.

The poem is written in two long irregular stanzas with a short linking stanza. The second longer stanza **delves more deeply** into ideas raised by the descriptions in the first, and comes to its conclusion about how we each arrive at knowledge.

Questions

1	What details make Bishop's descriptions in the first section of the poem particularly vivid and realistic?
2	List the religious references in the poem and offer an opinion as to why Bishop included them.
3	Compare and contrast the two encounters Bishop has in the poem – with the old fisherman and the seal.
4	How is the sea described? What do you think it might symbolise?
5	How is an air of mystery created in the poem? Explore Bishop's language and imagery in your answer here.
6	List two or three sound effects that particularly appealed to you in the poem and comment on the effect you found they had.
7	What images were particularly striking for you and why?
8	What does Bishop learn from the sea? Do you agree with her conclusion in the final six lines? Explain.
9	Which of the following most sums up the theme of the poem for you and why? ■ This is a poem about nature. ■ The theme of this poem is knowledge. ■ Feeling alienated and out of place is the theme of this poem. ■ This poem deals mainly with Bishop's difficult childhood.
10	Is there a place that brings back memories or evokes strong emotion in you? Write about this in any format you like (diary entry, personal essay, feature article, poem, etc.).
11	Using Bishop's description and symbolism as a model, create a description of another location, for example a forest, a desert, a city, the moon, the Arctic. Work in pairs or small groups.

Before you read

What do you know about the biblical parable of the prodigal son? In pairs, share your knowledge, research together and present your findings to the class.

The Prodigal

The brown enormous odor he lived by
was too close, with its breathing and thick hair,
for him to judge. The floor was rotten; the sty
was plastered halfway up with glass-smooth dung.
Light-lashed, self-righteous, above moving snouts,   5
the pigs' eyes followed him, a cheerful stare –
even to the sow that always ate her young –
till, sickening, he leaned to scratch her head.
But sometimes mornings after drinking bouts
(he hid the pints behind a two-by-four),   10
the sunrise glazed the barnyard mud with red;
the burning puddles seemed to reassure.
And then he thought he almost might endure
his exile yet another year or more.

But evenings the first star came to warn.   15
The farmer whom he worked for came at dark
to shut the cows and horses in the barn
beneath their overhanging clouds of hay,
with pitchforks, faint forked lightnings, catching light,
safe and companionable as in the Ark.   20
The pigs stuck out their little feet and snored.
The lantern – like the sun, going away –
laid on the mud a pacing aureole.
Carrying a bucket along a slimy board,
he felt the bats' uncertain staggering flight,   25
his shuddering insights, beyond his control,
touching him. But it took him a long time
finally to make his mind up to go home.

Glossary

Title	*Prodigal*:	a person who spends money wastefully and recklessly
1	*odor*:	unpleasant smell
10	*two-by-four*:	a piece of timber with a cross-section measuring two inches by four inches
20	*companionable*:	friendly, getting along together well
23	*aureole*:	a halo of light around the head, often shown upon a saint

Guidelines

Written in 1951, this poem is from the collection *A Cold Spring* (1955) and takes the form of a double sonnet.

Bishop had a **drinking problem** from her student days and regularly drank herself into such a state that she ended up in embarrassing situations, often having to move on from friends or accommodation out of **shame**. She wrote this poem inspired by an experience in Nova Scotia in 1946, when 'one of my aunt's stepsons offered me a drink of rum, **in the pig styes** at about nine in the morning'.

Commentary

Bishop chooses to set her poem in the sty the Prodigal shares with pigs during the time when he decides to return home. She **identifies with the marginalised alcoholic figure** of the Prodigal, with his **'rock bottom' situation** and **gradual realisation that recovery is possible**. The poem is written in the form of a double sonnet.

Sonnet 1. Lines 1–8

The appalling conditions of the sty are **juxtaposed** with images of beauty and hope in the first sonnet.

The stench of the pigs and their breathing, hair and dung pervade this octave. The Prodigal is at rock bottom and has lost all sense of judgement, so inured is he to his pitiful environment: 'The brown enormous odor he lived by / was too close'. The dung plasters the walls making them 'glass-smooth'. The description moves to a close-up of the pigs themselves, described sympathetically by Bishop as 'Light-lashed', with 'a cheerful stare', yet simultaneously 'self-righteous'. Are they judging the Prodigal and finding themselves to be above him? Although he is sickened by the sow which ate her young (and by his own drinking), he is still desperate for her companionship.

Lines 9–14

Against this degraded, awful existence there are **contrasting moments of beauty and hints at redemption** in the sestet. In the morning, despite his hangover, he notices how 'the sunrise glazed the barnyard mud with red; / the burning puddles seemed to reassure.' The beauty of the sunrise comforts the Prodigal; everything seems a little better in the morning and the Prodigal feels he 'almost might endure / his exile yet another year or more.' The word 'almost' creates doubt here. We see that **he has not faced up to the reality** of his alcoholism yet '(he hid the pints behind a two-by-four)', despite the reality that he has been totally debased and dehumanised by his situation.

Sonnet 2. Lines 15–20

'But' is used to begin sonnet two, a word which negates the conclusion reached at the end of the first sonnet. As night approaches, the Prodigal is less sure he can endure this life much longer. The image of 'the first star' come to 'warn' is ominous, and suggests that the nights were hardest for him, a time when he had to face his demons and his reality. **His isolation is emphasised in contrast to the animals** who are shut away, 'beneath their overhanging clouds of hay', 'safe and companionable'.

Lines 21– 28

'The pigs stuck out their little feet and snored'; the farmer's lantern recedes 'like the sun, going away', and the Prodigal is left in darkness, alone and fearful. The sun that brought the Prodigal comfort in sonnet 1 has deserted him. As he carries out his odious chores, 'Carrying a bucket along a slimy board', the erratic flying of the bats brings home to him the **hideousness of his alienation and debasement**. These 'shuddering insights' grip him 'beyond his control'. And yet despite the nightmarish quality of this experience, 'it took him a long time / finally to make his mind up to go home.' This underlines how difficult it can be to begin recovery from something like alcoholism. Home is a last resort. **Home itself is a difficult concept for the poet** who lacked parental love due to her father's early death, her mother's mental illness and the poet's lack of a permanent home in the following years. Note that 'home' doesn't fully rhyme with 'time' at the end of the poem.

Themes

Bishop's alcoholism is clearly a theme here and she draws **strong parallels** between herself and the central character in the poem. Her poetic treatment of him is fair; he is not overly sentimentalised but there is a

compassionate understanding at play. **Redemption and hope** are strong themes. Why might Bishop have used the story and character of the Prodigal rather than write herself into a straightforwardly autobiographical poem? Have you seen her do this elsewhere?

Imagery

Religious imagery abounds in the poem: the Prodigal, the Ark, aureole (aura or halo). Gross and deeply unpleasant images vie with more optimistic ones. The **contrast between light and darkness** is especially symbolic and meaningful. **Images often echo each other** even when the effect is contrasting, for example the dung glazes the sty walls while 'the sunrise glazed the barnyard mud'. The poem is **vivid in its descriptive power and atmosphere**.

Language

Again a **contrast between positive and negative** is very clear in the poet's language: 'cheerful', 'sunrise', 'reassure', 'companionable', 'little feet', 'aureole', 'home'; versus 'brown', 'odor', 'rotten', 'dung', 'ate her young', 'exile', 'dark', 'bats'. These contrasts are at the heart of the poem. Although very descriptive and evocative, the language is straightforward and accessible.

Form

A **sonnet** is a fourteen-line poem made popular by Petrarch and Shakespeare. Sonnet 1 takes the form of a Shakespearean sonnet, made up of three quatrains (four-line sections) and a rhyming couplet (the last two lines). The first eight lines present an issue, the third quatrain offers a deeper meditation on this issue, and the final couplet presents a solution. The terrible state of the Prodigal's life and dwelling is the issue. The description of the farmyard deepens this and provides the reason (the beauty of the sunrise) for the conclusion reached in the couplet, that the Prodigal might be able to survive another year of this.

The second sonnet is less ordered in its structure of form and thought. As night falls there is a sense of crisis; finally the Prodigal feels 'shuddering insights' and reaches a shaky resolution, 'finally to make his mind up to go home'. But **'time' and 'home' do not make a true rhyme** or rhyming couplet as 'endure' and 'more' do at the end of the first sonnet. Why might Bishop have done this? Does it create uncertainty, or suggest that the Prodigal isn't convinced by his decision?

Exam-Style Questions

Understanding the poem

1. Describe the living conditions of the Prodigal. Which details in particular successfully convey the squalor he lives in?

2. Did you like or dislike the pigs, based on Bishop's description of them? Explain your view.

3. What opinion of the Prodigal did you form in sonnet 1? Support your opinion with quotation and reference.

4. Do you think Bishop is fair in her description of the Prodigal? Explain.

5. How does the atmosphere of the second sonnet differ from that of the first?

6. Why, do you think, does Bishop use the character of the farmer here? What is his role?

Thinking about the poem

1. *Groupwork* In pairs, find images of light and darkness in the poem and comment on their effect. Use a grid to display your examples and ideas.

2. List examples of religious images in the poem and comment upon their effect.

3. Overall does the poem offer a positive or a negative point of view in your opinion? How?

4. What decision is made at the end of the poem and how does the Prodigal feel about this?

5. What, do you think, does the poet reveal about herself, her life and her experiences through the poem?

Imagining

1. Write the letter the Prodigal sends to his father asking if he may come home.

2. *Groupwork* In small groups imagine you were to make the poem into a short film. Draft a synopsis of this and / or draw a story board to show how your film would progress. You may also like to choose music or sound effects.

SNAPSHOT

- Double sonnet
- Prodigal's state of mind is conveyed
- Description of animals is realistic and sympathetic
- Images of light and darkness predominate
- Bishop's personal experience parallels the Prodigal
- Complex idea of 'home'
- Religious references

Before you read

Ask and answer these questions with the student beside you: Why do people like to travel? What aspects of travel do you find most enjoyable? Where would you most like to visit in the world and why?

Questions of Travel

There are too many waterfalls here; the crowded streams
hurry too rapidly down to the sea,
and the pressure of so many clouds on the mountaintops
makes them spill over the sides in soft slow-motion,
turning to waterfalls under our very eyes.   5
— For if those streaks, those mile-long, shiny, tearstains,
aren't waterfalls yet,
in a quick age or so, as ages go here,
they probably will be.
But if the streams and clouds keep travelling, travelling,   10
the mountains look like the hulls of capsized ships,
slime-hung and barnacled.

Think of the long trip home.
Should we have stayed at home and thought of here?
Where should we be today?   15
Is it right to be watching strangers in a play
in this strangest of theatres?
What childishness is it that while there's a breath of life
in our bodies, we are determined to rush
to see the sun the other way around?   20
The tiniest green hummingbird in the world?
To stare at some inexplicable old stonework,
inexplicable and impenetrable,
at any view,
instantly seen and always, always delightful?   25
Oh, must we dream our dreams
and have them, too?
And have we room
for one more folded sunset, still quite warm?

But surely it would have been a pity   30
not to have seen the trees along this road,
really exaggerated in their beauty,
not to have seen them gesturing
like noble pantomimists, robed in pink.
— Not to have had to stop for gas and heard   35
the sad, two-noted, wooden tune
of disparate wooden clogs
carelessly clacking over
a grease-stained filling-station floor.
(In another country the clogs would all be tested.   40

Each pair there would have identical pitch.)
— A pity not to have heard
the other, less primitive music of the fat brown bird
who sings above the broken gasoline pump
in a bamboo church of Jesuit baroque: 45
three towers, five silver crosses.

— Yes, a pity not to have pondered,
blurr'dly and inconclusively,
on what connection can exist for centuries
between the crudest wooden footwear   50
and, careful and finicky,
the whittled fantasies of wooden cages.
— Never to have studied history in
the weak calligraphy of songbirds' cages.
— And never to have had to listen to rain   55
so much like politicians' speeches:
two hours of unrelenting oratory
and then a sudden golden silence
in which the traveller takes a notebook, writes:

'Is it lack of imagination that makes us come   60
to imagined places, not just stay at home?
Or could Pascal have been not entirely right
about just sitting quietly in one's room?

Continent, city, country, society:
the choice is never wide and never free.   65
And here, or there . . . No. Should we have stayed at home,
wherever that may be?'

Glossary

11	*hulls*: main bodies of ships	
11	*capsized*: turned over in the water	
12	*barnacled*: covered with small stony shellfish	
20	*the sun the other way around*: the sun seen from the southern hemisphere	
22	*inexplicable*: cannot be explained	
23	*impenetrable*: cannot be seen through	
34	*pantomimists*: people acting in an over-the-top way; actors in a pantomime	
35	*gas*: car fuel, gasoline	
37	*disparate*: not similar	
45	*Jesuit baroque*: ornate seventeenth century architectural style often found in churches in Brazil	
51	*finicky*: overly fancy, with lots of small complex detail	
52	*whittled fantasies*: wooden items imaginatively carved, e.g. the birdcages in the poem	
54	*calligraphy*: the art of handwriting, often ornate and swirled	
57	*oratory*: public speaking, e.g. a politician's speech	
62	*Pascal*: Blaise Pascal, a French mathematician and philosopher (1623–1662)	

Guidelines

This is the title poem in the collection *Questions of Travel* from 1965.

Brazil is the 'here' of line 1, a place Bishop travelled to in November of 1951 intending to stay only two weeks, but where she found herself living for fifteen years with her lover Lota (to whom she dedicated this poetry collection). During this time she wrote to Robert Lowell, saying, 'I am extremely happy for the first time in my life', and the **quirky, upbeat** nature of this poem reflects this. It seems Bishop was a little overwhelmed by Brazil at first, according to the opening section of the poem. It is clear, however, that she comes to love the place, as she admires its churches, birdsong and even the sound of the clogs worn by the locals!

The poet **reflects on the idea of travel** and **wonders why** people want to experience different places and cultures. She is critical of the box-ticking nature of tourism whereby many view a famous sight and move on without really experiencing anything. Bishop concludes in a positive way, having questioned the rights and wrongs of travel and **examined the notion of home**, a **recurring theme in her work**.

Commentary

Lines 1–12

The speaker feels overwhelmed by the Brazilian landscape: the sheer volume of water, the 'crowded streams' becoming waterfalls, then clouds, and the process repeating eternally. Repetition and sibilance in this section emphasise the **weariness the poet feels** and the **repetitive relentless nature of this process**, 'spill over … in soft slow-motion', 'mile-long', 'travelling, travelling'. Mountains are compared to overturned ships. **Boats and water** are **recurring symbols** in Bishop's imagery. The **constant movement** is exhausting.

Lines 13–29

In the persona of a tourist, Bishop wonders whether travel is worth the effort: 'Think of the long trip home.' She wonders if remaining at home and simply dreaming of foreign lands might be better. She asks **eight questions** about travel in this stanza. She **queries the ethics** of watching locals and their customs as if it were a show put on to entertain: 'Is it right to be watching strangers in a play'? She asks whether it is childish to go halfway round the world just to see the sun 'the other way around' or to examine an old building or monument – 'some inexplicable old stonework'. The fact that sights are 'instantly seen' and pronounced 'delightful' clearly irks the poet.

Lines 30–46

The tone calms as the speaker becomes reflective, pondering the sights she has loved and truly savoured, not on the tourist trail. These are the ordinary sights and sounds in Brazil: 'the trees along this road', 'the sad, two-noted, wooden tune / of disparate wooden clogs', 'music of the fat brown bird', 'a bamboo church'. Look at how much **energy and close observation** are contained in these images.

> **Pascal on travel**
>
> **'All the unhappiness of men arises from one single fact that they cannot stay quietly in their own room.'**
>
> *Pascal*

Lines 47–59

The level of **detail** and use of **quirky comparisons** in this stanza really bring the place to life for the reader and Bishop's enthusiasm and humour is infectious, for example in her account of the birdcages which contrast so much with the clumsy big clogs worn by locals, or comparing the torrential rain to 'politicians' speeches: / two hours of unrelenting oratory'. It is clear that the poet has taken time to truly explore and observe this land, its people and culture, in contrast to the way the 'tourist' persona of the first section approaches their trip.

Lines 60–67

Two stanzas follow written in italics (giving the impression of handwriting in a journal) in which Bishop, as the traveller, asks, 'Is it lack of imagination' that makes people travel? Should we agree with Pascal and stay at home? However, for Bishop the question of travel carries her, as so often her poems do, to **the question of where and what home is**: 'Should we have stayed at home, wherever that may be?'

Is the idea of travel as exotic and exciting for someone like Bishop who never had a fixed home or family life?

Themes

'At the Fishhouses' and 'The Prodigal' also question the **idea of home**. It is clearly a very important theme for Bishop. Perhaps one has to live in a place with a loved one and make it a home to truly appreciate and understand its people and culture. She has clearly fallen for the charms of Brazil and it was to become her home for many years, the most permanent one she ever had.

Travel is a theme also; Bishop had won a scholarship in 1951 enabling her to travel to Brazil. She had also travelled to Europe and around the USA thanks to an inheritance from her father. **Notions of belonging** and of **how we interpret the world** are at play here. There are different, **contrasting and conflicting, points of view** in the poem. Which opinion most closely reflects your own stance on travel, home and belonging?

Baroque

Baroque is a sixteenth-century style of architecture which was highly ornamented and elaborate. When employed by churches it was a powerful statement of the wealth and power of the church. During the seventeenth century, the religious order the Society of Jesus (Jesuits) built churches in this style across Europe and South America. Interiors were busily adorned with stucco, painting and sculpture.

The **beauty of the everyday**, the ordinary, is central: the bamboo church seems to her 'Jesuit baroque', the trees are 'really exaggerated in their beauty,' even the rain and the 'golden' silence afterwards convey this. The **extraordinary nature of the ordinary** is a passion of Bishop's which, she shows us, we can discover if we stop a moment and bring close observation and imagination into play.

Imagery

Metaphor, symbolism and simile crowd the poem like the waterfalls of stanza 1 crowd the landscape. As ever with Bishop, the imagery is **carefully detailed and highly evocative**. Nature imagery features heavily: the waterfalls, birds, rain and trees **contrast** with imagery that is of man-made objects like the bird cages, the gas station and the bamboo church. Bishop's quirky originality is particularly strong in this poem. What details would you pick out as the most unusual?

Language and form

Poetic language laden with details and sound effects exists simultaneously with a conversational light-hearted tone. Effective use of sibilance, assonance, repetition and alliteration combine to bring the sights and sounds of Brazil to life – 'wooden clogs / carelessly clacking over / a grease-stained filling-station floor'. The **use of questions is a recurring feature** of Bishop's poetry and this poem is peppered with them, creating a sense of **wonder and fascination**, yet at the same time **uncertainty**.

Bishop's love of music

'I am in need of music that would flow
Over my fretful, feeling fingertips,
Over my bitter-tainted, trembling lips,
With melody, deep, clear, and liquid-slow.
Oh, for the healing swaying, old and low,
Of some song sung to rest the tired dead,
A song to fall like water on my head,
And over quivering limbs, dream flushed
   to glow!'

Elizabeth Bishop, Sonnet

The poem is made up of four irregular stanzas, the second and third being longer, and then in sharp contrast two regular italicised stanzas which rhyme. Bishop clearly wants these to be very different in form and style. Why might that be?

Questions

1	What picture of Brazil is conveyed to you in stanza 1? Do you find this landscape attractive? Explain.
2	List in your own words the eight questions asked by the poet in stanza 2. In small groups discuss the answers you would give and feed back to the class as a whole.
3	How does the poet's experience of her travels in stanza 3 contrast with that of the tourist persona in stanza 2? Which account do you prefer and why?
4	In stanza 3 choose the sound effects and images which appealed to you most and give reasons for your choices.
5	Write a brief answer to each of the two questions posed in stanza 5, giving your own opinion. Do you think the poet would agree with your answers?
6	'The choice is never wide and never free' (line 65). What does Bishop mean by this, do you think?
7	'Home wherever that may be?' Considering what you have discovered about Bishop's life, especially her childhood, what might Bishop mean here?
8	List the sounds described by the poet in the poem. Do you agree that the poem has a musical quality?
9	'Bishop's poems are full of vivid detailed description, often using quirky and original comparisons.' Analyse 'Questions of Travel' in the light of this statement.
10	What might the cages described in the poem symbolise?
11	What aspects of Bishop's personality are revealed in the poem to the reader?
12	Trace the tone of the poem and how it changes as the poem progresses.
13	Examine the use of personas in the poem. How many different voices do you think the poem contains? Who is speaking in the last two stanzas?
14	'Travel broadens the mind.' Have a class debate on this topic.

Before you read

What customs or traditions can you think of that may be harmful to nature? Research this with a classmate.

The Armadillo

for Robert Lowell

This is the time of year
when almost every night
the frail, illegal fire balloons appear.
Climbing the mountain height,

rising toward a saint   5
still honored in these parts,
the paper chambers flush and fill with light
that comes and goes, like hearts.

Once up against the sky it's hard
to tell them from the stars –   10
planets, that is – the tinted ones:
Venus going down, or Mars,

or the pale green one. With a wind,
they flare and falter, wobble and toss;
but if it's still they steer between   15
the kite sticks of the Southern Cross,

receding, dwindling, solemnly
and steadily forsaking us,
or, in the downdraft from a peak,
suddenly turning dangerous.   20

Last night another big one fell.
It splattered like an egg of fire
against the cliff behind the house.
The flame ran down. We saw the pair

of owls who nest there flying up   25
and up, their whirling black-and-white
stained bright pink underneath, until
they shrieked up out of sight.

The ancient owls' nest must have burned.
Hastily, all alone,   30
a glistening armadillo left the scene,
rose-flecked, head down, tail down,

and then a baby rabbit jumped out,
short-eared, to our surprise.
So soft! – a handful of intangible ash   35
with fixed, ignited eyes.

Too pretty, dreamlike mimicry!
O falling fire and piercing cry
and panic, and a weak mailed fist
clenched ignorant against the sky!   40

Glossary

Title	***Armadillo***: burrowing South American mammal, with bony armour-like skin
3	***fire balloons***: paper lanterns which contain a candle, as the air inside heats, they rise
7	***chambers***: rooms, referring here to the balloon part of the fire balloon; also links to the 'heart' image of line 8
13	***pale green one***: probably Uranus
16	***kite sticks of the Southern Cross***: a cross-shaped constellation in the southern hemisphere
35	***intangible***: cannot be touched
37	***mimicry***: imitation
39	***mailed fist***: the armadillo, when rolled into a protective ball, resembles a glove from a suit of armour

Guidelines

Robert Lowell was a close friend of Bishop and even proposed to her once. He said that this was one of her best poems; it appeared in the *Questions of Travel* collection of 1965.

The setting is Brazil, Rio de Janeiro on 24 June, which is the winter solstice there and the feast day of St John. Traditionally fire balloons were set off at night intended to float towards the saint's mountain shrine; however, many blew off course and landed in the forest wreaking havoc on the flora and fauna there by causing hugely destructive fires. This practice continued in spite of the government making it illegal. In the poem Bishop explores her reactions to this custom, shifting from admiration and wonder at first to outraged horror as the poem progresses.

Commentary

Lines 1–8

As usual Bishop begins with a brief account of what is happening, while providing a **context** for the reader. She **observes** the fire balloon custom rather than participating in it. At first the balloons seem fragile and 'frail' as they climb the 'mountain height'. As the paper balloons expand with heat and become illuminated by the fires within, they appear 'like hearts'. This refers to the red glow but also the pulsating effect of the flame which flickers inside.

Lines 9–20

The balloons rise so high that they seem to join the cosmos. Bishop emphasises those more colourful 'tinted' planets, such as Venus, the planet of love, and Mars, the red planet of war which is often linked to impending violence or catastrophe. The poet is **foreshadowing** the disaster to come. With her reference to 'the pale green one', the narrator endears us with her admission of a lack of complete knowledge, and the **tone is relaxed** and conversational as she admires the trajectory of the balloons; they seem to steer towards the 'Southern Cross'. As the balloons move farther away they abandon the watchers: 'forsaking us'. Then the tone changes dramatically as some balloons are caught by a breeze and blown earthwards.

Lines 21–36

The poet moves from a generalised account to a very specific event – the night before, a balloon had fallen to the ground and 'splattered like an egg of fire'. There is a suggestive **paradox** here: an egg is commonly a

symbol of birth and life, but here it brings death and destruction. Extending the egg simile, the first victims of the fire are a pair of 'ancient owls' whose nest has been destroyed. They fly off shrieking in panic, 'their whirling black-and-white / stained bright pink underneath'. In contrast to the 'we' of the poem, a lonely figure appears scuttling out of the undergrowth, 'Hastily, all alone, / a glistening armadillo'. He is 'rose-flecked' with scorching ash and determined to escape – 'head down, tail down'.

Our pity and horror are further engaged as a 'baby rabbit jumped out, / *short*-eared … So soft!' **Through her description of the rabbit, the poet reveals her emotions** concerning the fire: it is a 'handful of intangible ash', and fear shows in its 'fixed, ignited eyes'. The old, the lonely and the young have been displaced, traumatised and harmed.

Lines 37–40

As in 'Questions of Travel' the final stanza is italicised. Here the speaker **rails against the unfairness** of this unnecessary suffering. The balloons' prettiness has deceived her, their captivating charm a cruel ruse: '*Too pretty, dreamlike mimicry!*' In reality they have wrought destruction and doom: '*falling fire and piercing cry / and panic*'. The **language is almost Shakespearean** in this stanza compared to the modern conversational tone of the rest of the poem.

The poet concludes by returning to the image of the armadillo. He rolls into a protective ball, reminding Bishop of a '*weak mailed fist / clenched ignorant against the sky*'. His protest and defiance, and his attempt to survive this situation, are ultimately futile. He will surely die.

Themes

Mankind's disregard for nature is an obvious concern here. Despite the balloons being 'illegal', because of their danger to the landscape, the locals persist in the tradition. The **violence that religion has provoked** continues to be a huge issue in our world today. Do we have the right to cause destruction and death in the name of our beliefs? The **powerlessness** of those who suffer from oppression, and the **loss of home**, could both be seen as themes here. The tiny rabbit in particular symbolises this. Its fluffy fur offers no protection; it is totally **innocent and vulnerable**, reduced to 'a handful of intangible ash'. Even the armoured armadillo cannot withstand the onslaught of the flames. All of these animals have **lost their homes**. Like Bishop, the owls are **displaced** and must travel to find somewhere new to settle. The 'whirling' nature of their flight conveys their panic and distress.

On a deeper level Bishop **could be writing about poetry itself**, which is after all a '*pretty, dreamlike mimicry*' of the real world. Is Bishop criticising her own act of writing poetry as a pale reflection of reality, ultimately as powerless to change things as the tiny rabbit? What good can poetry do in the face of violence and injustice? Perhaps the poet sees herself in the armadillo; powerless, without a home and futilely railing against things she cannot change? Is there a more positive alternative interpretation for the ending of the poem?

Imagery

Images of the **balloons, nature and fire** dominate the poem. **Bishop uses adjectives and similes to bring her descriptions alive**: the balloons are like 'hearts' and 'stars', and the smashed balloon is like an 'egg of fire'. As the fire intensifies though, the descriptions become more straightforward, **heightening the immediacy and tension**. Where water has been a central image in Bishop's poems before, fire is the key image here. Perhaps compare Bishop's use of fire here with her use of water in 'The Bight' and 'At the Fishhouses'.

Language and form

The final stanza's **more formal and archaic language** raises the plight of the animals above mere description and hints that the poem's theme has more far-reaching and profound connotations than just a protest against this one traditional custom. It sounds like a **different speaker** is narrating the final lines, and the **two exclamation marks suggest powerful emotion**, for example frustration, anger or despair.

Only this poem and 'The Prodigal' so far have used **regular stanzas**. There are ten quatrains (four-line stanzas) with the last stanza **emphasised** by the use of italics. Every second and fourth line rhyme within each stanza. Why, do you think, does the poet use a stricter, more rigorous structure? Is it perhaps to **contain and shape a very emotional and upsetting experience**? Is it more difficult to write freely about upsetting things? The rhyming scheme falters slightly in stanza 6. Interestingly this is the point at which the fire balloon crashes causing havoc. Does the poet's lack of true rhyme in this stanza ('fell' / 'fire' / 'house' / 'pair') reflect the shock of what she has witnessed?

Questions

1	What information does the poet give us about the setting of this poem?
2	What is the purpose of the fire balloons?
3	How are the balloons described in the first four stanzas? Comment on the imagery used in these descriptions.
4	Where does the poet's tone change and why does this change occur?
5	What consequences do the fire balloons have for the forest and the animals who inhabit it?
6	What, do you think, is the poet saying in the final stanza of the poem? How is this stanza different to the ones before?
7	Why, do you think, did the poet choose 'The Armadillo' as the title of the poem? Choose an alternative title and justify your choice with reference to the poem.
8	In terms of symbols, what might the fire balloons and the forest creatures represent?
9	Identify the sound effects Bishop uses in the poem. List examples and comment on their effect.
10	Why might the last stanza be italicised? Is there a new speaker here? Whose voice might this be and what is their position on the events that have unfolded?
11	*Groupwork* In pairs, choose another poem where Bishop uses an animal as a central image, and compare it to this one.
12	How did you feel as you read this poem; what was your overall reaction to it?
13	Write a newspaper article for a tabloid or broadsheet newspaper reporting on the forest fire.

Sestina

September rain falls on the house.
In the failing light, the old grandmother
sits in the kitchen with the child
beside the Little Marvel Stove,
reading the jokes from the almanac,   5
laughing and talking to hide her tears.

She thinks that her equinoctial tears
and the rain that beats on the roof of the house
were both foretold by the almanac,
but only known to a grandmother.   10
The iron kettle sings on the stove.
She cuts some bread and says to the child,

It's time for tea now; but the child
is watching the teakettle's small hard tears
dance like mad on the hot black stove,   15
the way the rain must dance on the house.
Tidying up, the old grandmother
hangs up the clever almanac

on its string. Bird-like, the almanac
hovers half open above the child,   20
hovers above the old grandmother
and her teacup full of dark brown tears.
She shivers and says she thinks the house
feels chilly, and puts more wood in the stove.

It was to be, says the Marvel Stove.   25
I know what I know, says the almanac.
With crayons the child draws a rigid house
and a winding pathway. Then the child
puts in a man with buttons like tears
and shows it proudly to the grandmother.   30

But secretly, while the grandmother
busies herself about the stove,
the little moons fall down like tears
from between the pages of the almanac
into the flower bed the child   35
has carefully placed in the front of the house.

Time to plant tears, says the almanac.
The grandmother sings to the marvellous stove
and the child draws another inscrutable house.

Glossary

Title	*Sestina*: a poetic form (see below)
4	*Little Marvel Stove*: a brand of solid-fuel stove
5	*almanac*: a calendar that also forecasts the weather and other events on the basis of astrological calculations. For this reason, it was sometimes thought to have magic powers. It also contains jokes
7	*equinoctial*: at the time of the autumn equinox
39	*inscrutable*: cannot be understood

Guidelines

From *Questions of Travel* (1965), and set in Nova Scotia, this is **one of the first poems Bishop wrote exploring her difficult childhood directly**, although she was over fifty when she wrote it. The child deals with past loss as she draws a picture of a house and garden in her grandmother's kitchen, but the **seeds of grief are growing**, and the little girl will have more sadness.

> ### Sestina form
>
> A sestina is an old-fashioned poetic form consisting of six unrhymed sestets and a seventh stanza of three lines, called an envoy. The same six words end the lines of each stanza, but in a different order each time – 'house', 'grandmother', 'child', 'stove', 'almanac' and 'tears'. The last word in each stanza becomes the end word of the first line in the next. The envoy uses all six words.

Art therapy today is a recognised way to help children with trauma. The child in the poem uses drawing to express what she has lost and what she longs for – a father and a stable home. The **rigid and difficult structure** of a sestina is **reminiscent of a nursery rhyme in its repetition**, but the apparent simplicity is deceptive, and requires great skill to accomplish. **The strictness of the form allows Bishop to explore her grief in a contained and manageable way.** Bishop uses a controlled form in a similar way in 'The Armadillo'.

Commentary

Stanza 1

On the surface a cosy scene is described: grandmother and child sit beside the warm stove reading and laughing at jokes from the almanac. Beneath this seemingly happy activity though, there is pain and loss. There is no mother or father. It is raining and the light is fading. The grandmother is 'laughing and talking to hide her tears'. All is not well.

Stanza 2

The child believes the almanac has not only foretold the equinox, but the rain and the grandmother's tears also (she has not been successful in hiding them from the child). In the child's mind the grandmother is the only one who knows what the almanac has foretold. She is at the **centre of this child's world** and is the **holder of all knowledge**. Do you think this is typical of how young children see the adults who are central in their lives? **Comforting everyday routines** soften the sadness: the kettle 'sings' and food is prepared – 'She cuts some bread'. There is a **tension** in the poem **between what is happening on the surface**, and **the emotions which bubble underneath**.

Stanza 3

The sorrow grows despite the grandmother's efforts at cosy domesticity: 'It's time for tea now;' the child, 'watching the teakettle's small hard tears', is well aware of the sorrow that pervades the house. The stove that seemed so cute and toy-like earlier is now menacing, and the 'mad' dance of the kettle's tears might remind us that Bishop's mother had been committed to a mental institution. Outside too a **rain of tears** beats upon the house. **The grandmother's attempts to tidy up reflect the poet's own attempt to impose a rigid order onto this poem**, in an effort to cope with the difficulty of writing about that time. Is imposing order and routine a typical way to cope with difficult circumstances in life?

Stanza 4

The almanac is now hanging open above the child as she draws; it is compared to a bird. The grandmother is clearly upset, shivering with a 'teacup full of dark brown tears', but she perseveres in her efforts to make the house as cheerful and cosy as she can: 'puts more wood in the stove'. Bishop's maternal grandmother was clearly a loving and nurturing presence for the poet, and we know that Bishop was hugely distressed when her deceased father's parents came and abruptly took her away from Nova Scotia.

Stanza 5

The **personification of the household objects** intensifies as they speak to the child: 'It was to be', says the Marvel Stove', as if the loss of both parents was inevitable. But the almanac, which later sheds tears, answers 'I know what I know', is this grief? In a heart-breaking image the child draws what so many children draw – a house and garden and 'a man with buttons like tears'. This man is most likely **the poet's father, a man she never knew**. He died when she was an infant, the event which triggered her mother's breakdown.

Stanza 6

Even as a child Bishop clearly had the great imagination we see in her poetry. As her grandmother tidies, she draws a flower bed into her picture and fantasises that moons from the almanac drop 'like tears' into it, as if they are watering it. Nature has always been central to Bishop's work. Perhaps the flowerbed symbolises Bishop's future, her growth.

Stanza 7

The almanac says 'Time to plant tears', implying that more heartbreak and loss may be in store. The child will be ripped from this loving home, but **these experiences will grow into poetry**, which will be Bishop's life. The child continues to create – 'draws another inscrutable house', just as Bishop will continue to create art in the form of literature and painting (she was also a gifted artist). The final image gives some comfort: 'The grandmother sings to the marvellous stove'. The mood has lifted and all is well, for now.

Themes

Childhood, family and loss are central themes. The child acts as children do, drawing pictures and imagining that even household objects come to life, but in many ways the losses suffered by this family have affected the child. The tear-shaped buttons on the man she draws, and her understanding that her grandmother is grieving, convey this. There is a sense too that **the sorrow Bishop endured could not be avoided**. The **inevitability of death and grief** is apparent here: 'It was to be'. The **comforting power of art and creativity** lift the poem from complete pessimism and melancholy. Music and art comfort the grandmother and the little girl: 'The grandmother sings to the marvellous stove / and the child draws another inscrutable house.'

Imagery

Personification is used extensively in the poem. A **child's imaginary inner world brings everyday domestic objects to life**: the almanac is 'clever', the kettle sings and the stove speaks. **Pathetic fallacy**, where the weather mirrors the mood of the poem, is used effectively here too: the rain that beats upon the house reflects the **tears that seem to fall from everywhere** in the poem. The kettle, the tea, the grandmother and even the buttons of the man the child has drawn are tear-shaped. This creates an **overwhelming feeling of sorrow**.

Language and form

The language is simple and repetitive with an almost staccato rhythm, giving the poem **a deceptive air of simplicity** which sounds childlike. Although the child is clearly Bishop, **the poet distances herself from the scene**: 'the old grandmother', 'the child', 'a man'. The poet possibly needs to create this distance in order to cope with the trauma she's undergone while still being honest and objective. The repetition also builds in such a way that the reader comes to expect the words 'grandmother', 'child', 'stove', 'tears' etc. as the stanzas progress, emphasising the idea of inevitability discussed in 'Imagery' above, but also **giving comfort through steady rhythm**.

Questions

1	This poem was originally entitled 'Early Sorrow'. Why, do you think, was this title chosen and then replaced with 'Sestina' by the poet?
2	What is the tone of this poem? Does it change anywhere? Trace the tone through the poem.
3	The world described by Bishop is seen through the eyes of a young child. Has Bishop created this world effectively? What details worked particularly well to achieve this?
4	Describe the relationship between the two central figures in the poem.
5	Look at the six main words around which the poem is constructed. What meaning or symbolism might each have?
6	Recreate the child's drawing as a simple sketch and write a note explaining what you think it means for the poet.
7	Did you think that the sestina structure of the poem added to its meaning in any way? Why, do you think, did Bishop use this form?
8	This is one of Bishop's most revealing poems. What do you feel you have learned about the poet?
9	What effect does the use of personification have on the poem?
10	'... the child draws another inscrutable house.' What is your understanding of this line in the context of the poem as a whole?
11	Which character in the poem do you feel most sympathy for and why? Look closely at the language used around each character.
12	Write a diary entry where you explore a childhood memory.
13	Work with a partner to create a short dialogue between the grown-up child and her grandmother, where they look back on this time and discuss the issues raised in the poem.

Before you read

What poems or songs do you know that deal with the death of a child? How was this sensitive subject handled? For example, you may have studied 'Tich Miller' or 'Mid-Term Break' for your Junior Cycle.

First Death in Nova Scotia

In the cold, cold parlor
my mother laid out Arthur
beneath the chromographs:
Edward, Prince of Wales,
with Princess Alexandra,   5
and King George with Queen Mary.
Below them on the table
stood a stuffed loon
shot and stuffed by Uncle
Arthur, Arthur's father.   10

Since Uncle Arthur fired
a bullet into him,
he hadn't said a word.
He kept his own counsel
on his white, frozen lake,   15
the marble-topped table.
His breast was deep and white,
cold and caressable;
his eyes were red glass,
much to be desired.   20

"Come," said my mother,
"Come and say good-bye
to your little cousin Arthur."
I was lifted up and given
one lily of the valley   25
to put in Arthur's hand.
Arthur's coffin was
a little frosted cake,
and the red-eyed loon eyed it
from his white, frozen lake.   30

Arthur was very small.
He was all white, like a doll
that hadn't been painted yet.
Jack Frost had started to paint him
the way he always painted   35
the Maple Leaf (Forever).

He had just begun on his hair,
a few red strokes, and then
Jack Frost had dropped the brush
and left him white, forever.   40

The gracious royal couples
were warm in red and ermine;
their feet were well wrapped up
in the ladies' ermine trains.
They invited Arthur to be   45
the smallest page at court.
But how could Arthur go,
clutching his tiny lily,
with his eyes shut up so tight
and the roads deep in snow?   50

Glossary

1	*parlor*: a room for receiving guests
3	*chromographs*: coloured copies of pictures
4	*Edward*: a member of the British royal family (1841–1910)
5	*Alexandra*: Edward's wife
6	*King George*: King George V, also a British royal (1865–1936)
6	*Queen Mary*: wife of King George
8	*loon*: a species of water bird which has a crest and dives for food
14	*he kept his own counsel*: he kept his advice and opinions to himself
18	*caressable*: invites touch, you would want to caress it
25	*lily of the valley*: a fragrant winter plant with small white bell-like flowers
28	*frosted*: covered with icing
36	*Maple Leaf*: national symbol of Canada
36	*Forever*: refers to Canada's national anthem at the time, 'Maple Leaf Forever'
44	*ermine train*: long trailing back on a robe or dress trimmed with the fur of an ermine (a white stoat), and worn by royalty
46	*page*: a young boy servant
46	*at court*: in a palace

Guidelines

From *Questions of Travel* (1965). Psychoanalysis had helped Bishop deal with childhood issues such as those raised in 'Sestina'. In this poem, also set in Nova Scotia, Bishop writes about the death of her cousin Arthur. The poet was almost four at the time, and the poem is **written from the perspective of a child**, but this is coloured by an adult's retrospective interpretation.

As in 'Sestina', **ordinary objects in the house take on significance for the child,** and the poem contains a rare direct reference to Bishop's mother.

Nova Scotia.

Commentary

Stanza 1

The poet's mother has laid out her cousin Arthur in the 'cold, cold parlor'. The **repetition** here emphasises the atmosphere of grief and death that pervades the scene: Arthur is dead, as is the loon which sits stuffed on the table. Family is a central characteristic of the objects described, the pictures of the British royal family and the poet's; the poet's mother, her deceased cousin and his father are all mentioned. (Cousin Arthur's real name was Frank.)

Stanza 2

The loon is depicted as if it is a witness to the scene but keeps quiet out of discretion: 'Since Uncle Arthur fired / a bullet into him, / he hadn't said a word. / He kept his own counsel'. There is a dry if **macabre wit** to this. The loon is described in more detail, it is set on a white marble table resembling an ice-covered lake, and the white feathers of its breast are 'cold and caressable', its eyes of red glass are 'much to be desired'. The speaker seems fascinated with this stuffed bird and longs to touch it. In a macabre association, the body of her cousin is displayed as if it is an ornament, just like the loon.

Stanza 3

As Bishop's mother lifts her up to 'say good-bye' to her cousin, Bishop places the delicate white flower in his hands and notices how pretty his coffin looks; it reminds her of an iced cake, probably referencing the satiny lining the coffin may have had, and the carved painted white wood it was made of. The loon seems to be as impressed by it as the child is, he 'eyed it / from his white, frozen lake'.

Stanza 4

Bishop now goes on to give us a more detailed account of Arthur in his coffin. His tiny stature makes him seem doll-like to her, a comparison that is re-enforced for Bishop by how pale he is, 'all white, like a doll / that hadn't been painted yet.' **In trying to make sense of the scene, the child refers to a familiar image from nature**, the coating of winter frost on leaves: 'Jack Frost had started to paint him'. Using nature to represent and describe aspects of life and death is a technique Bishop uses extensively in her poetry.

Stanza 5

The child now imagines a fairy-tale ending for little Arthur, where the royals in the pictures from stanza 1 welcome him into their gracious world as a page: 'They invited Arthur to be / the smallest page at court', but the child wonders how he could ever get there, given that he seems to be sleeping, and 'the roads [are] deep in snow'. The poem ends on a note of innocent confusion.

Themes

Strong themes in this poem include **death, family and childhood**, and again **the idea of home** surfaces. Bishop has written another biographical poem, a very revealing one. Her family clearly experienced a huge amount of loss and deep sorrow. **Note that she is beginning to name relatives** – 'Arthur', 'Uncle Arthur', 'My mother'. This is a **step towards a more intimate and confessional style**, compared to the distance created in poems like 'Sestina', where the characters are 'The child' and 'The grandmother'. The child seems so comfortable in this home and with the objects around her, compared to her experience 'In the Waiting Room', where the more formal world of Massachusetts is patently unsettling for her.

Making sense of the world through description and unusual comparisons is something Bishop clearly began doing while young, and something she continued to do in her work. In this way, **knowledge and the creation of knowledge** is also a theme (as in 'The Bight'). There is a **tension between what the child knows and does not know**. On the surface it would seem that the child doesn't understand the finality of death, but if we examine the language closely we see there is a **deeper knowledge at play** in words such as 'cold', 'laid out', 'shot', 'white', 'frozen' and 'forever' which hints that the child subconsciously knows more about death than she realises.

The loon

The loon is the official bird of the province of Ontario and is considered a symbol of solitude in this region. It is now a protected species in many areas including the nature reserve of Abraham Lake in Nova Scotia, where this poem is set.

Jack Frost

Jack Frost is the personification of winter in folklore, often depicted as a mischievous, impish figure who brings snow, sleet and ice and is responsible for the pretty intricate lace-like patterns of frost on leaves, windows, etc.

Cousin Arthur

Cousin Arthur's real name was Frank. Bishop renames a relative in her poem 'In the Waiting Room' also — 'Aunt Consuelo' was in fact her Aunt Florence. Even in her most biographical poems, Bishop's need for privacy and the difficulty she had dealing with her traumatic childhood means she changes these factual details. Arthur of course was a famous king of England, according to legend, which fits Bishop's fantasy of her dead cousin being a page at the court of this king.

Imagery

As in the previous poem, **weather mirrors mood** extensively. The **snow and ice outside are brought into the room**, as the child imagines Jack Frost painting young Arthur white in death. **Colour is used symbolically**, white linking death with purity and innocence, and red suggesting death and danger: the loon's eyes are red while Arthur's hair has 'a few red strokes'. Both the loon and Arthur have died before their time.

There is a **surreal quality to the imagery as inanimate objects** – chromographs, stuffed bird – seem to **partake in the drama**. The creativity of a child's inner world is made apparent.

Lily of the valley.

Language and form

The **unusual juxtapositions** in the poem create a 'stream of consciousness' style, which effectively echoes how a child makes **seemingly random connections** to help make sense of what isn't yet understood. These include describing the coffin as if it is an iced confection, and the comparison of Arthur's deathly pallor to a frosted 'Maple Leaf'. The ending is ambiguous; will Arthur have a happy ever-after? The child thinks so, but sees obstacles to this happy ending. As in 'Sestina', the language is filled with **short lines and repetition**, particularly of key images, **which creates a childlike effect in the tone**.

There are five stanzas of ten lines each and although there are occasional rhymes, there is no regular rhyming scheme. Perhaps Bishop wants to keep the tone informal and conversational. The use of trimeter (three-stressed lines) as the metre of the poem adds to the naturalness of the voice used: 'He was áll whíte, like a dóll'.

The **increasing regularity of form and structure** in Bishop's poetry is something you may have noticed as your study of her work progresses. How might you explain this?

Questions

1	Why, do you think, does the poet use the phrase 'First Death' in the title?
2	List the objects the speaker notices in the parlour. What atmosphere does this description create? What might these objects symbolise?
3	What impressions do you form of the poet's mother, cousin and uncle from the poem?
4	Find examples of how the colours red and white are used in the poem. List and analyse the examples you find, mentioning what you think the meaning attached to them might be.
5	Do you think the poem effectively conveys how a young child might seek to make sense of death? Explain, giving examples.
6	What is the effect of ending the poem on a question, and of the long rhyme at the end? How do these create a sense of closure?
7	Which word best describes the speaker in the poem and why: naïve, confused, imaginative?
8	Why, do you think, does the child create her fantasy for Arthur at the end of the poem? Explain what this fantasy is in your answer.
9	Write about one of the following: the sound effects in the poem OR the imagery in the poem.
10	Compare and contrast this poem to 'Sestina'.
11	How did you respond to this poem? Was it strange, sad, amusing or perhaps something else? Discuss in pairs or groups.
12	How does the poet use repetition in the poem and what is the effect of this?
13	Write Bishop's mother's diary entry for the day described in the poem.
14	Take a memorable event from your childhood and turn it into a fairy tale.

Before you read

Having read that the title is 'Filling Station', describe the setting that comes to mind. Try to give as much detail as possible.

Filling Station

Oh, but it is dirty!
– this little filling station,
oil-soaked, oil-permeated
to a disturbing, over-all
black translucency.   5
Be careful with that match!

Father wears a dirty,
oil-soaked monkey suit
that cuts him under the arms,
and several quick and saucy   10
and greasy sons assist him
(it's a family filling station),
all quite thoroughly dirty.

Do they live in the station?
It has a cement porch   15
behind the pumps, and on it
a set of crushed and grease-
impregnated wickerwork;
on the wicker sofa
a dirty dog, quite comfy.   20

Some comic books provide
the only note of color –
of certain color. They lie
upon a big dim doily
draping a taboret   25
(part of the set), beside
a big hirsute begonia.

Why the extraneous plant?
Why the taboret?
Why, oh why, the doily?   30
(Embroidered in daisy stitch
with marguerites, I think,
and heavy with gray crochet.)

Somebody embroidered the doily.
Somebody waters the plant,   35
or oils it, maybe. Somebody
arranges the rows of cans
so that they softly say:
ESSO–SO–SO–SO
to high-strung automobiles.   40
Somebody loves us all.

Glossary

3	*oil-permeated*: oil has completely soaked into everything
5	*translucency*: an almost transparent shine
8	*monkey suit*: overalls
10	*saucy*: flirtatious in a cheeky or playful way
24	*doily*: lace-like napkin often placed under plants
25	*taboret*: a stool without a back or arms
27	*hirsute*: hairy
27	*begonia*: a plant with large, blousy flowers
28	*extraneous*: unnecessary, extra, not required
32	*marguerites*: daisies
33	*crochet*: a lacy form of knitting using a small hook
39	*so-so-so*: Bishop said this was a phrase used to calm horses

Guidelines

From *Questions of Travel* (1965), in this poem we see a **more fun-loving, humorous side** to Bishop. This is something she had hinted at in earlier poems but **this detailed description of a petrol station is particularly playful**, albeit with a poignant message at the end. The poem is set in California where 'gas stations' were becoming an everyday sight. In an allegorical sense, the **filling station may represent the world in general**, and the **importance of home and family as the key to making a disordered and sometimes unpleasant world bearable**.

Commentary

Stanza 1
Bishop speaks as an observer trying to make sense of the strange sights which greet her at the filling station. The tone here seems shocked on the surface, but perhaps the speaker is quite enjoying the grime that covers everything: 'Oh, but it is dirty! / – this little filling station'. The use of 'little' here gives the scene a cosy 'cuteness' and sounds affectionate. Everything appears soaked in oil, and although the speaker says this is 'disturbing', she throws in a jokey, 'Be careful with that match!'

Stanza 2
The poet goes on to describe the men who work there in equally playful terms. It belongs to a father and his sons: 'it's a family filling station'. These men seem happy in their work, the father a little overweight (his overalls cut him 'under the arms'), and the sons are 'quick and saucy' as they assist him. They are 'all quite thoroughly dirty', but the speaker seems to enjoy the energy and bustle of the scene.

Stanza 3
The poet is incredulous as she questions the idea that they live in the station, but concludes they must when she sees the evidence: 'grease- / impregnated wickerwork / … / a dirty dog, quite comfy'. The inhabitants seem quite at home in their grimy environment. The alliterative 'd's of 'dirty dog' sound lively and playful here.

Stanza 4
The only true colour she can see that isn't darkened by an oily layer is provided by some 'comic books'. Perhaps there's a younger child somewhere or perhaps the saucy sons like to amuse themselves with these. The effect is cheerful and devil-may-care. The focus becomes more magnified now as Bishop notices some unlikely

objects. The comics lie on 'a big dim doily / draping a taboret / (part of the set), beside / a big hirsute begonia'. These decorative and inessential items seem at odds with the petrol pumps, overall-clad men and the grease that permeates the filling station. The parenthesis not only shows the **poet's fine eye for detail**, but continues the **good-natured feeling of fun** in the poet's faux horror at what she sees – note the continued alliteration on 'd'.

Stanza 5

The poet pauses to reflect on the objects she has noticed in the last stanza. The repetition of 'why' emphasises her incredulity. Why would anyone bother to add these feminine and decorative touches to this busy, dirty place of work? Someone has even gone to the bother of embroidering daisies onto the doily.

Stanza 6

In this touching stanza, Bishop answers the questions she has posed in the previous one. Although the mother is absent from the scene in person, Bishop notices thoughtful touches everywhere. The plant is watered, the doily was embroidered, and the cans arranged uniformly. Bishop jokes that the plant might be oiled rather than watered, and admires the calming sound spelled out by the arrangement of the oil cans. She realises these decorative touches have been executed by an unseen presence in the filling station, a mother-figure, the 'Somebody' who 'loves us all'.

Themes

Family, the **effect of a mother's love** and the **importance of home** are themes in this poem. It is to the poet's credit that she remains very upbeat and cheerful, considering she grew up without her own parents around her, and felt the lack of a mother and a stable home very strongly. It is particularly touching when she asserts 'Somebody loves us all'. The 'us' here includes the speaker, and **perhaps Bishop felt ready to accept that her mother still loved her**, despite her inability to cope with Bishop's father's death and her mother's own subsequent nervous breakdown.

Language and imagery

The punctuation of the poem includes **exclamation and question marks which heighten the emotional reaction the speaker** has to what she notices about the filling station. The language is **deceptively simple and accessible**, and the poem is open to different interpretations. Is it about the presence of a mother making life happy, or is that mother absent and her maternal touches are fading beneath the grime? Is the final line positive and affirming, or sarcastic? The reader must decide.

There is a **contrast** within the imagery; the industrial masculine images of the pumps, the father and sons, cement and oil cans provide a foil for the traditionally feminine touches of the embroidered doily, taboret and plant. What does the covering of oil and grime over everything represent, and why might the comics be of interest? The presence of the contentedly curled up dog adds to the domesticity of this scene.

Exam-Style Questions

Understanding the poem

1. Do you think the poet likes or dislikes what she sees in the filling station? Why?

2. Describe the family who lives there.

3. Look at the sibilance (repetition of 's' sounds) in stanza 2 and comment on the effect of this.

4. Why do the decorative touches (the plant, doily, etc.) puzzle the speaker so much?

5. Comment on the phrase 'high-strung automobiles' in the last stanza.

6. 'Somebody loves us all.' What does Bishop mean here? Who is that 'Somebody'? Explain.

Thinking about the poem

1. What word best describes the speaker's personality revealed here and why: nosy, affectionate, playful, sad?

2. Do you agree that the absence of a mother in her own childhood makes Bishop more likely to notice a mother's presence elsewhere? Discuss with reference to this and other poems by Bishop.

3. Which of the following statements best sums up the theme of this poem for you?
   ■ Everybody is loved by somebody.   ■ Don't judge by first impressions.   ■ Life is full of surprises.

4. Would you agree that this poem is deceptively casual? Explain your answer.

5. Do you think the final line is a fitting and effective ending to the poem? Explain your answer.

6. Do you agree with the positive, upbeat interpretation of the poem in the commentary or is there another way to read the poem? Perhaps the speaker really is disgusted by what she sees? What do you think?

Imagining

1. Is this Bishop's most positive poem? Discuss this in groups and feed back your ideas to the class.

2. In general, what touches do you think a mother-figure brings to a home? Is this an outdated idea these days, in your opinion?

SNAPSHOT

- Vivid description
- Curiosity of speaker
- Conversational, playful tone
- Looks beyond the surface of things
- Family and home are important themes
- Personality of poet is revealed
- Disapproval and admiration

Before you read

What do people do to
pass the time in
waiting rooms? What
thoughts and feelings
might you have as you
sit waiting in one?

In the Waiting Room

In Worcester, Massachusetts,
I went with Aunt Consuelo
to keep her dentist's appointment
and sat and waited for her
in the dentist's waiting room.   5
It was winter. It got dark
early. The waiting room
was full of grown-up people,
arctics and overcoats,
lamps and magazines.   10
My aunt was inside
what seemed like a long time
and while I waited I read
the *National Geographic*
(I could read) and carefully   15
studied the photographs:
the inside of a volcano,
black, and full of ashes;
then it was spilling over
in rivulets of fire.   20
Osa and Martin Johnson
dressed in riding breeches,
laced boots, and pith helmets.
A dead man slung on a pole
– "Long Pig," the caption said.   25
Babies with pointed heads
wound round and round with string;
black, naked women with necks
wound round and round with wire
like the necks of light bulbs.   30
Their breasts were horrifying.
I read it right straight through.
I was too shy to stop.
And then I looked at the cover:
the yellow margins, the date.   35

Suddenly, from inside,
came an *oh!* of pain
– Aunt Consuelo's voice –
not very loud or long.
I wasn't at all surprised;   40
even then I knew she was
a foolish, timid woman.
I might have been embarrassed,
but wasn't. What took *me*
completely by surprise   45
was that it was me:
my voice, in my mouth.
Without thinking at all
I was my foolish aunt,
I – we – were falling, falling,   50
our eyes glued to the cover
of the *National Geographic*,
February, 1918.

I said to myself: three days
and you'll be seven years old.   55
I was saying it to stop
the sensation of falling off
the round, turning world
into cold, blue-black space.
But I felt: you are an *I*,   60
you are an *Elizabeth*,
you are one of *them*.
Why should you be one, too?
I scarcely dared to look
to see what it was I was.   65
I gave a sidelong glance
– I couldn't look any higher –
at shadowy gray knees,
trousers and skirts and boots
and different pairs of hands   70
lying under the lamps.
I knew that nothing stranger
had ever happened, that nothing
stranger could ever happen.
Why should I be my aunt,   75
or me, or anyone?
What similarities –
boots, hands, the family voice
I felt in my throat, or even

the *National Geographic*   80
and those awful hanging breasts –
held us all together
or made us all just one?
How – I didn't know any
word for it – how "unlikely" . . .   85
How had I come to be here,
like them, and overhear
a cry of pain that could have
got loud and worse but hadn't?

The waiting room was bright   90
and too hot. It was sliding
beneath a big black wave,
another, and another.

Then I was back in it.
The War was on. Outside,   95
in Worcester, Massachusetts,
were night and slush and cold,
and it was still the fifth
of February, 1918.

Glossary

1	*Worcester, Massachusetts*: where Bishop lived with her paternal grandparents, after being taken from Nova Scotia
9	*arctics*: overshoes to protect one's shoes from snow and rain
14	*National Geographic*: magazine about different places and peoples, famous for its photography
20	*rivulets*: small streams
21	*Osa and Martin Johnson*: a husband and wife explorer team
22	*riding breeches*: short tight trousers worn for horse riding
23	*pith helmets*: helmets used to protect against strong sun, often worn by explorers
25	*'Long Pig'*: name for a human who is to be eaten by cannibals
95	*The War*: First World War

Guidelines

This is the first poem in Bishop's last collection *Geography III* (1976). The poet remembers a seminal experience at six years old when she was taken to the dentist with her Aunt Florence (called Consuelo here). She disliked Worcester and the formal, distant ways of the family whom she felt had 'kidnapped' her from Nova Scotia. As she looks at photographs in a magazine she becomes **aware of her individuality, but also that she is part of a family and part of the female gender**. It is an important **epiphany** (sudden realisation), yet a **disorienting experience** for her.

Commentary

Stanza 1

The poet remembers how as a six-year-old she waited for her aunt at the dentist. It is winter and the locals are dressed appropriately for the weather. She seems to be the only child: 'The waiting room / was full of grown-up people'. Due to the long wait, Bishop reads and looks at the photographs in a *National Geographic* magazine, noting an erupting volcano; the image creates a sense of **foreboding** and the **atmosphere is tense**. She notices an explorer couple in their 'riding breeches, / laced boots, and pith helmets'. As usual **Bishop's eye for detail is precise**. The next image is a shocking one, a dead man hung on a pole ready to be roasted and eaten by a cannibal tribe. The tribe look very strange to the child; 'Babies with pointed heads / wound round and round with string' refers to a custom of binding babies' heads with string to force them to grow into a point. 'Black, naked women with necks / wound round and round with wire' also look strange to Bishop.

Some tribes consider long necks on women to be desirable so women have metal rings wound around their necks to extend them. These customs are very alien to the child and shock her; these people look so different to the conservatively dressed adults in the waiting room. The nakedness of the women mortifies her: 'Their breasts were horrifying.' She continues reading then stares at the cover to hide her shame.

> *National Geographic*
>
> **This is the official magazine of the National Geographic Society, first published in 1888, which brought to its readers photography and articles from all over the world, especially concerning nature and anthropology. In those days many parts of the world were still unexplored and readers were fascinated by information and images from other lands and cultures. The magazine is still published and read around the world today.**

Stanzas 2 and 3

She hears a timid cry of pain and thinks it is her aunt whom she has little regard for and is happy to ignore – 'I knew she was / a foolish, timid woman', then has the disconcerting realisation that it is her own 'oh!' she has heard in her aunt's voice, and she realises how much they sound alike. She is struck by this: 'I was my foolish aunt'. She feels faint; this strange moment has unsettled her: 'I – we – were falling, falling'. She tries to steady herself by staring at the magazine cover, noting the date 'February, 1918'. To try and compose herself further she focuses on concrete truths: 'three days / and you'll be seven years old. / I was saying it to stop / the sensation of falling off / the round, turning world'. It is a **moment of epiphany** for the poet as she realises that she is an individual: 'you are an *I*, / you are an *Elizabeth*'. She also realises that she is a women just like her aunt, just like those strange naked women in the magazine: 'you are one of *them*'. She wonders how this could be – '*Why* should you be one, too?' and glances around at the sedate, formally dressed occupants of the waiting room, too nervous to look above their knees. 'nothing stranger / had ever happened' – the moment we realise our individuality is a step on the road to adulthood, and the poet realises how important this moment is.

Bishop **continues to formulate questions**, wondering now about the arbitrary nature of where and what we are born into; that she should be from this repressed society while these tribal women endure painful rituals to be more beautiful is so strange. **She is amazed that humans are the same and yet so different**: 'What similarities / … held us all together / or made us all just one?' **The fact that everyone is an individual yet part of a family, and then a society and culture, is a revelation to her**. Bishop is amazed that she was there at that exact moment to see those photographs and then come to these conclusions and discoveries: 'how "unlikely". . . / How had I come to be here'.

Stanzas 4 and 5

The poet feels dizzy as if she is drowning; she seems to panic, 'sliding / beneath a big black wave, / another, and another'.

She is suddenly okay again; by focusing on the facts of the present she grounds herself: 'The War was on', 'night and slush and cold', 'the fifth / of February, 1918'. However, she is forever changed by a new knowledge that will carry her into adulthood. Mentioning the war shows an awareness of the bigger world outside her childhood concerns, and is a pessimistic note on which to end the poem.

Themes

Childhood and family are themes here. Just as in 'Sestina' and 'First Death in Nova Scotia', Bishop writes **candidly**, using childhood memories to explore incidents from her past. This poem goes beyond her personal life though, to explore **universal themes of individuality, societal customs and traditions, belonging and otherness**. This child who was so shocked by the magazine's content will go on to love travel and write of her experiences of different places and cultures.

The stuffy world of Worcester, Massachusetts is **symbolised by the waiting room** where the 'grown-up people' sit silently, dressed head-to-toe in sensible weather-proof clothes: 'arctics and overcoats', 'shadowy gray knees / trousers and skirts and boots'. This is a **massive contrast to the vibrancy and 'otherness' of the wider world beyond**, where volcanoes erupt, cannibals feast, adventurers explore, and naked women and babies change their shape with wire.

Imagery

Vivid description brings the waiting room and the images in the magazine to life for the reader. Bishop creates setting meticulously, **a sense of time and place**, so that the poem is **grounded in reality** and has a cinematic quality to it. In the first three stanzas the imagery is quite straightforward; the only simile is the comparison between the women's necks wound with wire and 'the necks of light bulbs'. The **images become more surreal, reflecting the disorientation Bishop feels**: 'round, turning world / into cold, blue-black space.'

Images of violence and death abound: the erupting volcano, the dead man about to be eaten, the mutilation of babies and women with wire and string. These **contrast sharply with the quiet sedate waiting room** where the poet is embarrassed to see pictures of breasts, and where a small cry of pain might be embarrassing. The images of slush, darkness and war in the final stanza are bleak and pessimistic. These may foreshadow the depression, alcoholism and ill-health that would beset Bishop as she entered adulthood.

Language and form

Full of **questions** and **short, clear descriptions**, the language gives **the effect of a child's perspective**, but the **older, wiser voice of Bishop**, now in her fifties, **informs these observations**. The **use of dashes** in stanza 2 onwards **conveys the shock and disorientation** the speaker feels as she thinks about culture, individuality and gender: 'Aunt Consuelo's voice', 'I – we – were falling', 'How – I didn't know any / word for it – how "unlikely"'.

Returning to a familiar structure, Bishop writes in long irregular unrhymed stanzas, with two shorter stanzas completing the poem. The statement of where and when the speaker is, and what is going on in the world, gives the poem a sense of closure: 'Then I was back in it. / The War was on.' The child has recovered her composure. Is she ready to face the world around her and the life ahead of her?

Questions

1	What is the atmosphere in the waiting room? What details in the poem convey this?
2	How does the waiting room contrast with the images in the magazine?
3	How does Bishop feel when she sees the pictures in *National Geographic*? Provide specific points and examples.
4	What, do you think, is the moment that triggers the child's epiphany in the poem?
5	Sum up the questions asked by the poet in the poem. Are they answered? Explain.
6	What images are used to show that the child feels she is losing her grip on reality?
7	How does the child try to recover her composure?
8	Compare this poem to the two others where Bishop recounts childhood memories. In which one, do you think, is she least happy? Why? ('Sestina' and 'First Death in Nova Scotia'.)
9	How might the title be symbolic in the poem? In groups or pairs discuss what a waiting room might represent.
10	Write an account of either the *theme* of this poem OR the *tone* of this poem.
11	Write the speaker's diary entry for that day.
12	Write a composition based on one of the photographs described by Bishop.

Exam-Preparation Questions

1   'I think geography comes first in my work.'
To what extent do you agree with Bishop's assessment of her poetry with regard to the poems you have studied by her?

2   'Elizabeth Bishop's narrative style and her use of conversational language make her poems accessible to the reader.'
Would you agree with this view?

3   Write the text of a presentation you would give entitled 'Elizabeth Bishop, Home and Away'. Here are some possible ideas you might use:
- Look at the theme of home in her poetry and how a sense of belonging or not belonging tends to be at the heart of many of her poems
- Bishop's poems concerning family or the lack of one (NB mother-figure)
- Poems about travel, unusual customs, different places and experiences

4   A critic once remarked on the 'deceptive casualness' of Bishop's poetry. Do you agree with this assessment of her work?

5   Bishop looks at ordinary things and sees the extraordinary, often finding beauty in what others might consider ugly or banal. Write about how this is true of the poems you have studied.

6   The natural world is celebrated and hugely symbolic in Bishop's poems. Write about how Bishop uses nature in her imagery and suggest what the different aspects of nature you've encountered in her work might symbolise.

7   Analyse the sound effects and references to music in Bishop's poetry.

8   'Her work is unusually personal and honest in its wit, perception and sensitivity.'
Do you agree with Randall Jarrell's description of Bishop's poetry?

9   Write about 'observation leading inward and onwards to epiphany' in the work of Elizabeth Bishop.

SNAPSHOT ELIZABETH BISHOP

- Highly descriptive
- Childhood trauma informs outlook and themes
- Nature closely observed and used symbolically
- Variety of forms; sonnets, sestina, lyric, narrative, etc.
- Highly original imagery, especially in terms of comparisons
- Sense of humour evident
- Celebration of the ordinary
- Situation closely observed which often leads to an epiphany
- Confessional poet

Sample Essay

'The poetry of Elizabeth Bishop appeals to the modern reader for many reasons.' Write an essay in which you outline the reasons why poems by Elizabeth Bishop have this appeal. (2002)

In my opinion the modern reader wants a poet with a lively, fresh voice and an original way of looking at the world, someone who isn't afraid to reveal themselves, but who has an ultimately positive and uplifting message for us. I feel Elizabeth Bishop is most definitely that poet. By creating vivid narratives using startling imagery, Bishop not only entertains but educates her audience with her thought-provoking and often wryly humorous poetry.

Introductory paragraph addresses question and defines terms, indicating areas that will be developed. Personal response clear by using 'I feel'

Aspects introduced in the opening paragraph are developed

'The Fish' is a vivid narrative where Bishop uses startlingly original imagery to convey a positive message. She conversationally recounts the tale of catching 'a tremendous fish', noticing that it has survived many battles before: 'from his lower lip / ... hung five old pieces of fish-line / … Like medals with their ribbons'. She uses a trio of adjectives as she describes this soldier-like, 'battered and venerable / and homely' fish, in a tone of admiration using unusual and amusing similes: 'his brown skin hung in strips / like ancient wallpaper, / … shapes like full-blown roses'. The assonance here adds to the lively sense of fascination. The more she notices about the creature the more the speaker's mood builds towards an elated epiphany: 'until everything / was rainbow, rainbow, rainbow!' This excited repetition engages the modern reader and leads up to the moment of decision: 'And I let the fish go.' The embattled, exhausted fish is given another chance at life and in this I think the fish represents Bishop herself. She had survived childhood grief, displacement and trauma, and struggles with her physical and mental health, including skin conditions, depression and alcoholism. I like to think that by letting the fish go free, Bishop is symbolically congratulating herself on being a survivor, and extending the message to us, that we all deserve another chance at life. This entertaining fable has taught us a valuable lesson and made us feel we know something of Bishop's personality.

Personal response continues

Opening of third paragraph links it with second

A very similar message is conveyed in 'The Prodigal', where the central character is an alcoholic swineherd living among the pigs he tends. He too gets another chance: 'it took him a long time / finally to make his mind up to go home'. Bishop teaches us that no matter how shameful or debased we have become, redemption is possible. The Prodigal lives in dire conditions – 'the floor was rotten; the sty / was plastered halfway up with glass-smooth dung'; but there is beauty and hope to be seen even here: 'the sunrise glazed the barnyard mud with red'. I find Bishop's original description and ability to see beauty in the most ugly or ordinary things refreshing and lively. Bishop had found herself in many embarrassing situations because of her drinking, and clearly identifies herself with the character of the Prodigal. Even though revealing this side of herself must have been painful for her, the poet can make us smile, for example describing the pigs contentedly sleeping cosily: 'The pigs stuck out their little feet and snored.' This reveals an ultimately optimistic personality and endears the modern reader to her work.

The 'modern reader' of the question is kept central to analysis

'This is the time of year / when almost every night / the frail, illegal fire balloons appear.' In 'The Armadillo', Bishop teaches us about the Brazilian custom of releasing fire balloons on St John's feast day, but goes further to warn about and criticise the terrible harm mankind inflicts on our environment. The balloons often crash to earth, described by Bishop in characteristically unusual and striking imagery: 'It splattered like an egg of fire / ... / The flame ran down.' She had admired the beauty of the lanterns, but upon witnessing the harm they inflict she is scathing in her criticism of them: '*Too pretty, dreamlike mimicry! / O falling fire and piercing cry / and panic*'. Her account of the suffering the forest creatures endure is what truly engages the modern reader's emotions: 'a baby rabbit jumped out, / *short*-eared... / So soft! – a handful of intangible ash'. The pair of owls whose nest has been destroyed, and the armadillo himself, rolled into a protective ball yet doomed to die, combine with the rabbit as startling symbols of the damage we needlessly inflict upon the natural world. So far all of these poems have used animals as central images to help the poet convey her message, in this case an environmental one. She loves nature and feels passionately about its preservation. I found I shared wholeheartedly her indignation and empathy.

Linking together the poems discussed so far

Personal engagement evident in closing sentence

In later poems Bishop revealed even more about her life, and dealt openly with painful childhood memories. 'Sestina', 'First Death in Nova Scotia' and 'In the Waiting Room' fall into this category. After reading these poems I felt I knew a lot about the poet and understood even more the messages of survival and determination her earlier poetry conveyed. In 'Sestina', Bishop uses this rigid and complex form to explore her childhood confusion at the grief and loss her family had suffered. Bishop's father died when she was an infant and while still a young child her mother was committed to a mental institution, where she was to die without the poet ever seeing her again. Images of tears pervade the poem, but Bishop does create a quietly playful element with the almost cartoon-like personification of domestic objects: 'the child / is watching the teakettle's small hard tears / dance like mad on the hot black stove'. Six key words are repeated in every stanza: 'house', 'grandmother', 'child',' stove', 'almanac' and 'tears'. This repetition emphasises the key symbols and characters while giving the poem a lively childlike rhythm, giving it energy despite the sad subject matter. The ending conveys that life will go on for the child and her grandmother; there is a future for them: 'The grandmother sings to the marvellous stove / and the child draws another inscrutable house.' Bishop offers another valuable lesson of hope, and she conveys her determination to survive by using the demanding structure of a sestina. She wants to understand, to put a shape on her past.

Clear background knowledge of poet's life used to inform analysis

'First Death in Nova Scotia' is the only poem to directly feature the poet's mother, as she lifts three-year-old Elizabeth up to place a flower into the hand of her dead cousin Arthur. It's another startling poem in terms of the painful memory it describes and the originality of the imagery used to vividly describe the scene. Bishop engages her reader's empathy. A stuffed white loon seems to gaze at Arthur's body echoing the colour of the snow outside, the ermine trim on the clothes of the royal family's pictures, the flower in Arthur's hand and the pallor of Arthur himself. Bishop imagines her little cousin becoming 'the smallest page' at the court pictured in the 'chromographs', conveying effectively how a child's imagination helps them to make sense of confusing and upsetting situations. By using the persona of the child, Bishop reminds us how we thought and felt as children – constantly trying to make sense of an often bewildering world – and does this in a similar way in 'Sestina'. Both poems use a rigid structure laced with repetition to impose an order on the chaotic and traumatic events the poet is dealing with. I felt great sympathy for her here and admired her lack of sentimentality and her skill as a poet. She has developed her style and been more

Knowledge of structural aspects of poem used to support observations about content and meaning

Keeping the idea of 'modern reader' from the question central in the answer

open in her content and mentions her mother directly. This shows a progress in Bishop, and perhaps she is coping better with the awful events of her past. I think seeing a growth and development like this appeals to the modern reader of poetry, allowing them to gain a deeper understanding of the poet and her work.

I feel I have come to know so much about Bishop from reading her poetry, and learned many valuable lessons along the way – that there is always a way forward, another chance to value and preserve nature, to examine the nature of identity and belonging, and more than anything that if we are optimistic, imaginative and keep our sense of humour we can survive anything. Bishop's lively fresh voice, candour and positivity entertain and educate us through vivid and original narratives, offering so much to the modern reader of poetry.

'All the untidy activity continues, / Awful but cheerful.'

I feel this quote sums up Bishop's work and her approach to life beautifully, and I was interested to learn that she chose this as her epitaph. She seems to say to me, 'Don't give up, look at the beauty of life, don't expect it to be perfect, find things to celebrate and deal with the pain as best you can.' It is this message more than anything that means the poems of Elizabeth Bishop appeal to me and so many other modern readers of poetry.

Overall conclusion reached and question addressed again

ESSAY CHECKLIST		Yes √	No x
Purpose	Has the candidate understood the task?		
	Has the candidate responded to it in a thoughtful manner?		
	Has the candidate answered the question?		
Comment:			
Coherence	Has the candidate made convincing arguments?		
	Has the candidate linked ideas?		
	Does the essay have a sense of unity?		
Comment:			
Language	Is the essay written in an appropriate register?		
	Are ideas expressed in a clear way?		
	Is the writing fluent?		
Comment:			
Mechanics	Is the use of language accurate?		
	Are all words spelled correctly?		
	Does the punctuation help the reader?		
Comment:			

Emily Dickinson

1830–1886

Biography

Emily Dickinson's life reads like a detective mystery. Until the age of thirty she lived a social life, meeting up with friends, attending parties in her hometown of Amherst, Massachusetts, USA and attracting the attention of several young men. By all accounts she was high-spirited and witty. In her early teens, she wrote, 'I am growing handsome very fast indeed!' – so fast that she expected to become 'the belle of Amherst when I reach my seventeenth year'. From about the age of thirty she increasingly withdrew from society, choosing to live most of her life as a recluse in her father's house, communicating with the outside world through a voluminous correspondence. After her death, in accordance with her wishes, her sister and sister-in-law destroyed all the letters she had received. Fortunately, the thousand or so poems her sister found hidden in Emily's writing desk were saved.

Family life

Emily Elizabeth Dickinson was born on 10 December 1830 in Amherst, a Calvinist town in Massachusetts. Apart from a brief period at Mount Holyoke Female Seminary, a trip to Washington and Philadelphia and a stay in Boston to receive treatment for an eye problem, all her life was spent there. She was the second child of Emily Norcross and Edward Dickinson. Her mother came from a prosperous family, and her father was a lawyer, a politician and, later, the treasurer of Amherst College. In a letter to Thomas Wentworth Higginson, Dickinson was less than flattering about her parents: 'My Mother does not care for thought – and, Father, too busy with his Briefs – to notice what we do – He buys me many Books – but begs me not to read them – because he fears they joggle the Mind.' However, as an older woman, she was greatly distressed by the death of both her parents. Emily had an older brother, Austin, and a younger sister, Lavinia. All three children were very close throughout their lives and all attended school in the one-room local primary school.

Education

Dickinson received a sound education at Amherst Academy and Mount Holyoke Seminary. Edward Dickinson encouraged his children in their education. In a letter, written when Emily was seven, he exhorted them to 'Keep school, and learn, so as to tell me when I come home, how many new things you have learned, since I came away.' Amherst Academy was a progressive school. It had a broad curriculum and the teachers were well-qualified and motivated. The school was connected to Amherst College and students could attend college lectures in astronomy, botany, chemistry, geology, natural history and zoology. This scientific emphasis is reflected in Dickinson's poetry in her fascination with naming, her detailed descriptions, her choice of words and the range of her imagery.

Religious belief

Dickinson entered Mount Holyoke Female Seminary when she was seventeen. The boarding school was run by a devout Christian headmistress called Mary Lyon and many of its graduates became evangelical missionaries. Evangelical fervour swept through the college and the students were invited to publicly declare their faith in God. Dickinson refused to do so and was put into a category of students who were 'without hope'. Unhappy and homesick, she returned to Amherst. Thereafter her attitude to Christian belief was one of positive

Congregationalism

The Dickinson family belonged to the First Congregational Church. As the name suggests, the congregation ran its own affairs and was not ruled by a bishop or other leader. For Congregationalists, God is head of the Church and no other leader is needed. Visiting preachers were invited to give sermons.

doubt. In 1850, when Amherst was infected with a bout of revivalist fervour, the nineteen-year-old Dickinson wrote: 'I am standing alone in rebellion'. Her rebellion, such as it was, was more private and interior than public in nature and found expression in her poetry. Although she never declared herself a Christian, Dickinson spent a lifetime exploring the nature of the soul and the spiritual life, her poems are influenced by the rhythms of Protestant hymns and the Bible is a major source of her diction and imagery.

Domestic life

As was the case with many unmarried daughters after the completion of their formal education, the future for Dickinson was one of domestic work. Her family was a prominent one in Amherst, so there were many visitors to the house. Not only were visitors to be received and entertained, there was also an obligation to return social visits. In a letter written in 1850 Dickinson exclaimed: 'God keep me from what they call households.' Although she baked bread and worked in the garden, she refused to clean and dust the house or make social calls (although she did maintain an active social life with her siblings and friends). When their mother's health began to decline in 1855, Emily and Lavinia took over the running of the house.

Dickinson's Irish maid

Margaret Maher, from a Tipperary family who emigrated to Amherst after the famine, was a maid in the Dickinson household. Dickinson described her in several letters as 'courageous', 'warm and wild and mighty' and 'good and noisy, the North Wind of the Family'. She stored bundles of her poems in Margaret's trunk. It is thought that Margaret had been instructed to destroy them after the poet's death, but she kept them safe. Margaret also preserved the only image we have of Emily Dickinson.

Dickinson also read widely. Among the novels that had an electric effect upon her was *Jane Eyre* and she may well have identified herself with the novel's heroine.

In 1850 Dickinson befriended Susan Gilbert, whose family also came from Amherst. Susan became her closest friend and then her sister-in-law in 1856 when she married Austin Dickinson. Austin and Susan set up home in an adjoining house and Emily spent many evenings in their company and in the company of their friends. One of these friends was Samuel Bowles, editor of the *Springfield Republican*, an influential newspaper in Massachusetts, who published some of her poems. Dickinson maintained a correspondence with Bowles and his wife over the course of twenty-five years.

Secret love

Dickinson travelled to Washington in 1855 to visit her father, who had been elected to the US House of Representatives. She went on to Philadelphia to visit a friend from school. There, it seems, she met Charles Wadsworth, a Presbyterian preacher. There is much speculation that Wadsworth was the great secret love of her life. Some critics, however, argue that she was in love with her married friend Samuel Bowles. An early biographer of Dickinson suggests that she formed 'extravagant attachments' and gave her love and devotion to a succession of friends, both male and female. More recent biographers speculate that Susan Gilbert may well have been the real love of her life.

Withdraws from society

While still in her twenties, Dickinson began to withdraw from society. Gradually she became a recluse, rarely if ever leaving her home. The myth of the mysterious woman dressed in white, glimpsed in her garden, was formed during her lifetime. Mabel Todd, who came to live Amherst in 1881 and became the lover of Austin Dickinson, wrote to her parents about the 'lady whom the people call the Myth': 'She has not been outside of her own house in fifteen years … she dresses wholly in white, and her mind is said to be perfectly wonderful. She writes finely, but no one ever sees her.'

There has been much speculation on the cause of her seclusion. Many early biographers favoured the explanation of disappointment in love. Charles Wadsworth visited her in 1860 and some biographers see a connection between this visit and her decision to withdraw from the world. The truth may have been more prosaic. Her brother, for example, thought that her seclusion was simply a pose. One commentator suggests that Dickinson suffered from epilepsy and this was the cause of her seclusion.

Relieved of the necessity of visiting and entertaining, Dickinson pursued her interest in writing. She wrote poems and she wrote letters to friends. Indeed, she regarded letter writing as a form of visiting, although more focused and intense than the polite social visits that were common in Amherst at that time. Some of the recipients of Dickinson's letters found them too intense and overwhelming in their expression of feeling. From an early age, her letters reveal a sharp wit and a grim sense of humour.

Although Dickinson withdrew from society, she did have friends. Apart from her sister and brother, Susan Gilbert was a trusted friend and one of her most important readers. Indeed, Susan may well have read all of Dickinson's poetry and many poems were written for her. (Despite living in neighbouring houses, Dickinson often preferred to write to Susan rather than meet her face to face.) Helen Hunt Jackson was another literary friend who encouraged Dickinson to publish her work. Dickinson was romantically involved with Otis Lord, a family friend, to whom she wrote ardent letters, but whose proposal of marriage she declined in 1880.

An audience for her poetry

In 1862 the thirty-two-year-old Dickinson wrote to writer and editor Thomas Wentworth Higginson enclosing four of her poems. She wanted to know if her verse was alive and if it breathed. Higginson was widely known as a man of letters and a prolific essayist and an essay of his in the *Atlantic Monthly* had prompted her to write to him. He was also a radical theologian, an outspoken supporter of women's rights and an advocate for the abolition of slavery. Although he had a reputation for encouraging young writers, Higginson did not really understand the nature of Dickinson's talent

---

Writing habits

Dickinson mostly wrote in her bedroom at a small cherrywood table that measured 18 inches by 18 inches. She had a corner room with four windows. At some point, she began to rise at three a.m. and wrote until midday. Her only task in these hours was to wake the household. In a dedication to a poem, she thanked her father for her morning hours. Her niece recalled her aunt sometimes working at a table in the dining room, where she could see the plants in the conservatory.

Letter to Higginson

Dickinson sent the following note with her poems:

'Mr Higginson,
Are you too deeply occupied to say if my Verse is alive?
The Mind is so near itself – it cannot see, distinctly –
and I have none to ask – Should you think it breathed –
and had you the leisure to tell me, I should feel quick gratitude –
I enclose my name – asking you, if you please –
Sir – to tell me what is true?'

or the scope of her achievement. Faced with her epigrammatical style, he tried to regularise and smooth her poems. Determined and certain, Dickinson refused to compromise. Despite not fully appreciating her peculiar genius, Higginson mentored and encouraged Dickinson for many decades and her correspondence with him was immensely important to her.

Fascicles

From 1858 Dickinson kept handwritten copies of her poems on folded sheets of paper. Each folded sheet created four pages. She placed several of them on top of each other, then punched two holes either side of the centrefold and tied them together with string. Mabel Loomis Todd called these homemade booklets 'fascicles'.

Interestingly, fewer than twenty of Dickinson's poems were published during her lifetime. However, she sent poems to nearly all her correspondents and, in this way, her poems circulated among her circle of friends. So, although little of her work was printed, she did have an audience for her poetry.

After Dickinson's death her sister, Lavinia, found a box containing 900 poems 'tied together with twine' in 'sixty volumes' or fascicles. A hundred poems were published in 1890, edited by Mabel Todd and Thomas Wentworth Higginson, with 'corrections' made by Higginson to rhymes, punctuation, rhythms and, in some cases, imagery. Because of copyright problems and family feuds over the ownership of the poems, it was not until 1955 that her collected poems were published in the way that she had written them.

Difficult years

Mabel Loomis Todd

Mabel was the young wife of a lecturer in astronomy appointed to Amherst College in 1881. She was vivacious and a talented singer and pianist. Very quickly she befriended Austin and Susan Dickinson and their family, and she and Austin became lovers. Their affair continued until Austin's death in 1885.

It is evident from the number of poems that she wrote in 1862 that Dickinson underwent some kind of personal crisis. Speculation suggests that this crisis was related to the failure of a love affair. Many of the poems written in this period explore despair and a depressed state of mind.

The three years between 1882 and 1885 were also particularly difficult for Dickinson. She lost her mother, Otis Lord, Helen Hunt Jackson and her young nephew, Gilbert. Her brother, Austin, began an affair with the writer Mabel Loomis Todd, a family friend, and Emily was torn between her brother and her sister-in-law, Susan. Austin's relationship with Mabel led to a split in the family and a feud that survived well into the twentieth century.

The real Emily

After Dickinson's death, Mabel Todd edited a selection of her letters, omitting nearly all references to Susan Gilbert. Later, Todd claimed it was Austin, Susan's husband, who insisted on this. Susan's daughter and Emily's niece, Mattie, then published a memoir that painted a different picture from the one given in the edited letters. There followed a series of rival publications and disputes over Dickinson's unpublished papers. The family feud continued through second and third generations, as each side sought to present the 'real' Emily Dickinson.

Death

In 1884 Dickinson suffered the first attack of the kidney disease that eventually caused her death in 1886, at the age of fifty-five. She left precise instructions for her funeral, specifying the white dress she was to be buried in and the route to be taken from her house to the churchyard. At her funeral service Thomas Wentworth Higginson read a line from her favourite Emily Brontë poem as her epitaph: 'No coward soul is mine.'

Social and Cultural Context

Although her father was a politician and she lived during the period of the American Civil War, there is little indication that the war had any significant influence on the poetry of Emily Dickinson. Nor do the poems give much indication that the era in which she lived was one in which the campaign for the rights of women began or that the campaign for the abolition of slavery, which led to the Civil War, dominated national politics. Dickinson's poetry does, of course, speak to the cultural and literary context of her day.

> **American Civil War**
>
> Although she did not write about the Civil War (1861–1865), Dickinson's family and friends were affected by it. In 1862, after the introduction of conscription, the family paid an Irish labourer $500 to fight in Austin's place. Austin's close friend Frazar Stearns was killed in the war. Her cousins from Georgia fought on the Confederate side. Her friend Thomas Wentworth Higginson became a colonel in the Union army and led a regiment of 900 former slaves into battle.

Status of women

The **position of women in society** in nineteenth-century New England is important to an understanding of Dickinson's poetry. Women were subservient to men. They were not expected to be full-time writers or intellectuals, or to be involved in public affairs. Their place was at home, living pious, domestic lives. While the bare facts of Dickinson's life suggest that she was content with a domestic role, her poetry speaks of extreme states of mind, hints at suppressed emotions and feelings, challenges religious orthodoxy and reveals an individual deeply at odds with the social and religious values of her day and who stood alone in rebellion.

Dickinson came from a well-off and respected family. The family hosted important visitors and was the centre of intellectual life in Amherst. However, the community in which she lived was conservative and, despite her privileged life, there were **few opportunities** for a woman of her talent to take part in the cultural and artistic life of the nation. With her father's consent, she devoted long hours each day to writing. She circulated her poems to friends and literary acquaintances, but she never published a collection. Publication carried risks. The acclaimed poet Julia Ward

> **Abolitionist movement**
>
> A social and political movement whose aim was to abolish the institution of slavery in America. Slavery was a feature of the economy of the southern states and many southerners resented the interference of 'Yankees' in their affairs. Dickinson's father was an abolitionist.

Howe was effectively censored by her husband, the politician and abolitionist Samuel Howe, after she published her collection *Passion Flowers* in 1854. He threatened to end the marriage and take their children because, in his view, the book was too passionate and personal.

In an early poem Dickinson imagined marriage as an obligatory martyrdom. She chose to avoid this fate. **By not marrying, Dickinson retained a modicum of personal freedom**, although she was financially dependent on her father and, later, her brother. Dickinson's closest friend, Susan Gilbert, tried to live an independent life by teaching but found that she could not survive on her salary. Marriage to Dickinson's brother, Austin, offered financial security; however, Susan was reluctant to marry. Her older sister, Mary, had died a few days after giving birth, ten months after her wedding, and so Susan feared childbirth.

Dickinson had the constant support of Susan Gilbert, her friend, adviser, reader and, on occasions, muse. Dickinson sent hundreds of letters to her and was in daily communication with her. They shared their reading, their writing and their concerns. Their friendship was close and loving, literary and intellectual.

Calvinism

The Calvinist tradition of her family and the writings of Henry David Thoreau and Ralph Waldo Emerson were important influences on Dickinson. Calvinism was brought to New England by the Pilgrim Fathers who settled there in the seventeenth century. It emphasised **sin and damnation and promoted a strict moral code**. All life, it seemed, was directed at preparing for the Day of Judgement. For this reason, individuals were encouraged to constantly examine their conscience. Calvinism created an atmosphere in which individualism was curtailed and in which artistic expression was viewed as, potentially, proud and sinful.

Although Calvinism was on the wane in the nineteenth century, its influence remained strong in Amherst. Indeed, when Dickinson was a student at Mount Holyoke Female Seminary, the headmistress instigated a series of Calvinist revivals, during which students were encouraged to declare their faith as Christians. Beset by doubts, Dickinson refused to do so and remained unconverted. Despite this, the language of Calvinism and of the Bible is evident in her poetry and provides a **rich source of imagery**, and the question of **everlasting life** was one to which she returned, again and again, in her poetry. A more playful use of imagery drawn from popular sermons on temperance is found in 'I taste a liquor never brewed'.

Ralph Waldo Emerson

Dickinson was certainly influenced by the group of writers known as **Transcendentalists**, the most famous of whom was Ralph Waldo Emerson. The Transcendentalists believed that **God dwelt or was immanent in nature and in humanity**. This outlook led to a celebration of the natural world as a sign of God's creative energy. Dickinson did not convert to Transcendentalism, but she did admire Emerson's emphasis on **self-reliance, the primacy of individual experience over tradition and the importance of the interior life**. Indeed, Dickinson's reclusive lifestyle and her exploration of what she referred to as 'the undiscovered continent' echo some of the themes she found in Emerson's writing.

Themes

Dickinson's poetry addresses big themes: **nature; life, death and eternity; religious belief and doubt; love, absence and loss; mental anguish and the workings of the mind**. The poems are wide-ranging in tone and mood and address the reader in ways that can be humorous, provocative, blasphemous or tragic. They are frequently surprising, riddling and abrupt. Although they often contain direct statements, 'I heard a Fly buzz – when I died', their meaning is rarely direct.

Dickinson's poetry is emotionally and intellectually engaged, but it is neither confessional nor autobiographical. She told her first editor that when she used 'I' in her poetry, she meant 'a supposed person'.

Dickinson was raised in a religious family but as an adult stopped attending church with them. She was drawn to the idea of immortality and the promise of the Resurrection, when she would be reunited with her loved ones. However, when she uses Christian imagery, she often reworks it to her own purpose. Her imagination was engaged by death, although she never solved the riddle of mortality. For her, **death remained disturbing and incomprehensible**. Not for her the Christian consolation of viewing death as the soul's transition into eternal life with God.

Her love poetry is equally unconventional, as much about **love lost** as love gained, with the critic Helen Vendler referring to Dickinson's 'stern poetry of heartbreak'.

> Faith
>
> '"Faith" is a fine invention
> For Gentlemen who see!
> But Microscopes are prudent
> In an Emergency!'
> While the young Emily attended services with her family at the local First Congregational Church, and her father gave her a gift of a bible when she was thirteen, she also lived in an age when science was starting to challenge some Christian beliefs.

Form

The majority of Dickinson's poems are written in hymn metre, i.e. four-line stanzas with four beats in the first line, three in the second, four in the third and three in the fourth, with a rhyme or part-rhyme between lines 2 and 4. What is astonishing is that Dickinson writes poems of such arresting power within what appears to be a **simple form**.

Dickinson was very **eccentric in her usage of punctuation and capital letters**. Generally, her odd use has the purpose of emphasis. She used the dash as a device to indicate her own sense of rhythm, which she felt was not adequately served by regular punctuation such as the semicolon and colon. However, it is more than a question of rhythm. The dash pushes phrases apart from each other and creates spaces for the reader to fill. It can create moments of suspense or dramatic pauses in the poems. It can also signal a break in the line of thought. When they occur at the end of a poem, they invite the reader to tease out the meaning of what is not said but is implied beyond the dash.

Timeline

1830	Born 10 December in Amherst, Massachusetts
1835	Attends local primary school with her brother, Austin
1840	Attends Amherst Academy
1847	Attends Mount Holyoke Female Seminary as a boarder; declines to profess herself a Christian
1848	Withdraws from Mount Holyoke due to ill health and homesickness
1850	Back in Amherst: 'I am standing alone in rebellion'
1855	Travels to Washington to visit her father and then to Philadelphia; probable meeting with Charles Wadsworth. Her mother's health begins to decline
1856	Austin marries Susan Gilbert and the couple live in an adjoining house
1858	Writing begins in earnest; assembles her poems into bound packets or fascicles
1860	Visit of Charles Wadsworth
1861	Suggestion of a personal 'major crisis'; withdraws more and more from the world. American Civil War begins
1862	Writes to Thomas Wentworth Higginson and encloses some poems. Writes 366 poems
1863	Writes 141 poems
1864	Writes 174 poems. Visits Boston for treatment for her eyes. May have met Judge Otis Lord who later proposes to her
1870	Thomas Wentworth Higginson visits
1874	Her father, Edward Dickinson, dies on 16 June
1875	Her mother now bedridden and paralysed
1878	Her friend Samuel Bowles dies
1880	Charles Wadsworth visits for a second time
1880	Judge Otis Lord proposes marriage but is turned down
1881	Austin and Susan befriend Mabel Loomis Todd
1882	Friendship with Susan strained by Austin's love affair with Mabel Todd. Mother dies. Charles Wadsworth dies
1883	Eight-year-old nephew Gilbert dies; she is heart-broken
1885	Bedridden with Bight's disease
1886	14 May writes to cousins 'Called Back'. 15 May dies
1890	First selection of her poems published
1955	First edition of her poems published as she wrote them

'Hope' is the thing with feathers

Before you read

How important is hope in your life? Share your thoughts with a fellow student. Revisit your discussion after you have read the poem.

'Hope' is the thing with feathers –
That perches in the soul –
And sings the tune without the words –
And never stops – at all –

And sweetest – in the Gale – is heard –   5
And sore must be the storm –
That could abash the little Bird
That kept so many warm –

I've heard it in the chillest land –
And on the strangest Sea –   10
Yet, never, in Extremity,
It asked a crumb – of Me.

Glossary

| 1 | *the thing*: although she gives 'Hope' some of the characteristics of a bird, Dickinson also wishes to be true to its abstract nature of 'hope' as a quality or disposition |
| 7 | *abash*: destroy the confidence of |

Guidelines

Dickinson wrote a number of 'definition poems' in which she used physical details to define what an abstract experience is or is not. Often her definitions consist of a series of comparisons. However, she does not use the word 'like'. Hope is not *like a thing* with feathers, it *is the thing* with feathers. The directness and confidence of the statement makes her definition vivid and immediate. As in religious symbolism, 'Hope' is imagined as having some of the characteristics of a bird – it is 'the thing with feathers'. Although 'Hope' may seem something slight (it is only a 'little Bird'), it is in fact something immensely powerful, persistent and comforting. The poem, written in 1861, during what was a difficult period for Dickinson, has an optimistic, buoyant mood.

Commentary

Stanza 1

In the first stanza Dickinson **introduces the metaphor**, 'Hope' is a 'thing with feathers' (i.e. something that can fly and that can lift the spirit) and begins to develop it by telling us that Hope sings. The use of the word 'feathers' suggests the warm, comforting nature of Hope. Hope, the poem asserts, resides in the soul. By describing the song of Hope as 'the tune without the words', Dickinson suggests that Hope goes beyond logic and reason and their limitations. Hope is resilient and unceasing. It never stops 'at all'.

Stanza 2

The warm comfort that Hope gives in times of distress and uncertainty – emotional, spiritual, psychological – is recorded in stanza 2. Its comfort is known to many. The phrase 'the little Bird' suggests the poet's affection and admiration for Hope. The stanza also conveys the courage and resilience of Hope, which is not abashed by gales and storms.

Stanza 3

The third stanza **records the poet's personal experience** of Hope, in times of personal anguish. Hope has come to her in the 'chillest land' and on the 'strangest Sea'. It is found in all places. The physical landscape and seascape suggest psychological or spiritual terrain. In these periods of crisis, Hope offered comfort, without seeking anything in return. Hope, in other words, is generous, asking nothing for itself. This final stanza strikes a solemn note, as if the poet wants to give Hope the dignified celebration she believes it deserves.

Themes and imagery

The **theme of hope and its persistence** is common in religious writing and sermons; however, in Dickinson's poem, God is not mentioned. The idea that hope 'never stops – at all' (line 4) is one that cannot be proven and is itself an expression of hope. The poem works on a series of comparisons. The voice of hope is 'sweetest' (line 5) in those situations that are the most extreme. Compare 'sweetest' with 'chillest' and 'strangest'; the phrases, 'chillest land' (line 9) and 'strangest Sea' (line 10) suggest psychological and spiritual states of anguish, including, perhaps, loneliness and depression.

Form and language

The poem is written in **four-line stanzas**. The opening statement of line 1 is dramatic. After that the poem settles into an **even rhythm**, which suggests the steadfastness of hope. The repeated use of 'And' gives a sense of strength and conviction to the statements made by the poet.

Definition poems

Dickinson wrote a number of definition poems in the manner of "Hope". They include: 'Renunciation — is a piercing Virtue'; 'Remorse — is Memory — awake'; and 'Eden is that old-fashioned House'. In all cases she makes definite statements though she is, in fact, making a comparison. In another poem Dickinson wrote, 'We see — Comparatively'. These definition poems are linked to Dickinson's fascination with naming plants and flowers and her close observation of the natural world.

By using the word 'thing' in the first line, Dickinson establishes an emotional distance, so that this 'thing' can be classified using a series of inner questions. What is it like? Where does it reside? How does it express itself? In what circumstances does it express itself?

The second and fourth lines of each stanza rhyme. The metre is based on the common metre of hymns and ballads, with four-beat and three-beat lines. Dickinson's punctuation, her use of slant rhymes and enjambment (run-on lines), and her skilled use of repetition and alliteration work to eliminate the sing-song effect of this metre.

Questions

1	How does the poet visualise hope?
2	What kinds of seascape and landscape are mentioned in the poem?
3	What is the most important quality of 'Hope', as suggested by stanza 1? What words or phrases capture this?
4	Why might a 'tune without the words' (line 3) be appropriate to 'Hope'? Explain your answer.
5	How is the strength and courage of 'Hope' suggested in stanza 2?
6	What is the effect of the adjective 'little' in line 7?
7	The poem becomes more personal in stanza 3. What has been the poet's experience of hope?
8	What is the effect of the words 'chillest' (line 9) and 'strangest' (line 10)? Explain your answer.
9	What, do you think, has the poet in mind in her reference to 'Extremity' in line 11?
10	Do you agree that this poem may offer consolation to a reader in some kind of distress? Give reasons for your answer.
11	Does the poem reveal anything of Dickinson's personality? Explain your answer.
12	Using this poem as a model, write your own definition poem on either 'Love' or 'Despair'.
13	Working in pairs, create a multimodal interpretation of the poem, using text, images and sound.

Before you read

Think of an adjective to describe the quality of sunlight in each of the four seasons. In your view, does the quality of sunlight affect our physical and mental wellbeing? Share your thoughts with your class.

There's a certain Slant of light

There's a certain Slant of light,
Winter Afternoons –
That oppresses, like the Heft
Of Cathedral Tunes –

Heavenly Hurt, it gives us –   5
We can find no scar,
But internal difference,
Where the Meanings, are –

None may teach it – Any –
'Tis the Seal Despair –   10
An imperial affliction
Sent us of the Air –

When it comes, the Landscape listens –
Shadows – hold their breath –
When it goes, 'tis like the Distance   15
On the look of Death –

Glossary

3	*Heft*: weight
10	*Seal*: mark or sign, as in the wax seal placed on a letter (the slant of light is the mark or sign of despair)

Guidelines

'There's a certain Slant of light' explores a state of mind in which the comfort of hope is absent. In its place there is the despair associated with a particular kind of winter light falling on the landscape. The speaker in the poem sees the light, coming from heaven, as an affliction, affecting the inner landscape of the soul. The poem was probably written in 1861, during the period when it is believed Dickinson suffered a major personal crisis.

Commentary

Stanza 1

The fall of a certain kind of winter light is oppressive, according to the first stanza of the poem, as oppressive as the 'Heft / Of Cathedral Tunes'. This is a striking simile. It links winter light and church music with a heaviness of the soul. What starts off as a visual image is now described in terms of music, and the music is, in turn, described in terms of weight. This blurring of the distinction between the senses (synaesthesia) creates a feeling of disturbance. What is also interesting is that hymns are described as having an oppressive effect.

Stanzas 2 and 3

Dickinson states that the slant of winter light gives 'Heavenly Hurt'. This hurt leaves no physical wounds or scars but affects the inner life or soul of the person and brings despair. One can interpret this stanza as suggesting that the relationship between humanity and heaven is marked by a certain cruelty on the part of heaven. It is suggested that this 'Heavenly Hurt' cannot be understood, taught or explained away. It is without remedy.

The winter light is the 'Seal Despair'. In the Calvinist tradition, the sacraments are seals of God's promise of salvation. Here, 'Seal' indicates the sign or symbol of despair and the hope of salvation is noticeably absent. 'Seal' also suggests the message of a royal personage, a closed communication, something beyond contradiction. This meaning is reinforced by the phrase 'imperial affliction', which implies that the hurt associated with the winter light is sent by a sovereign authority. Is the message of the winter light the message of human mortality that is beyond contradiction?

Winter

While Dickinson wrote over 200 poems on summer, only 30 mention winter. For Dickinson, winter is the season of grim reality. It is associated with depression and death. Much of her own writing was completed in spring and summer, when sunlight gave the writer feelings of optimism and hope. A summer's noon represents for Dickinson the highest point of hope and possibility. In periods of optimism, Dickinson imagined eternity as an unending summer's day. In periods of depression, eternity was imagined as a frozen winter.

Stanza 4

The winter light causes the world to be still and hushed, as if nature itself is in awe of heaven's light, and passive in the face of it. In other words, the light impresses as much as it oppresses. Note how the poem moves back from the inner landscape to an external one in this stanza. The passing of the light does not lift the feeling of despair. On the contrary, the passing of the light leaves a chill, as if we had looked on the distance between the present and our death. It is only when the light disappears that its full meaning becomes clear. The final dash in the poem suggests the unknown into which we all face.

Themes and imagery

The **theme of despair** contrasts with the hopefulness of '"Hope" is the thing with feathers'. Despair is both a psychological and a spiritual condition. In the Christian tradition, despair is a grave sin that prevents the salvation of the soul.

Light is often associated with renewal, hope and truth, but in this poem the truth of the light is a despairing one. The poem **moves constantly from the outside world to the inner world**; from the external light to the

inner hurt; from shadows to death. The critic Helen Vendler suggests that the impossibility of separating the sense of experience of landscape from the spiritual experience of despair is a central point of the poem.

The poem's imagery and diction are diverse, coming from religion ('Cathedral Tunes', 'Heavenly Hurt') and from nature ('Slant of light', 'Winter Afternoons', 'Landscape', 'Shadows'). Another set of words suggests physical injury ('Hurt', 'scar', 'affliction').

Metre

The metre of Dickinson's poems is based on that of the hymn. She writes in short lines, alternating 4-beat and 3-beat lines. However, the poems rarely sound monotonous or predictable. This is because of her use of punctuation; changes in word order; and her choice of unusual or ambiguous words, such as 'Heft' (line 3) or 'scar' (line 6) in 'There's a certain Slant of light'.

Form and language

The poem is written in **four-line stanzas with a regular rhyming scheme**. The sounds and rhymes of the poem add considerably to the feeling of seriousness and weighty matters. Note the use of final 't' sounds, which slow the rhythm and give a sense of definition and precision to the poem. The poem itself works as a seal – it is written in an authoritative style that brooks no contradiction.

Questions

1	What kind of sunlight is described in the poem?
2	On first reading, what kind of mood is captured in the poem?
3	What is the effect of a certain kind of winter light, according to the first stanza of the poem?
4	What state of mind might regard 'Cathedral Tunes' (line 4) as heavy or oppressive? Explain your answer.
5	What, according to stanza 2, is the effect of the light? Where is the difference made by the light noticed or felt?
6	In stanza 2, the words 'We' and 'us' are used by the poet. Might 'I' and 'me' have been more appropriate? Explain your answer.
7	What words or phrases in the third stanza suggest the powerlessness of those afflicted by despair? What, in particular, is the effect of the word 'Seal' in relation to despair?
8	Consider the phrase 'imperial affliction' (line 11). Does it suggest that the affliction is sent by a higher authority (God) or is the idea that affliction is itself majestic? Explain your answer.
9	What, according to the speaker, is the feeling or situation when the light goes?
10	Examine the rhymes and the rhythm of the poem. In your view, how important are they in expressing the poet's concerns?
11	Consider the three phrases 'Heavenly Hurt' (line 5), 'the Seal Despair' (line 10) and 'An imperial affliction' (line 11). What view of God emerges from them?
12	Discuss the poem as an expression of a religious crisis, in which the speaker feels betrayed by God.
13	What does this poem have in common with '"Hope" is the thing with feathers'?
14	'internal difference, / Where the Meanings, are – ' (lines 7–8). What, do you think, does this statement suggest about Emily Dickinson?
15	Working with images, sound and written text, create a multimedia text that captures the mood of the poem and the light that provokes it.

Before you read

Working in pairs, think about the kind of poem you expect to follow from the first line, 'I Felt a Funeral, in my Brain'. Consider the possible circumstances in which you might use these words to describe an experience.

I Felt a Funeral, in my Brain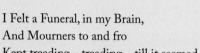

I Felt a Funeral, in my Brain,
And Mourners to and fro
Kept treading – treading – till it seemed
That Sense was breaking through –

And when they all were seated,   5
A Service, like a Drum –
Kept beating – beating – till I thought
My Mind was going numb –

And then I heard them lift a Box
And creak across my Soul   10
With those same Boots of Lead, again,
Then Space – began to toll,

As all the Heavens were a Bell,
And Being, but an Ear,
And I, and Silence, some strange Race   15
Wrecked, solitary, here –

And then a Plank in Reason, broke,
And I dropped down, and down –
And hit a World, at every plunge,
And Finished knowing – then –   20

Glossary

1	*Felt*: what the poet imagines is so vivid that it feels like a physical experience
4	*Sense*: waking consciousness; common sense
6	*Service*: church funeral service or ceremony
9	*Box*: coffin
11	*Boots of Lead*: the heavy tread of the mourners
12	*Space*: the outside world into which the imagined funeral cortège moves
13	*Heavens*: the sky; the firmament
19	*World*: place the poet imagines her soul passing through on its way to its destination
20	*Finished knowing*: the poet's knowledge of the beyond is finished at this point; or, the poet has finished her imagined funeral with the knowledge of something that she cannot express; or knowledge itself finishes

Guidelines

This celebrated poem gives an account of the progress of a funeral from the startling perspective of the person lying in the coffin. It was written during a difficult period in Dickinson's personal life, when she was beset by both religious and artistic doubts. In addition, there were also her complicated and disappointed feelings for Samuel Bowles, editor of the *Springfield Republican*. Some critics see the funeral described in the poem as a metaphor for the breakdown of consciousness, and relate the poem to Dickinson's personal crisis. They read the poem as one of Dickinson's definition poems, where the progress of a funeral is used to capture the process of falling into despair or undergoing a mental breakdown. Others take the poem at face value, regarding it as an unusual exploration of one of Dickinson's favourite themes: the transition between life and death, which she also explores in 'I heard a Fly buzz'. Some readers regard the poem as charting the failure of her poetic imagination, during a period when she was unable to write. More recently it has been suggested that the poem may describe: the experience of a bad migraine; the onset of a seizure associated with epilepsy; or an attempt to 'bury' a bad experience. Whichever interpretation is given, the poem sees Dickinson straining her imagination to the limits of its power. Most critics give 1861 as the likely year in which the poem was composed.

Commentary

Stanza 1

The speaker declares 'I Felt a Funeral, in my Brain'. The verb 'Felt' and the noun 'Brain' suggest an experience that is intense and physical. By using these words, Dickinson abolishes the traditional boundary between experiences of the mind and those of the body.

Stanza 2

The first-person narrative account of the progress of the funeral continues. When the mourners were seated, the service began. The stanza emphasises how hearing became the sense through which the 'I' received the world, encased as she is in a dark coffin. The transition from the noun 'Brain' in line 1 to 'Mind' in line 8 suggests, perhaps, that the physical intensity lessened and the experience became more psychological in character. However, Dickinson understood that there can be no absolute distinction between mind and body.

Stanzas 3 and 4

The word 'Soul' is introduced in stanza 3, indicating that the experience, which began as a physical one and then became more psychological in character, developed a spiritual quality as it proceeded. This development did not make the experience any clearer. In fact, the descriptions in stanzas 3 and 4 suggest that the 'I' became increasingly disoriented and the boundary between external and internal collapsed.

Furthermore, the experience was increasingly defined by a sense of contraction. Space was filled with the tolling of a bell and being was reduced to hearing. Just as bells mark time and differentiate one moment from another, so the tolling in the poem marks a decisive moment. The sense of contraction experienced by the 'I' was accompanied by an overwhelming sense of isolation. The 'I' is described as shipwrecked from life, cut off, along with silence, and left 'here'. The use of 'here' gives a startling immediacy to the experience.

Stanza 5

Before the 'I' and the reader can take stock of the situation and grasp the nature of the 'here' at the end of stanza 4, the poem is on the move again. 'Reason', the faculty that could help to make sense of the experience, did not hold up ('And then a Plank in Reason, broke') and the 'I' underwent a new sensation, that of falling, plunging deeper into the experience, plunging to new levels or worlds. And at the end of this plunging, we are told that the 'I' 'Finished knowing – then – '. Interestingly, the verb 'Finished' might suggest that the speaker chose to stop trying to make sense of her experience.

Themes and imagery

Death, madness and uncertainty are key themes in the poem, although critics do not agree on the exact relationship between all three.

Some critics read the 'plunge' as the coffin's descent into the grave and the 'here' of line 16 as death. (The word 'Plank' in line 17 may suggest the planks placed across the opened grave before the interment.) They see stanzas 4 and 5 as describing the experience of entering into death. Others interpret the final stanza as describing a mental breakdown, a descent into madness or despair; while yet more read the 'plunge' as a description of the loss of consciousness. For the critic Helen Vendler, the poem is an account of a mental breakdown that is indistinguishable from death.

The final line is highly regarded by critics, even as they disagree on its meaning. Some interpret it as a declaration that the plunge beyond reason yielded a new and deeper knowledge, although this knowledge is not expressed. At the end or finish of the fall, the 'I' had learned something, but this something is not revealed. Others read the final line as suggesting that thought and knowledge are lost in the fall. Another reading suggests that the poet, on the verge of gaining an imaginative insight into the nature of death, fails. However much she might desire to experience death, imaginatively, it is beyond the imagination's capacity to do so.

The imagery has the **eerie, disturbing quality of Gothic horror**: the altered consciousness of the speaker; the sense of entrapment in a coffin; the after-death experience; the speaker's loss of understanding; the terrifying plunge into the unknown. The speaker seems to be under attack in each stanza: from the treading of the mourners (stanza 1), from the beating of the service (stanza 2), from the boots of lead (stanza 3), from the threat of a shipwreck (stanza 4) and from the terrible plunge into unconsciousness in the final stanza.

> **Dickinson's funeral**
>
> **Dickinson left precise instructions for her funeral. Her coffin was white, with white lining, ribbons and handles. She was laid out in a robe of white flannel. Two sets of pallbearers carried the coffin. The first set took it out of the back door of the house and the second, made up of six Irishmen who had worked for the family, carried it to the graveyard. The funeral party circled her garden, walked through the barn and crossed the fields of buttercups to the cemetery.**

Form and language

Again, Dickinson uses the four-line stanza of the ballad or the hymn in this poem. The **rhythm is regular and insistent** throughout, and reinforced by the repeated use of 'And', especially in stanzas 4 and 5. This style creates a sense of **terrifying forward motion**, as if the 'I' was powerless before the experience. Another notable effect is the repetition of the words 'treading' (line 3) and 'beating' (line 7) and the use of the dash after each, which emphasises the insistent nature of the noise and creates the feeling of someone being driven mad by the incessant, beating sounds. Just as there are several ways of interpreting the poem, there are a number of possibilities for reading it aloud. For example, it can be read as a narrative of a terrifying nightmarish experience. In this reading, the dashes and punctuation may suggest the fragmented comprehension of the 'I'. In contrast, the fact that the poem is narrated in the past tense may suggest that a tone of calm, puzzled wonder might be appropriate.

> **SNAPSHOT**
> - Startling perspective
> - Description of funeral
> - Imagery of heaviness and contraction
> - Imagery of falling
> - Terrifying, isolating experience
> - Experience is physical, psychological and spiritual
> - Use of 'And' and other repetitions create sense of being overwhelmed
> - Theme of death and dying
> - Theme of breakdown
> - Ends on a note of uncertainty

Exam-Style Questions

Understanding the poem

1	What is the story that the poem tells?
2	Who tells the story?
3	What do you find most striking about the poem on first reading?
4	What, according to the speaker, happens in the opening two stanzas of the poem?
5	In the third stanza, the speaker says that the mourners creaked across her soul with 'Boots of Lead'. What feeling is created by this description?
6	Who, according to the speaker, is her companion in stanza 4?
7	The most dramatic moment of the poem occurs in stanza 5. Explain in your own words what happens.

Thinking about the poem

1	The poet uses the words 'Brain' in line 1, 'Mind' in line 8 and 'Soul' in line 10. How do these changes contribute to the meaning of the poem? Explain your answer.
2	Comment on the effectiveness of the following words in the poem: 'Felt' (line 1); 'creak' (line 10); and 'Wrecked' (line 16).
3	What is the effect of the repetition of 'treading' in line 3 and 'beating' in line 7? What, in your view, is the effect of the repeated use of the word 'And' in the poem? Give other examples of the effective use of repetition in the poem.
4	Consider two examples of the use of the dash in the poem and comment on their effectiveness.
5	'And Finished knowing – then – ' (line 20). What is your understanding of the final line of the poem?
6	In terms of a person in a coffin, does it make sense to suggest that the whole of one's being might be reduced to the sensation of hearing, as one moves from life into death (lines 13–14)? Explain your answer.
7	Which of the following statements is closest to your own interpretation of the poem? ■ It is a poem about a funeral. ■ It is a poem about a nervous breakdown. ■ It is a poem about the limits of the imagination. You may choose more than one but you must explain your choice.
8	Prepare a reading of the poem that is calm and reflective. Prepare another that is panic-stricken. Which reading, in your view, best captures the spirit of the poem?

Imagining

1	You have been asked to make a short film based on the poem. Write a note on the character of the speaker of the poem and how you visualise her (or him).
2	Suggest an alternative title for the poem. Explain your suggestion.
3	'I have lost the ability to understand anything.' Using this as a first line, write a short piece (poetry or prose) inspired by the poem.

Before you read

Have you ever watched a bird in a park or garden? What did you notice? How did the presence of the bird make you feel? Share your experience with another student.

A Bird came down the Walk

A Bird came down the Walk –
He did not know I saw –
He bit an Angleworm in halves
And ate the fellow, raw.

And then he drank a Dew   5
From a convenient Grass –
And then hopped sidewise to the Wall
To let a Beetle pass –

He glanced with rapid eyes
That hurried all around –   10
They looked like frightened beads, I thought –
He stirred his Velvet Head

Like one in danger, Cautious,
I offered him a Crumb
And he unrolled his feathers   15
And rowed him softer home –

Than Oars divide the Ocean,
Too silver for a seam –
Or Butterflies, off Banks of Noon
Leap, plashless as they swim.   20

Glossary

3	*Angleworm*: worm used as fish bait in angling
18	*Too silver for a seam*: the ocean's surface is so silvery that no division (such as may be made by oars) can be seen
20	*plashless*: making no disturbance

Guidelines

The poet observes a bird. She offers him a crumb. The bird flies away. In her poetry, Dickinson describes many small moments in life, especially in meetings of the human and the animal world, which have a feeling of accident, surprise and favour about them.

Commentary

Stanzas 1 and 2

In the first stanza the narrator tells us about a bird straying into the human realm by coming down 'the Walk'. The narrator is unobserved by the bird and registers an amused surprise at the bird eating a 'raw' worm. As presented by Dickinson, the narrator expresses mock-horror at the ungentlemanly behaviour of the bird.

The narrator continues to observe the bird in stanza 2. Having dined, the bird quenches its thirst by drinking from the dewy grass. By referring to 'a Dew' Dickinson particularises the image, and creates the impression of observing the event through a microscope, as a scientist might do. Having eaten and drunk his fill, the bird courteously steps aside to 'let a Beetle pass'. The bird's behaviour towards the beetle is in marked contrast to his actions with the angleworm. This image captures the **essence of Dickinson's technique** in the poem. On one hand she observes the bird with a scientist's eye, and on the other she treats the events in a humorous, whimsical manner by attributing human qualities and motives to the action of the bird.

Stanza 3

The third stanza brings a change in perspective. The bird is no longer the gentleman diner. The description here emphasises the non-human eyes and movement of the bird's head. The bird's actions suggest the nervousness of a creature who might itself fall prey to a predator. The phrase 'Velvet Head' accurately captures the texture and appearance of the head feathers and also suggests the beauty of the bird.

Stanzas 4 and 5

Sympathetic to the bird's fears, the observer moves to allay them by offering him a crumb. By using the word 'Cautious' to refer to both the bird and the observer, Dickinson creates a sense of identification between them. Despite this, the proffered gift is not taken and the bird flies away.

The flight is not undertaken in panic. The sense of grace and ease in the flight of the bird is mirrored in the language of lines 15–20, which create an impression of gentle motion. Although the bird flies away, there is little sense of disappointment in the poem's conclusion. The observer takes pleasure in their accidental encounter. The vocabulary of the final stanza ('Ocean', 'silver', 'Butterflies', 'Noon', 'Leap', 'swim') suggests a life of innocent, carefree pleasure. Like an impressionist painting, there is a harmony of air, water and light.

Themes and imagery

The poem **expresses a delight and relish in the natural world**. In describing the bird, Dickinson mixes accurate and poetic description. The accurate description captures the bird on the ground: a predator, who bites a worm in two and eats it 'raw' (line 4) and who is constantly on the alert for danger. The description of the bird's eyes as 'frightened beads' (line 11) is particularly effective. The poetic description is reserved for the bird in the air, taking flight.

The imagery of the last six lines is complex as the poet strives to **convey the silent grace of the bird** as it glides into the air. First the narrator suggests that the bird unrolls his feathers. Then the feathers are compared to oars dividing a silver ocean. However, she wants another comparison to capture the silent, graceful movement of the bird. In the last two lines the movement of the bird is compared to the 'swimming' of butterflies in the air, as they jump off 'Banks of Noon' (line 19). Now the bird, taking flight into the air, has become a symbol of the poet's delight in nature.

Form and language

The poem is written in **four-line, rhyming stanzas**. The dash is used to create pauses but it does not have the jarring effect here that is evident in other poems. The complex imagery of the last six lines is supported by the richness of the language. The succession of 'o' sounds ('unrolled … rowed … home … Oars … Ocean') in lines 15–17 is followed by the light-sounding, alliterative 'silver for a seam' (line 18) and what Helen Vendler calls Dickinson's buoyant 'Butterflies, off Banks of Noon' (line 19). The effect, as with the onomatopoeic 'plashless', is joyful and good-humoured.

Questions

1	The narrator observes a bird. What does the bird do?
2	How does the narrator move from being an observer to being a participant?
3	What is the reaction of the bird to the narrator?
4	What words and phrases in the poem convey the bird as (a) a predator, (b) a gentleman, (c) prey? What is the poet's attitude to the bird in each of these guises?
5	The use and placing of the word 'Cautious' in line 13 is often admired by critics. Why, do you think, is this so?
6	The poem concludes with images of rowing and swimming. What do they suggest about the flight of the bird? What do they tell us about Dickinson? Explain your answers.
7	Where, in your view, is the humour and amusement of the poet most evident in this poem?
8	What, do you think, do rhyme and punctuation contribute to the effectiveness of the poem?
9	'In the poem, we see how Dickinson views the world with the eye of a scientist and the eye of an artist.' Give your response to this assessment of the poem.
10	What impression of Dickinson do you form from reading the poem? Explain your answer.
11	Does the poem offer any interesting insights into the natural world? Explain your answer.
12	What, in your view, is the theme of this poem?
13	Follow Dickinson's example and write a short poem based on your close observation of a bird in your garden.

Before you read

Think about a deathbed scene that you have seen in a film. Working with a partner, describe how the characters in the scene related to each other. Describe the atmosphere of the scene. Keep that scene in mind as you read Dickinson's poem.

I heard a Fly buzz – when I died

I heard a Fly buzz – when I died –
The Stillness in the Room
Was like the Stillness in the Air –
Between the Heaves of Storm –

The Eyes around – had wrung them dry –   5
And Breaths were gathering firm
For that last Onset – when the King
Be witnessed – in the Room –

I willed my Keepsakes – Signed away
What portion of me be   10
Assignable – and then it was
There interposed a Fly –

With Blue – uncertain stumbling Buzz –
Between the light – and me –
And then the Windows failed – and then   15
I could not see to see –

Glossary

4	*Heaves*: wind surges
5	*Eyes around*: bedside mourners keeping watch
7	*last Onset*: final assault of death
7	*the King*: God
8	*witnessed*: inspired by their religious faith, all waited for the moment of death when, they believed, God would be present in the room. In the Calvinist tradition, the moment of death is the moment the soul faces the judgement of God
9	*Keepsakes*: mementoes; souvenirs
11	*Assignable*: could be left or bequeathed
13	*Blue*: there is no noun to follow the adjective 'Blue' so it carries over to 'Buzz' at the end of the line and suggests a confused or disturbed apprehension of the world

Guidelines

Dickinson's fascination with death provides the subject matter of this poem. The poem is written in the past tense, in the voice of a dead person, and describes the moment of death. This moment is dominated by the buzzing of a fly in the death-room. As the last act in the drama of life, the buzzing fly causes the moment of death to be grimly comic rather than spiritually uplifting.

Commentary

Stanza 1

The startling perspective in the poem is announced in the first line: 'I heard a Fly buzz – when I died – '. The poem is spoken by someone who has died and it explores the moment of death. The 'Room' is the death-room, where the dying person and the mourners await death. The repetition of 'Stillness' suggests the sense of waiting and expectation in the room. The 'Heaves of Storm' are the bouts of laboured breathing of the dying person. Between these 'Heaves', the dying person and the very air in the room are still.

Stanza 2

We are told that, as the moment of death approached, the mourners gathered themselves for 'that last Onset'. They had shed their tears of grief ('The Eyes around – had wrung them dry – ') and now waited for the moment of death. Inspired by their religious faith, they believed that 'the King', their God, would 'Be witnessed – in the Room – 'at the moment of death, when the dying person drew her last breath. The phrase 'Be witnessed' suggests the solemnity of a court. In the Calvinist tradition, the moment of death is the moment when the soul faces God's judgement.

Stanza 3

The speaker tells us that she has tidied up her legal affairs and thus prepared and waited for the moment of death. The 'portion' of her that was not 'Assignable' is her soul, the spiritual self, which awaited the arrival of God. However, it was not the presence of God, coming to claim her soul, that filled her consciousness, but a fly that 'interposed' between her and her expected salvation. The word 'interposed' suggests that the fly got between the dying person and the solemn moment of death.

Stanza 4

In the final stanza, as the moment of death is described, the phrasing is fractured, suggesting the failure of consciousness, as sight, movement and sound blur and become one. As a result the fly is described as coming 'With Blue – uncertain stumbling Buzz – '. Like a drunkard disturbing the solemnity of an important occasion, the stumbling, buzzing, blue-black fly comes between the dying person's consciousness and the expected light. And then, as suggested by the imagery of light and darkness, the dying person was plunged into the darkness of death, and sight failed. The final line, 'I could not see to see' suggests that, at the moment of death, both the physical sight of the dying person and her understanding of what is happening failed.

It is not clear from the final stanza whether the 'Windows' mentioned in the second last line of the poem refer to the windows in the room, or the dying person's eyes.

Themes and imagery

The poem seems to suggest that death, which many believe will be the moment when the soul is united with God, is not a momentous occasion.

The arrival of the fly, symbol of human decay and corruption, suggests that **death is something ordinary and insignificant**, and something that cannot be managed, arranged or ordered. The dying person had high expectations of death as a moment of spiritual enlightenment. Instead, the buzzing of a fly filled her last moments of consciousness. In this instance, the speaker did not find what she expected or hoped to find.

The ending of the poem, and the **anti-climax** it describes, suggests that humans have no way of knowing if the immortal life with God that their faith professes actually exists. It may even suggest that immortal life with God does not exist. The final line implies that the dying person is robbed of both sight and understanding, a finality emphasised by the rhyme of 'me' and 'see'. Is this the message of the voice from the dead – after dying, all is darkness and emptiness? Is that the significance of the dash that ends the poem?

As a symbol of death, **the fly represents human decay and the corruption of the body**. The poem has no symbol of the soul rising to heaven, or of divine light flooding the death-room. As such the poem would have seemed blasphemous to the members of Dickinson's Calvinist community as she has replaced the arrival of Christ the King with the arrival of a buzzing fly. There is also no sense of heaven in the poem and the voice speaking the poem does so from nowhere. For these reasons, some readers believe that the poem offers evidence of Dickinson's lack of faith in an afterlife with God.

Form and language

As befits a poem on a religious theme, 'I heard a Fly buzz' is written in the metre of a hymn: a four-beat line followed by a three-beat line in a four-line stanza with a regular rhyming scheme. However, the use of half-rhymes ('Room' and 'Storm'), the dash (with its effect of breaking up the phrasing) and run-on lines takes away the sing-song effect of the form.

The language captures the speaking voice, while the successive use of 'and then' (lines 11 and 15) creates a mounting sense of drama.

SNAPSHOT

- Written in the voice of a dead person
- Describes the moment of death
- Solemnity of death disturbed by the fly
- Ending almost comic
- Themes of death and faith
- Ambiguous on the issue of eternal life
- Written in four-line stanzas
- Use of dash, run-on lines and 'and then' for dramatic effect

---

Exam-Style Questions

Understanding the poem

1	What is the story that the poem tells?
2	Who tells the story?
3	In the second stanza, which of the following words best describes the attitude of the mourners as they wait for the death of the dying person: upset; excited; frightened; resigned? Explain your answer.
4	Who is the 'King' referred to in the second stanza?
5	What words or phrases in stanza three suggest that the speaker has prepared carefully for her death?
6	What happens at the end of the poem?
7	Given the ending, how would you describe the tone of the poem: amused, irritated, fearful, puzzled, disappointed? Explain your choice.

Thinking about the poem

1	'I heard a Fly buzz – when I died – ' (line 1). In your view, is this an effective opening to the poem? Explain your answer.
2	Pick two examples of words chosen by the poet that you think are particularly effective. Explain your choice.
3	Do you find any humour in the poem? Explain your answer.
4	Consider each of these readings of the poem. Which of them, if any, corresponds with your own? ■ The fly cheats the dying person of a glimpse of God before the moment of death. ■ The appearance of the fly is a reminder that death is about the decay of the body. ■ The buzzing of the fly suggests that death is not an important event. ■ The poem calls into question faith in God and an eternal life. Explain your choice.
5	The critic Helen Vendler suggests that the dying speaker realises that the insignificant fly is herself. Discuss this interpretation.
6	On the evidence of this poem, what kind of person do you imagine Emily Dickinson to have been? Explain your answer.
7	Which of Dickinson's other poems on your course bears the closest resemblance to this one? Explain your answer.

Imagining

1	Imagine you are one of the mourners in the room. Write a letter to a friend in which you describe the moment of death and the feeling in the room afterwards.
2	You are asked to make a video version of the poem. Describe as clearly as you can what your finished video will look and sound like.

Before you read

Groupwork

Think of a song that you feel deals in a vivid way with depression, joy and anguish. Share your choice with a fellow student. Discuss what makes the song so memorable. Then read the poem and compare it with your song choice.

The Soul has Bandaged moments

The Soul has Bandaged moments –
When too appalled to stir –
She feels some ghastly Fright come up
And stop to look at her –

Salute her – with long fingers –   5
Caress her freezing hair –
Sip, Goblin, from the very lips
The Lover – hovered – o'er –
Unworthy, that a thought so mean
Accost a Theme – so – fair –   10

The soul has moments of Escape –
When bursting all the doors –
She dances like a Bomb, abroad,
And swings upon the Hours,

As do the Bee – delirious borne –   15
Long Dungeoned from his Rose –
Touch Liberty – then know no more,
But Noon, and Paradise –

The Soul's retaken moments –
When, Felon led along,   20
With shackles on the plumed feet,
And staples, in the Song,

The Horror welcomes her, again,
These, are not brayed of Tongue –

Glossary

7	*Goblin*: an ugly demon
10	*Accost*: approach and speak to someone; also, solicit sexually
13	*abroad*: in different directions; also, out of doors
16	*Dungeoned*: imprisoned
19	*Soul's*: Soul has
20	*Felon*: convict, prisoner
21	*shackles*: rings fixed round a prisoner's ankles and joined by a chain
21	*plumed*: feathered; the image calls to mind the messenger of the Gods, Mercury, who had winged sandals
24	*These*: refers back to the 'retaken moments' of line 19
24	*not brayed of Tongue*: not spoken about or publicised

Guidelines

The poem explores depression and the contrasting highs and lows of the inner life. Images of horror and fright are contrasted with images of fulfilled happiness. Images of imprisonment are contrasted with those of freedom. The poem begins with the figure of Fright and ends with the figure of Horror, suggesting that the soul experiences more anguish than joy.

The poem may be read in a number of different, if related, ways; in psychological terms, as an exploration of depression and elation; in spiritual terms, as an exploration of despair and hope; in sexual terms, as an exploration of oppression and freedom; in artistic terms, as an exploration of the absence and presence of inspiration.

Commentary

Stanzas 1 and 2

The opening line suggests that the Soul has moments of hurt when she hides her wounds beneath bandages, but the reader is given no idea what causes these 'Bandaged moments'. In these times of vulnerability the Soul is paralysed and subjected to unwelcome attention. Many critics interpret the 'Fright' of stanza 1 as death or death's servant. In stanza 2 the Fright is described as saluting and caressing the Soul's freezing hair. The 'freezing hair' indicates the chill of fear and the coldness of death experienced by the Soul as the Fright pays her unwanted attention. The wounded soul is portrayed as a terrified woman, helpless before the attention of a predatory male. The verbs describing the action of the Fright create a mounting sense of dread: 'stop', 'look', 'Salute', 'Caress', 'Sip'. The dashes of line 5 capture the increasing fear of the Soul.

Lines 9–10 have an apologetic air, as though the speaker is ashamed at the image of the Fright sipping from the lips that 'The Lover' kissed. However, the placing of the word 'Unworthy' makes the subject uncertain. Does it refer to the Lover; the Fright; the Soul herself? Does the word refer to the erotic turn the poem takes at this point?

Stanzas 3 and 4

These two stanzas suggest an intense period of psychological elation and, perhaps, artistic energy. The poem breaks free of the atmosphere of threat, dread, claustrophobia and death that dominates the first two stanzas. Now the images suggest sensuous pleasure, freedom, warmth and fulfilment. The verbs hint at a manic energy: 'bursting', 'dances', 'swings'. The nouns 'Noon' and 'Paradise' suggest perfect happiness.

The memorable simile 'like a Bomb' strikes a note of caution. The Soul's escape is too exuberant, too ecstatic, too public. Like a bomb, it will explode and leave a sense of desolation. (In other poems, Dickinson used images of a volcano and of a loaded gun to suggest the dangerous potential she saw in herself.) Interestingly, the word 'Bomb' was used in the nineteenth century to describe the act of striking a bell. This meaning may link to the idea of the Soul swinging upon the rope of a church bell to mark the 'Hours'.

Stanzas 5 and 6

The moments of escape come to an end and, like a prisoner, the Soul is welcomed again by 'The Horror'. The imagery of shackles and staples is striking and contrasts with the imagery of flight often used by Dickinson to denote joy and happiness. The final two stanzas express the poem's despairing point of view that the interior

life – psychological, spiritual, artistic, erotic – is characterised by feelings of oppression and despair, punctuated by periods of respite.

The final line states that these, the 'Soul's retaken moments', 'are not brayed of Tongue'. This may suggest that depression and despair are not spoken of in public, and to do so would be to 'bray', to speak in a way that might be considered rough and uncouth. Thus, the experience of depression is, essentially, a lonely and an isolating one. However, the tone of the final line can also be read as a proud declaration of strength and pride. Despite the brave ending, the reader realises that the torments of the Soul will never end.

Themes and imagery

The central theme is one of depression, of the fragile nature of the soul and the suffering and torment to which the soul is subject. In the poem the soul fluctuates between hurt and ecstasy. The soul is like a convicted prisoner who experiences a brief moment of escape before being returned to confinement. In the poem, the soul, the innermost identity of the person, is kept in oppression. The imagery works by means of **contrast** as images of wounding, fright and imprisonment oppose those of joy and freedom.

The Gothic

The taste for the Gothic in both popular and literary culture in nineteenth-century America is reflected in Dickinson's 'Goblin poems'. Dickinson evokes the figure of the beautiful woman, vulnerable in both body and soul, who is held captive by the terrifying goblin. Her poems mirror the uncanny and supernatural qualities of Gothic fiction.

The personification of the soul as a woman and the fright as a seductive goblin lends a **Gothic** feel to the imagery of the opening two stanzas. The imagery is erotic and frightening. It is intended to inspire a feeling of dread in the reader. Equally appalling is the imagery of captivity in the final two stanzas, where the 'Soul' is held captive by 'The Horror' (line 23) and treated as a criminal.

Form and language

The poem departs from Dickinson's usual four-line stanzas with one verse of six lines and a concluding couplet. Structurally, it can be divided into three sections, each containing two stanzas. Each section describes a different condition of the soul. The first (stanzas 1 and 2) suggests constraint and violation; the second (stanzas 3 and 4) celebrates the delirium of freedom; the third (stanzas 5 and 6) describes the soul's recapture.

In the second stanza, the repetition of 'her', the alliteration and the hissing 's' sounds combine to create a feeling of dread. The dashes in the opening stanzas and the final dash of the poem also contribute to this sense of dread, of things that cannot be spoken.

The third-person narrative creates a distance between the narrator and the experiences she describes, although the imagery still has the power to shock and disturb.

Questions

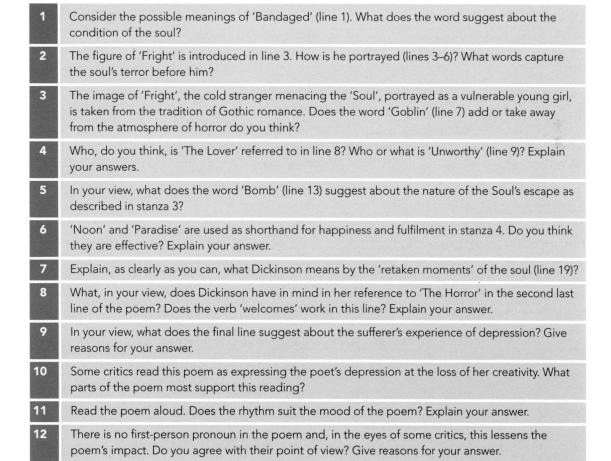

1	Consider the possible meanings of 'Bandaged' (line 1). What does the word suggest about the condition of the soul?
2	The figure of 'Fright' is introduced in line 3. How is he portrayed (lines 3–6)? What words capture the soul's terror before him?
3	The image of 'Fright', the cold stranger menacing the 'Soul', portrayed as a vulnerable young girl, is taken from the tradition of Gothic romance. Does the word 'Goblin' (line 7) add or take away from the atmosphere of horror do you think?
4	Who, do you think, is 'The Lover' referred to in line 8? Who or what is 'Unworthy' (line 9)? Explain your answers.
5	In your view, what does the word 'Bomb' (line 13) suggest about the nature of the Soul's escape as described in stanza 3?
6	'Noon' and 'Paradise' are used as shorthand for happiness and fulfilment in stanza 4. Do you think they are effective? Explain your answer.
7	Explain, as clearly as you can, what Dickinson means by the 'retaken moments' of the soul (line 19)?
8	What, in your view, does Dickinson have in mind in her reference to 'The Horror' in the second last line of the poem? Does the verb 'welcomes' work in this line? Explain your answer.
9	In your view, what does the final line suggest about the sufferer's experience of depression? Give reasons for your answer.
10	Some critics read this poem as expressing the poet's depression at the loss of her creativity. What parts of the poem most support this reading?
11	Read the poem aloud. Does the rhythm suit the mood of the poem? Explain your answer.
12	There is no first-person pronoun in the poem and, in the eyes of some critics, this lessens the poem's impact. Do you agree with their point of view? Give reasons for your answer.
13	'With shackles on the plumed feet, / And staples, in the Song' (lines 21–22). Write a short piece (poetry or prose) or create an image that conveys the idea of restriction suggested in these lines.

I could bring You Jewels – had I a mind to

I could bring You Jewels – had I a mind to –
But You have enough – of those –
I could bring You Odors from St. Domingo –
Colors – from Vera Cruz –

Berries of the Bahamas – have I –   5
But this little Blaze
Flickering to itself – in the Meadow –
Suits me – more than those –

Never a Fellow matched this Topaz –
And his Emerald Swing –   10
Dower itself – for Bobadilo –
Better – Could I bring?

Glossary

3	*St. Domingo*: San (or Santo) Domingo, capital of the Dominican Republic, a city given its name by Christopher Columbus
4	*Vera Cruz*: port in Mexico, founded by Cortés and known for its colourful houses and its tropical plants and flowers
5	*Bahamas*: island in the West Indies where Columbus first landed in 1492
6	*this little Blaze*: jewelweed, a green plant with tiny trumpet-shaped yellow and orange flowers, which are dusted with red speckles; also called touch-me-not
9	*Topaz*: a gem famous for its lustre and beautiful colours
10	*Emerald*: a precious stone, green in colour
11	*Dower*: gift, often used to describe the wealth brought to a man by a woman on their marriage
11	*Bobadilo*: Francisco de Bobadilla was sent by Isabella and Ferdinand, the Spanish monarchs, to St Domingo to take over from Columbus as governor of the Indies. He ordered Columbus to be returned to Spain in shackles and he seized his gold and treasures, giving himself enormous wealth

Guidelines

Although Dickinson is often described as a recluse, she had a wide circle of friends and corresponded with many of them throughout her life. Her letters often took the form of poems, and she enclosed poems with small gifts. These poems, many of them written as riddles, show the playful and humorous sides of Dickinson's personality. Some of the letters/poems were clearly intended as tokens of her love, although she took considerable pains to disguise the identity of her beloved. 'I could bring You Jewels' is a good example of her letter-poems. It was sent to Susan Gilbert in 1863, seven years after Susan's marriage to Austin Dickinson. Susan was Emily's closest friend and this is one of over 300 poems she wrote to her, even though the two lived next door to each other. Enclosed with the poem was a gift of the meadow flower jewelweed.

> **Writing to Susan**
>
> **Dickinson sent an astonishing range of writing to Susan Gilbert, ranging from jokes and comments about mutual acquaintances to poems on the theme of romantic love in the lives of women. She sent her letter-poems on faith and doubt; notes on the books they were reading (they both read widely); reflections on her father's rules; and a letter-poem of comfort and grief on the death of Susan's son, Gib, at the age of eight. In this correspondence, Dickinson experimented with punctuation, layout and illustrations, and both her humour and intellect are evident.**

The opening line of the poem strikes a **note of confidence and playfulness**, a note that is sustained to the end of the poem, making this the most joyful of the Dickinson poems on your course. The poem is also different in that it focuses on a relationship, rather than on the individual consciousness of the speaker.

Commentary

Stanzas 1 and 2

The speaker considers the gift she could offer her beloved, the 'You' of the poem. Different gifts are considered: jewels, perfumes, exotic colours and fruits. The place names mentioned are associated with the Spanish conquest of the Caribbean and South America and are intended to suggest somewhere exotic. She settles on a small meadow flower, 'this little Blaze', itself a jewel. The chosen gift is a mark of the speaker's freedom and uniqueness, and a reflection, perhaps, of her unshowy personality. The note of confidence and self-ease is striking in this choice. The luxury of considering exotic gifts is reflected in the long lines that Dickinson employs in stanza 1. As she settles on her gift, the lines get shorter, the tone more decisive.

Stanza 3

A jaunty, confident tone is evident in the use of the word 'Fellow' (line 9). The concluding rhetorical question suggests that the flower is the best gift she could offer, as valuable and priceless as the dowry a wife might bring to marry the extremely wealthy 'Bobadilo'. Notice how in this final stanza the assured, confident tone is emphasised in the use of the word 'Never' and in the rhyming of 'Swing' and 'bring', which closes her argument with a ring of authority. In its playful, assured way, the poem establishes that the true value of gifts and the true nature of riches cannot be measured in material terms.

Themes and imagery

Domingo

This island in the Caribbean (modern-day Haiti and the Dominican Republic) was a site of rum production, slave revolution and butterflies. It was often invoked during the American Civil War by those opposed to the emancipation of slaves as evidence that black people were primitive and ungovernable. To their way of thinking, the slave revolution of 1791 led to a descent into lawlessness and the killing of white settlers.

The central theme is one of love and friendship and the best gift to celebrate it. The poem is a study in contrasts between goods considered valuable (jewels), rare (perfumes and spices from St Domingo) and exotic (colours and fruits from the Caribbean) and goods that are simple, natural and homely, with no material value, such as a common meadow flower. The gift that the speaker chooses suggests that the friendship is as beautiful and natural as the little flower. It is typical of Dickinson's wit that she substitutes a flower called jewelweed for the jewels mentioned in line 1. Here, as elsewhere in her poetry, Dickinson uses images from the Caribbean and South America to suggest the bright and pleasurable aspects of life. Domingo, in particular, seemed to inspire her imagination.

Form and language

Dickinson employs the four-line stanza with the rhyme occurring between lines 2 and 4. Unlike other of her poems, there is a conversational feel to the opening lines, achieved by the length of the line and the phrase 'had I a mind to' (line 1). This is **Dickinson at her most relaxed**. As the poem proceeds, the tone becomes less conversational and concludes with the magisterial four-word last line, confident and joyous.

Questions

1	What do we learn about the central characters, the 'You' and 'I' of the poem, and their lives and circumstances, from 'I could bring You jewels – had I a mind to'? Explain your answer.
2	What, in your view, is the effect of the place names used in lines 3–5?
3	In the first five lines, a number of potential gifts are rejected. How does the gift that is eventually selected differ from them?
4	What does the choice of gift tell you about the 'I' of the poem? What does it suggest about the nature of the relationship between the giver and the receiver?
5	What view of riches is suggested by the poem? Explain your answer.
6	'The voice of the poem shows an absolute certainty and confidence in herself, in her choice of gift and in her beloved.' Give your response to this assessment of the poem.
7	Which of the following words best captures the tone of the poem: playful, joyous, romantic or serious? Explain your choice.
8	How would you feel if you received this poem and a gift of a meadow flower, such as a snowdrop or a bluebell, to go with it? Give reasons for your answer.
9	'The poem conjures up a vivid picture of an exotic world but settles for a homely pleasure.' Give your response to this view of the poem.
10	Using 'I could bring You Jewels' as a model, write your own love poem.

Before you read

Have a class discussion on the animals that cause feelings of fear or terror and try to identify the source of these feelings.

A narrow Fellow in the Grass

A narrow Fellow in the Grass
Occasionally rides –
You may have met Him – did you not
His notice sudden is –

The Grass divides as with a Comb –   5
A spotted shaft is seen –
And then it closes at your feet
And opens further on –

He likes a Boggy Acre
A Floor too cool for Corn –   10
Yet when a Boy, and Barefoot –
I more than once at Noon
Have passed, I thought, a Whip lash
Unbraiding in the Sun
When stooping to secure it   15
It wrinkled, and was gone –

Several of Nature's People
I know, and they know me –
I feel for them a transport
Of cordiality –   20

But never met this Fellow
Attended, or alone
Without a tighter breathing
And Zero at the Bone –

Glossary

6	*spotted shaft*: the long thin mottled body of the snake
13	*Whip lash*: the part of the whip used for striking or lashing
14	*Unbraiding*: untwining like the leather thongs of a lash
19	*transport*: strong emotion

Guidelines

This was one of the few poems published during Dickinson's life. It was published under the title 'Snake', although the word is not used in the poem. (In a letter discussing the poem, written in 1866, Dickinson did, however, refer to 'my Snake'.) Dickinson wrote many poems on small creatures that she observed in her garden. Her attitude to birds and animals is often one of amused fascination. However, the snake arouses a terrified response. The poem has the riddling quality that characterises many of Dickinson's poems.

Commentary

Stanza 1

The opening two lines of the poem strike an off-hand note, as if the reader has joined a casual conversation. The word 'Fellow', for example, creates a sense of easy familiarity, as though the speaker is referring to a neighbour. The tone alters with the abrupt fourth line, 'His notice sudden is', and the menacing 's' sounds it contains indicate an absence of fellow-feeling in the speaker for the snake. On second reading, it may well be the figure of the Devil on horseback that is brought to mind by the imagery.

Stanza 2

Stanza 2 hints at the secrecy, danger and unpredictability of the snake. The effect of the snake's movement, 'The Grass divides', can be seen but not the snake itself. The word 'shaft' suggests the danger and speed of an arrow-shaft.

Stanza 3

The third, eight-line, central stanza returns to the casual-seeming air of the opening line and describes the favoured habitat of the snake, 'He likes a Boggy Acre'. The use of the personal pronoun 'He' suggests a fellow-human. The poem changes direction in this stanza. There is a switch to the past tense as the narrator recalls an unsettling boyhood memory. The word 'Barefoot' suggests the vulnerability and simplicity of the boy, who is no match for the crafty snake. The snake's ability to transform from what seems an inanimate piece of leather, 'a Whip lash', into a living, writhing animal is recalled. The use of 'wrinkled' as a verb is noteworthy.

Stanzas 4 and 5

There is a definite change of tone and voice in the final stanzas. The speaker now sounds like the adult poet. He (she?) states that he knows 'Several of Nature's People' and they know him, and he professes for them 'a transport / Of cordiality'. This delightful phrase captures the whimsical air of this stanza. However, the snake stands apart from the 'Several of Nature's People' and the speaker's attitude to the snake is caught in the celebrated final stanza. Here the speaker relates that whether alone or with others, any encounter with a snake is terrifying.

The final line of the poem, 'And Zero at the Bone', evokes the inner terror caused in the speaker by this animal. The combination of the abstract 'Zero', with its association of void and emptiness, and the concrete 'Bone' captures the physical sensation of a terror that is almost beyond words. The use of the word 'Fellow' in the final stanza reads as a measured irony.

Themes and imagery

The poem explores **the relationship between humans and the natural world**. Elsewhere in her poetry, Dickinson describes chance encounters with birds and other creatures in her garden. These encounters evoke delight. In the case of the snake, the encounter is unnerving and evokes terror. The image of the grass dividing, 'as with a Comb' (line 5) to represent the movement of the snake, is an example of Dickinson's powers of observation.

Interestingly, **the poet represents herself as a boy** in the poem. In doing so, the poem hints at what Helen Vendler calls 'the freedom granted to boys and denied to girls'.

In responding to a poem about a snake, it is almost impossible to ignore the figure of the snake in the story of Adam and Eve. There, the serpent, the Devil in disguise, deceived Adam and Eve into acting against God's command. This story predisposes us to view the snake as an evil deceiver.

Form and language

Dickinson rarely strayed from the four-line stanza of the ballad or the hymn. When she does, as in the third stanza of this poem, there is very little innovation in the stanza form. Her success as a poet comes in the dramatic use of the dash, the changes in tone she achieves through the sound of words and her startling imagery, as evident in the final line of the poem. Cutting across the stanzas, the poem has three distinct sections. The first (lines 1–10) paints a general picture of the snake. The second (lines 11–16) recalls boyhood encounters with the snake. The third (lines 17–24) makes a distinction between the snake (and the feeling it evokes) and other creatures in nature.

Questions

1	The word 'Fellow' has a feeling of familiarity about it. Does it capture the speaker's attitude to the snake? Explain your answer.
2	In six lines (lines 3–8), Dickinson succeeds in suggesting the danger, unpredictability and secrecy of the snake. How, in your opinion, does she do this?
3	What, in your view, does the snake's habitat (lines 9–10) tell us about him?
4	In your view, which of the following are associated with the adjective 'Barefoot' in line 11: hardiness, innocence, vulnerability or foolishness? Explain your choice.
5	What do the words 'Whip lash' (line 13) suggest about the snake? Explain your answer.
6	What is the speaker's relationship with 'Nature's People', as described in stanza 4? In your view, is there anything contradictory in the idea of 'a transport / Of cordiality'?
7	What, do you think, is the effect of the 'But' placed at the opening of the fifth stanza?
8	Dickinson substitutes her phrase 'Zero at the bone' in the final line for the more usual 'chilled to the bone'. In your view, what does she gain by doing so?
9	Show how Dickinson uses rhythm and sound to capture the movements of the snake.
10	'In the poem, the representation of the snake moves from a familiar neighbour to a deeply disturbing, hidden presence.' Discuss this statement.
11	What, if anything, does the snake symbolise in the poem? Explain your answer.
12	Re-read the poem. Note any places where the voice of the speaker changes, and comment on the change.
13	'And Zero at the Bone – ' (line 24). Suggest a piece of music that you think resonates with this powerful phrase.

Before you read

Think of experiences that are accompanied by a natural high and that might be described as exhilarating and intoxicating.

I taste a liquor never brewed –

I taste a liquor never brewed –
From Tankards scooped in Pearl –
Not all the Vats upon the Rhine
Yield such an Alcohol!

Inebriate of Air – am I –   5
And Debauchee of Dew –
Reeling – thro endless summer days –
From inns of Molten Blue –

When 'Landlords' turn the drunken Bee
Out of the Foxglove's door –   10
When Butterflies – renounce their 'drams' –
I shall but drink the more!

Till Seraphs swing their snowy Hats –
And Saints – to windows run –
To see the little Tippler   15
Leaning against the – Sun –

Glossary

3	Vats: vessels for storing liquid such as wine
3	Rhine: a wine region of Germany. There is another draft of this poem in which line 3 reads, 'Not all the Frankfort berries'
5	Inebriate: intoxicated
6	Debauchee: person who pursues pleasure in a reckless way
8	Molten: melted; presumably, the shimmering effect on the blue sky caused by the heat of the sun
10	Foxglove: tall purple- or white-flowered plant
11	drams: small measures of alcohol
13	Seraphs: angels who guard God's throne
15	Tippler: frequent drinker of alcohol
16	In the other draft of the poem, the final line reads 'From Manzanilla come.'

Guidelines

This poem was first published anonymously on 4 May 1861 in the *Springfield Republican*, under the title 'The May Wine'. Two lines were altered by the editor to achieve an exact rhyme, and another line was changed to make the meaning clearer. The central metaphor of intoxication is ironic, given that Dickinson grew up in a Puritan household, and her father was a supporter of the Temperance League. A further irony is that the poem was written in the common rhythm of hymns.

> **Temperance movement**
>
> A social, religious and political movement that encouraged people to abstain from drinking alcohol. In the period before the American Civil War many temperance reformers were progressive and liberal and were involved in the movement to emancipate slaves and promote equality. For these reformers, every citizen had the right to control over their bodies.
>
> Interestingly, in a letter to Thomas Wentworth Higginson, Dickinson said she had tasted rum from Domingo and it could not be equalled.

Commentary

Stanza 1

The poem describes the speaker's sense of delight in the beauty of the world in summer. Dickinson strikes an exaggerated, playful tone, established from the first line, 'I taste a liquor never brewed'. The riddling quality of this line and the extravagance of the imagery capture the mood of dizzy happiness that infuses the poem. The 'Pearl' of line 2 refers to the frothy bubbles in the vats of alcohol. The speaker says that her non-drunken intoxication could not be equalled by drinking wine from the Rhine.

Stanzas 2 and 3

The idea of intoxication continues. The imagery in stanza 2 suggests a drunken person ('Inebriate') behaving without any restraint ('Debauchee') as he or she reels from pub to pub. The humour is that the speaker drinks in nothing more than the air, the dew from the grass, and the shimmering blue of the sky.

The imagery of flowers as inns or taverns and bees as drunkards in the third stanza maintains the vein of cartoon humour evident throughout the poem. The final line of the third stanza, 'I shall but drink the more!', appears as the comic rebellious declaration of a drunkard.

Stanza 4

Dickinson does not present the world's beauty as a sign of God's creativity. The inhabitants of heaven are presented as faintly ridiculous, enclosed and perhaps envious of the freedom of 'the little Tippler', whose pose, leaning against the sun, strikes a note of comic rebelliousness, applauded by the angels, as they swing their hats to honour her.

Some critics do not read this stanza as a celebration of excess and rebelliousness. Instead, they view the 'Sun' of line 16 as a symbol of Christ and consider that the speaker is announcing her intention to enjoy the beauty of the world until she comes into the company of Christ, where her arrival will be greeted by the watching angels and saints.

Themes and imagery

Richard Sewell, Dickinson's biographer, describes this poem as **'a rapturous poem about summer'**. In many of Dickinson's poems, the 'I' persona is shown as starving or thirsting. This poem is a rarity in her work in that it celebrates the joy of excess, a reckless, indulgent joy captured in the word 'Debauchee' (line 6). The sense of **happiness, excess and rebelliousness** of the poem is expressed through **images of drunken intoxication and indulgence**. A woman of Dickinson's class would have been expected to act in a restrained way and to exhibit exemplary behaviour in public. Dickinson clearly relishes portraying the speaker as someone who is drunk and unrestrained.

The imagery of the poem has a child-like, cartoonish quality. The poem is topsy-turvy in its celebration of intoxication over sobriety, with the 'little Tippler' (line 15) being envied by the angels and saints in heaven.

Form and language

The poem is written in the common metre of hymns and flows along without any of the dramatic pauses or changes of tone evident in many of her other poems. The use of alliteration as in 'Debauchee of Dew' (line 6) has a comic effect.

Questions

1	What kind of liquor is not brewed?
2	How can tankards be scooped in pearl?
3	What creature might be a 'Debauchee of Dew' (line 6)?
4	Is the association of drunkenness with bees (lines 9–10) apt? Explain your answer.
5	Identify the words and phrases that are associated with intoxication in the poem.
6	'The three most important words in the poem are "endless summer days"' (line 7). Do you agree? Give reasons for your answer.
7	'I shall but drink the more!' (line 12). What, in your view, is the tone of this declaration?
8	What image of heaven is presented in stanza 4? In your view, is it an effective image?
9	One critic remarked that the sun, in stanza 4, is treated as a celestial lamppost. Would you agree that the entire poem is marked by a similar spirit of whimsy and joy? Explain your answer.
10	Comment on the use of comic exaggeration in the poem. What phrases strike you as being particularly humorous?
11	What view of Emily Dickinson emerges from this poem?
12	Compare the celebration of the summer sun in this poem with the meditation on winter light in 'There's a certain Slant of light'.
13	Emily Dickinson's father, Edward, was stern in character, disciplined in his behaviour and a supporter of the Temperance League. Imagine a scene between father and daughter in which he speaks to Emily after reading this poem.

After great pain, a formal feeling comes

After great pain, a formal feeling comes –
The Nerves sit ceremonious, like Tombs –
The stiff Heart questions was it He, that bore,
And Yesterday, or Centuries before?

The Feet, mechanical, go round –   5
Of Ground, or Air, or Ought –
A Wooden way
Regardless grown,
A Quartz contentment, like a stone –

This is the Hour of Lead –   10
Remembered, if outlived,
As Freezing persons, recollect the Snow –
First – Chill – then Stupor – then the letting go –

Before you read

Think of a book, play or film that portrays a character numbed by grief or pain. How did the text represent or convey the suffering of the character? When you have read the poem, compare Dickinson's account of the aftermath of great suffering with the depiction in the text you chose.

Glossary

3	*bore*: could refer to bearing suffering, or to accepting the blame
6	*Ought*: anything
13	*Stupor*: state of near unconsciousness

Guidelines

This poem was written in 1862, a year in which Dickinson wrote 366 poems. Many commentators believe that she was on the edge of madness during this time. The poem explores the effects of anguish upon the individual. The source of the 'great pain' is not disclosed. It may be the result of loneliness, separation or bereavement, all of which Dickinson experienced. There is an absence of personal statement in the poem, which gives it a universal quality, as if the poet is speaking on behalf of all who have suffered great pain, distress and loss.

Commentary

Stanza 1

The opening line strikes a note of dignified solemnity. The nature of the 'great pain' is not described. It suggests that such pain leads not to a loss of control but to the constraint of formality. As with mourners at a funeral, the nerves and feelings are deadened, and ceremony and stiffness replace spontaneity. The victim's confusion is captured in lines 3–4. 'He' could refer to the 'stiff Heart', or to Christ, whose suffering is brought to mind by the experience of great pain. Feeling disoriented, her (or his) heart wonders when the suffering took place, unable to distinguish between recent time ('Yesterday') and past time ('Centuries before'), and whether it was she who endured it. The victim has no way of answering these questions.

Stanza 2

The sense of control is lost in the second stanza with its fragmented phrases and incomplete meanings. The stanza suggests that the sufferer is walking around. The use of the definite article in the phrase 'The Feet' suggests that the sufferer feels disconnected from her body, and the body moves in a mechanical, stumbling way, with little sense of where she is or what surrounds her: 'Of Ground, or Air, or Ought'. The three words of line 7, 'A Wooden way', may suggest the unnatural movements of a puppet, the mechanical movement of the sufferer, and the way in which suffering can dull our senses and make us insensible. It may also refer to the suffering of Christ on the Way of the Cross.

The phrasing and punctuation of this second stanza suggest a series of unconnected sensations and thoughts, and reflect the way in which pain interrupts the mind's ability to make sense of experience and derive meaning from it. The final line of the stanza suggests that great pain results in a stone-like insensitivity, which brings its own kind of contentment, 'A Quartz contentment, like a stone'. The word 'contentment' is almost ironic.

Stanza 3

The opening line of the third stanza defines the nature of this 'contentment' – it is the 'Hour of Lead', a period of heavy and deadening oppression when all human sensations become frozen. This period is not forgotten, even if the sufferer survives it. The memory of this oppression is likened to 'Freezing persons' recollecting 'the Snow'. The continuous present of the final line means that the reader cannot determine if the freezing person has survived the ordeal, or if it continues. Here, as in the rest of the poem, the thought is incomplete.

Themes and imagery

In this poem Dickinson again **explores the effects of anguish and pain upon the individual**. It describes the psychological and spiritual numbness that follows intense pain. To the sufferer, the experience will be remembered, if he or she survives it, as a death-like experience.

The poem captures the way victims of suffering cope by burying their feelings and acting in a formal and mechanical way. The imagery suggests the behaviour of mourners at a funeral, who have been numbed by their grief. The brilliant simile used in line 2, 'The Nerves sit ceremonious, like Tombs – ', merits close attention. It suggests that sufferers are so stunned by pain that their nervous system, the means by which thoughts and feelings move between the brain and the body, comes to a standstill, to the effect that they resemble a statue on a tomb more than a living person. Through this image, the poet establishes a chilling relationship between suffering and the death of the inner life.

This idea carries over to the concluding image of the poem (line 13), which suggests that sufferers, if they survive, when they recall their death-like paralysis will, in the words of Helen Vendler, 'Enact, in sequence, the stages of trauma.' These stages are: the 'Chill', as the body temperature drops; then the 'Stupor', as the cold causes the sufferer to fall into a state of near unconsciousness and to lose the sense of feeling; and then the 'letting go', as the sufferer surrenders to the snow and loses the will to live. What is remarkable is the logical exactness of this simile. Even in confronting the most difficult of human experiences, **Dickinson's intellect is fully engaged**. As with the simile of line 2, the effect is chilling.

Form and language

In keeping with the theme it explores, the poem moves away from the regularity of the ballad and hymn form. The opening stanza is composed of two rhyming couplets with ten-syllable lines. The long lines of the opening stanza, with their steady stoicism and harmonious sounds, are in contrast to the staccato movement of stanza 2, where the syntax (arrangement of words) and the use of the dash suggest a series of broken, jagged thoughts. Interestingly, even in these fragmented lines, Dickinson closes the stanza with a full rhyme ('grown' and 'stone'), which leads to the controlled thought of the final stanza. The final two lines of the poem form a rhyming couplet with ten syllables in each line. This form mirrors the opening lines of the poem and gives a sense of formal completion, even if the meaning of the final line is uncertain.

The poem is remarkable for its **compression of thought**, for the way in which Dickinson fits thoughts and ideas into the fewest possible words, no more so than in line 11, 'Remembered, if outlived'.

Questions

1	'After great pain, a formal feeling comes' (line 1). Explain, as clearly as you can, what is meant by 'formal', in this context.
2	What, in your view, is the effect of comparing the nerves, which convey feelings and sensations from the body to the brain, to 'Tombs' (line 2)?
3	The meaning of lines 3–4 is hard to unravel, due to the conciseness of the language. Give careful consideration to each of the following questions: (a) What does the adjective 'stiff' suggest about the heart? (b) If 'He' does not refer to the heart, does it refer to Christ? Could it refer to both? (c) Does 'bore' suggest suffering or blame? Might it suggest both? (d) Does the line 'And Yesterday, or Centuries before' suggest the heart's confusion, or the fact that Christ's suffering is both past and present? In each case, explain your answer.
4	How, in stanza 2, is the dazed condition of the victim of great pain suggested? What words are particularly effective?
5	Comment on the use of the word 'mechanical' (line 5).
6	In your view, what kind of contentment is a 'Quartz contentment' (line 9)?
7	How well, do you think, does the phrase 'Hour of Lead' (line 10) sum up the mental and physical condition of the sufferer? Give reasons for your answer.
8	The final image of the poem 'Chill – then Stupor – then the letting go – ' is much admired. Do you read it as a pessimistic or an optimistic ending? Explain your answer.
9	Read the poem aloud. What sounds contribute to the mood of the poem?
10	'What Dickinson describes in "After great pain" is the numbed feeling that is caused by emotional or spiritual pain.' Give your response to this statement.
11	Write a short piece (poetry or prose) inspired by the title 'Formal Feeling'.

Exam-Preparation Questions

1 'Emily Dickinson's poetry explores extreme states of mind and emotion in an unusual way.' Discuss this statement.

2 Discuss the view that Emily Dickinson's fascination with death leads to some of her best writing.

3 'It is less what Emily Dickinson has to say than her manner of saying it that is interesting.' Give your view of this statement.

4 From your reading of her poetry, do you agree that Emily Dickinson's poems offer us a glimpse into a fascinating mind and a fascinating writer?

5 'The loss of love and the loss of faith are dominant themes in Emily Dickinson's poetry.' Discuss this view.

6 'Even when she is dealing with serious themes, Dickinson's poetry is marked by a sense of wit and a sense of humour.' Discuss this view.

7 'In Dickinson's poetry we see the world through the eye of an artist and the eye of a scientist.' Discuss this view.

8 'Emily Dickinson's poetry is not hard to understand. It is, however, complex.' Give your response to this statement.

9 What, in your experience, is the effect of reading Emily Dickinson's poetry?

10 'Emily Dickinson's poetry is the poetry of small details and large ideas.' Discuss this view.

11 Write an introduction to the poetry of Emily Dickinson for readers new to her poetry. Your introduction should cover the themes and preoccupations of her poetry, and how you responded to Dickinson's use of language and imagery in the poems that you have studied. Some of the following areas might be covered in your introduction:
- Exploring extreme states of mind
- Exploring death and dying
- The importance of the soul
- A fondness for definition
- Observations of nature
- The power and freshness of her language
- Her epigrammatical style
- Her creative use of the dash and capitalised nouns.

12 'What Emily Dickinson's poetry means to me.' Write an essay in response to the above title. Your essay should include a discussion of her themes and the way she expresses them. Support the points you make by reference to the poetry on your course. Some of the following topics might be included:
- Her treatment of hope and despair
- Her search for definition
- Her attitude to death and mortality
- The psychological drama of her poems
- The lack of firm conclusions
- Her sense of nature
- The craft of her poetry.

13 Write a letter to a friend outlining your experience of studying the poetry of Emily Dickinson. In your letter you should refer to her themes and the way she expresses them. Support the points you make by reference to the poetry on your course. Material might be drawn from the following:

- Her family and religious background
- The contrast between her sedate life and the drama of her poetry
- Her tone and style
- Her interest in extreme emotions and psychological states
- Her preoccupation with death
- Her painter's eye for the details of nature
- The lines and images that stay with you.

14 Write an essay in which you outline your reasons for liking or not liking the poetry of Emily Dickinson. You must refer to the poems by Dickinson on your course.

Some possible reasons for liking the poetry:

- Unique poetic voice
- Striking perspective of many poems
- Vitality and energy of the writing
- Exploration of emotions and extreme states of mind
- Exploration of the experience of death
- The impact of the poetry upon the reader
- Dickinson's wit and intelligence
- Dickinson's skill as a poet.

Some possible reasons for not liking the poetry:

- Themes of death, isolation and despair
- Absence of happiness in many poems
- Sense of annihilation in many poems
- The obsession with her own mind
- Effect of the poems upon the reader.

SNAPSHOT EMILY DICKINSON

- Sets herself the task of definition (hope, despair, pain, joy)
- Sees the world in terms of comparisons and metaphors
- Mixes abstract concepts and concrete details
- Tone is confident and authoritative
- Centrality of the soul and of personal experience
- Exploration of death, mortality and immortality
- Travels in the mind and the imagination
- Delights in observing nature

- Describes private, psychological dramas
- Interest in extreme emotions and sharp contrasts (intoxication, despair)
- Endings of poems are often open
- Style is epigrammatical
- Meanings are compressed
- Unconventional use of capital letters and the dash to highlight words and ideas
- Language is fresh and original
- Rhythm based on the metre of hymns

Sample Essay

Write a letter to a friend outlining your experience of studying the poetry of Emily Dickinson. In your letter you should refer to her themes and the way she expresses them. Support the points you make by reference to the poetry on your course.

Uses appropriate register

Dear Jane,

Expressive use of language

We have just finished reading the poetry of Emily Dickinson in class. What an amazing experience it has been. I feel I have been on an exhilarating but exhausting rollercoaster. What a fascinating poet and woman. I think Emily Dickinson proves the old saying true: never judge a book by its cover.

Viewing her life from the outside, who could have guessed at the tumultuous seas of her mind? She came from a well-respected family in Amherst in New England. Her family were Calvinists, which makes me imagine a strict upbringing with a great deal of attention on saving your soul, but maybe our ideas of other religious traditions are never really accurate. It seems Emily enjoyed parties and visiting and dancing, and several young men were interested in her. That doesn't seem too strict. In the school she attended, Mount Holyoke Female Seminary, she was a bit of a rebel, refusing to declare publicly her faith in God. That must have taken some courage. And, if her poetry is anything to go by, I don't think she ever really settled the questions of belief in God and belief in the afterlife in her lifetime. She was a rebel in other ways, too. After she came home from boarding school, she opted out of some of the duties of someone in her position: receiving visitors and making endless social calls and doing mindless household chores. I like the sound of her – quietly determined and not bound by other people's rules. (She reminds me of you.) And then when she was about thirty, something significant happened to her, because she more or less withdrew into her own room and began writing in a furious kind of way, communicating with most of the outside world through letters. I know I've often wanted to lock myself in my room, but that doesn't last more than a few hours! And when I'm in a black mood it helps if I scribble in my diary, but she wrote 366 poems in 1862 alone. What could have happened to her? We don't know and that adds to the fascination. I read her poems looking for clues, but there are no definitive answers. Her sister destroyed all her correspondence after her death, as she had requested. I wish she hadn't! Luckily, she kept the thousand or more poems (a thousand poems!) they found in her writing desk.

Selective use of relevant biographical information

Discussion of biography has to be relevant to the poetry

Personal response

Writing as a reader of the poetry

And what poems they are – short, sharp meditations on the world around her and the places she travelled to in her imagination. Those journeys were to the 'chillest' lands and the 'strangest' seas and she made them bravely and in solitude. I think I understand why hope was so important to her. If you undertake the kind of dangerous psychological journeys she did, you need to have something to fall back on, something that 'never stops – at all – '. You want everything to turn out well for her. I almost cheered when I read 'I taste a liquor never brewed', how she drank in the happiness of summer days. Those moments of happiness are rare enough in her poetry. And you hope that when she sent her

Good use of quotation in this paragraph

Shows knowledge of the poetry and a personal response

beloved the little meadow flower, described in 'I could bring You Jewels – had I a mind to', her beloved sent her something equally charming back. Because, more often than not, the emotions in the poems are fearful and despairing. Even her little poem on the snake ends with the terrifying 'Zero at the Bone'.

Good sprinkling of quotations throughout the answer

The poems that have the greatest impact on me are the darker poems. 'After great pain, a formal feeling comes' is icy in its depiction of what I think was probably a broken heart and the numb feeling that comes with intense pain, so that you no longer want to cling to life: 'First – Chill – then Stupor – then the letting go – '. It is such a precise poem that you never doubt that Dickinson is writing about herself and her own experience, even if she writes in an impersonal way. I think the impersonal style is a way of dealing with what would otherwise be too difficult to write about. There is a similar feeling of chill in 'The Soul has Bandaged moments'. (Isn't that the best title ever?!) I love the image of the 'freezing hair' and the dread caused by the unwanted advances of the 'Fright'. Likewise the images of the 'shackles on the plumed feet' and the 'staples, in the Song.' It is as if Hope has been imprisoned and 'the little Bird that kept so many warm' is now abashed. Is it strange to say 'I love' such imagery? That is the funny thing about a poem – even when it deals with psychological pain, you can admire the mind and the skill of the poet who created it. I feel a similar kind of admiration for the stately, stoical tone in which Emily describes the 'Heavenly Hurt' that comes with 'a certain Slant of light'. The light carrying the 'Seal Despair' cannot be countered or stopped and so must be endured. But she writes with such certainty and force that the poem carries her own seal of authority. Her unusual punctuation adds to the sense that she will not be contradicted. She knows what she is talking about. It's as if she masters negative experiences by defining them so clearly.

Offers both interpretation and response

Good cross-reference

Good choice of adjectives to describe the tone

Interesting comment – could be developed

Paragraph well set up

Of course, Emily Dickinson doesn't always know what she is talking about. In her two great poems on death, she ends with the shuddering dash of 'I Felt a Funeral, in my Brain' and the darkness of 'I heard a Fly buzz – when I died'. That final dash is like a barrier that stops her and us from falling over a cliff. Somewhere beyond that dash is the place 'Where the Meanings, are', but despite her brave, maybe even her mad, efforts, she cannot get there. When she pushes her imagination to 'Extremity', she still comes up short, at the end of knowing, facing the blank space beyond the dash. Or a fly gets between her and the revelation she is waiting for! 'I heard a Fly buzz' is grimly comic, but I wonder how Emily felt when she finished 'I Felt a Funeral, in my Brain'? I think she must have felt as 'wrecked' and 'solitary' as the persona of the poem. To put all that effort into imagining and understanding something and then to finish with that emptiness, that 'Zero at the Bone'. I wonder did she take consolation from creating what I think is her finest poem? I hope she did. It's not the easiest poem to read or interpret. I think it is definitely an attempt to imagine a funeral from the perspective of the person in the coffin, before the moment when you are buried and lose the connection from the life you are departing. All your experiences contract and you can only hear the world ('And then I heard them lift a Box', 'Then Space – began to toll,' 'As all the Heavens were a Bell, And Being, but an Ear') and then you lose even that connection and plunge into death. But it is also a description of Dickinson the poet undergoing the experience of imagining the funeral in her brain and persisting and succeeding, even if it is a terrifying and disturbing experience, until the point when the connection with life is severed and her

Comment and interpretation

Not afraid to acknowledge difficulty of interpretation

imagination cannot travel any further:

> And then a Plank in Reason, broke,
> And I dropped down, and down –
> And hit a World, at every plunge,
> And Finished knowing – then –

Empathetic ← I'm not sure I'd have the courage to make that kind of psychological and imaginative journey and record it as carefully as she has done. How it must have exhausted her and left her depleted.

Please read these poems, Jane, and write back and let me know that you love them as much as I do! Having encountered them, 'I feel for them a transport / Of cordiality'. I hope you will, too.

Keeps task in mind in concluding the essay

Your friend,
Sarah

ESSAY CHECKLIST		Yes √	No ×
Purpose	Has the candidate understood the task?		
	Has the candidate responded to it in a thoughtful manner?		
	Has the candidate answered the question?		
Comment:			
Coherence	Has the candidate made convincing arguments?		
	Has the candidate linked ideas?		
	Does the essay have a sense of unity?		
Comment:			
Language	Is the essay written in an appropriate register?		
	Are ideas expressed in a clear way?		
	Is the writing fluent?		
Comment:			
Mechanics	Is the use of language accurate?		
	Are all words spelled correctly?		
	Does the punctuation help the reader?		
Comment:			

John Keats

1795–1821

Biography

John Keats was born in London on 31 October 1795. In his lifetime he was sometimes derided as a 'Cockney' poet, an attack on his perceived 'working-class' background in an age when recognised poets came from higher classes. In fact, his family was not as poor as that word would suggest. His father had married the daughter of the owner of a busy coaching inn and stables near the City of London, and soon took over running it. John Keats was the eldest of five children, one of whom died as an infant.

When Keats was eight his father died in a riding accident, and soon afterwards his mother abandoned the family, leaving the children to be brought up by their grandmother in Edmonton. John Keats and his brothers, George and Tom, were sent to Clarke's School, a private boarding school run by a man of strong but unorthodox, free-thinking Christian beliefs. The school was in Enfield, close to Edmonton, now districts of north-east London, but then villages surrounded by fields, so Keats grew up knowing and loving the countryside.

At school Keats didn't show any great intellectual ability, but he got a good education, even though it was not in the old-fashioned classical tradition. He did not study Greek, but he learned to read Latin, and his education benefited greatly from his friendship with Charles Cowden Clarke, the son of the headmaster, who was eight years older than Keats, and acted as a mentor or guide, encouraging his interest in poetry, music, theatre and classical myths. Though Keats was sensitive and imaginative, he also had a pugnacious streak, and developed a reputation for fighting.

Tuberculosis

Tuberculosis, or TB, was the killer disease of earlier centuries. It was known as consumption because it consumed or ate up the person who was infected and they wasted away. It was usually associated with coughs and breathing problems. In the nineteenth century, the disease killed tens of thousands every year in Britain and Ireland, especially among the urban poor. John Keats's mother and youngest brother died of the disease, and it is more than likely that he himself was infected while nursing Tom. The discovery of antibiotics in the mid-twentieth century finally provided a cure for TB.

He was thirteen when his mother returned to be with her children. She was gravely ill with tuberculosis (TB), but far from rejecting her, her eldest son made it his job to nurse her when he was at home. She died when he was away at school, leaving him an orphan at fourteen.

His life was now under the control of his guardian, Richard Abbey, who seemed more concerned to curb his enthusiasms and ration his money than nurture or protect him. It was decided that Keats should become a doctor. The decision does not seem to have been forced on him; he had already shown compassion in the way in which he nursed his mother. He was apprenticed to a surgeon shortly before his fifteenth birthday. His childhood was over.

His apprenticeship gave him freedom. He moved out of his grandmother's house and lodged with the surgeon. In some ways, it was the happiest period of his life. He had time for reading and writing and making friends. He gradually became more and more convinced that poetry was his true destiny.

After his apprenticeship, he went on to study medicine at Guy's Hospital in London from 1815. Although he qualified as an apothecary (in effect, a junior doctor) in 1816, he had made friends in the literary world and had started to have his poems published. He finally abandoned his medical studies at the end of 1816, at the age of twenty-one. He now dedicated his life to poetry.

Keats had formed strong friendships with men who gave him some access to London's artistic world of the time. There was Leigh Hunt, the poet and radical thinker, who edited the *Examiner*, the magazine which published some of Keats's early poems. There was William Hazlitt, a powerful literary figure of the day. There was also Benjamin Haydon, a painter who guided Keats around the ancient Greek artworks in the British Museum.

The years 1817 and 1818 saw Keats moving around in north London, living mostly in Hampstead, an expanding, increasingly fashionable suburb. It was an unsettled time, but a creative one. His first book of poetry was published in 1817, and the following year he published his first long poem, *Endymion*, on a mythological subject. It was hugely ambitious, but Keats knew he had not achieved what he had set out to do. It was savaged by the critics, and some commentators believe that the reviews destroyed him. His contemporary, the much-admired and very successful poet Lord Byron, claimed that he was 'snuffed out by an article'. But Keats was not really so feeble. As he wrote in a letter, 'I was never afraid of failure; for I would sooner fail than not be among the greatest.'

In any case, there were other things than bad reviews on his mind. His youngest brother Tom had developed TB, the same disease that had killed their mother, and Keats spent a lot of time and energy looking after him. In 1818, his other brother, George, to whom he had always been closest, married and decided to emigrate to America. Keats went to see him off from Liverpool, and then went on a walking tour with his friend Charles Armitage Brown to the Lake District and then Scotland. They often walked for more than twenty miles a day in all sorts of weather, and it was after a trudge in the rain across the Isle of Mull that Keats showed the first symptoms of the illness that was to kill him.

On his return from Scotland he devoted himself to nursing his brother Tom in his final illness. At the same time, however, he applied himself with renewed energy to his writing, conscious that his imagination was becoming more and more powerful and that he was mastering his craft as a poet. As he wrote in a letter in October, 'The faint conceptions I have of Poems to come brings the blood frequently into my forehead.'

This was the beginning of an extraordinary year. Between the autumn of 1818 and the autumn of 1819 he wrote almost all the poetry for which he is now remembered, and which gives him the place he craved among the great English poets. The work of this period, completed by the time Keats was twenty-four, includes 'The Eve of St Agnes', 'La Belle Dame Sans Merci', and the great odes 'On a Grecian Urn', 'On Melancholy', 'To a Nightingale' and 'To Autumn', as well as the epic fragment 'The Fall of Hyperion'.

Tom died in December 1818, his brother John by his side. At much the same time Keats met for the first time Fanny Brawne, an eighteen-year-old girl. Although he had vowed to avoid women so that they did not distract him from his art, and although he fought against it and concealed his feelings from his friends, who thought her unworthy of him, he was falling in love.

This was a tortured yet intensely creative time for Keats. He was in love but was always battling his feelings. Not only did he lack the financial means to marry Fanny, but by early 1819 he knew, with his medical training and personal experience, that his persistent sore throat was a sign that he had contracted the same disease that had killed his mother and younger brother: tuberculosis. These days a course of antibiotics could easily cure the illness, but there was no good treatment two hundred years ago. It was a death sentence. He could not feel easy marrying Fanny when he knew that he would soon leave her a widow.

He knew all this but could not fully accept it. He alternated between devoting himself to Fanny and pushing her away. His love for her was mixed up in his mind with his approaching death. He wrote in one letter to her:

> I have two luxuries to brood over in my walks, your Loveliness and the hour of my death. O that
> I could have possession of them both in the same minute.

Perhaps the knowledge of his approaching death concentrated his mind. He knew he had little time to turn himself into the great poet he wanted to be, so he wasted none of it. The spring and early summer of 1819 produced most of the great odes in which he meditated on joy and suffering and the creative imagination, but by the end of the year he was exhausted, and would write little more.

In February 1820 Keats started coughing up blood. It was, as he declared, his 'death warrant'. He knew that he could have no more than a year to live, and that he had no hope of marriage to Fanny, although they were engaged. In September he sailed to Italy, persuaded that the mild climate of that country might improve his health. He described the last few months of his life as 'a posthumous existence'. He lingered only until 23 February 1821, when he died painfully in Rome.

Social and Cultural Context

Romanticism

Keats is usually grouped with the **English Romantic poets**. They were writers who reacted against the very rational, often witty, but primarily public poetry of the so-called Augustans, such as Alexander Pope. William Wordsworth and Samuel Taylor Coleridge had led the way with the publication of their *Lyrical Ballads* in 1798. Lord Byron, Robert Southey, William Blake and Percy Bysshe Shelley were among the other poets associated with the movement.

Their politics were often radical, and they put ordinary people and their everyday language at the heart of what they wrote. Their poetry tended to focus on **the individual soul, the passions and the creative imagination**. As Shelley wrote, the imagination 'lifts the veil from the hidden beauty of the world'.

The **natural world** was a great inspiration and source of metaphors for their poetry. Wild landscapes and wild weather were appreciated for the emotions they could stir or suggest. Wordsworth did a great deal through his poetry to make fashionable the rugged grandeur of the Lake District in north-west England, where he came from and which he wrote about.

Keats lived through times of great political unrest, in the aftermath of the French Revolution, and had himself been brought up as a freethinker. He cared deeply about social justice and the plight of ordinary people. His first chief mentor in the literary world was Leigh Hunt, who co-founded and edited the radical magazine the *Examiner*, which published some of Keats's early poems. Keats believed that poetry could and should do some good in the world, and a great deal of the hostile reaction to his long poem *Endymion* came from conservative critics who disliked its **challenging political ideas**.

Little of this radical politics, however, is evident in the poems on your course. What is apparent is his love of the natural world, the high value he placed on the imagination and the truths it could reveal. His comment on Newton's scientific explanation of the colours of the rainbow reveals a great deal about his way of thinking. He said that Newton had 'destroyed all the Poetry of the rainbow by reducing it to a Prism'. He praised the 'sensual life of verse' and looked back to the older English poetic tradition of Chaucer, Spenser and Shakespeare rather than the Augustans of the previous century.

Classicism

Romanticism and Classicism are usually regarded as opposite poles, one representing passion and imagination, the other reason and order. Keats, however, was a great admirer of the **culture, art and literature of ancient or 'classical' Greece**, which is where this sense of the word 'classical' comes from.

The sonnet 'On First Looking into Chapman's Homer' takes as its subject his discovery of the beauties of Homer, the first and most revered of Greek poets. The 'Ode on a Grecian Urn' is fuelled by his love for classical visual art and sculpture. He spent many hours in the British Museum looking at its collection of ancient Greek and Roman objects. He responded above all to the pure, joyful beauty of classical form in Greek art, and if there are hints in the ode that he saw something cold in its perfection, his admiration of it was extremely passionate. His friend George Felton Mathew said that he 'invited comparison with the Greeks in that one of the main endeavours of his poetic career was to grow more Grecian'.

He loved **Greek mythology** too, and knew the stories intimately. Many of his poems use images and stories from Greek myths.

The letters

As well as his poems, Keats left us many long, thoughtful, passionate and spontaneous letters in which he revealed a great deal about his most private self, and also **discussed his beliefs about art, beauty, and the role of the poet**. They were written to his friends and family and often contained copies of his latest verses. In particular, he wrote long letters over extended periods to his brother George and his wife, Georgiana, in America. They act as a diary of his actions and inner life, and help us to understand his character, what he was thinking and what he was trying to achieve in his poetry.

One of Keats's central beliefs about poetry was that **the poet should be a sort of chameleon**, able to take on different personae or roles, and identify at the deepest levels with the subjects of his poems, human or otherwise. His model was Shakespeare. In a famous passage from a letter to his friend Benjamin Bailey, he discusses the power of the imagination and his capacity to lose his own identity entirely in the observation and contemplation of something outside himself: 'if a sparrow come before my window, I take part in its existence and pick about the gravel'. He also used the term **'negative capability'** to describe a similar capacity in the writer to suspend his judgement in order to let his imagination work. He described negative capability as 'when a man is capable of being in uncertainties, Mysteries, doubts, without any irritable reaching after fact & reason'.

In some ways his beliefs were a reflection of his personality. He always felt overwhelmed by other people. He wrote in a letter in 1818, 'When I am in a room with People … the identity of everyone in the room begins to press upon me.' But however difficult this was in his day-to-day life, he made this characteristic a virtue in his poetry. It meant that he was capable of exploring so much of life. As he wrote in a letter in October 1818, at the start of his greatest creative period, 'I feel more and more every day, as my imagination strengthens, that I do not live in this world alone but in a thousand worlds.'

Keats and women

Keats once wrote in a letter, 'I am certain I have not a right feeling towards Women'. As a boy, he said, he had idealised and idolised them. As a grown man he struggled with his feelings towards them. He was scared of letting them get too close in case they distracted him from his chosen destiny as a poet. He was scared of being humiliated or let down by them. He was also scared of letting them down. Despite his love for Fanny Brawne, he tried several times to break off the relationship or distance himself from it. He wrote to his brother George at one point, 'I feel I can bear any thing, any misery, even imprisonment – so long as I have neither wife nor child.' But he also wrote Fanny passionate love letters, one of which declared, 'Love is my religion – I could die for that – I could die for you.'

It is perhaps not surprising, given his early experiences, that he had **complicated feelings about women**. The first woman in his life was, of course, his mother, Fanny. She left her children after her husband died, and when she came back, Keats nursed her in her illness and lavished her with love. Then she abandoned him again by dying. His sister, also called Fanny, was much younger than him, and he never had a close relationship with her, a fact that sometimes made him feel guilty.

The conflicts in his attitude to women can be seen in 'La Belle Dame Sans Merci', where the lady is both bewitching and dangerous, and also in 'Bright Star', in which he seems to desire from his 'fair love' both sacred purity and the physical intimacy that might destroy that purity.

Themes

We have already touched on many of the themes of Keats's poetry. These include the **natural world** and, just as important, humankind's relationship with it. It is a theme that is present in many of the poems on your course, including 'To one who has been long in city pent', 'Ode to a Nightingale' and 'To Autumn'. Descriptions of the natural world abound in Keats's poetry, and where it is not the subject of the poem, the natural world is often a **rich source of metaphors and images**.

A closely related theme is **the relationship of life and art**, and the role of the artist in transforming one into the other. In both his letters and his poems, Keats focuses on the part played by the imagination that is needed for that transformation; and beauty, which is both the goal and the guarantee of the act of imagination, be it poem, painting, music or sculpture. He wrote in a letter to his friend Bailey in 1817:

> 'I am certain of nothing but of the holiness of the Heart's affections and the truth of Imagination – What the imagination seizes as Beauty must be truth – whether it existed before or not – for I have the same idea of all our Passions as of Love: they are all, in their sublime, creative of essential Beauty.'

It is his notion of **the imagination as the most precious gift of the creative artist** that most clearly identifies Keats as a Romantic poet. Closely linked to this belief is his thirst for intense, transcendent experience. This can be the excitement at the discovery of beauty, as in 'On First Looking into Chapman's Homer', the destructive passion of 'La Belle Dame Sans Merci', the tender, erotic intimacy of 'Bright Star', or the vision-like experience of 'Ode to a Nightingale'.

This can be viewed as a sort of escapism, a sign of Keats's desire to be free of the miseries and suffering of life that he knew so well. As he wrote in his first letter to Fanny Brawne, 'I have never known any unalloy'd Happiness for many days together'.

But Keats's poetry turns this desire into something more than mere escapism. It is a way of seeing the world that was central to Keats's imagination. Intense experiences and emotions that are normally seen as very different are often

closely related in his poetry: **suffering is close to joy; love is close to death**. It is most apparent in the 'Ode to a Nightingale', where the speaker's aching heart comes from 'being too happy', and he imagines death as a way of prolonging bliss:

> To cease upon the midnight with no pain,
>   While thou art pouring forth thy soul abroad
>   In such an ecstasy!

The knight's love for the lady in 'La Belle Dame Sans Merci' is intertwined with his suffering. The only imaginable alternative to the speaker's 'sweet unrest' lying blissfully in the arms of his beloved in 'Bright Star' is to 'swoon to death'.

You could argue that any intense experience in Keats's poetry contains an element of suffering, or a mixture of joy and suffering. This idea has a moral or philosophical dimension too. **Keats believed that suffering has a purpose.** In a letter to George and Georgiana, he wrote about the world as a school for the human soul, asking, 'Do you not see how necessary a World of Pains and troubles is to school an Intelligence and make it a soul?' Suffering is something to be faced and used rather than simply escaped.

Timeline

1795	Born in London. Father ran a coaching inn
1803	Starts as a boarder at Clarke's school in Enfield
1804	Father dies
	Mother leaves the family home
	Children looked after by their grandmother
1810	Mother dies
	Leaves school to be apprenticed to a surgeon
1815	Becomes a medical student at Guy's Hospital in London
1816	First poems published
	Abandons medical studies for a life as a poet
1817	First volume of poems published
1818	Long mythological poem *Endymion* published, to hostile reviews
	Brother George leaves for America
	Nurses brother Tom, who is dying of tuberculosis
	Feels first symptoms of his own tuberculosis
	Meets Fanny Brawne
1819	Writes the five great odes, three of which appear in this anthology
1820	Publishes volume of poems including the odes
	Goes to Italy hoping to improve his health
1821	Dies in Rome

Before you read

Do you prefer city or country life? Discuss in pairs, then share your thoughts with the class.

To one who has been long in city pent

To one who has been long in city pent,
    'Tis very sweet to look into the fair
    And open face of heaven,—to breathe a prayer
Full in the smile of the blue firmament.
Who is more happy, when, with heart's content,   5
    Fatigued he sinks into some pleasant lair
    Of wavy grass, and reads a debonair
And gentle tale of love and languishment?
Returning home at evening, with an ear
    Catching the notes of Philomel,—an eye   10
Watching the sailing cloudlet's bright career,
    He mourns that day so soon has glided by:
E'en like the passage of an angel's tear
    That falls through the clear ether silently.

Glossary

1	*pent*: confined, imprisoned
4	*firmament*: heavens, sky
7	*debonair*: elegant, light-hearted
8	*languishment*: pining, inactive unhappiness because of love
10	*Philomel*: nightingale
11	*career*: passing by
13	*E'en like*: even like, just like
14	*ether*: air, atmosphere; ether was believed to be an invisible element that filled all space

Philomel

According to the ancient Greek myth, Philomel (or Philomela) was a young woman who was raped by her sister's husband, King Tereus, who cut out her tongue to stop her telling. She was transformed into a nightingale, whose beautiful song is sometimes thought to express great sorrow.

Guidelines

This sonnet was written in June 1816 when Keats was still just twenty years old. At that time he was studying to be a surgeon at Guy's Hospital in the middle of London. According to his brother George, this poem was 'written in the fields' on one of his days off spent walking in the countryside around the city.

Keats was already considering a possible future as a poet rather than a surgeon, and he spent much of his spare time educating himself in classical literature and the great English poets of the sixteenth and seventeenth centuries, especially Spenser, Shakespeare and Milton. This poem's opening echoes some lines from Milton's

Guy's Hospital

Keats's studies at Guy's meant that he had to join crowds of other students pressing forward for a view of gruesome operations carried out with no anaesthetic except alcohol, or of dissections of dead bodies in suffocating and foul-smelling rooms. This was part of what he was escaping in his walks in the country celebrated in this poem, and what he would return to at the end of them. He gave up his studies at the end of 1816, determined to make his way as a poet.

Paradise Lost: 'As one who long in populous city pent, / Where houses thick and sewers annoy the air'. That vision of the city as a crowded, unhealthy place to be escaped from haunts Keats's poem, even though the city is never described in it.

Commentary

Octave (lines 1–8)

The first eight lines of the sonnet, the octave, express a simple thought and ask a simple question: in other words, it's great to get out in the open air on a nice day if you've been stuck in the city for a while (lines 1–4); and (lines 5–8) what could be better than lying back in the long grass with a good love story to read?

Sestet (lines 9–14)

The second part of the poem evokes the mood at the end of the day in the countryside, 'Returning home at evening'. There is a pleasure in the evening's beauty – the 'notes of Philomel' (a nightingale), the little cloud sailing by – but there is also a strong sense of sadness at the day's ending: 'He mourns that day so soon has glided by'. The final image, which is the most striking and original one in the poem, focuses and deepens this doubleness: the angel suggests perfection of a kind, but the tear indicates sorrow. It is an image of heavenly, almost sacred sadness, made all the more poignant and magical because the tear falls 'silently'.

Themes

This is a simple yet charming sonnet without the depth or complexity of Keats's finest poems, but many of the themes and moods of those poems are foreshadowed in it.

There is, first of all, the **strong sense of fleeting beauty** – a beauty that is so vividly perceived because of the awareness that it is transient and will be gone all too quickly. This **connection between beauty and melancholy** (sadness) is central to the poem's effect. As well as the melancholy awareness that this day has to end, there is a close relationship between pleasure and suffering in other details. Though the 'face of heaven' (line 3) may be 'open' and the 'blue firmament' (line 4) is smiling, the pleasure of lying down to read is linked with exhaustion ('Fatigued he sinks', line 6) and the tale he reads mingles love and 'languishment' – the pining unhappiness that is conventionally associated with love. Do you think that it might also be significant that Philomel is not simply a Greek term for the nightingale, but has a story attached?

The mood of the poem also looks forward to the great odes, several of which we are studying on this course. There is a feeling of tiredness, heaviness and pleasant indolence, especially in lines 5–8, where the 'Fatigued' subject 'sinks' into the grass and even the story he reads involves 'languishment'. This mood is associated with sensual pleasures: the touch of the 'wavy grass', the sound of the nightingale, the sight of the passing cloud.

The poem also depends on the **contrast between city and country**. Though it is not directly described, life in the crowded, dirty city haunts the poem, making this day in the country so precious. The word 'pent' (line 1) does a lot of work, implying as it does that life in the city is a sort of imprisonment.

Imagery and language

The imagery of the poem is mostly **subtle but conventional**: the idea of heaven as a smiling face; a passing ('sailing') cloud like a ship in the sky. Only the final image, discussed above, is memorable. The language of the poem contains some rather archaic words and phrases, showing the influence of Keats's reading of Spenser and Milton: 'firmament', 'debonair', 'E'en like'. Elsewhere, the language is conventionally poetic: 'very sweet'; 'heart's content'; 'gentle tale'. Keats had not yet found a poetic language of his own.

Form

'To one who has been long in city pent' is a **Petrarchan sonnet**, divided into octave and sestet, with a rhyme scheme of *abba abba cdcdcd*. The argument of the poem fits neatly into the conventional divisions: the first two sentences occupy four lines each, and the third takes up the remaining six lines. Despite that, the poem never feels constrained by its form. Keats handles it with dexterity and skill with plenty of run-on lines (enjambment) to break up the rigid patterns of the sonnet form. Notice too how he uses rhyme words to highlight key ideas: 'ear' at the end of line 9 and 'eye' (line 10) remind us of the different senses that are evoked in the poem.

The final word of the poem, 'silently', is interesting in this respect. The word is emphasised by being placed out of its normal sentence position in spoken English ('falls silently through the clear ether') and by being only a half-rhyme, and that on an unstressed syllable; speak it aloud and you will hear that the stress falls on the first syllable of the word: *śilently*. What, do you think, is the effect of this?

Questions

1	What do you think is the main theme of the poem?
	■ The contrast between city and country
	■ The beauty of nature
	■ The nature of pleasure
	■ The transience of beauty
	Or what other response would you give? Explain your answer.
2	How would you describe the mood of this poem?
3	Comment on the form of the poem.
4	In what ways would this poem be different if Keats had written 'nightingale' instead of 'Philomel'?
5	Comment on the final image of this poem.
6	Are there any signs in the poem that suggest its writer was to become one of the most admired poets in the English language?
7	Suggest an alternative title for the poem. Explain your suggestion.
8	Write a short piece, either prose or verse, with the title 'The Pleasures of Exhaustion'.

Before you read

Find out what you can about (a) Homer, the ancient Greek poet, and (b) George Chapman, who made an English translation of Homer's work.

On First Looking into Chapman's Homer

Much have I travell'd in the realms of gold,
    And many goodly states and kingdoms seen;
    Round many western islands have I been
Which bards in fealty to Apollo hold.
Oft of one wide expanse had I been told   5
    That deep-brow'd Homer ruled as his demesne;
    Yet did I never breathe its pure serene
Till I heard Chapman speak out loud and bold:
Then felt I like some watcher of the skies
    When a new planet swims into his ken;   10
Or like stout Cortez when with eagle eyes
    He star'd at the Pacific—and all his men
Look'd at each other with a wild surmise—
    Silent, upon a peak in Darien.

Glossary

Title	*Chapman's Homer*: George Chapman (c.1559–1634) was an English poet and dramatist whose verse translation of Homer's ancient Greek poems, the *Iliad* and the *Odyssey*, were published in 1616
1	*realms*: territories, kingdoms
2	*goodly*: fine, attractive
4	*bards*: poets
4	*fealty*: loyalty
4	*Apollo*: Greek God of the sun, music and poetry
6	*demesne*: territory, kingdom
7	*serene*: clear, calm (air); normally an adjective, but here used as a noun
10	*ken*: view, field of vision
11	*stout*: brave
11	*Cortez*: Spanish conqueror of Mexico; Keats is confusing him with Balboa, another Spanish adventurer, who discovered the Pacific in 1513
13	*surmise*: thought, guess
14	*Darien*: a neck of land joining North and South America; it is in present-day Panama, and has a chain of mountains running through it

Guidelines

One day in October 1816, Keats's friend, Charles Cowden Clarke, showed him a copy of a rare old book, Chapman's translation of Homer's *Iliad* and *Odyssey*. Keats had never read Homer before, and they sat up all night reading the book. Keats left Clarke at six in the morning, excited by his night's reading, composed this sonnet in his head as he walked home, wrote it down when he got in, and sent it to Clarke by the early morning postal messenger.

The poem is full of the excitement with which it was written.

Commentary

As the title indicates, the subject of the sonnet is the experience of reading a great poem in translation, and yet books are never actually mentioned in the poem. Instead Keats uses an extended metaphor, speaking of his reading in terms of travel and exploration.

Lines 1–4

The 'realms of gold' with their 'goodly states and kingdoms' represent the world of the imagination as expressed in great literature. These include the old English poets Keats loved and also the classics of ancient Greece and Rome, as the reference to Apollo implies. These Keats knows. In the poem's central metaphor, he has 'travell'd' these areas.

Lines 5–8

The metaphor is sustained, but the focus now narrows to one particular 'wide expanse', a 'demesne' or dominion greater than these others, 'ruled' by 'deep-brow'd Homer', most revered of all the ancient poets. Keats is referring to Homer's two great epic works: the *Iliad* and the *Odyssey*. He had 'been told' of this 'demesne', but had never visited it and breathed its 'pure serene' (i.e. read the poems) until now, when he 'heard Chapman speak out loud and bold' in his verse translation of Homer's works.

Lines 9–14

The rest of the poem describes Keats's feelings on reading Chapman's Homer ('Then felt I …'). He compares his thrill of discovery to that of an astronomer (a 'watcher of the skies') seeing a previously unknown planet in his telescope, and finally to that of a conqueror and explorer, 'stout Cortez' discovering the Pacific Ocean (though in fact he was thinking of Balboa: see Glossary).

Homer

The deep brows mentioned in the poem call to mind the busts of a serious-looking Homer. In fact, we know very little about the person who wrote the *Iliad* and the *Odyssey*. It is probable that both these works were composed to be recited aloud rather than read, and may not have been written down until long after they were composed. They may be the work of more than one person, and some have speculated that the poet was a woman.

The *Iliad* and the *Odyssey* are long, epic poems, full of heroes and gods and adventure. The *Iliad* tells the story of the Trojan War. The *Odyssey* tells the story of Odysseus, one of the Greek heroes returning from that war. It is a story of voyaging by sea among islands, and so is closely linked to the central metaphor of Keats's poem.

Notice how this reference to the conquest of Central and South America arises naturally out of the poem's opening metaphor of voyaging, especially its reference to 'realms of gold'. The Spanish *conquistadores* were both explorers and soldiers, drawn by the prospect of finding gold and discovering new lands – and conquering them.

The poem as a whole conveys the breathless excitement that Keats felt on reading Chapman's Homer. We know he wrote it quickly, and yet his poet's instincts for rhythm and phrasing keep his train of thought lucid. Notice how, in the final lines, the concluding image is held back by the aside about the soldiers ('and all his men / Look'd at each other …') so that the last line reaches a climax that is exalted (literally, high: 'upon a peak'), but also, after the rush of images in the poem, finally, magically, still: 'Silent'. Keats throws the emphasis on to this word by the line break before it, by the pause dictated by the comma after it, and also by the stress that falls on the first syllable of the word (*sílent*), breaking the iambic metre of the poem.

Themes

The clearest theme of the poem is **the world-changing joy and beauty to be found in great art** – in this case, the poetry of Homer. The 'realms of gold' stand for the domain of great art, which, like gold, is both beautiful and everlasting. Gold does not rust or tarnish so it is often associated with eternal or divine beauty. Think of gold leaf used on medieval religious paintings or on icons of the Greek or Russian Orthodox churches. Keats believed in the power of art, and of poetry in particular, to do good in the world, and this is a theme that runs through his poetry. He takes it up most directly in his 'Ode on a Grecian Urn', as we will see.

Beyond this simple celebration of timeless art, however, **this poem sees Keats reflecting on his own relationship with that art**. He was then a would-be poet who had not yet made the decision to commit his working life to poetry, and he was conscious that he was, to a great extent, an outsider in that world. He lacked the privileged background and classical education of Shelley or Lord Byron, who was at that time the most successful and widely read of the younger generation of poets. That meant, among other things, that he was unable to read Homer and other ancient classics in the original Greek. This sonnet acknowledges his shortcomings: he can read Homer only in translation, and can never know that 'demesne' directly. To some extent, he can only guess at the beauty of the original. The Pacific was distant and unknowable to Cortez/Balboa, just as Homer is to Keats. It is also surprising because the Spanish had expected to find Asia as they went west, not a vast ocean.

John Fuller has an interesting comment on this aspect of the sonnet:

> 'Keats's point is that just as Cortez (though Keats means Balboa, discoverer of the Pacific in 1513) discovers a continent through an ocean (i.e. that he is not in Asia after all), so Keats discovers Homer through Chapman's translation. This is what the 'wild surmise' of line 13 is all about: the discovery in each case is indirect.'

He was an outsider but he wanted to be an insider. You could see this sonnet as **Keats staking his claim to the poetic territory he wanted to occupy**.

Imagery

This poem works by means of its images. As discussed above, the **extended metaphor of voyaging and discovery**, including the discoveries of astronomy, is used to talk about discovering great poetry, even though books and poems are never actually mentioned. The explanation given by the poem's title is needed to interpret the metaphor. Though the same basic metaphor runs through the whole poem, notice how it develops from generalised travelling through the known world at the beginning to a specific, beautifully realised moment of discovery at the end, as 'Cortez' stands silent on a mountain peak, the first European to see the Pacific Ocean.

Form and language

Like 'To one who has been long in city pent', this is a **Petrarchan sonnet written in iambic pentameters**. Here, though, the form is treated a little more freely, conveying a great sense of urgency, especially in the sestet, the final six lines of the poem.

The sonnet is **beautifully constructed**. The octave divides neatly into two quatrains of four lines each. The first ends in a full stop, but the second concludes in a colon, which propels the reader into the sestet and helps create the sense of headlong excitement. The sestet divides unequally into two lines about the astronomer (9–10) and four about Cortez (11–14), so that the final four lines carry the impetus of the poem forward to the final, memorable and still final line: 'Silent, upon a peak in Darien'.

The language of the poem is conventionally poetic in some ways. It uses inversions in word order ('Much have I travell'd'; 'Yet did I never breathe'; 'Then felt I') and poetic diction (notably 'pure serene', line 7, where the adjective 'serene' is used as a noun). Yet some of its finest effects come from simple words used in a straightforward manner. The short words and hard consonants ('t', 'd', 'b') of 'Till I heard Chapman speak out loud and bold' (line 8) give us a feeling for the power of Chapman's verse, and the sheer simplicity of the final line, with its subtle repetitions of 'n' and 'p' sounds, is crucial to the atmosphere of breathless stillness.

Exam-Style Questions

Understanding the poem

1	What actual experience is Keats describing with his images of voyaging in the first four lines of the poem?
2	Was the speaker acquainted with the work of Homer before reading Chapman's version? Explain your answer.
3	What experience is being conveyed in lines 7–8?
4	What do the speaker and the astronomer mentioned in line 9 have in common?
5	What do Cortez and the speaker of the poem have in common?

Thinking about the poem

1	Keats begins the sonnet with images of voyaging and discovery. Show how these images are maintained throughout the poem.
2	What impression of Homer do you get from the poem?
3	What purpose is achieved by the final six lines of the sonnet in relation to the first eight?
4	Describe the emotions of the speaker of the sonnet.
5	Show how indirect experience, rather than direct experience, is a theme of the sonnet.

Imagining

1	Imagine you were one of the soldiers with Cortez 'upon a peak in Darien'. Describe the scene in your own words, concentrating on the reactions of Cortez to seeing the Pacific.
2	Describe an exciting journey you have taken or a view that you love. You can use verse or prose, or just share your experience with a partner in class.

SNAPSHOT

- Petrarchan sonnet
- Rich poetic language
- Metaphors of voyaging and discovery
- Records a moment of intense experience
- Sense of wonder and delight
- Theme of indirect discovery

Before you read

In groups or pairs, discuss what you might expect from a poem that starts 'When I have fears' written by a young, talented poet.

When I have fears that I may cease to be

When I have fears that I may cease to be
    Before my pen has gleaned my teeming brain,
Before high-pilèd books, in charactery,
    Hold like rich garners the full ripened grain;
When I behold, upon the night's starred face,   5
    Huge cloudy symbols of a high romance,
And think that I may never live to trace
    Their shadows with the magic hand of chance;
And when I feel, fair creature of an hour,
    That I shall never look upon thee more,   10
Never have relish in the faery power
    Of unreflecting love—then on the shore
Of the wide world I stand alone, and think
Till love and fame to nothingness do sink.

Glossary

2	*gleaned*: picked out the best bits from; the image is from harvesting, where gleaning is the process of picking through the harvested field to find ripe grains that have been left behind
2	*teeming*: filled with ideas, overflowing
3	*charactery*: writing or print
4	*garners*: granaries or barns, where the harvested grain is stored
11	*relish*: enjoyment
11	*faery*: magical, supernatural
12	*unreflecting love*: love untroubled by uncertainty; spontaneous love

Guidelines

This poem was written in late January 1818. Keats had had his first volume of poems published the previous year, but it had received little attention. His self-belief was not diminished, but he had come to understand how difficult was the life he had chosen. It had also become clear that his youngest brother, Tom, was ill with tuberculosis.

In this poem Keats contemplates his hopes and ambitions and confronts the fear that he may not live long enough to achieve them.

Commentary

The poem is a sonnet, but unlike the previous two poems, it is a Shakespearean sonnet, consisting of three quatrains (groups of four lines) and a final rhyming couplet.

The structure of the sonnet is simple. It is a single sentence. Each quatrain is a statement of a possibility (or conditional clause) introduced by 'when', and they are followed by a conclusion in the final two and a half lines, introduced by 'then'. The sentence's two main verbs do not arrive until line 13: 'I stand … and think'.

Lines 1–4

The first quatrain starts 'When I have fears …' and goes on to express those fears. The main fear is that he might die before he has been able to write and publish all the work he is capable of writing. The image here is of harvesting – his pen gleaning his 'teeming brain' as a peasant or farmer picks the ripe grains from the cut wheat (see Glossary), and then his words are turned into 'high-pilèd books', which Keats likens to stores of 'full ripened grain'.

He is confident that his imagination is rich and fertile enough for him to become a great poet and leave behind a significant body of work, if only he has time to write it.

Lines 5–8

The second quatrain, starting 'When I behold …', develops the main idea of the first. The speaker imagines looking up at the night sky and seeing in the stars the vague outline ('cloudy symbols') of a noble story ('a high romance'), and then he is struck by the thought that he may not live to compose this great work and turn those 'shadows' into poetic form. The 'magic hand of chance' is an ambiguous phrase. It seems to refer to the mysterious force of poetic inspiration, and yet at the same time it reminds us of the uncertain fate that hangs over the poet.

Lines 9–12

The third quatrain moves from poetry to love – another aspect of his life in which Keats had great, unfulfilled yearnings and also great fears. Perhaps the 'fair creature of an hour' is the woman he had glimpsed some years before in Vauxhall Gardens and wrote about then. Perhaps she is another woman he had met. But he is overwhelmed by the thought of never seeing her again and, more significantly, never experiencing 'the faery power / Of unreflecting love'.

Lines 12–14

The final thought – and the conclusion of the sentence – begins in the middle of line 12, before the last quatrain is complete: 'then on the shore …'. Keats has been thinking of how death can waste the talents of a poet like himself and how his dearest hopes and ambitions may be always unrealised. He imagines himself standing alone 'on the shore / Of the wide world', facing his hopes and fears, and thinking. If 'love and fame' are so vulnerable to time and death, they are nothing, he decides. You can read this as despair, but there is also a strength and determination to it. The speaker is not just a victim; it is in part his thinking that turns these worldly desires into 'nothingness'.

Themes

Given that we know that Keats had only three more years to live when he wrote this poem, his anxiety that he might not live long enough to write what he knew was in him is deeply poignant, and feels prescient, as if he already knew he would die young. It is true that he expresses that fear in a number of poems, but it is important not to let the fact of his early death overwhelm our reading of the poem. It is worth remembering that Keats had quit medicine about a year before and decided to make his living as a poet. Poetry has never been an easy path to success, and very few poets manage to make a living from their writing. Keats never did. So it is not surprising that he was full of anxieties about the life he had committed himself to. The decision faced him with the possibility of failure, and the necessity, as he saw it, to prioritise his art over love. He believed – at least at times – that he would never be able to combine poetry with a loving relationship with a woman, and so he had effectively denied himself the 'faery power / Of unreflecting love' (lines 11–12).

Keats's **powerful sense of the transience of beauty** is something that we saw in 'To one who has been long in city pent', and an important element in the great odes that we will be looking at (see pages 141–165).

Imagery

The image of **harvest** in lines 1–4, discussed above, looks forward to Keats's late poem, 'To Autumn'. The image of the **starry sky** in lines 5–8 is another one that runs through his poetry, from the 'watcher of the skies' in 'Upon First Looking into Chapman's Homer' to the central image of the sonnet 'Bright Star'.

The poem's final image, of the speaker himself standing 'on the shore / Of the wide world' recalls 'stout Cortez' looking at the Pacific in 'Chapman's Homer'. The wide world is like an ocean into which 'love and fame' sink and disappear, and the 'I' is left alone facing the universe. What feelings does this image evoke for you?

Form and language

Keats had been rereading Shakespeare's plays and sonnets around the time he wrote this poem, and this was his first attempt at a **Shakespearean sonnet**. Like a Petrarchan sonnet, a Shakespearean sonnet has fourteen lines, but the rhyme scheme is looser (*abab cdcd efef gg*) and leads to a natural division of the sonnet into three quatrains (groups of four lines) and a final rhyming couplet.

The ideas of this sonnet follow this structure very closely, with one clause/statement ('when I …') for each quatrain, except that the final clause with its main verbs ('stand … think') starts in the middle of line 13 ('then on the shore …').

As well as using the Shakespearean form, this sonnet tackles a theme that Shakespeare wrote about in several sonnets: **the destructive power of time**.

The vocabulary, as ever with Keats, is **rich with adjectives and full of unusual and resonant words**. There is not enough space to look at all these in detail, so we will concentrate on the first quatrain. Notice how the idea of the abundant harvest is suggested by the abundance of adjectives relating to abundance: 'teeming', 'high-pilèd', 'rich', 'full ripened'. The effect is strengthened by assonance in 'gleaned … teeming' and 'high-pilèd', and double pairs of stresses in 'rích gárners', 'fúll rípened' and, again, 'hígh-pílèd'.

Keats is never afraid to use unashamedly poetic language full of unusual words and an order of words that is dictated more by the requirements of rhyme than the natural forms of spoken English. The richness of the language can occasionally become cloying, but it is tempered by the clarity of the thought that the language expresses. There is always a strong through-line, and he never stops to wallow in the rich language for its own sake. Keats is also capable of **moments of moving simplicity**, as in the final couplet of this poem, where the words are plain and the only 'effect' is the alliteration and long vowel sounds of 'wide world', which together suggest the vastness the speaker is contemplating.

Questions

1	In your own words, what fear is the speaker expressing in the first four lines of the poem?
2	What mode of composing poetry is suggested in the second quatrain (lines 5–8)?
3	What fears is the speaker expressing in the third quatrain (lines 9–12)?
4	What gifts does the speaker value most? Why do these seem less valuable to him at the end?
5	Describe the mood in the final three lines of this poem.
6	The poem conveys the speaker's sense of the power of his imagination. Explore this idea.
7	Comment on the significance of the repeated use of 'never' in the poem.
8	The words 'shore' (line 12) and 'sink' (line 14) suggest the ocean, a traditional image of fate or eternity. How does this idea throw light on what the speaker has been saying?
9	It has been suggested that the 'fair creature of an hour' was a woman Keats once saw in a public place in London, and perhaps never spoke to, but could never forget. Imagine the scene, and write your own account from Keats's point of view.
10	Respond to this poem by expressing your own fears for the future in a poem.

Before you read

The next poem is a ballad. In groups or as a class, discuss what you know about what a ballad is and what you expect from a ballad.

La Belle Dame Sans Merci

O what can ail thee, knight-at-arms,
  Alone and palely loitering?
The sedge has wither'd from the lake
  And no birds sing!

O what can ail thee, knight-at-arms,   5
  So haggard, and so woe-begone?
The squirrel's granary is full
  And the harvest's done.

I see a lily on thy brow
  With anguish moist and fever dew,   10
And on thy cheeks a fading rose
  Fast withereth too—

I met a lady in the meads
  Full beautiful, a faery's child
Her hair was long, her foot was light,   15
  And her eyes were wild—

I made a garland for her head,
  And bracelets too, and fragrant zone:
She look'd at me as she did love
  And made sweet moan—   20

I set her on my pacing steed
  And nothing else saw all day long
For sidelong would she bend and sing
  A faery's song—

She found me roots of relish sweet   25
 And honey wild and manna dew
And sure in language strange she said
 'I love thee true'—

She took me to her elfin grot
 And there she wept and sigh'd full sore   30
And there I shut her wild wild eyes
 With kisses four.

And there she lullèd me asleep
 And there I dream'd—Ah woe betide!
The latest dream I ever dreamt   35
 On the cold hill side.

I saw pale kings and princes too,
 Pale warriors, death-pale were they all;
They cried 'La belle dame sans merci
 Hath thee in thrall.'   40

I saw their starv'd lips in the gloam
 With horrid warning gapèd wide
And I awoke and found me here
 On the cold hill's side

And this is why I sojourn here   45
 Alone and palely loitering;
Though the sedge is wither'd from the lake
 And no birds sing——

Glossary

Title	*La Belle Dame Sans Merci*: Keats borrowed his title from a medieval poem by Alain Chartier; it means 'the beautiful lady without pity'
1	*what can ail thee*: what is the matter with you?
3	*sedge*: coarse grass which grows in wet places
6	*haggard*: lean, hollow-eyed
10	*fever dew*: the sweat of fever
13	*meads*: meadows
18	*zone*: belt or girdle (of fragrant flowers); 'zone' is used here with its original meaning, which was rare even when the poem was written
21	*set*: put
25	*of relish sweet*: sweet-tasting
26	*manna dew*: sweet-tasting liquid; God provided manna as food for the Israelites in the desert
29	*elfin grot*: fairy cave (grotto)
30	*full sore*: very sorrowfully
35	*latest*: last
40	*in thrall*: in slavery
41	*gloam*: twilight
45	*sojourn*: stay for a while

Guidelines

Keats wrote 'La Belle Dame Sans Merci', one of his best-loved and most haunting poems, in April 1819. A lot had happened in his life since writing the sonnets we have previously looked at. It had been an agonising year. His long poem *Endymion* had received hostile and wounding reviews. His brother George, closest to him in age and affection, had left England with his new wife for a new life in America. His youngest brother, Tom, had died of tuberculosis in December 1818. Keats had spent many weeks nursing him, and was with him at the end; he was also showing the first signs of the same disease, which was to kill him less than two years later. He had also met and fallen in love with the eighteen-year-old Fanny Brawne. All of these events are reflected in the emotional landscape of this poem.

The earliest text of the poem is known from a letter Keats wrote to his brother George. When it was published in the *Indicator* magazine in 1820, it was revised by his friend Leigh Hunt. It is generally accepted that the version printed here is the better poem.

Keats used minimal punctuation when he wrote it out for his brother, and though some adjustments have been made, and a few commas and hyphens added for clarity, this version is more lightly punctuated than those found in most modern editions.

Commentary

'La Belle Dame Sans Merci' is a ballad. Ballads were originally a popular form, using simple vocabulary, rhyme and repetition to tell stories that are memorable and create effects that are often mysterious. Keats's poem is a literary version of the popular form.

Lines 1–12

The first three stanzas set the scene for the story: a solitary, unhealthy and unhappy-looking knight in a bleak, lifeless landscape. His forehead is white like a lily, and the rose-red in his cheeks is fading. The narrator asks what is wrong with him: 'O what can ail thee …?'

Lines 13–48

From the fourth stanza on, it is the knight who is speaking. He tells the story of meeting a beautiful, mysterious lady, 'a faery's child' (line 14), in the fields. He made her ornaments from meadow flowers and she seemed to love him, or so he thought. He put her on his horse and rode away.

At this point in the story she takes the initiative. She sang him songs and found delicious food for him and declared her love – or at least he thinks she did because it was 'in language strange' (line 27). She took him to 'her elfin grot' and, for reasons we are not told, 'wept and sigh'd full sore' so that he kisses her eyes, presumably to calm her down. But it is *she* who lulls *him* to sleep, and in his dream he sees kings and princes, presumably former doomed lovers of *la belle dame*. Their looks and their words warn him of his own fate, and when he awakes he is alone on 'the cold hill's side' (line 44).

The ending of the poem returns to its beginning, as the knight declares that the story he has told is the explanation for his being in this desolate place, 'Alone and palely loitering'.

Form and language

As noted above, 'La Belle Dame Sans Merci' is a **literary ballad**. It uses the common ballad form of four-line stanzas (quatrains) rhyming *abcb*. The metre is largely iambic, with four beats or stresses per line, except that the final line of each stanza is shorter, with just two main stresses. This creates a slightly deadened, **downbeat end to each stanza**, which adds to the melancholy mood of the poem.

Like many ballads, this poem makes much use of **direct speech**. Although Keats didn't use any quotation marks at all when he wrote out the poem, it is clear that the first three stanzas are not simply narration, but the narrator directly questioning the knight: 'O what can ail thee …?' The rest of the poem is the knight's reply.

The **syntax (word order) is straightforward and direct**, often using the simplest conjunction, 'and'. Look, for example, at lines 29–36, where the mysterious central events of the poem in the 'elfin grot' are narrated as a simple sequence linked by 'And there …'. The vocabulary is mostly plain, but it is heightened at times by obscure or unusual words that suggest the medieval and magical setting of the story: the 'fragrant zone' (line 18), the 'pacing steed' (line 21), the 'elfin grot' (line 29).

Another feature of the ballad, matching the simple narrative style, is **repetition**. Not only does the end of the poem echo the beginning, almost word for word, but there are many patterns of repetition with variation throughout. The second stanza mirrors the first, and they share an opening line: 'O what can ail thee, knight-at-arms'.

There is the simple repetition in 'wild wild eyes' (line 31) and the almost-repetition at a stanza's end at lines 36 and 44: 'On the cold hill side' / 'On the cold hill's side'. Read those two lines out loud. What difference does the added 's' make to the sound and mood?

This poem may not have the rich patterns of sounds and imagery that Keats employs in some of his poems, but it has a **haunting music of its own**. The repeated liquid 'l' sounds in the first lines of the poem – 'ail … / Alone and palely loitering' – are important in creating its seductive atmosphere. If you look through the rest of the poem you will find that Keats uses this letter prominently in every stanza.

Imagery

There is very **little use of metaphorical language in the poem**, except in the third stanza, where the 'lily on thy brow', standing for whiteness and sickness, and the 'fading rose' on the cheeks, standing for redness, blood and (fading) health, have an artful simplicity to them.

Otherwise **the imagery of the poem consists of the pictures the story paints**, and those are very vivid ones: the pale knight in the desolate landscape; the long-haired, wild-eyed lady; the flowers with which he adorns her; the foods with which she feeds him; the four kisses; the procession of ghoulish nobles and warriors.

The scene is given a certain glamour and distanced somewhat from everyday experience by the medieval trappings: the 'knight-at-arms', the 'steed', kings and princes and warriors. It is not surprising to learn that the poem was the inspiration for a number of paintings, especially later in the nineteenth century, when there was a revival of interest in the Middle Ages.

Interpretation and themes

The effect of the simple syntax, rhyme, metre and repetition is to create **clear, vivid impressions that are both mysterious and charged with emotion**. The mysteriousness of this poem is one of the glorious things about it. It can mean different things to different people. Nevertheless, a little information about what was happening in Keats's life at the time can provide hints of what emotions underlie the poem, and what he may have been writing about without even realising it.

Love is clearly central to the poem, and specifically a man's love for a woman. The story is seen from a male perspective, while the woman is mysterious, seductive, desirable, unpredictable and dangerous. What do we know about Keats's relationships with women?

The story of his childhood would suggest that he learned very early that they could let you down. His mother effectively abandoned her children after their father's death, when Keats was eight, and probably took up with another man. When she returned to the family several years later she was mortally ill with tuberculosis, and rather than looking after her children it was she who needed looking after. Keats appointed himself her carer, devotedly nursing her through her final illness until her death when he was fourteen. It has been pointed out that this pattern of loss–recovery–loss is mirrored in 'La Belle Dame Sans Merci', which starts and ends with the desolate, solitary knight.

This early experience certainly affected his attitude to women, which was full of contradictions – desire and idealisation on the one hand; distrust and fear on the other. He understood this about himself. As he wrote in a letter in 1818, 'I am certain I have not a right feeling towards women.'

Love is my religion

'Love is my religion – I could die for that – I could die for you. My creed is Love and you are its only tenet – You have ravish'd me away by a Power I cannot resist.'

Keats, letter to Fanny Brawne

He could be strongly attracted to women, but did not think himself capable of having a conventional relationship. As a creative artist he often saw marriage and children as a threat to the freedom he believed he would need to be a true poet.

'La Belle Dame' was written a few months after Keats met Fanny Brawne, the last and greatest love of his short life. At first he was dismissive of his feelings for her, at least to his friends, but part of him wanted to yield himself utterly to them. This poem could be seen as his attempt to work out his contradictory feelings about her and about love: the beautiful lady is at the heart of a sublime experience, but her power is also destructive.

The encounter of knight and lady carries a strong sexual charge, hinted at in the lady's 'sweet moan' and underpinned by the masculine symbolism of the 'steed' and the feminine symbolism of the lady's 'grot' or cave.

If love is one central theme of the poem, then surely **death** is the other. As in other poems, death is on Keats's mind. He had been with his brother when he died from tuberculosis, and must have been aware of the first signs of the disease in himself. The appearance of the knight – his fevered, white brow and flushed red cheeks – are those of a tuberculosis sufferer. Again, it is hard not to see a premonition of his own death in the pale, doomed knight.

Love and death are tightly bound together in the poem. The 'belle dame' promises love, but brings death. What does this mean? Should we read the poem as an expression of Keats's fear of women? Should we take it as his stark warning against love? And did Keats know what he was saying? It does not feel so simple as that. Whatever experience the knight has undergone, it has transformed him. He is not just a victim. When he awakens from his dream he doesn't run away, but chooses to remain or 'sojourn' on the 'cold hill's side'. He may be doomed, but he also seems to embrace his fate. Was this Keats's view of the poet's role – love as a form of suffering that would enrich his art?

In the end there is no one answer, and **different readers see different things in the poem**. As the poet Andrew Motion wrote in his biography of Keats, the poem 'creates surfaces of beguiling simplicity, through which readers peer into states of great emotional complexity'. We can only explore what those emotional states might contain.

SNAPSHOT

- Literary ballad
- Medieval setting
- Story told using two speakers
- Theme of the destructive power of love
- Theme of love and death
- Language simple, diction sometimes old-fashioned
- Simply told story with great emotional depth
- Natural world used to create mood

Exam-Style Questions

Understanding the poem

1. In your own words, describe what the first speaker sees in the first three stanzas?

2. From the fourth stanza onwards it is the knight who speaks. Tell his story in your own words.

3. What impression does the lady make on the knight to begin with?

4. How does this impression change later in the poem?

5. What is the knight doing at the end of the poem, and why?

Thinking about the poem

1. What kind of mood or atmosphere is created in the first three stanzas? How do the sounds of the words and the rhythms contribute to the mood?

2. The poem is divided between two speakers. Who are the speakers and what is achieved by dividing the poem between them?

3. How would you describe the knight's experience of love? What does the poem suggest about the relationship between love and happiness?

4. Consider the significance of nature images in the poem. How do these contribute to its overall meaning?

5. The poem features a most effective use of contrast. Examine the effects created by contrasting images throughout the poem.

6. The title of the poem suggests the contradictory nature of the lady. What does she represent?

Imagining

1. Write an account of what is described in the poem from the point of view of the woman ('la belle dame') mentioned in the title.

2. Imagine you are the first speaker. Tell your story of meeting the 'knight-at-arms' to a friend the next day.

Ode to a Nightingale

My heart aches, and a drowsy numbness pains
    My sense, as though of hemlock I had drunk,
Or emptied some dull opiate to the drains
    One minute past, and Lethe-wards had sunk:
'Tis not through envy of thy happy lot,   5
    But being too happy in thine happiness,—
        That thou, light-wingèd Dryad of the trees,
           In some melodious plot
Of beechen green, and shadows numberless,
    Singest of summer in full-throated ease.   10

O, for a draught of vintage! that hath been
    Cool'd a long age in the deep-delvèd earth,
Tasting of Flora and the country green,
    Dance, and Provençal song, and sunburnt mirth!
O for a beaker full of the warm South,   15
    Full of the true, the blushful Hippocrene,
        With beaded bubbles winking at the brim,
           And purple-stainèd mouth;
That I might drink, and leave the world unseen,
    And with thee fade away into the forest dim: 20

Fade far away, dissolve, and quite forget
    What thou among the leaves hast never known,
The weariness, the fever, and the fret
    Here, where men sit and hear each other groan;
Where palsy shakes a few, sad, last gray hairs,   25
    Where youth grows pale, and spectre-thin, and dies;
        Where but to think is to be full of sorrow
           And leaden-eyed despairs,
Where Beauty cannot keep her lustrous eyes,
    Or new Love pine at them beyond tomorrow.   30

Away! away! for I will fly to thee,
    Not charioted by Bacchus and his pards,
But on the viewless wings of Poesy,
    Though the dull brain perplexes and retards:
Already with thee! tender is the night,   35
    And haply the Queen-Moon is on her throne,
        Cluster'd around by all her starry Fays;
            But here there is no light,
    Save what from heaven is with the breezes blown
        Through verdurous glooms and winding mossy ways.   40

I cannot see what flowers are at my feet,
    Nor what soft incense hangs upon the boughs,
But, in embalmèd darkness, guess each sweet
    Wherewith the seasonable month endows
The grass, the thicket, and the fruit-tree wild;   45
    White hawthorn, and the pastoral eglantine;
        Fast fading violets cover'd up in leaves;
            And mid-May's eldest child,
    The coming musk-rose, full of dewy wine,
        The murmurous haunt of flies on summer eves.   50

Darkling I listen; and, for many a time
    I have been half in love with easeful Death,
Call'd him soft names in many a musèd rhyme,
    To take into the air my quiet breath;
Now more than ever seems it rich to die,   55
    To cease upon the midnight with no pain,
        While thou art pouring forth thy soul abroad
            In such an ecstasy!
    Still wouldst thou sing, and I have ears in vain—
        To thy high requiem become a sod.   60

Thou wast not born for death, immortal Bird!
    No hungry generations tread thee down;
The voice I hear this passing night was heard
    In ancient days by emperor and clown:
Perhaps the self-same song that found a path   65
    Through the sad heart of Ruth, when, sick for home,
        She stood in tears amid the alien corn;
            The same that oft-times hath
    Charm'd magic casements, opening on the foam
        Of perilous seas, in faery lands forlorn.   70

Forlorn! the very word is like a bell

    To toll me back from thee to my sole self!

Adieu! the fancy cannot cheat so well

    As she is fam'd to do, deceiving elf.

Adieu! adieu! thy plaintive anthem fades   75

    Past the near meadows, over the still stream,

      Up the hill-side; and now 'tis buried deep

        In the next valley-glades:

    Was it a vision, or a waking dream?

      Fled is that music:—Do I wake or sleep?   80

Glossary

2	*hemlock*: a poisonous plant, used as a powerful sedative
3	*opiate*: another sedative drug
3	*drains*: the dregs; the bottom of the bottle
4	*past*: ago
4	*Lethe-wards*: towards Lethe, the river of forgetfulness in the classical underworld
7	*Dryad*: a wood nymph
9	*beechen*: to do with beech trees
11	*a draught of vintage*: a drink of wine
13	*Flora*: Roman goddess of flowers and fertility
14	*Provençal song*: the reference is to a region in southern France, associated with music and romantic poetry
15	*warm South*: wine from the south
16	*Hippocrene*: the fountain on Mount Helicon whose waters inspired the Muses; Keats thought of its liquid as red wine rather than water, as is apparent from his calling it 'blushful'
23	*fret*: worry
25	*palsy*: a disease which causes limbs to tremble
32	*Not ... pards*: not under the influence of wine; Bacchus, the god of wine, was traditionally shown in a chariot drawn by leopards ('pards')
33	*viewless*: invisible, because flying too high
33	*Poesy*: poetry
35	*tender*: mild
36	*haply*: perhaps
36	*the Queen-Moon*: Diana, the moon goddess
37	*Fays*: fairies; Keats imagines the stars as fairies in the service of Diana
40	*verdurous*: green, leafy, full of vegetation
43	*embalmèd darkness*: darkness steeped in scents, like the 'incense' of the previous line
46	*eglantine*: sweet briar
49	*musk-rose*: small rose with distinctive scent
51	*Darkling*: in the dark
52	*easeful*: comforting
53	*musèd*: thoughtful; also, perhaps, inspired by the Muses
59	*have ears in vain*: be unable to hear
60	*To thy ... sod*: Keats is imagining the nightingale singing a requiem mass, which he will no longer hear, having returned to earth ('become a sod')
66	*Ruth*: in the Old Testament book which takes her name, Ruth is a lonely, unhappy exile, anxious to escape from her 'alien' environment
69	*casements*: window openings
70	*forlorn*: unhappy, lost
73	*fancy*: the imagination
75	*plaintive*: sounding sad or mournful
75	*anthem*: song, usually a setting of a religious text

Guidelines

The 'Ode to a Nightingale' is one of a series of odes Keats wrote in 1819, which all throw light on one another, and some of which he probably worked on at the same time. Taken together, they are generally agreed to be his greatest achievement as a poet. As well as the poems on this course, the odes 'on Indolence', 'on Melancholy' and 'to Psyche' are worth reading to get a fuller idea of Keats's preoccupations and to appreciate how he uses the form of the ode.

This ode was written around the beginning of May 1819. According to Charles Armitage Brown, a friend of Keats, with whom he was staying when he wrote it, it was written very quickly. Brown recorded that Keats sat for some hours in his garden, listening to the nightingale's song, then came into the house with some scraps of paper in his hand that 'contained his poetic feeling on the song of the nightingale'. Brown claimed that he and Keats arranged the stanzas from Keats's fragments, and the result was 'a poem which has been the delight of everyone'.

That account is probably not the whole truth, but this ode, more than any of the others, has a sense of urgency to it, as if it was written quickly, while the excitement of the experience it describes was still present. The poem does not pursue an argument, but follows the shifting moods, the changing thoughts and imaginative processes of the speaker. His experience of listening and letting his imagination wander is the core of the poem. Indeed, a recent biographer of Keats, Nicholas Roe, who believes the poet was addicted to laudanum (a form of opium) at this time, describes this poem as 'one of the greatest re-creations of a drug-inspired dream-vision in English literature'.

Commentary

Stanza 1
Keats puts himself and his emotions at front and centre from the beginning of the poem: 'My heart aches'. The feelings he describes suggest dullness and dejection ('drowsy numbness'), as if he had been drugged into a stupor, but his heartache isn't altogether negative.

He explains, from line 5, the cause of these emotions. He is listening to a nightingale, and he is not feeling bad-tempered out of envy for the joy he hears in the nightingale's song; his heartache comes from being 'too happy' in the happiness of the nightingale. As elsewhere in Keats, joy and pain are close together. He goes on to describe the bird's 'happiness', like a Dryad or tree spirit singing among the trees 'in full-throated ease'.

Stanza 2
Though he has said he does not envy the nightingale, he wishes he could in some way unite himself with it, or with its song. The second stanza imagines that a drink of wine ('a draught of vintage') might enable him to 'fade away' with the nightingale 'into the forest dim'. He wants to prolong his ecstatic state of mind, and imagines a drink of wine that could do so. Not any ordinary wine, this, but something cooled deep in the earth, yet with the warmth of the 'South'. He imagines it as being infused with all sorts of qualities: flowers ('Flora') and dance and song and 'sunburnt mirth' – even the sacred spring of the ancient Greek Muses, the Hippocrene. It is not, in other words, just a glass of wine he wants, but the inspiration of all the cultural associations he invokes.

Stanza 3

The next stanza pursues the idea of fading away and elaborates on the reason for wishing to do so. Now it is less a matter of maintaining his rapt state of mind than of escaping from the world. The spontaneous joy of the nightingale's unthinking, untroubled song is set against the human experience of suffering, which is what 'thou among the leaves hast never known'. This misery is described in stark phrases with many monosyllables: 'Here, where men sit and hear each other groan'. Keats uses personification – 'palsy' stands for a feeble old person, 'youth' for a young one, 'Beauty' for a beautiful woman whose beauty will fade, and 'Love' for someone newly in love whose love will also fade.

But perhaps the most affecting and significant lines are the most direct: 'Where but to think is to be full of sorrow'. This is the heart of the contrast between the speaker and

Keats Listening to the Nightingale on Hampstead Health, Joseph Severn, 1849. Image courtesy of Keats House, City of London.

the nightingale: being conscious, the speaker is weighed down by the world's suffering, whereas the nightingale's song is unburdened by that knowledge.

Stanza 4

'Away! away!' at the opening of the fourth stanza takes up the desire at the end of the second stanza to fade away with the nightingale. Now, though, Keats dismisses the idea of getting drunk in order to achieve this. He will fly not by drinking wine, represented by 'Bacchus and his pards', but, despite his 'dull brain', 'on the viewless wings of Poesy'. Here he seems to mean the imagination that creates poetry (Poesy) as much as poetry itself, for with a thought he is 'Already with thee'. He conjures a comforting, beautiful image of the scene: 'tender is the night'. He thinks of the 'Queen-Moon' and the stars, as if in an allegorical painting, but makes clear that he is separate from this imagined scene. He is under a tree and in the dark, with no light except what 'is with the breezes blown' to the green ('verdurous') place where he sits or lies.

Stanza 5

In this stanza he explores this green place. He can see nothing, only smell the flowers and imagine what they must be. Lovingly and sensuously, he lists them. He revels in the 'embalmèd darkness', and yet there is also the haunting sense that all this beauty is short-lived and at the mercy of time: the violets are 'Fast fading', and the musk roses will become the 'haunt of flies' as summer comes.

The nightingale is not mentioned in this stanza, but the eradication of all senses except smell, and above all the removal of sight in the darkness, concentrates his mind on the listening. We know the song is continuing, and the stanza creates a sense of the listener's trance.

Stanza 6

The opening of the stanza returns us to that listener in the dark ('Darkling I listen') before reflecting on his state of mind, both now and in the past. The thought of death is now uppermost: 'I have been half in love with easeful Death' and 'Now more than ever seems it rich to die'. It is a special sort of death that he imagines: 'To cease upon the midnight with no pain'. It is as if death is the logical end point of the fading away and dissolving into the nightingale's song that he longs for, a way of partaking in the 'ecstasy' of that song. He imagines that death: the nightingale is still singing, but he, the listener, has turned into a 'sod' of earth, so that the song becomes a requiem over his grave.

Stanza 7

With the speaker's self obliterated, his attention turns back to the nightingale and its audience. By calling the nightingale an 'immortal Bird' he does not mean, of course, the particular bird he is listening to, but rather its song – the 'voice' that has been heard throughout history by all types of people, 'emperor and clown'. He thinks of the song as having the power to comfort, and imagines the biblical figure of Ruth, exiled and unhappy, being soothed by the nightingale's song. Then in the final three lines of the stanza he goes on to picture the song as an inspiration to the imagination, as if the music could cast a spell ('charm') on a view of a fantastical landscape. There is no human audience now, but the 'perilous seas' and 'faery lands' suggest tales of magic and adventure. It is clear that Keats is implying a relationship between the nightingale's song and the artist's or poet's imagination.

Stanza 8

The final stanza picks up the last word of the previous one: 'forlorn'. We are back with the listener, but the mood has changed, and so apparently has the nightingale's song. Where it was happy in the first stanza, singing 'in full-throated ease', now the feeling is sad and the song is a 'plaintive anthem'.

The word 'adieu' rings through this final stanza. The speaker is bidding adieu both to the bird flying off into the next valley and to his intense experience. Whatever experience that was is fading now, and Keats's imagination ('fancy') is not enough to keep it alive. It cannot 'cheat so well'. After all his rich imaginings he is left alone and lonely, his 'sole self'. He isn't sure what he has been through – a 'vision' of some essential truth or a 'waking dream', which sounds less significant. It sounds like waking up from a vivid dream when you are still half-asleep, caught up in the images of the dream and confused: 'Do I wake or sleep?' There is a sense of loss. The music is gone, 'fled' with the singing bird. The dream-vision is over.

Themes and imagery

The emotional landscape

On one level, the poem can be read as what it appears to be: **the account of an intense experience of listening in the dark to the beautiful singing of a nightingale.** As noted above, Nicholas Roe has suggested that Keats may have been addicted to laudanum, and the first stanza hints at the possibility that he may have 'emptied some dull opiate to the drains' (line 3); laudanum is an opiate.

But whether or not his intense and fluctuating emotions on listening to the nightingale were drug-inspired, **Keats lets his imagination roam, and pursues it where it takes him.** The emotional landscape it reveals is familiar from his other poetry. Suffering and joy are closely related: the happiness he feels in the nightingale's beautiful song makes his heart ache with an emotion that contains both **pain and pleasure**. His soul responds to the nightingale's – or that is how he sees it when he describes the song as 'pouring forth thy soul … / In … ecstasy' (lines 57–58).

This **ecstasy is at the emotional heart of the poem**. The speaker wants to prolong and intensify his trance-like state as he listens, and to share in the nightingale's 'ecstasy'. That is why he imagines 'a draught of vintage' (line 11) that would enable him to enter more deeply into that state of mind. Keats imagines that state in terms of transcendence (literally, rising above) in the imagery of the fourth stanza: 'I will fly to thee' (line 31). But more often he thinks of it in terms of **his own dissolution** (dissolving) or annihilation. He wants to 'fade away into the forest dim' (line 20), and in the next line, 'Fade far away, dissolve'. The word 'fade' or its variants occurs four times in the poem, and even the forest he wants to fade into is 'dim'. Read through the poem and notice the other words that have to do with blurring sight, half-light and semi-consciousness.

The furthest extension of the desire to dissolve is **the idea of dying** that Keats explores in the sixth stanza, and which we have seen before, especially in 'When I have fears that I may crease to be'. As he writes, 'for many a time / I have been half in love with easeful death' (lines 51–52). This death, however, is imagined as a sort of union with the nightingale. He wants to 'cease upon the midnight with no pain' while listening to the song.

In part this desire to fade, dissolve and 'quite forget' (line 21) is linked with **his desire to escape the troubles of the world**, as the third stanza makes absolutely clear. It is easy to understand this in the context of Keats's life. In the past year, his brother Tom had died from tuberculosis, and his memory haunts line 26: 'Where youth grows pale, and spectre-thin, and dies'. His other brother, George, to whom he was very close, had left for America; his poetry had received savage reviews, and his own health was fragile.

There is always a tension, however, between the urge to fade and die, and the vivid, joyful life that the speaker perceives in the nightingale's song. On the one hand, there is the imagery of dissolving, darkness and dimness; on the other, there is the world of 'sunburnt mirth' (line 14) and 'full-throated ease' (line 10). This is explored with great power in the fifth stanza, with its sensuous evocation of the unseen flowers and their sweet scents. Yet even here death is present: the darkness is 'embalmèd' like a body awaiting burial, and the violets are 'fading'.

The imagery of the poem is often richly sensual, and like the emotional journey it is complex and ambiguous. 'Ode to a Nightingale' is one of Keats's best-loved poems because of this complexity and intensity of emotions and images. It describes **elusive states of feeling** that readers often respond strongly to, especially if they have been touched by joy and sorrow, and know the way in which great beauty can stir those emotions.

Art and music

Thinking about the role of beauty brings into focus another important element of this poem. As the critic Helen Vendler has suggested, this ode is also an **exploration of the power of art**, and specifically of music.

The nightingale is not just a bird, it is an 'immortal Bird' (line 61). The bird has become its song, and its song is timeless in the way that great art is timeless. The association of the nightingale's voice with great music becomes more apparent as the poem goes on. At first it is simply birdsong, but later that song is described as 'pouring out thy soul', as a human musician might. Then its song is described as a 'high requiem' and a 'plaintive anthem' – both of which imply human composition – until in the final line it is simply 'music'.

The focus on music is strengthened by the poem's increasing **focus on the sense of hearing**. The visual images of the poem's opening – the 'beaded bubbles', the 'purple-stainèd mouth' – disappear as the speaker is lost in darkness, listening. In the fifth stanza the flowers are only guessed at by their scent, and by the sixth all senses but hearing have been left behind ('Darkling I listen', line 51), and the focus is all on the listening.

Keats's use of classical imagery – Lethe and the Dryad in the first stanza, Flora and the 'blushful Hippocrene', sacred to the Muses, in the second – reinforces the association of the nightingale's song with the values of ancient culture. So, in another way, does the mention of the Mediterranean culture represented by 'Dance, and Provençal song' and 'the warm South'.

Seen from this perspective, the poem becomes **an exploration of the powers and purposes of art**. It can, first of all, stir the emotions: the speaker's 'heart aches' because of the nightingale's song. It can be an **escape from the cares of the world**, a way of forgetting the suffering that comes with human consciousness, 'Where but to think is to be full of sorrow' (line 27). The bird and its music are free of that knowledge.

Art can also **console or comfort**. Keats said of his role as a poet, 'I am ambitious of doing the world some good.' The sort of good he meant is suggested by the story of Ruth in the seventh stanza: here music (the nightingale's song) provides a comfort for her as 'She stood in tears amid the alien corn' (line 67).

As noted in the Commentary, the next three lines touch on the nightingale's song as **inspiration for the artistic imagination** – music with the power to cast a spell on 'magic casements, opening on the foam / Of perilous seas' (lines 69–70). The image of casements (sets of windows) is a common one for the imagination, and the fact that here they look out on such a romantic landscape feeds the idea that Keats is thinking of the nightingale's song as poetic inspiration.

Music, at least as Keats views it in this poem, is all bound up with the senses, as opposed to thought. That is why it can be an escape from this world where 'men sit and hear each other groan' (line 24). The final stanza, as the nightingale flies away, its music fades and the vision dissolves, hints that art as escape from the world is of limited value.

Form

The 'Ode to a Nightingale' is the first of Keats's odes that we are studying. **An ode is a poem of praise for a person or thing, in which the subject is directly addressed**, as in line 61: 'Thou wast not born for death, immortal Bird!' There is no standard form for an ode, but Keats writes most of his in **ten-line stanzas**. The form bears some resemblance to a sonnet: the first four lines of each stanza rhyme *abab* like a Shakespearean sonnet, while the last six lines of this ode rhyme *cdecde* like the sestet of a Petrarchan sonnet. The metre is iambic, but in this poem Keats adds variety by introducing one shorter line (the eighth in each stanza) that has three stresses rather than the usual five. This form allows Keats more flexibility than would the tightly woven form of the sonnet, and though there is often a natural break between the first four lines and the last six (see, for example, the first stanza), this is not always the case; the fifth stanza has no clear division in it, a factor that contributes to the sense of being overwhelmed by impressions.

As well as flexibility within the stanzas, the links between them that move the train of thought from one to the next are also important. For example, the image of the poet dying and becoming a 'sod' to the nightingale's 'high requiem' (line 60) sparks the contrasting idea of the nightingale's immortality at the start of the following stanza: 'Thou wast not born for death' (line 61). Notice too how **Keats repeats key words** in order to make the links: 'fade away' at the end of stanza 2 is picked up in the opening words of stanza 3, and then again in 'Away! away!' at the start of stanza 4.

Language

The **richness of the language** is one of the great pleasures of reading this poem. Keats relishes the resources of poetic diction. These include the direct address to the nightingale using the intimate second-person 'thou', which was unusual in ordinary speech even two hundred years ago: 'Thou wast not born for death' (line 61). **Exclamations** (e.g. line 11: 'O, for a draught of vintage!'), **inversion** of word order (e.g. line 80: 'Fled is that music') and the use of **personification** in the third stanza (see Commentary) are other examples of poetic diction.

The language of the poem is **highly charged**. The use of the first person and the present tense from the first line ('My heart aches') contributes to the poem's emotional charge. So do the numerous, often richly resonant adjectives, which include many compound ones: 'light-wingèd', 'full-throated', 'deep-delvèd', 'purple-stainèd', 'spectre-thin', 'leaden-eyed'. There is a richness too, both of meaning and of sound, to many of the nouns and adjective–noun combinations. To take one example, the sensuality of 'sunburnt mirth' (line 14) is conveyed in part by the assonance of doubled vowel sounds in '—burnt mirth' and the three consecutive stresses that the phrase requires when spoken. (Try saying it.) The nouns often have their own richness, particularly in the flower names of the fifth stanza. There Keats uses the adjective–noun combinations to create the heady atmosphere of the sense impressions that accompany the nightingale's song in the 'embalmèd darkness' (line 43): 'soft incense', 'white hawthorn', 'pastoral eglantine', 'dewy wine', 'murmurous haunt'.

As already noted, the language is also rich with **musical effects**, including alliteration ('<u>d</u>eep-<u>d</u>elvèd'; '<u>b</u>eaded <u>b</u>ubbles') and assonance. Yet for all the richness of the language, it is never overwhelming. It always takes its place within a clear syntax which is never constrained by the rhymes and line endings, but always flows easily within them. Enjambment (run-over lines) is used a lot (see, for example, the poem's first two lines), but never draws attention to itself.

Also, for all the sensuous richness of the language, some of the poem's most powerful effects are achieved through **starkness and simplicity**: the plain **monosyllabic** epithets of 'a few, sad, last gray hairs' (line 25), for example.

The metre is iambic (unstressed, stressed), but Keats often varies it in subtle ways for effect. The monosyllables of line 25 quoted above require equal stresses and slow down the line, bringing out the bitter sadness in the words. The very opening of the poem, on the other hand, with its double stresses on the long vowels of 'heart aches', grab the reader's attention as well as conveying something of the speaker's anguish.

Questions

1	Describe the speaker's mood as this is conveyed in the first stanza.
2	The second stanza begins, 'O, for a draught of vintage!' Explain, in your own words, why the speaker wants a drink of wine, and what that 'draught of vintage' means to him.
3	In the third stanza, the mood of the poem changes. Explain.
4	Why, as the speaker expresses it in lines 27–8 ('Where but to think is to be full of sorrow / And leaden-eyed despairs'), does he suggest that thinking is the enemy of human happiness? What is his alternative?
5	What mood is created by the fifth stanza? How does Keats create this mood?
6	In stanza 6, the speaker's imagination surrenders to the attractions of an easy, painless death. Does this finally satisfy him? Explain your answer.
7	Line 61 ('Thou wast not born for death, immortal Bird!') is the focus for the main issues raised in the poem. Comment on the implications of this statement about the nightingale. In what sense is it true, and in what sense is it false?
8	What experience is being described in the final stanza? How would you describe the mood?
9	The poem is partly about the power of the poetic imagination, and of art in general, to transform human experience. Develop this idea.
10	Examine the tension between opposites found throughout the poem: between life and death, pleasure and pain, escapism and reality, life and art, mortality and immortality.
11	This poem has been described as a record of a 'drug-inspired dream-vision'. Is this a good description of the poem, do you think? Is it a complete one?
12	Choose one image or line from the poem that you particularly like (or dislike) and try to explain why. Comment on the sounds of the words if that is appropriate.
13	In the draft of the poem, line 26 read, 'Where youth grows pale, and thin and old and dies'. Why do you think Keats changed it? Consider the rhythm and sounds of the line.
14	Imagine you are the poet. Write two or three diary entries dealing with the poem (for example, the inspiration behind it, your own assessment of its value).
15	Listen again to a recording of a nightingale, and decide for yourself whether the song is sad or happy. Give yourself ten minutes to write your own response, in prose or verse, as you listen.

Before you read

Have you ever looked at classical Greek vases and urns? Before you read the poem, find some pictures online of carved or painted vases to get an idea of what Keats was writing about in this poem.

Ode on a Grecian Urn

Thou still unravish'd bride of quietness,
    Thou foster-child of silence and slow time,
Sylvan historian, who canst thus express
    A flowery tale more sweetly than our rhyme:
What leaf-fring'd legend haunts about thy shape   5
    Of deities or mortals, or of both,
        In Tempe or the dales of Arcady?
    What men or gods are these? What maidens loth?
What mad pursuit? What struggle to escape?
    What pipes and timbrels? What wild ecstasy?   10

Heard melodies are sweet, but those unheard
    Are sweeter: therefore, ye soft pipes, play on;
Not to the sensual ear, but, more endear'd,
    Pipe to the spirit ditties of no tone:
Fair youth, beneath the trees, thou canst not leave   15
    Thy song, nor ever can those trees be bare;
        Bold lover, never, never canst thou kiss
Though winning near the goal – yet, do not grieve;
        She cannot fade, though thou hast not thy bliss,
    For ever wilt thou love, and she be fair!   20

Ah, happy, happy boughs! that cannot shed
    Your leaves, nor ever bid the spring adieu;
And, happy melodist, unwearièd,
    For ever piping songs for ever new;
More happy love! more happy, happy love!   25
    For ever warm and still to be enjoy'd,
        For ever panting, and for ever young;
All breathing human passion far above,
    That leaves a heart high-sorrowful and cloy'd,
        A burning forehead, and a parching tongue.   30

Who are these coming to the sacrifice?
    To what green altar, O mysterious priest,
Lead'st thou that heifer lowing at the skies,
    And all her silken flanks with garlands drest?
What little town by river or sea shore,   35
    Or mountain-built with peaceful citadel,
        Is emptied of this folk, this pious morn?
And, little town, thy streets for evermore
    Will silent be; and not a soul to tell
        Why thou art desolate, can e'er return.   40

O Attic shape! Fair attitude! with brede
    Of marble men and maidens overwrought,
With forest branches and the trodden weed;
    Thou, silent form, dost tease us out of thought
As doth eternity: Cold Pastoral!   45
    When old age shall this generation waste,
        Thou shalt remain, in midst of other woe
Than ours, a friend to man, to whom thou say'st,
'Beauty is truth, truth beauty,' – that is all
    Ye know on earth, and all ye need to know.   50

Glossary

1	*unravish'd*: not broken or violated; virgin
3	*Sylvan*: to do with the woods and trees; the story on the urn takes place in a woodland setting
7	*Tempe ... Arcady*: places in Greece traditionally associated with beauty and golden-age happiness
8	*loth*: reluctant, unwilling
10	*timbrel*: musical instrument resembling a tambourine
29	*cloy'd*: experiencing unpleasant feelings as result of overindulgence
30	*parching*: dried out; thirsty
36	*citadel*: stronghold; fortified building
41	*Attic*: Greek
41	*brede*: interwoven pattern
42	*overwrought*: very elaborately carved (by the artist), and also worked up to too high a pitch (with reference to the man and the maidens)
44	*tease us out of thought*: baffle us with its mystery; defy our attempts to think rationally about what the urn signifies

Guidelines

The 'Ode on a Grecian Urn' was written at much the same time as the 'Ode to a Nightingale', and the two can be viewed as a complementary pair, sharing many of the same concerns. Here, more obviously than in the nightingale ode, the subject is the nature and purpose of art, in this case visual art: an ancient Greek urn. Like the nightingale ode, this poem was first published in the *Annals of the Fine Arts*, a magazine aimed at readers interested in the visual arts in particular, and especially at those who valued ancient Greek art as the highest ideal of beauty.

Keats had become more and more interested in classical Greek art and culture. He had spent a lot of time reading its literature in translation, and also looking at the Greek antiquities in the British Museum in London. According to his friend George Felton Mathew, 'one of the main endeavours of his poetic career was to grow more Grecian'.

This poem may have owed its immediate inspiration to some articles contributed to the *Examiner* in May 1819 by the painter and art critic Benjamin Haydon, a friend of Keats. In these articles, Haydon discussed some of the works of ancient Greek artists. These works included marble statues, marble ornamental decorations on buildings and beautifully decorated urns. Some of these artefacts depicted ancient Greek religious ceremonies, one in particular featuring a garlanded heifer and robed worshippers with dishevelled hair (see stanza 4), a boy flute-player wholly absorbed in the harmony of his own music (see stanza 2), and a city where 'all classes were crowding to the sacrifice' (stanza 4).

Commentary

Greek (or Grecian) urns were large vases, usually with handles and flat bases, used originally for storing the ashes of a cremated body. Although the painted clay vessels, often decorated with red and black figures, may be more familiar, Keats's urn is a marble one, decorated not by painting but by carving: 'with brede / Of marble men and maidens overwrought' (lines 41–42). Keats had looked at many, and had made a drawing of the Sosibios Vase (left) from a book about Greek art, but the urn he describes in the poem is his own invention, and does not match any actual vessel.

Stanza 1

Keats begins by addressing the urn, the subject of his ode. It is worth looking carefully at the first two lines and the words he uses to name the urn. The object is humanised, and thought of as female, a 'bride of quietness'. This phrase speaks to the literal silence of the urn, in contrast to the very vocal nightingale, but also to the sense of something tender, even sacred, in that silence. It is 'unravish'd', on one level, because although it is two thousand years old or so, it is undamaged, but the word also suggests both the femininity and purity of the object. The word 'still' carries a double meaning: 'not yet', after all this time, but also, simply, 'motionless'. The fact that it and all the scenes depicted on it are frozen in time is central to the poem.

The layers of meaning in the second line are equally rich and dense. The urn is a 'foster-child' because its original maker is long dead, and its foster parents are 'silence and slow time', embracing both the centuries during which the urn has survived, unchanging, buried or hidden, and the urn's own silence.

The urn is also called a 'Sylvan historian' that can tell a tale of the woods 'more sweetly than our rhyme'. Lines 5 to 10, following the colon at the end of line 4, question the nature of that 'flowery tale'. The speaker is trying to understand the story he sees carved into the urn. Are the figures gods or mortals? Where are they? What is happening? The maidens (plural) are 'loth'; there is a struggle; there are musicians. The scene conveys some sort of 'wild ecstasy'. Is this one of the stories of gods overpowering and raping mortal women that are so frequent in ancient Greek myths?

Stanza 2

The mood changes in the second stanza. The questions have stopped and instead there is an intense focus on the scene described, and clear statements about it.

By John Keats.

The first four lines act as a transition between the stanzas, picking up on the pipes described in the first stanza. They start with a proposition: unheard melodies (like those we can imagine being played by the musicians on the urn) are 'sweeter' than heard ones, presumably because their beauty is limited only by the viewer's imagination. This unheard music plays to 'the spirit', not the senses.

The scene we see in this stanza seems to be different from that described in the first one: instead of the men, gods, maidens and struggle, there is one lover, one woman and one musician. Here Keats concentrates on the way the scene seems suspended in time because it is a carving of one moment: the trees always in leaf, the musician ('Fair youth') always playing. The lover will be always in love, always about to kiss the maiden, and she 'cannot fade' and will always be beautiful.

Stanza 3

Now the speaker begins to project emotions onto this frozen scene. The trees must be happy because they exist in an eternal spring. The piper never gets tired and plays songs 'for ever new'. Above all, the lovers are happy: 'more happy, happy love!' They are always young, always on the brink of enjoyment, never knowing disappointment or disillusion. They are 'far above' the reality of 'breathing human passion', which is always a let-down: 'That leaves a heart high-sorrowful and cloy'd, / A burning forehead, and a parching tongue.'

Do you find the repetition of 'happy' in this stanza convincing? Is the speaker responding with simple joy to what he sees on the urn, or does the reality of human passion weigh more heavily? Is he trying too hard to convince himself that the beauty of art can make up for the sad reality of human experience?

Stanza 4

The mood changes dramatically in the fourth stanza. The fevered excitement of stanza 3 is replaced by a solemn, questioning tone. The scene here is clearly a new one. Some sort of religious ceremony is taking place. A priest leads a heifer decorated with flowers to a sacrificial altar. As in the first stanza, the speaker questions the scene: 'Who are these …?'; 'To what green altar …?' From line 35, however, the questions have a different focus – not on what the urn shows, but on what it does not show. Keats imagines a 'little town' which must be empty because all its inhabitants have come out to take part in the ceremony. Like the urn, its streets will always be 'silent', the town 'desolate'. This unseen empty town casts a shadow over the poem.

Stanza 5

In the final stanza, Keats addresses the urn directly again. The language now is distancing, where it had been humanising ('bride' and 'child') at the start of the poem. It is an 'Attic shape', an 'attitude', a 'silent form'. The designs on it are 'Cold Pastoral'. There is admiration, but also perhaps a little frustration, even resentment, in the speaker's statement that the urn 'dost tease us out of thought / As doth eternity'. Thinking about the urn and its meaning is what the speaker has been doing, but thinking about it doesn't reduce it to something comprehensible, any more than thinking about the nature of eternity.

The final five lines, however, reassert the permanent value of the urn, as a positive force, 'a friend to man', and then, in an extraordinary reversal, the silent urn speaks to its human viewers/listeners ('ye') in the final two lines. What it says, and what exactly Keats meant by it, has been the subject of a great deal of controversy. Some critics, including the great poet T. S. Eliot, have regarded it as meaningless, but it would appear that the idea of beauty and truth being equivalent was not meaningless to Keats himself. As he wrote in a letter, 'I can never be certain of any truth but from a clear perception of its beauty'.

Quotation marks?

The final two lines can be punctuated in different ways. In the original printing of the poem there were no quotation marks, but the fact that the words are addressed to 'ye', which is plural, strongly suggests that the urn is imagined as speaking to those looking at it, and through them to all humanity. In Keats's *Poems* of 1820 there were quotation marks around just 'Beauty is truth, truth beauty'. It has been suggested that those words were put in quotation marks because they are a quotation from an essay by the artist Joshua Reynolds. One solution, using modern conventions of punctuation, would be to put quotation marks around the whole of the final two lines, but the solution we have chosen leaves it open for the reader to interpret.

Themes and imagery

The 'Ode on a Grecian Urn' is **a meditation on the power and beauty of classical Greek art**, and through it on the purpose and place of art in general. Its imagery derives primarily from what is being contemplated: a marble Greek urn and the figures carved on it that suggest stories while being set in stone, as if frozen in time.

Despite an ending ('Beauty is truth, truth beauty') which sounds as though it summarises and clinches an argument, there is **no one simple, coherent argument** in what the poem says about art. There is, rather, an intense concentration on the object of contemplation and an engagement with it that is both intellectual and emotional, full of ambiguities of thought and feeling.

The poem's **central contrast is between the ideal and the actual**: the still and silent, utterly beautiful urn, and the messy realities of human life. This contrast comes to a head in the third stanza, where the 'happy, happy' trees and people, 'For ever panting, and for ever young' (line 27), are set against – and 'above' – the reality of 'breathing human passion'. This, on one level, is art as escape from life, and is familiar from the third stanza of the 'Ode to a Nightingale' and the desire to 'forget / … The weariness, the fever and the fret'.

One question to ask yourself in reading the poem is what makes the stronger impression on you, or feels more heartfelt – the exclamations at 'happy, happy love' or the description of human passion, 'That leaves a heart high-sorrowful and cloy'd, / A burning forehead, and a parching tongue'. Certainly there is tension. The silent, timeless perfection of the 'ditties of no tone' (line 14) or the eternal 'winning near the goal' (line 18) of stanza 2 are set against the human experience of time and the fact that 'old age shall this generation waste' (line 46).

The fourth stanza is interesting in this respect. It begins with questions about what is happening, where, and to whom. They resemble the questions in the first stanza aimed at understanding the story that is depicted on the urn. But from line 35, Keats's attention shifts. **Instead of using his intellect to try to understand the urn,**

he uses his imagination, his 'negative capability', to enter into the scene, speculating on an imaginary 'little town' that must now be empty because all its inhabitants have gone to the sacrifice the urn depicts. This is an interaction of viewer and object which creates its own meaning for the work of art. It creates a mood too. The 'desolate' town resonates through the poem, perhaps reflecting Keats's own state of mind. In this ode, as in the nightingale ode, Keats's imagination is tormented by the spectre of time and change obliterating all mortal things.

> 'I am certain of nothing but of the holiness of the Heart's affections and the truth of Imagination – What the imagination seizes as Beauty must be truth – whether it existed before or not – for I have the same idea of all our Passions as of Love: they are all, in their sublime, creative of essential Beauty.'
>
> **Keats, letter to Benjamin Bailey**

The poem **plays with the idea that great art can triumph over time.** The beautiful figures carved into the urn are unchanging, immortal. But the speaker also discovers his doubts about the unmoving perfection of the ancient urn. It is a 'friend to man', but it is not an easy friendship.

The poem starts with an awed, spiritual response to the 'unravish'd bride of quietness' and the 'foster-child' in the first two lines. It moves, through questioning and speculation, to the more detached stance of the final stanza, where the urn is viewed with some uncertainty or suspicion as an object of cold marble saying something that may be profound, but which also sounds dismissive: 'that is all / Ye know on earth, and all ye need to know' might imply that humans are not capable of other kinds of knowledge.

As in most great poetry, **the tensions that give the poem its energy are never entirely resolved**.

Form and language

In this ode Keats uses much the same form that he used in 'Ode to a Nightingale', except that here there are no shorter lines, and the rhyme scheme of the last six lines varies somewhat. The layout of the poem will help you to see the rhyme patterns.

'Ode on a Grecian Urn' does not have the linguistic richness of 'Ode to a Nightingale'. Where the nightingale ode is sensuous and highly charged, **the language of this poem is, on the whole, much plainer**, lacking the profusion of adjectives of its companion piece. Despite the subtle and suggestive phrases used to address the urn at the start of the poem (see Commentary), the language of the poem is mostly to do with **interrogation** (questions) or **proposition** (statements). The syntax (sentence structure) is often repetitive, for example in the series of questions in the first stanza, or in the frequent use of phrases introduced by 'ever', 'never', and especially 'for ever' in the second and third stanzas.

Throughout the poem, Keats is trying to understand the meaning of the urn. Whereas listening to the nightingale is all about a sensory experience that takes him on an emotional journey, **contemplating the urn stimulates his mind to engage actively with what he sees**. Like the pipes in stanza 2, the urn appeals 'Not to the sensual ear' but 'to the spirit' (lines 13–14). As a result he asks questions about the figures on the urn in the first and fourth stanzas, or makes assertions about them in the second and third stanzas.

Naturally enough in a poem based on contrasts between the ideal and the real, art and life, time and eternity, stillness and action, those assertions are often framed as **paradoxes**, expressing truths through apparent contradictions. The most daring example of paradox is found in the opening of stanza 2, which states that unheard music is sweeter than music which is audible. This entire stanza is paradoxical. The action goes on although the actors are motionless. We have soundless sound ('ditties of no tone'), stationary growth (trees that can never be bare) and timeless time ('ever wilt thou love, and she be fair'). Can you find other examples of paradox in the poem?

The word music of this poem is less rich than that of 'Ode to a Nightingale', but there are **many subtle effects**. Notice, for example, how the double stress on 'slow time' (line 2) slows down the line to match its meaning. Notice, too, the play of sounds and rhythm in lines 13–14: 'Not to the sensual ear, but, more endear'd, / Pipe to the spirit ditties of no tone'. The key word 'ear' is echoed in 'endear'd', and in the next line the consonance of 'p' and 't' sounds, along with the short 'i' sounds in the first part of the line, creates a light, dance-like music that contrasts with the assonance of long 'o' sounds in 'no tone'.

Questions

1	What impression is created of the urn in the first four lines of the poem? How does Keats create that impression?
2	In what sense can the urn tell a story 'more sweetly' than a poem ('rhyme') can?
3	What impressions do you get of the scene described in lines 5–10? Do you think it is the same scene as that described in the second stanza? Give reasons for your answer.
4	In the third stanza, why are the boughs, the musician and the lovers described as happy?
5	How do the speaker's questions about the scene he is looking at in stanza 4 differ from the questions he asked about the scene in stanza 1?
6	How would you describe the speaker's attitude to the urn in the final stanza? How does it differ from his initial attitude to it? Give reasons for your answer.
7	In what sense can the urn remain 'a friend to man'?
8	In stanza 3, do you think the speaker seems anxious to overcome whatever doubts might have been suggested in lines 15–20? Consider the significance of the repeated use of 'happy' in this stanza.
9	Why, do you think, does Keats dwell on the imaginary empty 'little town' in stanza 4? What mood does he create and what does the stanza add to the poem?
10	It has been said that this ode represents the triumph of Keats's imagination. Do you think that this comment is justified? Give reasons for your answer.
11	Is this an optimistic poem? Is the ending reassuring? Give reasons for your answer.
12	Comment on the language of this poem. How does it differ from that of 'Ode to a Nightingale'?
13	In stanza 4, the speaker wonders about the people coming to the sacrifice, and about the 'little town' they have deserted. Create your own version of the deserted town, of the people who have deserted it, and of the activities of those people on 'the pious morn' (line 37).
14	In stanzas 2 and 3 Keats imagines that the figures on the urn have feelings. Find a painting or sculpture that you like and imagine the thoughts and feelings of a character in it. Write them as a monologue.

To Autumn

Season of mists and mellow fruitfulness,
    Close bosom-friend of the maturing sun;
Conspiring with him how to load and bless
    With fruit the vines that round the thatch-eves run;
To bend with apples the moss'd cottage-trees,   5
    And fill all fruit with ripeness to the core;
      To swell the gourd, and plump the hazel shells
    With a sweet kernel; to set budding more,
And still more, later flowers for the bees,
Until they think warm days will never cease,   10
      For Summer has o'er-brimm'd their clammy cells.

Who hath not seen thee oft amid thy store?
    Sometimes whoever seeks abroad may find
Thee sitting careless on a granary floor,
    Thy hair soft-lifted by the winnowing wind;   15
Or on a half-reap'd furrow sound asleep,
    Drows'd with the fume of poppies, while thy hook
      Spares the next swath and all its twinèd flowers:
And sometimes like a gleaner thou dost keep
    Steady thy laden head across a brook;   20
    Or by a cyder-press, with patient look,
      Thou watchest the last oozings hours by hours.

Where are the songs of Spring? Ay, where are they?
    Think not of them, thou hast thy music too,—
While barrèd clouds bloom the soft-dying day,   25
    And touch the stubble-plains with rosy hue;
Then in a wailful choir the small gnats mourn
    Among the river sallows, borne aloft
      Or sinking as the light wind lives or dies;
And full-grown lambs loud bleat from hilly bourn;   30
    Hedge-crickets sing; and now with treble soft
    The red-breast whistles from a garden-croft;
      And gathering swallows twitter in the skies.

Glossary

1	*mellow*: mature, ripe
4	*thatch-eves*: the part of the thatched roof that overhangs the wall
7	*gourd*: a large, fleshy fruit like the melon
7	*plump*: make fat
11	*o'er-brimm'd*: overflowed
14	*careless*: free from care
15	*winnowing*: to winnow is to expose grain to the wind or to a current of air, so that such lighter particles as chaff or other waste matter are separated or blown away; as Autumn is engaged in this work, her hair is blown in the wind
17	*poppies*: traditionally associated with sleep; the source of opium
18	*swath*: a width of grass or corn cut by a reaping-hook
19–20	*a gleaner ... brook*: a gleaner is one who gathers grains of corn left by the harvesters
21	*cyder-press*: a cider-press is used to squeeze out the juice of crushed apples
25	*barrèd*: streaked
25	*bloom*: decorate like flowers
26	*stubble-plains*: the fields after the grain has been cut
27	*gnats*: small stinging flies
28	*sallows*: willows
30	*bourn*: land bounding the horizon
31	*treble*: high note
32	*red-breast*: the robin, the bird of winter
32	*croft*: an enclosed, cultivated patch of land near a house

Guidelines

'To Autumn' was written in September 1819, shortly after a walk Keats took in the stubble fields near Winchester in the south of England where he was then staying. We know this from a letter he wrote to his friend Reynolds two days later:

> 'I never liked stubble-fields as much as now – aye, better than the chilly green of spring. Somehow a stubble plain looks warm – in the same way that some pictures look warm – this struck me so much in my Sunday's walk that I composed upon it.'

Keats's poem, however, is much more than a simple description of what he saw on that Sunday walk. That was never his method. At about this time he described the essential difference between himself and the famous contemporary poet Lord Byron in these words: 'He describes what he sees – I describe what I imagine.' He added, 'mine is the hardest task'.

Commentary

Stanza 1

The dominant impression given by the first stanza is of the ripeness and abundance of autumn. The setting seems to be a cottage garden with a small orchard of old trees ('moss'd cottage-trees'). Everything is ripe and ready for harvesting, but harvesting has not begun. The verbs are important in creating the sense of ripe abundance: 'load and bless', 'bend', 'fill', 'swell', 'plump', 'set budding'. They have to do with actions involved in growth, filling and ripening. Everything is on the brink, ripe but not yet overripe. Only in the final image of the honey-making bees does this fullness overflow itself: 'Summer has o'er–brimm'd their clammy cells.'

This 'mellow fruitfulness' is placed in a discreet semi-mythological framework, hinted at but undefined in the stanza's opening lines. Autumn is not just a season but a maternal figure, 'bosom-friend' to the sun (which is usually pictured as male, like the sun god Apollo in Greek mythology). Together, they 'conspire' to 'load and bless' the plants with their seasonal fruits. You could think of it as a marriage or sexual union, with the harvest as its offspring, but the language does not insist on that.

Stanza 2

The second stanza focuses on the figure of Autumn as a woman. She is the personification of the season, presumably a goddess of some kind, but it is her ordinary, humanity not her divinity, that is emphasised. She is treated as something everyday and normal, a familiar figure rather than an exotic one: 'Who hath not seen thee oft …?'

She appears in different guises – as a thresher sitting on the granary floor; as a reaper, asleep on the job; as a gleaner carrying her basket of grains on her head; as a cider-maker who is not turning the press but just watching the 'last oozings' of the cider. These are all roles involved in harvesting. The poem has moved on from the ripeness of what is ready to be harvested to the harvest itself: the grain from the fields and the cider from the orchard's apples.

The mood is sensuous, sleepy, satiated; concentrating not on the human efforts and actions involved in harvesting but on the feelings of satisfaction and deserved rest that come with a job well done (compare Frost's 'After Apple-Picking'). There is room for lazing, luxuriating, and a benign negligence: she spares 'the next swath and all its twinèd flowers', as if the grain harvest is so abundant that some corn can be left uncut in order to spare the flowers. The day is warm and sleepy, as if under the influence of 'the fume of poppies'. Time seems to have slowed down with the 'last oozings' of the apple juice.

Stanza 3

The opening phrase of the third stanza – 'Where are the songs of Spring?' – raises for a moment a question that the poem does not pursue. It is put aside because it is this moment, autumn, that is being celebrated: 'thou hast thy music too'. The stanza goes on to describe some of that 'music' in the sounds made by the creatures: the 'wailful choir' of the gnats, the bleating of the lambs, the crickets singing, the song of the 'red-breast' (robin), and finally the twittering of the swallows.

The harvest is over now, and the figure of Autumn we saw in the second stanza is absent. The wheat fields have become 'stubble-plains'. The midday heat of the previous stanza has given way to evening, and a beautiful sunset, as 'barrèd clouds bloom the soft-dying day'. It is a lovely scene, as we move outwards from the fields to the 'river sallows' to the 'hilly bourn' and eventually up to the swallows in the sky.

There is a sense of things ending – the gnats are 'wailful' as if in grief; the lambs are 'full-grown', so no longer really lambs; and the swallows may be gathering for their migration south. But although winter may be around the corner, it is not here yet, and for now there is the music of autumn to listen to and enjoy.

Themes and imagery

Readers have always recognised the difference between this, Keats's final ode, and all the other odes he wrote, including the two we have already looked at. This poem feels **calmer, more accepting, less tortured** than the others. It is instructive to examine what is absent in 'To Autumn'.

It lacks, most obviously, the questioning and striving after meaning or truth of those other poems. **It lacks abstractions and abstract language**, like 'Beauty', 'Truth', 'Love', 'Youth'. Although Autumn herself is very present, she is imagined in entirely human terms. She is not an allegorical figure or a classical deity; though she owes something to the fertility goddess Ceres, and to Eve in Milton's *Paradise Lost*, she is a creature of Keats's own imagination. In fact, although, as we have seen, his imagination was filled with figures from classical mythology, there are no overt references to that mythology or culture in the poem.

Perhaps most significant of all, there is **no defined, personalised speaker**, no 'I' from whom we as readers can distance ourselves, whose emotions and ideas we can observe: no figure sitting in the dark under a tree listening to the nightingale and yearning to be dissolved into its song; nobody studying the urn and interrogating it until he can make it give up its secrets.

The effect of this is that we are not witnesses to a drama, but are absorbed into the speaker's viewpoint. No other perspective is offered. Instead of ideas, we are presented with images. Or, to put it another way, **the ideas in the poem are embodied in its sensuous images**. Let us examine some of those images.

One thing to notice is that **all the senses are involved in the poem**. As well as sight and hearing, taste is referenced in the 'sweet kernel' of line 8, touch in the bees' 'clammy cells' (line 11), and smell in the 'fume of poppies' (line 17). As noted in the Commentary, the first stanza makes much use of verbs of ripening and expanding that are almost **tactile**: 'fill', 'plump', 'swell'. The second stanza is primarily **visual**, as the figure of Autumn is presented in a series of tableaux (still scenes) like paintings. The third stanza is dominated by **auditory** images that follow on from the idea of the 'songs of Spring' and autumn's own music in the first two lines.

It has been suggested that the 'stubble-plains' mentioned in the third stanza (line 26), like those that Keats saw on his walk near Winchester, are the originating image of the poem. He saw them on that walk as 'warm', and his poem captures that warmth superbly. But stubble means that the harvest is over and winter is coming. And yet winter is the only season not mentioned in the poem, and traditional ideas about the cycle of the seasons, which tend to see autumn as a prelude to winter, are also absent.

Nevertheless, we should be sensitive to the nuances of the poem's mood. It was written at a time when Keats could no longer ignore the fact that he was seriously ill; when his ambitions to make a career as a writer seemed to be going nowhere; when he knew he had to make a decision about his relationship with Fanny Brawne (see Biography, page 115). The death of his brother Tom still haunted him, and he was anxious about his brother George in America. **'To Autumn' celebrates the beauty and abundance of the season, but it can't entirely shut out darker emotions.** It is impossible to read 'Until they think warm days will never cease' (line 10) without an awareness that they will, in fact, cease; or to hear 'last oozings' without being reminded that something is coming to an end. In the final stanza, the day is 'dying', albeit softly; the gnats 'mourn'; the wind 'lives or dies'; the lambs are 'full-grown'; the robin is often associated with winter (think Christmas cards); and those swallows will be flying away soon, even if not today.

The life and beauty that the poem so wonderfully conjures is all the more precious for the knowledge that it will not last forever, and we are aware of that without its being overtly stated. Unlike the other odes, the word 'adieu' (goodbye) is never used in 'To Autumn', and yet the poem can be read as one long, lovely goodbye.

> **Integrated imagination**
>
> **'Magnificent portrait of an integrated imagination, haunted by the fear of rejection, suppression and failure.'**
>
> **Andrew Motion on 'To Autumn'**

One facet of the poem worth noticing is that it **explores the interaction of humans and nature**. The harvest of the cottage garden or the wheat fields is a result of humans' interaction with natural forces, as gardeners, beekeepers and farmers. It is **not a wild landscape but an agricultural, humanised one**, and the harvest is carried out and its products enjoyed by people. You can read this, as Helen Vendler does in her book on Keats's odes, as an image for the creative processes of art, and of writing poetry in particular. In Vendler's view, the voices of the creatures in the final stanza, the music of autumn, represent poetry. It is an image of art that focuses on its natural, organic processes – a counterbalance to the agonised debates in the nightingale and urn odes.

That is one person's interpretation. The marvellous thing about 'To Autumn' is how open it is to interpretation, but how little it insists on it. This has led some critics to dismiss it as lovely but meaningless. Others consider it Keats's greatest achievement. For them, it is complete in itself, its images fully realised, and the whole poem is holding in balance the different forces and emotions at play in it.

What do you think?

Form

'To Autumn' is written in iambic pentameters, all of which use end-rhyme. As always in his mature poetry, Keats handles the form with wonderful deftness, so that the thoughts flow easily within and between the lines. Each stanza is built on a single sentence, though the second and third stanzas pose a preliminary question before launching into theirs. In each case the syntax (sentence structure) works through a series of parallel phrases.

The syntax and imagery of the first stanza all hinge on the third line, 'Conspiring with him how to …'. The verbs that follow – 'load and bless', 'bend', 'fill', 'swell … and plump', 'set budding' – all depend on that phrase and all follow the same pattern. In the second stanza the structure is built around 'Sometimes … Or … And sometimes … Or …'. In the third, the basic structure is: 'While' x (the sunset), 'Then' a (the gnats) 'And' b (the lambs) 'and' c (the robin) 'And' d (the swallows). In each case there is both **repetition and variation**, as the abundance of autumn is listed in all its variety. **The accumulation of phrases mirrors the abundance of the season.**

The poem is written in **eleven-line stanzas**, rather than the ten-line ones of the other odes. The first four lines rhyme abab, as in the others, but there is an extra line in the second part, meaning that there is always a rhyming couplet immediately before the stanza's final line. This in turn means that the final rhyme is delayed, and a greater tension is built up before it is released with the final rhyme that we know is coming. It is as if just one extra thing is always being crammed into the storehouse of the poem.

Language

As already noted, the language of the poem is sensuous and physical. It lacks the abstract elements that we find elsewhere in Keats's poetry, and is always working to create images. It also has a closely worked pattern of sounds that enrich the sensuousness of the images in multiple ways. These run through the entire poem, and are too numerous and complex to explore in any detail here. Nevertheless, look at how soft 'f' sounds (including in the word 'soft') run through the poem; or listen out for the vowel sound '–ore', not just in 'core' and 'more' and 'store' and 'floor', but also in 'warm', 'o'er-brimm'd', 'mourn', 'borne' and 'bourn', and also, of course, in 'or'.

We will finish by looking at some smaller-scale examples of word music, beginning with lines 15–16:

> Thy hair soft-lifted by the winnowing wind;
> Or on a half-reap'd furrow sound asleep …

Notice how the gentle consonants of 'soft-lifted', which imitate the action of the gentle wind, are taken up in 'half-reap'd furrow'; the alliteration of 'winnowing wind'; and the internal rhyme of 'reap' and 'asleep', as well as the half-rhyme of 'wind' and 'sound'.

In other examples, notice how the long vowels of 'last oozings hours by hours' slow down the rhythm to match the slow oozings; how the line break in 'keep / Steady' (lines 19–20) suggests the action of stepping carefully 'across a brook'; and how the reversed stresses on 'blóom the' (line 25) – dúm-di, instead of di-dúm – work with the alliteration on the initial 'b' and the long vowel ('–oom') that follows to emphasise 'bloom', and make it a verb of rich sensuous power in the line, as the setting sun catches the low clouds and lights them up like a great flower, a suggestion that is reinforced by 'rosy' in the next line.

Questions

1	In the first stanza, the richness and fullness of autumn's gifts are conveyed through tactile images (images that appeal to our sense of touch). Expand on this idea, drawing attention to the sounds of words and the rhythm and movement of the verse as the means of achieving sensuous effects.
2	In the second stanza Autumn is presented as an individual female figure. What are her main qualities as these are reflected in her activities? Are there suggestions that the figure of Autumn has some of the attributes of a goddess? Explain your answer.
3	Describe the mood of the second stanza. How does Keats create this mood?
4	How does the final stanza differ in mood and tone from the first two? What other differences are there?
5	In many poetic accounts of autumn, the emphasis is on decay and change. Is this true of Keats's poem?
6	In what sense is 'To Autumn' a more positive and optimistic poem than 'Ode to a Nightingale' or 'Ode on a Grecian Urn'?
7	Do you think that 'To Autumn' is the work of a poet at peace with the world? Explain your answer.
8	What view of nature is presented in 'Ode to Autumn'?
9	In what ways does the speaker of this poem differ from those of 'Ode to a Nightingale' and 'Ode on a Grecian Urn'? What are the effects of these differences?
10	Comment on the imagery of the poem. How does it differ from stanza to stanza?
11	Choose two examples of how Keats uses word music and rhythm to create effects, and describe how they work.
12	*Groupwork* Your group wishes to make a short film of this poem. Describe what kind of setting, music, lighting, etc. you would use to convey the atmosphere of the poem to viewers.
13	What is your favourite season? Write a short piece about it, or some aspect of it, in verse or prose.

Before you read

Groupwork

What qualities do you associate with a star? Read the poem and see if any of these qualities are present in it.

Bright Star

Bright star, would I were steadfast as thou art—
    Not in lone splendour hung aloft the night
And watching, with eternal lids apart,
    Like nature's patient, sleepless Eremite,
The moving waters at their priestlike task   5
    Of pure ablution round earth's human shores,
Or gazing on the new soft-fallen mask
    Of snow upon the mountains and the moors—
No—yet still steadfast, still unchangeable,
    Pillow'd upon my fair love's ripening breast,   10
To feel for ever its soft fall and swell,
    Awake for ever in a sweet unrest,
Still, still to hear her tender-taken breath,
And so live ever—or else swoon to death.

Glossary

1	*steadfast*: constant
2	*aloft*: high up in
4	*Eremite*: an old word for 'hermit'
6	*ablution*: cleansing

Guidelines

'Bright Star' was probably written in October 1819, and is one of Keats's last poems. It has always been associated with Fanny Brawne, the eighteen-year-old Keats had met and fallen in love with the year before. Their relationship is the subject of the 2009 film *Bright Star*. Keats presented her with a copy of this poem, and seems to have regarded it as a declaration of love. It certainly marked a new resolution in his attitude to her. Shortly after writing the poem, he and Fanny became formally, though secretly, engaged.

Commentary

The poem is a sonnet addressed to the 'Bright star' in the night sky, and expresses one fundamental wish, announced in the first line: 'would I were steadfast as thou art'.

The next seven lines, up to the end of the octave of the sonnet, expand on the image of the star 'hung aloft the night', watching over the cleansing tides of the oceans (lines 5–6) or the snow-covered countryside (lines 7–8). However, the whole passage is governed by the 'Not' at the start of line 2. He does *not* want to be alone like the star, 'in lone splendour'. Because of that 'Not' it is unclear how much of this image he admires or desires.

What he does desire is the 'steadfast' and 'unchangeable' nature of the star (line 9). The 'No' at the start of line 9, introducing the sonnet's sestet (final six lines), refers back to 'Not' in line 2: he wants to be steadfast not in splendid isolation like the star, but in his relationship with his lover, his head 'Pillow'd upon my fair love's ripening breast'. He wants to be unchanging in his love, and the lines imply something in addition to that: he wants this moment, as he lies there, feeling the 'fall and swell' of her breathing, to last for ever. Either that or, he declares in the poem's final phrase, to 'swoon to death' in the midst of this intense, heightened state of being. The eroticism of the passage is subtly underlined in this last image, with its suggestion of a fulfilment other than death: the phrase *la petite mort* ('little death') has long been used in reference to orgasm.

Themes and imagery

The heart of the poem is the **contrast between the bright star in the octave and the lover resting on his beloved's breast in the sestet**. You could imagine that he can see the star from where he lies and compares his situation with that of the star.

Let us examine the image of the **star** to begin with.

The star is a traditional image of **steadfastness and constancy**. But though the speaker admires its constancy, other qualities of the star are just as prominent in this sonnet.

The star has a **remote grandeur**, 'in lone splendour hung aloft the night' (line 2). Keats imagines it as a 'sleepless Eremite' or hermit. Hermits are people who have withdrawn from the world to pursue a solitary life devoted to self-denial, dedicated to avoiding the temptations of the flesh. The watching Eremite is associated with two natural forces distinguished for their purifying influence – the sea and the snow. The star presides over these with constant watchfulness, like a hermit keeping a prayerful vigil. The action of the sea around the shores of the world is seen as a cleansing ('pure ablution'), ritually performed by a 'priestlike' agent. The freshly fallen **snow** is another image of **natural purity**. Together they suggest a passionless purity, free from disturbing desire.

What are we to make of these images of remoteness and purity? The description of the star is preceded by 'Not' (line 2), which applies grammatically to the entire passage, and yet despite that 'Not', there is an aching beauty in the description that suggests that the speaker is also attracted by it. Does the star represent Fanny, or how Keats imagined her, both pure and compassionate? Does it express the purity and compassion he wished to feel in his love for her? If he asks for steadfastness, is it because he has a passionate, unsteady temperament and is not as constant as he would like to be?

Is the sonnet based on the ancient **conflict between lust and love**? This idea is supported by a comment Keats made on that subject at about the same time the sonnet was composed. He referred to 'lustful love' as 'the old plague spot and the raw scrofula' (a form of tuberculosis), and something that 'disgraces me in my own eyes'.

If the imagery of the octave represents perfect purity, the imagery of the sestet suggests another ideal, emphasising qualities the speaker finds lacking in the star. In contrast to the untouchable star is the image of the speaker with his head on his beloved's 'ripening breast' (line 10). It is **physically intimate and richly sensual.** The 'fall and swell' is now associated with his lover's breast rather than with the ebb and flow of the sea. The 'sweet unrest' of her embrace contrasts with the sexless, calm detachment of the star.

There is a **tension** between the two charged poles of purity and sensuality that the poem does not entirely resolve. Both are attractive in their different ways, and although the speaker chooses the holiness of physical love over the holiness associated with the star, the steadfastness or constancy he can experience in his lover's arms is of a very different sort from the steadfastness of the star. **He pictures it as an eternal continuation of his 'sweet unrest', and wants his heightened, aroused state to last for ever.** The word 'ever' is used three times in the last four lines.

That eternity is hard to imagine in the real world, which may be why he offers the alternative of swooning to death. Perhaps it was, in the end, unimaginable except as a sort of death, a dying into the moment, just as he had imagined in 'Ode to a Nightingale', prolonging a moment of happiness into eternity – 'to cease upon the midnight with no pain' while the nightingale sings.

Form and language

'Bright Star' is a **Shakespearean sonnet** with a rhyme scheme of *ababcdcd efefgg*, ending in a rhyming couplet. It divides naturally between the octave (first eight lines), which describe the star, and the sestet (last six lines), which describe the speaker lying in his beloved's arms. It consists of just **one sentence**, with the main idea announced in the first line, and the rest of the sentence stitched together by 'Not' in line 2, which introduces the image of the star, and 'No' in line 9, which links back to 'Not' and introduces the second image.

The ideas and images fit quite neatly into the lines. Although some of the images (e.g. lines 2–6) run over several lines, there is no jarring enjambment (run-on lines) to disrupt the flow. In the sestet, each element of the image fills a single line, with a comma at the end, until the final line, which contains the poem's only strong caesura (mid-line break), marked by the dash before 'or else swoon to death'.

The final rhyming couplet gives the poem a sense of completion or resolution that you could argue it does not quite deserve. Is the idea of swooning to death a natural completion, or is it a way out of a situation that cannot be resolved?

The language matches the subject matter. In the octave it has a restrained grandeur. The **paired stresses** of 'lóne spléndour' (line 2) and the pattern of 'l's and 'n's that is picked up in the words that follow, 'hung aloft the night', give a wonderful sense of the star's glory. The lines describing the 'sleepless Eremite' have a stately, unruffled rhythm.

In the sestet the language is more sensual, and the sounds of the words and their rhythm respond to the new mood. In line 10, the three consecutive stresses on 'fáir lóve's rípening breast' make the reader linger on the image and relish in particular the striking word 'ripening'. In the next line, the play of 'f' and 'l' sounds in 'feel for ever its soft fall and swell' conveys the **gentle sensuality** of the image.

The sestet also uses a lot of **repetition** – of 'ever' and 'for ever', and of 'still' – to suggest the urgency of the speaker's desire to make the moment last. Notice in particular how the repetition of 'still' in line 13 almost stops the forward movement of the verse, as if he wants to stop time.

Questions

1. What impression do you get of the star in the first eight lines of the poem? What words and images are most important in conveying this impression?

2. The star is a traditional image of steadfastness or constancy, which is what the speaker of the poem desires. Why, in that case, does he not find in the star a satisfying image of his ideal?

3. What is the speaker's more perfect image of his ideal, as described in the final six lines?

4. The sonnet suggests that even the most satisfying human experience is imperfect. How does it do this?

5. Compare and contrast the language used in the second part of the poem with that used in the first. How does Keats use the sounds of the words to bring out this contrast?

6. In 'Ode on a Grecian Urn', Keats contrasts 'breathing human passion' (line 28) with the 'Cold Pastoral' of 'marble men and maidens' (lines 45 and 42). Consider the relevance of this kind of contrast to that on which 'Bright Star' is based.

7. Do you find this poem happy or sad? Explain your answer.

8. Based on your reading of the poem, what kind of person do you think the poet is? Discuss this in pairs or small groups.

9. Keats sent a copy of this sonnet to Fanny Brawne, the 'fair love' mentioned in line 10. Compose a letter that she might have written on receiving the sonnet.

SNAPSHOT JOHN KEATS

- Poems display rare imaginative power
- Remarkable descriptive power
- Master of the musical use of language
- Lacking in wit and humour
- Poems often explore the significance of art
- Deep understanding of the tragic aspects of human experience
- Imagery often drawn from nature and country life
- Love of classical culture and art
- Poems reveal a troubled personality
- An escapist tendency in some poems
- Poetry is sensuous and passionate
- Drawn to intense, transformative experiences

Exam-Preparation Questions

1. 'In his poetry, Keats explores the relation between pleasure and pain, happiness and melancholy, imagination and reality, art and life, with brilliant poetic force.'
   Is this is a good description of Keats's poetry on your course, do you think? Refer in your answer to at least three of the poems.

2. 'John Keats presents abstract ideas in a style that is clear and direct.'
   To what extent do you agree or disagree with this assessment of his poetry? Support your points with reference to the poetry on your course.

3. Often we love a poet because of the feelings his/her poems create in us. Write about the feelings John Keats's poetry creates in you and the aspects of the poems (their content and/or style) that help to create those feelings. Support your points by reference to the poetry by Keats that you have studied.

4. 'While Keats's poetry celebrates life, it also acknowledges life's limitations.'
   Discuss this statement, supporting your answer by reference to the poems by Keats on your course.

5. 'In the poetry of Keats we see the poet striving towards a satisfying notion of permanence.'
   Discuss this view, supporting your answer by reference to the poems by Keats on your course.

6. 'Keats is one of the greatest descriptive poets.' Write a response to this comment.

7. You have been asked to give a talk with the title: 'An introduction to Keats's poetry'. Write out the text of the talk you would give.

8. Would you agree that after reading the poetry of Keats, we are left thinking that neither the beauty of nature nor the beauty of art can console us for the miseries of life?

9. Some readers may feel that Keats lays too much emphasis on the darker aspects of human experience, and that his poetry lacks joy. Basing your comments on the prescribed poems, say what you think of this idea.

10. 'Keats's poetry is essentially escapist. He is always trying to fly away from or forget the miseries of the world. For him, even death is a form of escape.'
    Is this a fair summary of Keats's poetry? Discuss the question with detailed reference to the poems on your course.

11. Explore the ways in which Keats uses rhythm and word music (alliteration, assonance and other techniques) to create effects that are central to the meaning of his poems. Use detailed examples from the poems on your course.

Sample Essay

'Keats uses sensuous language and vivid imagery to express a range of profound tensions.' To what extent do you agree or disagree with this statement? Support your answer with reference to the poetry of John Keats on your course.

Addresses the question immediately → It is hard to disagree with this description of Keats's poetry. Keats's language is not always sensuous, nor his images always vivid, but his poetry is full of both, and there are always tensions and ambiguities in what it is expressing. It is true too that a great range of tensions can be found in his poetry, but the ways in which his language and imagery express those tensions are varied. I will look at three of Keats's poems in some detail in order to explore this variety. ← *Adds qualification to first response*

Discussion of first poem uses key words from question → 'Ode to a Nightingale' is the poem which this quotation brings immediately to my mind. Here Keats's language is at its most rich and sensuous, the imagery vivid and varied. Here, too, the emotional tensions expressed by the speaker are at the heart of the poem. 'My heart aches', declares the speaker at the beginning, 'and a drowsy numbness pains my sense'. But this is a paradoxical heartache, brought on not by grief or envy but because he is 'too happy in thine happiness'. As so often in Keats, pain and pleasure are bound *Uses short quotations throughout* → closely together, held in a tension that enriches them both and that is central to the poem's meaning. The sublime beauty of the nightingale's song provokes apparently contradictory responses in the speaker: a profound melancholy and a joyous exhilaration; a desire to let his imagination fly like the bird and a longing to die. The song itself can sound both happy, as the bird sings in 'full-throated ease' in the first stanza, and sad, in the 'plaintive anthem' of the final stanza.

Addresses one element of the question (imagery) → The imagery has great variety – from the classical references to Flora and the Hippocrene in the second stanza, to the personifications of youth, love and beauty in the third, to the simple visual image, drawn from the Bible, of Ruth standing 'in tears amid the alien corn'. Perhaps the most vivid and sensuous imagery comes in the fifth stanza with Keats's description of the flowers that he can only guess at in the darkness. Their names – 'White hawthorn, and the pastoral eglantine' – help to convey an idea of the richness of the sensory experience, and of the abundance of the plant life, but Keats uses carefully chosen words to add an unease to that abundance. The darkness is 'embalmèd', and the scent of the flowers is described as 'incense', words that have overtones of death. All these details remind ← *Detailed analysis of the words used* us of decay and death in the midst of luxuriant life. The texture of the language holds the tension between life and death that is set up earlier in the poem, with the strong contrast between the celebration of life in the 'draught of vintage' tasting of 'Dance, and Provençal song, and sunburnt mirth', and this death-haunted world 'Where youth grows pale, and spectre-thin, and dies'.

Addresses the second element of the question (language) → And yet, for all its vivid imagery, it is the language of the poem that I find most remarkable. It is full of memorable phrases, and although it is often ← *Personal view* very sensuous, especially in its musical use of sounds, it has great delicacy and variety.

Keats's language is acutely sensitive to the changing moods: the delighted relish conveyed by the alliteration of 'beaded bubbles winking at the brim', or the slow, dirge-like monosyllables of 'a few, sad, last gray hairs'. At the same time, the mood of the poem as a whole is created in part by the use of the soft initial 'f' that recurs throughout the poem in key words such as 'fade', 'forget', 'fly', 'forest', forlorn', 'Flora', 'flowers', 'faery', and 'Fled', which begins the final line with a strong stress. It is a gentle, breathy sound that suggests the idea of fading and dissolving that is central to this poem, and it is often accompanied by the similar 'v' and 'th' sounds, as in 'the fever, and the fret' or 'Fast fading violets cover'd up in leaves'.

Use of quotation to analyse the sounds of words

But although Keats's use of sound is very sensuous, it seems to me that some of the most powerful effects in the poem are created by the simplest, plainest language. For example, 'Where but to think is to be full of sorrow' is a statement that is moving because it is so stark and simple. The beautiful description of the nightingale's disappearance in the final stanza is not sensuous, but merely a series of short phrases whose simple syntax seems to mirror the bird's journey: 'Past the near meadows, over the still stream, / Up the hill-side; and now 'tis buried deep / In the next valley-glades'.

Returns to the terms of the question

Has there been too much discussion of one poem?

A similar combination of simplicity and power is evident in 'La Belle Dame Sans Merci'. Here, though, it is the imagery rather than the language that is most striking.

Link to next poem to be considered

The poem is a ballad, and in keeping with the story-telling style of this genre, the language and syntax are simple, almost childish, with the repeated use of 'and'. For example, the knight's description of meeting the lady uses conventional language in a simple way: 'Her hair was long, her foot was light, / And her eyes were wild'. Carefully chosen details are used to build up vivid images. The bleak setting is established by the detail that the 'sedge has wither'd from the lake', and the solitary knight is depicted strikingly in white and red – a lily on his brow and a 'fading rose' on his cheeks. There is the 'lady in the meads' with her 'wild' eyes, and the description of their courtship: his gifts of the garland and bracelets, the journey on the 'pacing steed', her gifts of 'honey wild and manna dew'; her weeping, his kisses; and then the dream of the 'pale kings and princes'. The narrative is constructed from these vivid images.

Continued use of short quotations

Unlike the 'Ode to a Nightingale' there is no clearly defined 'I' at the centre of the poem whose shifting thoughts and emotions we are privy to. There is no description of motivation or the interior life of either of the two main 'characters', but everything is seen from the outside. We know 'she wept and sigh'd full sore', but we are not told why. We know that he 'shut her wild wild eyes / With kisses four' but we do not know what he was feeling. This creates a sense of mystery. There is a sense of the importance of the details – the possible symbolism of the lily and the rose, of honey and manna, of the 'pacing steed' or the 'elfin grot', but nothing is defined.

Contrasts one poem with another

What is certain is that there is a profound tension at the centre of the poem. The lady is beautiful and she seems to be loving, but her love is fatal. She is both vulnerable (weeping and sighing) and powerful, having the knight 'in thrall'. She is the object of love but also the bringer of death, something to be both desired and feared. This fundamental ambiguity reflects a powerful ambivalence in Keats himself, who remarked in a letter that he did not have 'a right feeling towards women'.

Returns to the terms of the question

Use of biographical information relevant to the poem

Introduction of third poem links it to the second

The tension in 'Bright Star' also concerns a woman, and is focused on the two contrasting primary images – of the distant star in the octave and the intimate embrace of the lovers in the sestet.

The remote grandeur of the star is given an aura of purity and spirituality. It is a 'sleepless Eremite' or hermit, withdrawn from all the pleasures of the world, watching over the oceans and the fresh snow, whose whiteness also implies purity. Keats's language is in keeping with the austerity of the image. The vocabulary suggests spiritual purity: the star watches with 'eternal lids'; the oceans perform a 'priestlike task' of 'pure ablution'. The rhythm is measured and solemn, made stately by the long vowels and strong stresses in a line such as 'Like nature's patient, sleepless Eremite'.

The image of the speaker in his beloved's arms, however, is intensely sensuous. Whereas the image of the star is primarily visual, the sense of touch is primary here. The word 'Pillow'd' evokes a familiar physical sensation, and the experience of lying against her 'ripening breast' is conjured in the next line: 'To feel for ever its soft fall and swell'. The repeated 'f', 's' and 'l' sounds add a great deal to the sensuality of the image. The rhythm too responds to the emotional intensity, with the repetition of 'Still, still' at the beginning of the line seeming to prolong this intense moment.

Quotation and detailed analysis of language

The tension of the poem hinges on the speaker's desire to bring those two images together – to have the 'unchangeable' steadfastness of the star while lying in his lover's arms, as if that moment could be extended for ever. At some level, he knows and the reader knows that that is impossible. I think that the poem's final phrase, 'or else swoon to death', is really an admission of that impossibility. The everlasting intensity of experience he desires can only be imagined as a sort of dying, just as Keats had imagined that he could 'cease upon the midnight with no pain' in the 'Ode to a Nightingale', and so make the ecstatic moment a final fulfilment.

Personal interpretation backed up by argument

As a man, Keats was full of contradictions, and subject to impulses which pulled him in different directions: towards sensuality and towards purity; towards a celebration of life and towards a longing for death. The tensions between these different impulses give his poems their special power. Even when he celebrates life most, as in 'To Autumn', a sense of life's transience (the swallows gathering for their migration) ensures that the poetry is full of tensions, and all the richer for it. Keats was a master of poetic language, and although it is often sensuous in its vocabulary and in the music of the words, its power can also come from simplicity. Vivid images are sometimes evoked in the plainest language. I would say that the statement in the question is true, but it is not the whole truth.

Is this too vague? Could it have been developed?

Brief mention of a fourth poem

Final sentence summarises the answer to the question

ESSAY CHECKLIST		Yes √	No ×
Purpose	Has the candidate understood the task?		
	Has the candidate responded to it in a thoughtful manner?		
	Has the candidate answered the question?		
Comment:			
Coherence	Has the candidate made convincing arguments?		
	Has the candidate linked ideas?		
	Does the essay have a sense of unity?		
Comment:			
Language	Is the essay written in an appropriate register?		
	Are ideas expressed in a clear way?		
	Is the writing fluent?		
Comment:			
Mechanics	Is the use of language accurate?		
	Are all words spelled correctly?		
	Does the punctuation help the reader?		
Comment:			

Brendan Kennelly

b. 1938

Biography

Early life and education

Brendan Kennelly was born in Ballylongford, a close-knit village on a crossroads in Co. Kerry, in 1936. His parents Tim Kennelly and Bridie Ahern, a nurse, had met at a dance in nearby Ballybunion, and married in June 1932. Brendan was one of seven children: five boys and two girls. He said it was often tough to be in such a big family: 'sometimes you don't feel loved'. At two years of age he was sent to live with an aunt for eighteen months to take some pressure off his mother. The Kennelly family ran a pub in the village where singing and storytelling was to inspire Brendan's fascination with words and sound, and was a contributing factor to Kennelly's love of the Irish oral tradition, which led to translations such as 'A Cry for Art O'Leary' and 'Saint Brigid's Prayer'.

Kennelly was educated at St Ita's College, Tarbert, Co. Kerry, a school run by Jane Agnes McKenna, to whom he would dedicate a 1992 collection of his early poetry, *Breathing Spaces*. He spoke highly of the education he received there for three pounds a term. He loved sport and was on the Kerry minor football team of 1954.

Kennelly spoke of his poetic talent as 'a gift that took me unawares'.

Trinity College, early work and influences

Statue of Patrick Kavanagh, who was a huge influence on Kennelly.

Kennelly went to Trinity College, Dublin on a scholarship and attended Leeds University for a time also. At the age of twenty-five he achieved joint first-class honours in English and French at Trinity and met his friend Rudi Holzapfel, who was to collaborate on Kennelly's first four books of poetry between 1959 and 1963. Holzapfel went on to run a bookshop in Cashel, Co. Tipperary, and said of Brendan about his early Trinity days: 'He was like the proverbial culchie – he had a belted mac, a little cap down over his eyes.' He was certainly not the typical wealthy Protestant Trinity student of the time; he was a rural GAA-playing Catholic, but he took to life in Dublin easily without forgetting his roots; he has said, 'I call myself a culdub – a culchie and a Dub.'

During his time in England, Kennelly worked as a bus conductor and was amazed to find himself becoming friends with a former Black and Tan, Will Flynn. This experience led Kennelly to question our perception of the villainised figures of Irish history, and to explore our national preoccupation with our subjugation. In 1963 Kennelly returned to Dublin from Leeds to complete his doctorate, which he was awarded in 1966. His thesis, 'Modern Irish Poets and the Irish Epic', reflected his fascination with Irish poetry of all eras and styles and he examined the work of Yeats, Russell and Clarke among others. In his early days as a student, Kennelly wrote out by hand Patrick Kavanagh's great epic poem 'The Great Hunger'. Kennelly loved Kavanagh's work and felt a deep affinity with his voice and his themes. He met the poet in Trinity and said he was 'witty in a mix of the country way and the city way'. Both were from rural small towns and came to live in Dublin. John McDonagh writes about the two poets, commenting on their **'natural empathy with and deep understanding of their respective birthplaces,** although the **poetic desire to see beneath and beyond the surface of an apparently idyllic rural**

existence soon emerges'. Kennelly took part in a 2012 RTÉ Radio 1 programme about Kavanagh entitled 'On the Street Where He Lived'.

Kennelly and Peggy O'Brien met in the Shelbourne Hotel around 1967. They were married in 1969 and walked from the church to the wedding reception at the Shelbourne. They were on the front page of the *Evening Press* newspaper and were considered an 'It Couple' of the time. They separated when their daughter Doodle, who was born on 16 March 1970, was eleven.

Kennelly has lectured at the University of Antwerp, at Barnard College New York and at Swarthmore College in Pennsylvania. He was appointed Professor of Modern Literature at Trinity College, a post specially created for him, and held that post from 1973 until his retirement in 2005. He continues to live in Trinity where he is now Professor Emeritus (a title given to a retired professor). To make room in his small lodgings, Kennelly sold a large portion of his private papers to Trinity, where they are currently being catalogued.

Kennelly's influences include Baudelaire, Rimbaud and the famous Beat poet Ginsberg, all of whom challenged societal norms in their work, just as Kennelly has strived to do. His poems *Cromwell* and *The Book of Judas* do just that, forcing us to challenge our preconceptions.

One of the things Kennelly is most famed for is the sheer volume of his output. He has published over forty books of poetry, two novels and several dramas, including translations of the ancient Greek tragedies *Antigone* and *Medea*. Kennelly has also written for the media, penned critical essays, appeared on radio and TV, and even in a car advertisement (something he was widely criticised for given that he wasn't a driver and was often critical of our consumerist society). Kennelly is also a widely respected editor and has edited many texts including *The Penguin Book of Irish Verse* (1970), *Landmarks of Irish Drama* (1988) and *Between Innocence and Peace: Favourite Poems of Ireland* (1993). Indeed such has been his output that Augustine Martin once called him 'recklessly prolific'.

Later life

Kennelly gave up alcohol in 1986 after drinking heavily for years. It was on the advice of a doctor who told him he would be dead within the year if he didn't stop. One change he found in being sober was that he was writing longer poems. He has found that 'The question of who I am never dies away. Maybe poetry is a constant search for an answer that it never finds.' Kennelly became associated with the powerful in Ireland, for example Charles Haughey, which many found at odds with the subversive messages in his poems. Haughey had created Aosdána, an association for artists and writers, and he exempted artists from tax.

Kennelly was certainly always available to the public, who found him very approachable and sociable. Appearances on TV and radio furthered this accessibility. His biographer and colleague Sandrine Brisset writes that he became 'the people's poet' by 'assuming the features of an Irish bard … jovial, alcoholic, roguish, promiscuous and charming'. He launched a book by Terry Keane, with whom Haughey was having an affair, likening it to *Ulysses* by James Joyce, and became friendly with Bono, mentioning him three times in a short collection of poetry published in November 2006.

Kennelly's voice

Kennelly was once voted 'the most attractive voice in Ireland' – listen to him reading poems online and see what you think!

In October 1996 he underwent a quadruple heart bypass and had hallucinations or visions afterwards of a man made of rain with whom the poet conversed. In 1998 he turned this experience into a collection of poems, *The Man Made of Rain*, from which the poem 'Saint Brigid's Prayer' comes. He seems to have become more religious; his daughter Doodle told the *Irish Independent*, 'He speaks as if he has an umbilical cord coming straight from mother Mary herself … he is the most holy person I know', while Kennelly says he goes to church in Clarendon Street every Sunday – 'I think I got married there as well.'

Kennelly's niece Mary once asked him how he'd like to be remembered, to which he replied, 'Maybe someday if an old man asks his grandson to read a poem, it might be one of mine.'

Style and Themes

In his poems Kennelly **closely observes his subjects**, often **adopting personas** which sometimes interact with and question each other. The poems in this anthology include personas as diverse as Oliver Cromwell, St Brigid and an ear of wheat. 'There is objectivity and then there is [sic] the voices. I think they are connected. You are objective as well as being open to absorbing another identity.' He is also interested in the real person behind the historical mask; as his collections exploring Judas and Cromwell attest, he became increasingly fascinated with **giving the 'scapegoats' of history a chance at presenting to us a more rounded view of themselves**. He has strived to teach us not to blindly accept the general viewpoint but to question and investigate, to come at things differently and less judgementally. The sonnet form is often used in his work to do this. It is no wonder that so many of his poems are peppered with questions; for example, 'Poem from a Three Year Old' and 'Things I Might Do'. Looking at the villains of history and religion with fresh, more sympathetic eyes makes Kennelly a very interesting and refreshing voice. Just as Kennelly explores a myriad of subjects, he also writes using many **different rhythms, metrical structures and forms, including** sonnets, dialogues, laments, prayers and epics. He has famously said that his poems come 'from the byways, laneways, backyards, nooks and crannies of the self'. He celebrates rural life but always with an eye for realism, careful not to mythologise the drawbacks of rural life. 'I See You Dancing, Father' is an example of this where his father's lively and cheerful attitude contrasts with his deterioration as he became old and more frail.

Kennelly's poetry covers the gamut of human emotion and experience, **exploring themes from love to hatred and violence, desire and jealousy, life and death, creation and destruction**. He is interested in exploring the **fine line between good and evil**, and makes us ponder the grey areas: can we have sympathy for Cromwell in his personal and public life, or think about how the women in Judas' life feel about his name being a byword for treachery? **Thus the reader is challenged to question their preconceptions.** In these epics Kennelly uses the voices of Cromwell, Spenser and William of Orange, who appear in many incarnations, including modern ones such as a taxi-driver in Kerry, an auctioneer and a furniture polisher; in this way **he plays with chronology and form**. His poems also explore **loneliness** and the **loss of faith and love**.

Social and Cultural Context

Kennelly's work stems from an emerging Ireland. Religion, patriarchy and parochialism were losing their grip on this emerging nation and this progression was further informed by Kennelly's stints working and travelling in the UK and USA. He was unafraid to interrogate society and attempts to turn Irish opinion and media away from their habit of blaming others (for example, our history with Britain) to look within itself to find the reasons for our unhappiness, often bringing him criticism. Poetry should be **'adventurous, daring, even offensive'**, Kennelly commented in 1994. He likes to challenge the socio-economic status quo and says **he loves Irish poetry because of its 'hard, simple, virile, rhetorical clarity'**. His vibrant, sensitive translations of poems like 'A Cry for Art O'Leary' and 'Saint Brigid's Prayer' are examples of this.

Timeline

1936	Born 17 April in Ballylongford, Co. Kerry
1948	Attends Jane Agnes McKenna's school in Tarbert
1957	Wins scholarship to Trinity College Dublin where he studies English and French
1959	Publishes poetry collection *Cast a Cold Eye* with Rudi Holzapfel
1961	Achieves a first-class honours degree in English/French and publishes *The Dark About Our Loves*
1963	Publishes a novel, *The Crooked Cross*, about his home town, having returned from Leeds University where he began his PhD
1966	Completes his PhD at Trinity College and publishes Collection One: Getting Up Early
1967	Wins the AE Memorial Prize for Poetry; censorship formally abolished in Ireland
1969	Marries Peggy O'Brien, a poet and academic from Massachusetts
1970	Edits the *Penguin Book of Verse*; daughter Doodle (Kirsten) born in Sandymount
1971	Publishes *Bread* and *Selected Poems*; on sabbatical in the US in 1971–2
1972	Publishes Love Cry, which includes the poem 'Dear Autumn Girl'
1973	Appointed Professor of Modern Literature at TCD
1980	Takes rooms in Trinity
1981/82	Separates from wife, Peggy
1983	Publishes *Cromwell: A Poem*
1988	Wins Critics' Special Harvey's Award
1995	Publishes the hugely successful collection *Poetry My Arse*, including 'The soul's loneliness'
1996	Undergoes major heart surgery, a quadruple bypass
1999	*Begin* published
2002	The *Little Book of Judas* published
2005	Retires from professorship at Trinity College; now Professor Emeritus; continues to live there
2011	The collection *The Essential Brendan Kennelly* published, edited by Terence Brown and Michael Longley
2015	Bronze bust of the poet unveiled in his home town of Ballylongford
2016	Special Day of Celebration to mark the 80th birthday of Kennelly held during Listowel Writers' Week

Before you read

List the things you see and hear on your way to school each morning. Be as descriptive as you can!

Begin

Begin again to the summoning birds
to the sight of the light at the window,
begin to the roar of morning traffic
all along Pembroke Road.
Every beginning is a promise   5
born in light and dying in dark
determination and exaltation of springtime
flowering the way to work.
Begin to the pageant of queuing girls
the arrogant loneliness of swans in the canal   10
bridges linking the past and future
old friends passing though with us still.
Begin to the loneliness that cannot end
since it perhaps is what makes us begin,
begin to wonder at unknown faces   15
at crying birds in the sudden rain
at branches stark in the willing sunlight
at seagulls foraging for bread
at couples sharing a sunny secret
alone together while making good.   20
Though we live in a world that dreams of ending
that always seems about to give in
something that will not acknowledge conclusion
insists that we forever begin.

Glossary

7	*exaltation*: a feeling or state of extreme happiness
9	*pageant*: a spectacular procession or celebration; a beauty contest
18	*foraging*: to wander in search of food or provisions

Guidelines

'Begin' is from Kennelly's poetry collection *Good Souls to Survive,* published in 1968. It has a cinematic quality as if a camera captures the morning routine the speaker describes. The poem reflects the sentiment described in this extract from an interview Kennelly gave to *The Independent* newspaper in 2012: 'I like that old Kerry saying: "Once you get up in the morning and stick your old leg out, you should be grateful".' In a newspaper interview Kennelly said, 'the quality which has stood most by me is determination, a determination to begin again.'

Commentary

Lines 1–4

The opening words urge us to begin a fresh day – to start anew: morning awaits and is worth rising for. There may be a suggestion that the poem's intended reader is finding it hard to go on and needs encouragement. Do you agree?

'Begin again' suggests a new start, a fresh chance to change and appreciate the sights and sounds of our daily routine. The birds call us into the world again, 'summoning' and beckoning us 'to the sight of the light at the window'. The poem is placed firmly in urban Dublin with the 'roar of morning traffic / all along the Pembroke Road'. Already **our senses are engaged** – we see the birds and the light; we hear the traffic.

Lines 5–8

Kennelly tells us that each morning is a promise that may not be kept: 'born in light and dying in dark'. It is spring, a time of new beginnings, fresh starts, the birth of things, and brighter days. This energy is captured in the lines 'determination and exaltation of springtime / flowering the way to work'. We are committed to this new beginning and the celebratory feeling springtime brings adds to this. The almost cartoon-like image of flowers popping up at our feet as we walk to work is so cheerful and positive that it cannot help but raise a smile and perhaps disguise a little the darkness that lies at the edges of the poem.

Lines 9–12

We pass girls queuing – perhaps at a bus stop or a coffee shop? They are a 'pageant' – beautiful and on show perhaps? To be judged?

The swans in the canal are arrogantly lonely, a strange description: are they masking their loneliness with this haughty demeanour or actually proud of their singlehood?

Either way they are a common sight on the canals of Dublin and help to set the scene. The canal bridges link to the image of the swans, but also are **a metaphor for our own links with friends** perhaps gone but not forgotten – they are with us in spirit, while there are future friends waiting for us too: 'bridges linking the past and future / old friends passing though with us still'.

Kavanagh, Kennelly and canals

Like his poetic hero Patrick Kavanagh, Kennelly uses the canals of Dublin to symbolise important issues in our lives and to provide a setting for the poem. For Kavanagh, the canal and its banks have redemptive qualities and symbolise rebirth and a love of nature.

Lines 13–20

The second half of the poem is **less positive and more tentative**: 'Begin to the loneliness that cannot end'. Kennelly turns this into something positive by saying it is loneliness that makes us go out into our world to explore it, to notice things such as the faces of strangers, the plaintive sound of birds crying at a sudden shower or hunting for scraps of food, branches still bare in the sun that 'wills' leaves to shoot from them, lovers sharing confidences – people alone together 'while making good'. They are making the most of what they have, **seeing the beauty in ordinary things**.

We can see very clearly in this poem the **influence that the Irish poet Patrick Kavanagh had on Kennelly**. Kavanagh also wrote of Dublin's Grand Canal as a place of re-birth and hope, redemption and love, and was a poet who **celebrated the fact that ordinary things have an extra-ordinary nature**, if we just open our eyes to them. Kavanagh also used **light, bridges and swans as central images**. Why does Kennelly use birds in his imagery so often? Look at 'Fragments' for a comparison.

Lines 21–24

What do you make of the poet's reference to a world that 'dreams of ending'? Is this a reference to natural forces such as death, night and winter? Bear in mind that the poem was written at a time when the threat of nuclear holocaust was real and ever-present; perhaps this self-destructive aspect of human nature is what the poet refers to. Nonetheless, he asserts there is something in the human spirit that keeps us trying again, something that rejects endings however inevitable they may be, something that insists we 'begin again': 'something that will not acknowledge conclusion'. Using **'Begin' as the first and last word** brings the poem full circle and adds a sense of urgency to the speaker's command.

Themes and imagery

A sense of place and time underpins this poem. It is morning in the city by the canal and the bustle of morning abounds. It is up to the reader to decide whether this is a positive optimistic meditation on the indomitable nature of the human spirit or a hollow-sounding, half-hearted attempt to tell us to go on in the face of the inevitability of death and change.

The repetition of 'Begin again, 'Begin to', 'Begin to' and 'forever begin', and the fact that this is the title of the poem creates a **mantra, a chant we can repeat to calm ourselves and infuse our day with positivity**.

The **poet uses personification to add life and energy to his imagery**: the traffic *roars*, days are *born* and *die*, the swans are *arrogant*, birds *cry*, the sunlight *wills* branches to bloom and the world *dreams* of ending. **Everything is infused with extra life and purpose here. Birds** are mentioned four times in the poem and are obviously an important motif for the poet. In the first line they are 'summoning' us to begin the day; the swans appear in line 10 seeming haughty and proud of their single status; in line 16 the birds cry at the shock of a sudden shower, and in line 18 seagulls search for food. The different attitudes and actions of the birds reflect the variety in the activities of the people in the city.

In line 11 **bridges are a metaphor for those we are bound up with in our relationships**, 'linking the past and future' – those who have died and those we have yet to meet.

Language

Several **sound effects** are used by Kennelly in the poem. 'In' **sounds are repeated** in the first line – 'Begin again to the summoning birds' – creating a kind of half rhyme that gives the poem an **upbeat, lilting opening**. There is lovely **internal rhyme** in line 2, which is also quite bouncy and cheerful in tone: 'to the sight of the light at the window'. **Alliteration** is used also, including 'dying in dark / determination' – quite a sombre and serious effect compared to the more cheerful 'way to work'. **Sibilance** is used in the lines 'loneliness of swans' and 'couples sharing a sunny secret', but with quite different effects; the former seems plaintive while the latter is more upbeat.

Form

The structure is very straightforward; there are **no stanzas to interrupt the flow and urgency of the poem**. In the twenty-four lines there are four sentences, the first three telling us to begin and the last one stressing the inevitability that we will begin – it is in our nature: 'something … / insists that we forever begin'.

Although the tone of the poem is mainly positive there is a darker side to the poem too, and examining the **opposites and contrasts in the poem** will reveal this, for example 'born in light and dying in dark'.

All of these elements lead us to the theme. Possible interpretations of this include the notion that no matter what the obstacles or conditions, living things on earth are programmed to keep going – it's what we do. The swans cope with their loneliness by seeming arrogant, seagulls come inland to search for food, the sun encourages leafless branches into bud and we wonder at all these things. **Despite our certainty that everything ends and death is inevitable, we keep going.** Whether this is an optimistic or fatalistic point of view is up to the reader.

SNAPSHOT

- Positive outlook
- Personification
- Voice in poem is gently insistent, urging the reader to 'Begin'
- Urban and nature imagery
- Idea of redemption linked to water
- Encouraging
- Mantra-like quality
- Cyclical nature of poem – 'begin' is first and last word

Exam-Style Questions

Understanding the poem

1 What three things does the speaker encourage the reader to 'Begin again'?

2 What may be suggested by using the word 'again'?

3 Birds are used a lot in the imagery. What might they symbolise in the poem? Explain.

4 'Every beginning is a promise'. What might beginning a new day promise us?

5 List the contrasts in the poem. What opposites can you find (e.g. the <u>loneliness</u> of the swans and the <u>togetherness</u> of the couple)?

Thinking about the poem

1 What images can you find from the natural and urban worlds?

2 'Begin to wonder at unknown faces'. What, do you think, does the poet mean by this? Look at the previous lines – what does he say is the cause of this wonder?

3 What, do you think, is the overall mood of the poem? In what lines or phrases is this mood evident?

4 What is this poem about?
- How great life is
- How difficult life is but we must keep going
- Something else

Explain and back up your answer.

5 There are several examples of personification in the poem. Which did you like best and why?

6 John McDonagh writes about Kennelly, admiring how he shows the 'ability of the human spirit to triumph over adversity'. Do you think this poem is a good example of this? Explain.

Imagining

1 On RTÉ's *The Late, Late Show*, Brendan Kennelly recited this poem following an incident where a woman had phoned in very upset and revealed her daughter had died in a car accident. Why, do you think, might this poem have been appropriate or comforting in this situation?

2 'This poem is a celebration of the ordinary.' Give your reaction to this statement.

3 Using some ideas from the Before you read exercise, write your own version of this poem, substituting the things you see, hear and wonder at on your morning journey to school.

4 Suggest an alternative title for this poem.
Explain and justify your suggestion to another student.

5 Source some images for this poem. Draw or cut them out and stick into your copy beside the words or phrases from the poem that inspired them.

6 Compare the images of birds in this poem to the birds at the end of 'Fragments' on page 228.

Before you read

If an ear of wheat or corn told its story from harvest to becoming bread, what stages would it describe? Write a brief and simple narrative where the grain tells its tale.

Bread

Someone else cut off my head
In a golden field.
Now I am re-created

By her fingers. This
Moulding is more delicate   5
Than a first kiss,

More deliberate than her own
Rising up
And lying down,

I am fine   10
As anything in
This legendary garden

Yet I am nothing till
She runs her fingers through me
And shapes me with her skill.   15

The form that I shall bear
Grows round and white.
It seems I comfort her

Even as she slits my face
And stabs my chest.   20
Her feeling for perfection is

Absolute.
So I am glad to go through fire
And come out

Shaped like her dream.   25
In my way
I am all that can happen to men.
I came to life at her finger-ends.
I will go back into her again.

Guidelines

'Bread' is from Kennelly's 1971 collection of the same name. It has been featured in many anthologies and is a poem in praise of the poet's mother and grandmother, who would often make bread. The poet said he found himself fascinated by the action of their hands as they kneaded dough.

Commentary

Stanzas 1–3

The speaker is the wheat which will change shape and become transformed into bread as the poem progresses. 'Someone else cut off my head / In a golden field' describes the harvesting of the wheat which will be milled into flour to become the central ingredient in bread. Although the image seems violent, the speaker is keen to point out that the woman who will make the bread wasn't responsible for this; it was done by 'Someone else'. The wheat has been totally 're-created' by the woman's fingers into dough. The description of the kneading process **is almost erotic** and **certainly involves love**. The dough feels her gentle touch which is 'more delicate / Than a first kiss'. **'Moulding' (line 5) is an interesting word**: the woman is shaping the wheat into a dough which will rise and become **something that sustains us**. Perhaps this is **like the process of creating art; a poet, for example, takes basic words and shapes them**, crafting them into something worthwhile and something beautiful.

This kneading action is done with more care and thought than the woman getting up and going to bed. Two things are at play here. On a practical level bread is often 'proved', which involves allowing it to rise in a warm place and then knocking the air out of it before allowing it to rise and increase a second time. On another level the woman rising and lying back down has sexual connotations which further the erotic image of the delicate kiss in stanza 2.

> **Bread and love**
>
> Kennelly's mother and grandmother were great cooks; so too was his wife Peggy. These women influenced Kennelly greatly, for example he has said that one of the most important things he was told was when as a young boy he asked his mother what the secret of life was and she replied 'To love as much as you can.' Love and its link to creation are clearly strong ideas in this poem.

Stanzas 4 and 5

The wheat is impressed by its transformation into dough and boasts 'I am fine / As anything in / this legendary garden'. This may be a reference to the Garden of Eden from the Bible, a paradise where the Judaic God's first creations dwelt. **Bread is an ancient and primitive food**, making this comparison – between a kitchen where bread is created and Eden – an effective one. The wheat quickly retracts its earlier boast by asserting that it would be 'nothing' without the creative fingers of the woman who 'shapes me with her skill'.

Stanzas 6–9

The wheat looks forward to becoming bread, sounding pleased that its shape will become 'round and white'; this shape is also reminiscent of the swelling belly of a pregnant woman. People often find baking therapeutic, and this seems true for the woman, who the grain feels is comforted by making this bread, 'Even as she slits my face / And stabs my chest'. These violent actions seem shocking and bring us back to the extreme image of line 1, where the wheat is 'decapitated'. These actions are a normal part of bread-making, especially where a cross shape is cut into Irish soda bread before baking, to make it easier to divide into four sections. The woman wants the bread to be perfect and has an innate 'feeling' for how to achieve this. The bread decides that it is happy to endure the 'fire' of the oven in order to be as perfect as the woman wishes it to be: 'And come out / Shaped like her dream'. There is **an obvious association with childbirth here**, often an agonising experience but one which brings great joy also; basic 'ingredients' (an ovum and a sperm) are transformed over time in a mother's womb to become something completely different that seems miraculous.

A slightly cryptic statement ends the poem. The bread attests that it is 'all that can happen to men'. Does this mean the only thing that can happen or the very best thing a man can experience? Is the poet saying that women are the only true creators because they carry and give birth to new life? The bread sums up the journey it has undergone: it 'came to life' at the hands of the woman and 'will go back into her again'. **There is more than one way to read the last line**: as a literal description of being eaten as bread to sustain and nourish the woman, or, in an extension of the 'men' image, a reference to the sexual act and its role in procreation.

Themes and imagery

The act of creation is at the heart of this quirky poem. It is up to you to decide whether the act being described is simply baking, the creation of art (like poetry or sculpture), a religious idea of creation, or is it human procreation that is being described through the **metaphorical journey of the wheat's transformation from grain to dough to bread**? Of course, more than one or even all of these are valid interpretations. Perhaps there is another reading of the poem that springs to mind?

By making the wheat narrate its journey, the poem takes on an **allegorical** feel, and we follow the grain's radical change at the skilled fingers of the woman. **The focus is mainly on her hands, those creative tools which have a sensual and almost magical ability to create and transform. Bread in itself is a strong religious symbol**: think, for example, of the body of Christ the Eucharist represents, or the importance of bread on the table at a Jewish Friday evening meal. Add to this the idea of a 'legendary garden', and the violent imagery of the bread being 'slit' and stabbed (calling to mind the sufferings of the last days of Jesus), and it is clear that there are religious undertones here. The wheat is not just instantly 'born' into its incarnation as bread, it is pummelled, kneaded and **transformed more than once**: into flour, into dough, then proved and 'slit', before it is put through fire to take on its ultimate form. **Perhaps this is the extent of how artists must transform their material before it can become art, or what love might do to those who love fiercely and passionately.**

Eating and pregnancy

A more pagan reading of the poem links back to religion: in ancient Irish myth eating and pregnancy were often related. Sandrine Brisset, Kennelly's biographer, makes this point, citing 'The Wooing of Étaín' as an example. In the myth Étaín has been turned into a purple fly. She lands in a gold cup being used by the wife of Étar, a warrior of the Ulaid. When Étar's wife drinks from the cup, she swallows the fly and becomes pregnant. Thus, Étaín is reborn.

The imagery here strongly suggests the role of women in childbirth as a theme. Kennelly very deliberately casts a woman in the role of bread-maker; she has the power and the wheat seems subserviently grateful for her manipulations: 'I am nothing till / She runs her fingers through me / And shapes me with her skill.' Women are generally quite powerful figures in Kennelly's poetry. 'A Cry for Art O'Leary' and 'Saint Brigid's Prayer' are two of Kennelly's translations where this is apparent.

Language and form

The **language is very straightforward and accessible** (which is why we need no glossary!). The opening lines are reminiscent of a children's rhyme

> 'Someone else cut off my head
> In a golden field.'

There is a **close relationship** between the adoring 'I' persona of the wheat and the 'her'/'she' figure of the female baker. Their love grows from a 'delicate / … first kiss' to the much more sensual relationship when the woman kneads the bread vigorously, and then this sensual touch becomes violent as she slits and stabs the bread.

Most of the poem is written in eight tercets, a form also favoured by Sylvia Plath. Kennelly uses **run-on-lines** (or enjambed lines) and **occasional rhyme** to give the poem a **flow and pace** without making it sound too formulaic or lyrical. **Thus the voice of the wheat seems animated and believable.** The ninth stanza, however, is five lines long, with 'I' beginning the last three lines. Is this because the bread needs more time to reach its conclusion both in terms of being baked and eaten, and in terms of realising this is the best outcome a man can hope for? **Do the two added lines have a particular emphasis regarding the importance of the message** at the end of the poem? We will explore this further in the questions which follow.

SNAPSHOT

- Journey of wheat from field to finished bread
- Notion of creation central in poem
- Violent imagery contrasts with images of love and affection
- Allegorical
- The woman figure is empowered
- Cinematic quality to poem
- Imagery: religious, sexual, related to birth
- Voice of wheat is male
- Ambiguous ending

Exam-Style Questions

Understanding the poem

1	What has happened to the wheat in the first three stanzas?
2	What do you imagine from the lines: 'In a golden field' and 'This legendary garden'? If these places are symbolic, what might they symbolise?
3	How is a sensual or romantic relationship between the woman and the speaker suggested in the first five stanzas?
4	'The form that I shall bear / Grows round and white.' What does this image suggest to you?
5	Why, do you think, is the bread 'glad to go through fire / And come out // Shaped like her dream'? Comment on what you think the last line of this quote means.
6	Why, do you think, is the last stanza two lines longer than the previous eight?

Thinking about the poem

1	What is the effect of giving the wheat a voice?
2	'The woman in the poem holds all of the power but the male persona of the wheat is happy about this.' Discuss this statement agreeing or disagreeing with the analysis offered. Describe your perception of the relationship described.
3	Comment on the images of violence in the poem. Examine how they contrast with the other images of touch in the poem.
4	Choose three sound effects that stood out to you after reading the poem aloud. Why did you choose these sounds? What was the effect of each one? (You may notice rhyme, rhythm, alliteration, sibilance, assonance or another sound effect.)
5	Explain what you interpret the last three lines to mean.
6	Which of the following, in your view, best sums up the central theme of the poem? Explain. ■ It is a poem about baking.　　　　　■ It is a poem about the act of creation. ■ It is a poem about birth, rebirth and life.　　■ It is a poem about love.

Imagining

1	Write a response to the wheat in the voice of the woman, either as a letter or a poem. Refer and respond to the ideas expressed in Kennelly's poem.
2	Make a simple cartoon strip with images and captions which show the stages the wheat goes through in the poem.

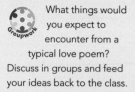

Before you read

What things would you expect to encounter from a typical love poem? Discuss in groups and feed your ideas back to the class.

Dear Autumn Girl

Dear Autumn girl, these helter-skelter days
When mad leaf-argosies drive at my head,
I try but fail to give you proper praise
For the excitement you've created
In my world: an islander at sea,   5
A girl with child, a fool, a simple king,
Garrulous masters of true mockery –
My hugest world becomes the littlest thing

Whenever you walk smiling through a room
And your flung golden hair is still wet   10
Ready for September's homaged rays;
I see what is, I wonder what's to come,
I bless what you remember or forget
And recognise the poverty of praise.

Glossary

1	*helter-skelter*: in confused and disorderly haste
2	*leaf-argosies*: the shape of the leaves falling in the blustery wind is like 'argosies' – ancient boats often used by exploring heroes such as the Greek adventurers of ancient legend, Jason and the Argonauts
7	*Garrulous*: chatting excessively especially about banal or trivial matters
11	*homaged*: respected, praised

Guidelines

This poem comes from the collection *Love Cry* (1972). Kennelly had been on sabbatical in the USA in 1971 and '72, and the following year he was offered the Chair of Modern Literature at Trinity College Dublin.

Perhaps the apologetic tone of the poem comes from the fact that Kennelly was a heavy drinker, and had a reputation for being a womaniser.

Commentary

Lines 1–8

The poem opens like a love-letter – 'Dear Autumn girl' – as the speaker apologises for failing to 'give you proper praise', though he has tried. This confession is set against blustery autumn weather where the speaker feels confused and lacking control: 'helter-skelter'. Leaves seem to 'drive' at his head like ships ('argosies'), adding to the confusion and happiness he feels. He is trying to thank her for bringing excitement into his life, and he lists the joys she has brought him: he is like 'an islander at sea', someone ready to leave his insular world and have an adventure, explore. Perhaps 'a girl with child', refers to the birth of his daughter Doodle Kennelly who was born in 1970. He continues his list with 'a fool' and 'a simple king', which are reminiscent of the two central characters in Shakespeare's *King Lear*, in which the king was actually the foolish one while the fool had wisdom. Does the speaker see himself as an amalgam of the two? The next line is ambiguous – 'Garrulous masters of true mockery'. Who are these chattering experts in mockery? Perhaps the journalists who liked to write about Kennelly's drinking and philandering? It could also represent poets and intellectuals by whom Kennelly was surrounded. His wife Peggy was also an academic and poet.

He feels that the 'hugest' things in his life become 'littlest' compared to how she makes him feel.

Lines 9–14

This happens when his 'Dear Autumn girl' walks 'smiling through a room'. He admires her 'flung golden hair' which 'is still wet'. She seems to have a devil-may-care attitude to life that the speaker finds captivating: she is ready to go out into the September sun despite her wet hair; she is a girl who doesn't worry about such things. He assures her that he appreciates all of how wonderful she is now – 'I see what is', and he is curious about their future together – 'I wonder what's to come'. He uses religious language to 'bless what you remember or forget'; perhaps she can be absent-minded, caught up in enjoying the moment, loving the 'now'. The final line seems an apology again for the inadequacy of his words to capture her spirit and to profess his ardent love for her: 'recognise the poverty of praise'.

Themes and language

Love is obviously a theme here; the speaker seems unsure, anxious that he may not be communicating effectively enough the strength of his passion for his 'Autumn girl'. His **words and images almost trip over each other** in his rush to convince her of his love and to tell her how she has transformed his life. His apologetic opening becomes a confused list of new experiences which this exciting girl has brought him: 'an islander at sea, / … / Garrulous masters of true mockery'.

He assures her that she is beautiful to him, and admires her joie de vivre: 'your flung golden hair is still wet / Ready for September's homaged rays'. He seems excited yet anxious about their future: 'I wonder what's to come', and apologises again for the inadequacy of his words.

It seems that the first bloom of love has passed (summer), and they are **entering the next phase in their relationship** (September and autumn dominate the imagery). Certainly a theme here is also inadequacy. He has cause for **worry**: will he be able to keep up with this whirlwind of a girl?

Form

This poem is written as a **Petrarchan sonnet**; in other words, it is organised into an octave (an eight-line stanza) and a sestet (a six-line stanza). Petrarchan sonnets were often love poems. In a sonnet the octave usually describes a situation, setting the scene for the poem; the first four lines of the sestet develop this and comment on it, before the rhyming couplet at the end comes to a conclusion of some sort. **Here the final couplet is used to reassure his beloved of his unshakeable love for her, and to assure her that he realises these words are a barely adequate expression of this.** The rhyming scheme (*ababcdcd efaefa*) adds **lyricism and pace** to the poem in line with the excited outpouring of his emotion. The rhymes help to put a shape on his words lest they become as 'helter-skelter' as the autumn days they describe.

Questions

1	What is the effect of the phrases/images 'helter-skelter days' and 'mad leaf-argosies'? What mood do they create?
2	'I try but fail to give you proper praise'. What is the speaker apologising for here?
3	What does the speaker wish to praise the 'Dear Autumn girl' for in lines 4–7? What, do you think, do the items in this list represent for the speaker?
4	Kennelly uses a run-on-line between the octave and sestet of the poem. Why, do you think, has he done this and what effect does it have?
5	What is your impression of this girl from your reading of lines 9–11?
6	What is the speaker saying in the last three lines?
7	Do you agree that his poem is poor or inadequate in its praise of his love? Why, do you think, does he repeat this apology?
8	Choose two images from the poem which you found to be particularly effective. In pairs or groups explain what they represent and why you chose them.
9	What, do you think, is the overall mood of the speaker in the poem? ■ Excited ■ Anxious ■ Passionate ■ Something else
10	Compare this poem to 'Bread' in its portrayal of a dominant female character.
11	Imagine you are the 'Autumn girl' and you've read the poem. Write your response. It may be a poem or perhaps a letter. Do you reassure your love, and reciprocate his feelings or do you find his neediness tiresome?

Poem from a Three Year Old

And will the flowers die?

And will the people die?

And every day do you grow old, do I
grow old, no I'm not old, do
flowers grow old?   5

Old things – do you throw them out?

Do you throw old people out?

And how you know a flower that's old?

The petals fall, the petals fall from flowers,
and do the petals fall from people too,   10
every day more petals fall until the
floor where I would like to play I
want to play is covered with old
flowers and people all the same
together lying there with petals fallen   15
on the dirty floor I want to play
the floor you come and sweep
with the huge broom.

The dirt you sweep, what happens that,
what happens all the dirt you sweep   20
from flowers and people, what
happens all the dirt? Is all the
dirt what's left of flowers and
people, all the dirt there in a
heap under the huge broom that   25
sweeps every thing away?

Why you work so hard, why brush
and sweep to make a heap of dirt?
And who will bring new flowers?
And who will bring new people? Who will   30
bring new flowers to put in water
where no petals fall on to the
floor where I would like to
play? Who will bring new flowers

that will not hang their heads   35
like tired old people wanting sleep?
Who will bring new flowers that
do not split and shrivel every
day? And if we have new flowers,
will we have new people too to   40
keep the flowers alive and give
them water?

And will the new young flowers die?

And will the new young people die?

And why?   45

Guidelines

Importance of questions

Kennelly's personas' chief function is to question. As in Elizabeth Bishop's work, the questions are important; more important than the answers, in fact. The three-year-old here is Kennelly's youngest interrogator!

Like 'Fragments' (page 228), this poem is structured around a series of questions – sixteen in all; but the voice asking the questions is that of a three-year-old child whose innocent wonderings open up a **meditation on death, ageing and what we value in life**.

Commentary

Lines 1–18

'And will the flowers die? / And will the people die?' The word 'And' gives the sense that we have entered a conversation that has already begun; it also creates **a childlike voice, impatient and full of curiosity**. Straightaway death is the theme, and the 'child' knows enough to realise that as part of the natural order of living things flowers and people will meet the same inevitable fate. The next set of questions probes the idea that even though the speaker is young they are also growing older each day. How can the child be called old if they are young, how can they be growing older? The child asks whether flowers age too. When flowers wither they are thrown out; do we apply the same logic to everything that ages, including people? Perhaps as a society we are being asked by Kennelly to consider how we treat the elderly.

The next section grows confused and confusing as the child persona and perhaps an adult voice discuss these ideas further. We can tell that a flower has grown old when its petals fall. With 'do the petals fall from people too' might there be an exploration into the signs of ageing? A slightly surreal passage follows where the child complains that the floor it wishes to play on is becoming obstructed by 'old / flowers and people'. The adult seems to come and sweep this debris from the floor 'with the huge broom'.

Lines 19–45

The child wonders what becomes of all this discarded 'dirt you sweep'; why is the adult working 'so hard' to make 'a heap of dirt'? The logic progresses to consider birth: 'who will bring new people? Who will / bring new flowers'? Will the new people keep the new flowers alive?

In the last three lines the **cyclical** nature of birth, life and death is addressed as the child asks: 'And will the new young flowers die / And will the new young people die'? The answer of course is 'yes'. The final question might seem the simplest and most childlike, but is also the deepest, the most philosophical conundrum: 'And why?'

Themes and imagery

Most children struggle to cope with **change**; they do not wish to think of those they love ageing and dying.

They are also full of **wonder**, **deeply curious** about the things they notice around them. 'Out of the mouth of babes' is an adage that could sum up this poem; in their **lack of guile** and **innocent honesty** children's questions often cut to the heart of things, things that adults might prefer to keep them in the dark about, or not think about themselves. **The images compare flowers and people, linking us to the natural order of things.** Why then has Kennelly decided to use the persona of a child to pose these questions? What does this bring to the poem that an adult voice would not? We will explore this further in 'Language and form'.

Birth, death and ageing are the main concerns of this curious child who seeks to understand what happens to the things that die and seem to disappear: where do old and dead things go? To the child the adults in its life seem to treat old and dead things like rubbish, to be unceremoniously swept into a heap and discarded: 'all the dirt there in a / heap under the huge broom that / sweeps every thing away'. The child wonders at the fact that new things will become old and wishes it were not so: 'Who will bring new flowers that / do not split and shrivel'. Earlier the child had considered their own mortality: 'do I / grow old, no I'm not old … / Old things – do you throw them out?' Perhaps now the child realises this is the way of things: 'And will the new young flowers die?' and questions a world where this apparent waste can occur and recur: 'And why?'

How we treat our elderly is an issue raised here; the idea of sweeping them into a heap like fallen petals chides us for marginalising our old people. The **simile** of the flowers hanging 'their heads / like tired old people wanting sleep' might suggest a nursing home or hospital setting. It combines the two main images for life and death in the poem, the old people and the flowers.

The **floor and the huge broom are clearly symbolic** also. The floor is the space the child has to play upon, it is becoming clogged with petals and old people and these must be cleared to make way for youth. So as people die, people are born. Who then holds the 'broom' that makes room for the next generation? Is it God? Is it mortality or entropy? Is the broom time, old age or death?

It is a **deceptively simple poem which challenges us to address the biggest questions**, such as why we are here, why we die and what happens to us afterwards?

Language and form

Kennelly often **peppers his poetry with questions, and uses a persona to interrogate a concept** with these questions. He has said, 'You are constantly searching for the marriage of two voices – the one within you and the one outside you. You put them together. That creates a lot of poetry for me.' The **repetition of key images**; flowers, people and the broom **coupled with the constant interrogation** produce an **unrelenting exploration of our mortality and attitude to death**, while lifting **and making lighter** these **profound and disturbing** ideas through the use of **a child's voice**. Thus using this child persona creates a voice that interrogates doggedly, without guile or preconception, to expose and explore issues that are fundamental to us all: birth and ageing, life and death.

The three central sections are framed by these quick-fire questions, while the repetition of 'And' suggests that **we have far more questions than we do answers**, but Kennelly has often spoken and written about the importance of asking questions. His biographer Sandrine Brisset has written about Kennelly's 'democratisation' of poetry. He wants to write for ordinary people and does this, according to John McDonagh, by 'operating at the extremities of form, theme and chronology to **speak to the centre by expressing the margins**'. The use of the child's voice here achieves much of this ambition. Kennelly can make us question our attitudes to youth, old age and death as well as the 'throw-away' nature of modern society with this **deceptively simple poem**, which is accessible **yet thought-provoking**.

Questions

1	Who do you imagine the child is talking to in the poem? Give a reason for your answer.
2	How are the wilting flowers and ageing people connected in the mind of the child? Are flowers an effective image in the poem? Explain.
3	Offer some suggestions as to what the floor, the child playing and the broom might represent. Explain how you formulated your ideas.
4	'What happens all the dirt?'; 'who will bring new people?' What, do you think, are the answers to these two questions? Are the answers connected? If so, how?
5	If we have new flowers that 'do not split and shrivel', what will be needed to ensure this?
6	Reading lines 37–42, what does the water for the flowers represent, do you think?
7	Comment on the meaning and effect of the last three lines of the poem.
8	Why, do you think, has Kennelly used the voice of a three-year-old child to pose these difficult questions? Has this technique been effective? Explain.
9	Did you like this poem? In pairs discuss this and feed back your partner's answers and reasons.
10	Trace the tone of the poem? Does it change as the poem progresses?
11	Write 'Poem from an Eighty Year Old', where you respond to the child's questions and add your own observations on life and death.

Before you read

What do you know about the historical figure Oliver Cromwell? How is he regarded in Ireland?

Oliver to His Brother

Loving brother, I am glad to hear of your welfare
And that our children have so much leisure
They can travel far to eat cherries.
This is most excusable in my daughter
Who loves that fruit and whom I bless.   5
Tell her I expect she writes often to me
And that she be kept in some exercise.
Cherries and exercise go well together.
I have delivered my son up to you.
I hope you counsel him; he will need it;   10
I choose to believe he believes what you say.
I send my affection to all your family.
Let sons and daughters be serious; the age requires it.
I have things to do, all in my own way.
For example, I take not kindly to rebels.   15
Today, in Burford Churchyard, Cornet Thompson
Was led to the place of execution.
He asked for prayers, got them, died well.
After him, a Corporal, brought to the same place
Set his back against the wall and died.   20
A third chose to look death in the face,
Stood straight, showed no fear, chilled into his pride.
Men die their different ways
And girls eat cherries
In the Christblessed fields of England.   25
Some weep. Some have cause. Let weep who will.
Whole floods of brine are at their beck and call.
I have work to do in Ireland.

Glossary

16	**Burford Churchyard**: church in Oxfordshire, England, site of the execution of three 'levellers' in Cromwell's army
16	**Cornet Thompson**: a rebel in Cromwell's New Model Army who was executed in Burford Churchyard on 17 May 1949
27	**brine**: salt water

Guidelines

This poem is part of Kennelly's 1983 epic *Cromwell: a Poem*. In it the poet imagines Oliver Cromwell writing to his brother, who is looking after Oliver's son and daughter while he deals with a rebellion in his army and prepares to go to Ireland.

In his preface to the poem, Kennelly says: 'This poem tries to present the nature and implications of various forms of dream and nightmare, including the **nightmare of Irish history**.' In the collection, a persona called M. P. G. M. Buffún Esq. engages in dialogues with several so-called villains of Irish history, including William of Orange, Edmund Spenser and Oliver Cromwell. Buffún says, 'I invited the butcher (Cromwell) into my room and began a dialogue with him'. Kennelly is interested in looking at how **the Irish have possibly made 'scapegoats' of some historical figures**, and explores them not as one-dimensional personifications of evil, but as fully rounded individuals with whom he can converse and explore the Irish psyche.

'Because of history, an Irish poet, to realise himself, must turn the full attention of his imagination to the English tradition'; Kennelly is interested in how we often define ourselves as a nation through our colonisation and rebellion by and against the English. Cromwell says to Buffún in the first poem in the collection 'Measures': 'you too are blind in your way and now you use me to try to justify that blindness'.

Commentary

Lines 1–15

> **To his son**
>
> In the poem 'Oliver to his Son', Cromwell rebukes his son for how fat he has grown and the debts he has accumulated, but assures him that he is only telling him these things because he loves him.

The persona of Oliver greets his 'Loving brother' at the beginning of this letter, telling him that he is happy both that his brother is well and that their children have enough time on their hands to 'travel far to eat cherries'. The **tone here seems sarcastic**, a thinly veiled criticism of his brother's lack of a Protestant work ethic. He excuses such extravagance in his daughter, the subtext being that he doesn't excuse such behaviour in men, namely his son. Oliver tells his brother to ensure that his daughter writes to him and is kept 'in some exercise'. His leniency disappears when he moves on to mention his son, using the odd phrase, 'I have delivered my son up to you'. This sounds almost sacrificial rather than a request to simply look after the boy. He hopes his brother will provide his nephew with good 'counsel' – 'he will need it', and follows this with the convoluted 'I choose to believe he believes what you say'. What does Oliver mean here? Does this imply mistrust or a lack of faith in his brother? Is he admitting he does not have much influence on his son? Is theirs a fractious relationship? He is certainly less sure of his son than he is of his daughter. There is definitely some doubt here about his brother's ability to manage Oliver's children in the Puritanical fashion their father would wish.

This section of the poem culminates in Cromwell sending his 'affection' to his brother's family, and advising that 'sons and daughters' must 'be serious', because 'the age requires it'. This could be to do with the age of the children, but most likely refers to the **events happening in England at the time**: there is civil war, and Cromwell is trying to eradicate the monarchy and Catholicism, to replace it with a very Puritanical version of Protestantism. 'I have things to do, all in my own way', introduces Oliver the soldier and political leader, who has crushed a rebellion in his army over pay and political demands. He will go on to observe the execution of the rebels. The **tone here is therefore quite assured, measured and cold**: 'I take not kindly to rebels'.

Lines 16–22

Oliver now gives an account of how three rebels were executed in Burford Churchyard. The first is 'Cornet Thompson' who 'died well' because he 'asked for prayers'. Then Corporal (Perkins) 'Set his back against the wall and died', while the third (Private Church) was commendably brave and dignified in death: he 'chose to look death in the face, / Stood straight, showed no fear' and Cromwell seems to admire his resolute composure.

Lines 23–end

Oliver reflects on these deaths, ruminating that 'Men die their different ways / And girls eat cherries / In the Christblessed fields of England'. Is this a coldly matter-of-fact observation; or is it flippant, callous, sardonic, regretful? The picture painted of girls seems a vacuous one, and if men are supposed to die fighting for a cause, how does this reflect on Cromwell's own son, who seems to be eating cherries along with his sister?

The word 'Christblessed' implies that England is a land beloved by God, and **foreshadows** the final line, where Oliver announces that he will turn his attention to Ireland now, which is certainly not, in his mind, 'Christblessed'. Cromwell, nick-named 'Old Ironsides', realises his actions have brought grief to some – 'Some weep' – but believes not all are entitled to weep: 'Some have cause.' He furthermore appears to dismiss all of this mourning with the line 'Let weep who will. / Whole floods of brine are at their beck and call.' The sentiment is 'let them cry all they want, I have bigger things to worry about' – 'I have work to do in Ireland.' This determination and sense of purpose is very much at odds with the actions of his children and brother's family, with their 'leisure' and easy, safe existence, their 'welfare'. The **contrast** deepens Oliver's implied criticism of his son and brother.

Using the word 'work' to represent the slaughter and subjugation of so many Irish **allows us to see this thought through Cromwell's eyes**. To him it is a job that must be done; rebels must be dealt with and doing the work of 'God', which Cromwell fervently believed he was, freed him from any doubt that this 'work' was anything but right, necessary and just.

In the next poem in the sequence, 'According to the Moderate Intelligencer', Cromwell sets out for Ireland to

> 'propagate the Gospel of Christ
> … Among the barbarous, bloodthirsty Irish
> Whose cursing, swearing, drunken ways
> Dishonour God by sea and land.
>
> Visit them Oliver, like God's right hand'

The Levellers

Cornet Thompson, Corporal Perkins and Private Church were three men in Cromwell's 'New Model Army' who were part of a movement called 'The Levellers'. The Levellers tried to secure better pay and conditions for the army, and they also had a number of political demands. Despite an agreement to negotiate, Cromwell attacked their four-hundred-strong group at night and had these three leaders shot four days later, an action which destroyed The Levellers movement and quashed any further rebellion.

Cromwell's mission

In the previous poem in this epic sequence, 'Thanksgiving', Cromwell has survived an attempt on his life and sums up his mission at a celebratory feast: to protect 'a people fearing God / Through laws and statutes close to the Laws of God, / A good God whose Hand supports this Nation / Rebuking all who would rebuke this Nation'. Those mentioned at the end of this list are the rebels whom Cromwell must deal with.

Historical context

Oliver Cromwell, First Lord Protector of England, signed the death warrant of Charles the First and led his New Model Army in a civil war against royalists and Catholics. He came to Ireland in August 1649 and left in May 1650, and his mission was to reconquer the country following a rebellion in 1641. In his time here he came to be called 'The Butcher of Drogheda'. He passed a number of **penal laws** against Roman Catholics, some of which are significant for the lament 'A Cry for Art O'Leary' (page 207). He confiscated huge tracts of land, and told those he had dispossessed they could have land in Connaught as compensation. The repercussions of the penal laws contributed to the famine, and the population was further decimated by the deportation of fifty thousand people to the West Indies. Many battles and sieges were fought, such as The Sieges of Drogheda and Limerick, and The Battle of Rathmines. Catholics, as well as having their land taken, were not allowed to live in towns; bounties were put on priests' heads and the practice of Catholicism was banned. Neither could Catholics hold public office.

In the poem 'In Dublin' which closely follows this poem in the collection, Oliver vows

'I will change the ways of this reeking town
For the Good of the Irish poor
… Let Protestant honesty come into its own'

Cromwell famously called the Irish 'barbarous wretches', but modern historians argue that the figures attributed to Cromwell in terms of slaughter are grossly inflated, and that as a military and political leader he was no more tyrannical or unjust than any other of the time.

Cromwell died of pneumonia in September 1658. In 1660 his body was exhumed and his head was displayed on a pole.

Themes

Kennelly is interested in showing us a **different side** of Cromwell, who in Irish history is viewed as a merciless villain who massacred countless people and denied the nation its religion, land and language. He is presented here as **a zealot** who truly believes what he is doing must be done, that he has right and God on his side. Oliver in this poem is **in supreme control of himself**, except perhaps when it comes to his son (possibly his son Richard, who eventually succeeded Cromwell, quite ineffectually). Thus we are given a possible insight into what would drive a man to do what Cromwell did.

Duty is a major theme, similar to Aeneas in Virgil's *Aeneid*; here is a man who does his military, national and religious duty at the expense of his own family and comfort.

The damage and destruction caused by killing in the name of religion is as relevant now as it was in the 1600s. The **harm done in the name of religion is something Kennelly has written about**. He speaks of the beatings that went on in Ireland's religious schools, something he experienced himself first hand in his youth. He was very vocal about the sexual-abuse scandals of the 1990s, the casual violence of clergy in the teaching profession and their lack of engagement with their pupils – 'there was no discussion, only questions and answers'. Kennelly does not paint all clergy with the same brush, but speaks openly of what he saw and experienced in Ireland from the 1950s to the present day. In the poem 'Sounds' he writes of 'The first time a teacher beat me / With a stick that sang through the air / Like a lark packed with venom.'

Imagery

The **image of the cherries** is an interesting contrast to the bleak and dark images of execution and work. They represent leisure, pleasure and decadence, quite at odds with Oliver's sense of duty and puritanism.

The Oxfordshire churchyard of Burford is an interesting site for the execution of The Levellers: a place of God, a God who says 'Thou shalt not kill', is the scene for the shooting of these men. On the same note, religion itself is the main justification for the slaughter that the English Civil War and the Irish 1641 rebellion led to.

Katleyn Ferguson writes, 'Kennelly both upholds and destabilises the popular myths of Oliver Cromwell as a villain and enemy of the Irish people by portraying him in a variety of guises'. This poem's image of Cromwell is a man who has much on his mind: family issues, civil war at home and a campaign in Ireland to face. His **measured and detached tone** is perhaps a way of dealing with all of this pressure and remaining calm; after all, he 'knows' that he has God on his side. Kennelly has written of the 'dangerous idea' that religion too easily gives of dividing life too glibly into heaven and hell, good and evil, heroes and villains. Kennelly wants to **debunk the myths** attributed to the 'scapegoats of history', because he often finds the Irish as a people likely to blame our issues on these 'scapegoats' rather than looking at our own failings throughout history and today.

Language and form

The letter to Oliver's brother is divided between concerns about the family and Oliver's account of his duty to deal with a rebellion. In **both spheres he seems to have lost some control** – control of his son and control of his own army. He has dealt with the army by executing the leaders of the rebellion, but he leaves his son's issues to his brother. This offers **an interesting picture of the man who may not be as assured and commanding as he first seems**. If one looks at the language used, it sometimes **drips with sarcasm**, such as in the phrase, 'I am glad to hear of your welfare / And that our children have so much leisure / They can travel far to eat cherries'. Often it's revealing to look at what Oliver **omits** just as closely as what he includes, for example 'This is most excusable in my daughter / ... whom I bless'. Of course this clearly implies that it is not excusable in his son, whom he does not bless; he seems not to trust him either: 'I have delivered my son up to you'. Cromwell even sends his affection to his brother's family; only his son is neglected. This speaks volumes without stating the facts baldly.

We must ask why Kennelly has chosen to write in the voice of Oliver Cromwell here. Although our perception of Cromwell as a violent man has not changed, we **are challenged** to take a closer look at him. He has a family, he loves his daughter and clearly worries about her, yet he has problems with his son. He does not enjoy the executions and seems to admire the dignity and courage the men show as they face death. He sees his imminent campaign in Ireland as 'work to do' rather than sounding thirsty for blood and vengeance. He is therefore not the two-dimensional villain that Irish history often presents.

Questions

1	What is Oliver Cromwell glad to hear of in lines 1–3? Do you believe that he is really 'glad'? Explain.
2	Describe his attitude to his daughter in the first eight lines.
3	Contrast this with his attitude to his son in lines 9–11.
4	What, do you think, do the words 'cherries' and 'exercise' suggest about the lifestyle of Cromwell's children? What is his tone here?
5	'Let sons and daughters be serious; the age requires it.' What does this line mean? Comment on the possible pun here.
6	'I have things to do, all in my own way.' What are these things and what might define Cromwell's own way?
7	Describe and compare the deaths of the three Levellers in the poem (lines 15–22).
8	'Men die their different ways / And girls eat cherries / In the Christblessed fields of England'. What is the tone here in your opinion? <ul><li>Flippant</li><li>Matter-of-fact</li><li>Callous</li><li>Regretful</li><li>Something else</li></ul> Consider all of the options in your answer.
9	What does the word 'Christblessed' suggest about Cromwell's attitude to England? Does it offer an insight into how he views Ireland?
10	'Let weep who will.' How does Cromwell seem to feel about those he has made weep?
11	Explain and comment on the last line of the poem.
12	What impression have you formed of Oliver Cromwell as a father, as a brother and as a political, military and religious leader? In pairs or groups, share your opinion, giving evidence from the poem.
13	What, do you think, is Brendan Kennelly trying to achieve in this poem? <ul><li>To show the humanity of an unjustly vilified historical figure</li><li>To explore the concept of duty</li><li>Something else</li></ul> Consider all the options in your answer.
14	Why, do you think, did Kennelly choose to structure this poem as a letter? What effect does this have? What does it allow the poet to do with his persona's voice?
15	Imagine you are Oliver's brother, and write a letter in reply.
16	Write a newspaper article, tabloid or broadsheet, describing the executions and the attitude of the man who ordered them.

Before you read

Write or talk about a fond memory you have of a family member, perhaps someone who is elderly or no longer living.

I See You Dancing, Father

No sooner downstairs after the night's rest
And in the door
Than you started to dance a step
In the middle of the kitchen floor.

And as you danced   5
You whistled.
You made your own music
Always in tune with yourself.

Well, nearly always, anyway.
You're buried now   10
In Lislaughtin Abbey
And whenever I think of you

I go back beyond the old man
Mind and body broken
To find the unbroken man.   15
It is the moment before the dance begins,

Your lips are enjoying themselves
Whistling an air.
Whatever happens or cannot happen
In the time I have to spare   20
I see you dancing, father.

Glossary

11	*Lislaughtin Abbey*: a friary built in 1478 which now houses a cemetery beside Ballylongford, the village the Kennelly family are from

Guidelines

From *A Time for Voices: Selected Poems* (1990). Kennelly, in an interview with the *Irish Independent* in 2012, said his father was 'a big strong man. Mad Fine Gaeler. He was a relaxed individual. He used to begin the morning every day down the stairs into the kitchen and he'd do a little dance.' This poem is about Kennelly **holding onto this memory** of his father; trying not to let his father's final days, when he had become ill and frail both physically and mentally, be his abiding memory of the man.

A newspaper article commented on the poet's drinking and how it caused him to neglect his family relationships: 'Kennelly has talked publicly of his guilt in this respect, in particular with reference to his neglect of his father.'

Commentary

Kennelly and his father

In Kennelly's poem 'Night Drive', the poet describes the drive he often took with his brother Alan to visit his father in hospital, and examines the guilt he felt about how he may have neglected his father over the years as a result of his alcoholism. The brothers fret at their father's steep decline: 'In the suffocating darkness / I heard the heavy breathing / Of my father's pain'; but all the while their father remains positive: '"I think I'll make it"'.

The poet recollects how his father danced each morning while whistling his own tune, as soon as he entered the kitchen, his feet in perfect harmony with this whistled music: 'Always in tune with yourself.' He speaks directly to his father, and the tone is conversational as the poet remarks – 'Well, nearly always, anyway' – for his father was to become ill and die. He still addresses his father directly, even though 'You're buried now', but whenever the poet thinks of him, he prefers to skip over the time when his father ailed – 'Mind and body broken' – to recollect instead a time when the man still danced in the kitchen whistling his own tune.

The **poet now thinks of his own mortality**; he too is ageing, but is determined in the time he has left – 'In the time I have to spare' – to recall his father in his prime: 'I see you dancing, father.'

Imagery

The image of the poet's father dancing first thing each day conveys an **impression** of a cheerful man, full of pep, who was happy to express himself in front of his family. It's a **joyful memory** and one Kennelly prefers to ponder rather than dwelling on his father's illness. In Kennelly's reminiscence, his father is whistling: 'Always in tune with yourself', showing that this was a man who was sure of himself, who coped admirably with life, and indeed seems to have celebrated each new day. He perhaps embodied the spirit of Kennelly's earlier poem 'Begin', in that he faced each new day with optimism.

This image contrasts with how out of tune with himself his father became as ageing and illness robbed his 'Mind and body' of the joyous harmony he'd once enjoyed. Even as the image of his father's demise and death interrupts the memory of his morning dance, Kennelly determinedly rejects it, forcing his mind 'back beyond the old man' to 'the moment before the dance begins'. He copes with the bereavement by recalling this happy time, and finds solace in that. His fears for the future of his own mind and body are hinted at: 'Whatever happens or cannot happen / In the time I have to spare'.

The poet is determined to preserve this special memory which defines all that was great about the man: 'I see you dancing, father.' This line **moves from a sense of the past in the title, to a continuous present in the last line**.

By writing the poem Kennelly has surely achieved this and provided comfort for many other bereaved sons and daughters in this, one of his most popular poems.

Form and language

The poem is a **simple and heartfelt elegy** to remember the poet's father. The poem has a **lyrical quality** in keeping with his father's natural **harmony**, while sounding **very natural and conversational** – 'Well, nearly always, anyway'. There are rhymes – 'door' and 'floor', 'air' and 'spare' – and half-rhymes – 'anyway' and 'Abbey', 'now' and 'you'. In the second-last stanza, however, the sounds become **less 'easy' and natural sounding**. This **awkwardness** reflects the struggle the poet is having with trying to 'go back beyond the old man' to get to an earlier memory of his father 'To find the unbroken man'. The 'b' and 'm' **alliteration** here use harder sounds, and seem **stilted**, which reflects the **dissonance** that illness has brought to this previously harmonious man. The quatrains are verse-like and remind us that Kennelly grew up in a village pub in Ballylongford, Co. Kerry where **recitations and singing were a regular occurrence**.

Tim Kennelly

The poet's father emigrated to America. He returned for what was to be only a visit, but he met Kennelly's mother at a dance in Ballybunion (he had always loved dancing) and soon the two were married.

It is an **unusually direct and autobiographical poem** for Kennelly, who tends to use personas in his work. The rarity of hearing the poet's own voice speak so clearly of his love and grief makes the poem all the more touching. His use of **colloquial phrases** like 'dance a step' add to the **naturalness and relatability** of the poem. Professor Declan Kiberd remembers his student days in Trinity and attending lectures Kennelly gave where he 'praised Keats … for putting commonplace snatches of talk into his poems'.

The extra line in the final stanza brings the poem back to the title and tells us that the speaker has been successful in his quest to move his abiding memory of his father back before illness had 'Mind and body broken'.

Questions

1	What does the poet's father do each morning? What does this say about his father's personality?
2	'Dance a step' is a colloquial way of describing his father dancing. What is the effect of using this in the poem? Can you find other examples where Kennelly uses the rhythm and phrasing of everyday speech in his poem? Comment on the effect produced.
3	'Always in tune with yourself.' Kennelly's words here can be interpreted both literally and metaphorically. Explain the two possible meanings this phrase might have.
4	Explain the poet's thought process in stanzas 3 and 4. What two memories of his father are in conflict here?
5	In the final stanza the poet's thoughts turn to his own mortality. How is this conveyed in the poem?
6	Why, do you think, did Kennelly add an extra line to the final stanza?
7	Although his father is dead, the speaker addresses him directly. Why, do you think, does he do this? What effect is achieved?
8	How would you describe the tone of this poem? Is it sad, joyful, nostalgic, melancholy or something else? Perhaps it is a combination of some of these?
9	Choose a character from one of your paper two texts who dies. What would your abiding memory of that person be? Write your response like a stanza from this poem beginning 'I see you …'

A Cry for Art O'Leary

(from the Irish of Eibhlín Ní Chonaill)

Before you read

What do you know about the ancient Irish tradition of keening? Do some research and share your findings with the class.

My love
The first time I saw you
From the top of the market
My eyes covered you
My heart went out to you   5
I left my friends for you
Threw away my home for you

What else could I do?

You got the best rooms for me
All in order for me   10
Ovens burning for me
Fresh trout caught for me
Choice meat for me

In the best of beds I stretched
Till milking-time hummed for me   15

You made the whole world
Pleasing to me

White rider of love!

I love your silver-hilted sword
How your beaver hat became you   20
With its band of gold
Your friendly homespun suit
Revealed your body
Your pin of glinting silver
Glittered in your shirt   25

On your horse in style
You were sensitive pale-faced
Having journeyed overseas
The English respected you
Bowing to the ground   30
Not because they loved you
But true to their hearts' hate

They're the ones who killed you
Darling of my heart

My lover   35
My love's creature
Pride of Immokelly
To me you were not dead
Till your great mare came to me
Her bridle dragging ground   40
Her head with your startling blood
Your blood upon the saddle
You rode in your prime
I didn't wait to clean it
I leaped across my bed   45
I leaped then to the gate
I leaped upon your mare
I clapped my hands in frenzy
I followed every sign
With all the skill I knew   50
Until I found you lying
Dead near a furze bush
Without pope or bishop
Or cleric or priest
To say a prayer for you   55

Only a crooked wasted hag
Throwing her cloak across you

I could do nothing then
In the sight of God
But go on my knees   60
And kiss your face
And drink your free blood

My man!
Going out the gate
You turned back again   65
Kissed the two children
Threw a kiss at me
Saying 'Eileen, woman, try
To get this house in order,
Do your best for us   70
I must be going now
I'll not be home again.'
I thought you were joking
You my laughing man

My man!   75
My Art O'Leary
Up on your horse now
Ride out to Macroom
And then to Inchigeela
Take a bottle of wine   80
Like your people before you
Rise up
My Art O'Leary
Of the sword of love

Put on your clothes   85
Your black beaver
Your black gloves
Take down your whip
Your mare is waiting
Go east by the thin road   90
Every bush will salute you
Every stream will speak to you
Men and women acknowledge you

They know a great man
When they set eyes on him   95

God's curse on you, Morris,
God's curse on your treachery
You swept my man from me
The man of my children
Two children play in the house   100
A third lives in me

He won't come alive from me

My heart's wound
Why was I not with you
When you were shot   105
That I might take the bullet
In my own body?
Then you'd have gone free
Rider of the grey eye
And followed them   110
Who'd murdered me

My man!
I look at you now
All I know of a hero
True man with a true heart   115
Stuck in a coffin
You fished the clean streams
Drank nightlong in halls
Among frank-breasted women

I miss you   120

My man!
I am crying for you
In far Derrynane
In yellow-appled Carren
Where many a horseman   125
And vigilant woman
Would be quick to join
In crying for you
Art O'Leary
My laughing man   130

O crying women
Long live your crying
Till Art O'Leary
Goes back to school
On a fateful day   135
Not for books and music

But for stones and clay

My man!
The corn is stacked
The cows are milking   140
My heart is a lump of grief
I will never be healed
Till Art O'Leary
Comes back to me

I am a locked trunk   145
The key is lost
I must wait till rust
Devours the screw

O my best friend
Art O'Leary   150
Son of Conor
Son of Cadach
Son of Lewis
East from wooded glens
West from girlish hills   155
Where rowanberries grow
Yellow nuts budge from branches
Apples laugh like small suns
As once they laughed
Throughout my girlhood   160
It is no cause for wonder
If bonfires lit O'Leary country
Close to Ballingeary
Or holy Gougane Barra
After the clean-gripping rider   165
The robust hunter
Panting towards the kill
Your own hounds lagged behind you
O horseman of the summoning eyes
What happened you last night?   170
My only whole belief
Was that you could not die
For I was your protection

My heart! My grief!

My man! My darling!   175

In Cork
I had this vision
Lying in my bed:
A glen of withered trees
A home heart-broken   180
Strangled hunting-hounds
Choked birds
And you
Dying on a hillside
Art O'Leary   185
My one man
Your blood running crazily
Over earth and stone

Jesus Christ knows well
I'll wear no cap   190
No mourning dress
No solemn shoes
No bridle on my horse
No grief-signs in my house
But test instead   195
The wisdom of the law
I'll cross the sea
To speak to the King
If he ignores me
I'll come back home   200
To find the man
Who murdered my man
Morris, because of you
My man is dead

Is there a man in Ireland   205
To put a bullet through your head

Women, white women of the mill
I give my love to you
For the poetry you made
For Art O'Leary   210
Rider of the brown mare
Deep women-rhythms of blood
The fiercest and the sweetest
Since time began
Singing of this cry I womanmake   215
For my man

Glossary

Line	Entry
Title	*cry*: this refers to keening or *caoineadh*, the Irish tradition of lament; a song of grief sung at a wake by the women there; keeners were often professional and hired by families to sing these laments at the wake of a loved one
22	*homespun*: homemade, woven at home
37	*Immokelly*: place name; Eibhlín Dubh Ní Chonaill was known as 'the pride of Immokelly'
40	*bridle*: the headgear of a horse to which the reins are attached
54	*cleric*: priest, member of the clergy
78	*Macroom*: town in Co. Cork
79	*Inchigeela*: named around 1170 when the O'Learys became lords of this valley in Cork
123	*Derrynane*: O'Connell's native town in Kerry
124	*Carren*: area in Co. Cork
126	*vigilant*: to be on the lookout but also may apply to the idea of holding vigil over the dead
151-3	*Conor, Cadach, Lewis*: ancestors of Art O'Leary
163	*Ballingeary*: a village in the Shehy Mountains in Co. Cork
164	*Gougane Barra*: scenic and sacred area in Cork
215	*womanmake*: made by women

Guidelines

Kennelly read this translation in his well-known and widely regarded talk on 'Poetry and Violence', where he examines both concepts through many different poems and traditions including Yeats, Longley and James Simmons.

This poem is a translation of a lament in the **Irish oral tradition** first 'sung' by Eibhlín Ní Chonaill over her husband Art's dead body in 1773. Many Irish writers have translated this poem or parts of it, including Thomas Kinsella, Paul Muldoon and Frank O'Connor (whose version Kennelly included when he edited *The Penguin Book of Irish Verse* in 1970).

Art O'Leary's wife, Eibhlín, sings this lament with a group of women over his body following his murder. She didn't write this down, but famously composed it as a keening at his wake, and it remained part of the Irish oral tradition of *Sean Nós* and *Caoineadh* (laments), until it was eventually transcribed. Kennelly was influenced by the oral tradition in Ireland and would have heard songs and poems like this performed in his family's pub from an early age.

> **Eibhlín O'Connell**
>
> Art O'Leary was Eibhlín's second husband; her first died when she was only fifteen. They eloped to Macroom in December 1767 due to her family's disapproval of the match. She was from the renowned O'Connell family of Derrynane in Co. Kerry, Kennelly's native county, and was the aunt of Daniel O'Connell. Her family were known for their low-key resistance to the penal laws imposed on Roman Catholics by their British occupiers.

Commentary

Lines 1–34

Eibhlín recalls the first time she saw Art O'Leary in the marketplace, and tells of how she desired him instantly. Her family disapproved, so they ran away together – 'What else could I do?' She had to follow her heart. Art was a good provider, giving her a lovely home, fine food to eat, and 'the best of beds'. They lived a life of domestic bliss: 'You made the whole world / Pleasing to me', and she was happy to do her share: 'Till milking-time hummed for me'. The intensity of her passionate love for Art is clear from the ardent line 'White rider of love!'.

Eibhlín admires the sword and elaborate uniform of her husband, and notes with sarcasm that 'The English respected you', though really this was a thinly disguised jealousy: they would later seize upon the chance to kill him.

> **O'Leary's horse**
>
> O'Leary famously brought a beautiful brown mare back from Vienna following his time fighting with the Austrian Army. The horse had a white star on her forehead and, according to legend, beat the horse of Abraham Morris, High Sherriff of Cork, in a race in Macroom. Morris begrudged O'Leary his popularity and demanded he sell the horse for five pounds. Under the penal laws no Catholic could own a horse worth more than £5 and had to sell it to a Protestant if they demanded it. Art refused, so Morris had a bounty put on his head.

Lines 35–95

Eibhlín tells how her husband's famous horse returned with no rider and a bloodied saddle, so, seized with panic she leaps from their bed onto the horse which takes her to her murdered lover's body, 'Dead near a furze bush'. She is saddened that Art, a Roman Catholic, had no last rites; no priest was on hand to deliver this sacrament: priests were hunted under the **penal laws**, and the practice of Roman Catholicism was outlawed. There was only an old crone, who covered his body with her cloak. The new widow tells of how she knelt at Art's side to kiss him, tasting the blood which still flowed freely from his wound.

She thinks of the last time she saw him alive – 'Going out the gate / You turned back again / Kissed the two children / Threw a kiss at me'. It seems to her now that he knew he would be killed: 'I must be going now / I'll not be home again'. She had no idea that his words would be the truth – 'I thought you were joking', as it seems he was often a joker: 'You my laughing man'.

She begs him to rise and ride again (the first stage of grief so often being denial) and wear his beautiful uniform, imagining the welcome all would give him, even the things of nature: 'Every bush will salute you / Every stream will speak to you / Men and women acknowledge you // They know a great man'.

Lines 96–137

She turns her thoughts now to the man responsible for O'Leary's death, Abraham Morris, High Sheriff of Macroom, cursing his treachery. He has robbed her of her man and the father to three children, one yet to be born: 'A third lives in me'. She suggests that this last child will not survive her grief: 'He won't come alive from me'.

> **Ambush**
>
> **On 4 May 1773, O'Leary was riding home-wards across the river Keel near Macroom, when he was ambushed by Morris and his men, who shot at him. The first shot, fired by a soldier named Green, hit O'Leary, who was left bleeding on the side of the road. He died lying there alone. He was 26 and his wife was pregnant with their third child.**

Eibhlín wishes she'd been there to take the bullet for her husband, imagining him riding after her killer in pursuit of vengeance.

We realise all this is being sung at O'Leary's wake, for she looks down at him in his coffin, recalling how he enjoyed life, fishing and drinking. He seems to have been something of a carouser: 'Drank nightlong in halls / Among frank-breasted women', but she doesn't seem jealous; rather she admires his spirited approach to life: 'I miss you // My man!' The men and women of the surrounding towns will be crying for her 'laughing man', and she urges the women to continue keening for him until he 'goes back to school'. She seems to imply here that this 'school' is his burial, an education of 'stones and clay'. Perhaps his death will teach others to avenge the persecution and subjugation of the Irish under the English Crown.

Lines 138–188

A more **metaphorical** section follows. Although there is still food in plenty: 'The corn is stacked / The cows are milking', her heart is 'a lump of grief'. This is a contrast to the beginning of the poem where the milking 'hummed' to her. She will feel this way until she is reunited with him in death. Until that time she is 'a locked trunk' which must wait until death and decay – 'rust' – 'Devours the screw' that keeps her from him. She says he was her 'best friend'. She proudly lists his ancestors and describes the beauty of the area he hailed from, a place of plenty where 'rowanberries grow / Yellow nuts budge from branches / Apples laugh like small suns'.

Eibhlín wouldn't be surprised to find bonfires in honour of Art littering the area, to mourn this skilled hunter 'of the summoning eyes'. She questions the reality of his death; she feels disbelief: she had always thought him invincible, especially with the protection of her love. To have this notion disabused causes her anguish: 'My heart! My grief!' She tells of a vision of his death in Cork, where the landscape is very different than the one she's just praised. Contrasting with the fruitfulness of his home place, his place of death is a 'glen of withered trees / A home heart-broken'; the hounds he once outran while hunting are 'Strangled'; and she can see his 'blood flowing crazily / Over earth and stone'. This echoes her earlier words of line 137: 'But for stones and clay'.

Lines 189– end

The widow insists that she won't wear the garb of mourning nor display its signs on her house. Instead she will go to the king seeking justice. Eibhlín promises that if she doesn't secure justice through legal means, she will find another way; she will find a man 'in Ireland / To put a bullet through your head'.

Finally the widow addresses the women keening with her, expressing her love for them. They have helped her to sing this lament, which is so special because of the **passionate grief of their keening** – 'Deep women-rhythms of blood' – is 'The fiercest and the sweetest / Since time began'. So Eibhlín and her women friends sing, 'this cry I womanmake', for her beloved, 'For my man'.

> **Murder**
>
> There was an inquest into O'Leary's death, but Morris and his men were cleared of murder. In fact, Green, the soldier who shot O'Leary, was commended for his action.
>
> Soon after, Art's brother Cornelius shot Morris through a window. Morris died of his wound.

Themes

Love and grief combine in this angry outpouring of emotion. The **tradition of the lament**, especially as a **female art-form, is celebrated**, particularly at the end of the poem.

Violence is also a major theme and is something Kennelly explored in detail both in his own poetry and in the work of other Irish poets. In a talk called *Poetry and Violence,* Kennelly recited his translation of this poem and said: 'The kind of violence I'm talking about now, the violence engendered by history, is the violence of hatred. Hatred is a dynamic force, a stimulating, animating power. Hatred hates indifference. Hatred loves its own annihilating expression, wiping out distinctions between innocent and guilty, adult and child, man and woman. Hatred tolerates no human hierarchies of kindness, gentleness, affection, considerateness. Hatred sneers at the futility of intellectual subtlety. And hatred is, above all, a devoted servant to a cause. Hatred revels in devotion, in an act of unswerving service to a cause. In serving that cause, whatever it be, hatred is exemplary in its attention to its own unshakeable purpose. Yeats captured the situation when he wrote:

> 'Out of Ireland have we come:
> Great hatred, little room
> Maimed us at the start;
> I carry from my mother's womb
> A fanatic heart.'

Murders like O'Leary's and the treatment of Catholic Irish people under the penal laws is still something that **rankles in the Irish psyche**. **Vengeful and strong women** are also themes close to Kennelly's heart, and are explored in his translations and staging of the three Greek tragedies *Antigone*, *Medea* and *The Trojan Women*. **The strength of women is a recurring theme** in Kennelly; look at St Brigid's determination in her prayer, and the creative power of the baker in 'Bread'.

Murder avenged

'[Art's brother Cornelius] rode into Cork city on the 7th July … he saw Morris at a window and fired three shots at him, wounding him. The shots were not fatal, but Morris survived for only two more years, dying in September 1775.' Cornelius escaped to France and from there went to live in America, so Ní Chonaill's desire for revenge is eventually fulfilled. (From the text of a Cumann Staire talk given by Peter O'Leary)

Kennelly also explained why he decided to translate this lament: 'I chose this poem because it is a poem about various forms of **violence** – sexual, religious, political, forms of violence that occur again and again throughout Irish writing. But it is far more than that: here, the woman's passion is fiercely real; **this fierce, passionate, violent reality creates the poem's momentum, its primal, driving, driven rhythms**. It is, above all, a cry – a violent cry, beyond words, put into words. It intrigues me most of all for **the way the woman's violent feelings are somehow changed even as they are expressed** in this unrelenting rhythmical momentum.'

Kennelly therefore finds Ní Chonaill's voice fascinating because of its **power**: her grief is primitive and almost **tangible in its force**. It answers Cromwell's dismissive 'Let weep who will' (from 'Oliver to his Brother') with the very opposite of his male measured detached voice. She is a woman keening; this is 'The fiercest and the sweetest' expression possible and shows the ragged horrible grief that hatred and murder 'for a cause' engenders. Is Kennelly commenting that while men are often the war-mongers it is the women who suffer?

Language and form

The **lament form often contains repetition and fervent expressions of anguished grief**, for example 'My man!' and 'White rider of love!'

The poem also **tells a story**; it is a narrative made all the more poignant by the setting: **Eibhlín stands over her husband's body singing her grief and pain and promising vengeance**.

The recurring mentions of **blood, earth and stone** emphasise the **tragedy** of this young man's death, and it's no wonder that songs such as these incited more and more men to rebel against their English colonisers. A country where the earth is soaked in blood will grow more violence in a vicious cycle of birth, hatred and death.

The **contrast** between the couple's idyllic life together and the widow's current broken-hearted existence is tragic in the extreme. It is interesting to note how powerful the voices of women are in Kennelly's poetry, how **decisive and sure of themselves** they are compared to his male personas. Ní Chonaill is absolutely certain of her deep love for O'Leary, convinced that they will be reunited in death and **resolute** in her determination to secure justice for his murder.

Questions

1	What kind of husband was O'Leary according to the first eighteen lines of the poem? Describe the couple's life together.
2	What impression do you get of O'Leary in lines 19–28? How do you imagine him?
3	Why did the English 'respect' him according to lines 28–32?
4	Retell briefly the story of how Eibhlín discovered her husband's death and body, using lines 38–62.
5	Sum up Eibhlín's last exchange with her husband as he leaves their home for the last time. How is our sympathy elicited here?
6	Read lines 75–95 and explain how Eibhlín imagines the various reactions to her husband's 'resurrection'.
7	How does the tone change at line 96 and why does this change occur?
8	What wish is expressed in lines 103 to 111?
9	How do you perceive O'Leary after reading lines 117–120? Has this changed your previous opinion of him in any way? Explain.
10	Offer an explanation of what you think Ní Chonaill is trying to convey when she talks of Art returning to school in lines 131–137.
11	Write out and explain the two metaphors Ní Chonaill uses to describe herself in lines 145–148.
12	What was Ní Chonaill's 'only belief' (lines 171–173)? Describe the vision she has in Cork (lines 176–188).
13	Why won't the widow observe the usual symbols and traditions of mourning (lines 189–204)? What are these symbols?
14	In your own words sum up what O'Leary's widow says, in the last ten lines of the poem, to the women keening with her. Comment on her tone here.
15	What, do you think, is the main theme of this poem? ■ Love ■ Revenge ■ Grief ■ History – Ireland in the Penal Times ■ Womanhood ■ Something else
16	Why, do you think, did Kennelly choose to translate this lament? What does assuming Ní Chonaill's voice allow him to explore? In your answer think about what relevance Ní Chonaill's story has for us today.
17	From your reading of the poem, what is your overall impression of the speaker and her husband? In pairs or groups, discuss.
18	Write a newspaper article in a tabloid style reporting on these events OR compose a similar (possibly shorter!) lament about someone famous, real or fictional, who has died (e.g. Nelson Mandela, Gatsby, a character from Shakespeare, David Bowie, Sylvia Plath, etc.).

Before you read

Can you think of any
famous traitors in religion
or history? Make a list.

Things I Might Do

I thought of things I might do with my heart.
Should I make it into a month like October,
A chalice for the sad madness of leaves
That I might raise in homage to the year's end?

Should I make it into a small white church in   5
A country-place where bells are childhood prayers?
Or a backroom of a brothel in Dublin
Where the trade of somethinglikelove endures?

Should I make it a judge to judge itself?
Or a caring face in a memory-storm?   10
Or a bed

For Judas dreaming of the tree:
     'There now, there now, rest as best you can,
     Darling, rest your treacherous head
     And when you've rested, come home to me'.   15

Glossary

3	*chalice*: a goblet, often ornate, used in religious ceremonies, particularly to carry the bread and wine that represent the body and blood of Christ in the Catholic mass
4	*homage*: respectful praise, honour

Guidelines

From *The Book of Judas* (1991), this is actually a small part of an epic poem (similar to *Cromwell*) where Kennelly explores 'the Judas voice': 'I wished to create the voice of a condemned man writing back to me.' The epic consists of hundreds of smaller poems and took Kennelly eight years to write. John McDonagh wrote about how Judas is an 'internationally recognisable icon of betrayal whose popular treatment parallels the specifically Irish demonisation of Oliver Cromwell'. The collection of poetry that is this epic is a fine example of Kennelly's **dialogic style of writing**, where he is often in **conversation with his personas** and they converse with each other. This poem has **two voices; who they are is not entirely clear**: is it Kennelly speaking and Judas answers him, or is Judas speaking and a lover answers him? Christ has been suggested here also as one of the voices. It is up to the reader to decide.

Commentary

Stanza 1

The poem opens simply: the speaker introduces us to a list of options, possible things he 'might do with my heart' ranging from the religious to the sleazy. The first suggestion is to 'make it into a month like October'. This time of year is sacred, leading to All Hallow's Eve when the souls of the dead are prayed for and it is a time when autumn begins to fade into winter bringing darker days and death. He suggests that this 'October heart' would be a chalice, a sacred receptacle for 'the sad madness of leaves', the blustery breezes of the season causing a flurry of leaves which seem manic and melancholy. He would use this chalice to raise a toast and pay his respects to the year that has passed. **Secular and religious ideas intertwine here.**

> **Kavanagh**
>
> Patrick Kavanagh, a great influence on Kennelly, often wrote about the idea of rediscovering one's childhood innocence to be closer to God, in poems such as 'Advent'. The bells of the speaker's childhood in the poem hark back to a time when faith was just accepted and the uncertainty of adulthood was not an issue.

Stanza 2

The religious and secular mixture continues here beginning with the speaker's second proposal, that his heart be 'a small white church' suggesting a modest place to pray. Perhaps the speaker wishes to be more religious, more devout while exploring a more childlike and innocent idea of prayer when things were less complicated, 'A country-place where bells are childhood prayers'.

The speaker seems to look to the reader or to another to advise him on what to do. In direct contrast with the idea of the church, the speaker's next option is sordid, the opposite of innocent prayer; to make his heart a 'backroom of a brothel in Dublin'. The speaker acknowledges the insincerity of the 'affection' he might find in such a place: 'Where the trade of somethinglikelove endures'. Using the word 'endures' suggests something that lasts but also something that must be borne, a **burden**.

> **Judging judgement**
>
> In the poem following this one in the collection, Judas says: 'The judging world finds judging easy. / If I happen to be in a house of ill-repute, / Low dive, dirty pub, grotty café or sleazy / Joint, I'm judged and sentenced in a minute.' Like Judas, prostitutes would be considered sinners but Christ forgave sinners and welcomed them into his kingdom. Who are we to judge them? A lot of the Judas poems criticise modern society for its judgemental nature.

Stanzas 3 and 4

'Should I make it a judge to judge itself?' We must ask why the speaker feels his heart should be judged — has he sinned?

Betrayed another? Has there been a crime that demands atonement? The suggestions come faster now: could it be the face of someone who had cared from a plethora of memories or perhaps a bed for Judas? The speaker imagines that Judas is 'dreaming of the tree', i.e. the method by which he would commit suicide, unable to live with the fact that he had betrayed Christ for thirty pieces of silver.

At this point **another voice enters the poem. It is unclear who it belongs to but it offers comfort**: ' "There now, there now, rest as best you can" '. 'Darling' suggests a very close, possibly even romantic relationship, and 'come home to me' tells us this is someone Judas was close to in the past, perhaps a mother or a lover? What do you think? The comfort and affection offered is tempered by the phrase 'treacherous head' but the overall sentiment is **forgiveness and acceptance**.

Themes and imagery

In the preface to this collection Kennelly cited the playwright Ibsen's belief that **'poetry is a court of judgment on the soul'**. This is certainly at play here and in the next poem from *The Book of Judas*, 'Gizzard', says 'The judging world finds judging easy … I ask myself if it was I closed the door on myself.' **Judgement is certainly a theme here.** The speaker seems sure of one thing: that he must do something new with his heart, change is needed. 'Gizzard' ends with the line: 'So. There's hope. There's rope. Hope rope rope rope'. This links strongly with the image of the tree in the poem, the place in the Garden of Gethsemane where Judas, according to the Bible, would hang himself, the thirty pieces of silver he'd been paid for betraying Christ lying at his feet. **Just as Judas is tormented by his crime the speaker's heart seems tormented and crying out for love and redemption.**

Religious imagery contrasts with more secular images, chalices hold leaves in a rather pagan image while a church and a brothel are side by side in stanza 2. The 'sad madness of leaves' has an **assonance** that produces a rather **melancholy** effect, while the image of the leaves echoes the earlier poem 'Dear Autumn Girl – 'When mad leaf-argosies drive at my head'. **The heart links the two sets of images, religious and secular.**

Kennelly likes to **subvert conventions** in his poetry and to **represent a life**, an existence that is explored without prejudice or a slavish, sheep-like adherence to convention. Thus we have this portrayal of Judas at the end. His name is a byword for treachery but somebody loves him, he is somebody's 'Darling'. Like 'Oliver to His Brother', this poem explores how the characters famous for evil and villainy were people too with families and loved ones. Kennelly in the book's preface was critical of how the Irish are fond of 'saying that everybody must be labelled … you needn't bother yourself with further enquiry into their characters or minds'. **He felt that the 'electricity … that burns the labels and restores the spirit of investigative uncertainty' is poetry.**

Language and form

Kennelly is known for **using the sonnet format to investigate and question himself, society and the subjects** of his poems often using two personas to drive this exploration. He begins conventionally enough with two quatrains but the third stanza takes an **unexpected line break** at the word 'bed' and then continues the line at the start of the last quatrain. Why, do you think, does Kennelly do this? Is he pausing to think who the bed might be for – who deserves it? Or is there another possibility?

There is a **dreamlike quality** to the **repetitious** last three lines which contrasts with the straightforward questioning of the poem thus far. The **title** is interesting; the speaker seems to want change but is confused about which path to follow; 'might' in the title is equivocal and it may be that the speaker will do nothing.

By allowing Judas to rest in his heart is he advocating treachery or forgiveness? Is the 'bed' in line 11 linked to the 'brothel' in line 7? The poem **makes us think about our preconceptions** and we question who is speaking and to whom.

Again the identity of the voices here is problematic, but really the important aspects of the poem are the **issues raised** by the speaker. What should we do with our heart, especially if we have sullied it with sin or emptied it of love; how can we be fulfilled; where can we seek redemption? Judas was so guilt-ridden and tormented by his betrayal of his friend that he took his own life. Is the speaker similarly anguished? Does the voice at the end of the poem offer consolation? Is the poem about forgiveness or despair?

Heart and soul

The heart of this poem is very like the soul in Kennelly's 'The soul's loneliness' (page 232). Both seem alone and lost, and search for companionship or redemption. Both consider religion as a possible source of comfort and neither resolve or improve their situation by the end of the poem.

Questions

1	Outline the speaker's suggestion for what he might do with his heart in stanza 1.
2	What might be the significance of the month of October, and what, do you think, is implied by the phrase 'sad madness of leaves'?
3	Think about the poet's use of the word 'chalice' here. What effect does it have on this stanza as a whole and what will he do with this 'heart chalice'?
4	Compare and contrast the two options the speaker puts forward for his heart in the second stanza.
5	'Somethinglikelove'. Explain what the speaker means by this and say why he might have made it into one word.
6	In the third stanza the speaker asks 'Should I make it a judge to judge itself?' Why might he feel his heart needs or deserves judgement? What does this reveal about the speaker?
7	What, do you think, is the poet describing through the metaphor 'memory-storm'? Might this image relate in any way to line 3?
8	There is a line break between 'bed' and 'For Judas' (stanzas 3 and 4). What effect does this have? Why, do you think, has Kennelly done this?
9	Why might Judas need a bed in the speaker's heart? Explain the significance of 'dreaming of the tree'.
10	Describe the speaker from what he has said in the first twelve lines of the poem. In your answer comment on his tone as the poem progresses, and what his use of and attitude to the figure of Judas says about him. Is this Judas talking to and about himself?
11	Who might be speaking in the final three lines? Could it be: ■ Christ offering understanding and forgiveness ■ A mother or a lover ■ The heart of the speaker ■ Someone else?
12	Which of the following, do you think, most closely describes what the poem is about? ■ Loneliness ■ Redemption ■ Atonement ■ Judgement
13	Compile a list of four or five questions you would like to ask the poet about this poem. Discuss your questions in groups or as a class and offer some possible answers.
14	Write a letter to the speaker advising him which option you think he should take for his heart and explain why. In it identify who you think the speaker is – Judas, Christ, the poet himself or another persona.

A Great Day

She was all in white.

Snow
Suggests itself as metaphor

But since this has been so often said
I may be justified in considering it dead.   5
Something about snow is not quite right.

Therefore, she was all in white.

He was most elegant too
All dickied up in dignified blue.

They came together, as is habitual   10
In that part of the world,
Through a grave ritual,

Listening
With at least a modicum of wonder –
What God has joined together   15
Let no man put asunder.

Man in woman, woman in man.
Soon afterwards, the fun began.

It was a great day –
Long hours of Dionysiac festivity.   20

Songs poured out like wine.
Praises flowed as they had never done.

The people there
Seemed to see each other in a new way.
This added to the distinction of the day.   25

And all the time she was all in white
Enjoying every song and speech
Enjoying every sip and every bite.

Such whiteness seems both beautiful and true
He thought, all dickied up in dignified blue.   30

He looks so good in blue
(This warmed her mind)
Blue suits him
Down to the ground.

At the table where they sat   35
Things seemed to fit.

And the loud crowd sang and danced
The whole day long, the whole night long.
There could never be anything but dance and song.

I must change, she whispered,   40
I must change my dress.

He never saw the white dress again.

In the train, the trees wore their rainy veils
With a reticent air.

It's good to get away, she whispered,   45
Touching her beautiful hair.

She closed her eyes, the trees were silent guests,
A tide of thoughts flowed in her head,
In his head.

'Darling, it was a great day,' she said.   50

Glossary

9	*dickied up*: dressed unusually elegantly
14	*modicum*: a small amount
16	*put asunder*: tear apart; break
20	*Dionysiac*: hedonistic, after the Greek god Dionysus, indicating a celebration involving large quantities of alcohol and a complete loss of inhibition
44	*reticent*: reluctant

Guidelines

From *Breathing Spaces* (1992). The poem describes a wedding day from the perspective of **an omniscient observer** who knows the thoughts and feelings of the couple and their guests. The poem explores the **ritual of marriage** as well as the festivities afterwards. Although marriage is often seen as the closest two people can be, the ending suggests that we never truly know what someone else is thinking or feeling.

Commentary

Lines 1–9

A bride is described in the first line, 'all in white'. The poet considers 'Snow' as a metaphor for the whiteness of her dress, but rejects it by line 4, 'since this has been so often said'. He admits it is a cliché, 'considering it dead'. 'Something about snow is not quite right', perhaps because snow is part of winter, things ending, death, and this is a wedding, something celebrating love and life. Or perhaps the poet hints that the innocence signified by white is not appropriate in the case of this wedding. The speaker begins again, and matches the description of the bride by remarking upon the elegance of the groom,

'dickied up in dignified blue'. The colloquial language of 'dickied up' coupled with the speaker's conversational tone and easy change of mind, creates **a relaxed feeling in the narration** of the poem.

Lines 10–25

The wedding ceremony is a 'grave ritual', the **pun** here suggests first something very serious, but also a reference to death which links back to the rejected 'snow' metaphor. There is wry humour as the speaker tells us the congregation to listen to the ceremony with 'at least a modicum of wonder': they have heard it many times before but still appreciate the specialness of the day. The couple become formally married with the words, 'What God has joined together / Let no man put asunder.' The celebrations begin and the wedding reception is 'Dionysiac', referring to the Greek God of wine and feasting, Dionysus. As people drink, their tongues loosen both to sing and to heap compliments on each other: 'Songs poured out like wine. / Praises flowed as they had never done'; the poet feels the wedding atmosphere is enhanced by how nice people are being to each other.

Lines 26–39

The bride enjoys seeing this companionable revelry, and remains in her white dress, admired by her new husband just as she admires him; they particularly like each other's attire. They sit at their table and survey the festivities, which continue unabated into the night. Note that the newlywed couple are happy to watch their guests enjoy the party, but **don't appear to take part themselves**, remaining content to observe.

Lines 40–50

The jovial, celebratory tone ends abruptly here as the bride decides its time they leave – 'I must change my dress'. We are told that 'He never saw the white dress again'. The couple have boarded a train, probably to begin their honeymoon. Nature is the guest here in the guise of the **personified trees** who wear veils of rain and are silent – 'With a reticent air', in stark contrast to the joyous revelry of the wedding reception guests.

Table motif

The table is a recurring motif in Kennelly's poetry. He deploys it through an array of images, from a scene of animal sacrifice to a sedate dinner party, from the Last Supper to this as the 'top table' at a wedding. The table often acts like an altar in Kennelly's work, sometimes pagan, sometimes Christian.

The bride seems to have been looking forward to being alone with her new husband: 'It's good to get away', and perhaps flirts a little, 'Touching her beautiful hair'.

Both are taken by a 'tide of thoughts' as the trees look on silently. Are they thinking back over their wedding day or perhaps forward to the consummation of their marriage?

The bride sums up the whole experience with the title of the poem: … 'it was a great day'.

Themes and imagery

Innocence, virginity and newness are summed up in the white dress worn by the bride and so admired by her husband. The fact that he never sees it again after that night is possibly a reference to her loss of innocence.

> **Dionysus**
>
> **Dionysus was the god of feasting, wine and drama in ancient Greek mythology. His cult had fiercely devoted female followers called Maenads who had mysterious and quite extreme initiation rites. These women would drink themselves into a frenzy of worship for this raucous God.**

Is there a melancholy here, a touch of sadness? Consider the phrase 'rainy veils'. Is the loss of virginity, innocence or youth being **mourned** through this poem? Perhaps the innocent phase of their love ends with marriage.

Marriage and the joy that these kinds of celebrations bring to the whole family, indeed community, is conveyed in the 'Dionysiac festivity' enjoyed by all. They are so affected by the jubilant mood of the drinking, singing and dancing it feels as if 'There could never be anything but dance and song'. There is a **very simple enjoyment** by the couple **of the different minute elements of the celebration**: 'Enjoying every song and speech / Enjoying every sip and every bite.'

Language and form

The poem is very **simple and straightforward**, with a relaxed speaker who uses phrases like 'dickied up', and easily changes his mind about using a metaphor. This lends a **conversational tone** to the poem and has the effect of suggesting that our narrator does not want to seem too 'poetic'. Perhaps he is concerned that we may doubt the veracity of his account if it seems too contrived. (Is 'dickied up' poking fun at the groom? Does he look incongruous in his blue suit for some reason?) This **informality** warms us to our narrator, and we might imagine him as a guest fondly watching the diversion of the event. **Even the rhymes are quite playful** and add a **lyrical**, **lilting effect** to the poem: 'habitual' and 'ritual', or 'loud crowd', for example. This casual effect contrasts with the almost grim formality in the words of the wedding ceremony: 'What God has joined together / Let no man put asunder.'

The tone throughout the account of the wedding suggests a **happiness to dwell in the moment**; contrast this with the urgency of the word 'must' (lines 40, 41). However, the rest of the poem, taking place in the train, is much calmer, even demure.

Note that the groom doesn't speak in the poem; we are only told his thoughts.

Does the simple and straightforward tone of the language conceal a darker subtext? Is the wedding day as much of an occasion for the couple as it is for their guests? They seem to observe the fun but we don't see them partake.

Questions

1	Why does the speaker reject snow as a metaphor for the bride's white dress in lines 1–6 of the poem?
2	How is the groom dressed? What is the effect of the word 'dickied'? Could the colour blue have any symbolism attached to it in the way that white often does?
3	Describe the mood and atmosphere of the wedding ceremony in lines 10–16 of the poem.
4	'Soon afterwards, the fun began.' Contrast the wedding reception with the church ceremony in terms of mood and atmosphere. Look closely at the poet's language in both sections.
5	How are the wedding guests seeing each other 'in a new way'? What factors, do you think, have brought about this change in them?
6	In lines 26–34, the bride and groom regard each other and observe the party. Describe and comment on this section.
7	'I must change'. The poem changes in terms of setting, mood and action at this point (line 40). Why does this change occur? Show how the poet conveys these changes in terms of his imagery and language.
8	'He never saw the white dress again' (line 42). What, do you think, does the white dress symbolise and consequently what is the significance of the groom's never seeing it again? Do you think this is a positive or a negative statement? Is the mood regret, contentment or something else?
9	Why, do you think, are the trees personified in lines 43–47, and what might they represent? Comment on the effect of their presence. Why are they 'reticent' and wearing 'rainy veils'?
10	'A tide of thoughts flowed'. What do you imagine the bride and groom are thinking in this section of the poem? Is the metaphor of a tide flowing effective?
11	In your opinion what is the effect of the last line? Is the bride content: are her words insincere and lacking enthusiasm or are they full of love? What do you think, and why?
12	What would you say is the main theme of the poem? ■ Love ■ Celebration ■ The importance of ritual ■ We can never truly know another ■ Something else
13	Compare and contrast this poem to 'Dear Autumn Girl'. Which did you prefer and why? Discuss in pairs or groups.
14	Imagine you were a guest at the wedding, and write your diary entry for the day.

Before you read

What does the word
'Fragments' suggest
to you?

Fragments

What had he to say to her now?
Where was the woman he believed he had known
In a street, out walking, by the sea,
In bed, working, dancing, loving the sun

And saying so, always for the first time?   5
Who was this stranger with the graven face?
What led to the dreaming-up of a home?
And what was he, at sixty? Who was

That man lifting the blackthorn stick
With the knobbed top from its place   10
At the side of the fire, quietly dying?

He listened to his own steps in the walk
Past the reedy mud where plover rose
And scattered, black fragments, crying.

Glossary

6	*graven*: serious, solemn; can also relate to a 'graven image', an idol carved from wood or stone and worshipped, i.e. a false god
13	*plover*: a type of wading bird with a short bill. A group of plover may be referred to as a stand, wing, or congregation

Sonnet

A sonnet is a fourteen-line poem made famous first by the Italian poet Petrarch and later by Shakespeare. The first eight lines generally outline a situation or problem while the last six offer some sort of deeper insight and / or offer a solution. Rather than offer a solution here, the man slowly and alone leaves the embers of his dying fire and walks alone out to the marsh thus enhancing his loneliness and despair.

Guidelines

'Fragments' is a sonnet where Kennelly uses **a series of questions** to explore the end of a relationship. If taken as a sequence to end 'Dear Autumn Girl' and 'A Great Day', the three poems seem to trace **the trajectory of a relationship** from courtship to demise.

Kennelly's marriage to Peggy O'Brien took place in 1969 and broke up in the early 1980s, perhaps inspiring these poems.

Commentary

Lines 1–7

A **rhetorical question** opens the poem, the first of six that the speaker will ask: 'What had he to say to her now?' The implication is that he can think of nothing. This causes the speaker to think back on their relationship, how it was and where it is now.

Here is a couple who have grown apart to the point where the man does not seem to recognise who the woman is now, and cannot recollect why they married. He recalls the energy and enthusiasm this woman brought to every part of her life; the use of **present participles** ('ing' words) creates a sense of **action and purpose**: 'walking', 'working', 'loving', 'saying'. This energy and love of the sun is reminiscent of the woman in 'Dear Autumn Girl'.

The woman used to tell him about her life but now they don't communicate; she has become a 'stranger with the graven face'. 'Graven' indicates that she has become serious, solemn, and she has lost her joy.

The speaker wonders what could have made them decide to get married; it now seems a crazy idea: 'What led to the dreaming-up of a home?' By saying 'dreaming' rather than 'setting', for example, the speaker seems to think their marriage was a flight of fancy, an idealistic whimsy rather than a decision based on good sense.

Lines 8–14

The focus in the sonnet now turns to the man, and the questions continue: who is this man, now sixty, who needs a stick and sits by a fire? The poet suggests that the man, like the fire, is quietly dying. In the final tercet the questions cease and the man goes out walking, hearing his own footsteps echo, totally alone. Out of the marsh a flock of plover rises into the air and scatters, looking like shattered pieces of something that was once whole, their screeching sounds like 'crying'.

Themes

The poem is about **the end of a relationship** and the strangeness of how two lovers can grow so far apart that they become strangers to each other, and even to themselves. Is **our memory so unreliable**, do we change so much that we cannot remember who we were and why we fell in love? For the speaker, it would seem that the answer is yes.

Time has passed and a couple have aged: her face is 'graven', and he is a sixty-year old man who must lift 'the blackthorn stick' to walk. **Phrasing his thoughts as questions** adds to the sense of **confusion and disbelief** the man feels at the changes time has wrought.

The pain of losing love is apparent, and so is the pain of ageing. The man, left alone and becoming more frail – like the fire, 'quietly dying' – has lost not only love and companionship, but also a sense of who he has become: 'What was he, at sixty?'

Language and form

Kennelly regularly uses **the sonnet form as a mode of interrogation**; here it explores the aftermath of a relationship which has shattered into 'Fragments'.

This sonnet is divided into two quatrains followed by two tercets, with only the final tercet absent of questions. **The poem is built on these questions**, which convey the disbelief and confusion of someone wondering where their life and their love have gone: 'What had he to say to her now?', 'Where was the woman … he had known'?, 'Who was this stranger'?, 'What led to the dreaming-up of a home?', 'what was he'?, 'Who was / that man'?

The poem is also **structured around present participles**. There is a striking contrast between those that pertain to the woman, which are **lively and upbeat** ('walk<u>ing</u>', 'work<u>ing</u>', danc<u>ing</u>', 'say<u>ing</u>'), and those that pertain to the man, which are much more **sedate** ('lift<u>ing</u> the blackthorn stick', 'the fire, quietly dy<u>ing</u>' and 'plover / … cry<u>ing</u>'). **The participle linking the two is 'dreaming'.** Is the speaker saying that this couple must have been too idealistic; perhaps even deluded, to think their relationship could have lasted forever?

The **plaintive rhyme**, in the final four lines, of 'dying' and 'crying' ends the poem on **a note of despair and regret**.

Imagery

The title represents the fragments of this relationship, something **once whole but now broken into pieces**. The man cannot comprehend how things have changed so utterly; **his memory is also a series of fragments**. He remembers how this woman once was in the past, but not how she became a stranger to him.

Our image of the woman in her youth is of someone who loves life, who has infinite energy and who doesn't lose an ounce of enthusiasm: 'loving the sun / And saying so, always for the first time'. But she has become a 'stranger' with a 'graven face'. The word 'grave' was used to describe the language of the wedding ceremony in 'A Great Day', so it is interesting that Kennelly should use it again as he describes a marriage that has died. A 'graven image' is a biblical term for a false idol that is worshipped in place of the true god, if Kennelly intended this connotation, what might it say about how the speaker views this woman now?

Three symbolic images are used for the man in the second part of the poem: the 'blackthorn stick', 'the fire, quietly dying', and the 'plover' which 'scattered' into 'black fragments, crying'. The stick is 'knobbed' – perhaps like the ageing man it is gnarled, twisted out of shape, **so too is the relationship** that has failed. Fire is often a symbol for life and passion, but **this fire is slowly going out** with no one tending to it and, as the word 'quietly' suggests, without a fuss. There is **an air of tired resignation to the image**. The plover too represents something broken and spent, silhouetted against the sky they are 'black fragments'; the blackthorn stick is also black, as are the dead embers of the fire. The **absence of colour** reflects the lack of love and passion in this man's life now.

Questions

1	'What had he to say to her now?' What, do you think, does the speaker mean by his first question?
2	From reading lines 2–5, what impression have you formed of the woman in her youth? Explain what you think line 5 means: 'And saying so, always for the first time'?
3	How has this woman changed? What, do you think, is suggested by 'this stranger with the graven face?' What might have caused this change?
4	'What led to the dreaming-up of a home?' Identify the tone here and comment on the use of the phrase 'dreaming-up'.
5	Look at the fifth and sixth questions asked in the poem (lines 8–11). What picture do they paint of the man in the relationship and what he has become?
6	'He listened to his own steps'. How does this image strike you? Does it imply loneliness, selfishness or something else?
7	Examine the images of the stick, the fire and the plover. What, do you think, do they represent? Are they connected in any way?
8	Why is the poem called 'Fragments'? Is it an effective title? Explain.
9	Look at the participles in the poem. Which are definite and which are ambiguous? Explain.
10	What is the tone of the poem? Does it change as the poem progresses? If so, where does it change and why?
11	The poem looks at the demise of this relationship largely from the man's point of view. Imagine you are the woman in the poem. Write an answer to each of the six questions asked in the poem, offering your perspective.
12	Read this poem as if it were the final instalment of the story told in 'Dear Autumn Girl' and 'A Great Day'. Working in groups or pairs, construct the story of the relationship, and investigate any signs that this relationship might not end well.

Before you read

Think about a poem you learned as a child that you have always remembered. It could be in a nursery rhyme or even a song. Write about it and explain why you think it has always remained with you.

The soul's loneliness

it's nothing to go on about
but when I hear it
in the ticking of the clock

beside the books and photographs
or see it in the shine   5
of an Eason's plastic bag at midnight

or touch it in the tree I call
Christ there outside my window
swaying in the day's afterglow

I shiver a little at the strangeness   10
of my flesh, the swell of sweat,
the child's poem I'll never forget

and find my eyes searching the floor
for a definition of grace
or a trace of yourself I've never noticed before.   15

Guidelines

From *Poetry My Arse* (1995). Pat Boran wrote in the *Irish Independent* about this collection that 'Much of Kennelly's power as a poet derives from his ability to explore the troubled psyche of a cast of characters (Cromwell and Judas are the best known of them, but there is also his poetic alter ego from his third 'epic' work, *Poetry My Arse*)'. This alter ego is 'the querulous anti-hero central character' Ace de Horner (a pun on Aosdána, a council of the elite of Irish artists and writers).

This poem like 'Things I Might Do', explores the situation of a speaker who seems **lost and in despair** at the state of his life.

Commentary

Stanzas 1–3

The opening line is conversational: 'it's nothing to go on about'; the poet almost dismisses what he is about to say before he says it. 'But' in line 2, however, intimates that this is something the speaker actually needs to discuss. We can take it that the 'it' in 'when I hear it' refers to the matter of the title, 'The soul's loneliness'. But is 'it' the soul or its loneliness? Clearly this is something the poet is sensing in everything around him, even the most mundane and familiar objects, all are infused with the loneliness of the speaker's soul.

He hears it 'in the ticking of the clock' which is 'beside the books and photographs'; he sees it in the glossy carrier bag of a bookshop in the middle of the night. He even feels it in the texture of a tree which is just 'outside my window'. This **list of senses** (hearing, sight, touch), and items (clock, bag, tree) tells us that the speaker is **experiencing a continual deep loneliness and anxiety**. He is awake 'at midnight' sensing it, and seeing it in 'the day's afterglow'. The fact that he calls the tree 'Christ' may imply **a spiritual need**, an emptiness that is causing him emotional pain.

Stanzas 4 and 5

This descriptive litany of the first three stanzas becomes **a more intense and frank expression of feeling**. The pretence of not-caring has worn through. The poet is very ill at ease with the loneliness of his soul: it causes a physical shaking and makes him perspire and feel as if he does not know his own physicality at all: 'I shiver a little at the strangeness / of my flesh, the swell of sweat'. Memories of a more innocent time, when life was perhaps simpler and more certain, cause this fevered reaction: 'the child's poem I'll never forget'.

The speaker finds himself scanning the floor, anxiously searching for 'a definition of grace'. He seems to be fervently seeking redemption, forgiveness, the blessing of God or perhaps love. He hopes to see 'a trace of yourself I've never noticed before'. Has a lover left him feeling lonely and abandoned, or is this a more spiritual search? Is he looking for Christ here, the comfort of faith? It is certainly a very **lonely poem** with the speaker just as unfulfilled at the end as he was from the title onwards.

Religious allusions

The speaker clearly seeks religious comfort to try and ease his 'soul's loneliness'. He looks to Christ, embodied in the tree outside, and searches for 'grace', a state of being blessed by God's love.

Themes

The **search for comfort and fulfilment** pervades the poem, set against a deep emptiness which dominates the speaker's life. He senses it all around him, especially as the day ends ('the day's afterglow') and he faces the night and evening alone: 'at midnight'. Religion is clearly bound in with this theme too; the mention of 'Christ' and 'grace' make this clear. These are not yet present in his life but he yearns for them to be: he has a 'tree I call / Christ', and his 'eyes searching the floor for … grace'. When we see how serious and painful the speaker's predicament is we must revisit the first line and wonder whether it's really 'nothing to go on about'. The very Irish trait of reserve is active here. Is Kennelly drawing our attention to **how the Irish find it hard to discuss feelings**, to have an open dialogue about depression and spirituality? He has been very critical of the 'half-heartedness' of the Irish nation and perhaps this poem challenges that. Actually depression, loneliness, emptiness is something 'to go on about', and the poem, which depicts a very lonely speaker suffering, 'shivering' and sweating alone at home in the middle of the night, emphasises the need to make it easier and more acceptable to have a frank and open dialogue about these issues.

Imagery and language

The sound of the clock's ticking indicates that time itself is full of 'The soul's loneliness'. Time moves interminably forward without any relief or comfort for the speaker. The 'books and photographs' don't appear to offer any comfort either. Kennelly wrote many books of poetry, fiction and drama. He was also a regular sight in the bookshops of Dublin as the 'Eason's plastic bag' shining on the floor reminds us. Is he saying that ultimately even the comfort of literature, writing or reading it, is not fulfilling him? The photographs suggest family, and **Kennelly's family life was another source of pain and loneliness**: his marriage had failed, his wife was living and working in the USA, and his daughter had moved there for a time.

Of course the speaker persona may not be Kennelly at all. It's rare to get a glimpse of the poet laid bare in his poems; it's more usual for him to create personas that engage in dialogues with each other to explore and often subvert societal conventions. This poem stands out as a **very simple and open admission of loneliness and pain**.

Soothing depression

In his blog on mental health issues, Anthony Wilson calls Kennelly's poems 'Lifesaving' and notes their 'redemptive healing qualities'. Here is a snippet of such a poem:

from **'A Time For Voices'**

**'May the silence break
and melt into words that speak
of pain and heartache**

**and the hurt that is hard to bear
in the world out here …**

**and the war on silence will end in defeat
for every heart permitted to beat
in the air that hearts make sweet.'**

The **lack of capitalisation**, even in the title, is striking. Capitals appear only for proper nouns: 'Eason's' and 'Christ', and for 'I'. This **makes the poem appear smaller, somehow diminished and laid bare**, just like the admissions of the speaker. The swaying tree that 'I call / Christ' combines religion and nature, and offers small comfort to the speaker in his deep need: 'when I / … touch it in the tree … / I shiver a little'. Here is a man **yearning** for something; but literature, family, religion, nature and love fail to fill the deep aching void inside his soul. These are all most likely things that did fulfil the speaker at one time. He finally finds himself searching the floor hungrily for a trace of solace, but the poem leaves him there: we don't see him find anything.

Questions

1	'it's nothing to go on about'. What, do you think, does the speaker mean by this? Why, do you think, has Kennelly not used a capital here?
2	What three senses are described in stanzas 1–3?
3	What, do you think, do the clock, the bag and the tree represent in the poem?
4	Comment on the effect of 'midnight' in line 6. Why, do you think, has the poet specified this time?
5	Why might the speaker have named the tree 'outside my window' Christ?
6	What effect does hearing, seeing and touching these objects have on the speaker in stanza 4?
7	Why does he mention 'the child's poem'?
8	As the speaker finds himself 'searching the floor' what two things is he searching for? Explain in detail and refer to the poem as a whole to explore why he might be searching for these things. What is the overall tone and effect of these last two lines?
9	Find three examples of sound effects in the poem and comment on their effect. You might notice rhyme, rhythm, sibilance, alliteration or assonance.
10	Why, do you think, has the poet used so few capital letters? Give examples from the poem in your discussion of this, remembering to include the title. Could the answer be in some way related to the first line of the poem?
11	What is the main theme of the poem in your opinion?
12	Write a letter to the speaker giving him advice and reassurance.
13	Compare the soul in this poem to the heart in 'Things I Might Do'.
14	Have a class discussion or debate on the topic of mental health in Ireland and the need for a more open dialogue around this.

Before you read

What is your idea of the place heaven? Describe.

Saint Brigid's Prayer

(from the Irish)

I'd like to give a lake of beer to God.
    I'd love the Heavenly
Host to be tippling there
    for all eternity.

I'd love the men of Heaven to live with me,   5
    to dance and sing.
If they wanted, I'd put at their disposal
    vats of suffering.

White cups of love I'd give them
    with a heart and a half;   10
sweet pitchers of mercy I'd offer
    to every man.

I'd make Heaven a cheerful spot
    because the happy heart is true.
I'd make the men contented for their own sake.   15
    I'd like Jesus to love me too.

I'd like the people of Heaven to gather
    from all the parishes around.
I'd give a special welcome to the women,
    the three Marys of great renown.   20

I'd sit with the men, the women and God
    there by the lake of beer.
We'd be drinking good health forever
    and every drop would be a prayer.

Guidelines

From Kennelly's 1998 collection *The Man Made of Rain*, which was written after the poet had major heart surgery. The collection is named after a vision of Kennelly's: he woke up after his operation to see a man made of rain, whom the poet began to converse with. Like 'A Cry for Art O'Leary', this poem is a translation by Kennelly from an Irish tenth-century poem attributed to the saint. Previously damning in his condemnation of the Catholic Church, Kennelly has grown more religious since his surgery and told a newspaper in an interview that, 'He goes to Mass in the church on Clarendon Street every Sunday. "I think I got married there as well."'

St Brigid was especially associated with beer. One legend concerning this was recorded by Cogitosus, an Irish monk who wrote the oldest existing account of her life, the *Vitae Sanctae Brigidea* (650 AD). The story goes that Brigid, a well-known beer lover and brewer, was approached by thirsty lepers who asked her for beer. Having none she noticed some baths full of water and blessed this. The water became beer and all drank gratefully from it. In the poem she extends her offer of beer to all those in heaven. **Kennelly was an alcoholic for many years** and often apologised publicly for things he had said or done while drunk. He has admitted to drinking up to 'three bottles of whiskey a day', until a doctor told him he would be dead within the year if he didn't stop. He gave up alcohol in 1986.

Commentary

Stanzas 1–3

Brigid speaks, expressing her wish to 'give a lake of beer to God', so that all those in heaven could 'be tippling there' forever. She'd like to live in heaven with God and all the men there, and imagines them singing and dancing. Brigid has not forgotten the suffering she will have left behind on earth, and will offer 'vats' of this to those who dwell in heaven.

The 'White cups of love' she would offer to those in heaven, 'with a heart and a half', may be a reference to the 'white martyrdom' – a voluntary exile Christian men and women would endure to bring them closer to God. The idea was that the loneliness and denial of withholding from oneself comfort, nourishment and companionship led to a purification of the soul, making it ready to accept God, do his work and dwell with him in heaven. The plentiful drink and friendly company in heaven were a just reward for this. 'Sweet pitchers of mercy I'd offer / to every man' reflects Brigid's famous **hospitality**, especially her **kindness** to the poor and to society's outcasts. Kennelly seems to find these attributes worthy of translation and inclusion in his collection, and Brigid's **all-encompassing welcome** is a stark contrast to the bleak loneliness of poems like 'Things I Might Do', 'The soul's loneliness' and 'Fragments'.

> **Brigit and St Brigid**
>
> St Brigid, whose feast day is celebrated on 1 February, was thought to have been born in 453 AD, the daughter of an Irish chieftain or druid. She went on to found many monasteries and was renowned for her hospitality and generosity to the poor. The most famous monastery was in Kildare (*cill dara*: the church of the oak hill), where nearby there is a pagan shrine to her (as Brigit), for Brigit was a pagan goddess of spring before her Christian incarnation. A number of wells in Ireland are named after her and many Irish homes still have a Brigid's cross hanging on a wall, especially above a door.

Stanzas 4–6

Brigid envisions a lively heaven; she'd make it 'a cheerful spot' where the men would be content and therefore honest, 'because the happy heart is true'. She thinks that making others happy, content and true would help 'Jesus to love me too'. Brigid's vision of heaven is inclusive: she's happy to welcome all, including those 'from all the parishes around' and especially 'the women, / the three Marys of great renown', i.e. Mary the mother of Jesus, his aunt Mary and Mary Magdalene.

All would sit together drinking and wishing each other good health eternally. From 'every drop would be a prayer', we can see that this is not a hedonistic vision of heaven, but one where **self-denial is at an end, and the spirit is rewarded with companionship and plenty**, while still cognisant of the importance of spirituality.

Themes

Generosity and inclusivity are strong themes here. Brigid's vision welcomes all, and her message is a simple one: our trials on earth, our good works and our efforts to please God and be closer to him will be rewarded with a very happy eternity at his side in heaven. The God and Jesus she depicts are happy to sit and drink side by side with men and women. Brigid acknowledges the suffering and sacrifices people have endured in the secular world to put their religion first, and will transform these 'vats of suffering' into vessels that contain her beer – 'White cups of love' and 'sweet pitchers of mercy'.

The **importance of companionship** is clear; there is a great sense of hospitality and togetherness and it seems to be this **friendly open sharing** that will make 'the happy heart' true. **Perhaps this is Kennelly's answer** to the predicament of the heart in 'Things I Might Do', and the soul in 'The soul's loneliness', both of which depict a painful void and a lonely yearning for joy and fulfilment, particularly in terms of spirituality.

Perhaps Brigid's vision appeals to Kennelly, who gave up alcohol in the mid-eighties. After this self-denial, maybe he can enjoy a drink again when he gets his reward in heaven.

Language, imagery and form

The repetition of 'I'd' emphasises Brigid's determination and her deep desire to see her happy vision of heaven realised. The many references to happiness create a joyful and cheerful mood, something we don't see too often in this selection of Kennelly's poems, where even those who do enjoy a modicum of happiness find it tempered by doubt and ambiguity. 'I'd love', 'tippling', 'dance and sing', 'cups of love', 'sweet pitchers', 'happy heart', 'contented' are examples and **every stanza contains this positivity and joy**, giving the character of Brigid an infectious exuberance and a generosity of spirit.

> **Imbolc**
>
> Brigid's feast day, 1 February, was a festival called *Imbolc* in pagan times. The Christian tradition often appropriated pagan deities, rituals and celebrations to make conversion to Christianity easier for people. Imbolc literally translates as 'i mbolg' – in my belly; the arrival of spring was celebrated with feasting and revelry. Some elements of Imbolc are also present in Shrove or Pancake Tuesday where people feast to prepare for a time when they will willingly go without in order to somehow purify themselves.

The **main image in the poem is of a feast**: there is a literal lake of beer with all of the 'Heavenly Host' gathered around companionably, toasting each other's 'good health forever'. This is quite a **pagan image**, reminding us that originally Brigid was a pagan goddess.

The beer and the vessels that contain it may have **metaphorical resonance**: the **beer representing the nourishment of spirit** and closeness to god in heaven, and the **vessels standing for the denial** and **suffering here on earth that will earn us that heavenly reward**.

In the six quatrains, the second and fourth lines rhyme (excepting stanza 3), giving the poem **a lyrical quality**. In fact the poem is **often set to music**, and several versions are available online.

Exam-Style Questions

Understanding the poem

1	What image of heaven is presented in lines 1–6? Were you surprised by this? Explain.
2	What vessels would St Brigid offer the men of heaven to drink their beer from? What does each represent?
3	How does Brigid intend to make heaven 'a cheerful spot'?
4	List the people that would be welcome to Brigid's lake.
5	How does Brigid ensure in the final stanza that the spiritual side of heaven is not neglected?

Thinking about the poem

1	What is the atmosphere of the poem? Is it completely positive and joyous or is there a darker side?
2	Does Brigid's vision of heaven appeal to you? Give a reason for your answer.
3	Do you feel that men and women are treated equally in Brigid's prayer? Explain.

Imagining

1	Where else in Kennelly's poetry have you encountered references to (a) religion and (b) strong women? Compare and contrast to this poem.
2	Compare Kennelly's translation to this version by Lady Gregory. Which do you prefer? Why?

'I would wish a great lake of ale for the King of Kings;
I would wish the family of heaven to be drinking it throughout life and time.
I would wish the men of Heaven in my own house;
I would wish vessels of peace to be given to them.
I would wish joy to be in their drinking;
I would wish Jesu to be here among them.
I would wish the three Marys of great name;
I would wish the people of heaven from every side.
I would wish to be a rent-payer to the Prince,
The way if I was in trouble He would give me a good blessing.'

SNAPSHOT

- Prayer
- Contrasts reward in heaven with sacrifices on earth
- Unusual image of heaven
- Joyous
- Pagan undertones
- Translated from the Irish
- Generosity
- Men and women equally welcome?
- Strong female voice

Exam-Preparation Questions

1	Compare and contrast the male and female voices and perspectives in the poetry of Brendan Kennelly.
2	Kennelly's biographer, Brisset commented on how Kennelly's poetry often 'emphasised the proximity between poems and prayers', and how he explores the 'Catholic faith but his verse is essentially pagan'. Would you agree with this assessment of Kennelly's poems?
3	Imagine you must choose five of Brendan Kennelly's poems for inclusion in a Leaving Cerificate Anthology. Which five poems would you choose and why?
4	Explore Kennelly's use of the sonnet form in his poetry.
5	Examine the theme of loneliness in Kennelly's poetry.
6	The function of poetry for Brendan Kennelly is to express 'the hope of connection both with oneself and with the outside world', according to J. McDonagh. Analyse Kennelly's poetry in the light of this statement.
7	How does Kennelly use nature in his imagery?
8	Write a letter to Kennelly in which you address the questions prompted for you from your study of his poetry. Refer extensively to his poems and your reactions to them.
9	The journalist Barry Egan commented after interviewing Kennelly that he was a 'potent amalgam of gentle charm, uplifting wit, joy, mystical inner voices and heart-breaking pathos, with a touch of the ribald, of the religious'. Do you agree with this in terms of Kennelly's poetry? In your answer refer to some or all of the qualities listed.

SNAPSHOT BRENDAN KENNELLY

- Religious language and imagery
- Variety of form including sonnets, lyric, letter, lament, etc.
- Explores human condition
- Use of a variety of personas
- Asks questions to explore themes and issues
- Strong females
- Relationships, loneliness and death strong themes
- Intense and introspective quality
- Powerful imagery

Sample Essay

Compare and contrast the male and female voices and perspectives in the poetry of Brendan Kennelly on your course.

Kennelly's women are far more confident, vibrant and sure of themselves than their male counterparts, who present as lonely, apologetic, lost and pitiful. The contrast is striking and I wondered why this was so. 'Bread' is a good poem with which to begin this analysis, as it has a male speaker (albeit an ear of wheat!) and a female persona. The male voice of the grain says, 'I am all that can happen to men. / I came to life at her finger-ends'. This seems to be the tale told by Kennelly's male characters: without women they are lost. The male voice wants to be moulded by the female baker, he longs for her to shape him and will endure mutilation and pain to achieve this: 'Even as she slits my face / And stabs my chest / Her feeling for perfection is // Absolute. / So I am glad to go through fire'. Kennelly's women are creators; they DO, they run, dance and love like 'Dear Autumn Girl'; they give and celebrate like St Brigid. Even in grief they are impressive in their determination and strength, like Eibhlín Ní Chonaill in 'A Cry for Art O'Leary'. While his men weep and bemoan their lot ('Fragments', 'Things I Might Do', 'The soul's loneliness'), Kennelly's women get on with the business of living. They have embraced the message at the end of 'Begin':

Straight into the heart of the question

Poems to be used are identified

'Though we live in a world that dreams of ending
that always seems about to give in
something that will not acknowledge conclusion
insists that we forever begin.'

This quotation will be repeated at end of answer as evidence of forethought and planning

Like the grain in 'Bread', the male voice in 'Dear Autumn Girl' is submissive and seems a poor match for the whirlwind of energy and action that is the woman he adores: 'I try but fail to give you proper praise'. She's made him feel alive, like 'an islander at sea' – she is an adventure for him. He is captivated by her zest for life and devil-may-care attitude: 'you walk smiling through a room / And your flung golden hair is still wet / Ready for September's homaged rays'. What has he to offer this wonderful woman? An apology and a blessing – 'I bless what you remember or forget / And recognise the poverty of praise'. This rather limp offering is not going to be enough for this woman and her 'helter-skelter' ways.

Clear contrast shown between male and female

In 'A Great Day', it seems to me that this relationship has moved on and the couple are getting married. The bride is stunning in her white dress – 'Such whiteness seems both beautiful and true', while the groom seems to me to be ill at ease in his unusually dapper attire – 'all dickied up in dignified blue'. It is the woman who makes the decision to leave and begin the wedding night; she wishes to be more than a virginal token of femininity and takes command of the situation: 'I must change, she whispered, / I must change my dress'. Her repetition of 'must' conveys her determination. By not giving the groom a voice in the poem (we hear only his thoughts, which are about how beautiful his wife is), Kennelly shows again that it is the female perspective which is the active one; the bride has the power here and the last word: '"Darling, it was a great day", she said.'

Dialogue used as example to support stance taken

'Fragments' is a poem from the male perspective which seems to take this relationship to the next stage. The marriage has broken down and the couple have grown apart, estranged from each other. The woman has grown resentful, while the man helplessly tries to figure out where it all went wrong. The man is bewildered by what has happened: 'What led to the dreaming-up of a home?' The first six lines describe his wife as she first was; very like the subject of 'Dear Autumn Girl', she is active and enthusiastic about life: 'the woman he believed he had known / In a street, out walking, by the sea, / In bed, work<u>ing</u>, danc<u>ing</u>, lov<u>ing</u> the sun // And say<u>ing</u> so, always for the first time'. But the man could not hold onto her, couldn't make her happy: 'Who was this stranger with the graven face?' If this man is the same one as the apologetic persona in 'Dear Autumn Girl' then it is no surprise the relationship ended. The portrayal of this man in the second half of the poem is a lonely one. He is broken by this loss of love, unlike Eibhlín Ní Chonaill in 'A Cry for Art O'Leary', which I will discuss in more detail later. The man takes up his 'knobbed' walking stick and leaves the fireside where he has been sitting, to walk by a marsh. Like himself and the passion in his marriage, the fire is 'quietly dying'; he goes out and sees the plover scatter in the sky, 'black fragments' like the shattered pieces of his life and love. Perhaps like him too the plover are 'cry<u>ing</u>'. Notice the difference in the hanging participles used about the woman and the man. His are laced with exhaustion, they signify his sadness and frailty and sit in stark contrast to the energy and action of those used for his wife.

The male voice and perspective becomes the focus now to provide balance

Clear comparison made between perspectives of genders

Imagery referred to – metaphor

Effective example using grammar to emphasise contrast between genders

'Fragments' offered its male persona no resolution, no option, no alternative to his lonely existence. Two poems where the male persona is similarly bereft are 'Things I Might Do' and 'The soul's loneliness'.

Progression and planning of argument

In 'Things I Might Do' the male speaker offers the reader a list of possibilities, as if seeking advice on what he should do with his damaged heart. He might fill it with October leaves like a chalice (a combination of pagan and Christian imagery that is typical of Kennelly) and use it to toast the end of the year. He could make it 'a small white church', or possibly something sexual rather than spiritual – 'a backroom of a brothel in Dublin'. What he can't give his heart is real love. He acknowledges that only 'somethinglikelove endures'. His heart might be a judge for itself, implying that there's a need for judgement. Does the speaker feel he has wronged someone? The final option for his heart is to be a bed for Judas as he dreams of suicide: 'dreaming of the tree'. Just as the owner of the heart sounds despairing, so is the figure he offers his heart to, Judas. After all of this torment and anguish a voice of solace interjects and offers a solution; this voice perhaps is female. It seems to be a mother or perhaps a lover: '"rest as best you can, / Darling … / And when you've rested, come home to me".' Although she is comforting, the female voice is also strong and unafraid to judge the man's 'treacherous head'.

Another poem where a lonely man searches for options and solace is the very bleak 'The soul's loneliness'. There is no female presence here to offer solace or solution. All we have is a bleak outpouring of loneliness and a fruitless search for meaning and love: 'searching the floor / for a definition of grace / or a trace of yourself'. The long poignant rhyme of 'trace' and 'grace' emphasises the speaker's despair. The soul here, much like the heart in the previous poem, seems lost and empty. The male voice and perspective in Kennelly's poetry often seems introverted; his

More development of poem needed here. This is not a 'well developed paragraph'

men gaze inward, contemplating their pain and loneliness. His women on the other hand seem to get on with the business of living without time for soul-searching or self-pity.

Take, for example, the robust no-nonsense voice of St Brigid in 'St Brigid's Prayer'. She is a joyful, enthusiastic character whose benevolent dream is to make heaven a companionable, fun and celebratory experience for the people there. Spirituality can be a social thing here, unlike the heart and soul's search for something spiritual in the last two poems, which were full of isolation and disappointment. Brigid welcomes all 'the men, the women and God' to sit by 'the lake of beer' she will provide, and 'be tippling there / for all eternity'. There's infectiousness about her energy and positivity, her zest for life (or afterlife) and her ability to see spirituality as something slightly pagan, where feasting and fun are totally valid ways of praising God. Brigid is not some unrealistic idealist either; she knows hardship exists in 'vats of suffering', but chooses to dwell on

Plenty of relevant quotation in this paragraph

the reward those who suffer for their belief will enjoy. It is hard to imagine Kennelly's male voices doing this. They seem to almost wallow in their pain. Brigid plans to turn heaven into a party where all are welcome and no heart is lost or empty, 'because the happy heart is true'.

Another, very different, female voice and perspective is that of Eibhlín Ní Chonaill, but she is equally active and robust in her attitude to life. She is also a force to be reckoned with in her heartfelt and powerful lament, 'A Cry for Art O'Leary'. Kennelly translated this 'caoineadh' of passionate love and thirst for vengeance from the Irish. Eibhlín has lost her love: he's been murdered by the men of the sheriff of Cork, Abraham Morris. Her heart is broken but she makes a conscious choice not to dwell on this or waste time mourning: 'I'll wear no cap / No mourning dress / No solemn shoes / No bridle on my horse / No grief-signs in my house / But test instead / The wisdom of the law'. Instead of the inertia we see in Kennelly's male characters, she is filled, or fills herself, with a resolute purpose to 'speak to the King', and if she doesn't get justice for her husband, Art, then she will 'find the man / Who murdered my man' and then have someone 'To put a bullet through your [Morris'] head'. Ní Chonaill's comment at the end of the poem is very pertinent to my analysis of Kennelly: she thanks the other women who have helped her compose and sing this lament, asserting that the poetry created by women is 'Deep women-rhythms of blood / The fiercest and the sweetest / Since time began'. Like the female baker in 'Bread', women are the primary force of creation in Kennelly's work.

The question has been addressed throughout and real knowledge of Kennelly's work is clear

Perhaps this emasculates his male personas, who don't feel as powerful or as in control.

I found Kennelly's men pitiable: they gaze ever inwards upon their pain and loneliness, doing very little to make their plight any better. His women on the other hand are captivating characters. I particularly enjoyed Ní Chonaill's intensity and Brigid's sense of sociable fun. Either of these could have been the 'Dear Autumn Girl' or the baker in 'Bread'. The only 'male' voice that was inspiring to me was the poet's own voice in 'Begin' –

'Though we live in a world that dreams of ending
that always seems about to give in
something that will not acknowledge conclusion
insists that we forever begin.'

If only the men in Kennelly's poetry had taken this sage advice! His women clearly don't need it!

*Notion of women and
creation explored well*

ESSAY CHECKLIST		Yes √	No ×
Purpose	Has the candidate understood the task?		
	Has the candidate responded to it in a thoughtful manner?		
	Has the candidate answered the question?		
Comment:			
Coherence	Has the candidate made convincing arguments?		
	Has the candidate linked ideas?		
	Does the essay have a sense of unity?		
Comment:			
Language	Is the essay written in an appropriate register?		
	Are ideas expressed in a clear way?		
	Is the writing fluent?		
Comment:			
Mechanics	Is the use of language accurate?		
	Are all words spelled correctly?		
	Does the punctuation help the reader?		
Comment:			

D. H. Lawrence

1885–1930

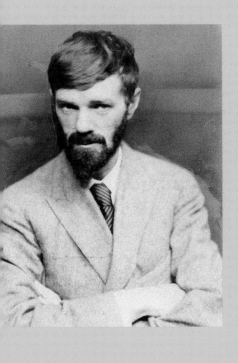

Biography

Early life

David Herbert Lawrence was born on 11 September 1885 in the small coal-mining town of Eastwood in Nottinghamshire in the midlands of England. His father, Arthur, was a miner, his mother, Lydia, worked at home making lace. It was not a happy marriage. Arthur could be violent, especially when he was drunk. Lydia was well educated, from a lower-middle-class background, and considered herself his social superior. She loved books, and encouraged her children to love them. Bert, as the future writer was then known, was very close

to his mother and so he did learn to love them. He was a frail boy, often in poor health, and preferred talking to fighting or sports. He got a scholarship to Nottingham High School but did not do particularly well there. After leaving school in 1901, he spent three years as a 'pupil-teacher' back in Eastwood.

His first serious attempts at writing were supported by Jessie Chambers, a girl from a nearby farm to whom he had become very close. As well as the prose fiction he was already writing, she encouraged him to write poetry. He studied for his teacher's certificate at University College, Nottingham, and in 1908 he went to take up a post as a teacher in Croydon, in the southern outskirts of London. He wrote energetically in the evenings and holidays, and in 1909 the *English Review* printed some of his poems that Jessie had sent in.

Lawrence was born into a mining town.

His first novel, *The White Peacock*, was accepted for publication in 1910, but his mother was dying of cancer and did not live to see it published. When she died in December, Lawrence was devastated, as you can see from 'Call into Death'. In November 1911 he became seriously ill with double pneumonia, the first clear sign of the tuberculosis that eventually killed him. He nearly died, was forced to give up his job as a teacher, and determined to make his way as a writer.

New life

In March 1912 he met Frieda, the wife of his Nottingham professor, Ernest Weekley, and fell in love. She was six years older than him, and from an aristocratic German family; her maiden name was von Richthofen, like the 'Red Baron', the ace fighter pilot of the First World War, to whom she was related. When she went to Germany that May, Lawrence went with her, determined to persuade her to leave her husband and children and stay with him. He eventually succeeded. Theirs was a passionate but stormy relationship, full of arguments and reconciliations. They finally married in July 1914 and Lawrence charted the progress of their love and marriage in a volume of poems, *Look! We Have Come Through!* The title says it all. He felt he was a new man with a new life, and most of his poems in this volume and later leave behind the old-fashioned metres and stanza forms that his early poetry had wrestled with, in favour of unrhymed 'free verse'.

The outbreak of war in 1914 saw the Lawrences trapped in England. His autobiographical novel *Sons and Lovers* had been published in 1913, and in 1915 *The Rainbow* appeared, but was swiftly banned. These novels are set in the industrial midlands of England where he had been brought up, but their power lay in how they explored human relationships at the deepest, most instinctive levels, laying bare the desires and conflicts previous novels had hardly more than hinted at.

The Lawrences moved to Cornwall, in the far south-west of England, but in 1917 they were expelled because there were suspicions that, Frieda being German, they might be spies. They were short of money and moved from place to place, often helped by friends and family, until the war ended.

Savage pilgrimage

Then, in 1919, they scraped together what money they could and set out on what Lawrence was to call his 'savage pilgrimage' in search of lives and cultures more in harmony with nature and instinct than the one he had grown up in. The first stop was Italy; then they moved ever further south until in February 1920 they came to Sicily and took a villa on the outskirts of Taormina, in the shadow of the volcano Mount Etna. There they stayed for two years and there Lawrence wrote many of the poems that became *Birds, Beasts and Flowers*, including 'The Mosquito', 'Snake' and, probably, 'Humming-Bird'. Bert Lawrence was now known as 'Lorenzo'. It was while they were there that *Women in Love*, generally considered Lawrence's finest novel, was published.

But the plan had always been to go to America, so in February 1922 they set sail for Ceylon (now Sri Lanka), taking the long way round the world. They stopped in Australia for a while, where Lawrence wrote the novel *Kangaroo*, and then went on to the United States, settling in Taos, an artists' colony in New Mexico.

There they stayed, setting up a ranch and taking journeys into Mexico to study the local culture, but Lawrence's tuberculosis had never gone away, and after a bad attack on a visit to Mexico in March 1925, the condition was finally and definitely diagnosed – although Lawrence would never really accept the truth of it. Because of his condition, the US authorities would not renew Lawrence's visa, so he and Frieda returned to Europe in September, where they settled for a while in northern Italy, near Florence.

Final years

The rest of Lawrence's life was overshadowed by his illness, which restricted his ability to travel and yet led to quite a lot of moving about in search of a climate or a doctor that might help him get better. It is a testament to the vitality that was still in him that he kept working so hard. He started to paint, and in 1926 he began work on his last, and most notorious, novel, *Lady Chatterley's Lover*. He also wrote *Etruscan Places*, a book about the burial customs of an ancient Italian culture, and *The Escaped Cock,* about Jesus after the resurrection. Death was clearly on his mind, but both those books focus on life – **the importance of the body and the life of the senses**.

In 1928 Lawrence and Frieda moved to a small hotel by the sea in Bandol, in the South of France. It was here that he wrote most of his late poetry, including *Pansies, Nettles* and the poems published posthumously as *Last Poems*.

After it was banned on its first publication in 1928, *Lady Chatterley's Lover* was unavailable for decades. Then, in 1960, Penguin published a cheap paperback edition in the UK. The publisher was prosecuted under the Obscene Publications Act, and a landmark trial took place, at which it was decided that the book was not obscene because it was a work of 'literary merit'. It marked the start of a more liberal attitude in publishing, and in society in general.

But Lawrence was still in conflict with authority. He was always determined to speak the truth as he saw it, however unpopular that sometimes made him. *Lady Chatterley's Lover* was published in Italy, but banned in the UK and the USA. His manuscript for *Pansies* was seized and cuts were demanded for the sake of decency. An exhibition of his paintings took place in London in 1929, but it was raided by the police and thirteen of the pictures confiscated because they were considered obscene: some of the images were sexual, and showed pubic hair.

The Lawrences visited Majorca, France and Bavaria in an attempt to find a place where his health might improve, but they returned to Bandol in September 1929. After a brief stay in a sanatorium in Vence, in the hills above the French Mediterranean coast, he moved himself out to a rented house, where he died the next day, 2 March 1930.

Social and Cultural Context

Lawrence as prophet

D. H. Lawrence was a one-off, as a man and as a poet. His working-class mining-town background did much to form him as well as provide material for his earlier writings, but he moved away from that background as a young man and kept on moving across the world for most of his life, following his instincts and impulses, **in pursuit of different ways of being**. As a poet, although he was at different times associated with both the 'Georgian' poets and the Imagists, he never saw himself as part of any movement. He knew and befriended – and often fell out with – many of the best-known writers and artists of his day, but he always went his own way.

In some ways he most resembles the great English poet and artist William Blake (1757–1827). Both were from working-class backgrounds, both wrote poetry and painted, and both were visionaries whose deeply personal and deeply held beliefs, both social and religious, ran against the current of their times.

What Lawrence believed, he believed with his whole being, sometimes against all the available evidence. This can make some of his pronouncements sound slightly crazy – all matter, he insisted in one book, including the sun and the moon, was formed of dead particles that had once been living things – but his conviction is always persuasive. When he writes about the inner life of a tree or a tortoise or a snake, he convinces you he knows what he is talking about – at least he absolutely believes he does. He was, perhaps, a prophet with a message for human beings about how they lived. He saw what he felt was wrong, and wrote in order to make it better. As he once said to a friend, 'If there weren't so many lies in the world … I wouldn't write at all.'

Lawrence the man

Being such **an isolated figure** in many ways, Lawrence's life and character are perhaps the best context in which to understand his writing.

His isolation had its roots in his childhood. He was a clever boy from a working-class background. As an adult, he never felt quite at home either among the more cultured people into whose world he was drawn or among the working classes whom he had left behind. The **tension** was there from the beginning, in the heart of his family, as a late poem makes clear:

> 'My father was a working man
>   and a collier was he,
> at six in the morning they turned him down
>   and they turned him up for tea.
>
> My mother was a superior soul
>   a superior soul was she,
> cut out to play a superior rôle
>   in the god-damn bourgeoisie.
>
> We children were the in-betweens
>   little non-descripts were we,
> indoors we called each other *you*,
>   outside, it was *tha* and *thee*.'

His relationship with his fellow men and women was never easy. Although he was a **passionate believer in the potential of human beings,** he was disappointed over and over again in the actuality of most of them, and he often found it hard to be among them. He could be wilful, arrogant, quarrelsome, and tended to push people away; but he was also passionate, energetic, charismatic and, to judge by the comments of those who knew him, very lovable.

Politically, he was torn. He could feel great sympathy for the plight of working people, whose lives he knew and understood better than most writers, but was disgusted by them at the same time; you can see the tensions at work in 'What Have They Done to You?' He was **not a believer in democracy** because he thought that people needed strong leaders to guide them. At the same time, he was no fascist, and despised Mussolini, the Italian fascist leader who came to power while he was living in Italy.

His **sexual politics** have come in for criticism in recent decades. His belief in the importance of sexual relationships, and his courage in writing about them, shocked many people at the time, but he did not advocate promiscuity. He considered sex a natural expression of a loving relationship, which should be free from shame. The fact that he viewed male and female roles as essentially different, and often in conflict, has drawn criticism from feminist critics. He liked to dominate, and could be a bully, but he didn't like subservient women. As he said of Frieda, she was 'the one possible woman for me, for I must have opposition – something to fight'.

Lawrence's **instinctive sympathy with the natural world** was free from the awkwardness of his dealings with people. Animals were always themselves or, as a late poem puts it: 'If men were as much men as lizards are lizards / they'd be worth looking at'. He developed his interest in the world of nature as a boy. Eastwood may have been a mining town, but it was surrounded by farms, and it was only a short walk to the fields or the woods, where the young Lawrence liked to spend his time. It is no coincidence that many of his finest poems are about animals, and his recognition of the **importance of man's relationship with the natural world** made him a pioneer of ecological thinking.

Free verse

When Lawrence started to write poetry he assumed poems should be like the neat Victorian verses he had grown up with: rhymed and metrical. But from the beginning **his instincts fought against this constriction**. He had things to say that did not always fit traditional forms.

His discovery of the work of the great American poet Walt Whitman (1819–1892) opened his eyes to another way of doing things. Whitman wrote about himself and the world he saw in **long, flexible, unrhymed lines**, which seemed **able to tackle any subject**. He is often known as the **father of free verse**.

Lawrence soon decided he didn't want to make neat poems perfectly shaped like gems or, to use an image he used himself, billiard balls – hard and clean-edged and separate from the world around them. **He wanted poems to open out, to respond to the moment-to-moment flow of thoughts and feelings, to be records of an engagement with something outside himself.** As Lawrence describes it in his essay 'Poetry of the Present':

> 'There must be the rapid momentaneous association of things which meet and pass on the forever incalculable journey of creation: everything left in its own rapid, fluid relationship with the rest of things.'

This is why free verse was his proper form. His voice can be heard, with all its assertiveness and humour. He can take hold of an image or a word and worry at it like a dog with a bone until it opens out and reveals its depths or another thought emerges out of it. In his poems **you can hear him in the process of discovering what he thinks and feels**, giving his subject his full attention, letting his imagination – his soul and mind and body – work. As he explained it, 'free verse is, or should be, direct utterance from the instant, whole man. It is the soul and the mind and the body surging at once, nothing left out.'

Free verse is not formless. Although Lawrence rejected the traditional metres and rhymes with which he had been brought up, he knew that **any good verse has a music and a shape of its own**, which should correspond with the thought or feeling it is expressing: 'I have always tried to get an emotion out in its own course without altering it. It needs the finest instinct imaginable, much finer than the skill of the craftsman.' By the 'craftsman' here, Lawrence means the sort of poet who makes verses in a traditional form.

Lawrence uses **repeated words and phrases to give shape to his poems**, and the music that comes from the **interplay of consonants and vowel sounds** is often very rich, and consists of much more than alliteration and assonance. Though there may be no definable metre, **there is always rhythm**, and the varying line lengths and line breaks that help to create those rhythms are skilfully handled.

In his best poems, where the thought or feeling has found its true expression, **form and content are in harmony**, and it is impossible to separate one from the other. That is not always the case, however, and sometimes it feels as though a thought has been put down in lines that might just as well be prose.

Themes

In the preface to his *Collected Poems* of 1928, Lawrence explained that he had tried to put the poems in chronological order 'because many of the poems are so personal that, in their fragmentary fashion, they make up a biography of an emotional and inner life'. He wrote many hundreds of poems, and all his thoughts and ideas and emotions were poured into them, so it is not easy to pick out individual 'themes' that run through them; there are just too many.

The cabin where Lawrence and Frieda lived in Taos, New Mexico in the 1920s.

Certain events, like the death of his mother or his love affair with Frieda, affected him deeply and he wrote about them in many poems. Other poems explore particular **encounters** – with a baby, a mosquito, a snake, even a bunch of gentians. He wrote, too, about sex, death, god, loneliness, industrialisation. What his poems have in common is **a fierce and passionate attention to the world, both inner and outer**:

> 'How marvellous is the living relationship between man and his object! be it man or woman, bird, beast, flower or rock or rain; the exquisite frail moment of pure conjunction.'

He wanted to find **his true relationship with himself, other people, animals, and the natural world** – to explore their otherness but also to understand his right relationship with them. And he wanted to bring his whole self to that exploration, body and spirit and soul. His outlook was always essentially religious, not materialist, but he was a pagan: **he saw multitudes of gods, and looked for gods in others**. He is focused on the snake's godhead in 'Snake', on the baby's in 'Trailing Clouds', the supreme godhead in 'Absolute Reverence', even his own in 'Bavarian Gentians'. He sees all creatures and all humans as sacred in their true nature.

> 'All things are relative, and have their sacredness in their true relation to all other things.'
>
> D. H. Lawrence, *Kangaroo*

Timeline

1885	Born on 11 September in Eastwood, Nottinghamshire, England
1901	Leaves school; meets Jessie Chambers
1902–06	Works as pupil-teacher in Eastwood
1906–08	Studies for teaching certificate at University College, Nottingham
1908–11	Teacher in Croydon
1910	December: mother dies
1911	January: first novel, *The White Peacock*, published; November: breaks down with tubercular pneumonia
1912	Meets and elopes with Frieda Weekley
1913	First poetry book, *Love Poems and Others*, published; *Sons and Lovers* published
1914	Marries Frieda, 13 July
1915	*The Rainbow* published, and banned for obscenity
1916	Moves to Cornwall; *Amores* published
1917	Publication of *Look! We Have Come Through!*; ejected from Cornwall
1919	November: 'savage pilgrimage' begins, first to Italy and Sicily
1920	*The Rainbow* and *Women in Love* finally published
1922	Visits Sri Lanka and Australia on the way to the United States; settles in Taos, New Mexico
1923	*Birds, Beasts and Flowers* published
1925	Diagnosis of tuberculosis; returns to Europe, settles in Italy
1926	Begins work on *Lady Chatterley's Lover*
1928	Publication of *Lady Chatterley's Lover*, banned in UK and USA; moves to Bandol in south of France
1929	Exhibition of his paintings in London
1930	Dies in Vence, 2 March

Before you read

What images are suggested to you by the idea of a sleeping baby? What feelings do these images bring with them? Discuss in small groups, then read the poem below to see how far the images and feelings in it overlap with the ones you talked about.

Baby-Movements II
'Trailing Clouds'

As a drenched, drowned bee
Hangs numb and heavy from the bending flower,
    So clings to me,
My baby, her brown hair brushed with wet tears
    And laid laughterless on her cheek,   5
Her soft white legs hanging heavily over my arm
    Swinging to my lullaby.
My sleeping baby hangs upon my life
    As a silent bee at the end of a shower
    Draws down the burdened flower.   10
She who has always seemed so light
    Sways on my arm like sorrowful, storm-heavy boughs,
Even her floating hair sinks like storm-bruised young leaves
Reaching downwards:
    As the wings of a drenched, drowned bee   15
    Are a heaviness, and a weariness.

Guidelines

When Lawrence left his home county to live and work as a teacher in Croydon, in the southern outskirts of London, in autumn 1908, he lodged with Mr and Mrs Jones, who had a baby daughter named Hilda May. He became devoted to the baby, and wrote a series of poems about her, of which this is one. It was first published in the *English Review* in November 1909, along with another of the baby poems called 'Running Barefoot'.

Commentary

Title

The first thing to notice is that the title of this poem is in quotation marks: 'Trailing Clouds'. This is a clue that the title is taken from a well-known line of a well-known poem, 'Intimations of Immortality' by William Wordsworth (1770–1850). In that poem Wordsworth writes about the innocence and even wisdom of childhood, putting forward the belief that an individual soul exists before birth, so that children are closer to God and more able than adults to see the divine in nature. So, in the words of Wordsworth's poem, children are born '*trailing clouds* of glory … / From God, who is our home'. This idea is discussed below under 'Themes'.

Lines 1–7

The poem consists of three sentences, which we will look at in turn.

The first seven lines make up one sentence, which takes the form of a simile: 'As … / So …'. The comparison is between a 'drenched, drowned' bee hanging from and weighing down a 'bending flower' (lines 1–3), and the baby clinging to the speaker, her hair wet with tears and her legs 'hanging heavily over my arm' (line 6) while the speaker sings a lullaby. The baby is closely observed: the damp brown hair on her cheek, and the 'soft white legs' which are 'Swinging', presumably to the rocking motion that accompanies the lullaby.

Who is speaking?

It is natural to think of the mother as the speaker of the poem; the baby, after all, is called 'My baby'. Lawrence, however, usually wrote in his own voice and of his own experiences. He was also, apparently, very attached to Hilda, and spent a lot of time playing with and caring for her and her sister, so it is quite possible that he may sometimes have thought of her as 'his' baby. Equally, he may have been fascinated with the bond between mother and baby, and adopted the **persona** of a mother in order to imagine himself into that place. What do you think?

Lines 8–10

The poem's second sentence reworks the image of the first seven lines. The baby is asleep, but the focus has shifted slightly to create the idea of the baby being a burden. The simple but strong statement of line 8 – 'My sleeping baby hangs upon my life' – may well suggest that this is the mother speaking. The sense that a mother feels the responsibility for, as well as the weight of, the baby is reinforced by the use of 'burdened' in the simile: if the baby is the bee, then the mother is the 'burdened flower'.

Lines 11–16

The final section of the poem again reworks the primary image, but develops and elaborates it. We learn that the baby 'has always seemed so light', in contrast to the heavy sorrow that is in her now. A new simile is introduced in line 12: the baby 'Sways on my arm like sorrowful, storm-heavy boughs', and her hair 'sinks like storm-bruised young leaves'. These images connect naturally with the image of the 'drenched, drowned bee', as they share the idea that a storm has passed, drenching and battering everything. What sort of storm was it? Does it have to do with the 'wet tears' that still cling to the baby's hair? Notice that, in this context, the poem's title might suggest a storm or a 'cloudburst'.

The final two lines return to the image of the 'drenched, drowned bee', focusing on its wings that are like the baby's damp hair. The last line uses two words that could be seen as defining the **emotional atmosphere** of the poem: 'heaviness' and 'weariness'.

Themes

One of the themes of the poem is the **burden of motherhood**, if we assume that it is the mother speaking. The baby is heavy in her arms, emotionally as well as physically; she 'clings to me' (line 3) and 'hangs upon my life' (line 8). The 'heaviness' and 'weariness' of the final line could describe a mother after dealing with her child's inconsolable tears.

The main focus of the poem, however, is on the baby. The 'heaviness' and 'weariness' are also hers. The speaker's attention is all on the her. There is **love** in the contemplation of the baby, and in the **delicate images from nature** with which she is described. But there is also distance. The baby isn't her normal self; she is 'laughterless', heavy instead of light, and her 'floating hair' is now sinking downwards. There is something **mysterious and unreachable** about the sleeping baby in this mood, and seeing her as a bee or the branch of a tree suggests that the life in her is more than – or other than – human.

This brings us back to the title of the poem, and the quotation from William Wordsworth discussed above. A child comes into the world 'trailing clouds of glory'. The idea that a child's soul exists before its birth implies that a baby has knowledge, experience, or a **divine innocence** that it is not conscious of. This perhaps, the title suggests, is the source of the mystery that the baby seems to hold for the speaker. There is **a loving wonder at the unknowable sleeping child** that balances the weariness.

Imagery

This poem works primarily through its images. You could almost say that the images are the poem. They convey a range of ideas and feelings. To take the central image of the bee on the flower: the bee is 'drenched', 'drowned', 'numb', 'heavy', 'silent'; all these adjectives describe **qualities that suggest the emotional as well as the physical state of the baby**. The relationship of bee and flower is also very suggestive. The bee drags the flower down with its weight; it is a burden, 'a heaviness, and a weariness'. The image of the bee at the flower suggests a baby suckling at her mother's breast. But a bee visits flowers to pollinate them as well as

Imagism was a movement among English and American poets in the early twentieth century that did not last long, but that influenced many of the major poets of the century, including T. S. Eliot, Wallace Stevens and Elizabeth Bishop. It rejected the forms and subjects of Victorian poetry, and aimed instead at clarity and concentration; poetry should be hard and clear and usually brief. The Imagists believed in using the language of common speech and they rejected regular metre in favour of free verse that could respond like a musical phrase to a particular image or idea.

take the nectar; the flower needs the bee as much as the bee needs the flower. So the image of the bee and the flower is powerfully suggestive of the bond between mother and child in both its negative and its positive aspects.

Lawrence was, for a while, associated with a group of poets who called themselves 'Imagists'. They believed in the power of the image to convey both emotions and ideas. Ezra Pound, a leading Imagist, wrote:

> 'An "Image" is that which presents an intellectual and emotional complex in an instant of time.'

'Trailing Clouds' could be described as an Imagist poem.

Form and language

Like other Imagist poems, 'Trailing Clouds' is written in 'free verse'. Although there is no regular metre, the sounds and rhythm of the poem have a distinct music of their own. Lawrence uses **clusters of long monosyllables**, often reinforced by alliteration, to give the effect of slowness and heaviness: 'drenched, drowned bee' (line 1); 'brown hair brushed' (line 4); 'soft white legs' (line 6); 'Draws down' (line 10); 'storm-bruised young leaves' (line 13). He also uses longer words and phrases where the stresses fall on the first syllable, creating **a falling quality** that suits the poem's mood: 'hánging héavily' (line 6); 'sórrowful, stórm-heavy bóughs' (line 12); 'héaviness … wéariness' (line 16).

Curiously, there is just one strong rhyme in the poem: 'shower' / 'flower' (lines 9–10). It seems almost accidental, as if Lawrence couldn't resist it. There is also a rhyme between 'bee' (line 1) and 'me' (line 3), but that is less obtrusive. Does the rhyme have a definite purpose, do you think? Or is Lawrence still struggling to escape from the conventions of traditional rhymed verse? This is an early poem. Perhaps what is most remarkable is how assured he is in using a non-traditional rhythm and form so early in his career as a poet.

The language of the poem is **rich in adjectives that give colour to the images**: there are five in the first two lines alone. The syntax is for the most part natural, and would make **good, clear descriptive prose**. The slight exception is in lines 3–4 'So clings to me, / My baby', where 'so my baby clings to me' would be more natural. Again, perhaps this is a trace of the 'poetic' language that Lawrence is trying to move away from.

One final feature to notice is Lawrence's **use of repetition**, a device which becomes more important in his later poetry, but which can already be seen in use here. The words 'heavy', 'heavily' or 'heaviness', 'hang' or 'hanging', and 'storm' are all repeated, as well as the phrase 'drenched, drowned bee'. The repetitions hammer home **key ideas** in the poem, and help to give it its **shape**.

Exam-Style Questions

Understanding the poem

1. Is the comparison of the baby to 'a drenched, drowned bee' a good one, do you think? Explain your answer.

2. What, do you think, has happened in the period of time leading up to the moment the poem depicts? Give reasons for your answer.

3. What state is the baby now in? Find words that support your answer.

4. What is the state of mind of the speaker of the poem? Give reasons for your answer.

Thinking about the poem

1. What is this poem about?
   - Parental exhaustion
   - Parental love
   - The glory of a baby
   - The mystery of a baby

2. How would you describe the mood of this poem?

3. Comment on the use of rhyme in lines 9–10 ('shower / … flower'). What is the effect of this rhyme?

4. Comment on the use of alliteration in this poem.

5. How would your reading of the poem change if you thought of it as being spoken by a man instead of a woman?

Imagining

1. Write a diary entry for the speaker of this poem describing the events of the day described in the poem.

2. Draw or paint a picture of the scene in this poem, or one inspired by the images of this poem.

SNAPSHOT

- Theme of the mother–child relationship
- The mystery of the baby 'trailing clouds of glory'
- Mood of heaviness and weariness
- Free verse with a distinct music
- Poem works primarily through its images
- Use of repetition for key ideas

Before you read

What does the title 'Call into Death' suggest to you about what the subject of the poem might be? How might it be different if it was called 'Call to Death'?

Call into Death

Since I lost you, my darling, the sky has come near,
And I am of it, the small sharp stars are quite near,
The white moon going among them like a white bird among snow-berries,
And the sound of her gently rustling in heaven like a bird I hear.

And I am willing to come to you now, my dear,   5
As a pigeon lets itself off from a cathedral dome
To be lost in the haze of the sky; I would like to come
And be lost out of sight with you, like a melting foam.

For I am tired, my dear, and if I could lift my feet,
My tenacious feet, from off the dome of the earth   10
To fall like a breath within the breathing wind
Where you are lost, what rest, my love, what rest!

Glossary

10   *tenacious*: something that keeps a firm hold; determined

Guidelines

This is one of many poems Lawrence wrote in response to the death of his mother, to whom he was extremely close, in 1910. It is not known exactly when this poem was written, but it was first published, under the title 'Elegy', in *Amores* in 1916. The title was changed when the poem was included in Lawrence's *Collected Poems*, published in 1928.

Commentary

The poem is addressed to 'you', who is called 'my darling', 'my dear' and 'my love' at different points. Although we know that Lawrence was writing about his mother, the language that he uses could also suggest a lover. When you read the poem, who do you imagine is being spoken to?

Stanza 1

The poem opens by evoking the feelings that the loss of a loved one ('my darling') has brought, using **a strange and striking image**: he feels as if 'the sky has come near', and that he is 'of it' – in other words, part of it. It is as if he is up in the heavens, with the stars close around him and the moon like a bird among the white 'snow-berries', as he describes the stars. There is something **hallucinatory** about the image, which is both somewhat **surreal and intensely vivid**; he even imagines he can hear the moon 'gently rustling'.

Stanza 2

The second stanza introduces the idea of coming to the dead person, and so by implication joining her in death. The speaker says he is 'willing' to do this. That word could be read in two ways – either as passive resignation (he is willing to let himself be taken) or as active intent (he is positively willing – wanting – that to happen). Which reading, do you think, best suits the mood of the poem? The image he uses here is of a pigeon taking off from the dome of a cathedral and being 'lost' in the sky. The word 'lost' is repeated in the next line when he says he would like to be 'lost out of sight with you' and dissolve 'like a melting foam'.

> **Mourning his mother**
>
> 'Then, in that year [1910], for me, everything collapsed, save the mystery of death, and the haunting of death in life. I was twenty-five, and from the death of my mother, the world began to dissolve around me, beautiful, iridescent, but passing away substanceless. Till I almost dissolved away myself, and was very ill.'
>
> D. H. Lawrence, Foreword to *Collected Poems*

Stanza 3

The third stanza explains the speaker's state of mind a little further: he is 'tired' and longs for 'rest' – the word that ends the poem. Lines 9–10 return to the image of the pigeon taking off, but now the dome is 'the dome of the earth' and the feet on it are human and 'tenacious': they cling to the earth and to life in spite of the speaker's desire to be lost in death. That desire is again expressed in line 11 with the image of a breath being engulfed by the 'breathing wind'. Notice that he speaks of falling – 'To fall like a breath' – where earlier the imagery had been of taking off. Is this a failure of the poet's control over his material, do you think, or is the disorienting reversal of up and down a deliberate effect?

Themes

The main theme of the poem is **death**, and **the reaction to the death of somebody deeply loved**. But rather than the outpouring of grief and despair that one might expect, the pain of bereavement has brought the speaker to a place where he imagines himself in a **new, expanded relationship with the world**. The pain is in the background, and the feelings Lawrence explores have to do with **lightness and bigness**. They bring with them the possibility of a sort of spiritual union, not just with the dead person but with the world itself, in which

the self is dissolved into the universe. Death is one of Lawrence's recurring themes, as we will see especially in 'Bavarian Gentians', one of his final poems, but it is remarkable that even in this early poem he sees death as a source of beautiful mystery, even comfort, and not just of terror. Note that the title of the poem is 'Call **into** Death', as if death were something in which you could be embraced or engulfed.

Imagery

The images used have been discussed in the Commentary section on page 259, as they are absolutely central to the poem, and are the main means by which it achieves its effects. Each image powerfully suggests the grief-stricken, sensitised, yearning state of mind of the speaker. The main images are of the **heavens** – the sky, stars and moon; the white bird and berries; the pigeon taking off and disappearing; **a breath** in the wind. They are all to do with **air** and/or the **sky**, in one way or another; there is a **lightness and expansiveness** to all of them, a lightness which increases as the poem goes on, so that the final image is of pure air: 'a breath within the breathing wind' (line 11). Many of them also involve the idea of dissolving or disappearance: the pigeon being 'lost in the haze of the sky', the 'melting foam', the single breath vanishing into the 'breathing wind'.

Form

'Call into Death' is written in three four-line stanzas (quatrains). Lawrence does not adhere to a strict form, however. There is no regular metre, but a slow, rather **languid** rhythm that tends to **fall away** towards the ends of the lines and helps create the sense of tiredness that is expressed at the end of the poem.

The use of rhyme is odd. The first stanza has a tight *aaba* pattern. The second takes up the *a* rhyme with 'dear' in line 5, and then all three other lines rhyme (*accc*), although 'come' (line 7) is really a half-rhyme. In the third stanza, however, none of the end words rhyme with each other or with words in the first two stanzas. You could argue that this mirrors the sense of **dissolution** (dissolving) that the poem describes.

We should also take into account Lawrence's ongoing engagement with rhyme in his poems. Most of his early poems use rhyme. The poetry he was brought up with used rhyme, and when he started writing poems he naturally followed the models he knew, assuming that poems should rhyme and have a clear form. In this poem he seems to have begun in this mode; in fact, he uses a rather awkward 'poetic' inversion of the word order in line 4, where it would be more natural to say 'And I hear the sound …', simply for the sake of the rhyme on 'hear'. Similarly, in the second stanza, you might think that the image of 'melting foam' is chosen more for the rhyme than its appropriateness, as it does not quite fit with the imagery of sky and air elsewhere. In his mature poems, however, Lawrence avoids rhyme or any sort of regular metre, and finds a loose style that suits what he wants to say and how he wants to say it. Perhaps, in the third stanza of 'Call into Death' he has simply **let his need to express what he wants to say take precedence over his desire to craft a 'well-made' poem.**

Language

The language of the poem is **intimate**, conversational, sometimes almost banal (the stars are 'quite near', line 2), and the striking images are expressed in **plain words**. There is even something childlike about the simple expression of the speaker's thoughts and desires: 'the sky has come near'; 'I am willing to come to you now'; 'I would like to come'; 'I am tired'.

There is something quite innocent, too, about the repetition of certain key words: 'near', 'white', 'bird', 'sky', 'lost', 'feet', 'rest'. Repetition was to become a key stylistic feature of Lawrence's later poetry, and we can see here how he is learning to use it to **keep the ideas of a poem fresh**, and give them the feel of being thought out **in the moment** of the poem's creation.

Questions

1	In your own words, describe the feelings expressed in the first stanza.
2	What impression do you get of the speaker from the first stanza?
3	In stanza 2, how does the speaker imagine he will 'come to you'? What sort of emotion does that suggest?
4	What is the overriding mood of stanza 3?
5	What is the effect of the word 'tenacious' (line 10)? What does it tell you about the speaker?
6	If you didn't know that this poem was about the poet's mother, do you think you could guess that from the poem? Why or why not?
7	In your own words, how does the speaker imagine the experience of reunion with the beloved?
8	Pick one image from the poem and say why you like it (or don't like it) and what it makes you feel.
9	Comment on the use of rhyme in the poem.
10	Are there any parts of the poem that ring false or feel 'wrong' to you? If so, explain why.
11	Imagine that Lawrence's dead mother could read this poem and respond to her living son. What would she say to him?
12	Have you ever felt the wish – or the need – to dissolve or disappear for any reason? Write your own poem about that feeling.

Before you read

Sounds, tastes and smells can often trigger memories. Discuss, in pairs or small groups, any experiences you have had when a sound, taste or smell has brought back a memory from your past.

Piano

Softly, in the dusk, a woman is singing to me;
Taking me back down the vista of years, till I see
A child sitting under the piano, in the boom of the tingling strings
And pressing the small, poised feet of a mother who smiles as she sings.

In spite of myself, the insidious mastery of song   5
Betrays me back, till the heart of me weeps to belong
To the old Sunday evenings at home, with winter outside
And hymns in the cosy parlour, the tinkling piano our guide.

So now it is vain for the singer to burst into clamour
With the great black piano appassionato. The glamour   10
Of childish days is upon me, my manhood is cast
Down in the flood of remembrance, I weep like a child for the past.

Glossary

2	*vista*: a far-reaching view
4	*poised*: neatly balanced
5	*insidious*: something harmful that works gradually without being noticed
8	*parlour*: a room usually set aside for entertaining guests
9	*vain*: useless
9	*clamour*: loud, emotional noise
10	*appassionato*: Italian musical term meaning 'full of passion'
10	*glamour*: enchantment; magical spell
11	*cast*: thrown

Guidelines

'Piano' is one of the most accomplished, and best known, of Lawrence's early rhyming poems. In it he recounts an experience of listening to a woman singing at the piano, which brings back memories of his mother playing the piano when he was a child. The first version of the poem was written in 1908, when his mother was still alive. He revised it in 1916, and again in 1918 for publication in *New Poems*, when its title was changed from 'The Piano' to 'Piano'.

Commentary

Stanza 1

The first line establishes a mood, with a woman singing 'softly'; it is evening ('dusk') and there is a sense of intimacy: she is singing not to a roomful of people but 'to me'. Line 2 describes a common but powerful sensation – a memory from years before evoked by the senses. Sometimes a smell or the taste of food can do it; here it is music. Lawrence sees himself as a child 'sitting under the piano, in the boom of the tingling strings'. 'Boom' and 'tingling' may appear strange words to describe the sound of a piano, but

> **'Piano'**
>
> The first word of the poem, 'Softly', is a translation of the poem's title. As well as being the name of a musical instrument, 'piano' is the Italian word for softly or gently. So the title of the poem indicates the mood at the beginning, as well as naming the central object in it.

if you imagine it as an upright piano, with the child squeezed in under the keyboard, his back to the wooden sounding board, it makes sense. Those words describe the **physical sensation** of the piano felt through his back rather than heard through the ears. Lawrence had an extraordinary memory for details of things he had seen, heard or felt. He didn't use notebooks to jot things down, but relied on his memory.

The fourth line tells us that in this memory his mother is playing the piano and singing – a quite different woman from that in the first line. The memory seems a comforting one: his mother is smiling, her feet are 'poised' and the child is 'pressing' them. The image suggests how much he **depends** on her reassuring presence.

Stanza 2

The second stanza describes the speaker being **overpowered** by the memory that the music has awakened in him. He longs to be that child again, and to 'belong' (line 6) to that comforting old life.

Notice, though, that he struggles against this desire, and regards it as a negative thing. He is emotionally affected 'In spite of myself', calling the powerful effect of the woman's singing 'insidious' – a word that always implies a harmful outcome. The song of line 1 'Betrays me back': he doesn't want to get sentimental about the past, it is a betrayal of his adult self, but he can't help it.

Despite himself, the feelings that the memory evokes are very strong: 'the heart of me weeps' with the desire to be a child again. This is nostalgia – the yearning for a happy time that is past. But nostalgia is always for something idealised and unreal. Lawrence did not have a happy childhood. His often drunk and sometimes violent father is not in the picture in this poem, nor are his parents' rows. Their parlour was not always 'cosy'. But in this mood he remembers what he wants to remember: family hymn-singing in a warm room, with his mother playing the piano as 'guide' to the singers.

Stanza 3

Line 9 brings us back to the present, and now the singer from the poem's opening breaks into a different song, a loud ('clamour') and passionate one, to judge by the words Lawrence uses. We get a glimpse of the 'great black piano', a grand piano rather than the upright one his mother played, that is now playing 'appassionato'. But the speaker is unmoved by this, caught up in his memories. It is like **a magic spell or enchantment** – a 'glamour' – and he is powerless to resist. His 'manhood' is 'cast / Down' (notice the lurching effect of the line break between those two words); memories overwhelm him like a 'flood' and he weeps 'like a child for the past'.

Themes

It is easy to misread 'Piano' as a sentimental poem that wallows in nostalgia. That is because it evokes very powerfully the **experience of being overwhelmed by nostalgia**, an experience most of us can recognise and which we know can be overpowering. In reading the poem, it is easy to give way to the sentimentality it evokes, just as it was impossible for Lawrence to resist its pull in the scene he describes in the poem. Perhaps it is better to think of 'Piano' as a poem *about* sentimentality. Certainly it is a more **conflicted**, even tortured, poem than it might at first appear. The second stanza gives the clearest evidence of this, as discussed above.

One of the poem's main themes is the **conflict** between the adult man and the child he had been and still sometimes wishes he could be. Like most of Lawrence's poems, 'Piano' is autobiographical. Behind it lies a personal history, which Lawrence wrote about in his great novel *Sons and Lovers*, of his close relationship with his mother and his long struggle to break free of her influence and become 'his own man'. This occurred primarily through his relationship with other women – notably the one he calls 'Miriam' in *Sons and Lovers* – until he met and eloped with Frieda Weekley in 1912. In 'Piano', the woman singing 'to me' at the beginning and later

'burst[ing] into clamour' (line 9) with the piano 'appassionato' (full of passion) can be seen as standing for **the possibility of an adult sexual relationship**. His mother clearly represents the draw of his childhood self. In the poem the childhood self wins and his 'manhood' is defeated, much to the speaker's regret.

Lawrence wrote the final version of the poem many years after his mother's death, after his marriage to Frieda and the volume of poems which charts his escape from his old self, *Look! We Have Come Through!* (1917). 'Piano' records a conflict in himself which the mature Lawrence had gone beyond, but which he remembered and respected well enough to bring vividly to life. Perhaps it was also his way of saying goodbye to his old self.

Imagery

We have already looked at the two main images of the poem: the contrasting scenes of the woman singing to the grand piano in the present and the mother leading hymn-singing at the upright piano in the past. You could say that the two images represent the **conflicting claims on the speaker's soul**.

Another thread of imagery that runs through the poem is to do with the **movement from the present towards the past** that the speaker undergoes. 'Taking me back' in line 2 contains the idea of being taken on a journey or transported, just as people sometimes say that they were 'transported' by an emotion. In the second stanza, 'Betrays me back' carries the same idea. Its culmination comes in the final stanza when the force that is carrying the speaker back becomes a 'flood of remembrance' (line 12) that carries away his 'manhood'. That flood is also perhaps connected to the weeping mentioned in line 6 and the tears at the end. The **flood of memory** and the weeping become almost the same thing.

Form and language

'Piano' is written in three four-line stanzas (quatrains) rhyming *aabb*. It has a basic metre that is anapaestic; in other words it is largely made up of **anapaests**, which are metrical feet consisting of two unstressed syllables followed by a stressed one. You can see that most clearly in the second line, which is regular except that it starts with a stressed syllable: 'Tákǐng mě báck dǒwn thě vístǎ ǒf yéars, tǐll Ǐ sée'. There are five stresses in most lines, but six in the fourth line of each quatrain (as well as line 3), with a definite **caesura** (pause) in the middle of the longer lines. The metre is handled flexibly, but it does give the verse **a soothing, lilting rhythm**. In fact, it is notable how well Lawrence contains his ideas in this poem within a relatively strict verse form.

While the language in 'Piano' doesn't have the ease or the characteristic conversational voice of his mature poetry, it is not filled with 'poetic' vocabulary. Though there are some conventional phrases, like 'vista of years' (line 2), the words are **carefully chosen**. Look at line 8, where the words 'cosy' and 'tinkling' are both rather childish. Is Lawrence being drawn into the sentimental picture of the happy hymn-singing in the warm parlour, or is he using those words to indicate that he knows that the picture is sentimental, and that he can see through it?

Questions

1	In your own words, describe the two scenes – present and past – that Lawrence depicts in this poem.
2	How would you describe the mood in stanza 1?
3	In stanza 2, what is there to indicate that Lawrence would like to resist the power of his memory?
4	What is there in the language to suggest that the memory of Sunday evenings in the parlour might be a false, or at least an incomplete, one?
5	Why is it 'vain' for the singer to 'burst into clamour' (line 9)?
6	How would you describe the mood at the end of the poem?
7	Do you think that this is a sentimental poem? Explain your answer.
8	Why, do you think, does Lawrence write 'A child' and 'a mother' in stanza 1, rather than 'myself' and 'my mother'?
9	Comment on the use of the word 'clamour' in line 9. Is it a good choice of words?
10	In line 11 Lawrence might have written 'childhood days' instead of 'childish days'. Comment on the effect of the word he actually chose.
11	Write a diary entry for the speaker for the evening on which the experience described in the poem occurs.
12	Write about your earliest clear memory, or an important early memory, in as much detail as you can.

The Mosquito

When did you start your tricks,
Monsieur?

What do you stand on such high legs for?
Why this length of shredded shank,
You exaltation?   5

Is it so that you shall lift your centre of gravity upwards
And weigh no more than air as you alight upon me,
Stand upon me weightless, you phantom?

I heard a woman call you the Winged Victory
In sluggish Venice.   10
You turn your head towards your tail, and smile.

How can you put so much devilry
Into that translucent phantom shred
Of a frail corpus?

Queer, with your thin wings and your streaming legs   15
How you sail like a heron, or a dull clot of air,
A nothingness.

Yet what an aura surrounds you;
Your evil little aura, prowling, and casting a numbness on my mind.

That is your trick, your bit of filthy magic: 20
Invisibility, and the anaesthetic power
To deaden my attention in your direction.

But I know your game now, streaky sorcerer.
Queer, how you stalk and prowl the air
In circles and evasions, enveloping me,   25
Ghoul on wings
Winged Victory.

Settle, and stand on long thin shanks
Eyeing me sideways, and cunningly conscious that I am aware,
You speck.   30

I hate the way you lurch off sideways into air
Having read my thoughts against you.

Come then, let us play at unawares,
And see who wins in this sly game of bluff.
Man or mosquito.   35

You don't know that I exist, and I don't know that you exist.
Now then!

It is your trump,
It is your hateful little trump,
You pointed fiend,   40
Which shakes my sudden blood to hatred of you:
It is your small, high, hateful bugle in my ear.

Why do you do it?
Surely it is bad policy.

They say you can't help it.   45

If that is so, then I believe a little in Providence protecting the innocent.
But it sounds so amazingly like a slogan,
A yell of triumph as you snatch my scalp.

Blood, red blood
Super-magical   50
Forbidden liquor.

I behold you stand
For a second enspasmed in oblivion,
Obscenely ecstasied
Sucking live blood,   55
My blood.

Such silence, such suspended transport,
Such gorging,
Such obscenity of trespass.

You stagger   60
As well as you may.
Only your accursed hairy frailty,
Your own imponderable weightlessness
Saves you, wafts you away on the very draught my anger makes in its snatching.

Away with a paean of derision,   65
You winged blood-drop.

Can I not overtake you?
Are you one too many for me,
Winged Victory?
Am I not mosquito enough to out-mosquito you?   70

Queer, what a big stain my sucked blood makes
Beside the infinitesimal faint smear of you!
Queer, what a dim dark smudge you have disappeared into!

Glossary

4	*shredded shank*: legs like shreds
5	*exaltation*: here, an elevated thing
7	*alight*: land
13	*translucent*: semi-transparent
14	*corpus*: here, body
18	*aura*: atmosphere or energy that surrounds a particular thing
21	*anaesthetic power*: power of putting to sleep or making something unconscious
24	*stalk and prowl*: follow and move about quietly (while hunting)
38	*trump*: trumpeting sound
46	*Providence*: fate
47	*slogan*: here, war cry
53	*enspasmed*: put into spasms
54	*ecstasied*: made ecstatic, i.e. extremely happy, even to the point of excess
57	*transport*: extremely pleasurable emotion
58	*gorging*: greedy eating or consuming
63	*imponderable*: something that cannot be weighed or evaluated
65	*paean*: hymn (usually of praise)
65	*derision*: ridicule or mockery
72	*infinitesimal*: extremely small

Guidelines

Genesis of the poem

The first draft of 'The Mosquito' was written in Siracusa in Sicily. Lawrence and Frieda stayed in the Grand Hotel there, which he described as 'a rather drear hotel – and many bloodstains of squashed mosquitoes on the bedroom walls'.

'The Mosquito' was written in Sicily in May 1920, and first published in the collection called *Birds, Beasts and Flowers* (1923). In this volume Lawrence focuses his attention on different animals and plants, imagining his way into **an understanding of their nature**. He wrote these poems in free verse that gives a sense of his mind working and his voice speaking. They are generally regarded as some of his finest poems.

Commentary

In this poem Lawrence observes a mosquito, and explores his feelings about and relationship with it. Notice, though, that it also tells the story of the **encounter** between man and mosquito, ending with the insect's death.

Lines 1–8

The poem starts with a series of questions addressed to the mosquito. He calls the mosquito 'Monsieur', and what he does 'tricks'. His attitude is ambiguous: 'tricks' suggests something underhand, whereas 'Monsieur' might suggest respect, but it might also be mocking. Think about what the word conjures up for you.

Lawrence is clearly looking closely at the mosquito, wanting to know why his thin legs ('shredded shank') are so long. He finds another word for him: 'exaltation' (line 5). Though the word is usually used to describe a feeling of joy, it also carries the meaning of something elevated, which is presumably what the poet is thinking of here, as he goes on to consider how the mosquito's long legs raise up the insect's body – its 'centre of gravity' – and make it so light that it cannot be felt on his skin. He is trying to understand how a mosquito operates.

Lines 9–17

As he watches and thinks, other ideas and observations occur to him. Another name is added to the growing list he has given the mosquito: 'Winged Victory'. This is a reference to a famous ancient Greek statue in the Louvre Museum in Paris. Unlike that statue, however, the mosquito has a head, which is turned towards its tail. Lawrence imagines that it smiles. It is clear from the following line what sort of smile he thinks it is – one of 'devilry' (line 12). He is **projecting human motivations and characteristics onto the insect**. He is fascinated by the creature, but far from friendly towards it.

The mosquito must have taken off because in lines 15–17 Lawrence observes it in the air, and tries to find images or words to define it. It is like a heron, which also flies with its legs trailing behind it; but this is immediately followed by another, very different image – 'a dull clot of air' – and then just a 'nothingness'. All the images are prefaced by the word 'Queer' (line 15), which suggests the non-human strangeness of the creature and also carries a slight sense of distaste.

Lines 18–23

In these lines Lawrence seems to reach an insight into what makes the mosquito 'tick'. He writes of an 'aura' in line 18, and repeats the word in the next line, making it clear how he feels about it: 'Your evil little aura'. What is this aura? It seems to be something like a spell that casts 'numbness' on his mind. Lines 21–22 define it further: 'Invisibility, and the anaesthetic power / To deaden my attention in your direction'. It is as if it hypnotises him. This, he says, is the mosquito's 'trick', a 'bit of filthy magic'. Notice how the words here pick up on each other, and on ideas from earlier in the poem: 'trick' is linked with 'magic' (as in a 'magic trick') and the idea of 'casting' a spell, and the latest term for the mosquito is 'sorcerer' (line 23).

'Queer'

The word 'queer' has shifted in meaning a good deal over the past hundred years. Its original meaning was 'strange', 'odd', 'peculiar', and this is the primary meaning Lawrence has in mind in this poem. In the course of the twentieth century, the word came to be used in an insulting (pejorative) way to refer to homosexual men, and more recently it has been reclaimed as a neutral or positive word by LGBT people.

There is a grim satisfaction in the declaration that 'I know your game now'. It is becoming more and more clear that the mosquito is an enemy.

Lines 24–32

Lawrence continues to observe the mosquito as it 'stalk[s] and prowl[s] the air'. He seems to be preparing for a battle. In line 28 the mosquito has landed and stands on its 'long thin shanks'. He imagines the mosquito as 'cunningly conscious' of the game they are playing, 'Eyeing me sideways' just as he is eyeing the insect.

Lawrence's hatred seems to be growing. You can feel it in the short line, 'You speck', which sounds as if it has been spat out. He also says he hates 'the way you lurch off sideways into air' (indicating that the mosquito has taken off again).

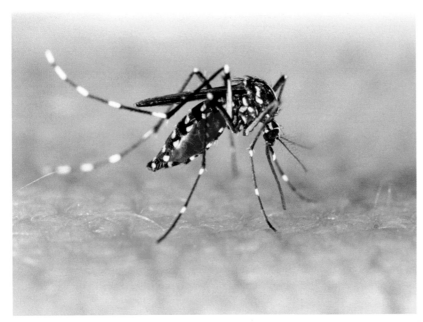

Lines 33–37

Now he talks directly to the mosquito: 'Come then, let us play at unawares'. It is, he says, a 'game of bluff' played between man and mosquito. They are both pretending that they have not noticed the existence of the other: 'You don't know that I exist, and I don't know that you exist'. The poet throws down a challenge: 'Now then!' In other words, let's see who wins.

Lines 38–48

This section begins with a sudden new thought, in short, urgent lines: 'It is your trump / It is your hateful little trump'. He is thinking about the high-pitched sound the mosquito makes – the 'small, high, hateful bugle in my ear'. This, he realises, is what 'shakes my sudden blood to hatred of you'.

He wonders why the mosquito does it; it must be 'bad policy' because it would warn victims of the insect's approach. He answers himself: 'They say you can't help it.' In that case, Providence protects the innocent by giving the victims a warning. But that thought doesn't satisfy him because the 'trump' sounds 'like a slogan' – meaning here a war cry of a Scottish clan, which is the origin of the modern uses of the word. It is the 'yell of triumph' of line 48: the high whine you hear when a mosquito is hovering near your ear, moving in to 'snatch' at your scalp.

Lines 49–59

In the storyline of the poem, this is the moment when Lawrence is bitten by the mosquito, resulting in 'Blood, red blood', the 'Forbidden liquor'. The **short lines and repetitions** in this section seem to **slow down the moment** of the biting, and Lawrence watches, fascinated and appalled, as the insect sucks his blood, 'enspasmed in oblivion, / Obscenely ecstasied'. **The words are invented** rather than chosen: 'enspasmed' and 'ecstasied' are adjectives created from nouns that have been treated as if they were verbs. Lawrence is reaching for the right way of describing what he sees as the almost sexual rapture of the mosquito as it drinks his blood. It is, for him, obscene.

Lines 60–70

Now the mosquito has had its fill of blood, and it staggers as if it is drunk. Lawrence tries to swat it, but the draught made by his hand blows the insect away. It is saved by its 'imponderable weightlessness' – 'imponderable' both because it is so light it cannot be weighed, but also because it cannot be grasped by thought (i.e. pondering).

It sounds to Lawrence as if the mosquito is mocking him with its 'paean of derision' (line 65) as it flies away. It seems for the moment as if he has lost the battle and the mosquito deserves the name 'Winged Victory'. But he has not given up trying to defeat it.

Lines 71–73

Apparently, he succeeds. He has killed the mosquito, and is now looking at the stain it makes – most of which is his own blood, while the insect's body is just an 'infinitesimal faint smear'. He still finds the whole experience strange, using the word 'Queer' twice more to sum up his feelings. He doesn't seem to feel the triumph of victory, and is left contemplating the 'dim dark smudge' that had been his mortal enemy.

Themes

It is hard to separate out the themes of this poem. It is fundamentally about what it says it is about: 'The Mosquito'. As in most of the poems in *Birds, Beasts and Flowers*, Lawrence uses his imagination to try to understand the non-human life of the thing he is writing about. What is unusual in this poem is that he treats the mosquito as an enemy, and his proper relationship with it as a battle, to such an extent that he has no reservations or remorse about killing it.

What is the reason for Lawrence's intense and unquestioning hatred? The critical moment seems to be when the mosquito bites him and sucks his blood, the 'Super-magical / Forbidden liquor' (lines 50–51). It has violated his body and taken the blood that is his essence; he calls it an 'obscenity of trespass', and that is when he stops watching the insect and tries to kill it.

It is not easy to pin down his attitude to the mosquito. As well as intense hatred, there is **respect**. It is an enemy, but he takes it seriously as an opponent. The fact that he sometimes gives it human characteristics – smiling at him, playing a game, even mocking him – may be because he sees it as a sort of equal.

There is also a **parallel** touched on in the poem **between outwitting the mosquito and writing a poem about it**. Both activities involve **observing it intensely** and trying to understand how it operates. In line 70 he asks, 'Am I not mosquito enough to out-mosquito you?' This implies that in order to defeat the mosquito he must become like it, and imagine himself inside it – exactly what he is doing in writing the poem. At the end the mosquito has 'disappeared' into 'a dim dark smudge'. Killing it doesn't seem to have lessened the mystery of the mosquito; in its dimness and darkness, it still escapes his mind's grasp.

Imagery

'The Mosquito' is **full of images, often in rapid succession**, as Lawrence tries one way after another of 'capturing' the insect in words. Some images are straightforward physical descriptions – e.g. 'with your thin wings and your streaming legs' (line 15) – while others are metaphorical, including the line that follows: 'How you sail like a heron, or a dull clot of air'.

As we have seen, there are underlying metaphors too. One that runs through the poem is the **idea of magic**, and the mosquito as a magician with his magic 'tricks'. We have noted its presence in lines 18–23 (see above).

Form and language

The form of this poem is quite different from the ones we have previously looked at, but typical of Lawrence's mature style. He writes in lines of uneven length and with no rhyme or traditional metre. The phrasing suggests **a mind at work in the moment**, wrestling with observations and ideas, considering and reconsidering. It is often **fragmentary, as thoughts are**, and many sentences lack verbs. The poem is broken up on the page into short sections as each new thought occurs. **Repetition** is often used, as a thought or feeling strikes him, and seems important, as if it won't go away. Look at the repetition of the word 'Queer' throughout the poem, or 'blood' in lines 49–56.

'Poetry of the Present'

In an essay from 1918 he called 'Poetry of the Present' Lawrence contrasted conventional poetry, which aims at formal elegance, with the sort of poetry he was now trying to write, which he called 'poetry of the present'. He described it in terms of change and movement rather than fixed perfection: 'There must be the rapid momentaneous association of things which meet and pass on the forever incalculable journey of creation: everything left in its own rapid, fluid relationship with the rest of things.'

It is worth finding that essay and reading it if you want to understand what Lawrence was trying to do as a poet.

Though there is no regular metre, there is a **rhythm** that responds to the changing thoughts and moods of the poem. Look, for instance, at the difference between the short lines beginning at 'Blood, red blood' (line 49), with their **strong stresses**, and the long line, 'Saves you, wafts you away on the very draught my anger makes in its snatching' (line 64). **The long line feels light** and seems to imitate the action of the mosquito being wafted away. Reading the lines out loud will help you to sense the differences.

The language suggests **a speaking voice**, but a very particular one. Lawrence writes simple phrases – 'What do you stand on such high legs for?' – but with a very **distinctive and inventive choice of words**. For example, he uses names or labels to try to capture something of the mosquito's nature – 'phantom', 'speck', 'Winged Victory', 'Ghoul on wings', 'winged blood-drop', 'exaltation', 'streaky sorcerer', 'pointed fiend'. Do you sense the relish in the way he comes up with these names?

Lawrence seems to let words bubble up uncensored, and even changes them around when he needs the right word to express his thoughts: 'ecstasied' and 'enspasmed', for instance, are invented words that re-energise the concepts in the original words 'ecstasy' and 'spasm'. There is great energy in his phrase-making, often reinforced with strong stresses and alliteration, e.g. 'shredded shank' (line 4) and 'dim dark smudge' (line 73).

Questions

1. The poem starts with the speaker observing a mosquito at rest, and ends with the mosquito's death. In between, it implies a series of actions. In your own words, tell the 'story' of the poem, backing it up with references to the text.

2. How would you describe the speaker's attitude towards the mosquito at the start of the poem? Explain your answer.

3. In line 20, the speaker declares 'That is your trick, your bit of filthy magic'. What, in your own words, is this 'trick'?

4. Lawrence sometimes projects human characteristics and motivations on to the mosquito. Give two examples, and comment on what this suggests about his attitude to it.

5. Why, in line 46, does Lawrence say 'I believe a little in Providence protecting the innocent'?

6. What is the speaker's attitude to the mosquito as it sucks his blood? How does Lawrence make it clear how he feels?

7. Has the speaker's attitude towards the mosquito changed by the end of the poem? Explain your answer.

8. Comment on the use of the term 'Monsieur' to address the mosquito in line 2.

9. Choose three words or phrases that Lawrence uses to label the mosquito, and comment on what they tell you about the mosquito and/or about Lawrence.

10. How different is the experience of reading this poem compared to the earlier ones we have looked at? Can you describe the differences, and say what you like or don't like about this poem?

11. Choose one unexpected word that Lawrence uses in the poem. In pairs or groups, explain why you do or don't like it.

12. Write your own animal (or bird or insect) poem. Take time to look at the creature and imagine your way into its mind and body. Write down, in any form you want, the thoughts, images and observations that occur to you.

Before you read

Have you ever seen a humming-bird, on film or in real life? In pairs or small groups, discuss your impressions of the bird.

Humming-Bird

I can imagine, in some otherworld
Primeval-dumb, far back
In that most awful stillness, that only gasped and hummed,
Humming-birds raced down the avenues.

Before anything had a soul,   5
While life was a heave of Matter, half inanimate,
This little bit chipped off in brilliance
And went whizzing through the slow, vast, succulent stems.

I believe there were no flowers then,
In the world where the humming-bird flashed ahead of creation.   10
I believe he pierced the slow vegetable veins with his long beak.

Probably he was big
As mosses, and little lizards, they say, were once big.
Probably he was a jabbing, terrifying monster.

We look at him through the wrong end of the long telescope of Time,   15
Luckily for us.

Glossary

2	*Primeval*: belonging to the earliest time in history
6	*inanimate*: showing no sign of life
8	*succulent*: juicy; thick and fleshy and moist

Guidelines

'Humming-bird' was written in Italy, probably in June 1920, after Lawrence read about humming-birds in a book by the American writer Crèvecoeur. At that time he had never seen a humming-bird. He must have been a bit embarrassed about this, as when the poem was published in *Birds, Beasts and Flowers* (1923), he indicated that it had been written in Española in New Mexico, where he had by then seen plenty of humming-birds. Thus, unlike most of the poems in this volume, this is not a poem of observation but of **imagination**. In it, Lawrence indulges in **a flight of fancy** about the existence of the bird at the very beginning of geological time.

Commentary

'I can imagine', starts the poem, telling us we are being taken on an imaginative journey. The journey is back in time, to an 'otherworld / Primeval-dumb', when nothing had a soul and 'life was a heave of Matter', gasping and humming like something only half-alive. In this 'awful stillness' the only real, distinct life is the humming-bird.

There is a wonderful contrast between the dumb, 'half inanimate' matter and the speed and brilliance of the humming-bird, 'whizzing through the slow, vast, succulent stems'. It is a vivid and extraordinary image which has no basis in science, but that does not put Lawrence off. **'I believe' he says twice**, and what he believes in is a world without flowers to provide the nectar on which modern humming-birds live. Instead he imagines that their long beaks 'pierced the slow vegetable veins' and sucked the sap inside. Whatever science may say, this vision has, for Lawrence, an imaginative truth.

You get the feeling that these thoughts are written down as fast as they occur to Lawrence, without being censored or changed. He lets his imagination go its own way, and now it takes another step: 'Probably' the humming-birds were giants, just as modern lizards are related to the dinosaurs that once dominated the world. Can you imagine a giant humming-bird? It would be, as he suggests, 'a jabbing, terrifying monster' (line 14).

The poem ends with a humorous twist. Lawrence suggests that it is as if we were looking at the humming-bird through the wrong end of a telescope – 'the long telescope of Time'. That is why it is so small. 'Luckily for us', he adds.

Themes

Lawrence is letting his imagination have free rein and **keeping the tone light**, but there are some serious things to take away from the poem. The poem might make us wonder about creation and evolution – how things have changed and will change, and where we as humans stand in relation to it. Our place is not as assured and stable as we sometimes like to think.

Imagination

The humming-bird is a fierce creature as well as a beautiful one. What does he represent? **He could stand for the imagination, taking life** from the 'slow vegetable veins' and transforming it into flashing brilliance. He could be Lawrence himself, with his **vivid individuality and creative force**, unafraid to stick his beak in and upset conventional society, much of which regarded him as a 'jabbing, terrifying monster' and wanted to censor his books and confiscate his paintings.

Individuality

The poem can also be seen as a **myth**, and has similarities to other accounts in Lawrence's prose of individual souls emerging from a formless mass. In this poem the creation myth of the humming-bird can be seen as a way of explaining the making of an individual soul, and for Lawrence, **the whole purpose of existence is to become an individual as fully and brightly as possible**. In this reading, the humming-bird stands for the individuality of any creature, human or otherwise.

The bird itself

But the poem is also about humming-birds in themselves. Even though Lawrence had not seen one, he was struck by descriptions of their beauty and what he called, in his essay on Crèvecoeur, 'their dark, primitive, weapon-like souls'. This poem is Lawrence's attempt to imagine his way into the humming-bird's soul and understand its origins.

Imagery

The imagery of the poem has already been discussed in the Commentary. At its heart is a **fundamental contrast between the 'heave of Matter' and the humming-bird**. Slowness is contrasted with speed, vastness with smallness, darkness with brightness, and softness with hardness.

In lines 12–14, we suddenly see the bird close up and huge, as a 'monster', but he is restored to normal size, as it were, with the image of looking through the wrong end of the 'long telescope of Time'. For a moment, it is as if we are looking back through time when we see the humming-bird.

Form and language

Like the other poems in *Birds, Beasts and Flowers*, 'Humming-Bird' is written in **free verse**, with varying line lengths, using no rhyme or stanza form, but dividing the poem on the page into what might be called '**verse-paragraphs**'.

The poem gives a strong sense of the speaker **thinking in the moment**, as his imagination works. This is partly down to the flexible lines, which match the changing, sometimes sudden **movements of the mind at work**. You also hear the speaker's voice through the use of repetition: 'I believe … / I believe …'; 'Probably he was … / Probably he was …'.

The sounds of the poem also help to create the contrasts mentioned above (see Imagery). The **short vowels** ('i') and **hard consonants** ('b', 'p' and 't') of the 'little bit chipped off in brilliance' are set against the **long vowels, sibilance and clusters of consonants** in a phrase like 'slow, vast, succulent stems'. There, Lawrence's use of **multiple adjectives** in describing the primeval world slows down the pace, whereas the active verbs associated with the humming-bird ('raced', 'chipped', 'flashed', 'pierced') **break through** the stillness of the setting.

Exam-Style Questions

Understanding the poem

1 How does Lawrence picture the primeval 'otherworld' in which the humming-bird first lived? How is it different from today's world? Give as much detail as you can.

2 In your own words, explain the contrast between the humming-bird and the primeval world.

3 In what ways is the ancient humming-bird Lawrence imagines different from a modern one? Give as much detail as you can.

4 Why is it lucky for us that we see the humming-bird 'through the wrong end of the long telescope of Time'?

Thinking about the poem

1 In the first line, Lawrence imagines an 'otherworld'. How would it have been different if he'd written it as two words: 'other world'?

2 Choose one line or phrase that you like the sound of, and try to explain how the sounds in it work. You might think about alliteration, assonance, vowel length and rhythm.

3 What, do you think, does the humming-bird in the poem represent?
■ D. H. Lawrence
■ The creative imagination
■ The individual soul
■ Just a humming-bird

Or something else? Give reasons for your answer.

4 What does the poem tell you about its author?

Imagining

1 Imagine that some ordinary, familiar animal – a dog, a cat, a spider, a snail or whatever you like – has been turned into a giant version of itself. Write about your encounter with that creature.

2 Your group has been asked to prepare an audio-visual programme to accompany this poem. Discuss what music, sounds and images you would want to use.

SNAPSHOT

■ **Flight of the imagination**
■ **Free verse following the working of the poet's imagination**
■ **Central contrast between humming-bird and primeval world**
■ **Sounds of words often help to create the contrast**
■ **Jewel-like beauty and fierceness of the humming-bird**
■ **Humming-bird as the individual soul**

Before you read

Have you ever seen a snake in the wild? In Ireland, probably not. If you have, share your experience with the class or a group. Then discuss the associations we have with snakes – negative and positive – and the reasons for them.

Snake

A snake came to my water-trough
On a hot, hot day, and I in pyjamas for the heat,
To drink there.

In the deep, strange-scented shade of the great dark carob-tree
I came down the steps with my pitcher 5
And must wait, must stand and wait, for there he was at the trough before me.

He reached down from a fissure in the earth-wall in the gloom
And trailed his yellow-brown slackness soft-bellied down, over the edge of the stone trough
And rested his throat upon the stone bottom,
And where the water had dripped from the tap, in a small clearness, 10
He sipped with his straight mouth,
Softly drank through his straight gums, into his slack long body,
Silently.

Someone was before me at my water-trough,
And I, like a second comer, waiting. 15

He lifted his head from his drinking, as cattle do,
And looked at me vaguely, as drinking cattle do,
And flickered his two-forked tongue from his lips, and mused a moment,
And stooped and drank a little more,
Being earth-brown, earth-golden from the burning bowels of the earth 20
On the day of Sicilian July, with Etna smoking.

The voice of my education said to me
He must be killed,
For in Sicily the black, black snakes are innocent, the gold are venomous.

And voices in me said, If you were a man   25
You would take a stick and break him now, and finish him off.

But must I confess how I liked him,
How glad I was he had come like a guest in quiet, to drink at my water-trough
And depart peaceful, pacified, and thankless,
Into the burning bowels of this earth?   30

Was it cowardice, that I dared not kill him?
Was it perversity, that I longed to talk to him?
Was it humility, to feel so honoured?
I felt so honoured.

And yet those voices: 35
If you were not afraid, you would kill him!

And truly I was afraid, I was most afraid,
But even so, honoured still more
That he should seek my hospitality
From out the dark door of the secret earth.   40

He drank enough
And lifted his head, dreamily, as one who has drunken,
And flickered his tongue like a forked night on the air, so black,
Seeming to lick his lips,
And looked around like a god, unseeing, into the air,   45
And slowly turned his head,
And slowly, very slowly, as if thrice adream,
Proceeded to draw his slow length curving round
And climb again the broken bank of my wall-face.

And as he put his head into that dreadful hole,   50
And as he slowly drew up, snake-easing his shoulders, and entered farther,
A sort of horror, a sort of protest against his withdrawing into that horrid black hole,
Deliberately going into the blackness, and slowly drawing himself after,
Overcame me now his back was turned.

I looked round, I put down my pitcher,   55
I picked up a clumsy log
And threw it at the water-trough with a clatter.

I think it did not hit him,
But suddenly that part of him that was left behind convulsed in undignified haste,
Writhed like lightning, and was gone   60
Into the black hole, the earth-lipped fissure in the wall-front,
At which, in the intense still noon, I stared with fascination.

And immediately I regretted it.
I thought how paltry, how vulgar, what a mean act!
I despised myself and the voices of my accursed human education.   65

And I thought of the albatross,
And I wished he would come back, my snake.

For he seemed to me again like a king,
Like a king in exile, uncrowned in the underworld,
Now due to be crowned again.   70

And so, I missed my chance with one of the lords
Of life.
And I have something to expiate;
A pettiness.

Taormina

Glossary

4	*carob-tree*: evergreen tree native to the Mediterranean region
5	*pitcher*: large jug
7	*fissure*: long, narrow opening
21	*Etna*: volcano on the island of Sicily, close to Taormina, where this poem was written
29	*pacified*: made calm
32	*perversity*: deliberate desire to act in an unreasonable way
33	*humility*: modesty, lack of pride
47	*thrice adream*: in a trance, as if dreaming deeply
64	*paltry*: petty, trivial
66	*albatross*: a reference to Samuel Taylor Coleridge's 'Rime of the Ancient Mariner' (see Commentary)
73	*expiate*: make amends for (usually a sin)
74	*pettiness*: something small-minded or mean-spirited

Guidelines

'Snake' was written while Lawrence and his wife Frieda were living in Taormina in Sicily (1920–21). It was first published in a magazine in 1921, and appeared in the collection *Birds, Beasts and Flowers* (1923). It is probably the best known and best loved of all his poems.

Commentary

The poem relates an encounter between a man and a snake. The poem is set in Sicily in July. It has usually been assumed that the poem describes something that actually happened to Lawrence in July 1920, but, as Lawrence scholar Keith Sagar points out, there is good evidence to suggest that 'Snake' was written in January

1921, and there is a surprising absence in his letters of any mention of the incident. As Sagar explains, the poem draws on ideas about snakes and the symbolism of snakes that Lawrence had been developing elsewhere in his writings, and the 'I' of the poem is much more anxious about snakes than Lawrence really was at this point in his life. We should be wary, therefore, of treating the poem as a simple story.

Lines 1–21

The first three lines set the scene: a 'hot, hot day'; the snake coming to drink at the trough; the speaker, rather comically, dressed in pyjamas.

The next few groups of lines shift the focus back and forth between speaker and the snake. Lines 4–6 tell the speaker's story: he comes down the steps to fetch water to find the snake is already there, so he must 'stand and wait'.

The following section describes what the narrator sees. The snake emerges from a 'fissure' in the earth-wall to drink in the stone trough. The scene is observed with care: the 'slack long body' of the snake, the 'small clearness' of water that has dripped from the tap, the 'straight mouth' of the drinking snake. **The atmosphere is mysterious and almost suspended in time**, as if the speaker were holding his breath. The word 'Silently' on its own at the end of this group of lines sets the tone for the whole scene.

The next two lines (14–15) return to the overall scene and remind us that the speaker is still 'waiting'. He is described as 'a second comer', which has resonances of the Second Coming of Christ (see also Yeats's poem 'The Second Coming', page 461) and adds to the sense that something of great importance is taking place.

Lines 16–21 return to the snake and describe him lifting his head, flickering his tongue and then stooping to drink more. The atmosphere is still and slow and quiet and hot. Do you get the sense that there is something ominous in this?

Lines 22–40

At line 22 the poem suddenly changes. We return to the narrator, but now there is urgency and uncertainty. The 'voice of my education' – the things he has been brought up to believe and to think – tells him this is a poisonous snake and that poisonous snakes must be killed. His courage as a man is also challenged: 'If you were a man' you would kill him.

But the speaker is conflicted. He questions his own motives and admits his fear: 'I was most afraid' (line 37). He is 'glad' the snake has come 'like a guest' to drink at his water-trough. He feels 'honoured' to have such a guest from another world: 'From out the dark door of the secret earth'.

Lines 41–62

The next section brings the focus back to the snake. What is described is simple – the snake raising his head, turning and slowly moving back towards the hole he had come from. But there is **a hypnotic fascination** in the description. Everything is slow and dreamlike. The word 'slowly' is used three times; 'slow', 'dreamily' and 'adream' once each.

The final part of the story of the encounter begins at line 50. As the snake begins to enter the hole a powerful feeling overcomes the speaker: 'A sort of horror, a sort of protest'. It is not a horror at the snake itself, but at his 'withdrawing into that horrid black hole'. Notice there the word 'horrid'; like 'dreadful' in line 50, it is a rather childish, even comical word to use, suggesting perhaps that the speaker's horror is a bit foolish.

Lines 55–57 have a very different energy from what has gone before. Instead of the slowness of long sentences with qualifying phrases, these three lines describe definite actions, one after the other. The speaker throws a log at the disappearing snake, and the atmosphere is broken. In the following few lines we see the 'undignified haste' of the snake as it instinctively disappears as fast as it can into the 'earth-lipped fissure', leaving the speaker to stare 'with fascination'.

The albatross

In Samuel Taylor Coleridge's poem 'The Rime of the Ancient Mariner', an albatross follows the ship in which the Mariner is sailing. When he kills the albatross with his crossbow, and the ship is becalmed in the burning tropical heat, the other sailors curse the Mariner and hang the dead albatross around his neck as a sign of his guilt. It is only after the rest of the crew is dead, when the Mariner sees the beauty of the water-snakes swimming by the ship and blesses them without thinking, that the albatross falls from his neck and the curse is lifted.

Lines 63–74

The final part of the poem describes the speaker's reaction to what he has done. He has done something 'paltry', 'vulgar' and 'mean', and he blames the 'voices of my accursed human education'. In lines 66–67 he thinks of the story of the Ancient Mariner in Samuel Taylor Coleridge's poem, who was cursed for shooting the albatross that had brought good fortune to his ship. Now he thinks of the snake as a 'king in exile', 'one of the lords / Of life'. He, though, is cursed; he has a sin on his conscience that he must do something to make amends for – to 'expiate'. It is not a great crime, though, but a 'pettiness'.

Themes

This poem is about an **encounter** between a man and a snake, and its fundamental theme is the **relationship between human and reptile**. In the course of the poem, the man gives in to a petty impulse and throws a log at the snake, then realises something important about what should be his proper, respectful relationship with the creature.

Lawrence is also exploring the relationship between man and snake on a deeper, more symbolic level. **The two come from different worlds** – the man down the steps from the house, the snake up from 'the dark door of the secret earth' (line 40). The man walks upright; the snake is on his belly. The snake, it seems, is in his proper place, whereas the man is an intruder who 'must stand and wait' for the snake to finish. The man is, somewhat comically, in pyjamas; the snake is 'like a god'.

The speaker in the poem could be seen as Lawrence as a younger man, more inhibited by the 'voices of [his] accursed human education' than Lawrence actually was at this stage in his life. In contrast, Lawrence emphasises the symbolic significance of the snake. He is associated with 'the burning bowels of the earth' (line 20), of which the smoking volcano Etna is an ever-present reminder. He is 'like a god', an honoured guest in the human world, or 'a king in exile' (line 69).

What, then, does the snake represent? Lawrence wrote of the 'dark gods', the **powers that Christianity and Western culture had denied or neglected and which human beings need to acknowledge and embrace**. Sexuality is an important element of those powers, though not the whole of them. In the Christian tradition, the snake is associated with the temptation of Eve in the Garden of Eden, and so is a creature to be feared, avoided or killed. For Lawrence, its association with the earth and the underworld (in line 69) suggests that it may be one of the 'dark gods'. The snake comes out of a 'fissure' in the earth. In his poem about the pomegranate he makes a connection between the 'fissure' of the fruit and the vagina, representing female sexuality. So the snake might be seen as a 'dark god' of sexuality. How does this idea affect your reading of the poem?

In the poem, the speaker is touched by the power that the snake represents, but he is not ready to embrace it. The snake may be 'a king in exile' who is 'due to be crowned again' (line 70) when humans acknowledge the power he represents, but the speaker in the poem misses his chance; he still has something to learn.

> **Symbolism of snakes**
>
> The most familiar association of the snake in Western Christian tradition is as a symbol of evil and corruption, largely because of the part the snake plays in the fall of Adam in the Bible story of the Garden of Eden. That association is part of what Lawrence calls his 'accursed human education', reinforced by the fact that many snakes are poisonous. But in more ancient mythologies the snake is often seen as a symbol of life – due partly to its fluid shape and movement, like a life-giving river, and partly to its association with the male sexual organ. It was sacred to Asclepius, Greek god of healing, and is still seen twining around a bowl or staff in signs outside many pharmacies.

Imagery

The main group of images concerns the snake, the earth and the underworld, gods and kings, and the fissure, as discussed above.

There are other very vivid, but more incidental images, mostly in the form of **similes that describe the snake**. These include the way he lifts his head from drinking 'as cattle do' (line 16), his tongue flickering 'like a forked night on the air' (line 43) and his tail that 'Writhed like lightning' (line 60) when he left.

Form and language

'Snake' is written in free verse that is beautifully crafted, with a **subtly varied music** that **responds to the changing images and moods of the poem**. The long lines that describe the movements of the snake have a **slow sinuousness** that matches those movements. Notice, for example, that it is impossible to read 'trailed his yellow-brown slackness soft-bellied down' (line 8) quickly. There are long vowels ('trailed', 'brown', 'down'), but it is also the groups of consonants that slow down the line: the sibilance of 'slackness' followed by 'soft' forces you to take the time to make the double 's' sound, for example (and also suggests the hissing of the snake). Can you find other examples of these **long, lingering syllables**?

The poem is divided into groups of lines of varying number, the great majority of which consist of just one sentence. It is noticeable that the longer **groups describe the snake, in long sentences**, with a simple structure in which the actions are linked one after the other with 'And' at the beginning of the lines, but slowed down by descriptive words and phrases, often using repetition (e.g. 'as cattle do, / … as drinking cattle do', lines 16–17).

The language is **rich in adjectives, adverbs and similes** when the scene and the action are being described, creating a **powerful, mysterious, rather ominous atmosphere**; even in line 4 there is a hint of something sinister in 'the deep, strange-scented shade of the great dark carob-tree'. The phrasing is sometimes used to reinforce this sense of mystery: instead of 'On a July day in Sicily', he writes 'On the day of Sicilian July' (line 21), which adds to the ominous quality of 'Etna smoking'.

By contrast, the internal debates of the speaker (e.g. lines 22–40) are written in shorter, more urgent lines, full of questions and qualifications.

Questions

1	How would you describe the atmosphere created in the first 21 lines of the poem? Can you explain some of the ways in which Lawrence creates it?
2	Why, do you think, does the speaker 'stand and wait' for the snake (line 6)?
3	What impression do you get of the snake in the first 21 lines?
4	How would you describe the 'voices in me' mentioned in line 25? Where do they come from?
5	In your own words, explain the conflict within the speaker in lines 22–40.
6	Why exactly, do you think, does the speaker throw the log at the disappearing snake (line 57)?
7	Does this poem have a moral? If so, what is it? Explain your answer.
8	What impression do you get of the speaker in the poem? Explain your answer.
9	Comment on the use of repetition in 'Snake'.
10	The word 'Silently' (line 13) is on its own at the end of a group of lines. What is the effect of placing the word here?
11	Choose a line or two whose sounds and rhythms you particularly like, and try to explain what you like about it/them.
12	What, do you think, does the snake represent in the poem? Explain your answer.
13	Nowadays we hear a lot about mankind's responsibility for the non-human life on the planet. Would this be a good poem to include in an anthology about man's relationship with the natural world? Why, or why not?
14	*Groupwork* Your group has been chosen to create an audio-visual accompaniment to a reading of 'Snake'. What sounds and images would you use?

Pansies and *More Pansies*

Towards the end of 1928, suffering from the recurrence of the tuberculosis that had affected him since he was a schoolteacher, living in France and confined to his bed for much of the day, Lawrence started to write the poems he called *Pansies*. He no longer had the energy to write novels, or even the sustained animal poems of a few years before, so his new poems were brief and written quickly, often several at a time.

He thought of the word 'pansies' as deriving from the French word *pensées* (thoughts), and these poems are short, like single thoughts, but not, as Lawrence insisted, in the least intellectual. Each poem, he said in his introduction to *Pansies*, is:

> 'a true thought, which comes as much from the heart and genitals as from the head. A thought, with its own blood of emotion and instinct running in it like the fire in a fire-opal.'

As he wrote elsewhere, true thought is 'a man in his wholeness wholly attending' ('attending' here means paying attention).

The word 'pansies' is also appropriate for these poems because, like the flower, they are often small and delicate and beautiful, and he didn't want them to be taken too seriously but to give the reader a moment's pause to reflect. He intended them to be 'fleeting as pansies, which will wilt soon, and are so fascinating with their varied faces, while they last'.

Lawrence also gave an alternative, fanciful derivation of the word 'pansy', from the French *panser*, to dress or soothe a wound, explaining that the poems 'are my tender administrations to the mental and emotional wounds we suffer from'.

The poems often come in groups which share an idea or an image, and thus cast light on one another. Lawrence made it clear that they were meant to be read together so as to create a picture of 'a complete state of mind'. If you can find a copy of Lawrence's *Complete Poems* you can get an idea of what was going on in his mind when he wrote the poems you are studying, by reading those before and after them.

Pansies was published in 1929, and then between May and September of that year Lawrence wrote more poems of the same kind, which were published after his death under the title *More Pansies*. All the poems we will be looking at next come from the latter collection.

> 'Live and let live, and each pansy will tip you its separate wink. The fairest thing in nature, a flower, still has its roots in earth and manure; and in the perfume there hovers still the faint strange scent of earth, the under-earth in all its heavy humidity and darkness. Certainly it is so in pansy-scent, and in violet-scent; mingled with the blue of the morning the black of the corrosive humus. Else the scent would be just sickly sweet.'
>
> **D. H. Lawrence, Introduction to *Pansies***

Intimates

Don't you care for my love? she said bitterly.

I handed her the mirror, and said:
Please address these questions to the proper person!
Please make all requests to head-quarters!
In all matters of emotional importance   5
please approach the supreme authority direct!
So I handed her the mirror.

And she would have broken it over my head,
but she caught sight of her own reflection
and that held her spellbound for two seconds   10
while I fled.

Guidelines

'Intimates' is one of a group of poems in which Lawrence comments on the self-importance and self-absorption of other people, and how it bores him. Many of these poems, including this one, centre on an encounter between himself and an unnamed person: 'a certain friend', 'a young man', a 'lovely young lady'. Here it is just 'she'. Given his stormy relationship with his wife, Frieda, and the fact that he wrote about that relationship at length in earlier poems, it is tempting to think of 'she' as Frieda, but the style of the poems in the group would suggest otherwise. The poem 'Sphinx' (below) is one of them.

Sphinx

But why do I feel so strangely about you?
said the lovely young lady, half wistful, half menacing.

I took to my heels and ran
before she could set the claws of her self-conscious questioning in me
or tear me with the fangs of disappointment
because I could not answer the riddle of her own self-importance.

Commentary

'Intimates' starts **dramatically** with a spoken question: 'Don't you care for my love?' It is 'she' speaking. The tone, apparently, is bitter. Is this a couple in the middle of an argument? Or has the question come out of the blue?

The speaker's answer is to hand her a mirror, and make some requests in **mock-official language**, asking her to speak to 'the proper person', 'head-quarters' or 'the supreme authority'. In other words: herself. These are harsh words if this is supposed to be a loving relationship.

What is the speaker implying? One way of interpreting it is that he is saying that she needs to look at herself (in the mirror) and learn to love herself before she can love him properly. But the tone is scathing rather than compassionate, and this idea is not present elsewhere in the group of poems to which 'Intimates' belongs. Another way of looking at it is that he is trying to tell her that she is more interested in herself, and what he calls in 'Sphinx' her 'self-conscious questioning', than in him. It's all about her, you could say.

The final section (lines 8–11) tends to confirm the second idea. Instead of breaking the mirror over his head in anger at his words, she 'caught sight of her own reflection' in the mirror and is held 'spellbound'. The implication seems to be that she is so entranced by her own image that, in a neat and humorous twist to the end of the poem, the speaker has time to make his escape.

Themes

You could regard this poem as a **scene – or a skirmish – from the battle of the sexes**. As the poem's title implies, this is a poem about two people who are intimate. More than ten years earlier Lawrence had written a long sequence of poems about his relationship with Frieda, charting the conflicts as well as the harmonies of their time together. It was published as *Look! We Have Come Through!* (1917). For Lawrence, the **conflict** was a proper part of a good marriage. He liked to quote the ancient Greek philosopher Heraclitus: 'in the tension of opposites all things have their being'.

And yet, in the group of poems to which 'Intimates' belongs the main focus is on the self-absorption of people, because of which they cannot really connect with others as they are always thinking primarily of themselves – what we often refer to as the ego. 'Most people, today,' he says in another poem from this group, are 'just fantasies of self-importance'. Self-importance bored him. Perhaps he would have preferred it if the woman *had* broken the mirror over his head; at least that would have been a real connection.

Imagery

'Intimates' depicts a short scene and **relies on dialogue and plain description rather than imagery**. There is one crucial image, however: that of the **mirror**. It could be thought of as a stage prop that the scene requires, and the repetition of 'I handed her the mirror' (lines 2 and 7) ensures that the reader is always aware of its presence. Potentially, it has **a double function**: it can be the glass wherein you see who you truly are, or it can be the surface in which you admire your own fascinating reflection. Which do you think is uppermost here?

Form and language

'Intimates' is written in free verse but, unlike the animal poems we have looked at, it is **plain** and unadorned by rich patterns of sound and rhythm. Curiously, there is one thread of rhyme running through it ('said' / 'head' / 'fled'), which feels almost accidental but helps to point to the humour of the short final line.

The language lacks the colourful adjectives and adverbs that we have seen in earlier poems. Rather, in the middle section Lawrence uses a formal register of rather **pompous 'official' language**, as if he is fobbing off a letter of complaint: 'Please make all requests to head-quarters' (note that the head is where the ego resides, or is 'quartered'). It is meant to mock and undermine the woman's bitter questioning, which he regards as false – we might today call it 'emotional blackmail'.

Questions

1	Do you think Lawrence is writing about an incident that really happened? Explain your answer.
2	Why, do you think, does the speaker hand the woman the mirror? What is he trying to say?
3	What impression do you get of the speaker of the poem? Are you sympathetic to him or not? Explain your answer.
4	What is the significance of the fact that catching sight of herself in the mirror holds her 'spellbound'?
5	Do you find this poem funny? Why, or why not?
6	What, do you think, is the real subject of this poem? Explain your answer.
7	Could the speaker, the 'I' in the poem, be a woman? Lawrence did not intend it to be, but how would it affect your reading of the poem if it were? What if the genders were reversed, or they were both men? Discuss in small groups.
8	In pairs – or perhaps threes – try acting out the 'scene' in this poem, using the words of the poem. Decide how best to divide the words between you. If you have time, try improvising what happens next – when she catches him running away.

Delight of Being Alone

I know no greater delight than the sheer delight of being alone.
It makes me realise the delicious pleasure of the moon
that she has in travelling by herself: throughout time,
or the splendid growing of an ash-tree
alone, on a hillside in the north, humming in the wind.   5

Guidelines

When Lawrence wrote 'Delight of Being Alone' he was **a dying man** and knew it. He had no patience for people he didn't want to see or things he didn't want to do; his time was too precious. He wrote many poems expressing his irritation with other people and his wish to be left alone, which are both apparent in 'Intimates', but in this poem he lets himself dwell on the positive and lets his imagination embrace the natural world.

Commentary

The poem is **direct and personal**. There is no doubt that the 'I' of the poem is Lawrence himself. You can imagine him writing this alone, feeling well enough to enjoy the luxury of it.

The first line is a simple statement of his theme: being alone is a 'sheer delight'. He goes on to imagine that aloneness on a grander scale, in the heavens. He thinks of what it must be like to be the moon, imagining it as female. He contemplates the 'delicious pleasure' the moon must have in 'travelling by herself', and not just in space but 'throughout time'. Then he thinks of an ash tree, alone 'on a hillside in the north'. Perhaps he is thinking of a landscape he knew as a boy in England, and finding comfort in that thought (though see the note on Yggdrasil overleaf). Notice that he thinks of the ash tree 'growing' and 'humming'. He is connecting not just with its aloneness, but also with **the life that is in it**.

Themes and imagery

The title announces the primary theme: the delight of being alone. It is a poem that celebrates being alone through **a daring leap of the imagination** out into the big world and the heavens. But perhaps there is

Yggdrasil

In Norse mythology, Yggdrasil is the immense, holy tree at the centre of the world. It is an ash tree. Might this myth have some relevance to 'Delight of Being Alone', do you think? The mention of roots and 'the centre of all things' in the poem 'Loneliness' by Lawrence below suggests that it might.

something else going on, and it is well to remember what state Lawrence was in when he wrote this poem. Lawrence is **imagining himself out of his own dying human body** and into completely different forms of being. Is this a form of escapism? Is his poet's imagination here the last refuge of a dying man?

Whatever you think about that, the images he conjures are beautiful. The two forms of life he imagines – the moon and the ash tree – are connected by being alone. In other ways there is great **contrast**: the moon is a traveller, the ash tree is rooted in one spot; one is of the heavens, the other of the earth; one is female, the other possibly male.

Language

As noted above, **the voice of the poem is clearly Lawrence's own**, as nearly as that can be said of any poem. The ideas in it may be daring, but the **language is restrained**, although full of relish. A lot of work is done by simple adjective–noun combinations that all emphasise the delight in the solitary self: 'sheer delight', 'delicious pleasure', 'splendid growing'. The beauty of the poem comes from **powerful, surprising thoughts stated with simple conviction** and no great verbal fireworks.

Nevertheless, Lawrence shows his mastery of the free verse form. Notice, for instance, that **the first line is also a complete sentence**; it makes the opening statement all the more definite. Notice too the way the **line break** after 'ash-tree' (line 4) isolates the repeated word 'alone' at the beginning of the next line, thus suggesting aloneness.

Loneliness

I never know what people mean when they complain of loneliness.
To be alone is one of life's greatest delights, thinking one's own thoughts,
doing one's own little jobs, seeing the world beyond
and feeling oneself uninterrupted in the rooted connection
with the centre of all things.

Questions

1	Comment on the two images Lawrence has chosen – the moon and the ash tree. Why, do you think, did he choose these particular images? What do they suggest, and how do they make you feel?
2	Comment on Lawrence's use of the free verse form in this poem.
3	Do you like this poem? Why, or why not?
4	Write your own poem (or prose), either in praise of being alone or against it.

Absolute Reverence

I feel absolute reverence to nobody and to nothing human
neither to persons nor things nor ideas, ideals nor religions nor institutions,
to these things I feel only respect, and a tinge of reverence
when I see the fluttering of pure life in them.

But to something unseen, unknown, creative   5
from which I feel I am a derivative
I feel absolute reverence. Say no more!

Glossary

1	*reverence*: deep respect and honour, especially for things that are sacred
6	*derivative*: something which has its origins in something else, from which it is 'derived'

Guidelines

'Absolute Reverence' comes from a group of poems in *More Pansies* in which Lawrence ponders questions of **spirituality and belief**.

Commentary

In this poem we see Lawrence trying to work out and define his feelings and beliefs as clearly as possible. He is dealing in **definitions and discriminations**, trying to understand what he means by 'absolute reverence' by examining his own feelings and contrasting it with that which it is not, which he calls 'respect'.

The first four lines deal with the negative – what he does not feel 'absolute reverence' for. The key idea is 'nothing human', including people, their ideas and their institutions. These he gives 'respect' to, and only 'a tinge of reverence' if he sees 'the fluttering of pure life' in them. This is a clue – to him and to us – about what does deserve reverence, even if it is not 'absolute': **life itself**.

The final three lines deal with the positive – the 'something' for which he does feel 'absolute reverence'. He cannot define it, but he **approaches what he means through what it is not**: it is 'unseen, unknown'. It is also 'creative', and he feels that he himself is a 'derivative' of this **creative power**; in other words, he is in some way part of it or owes his being to it.

And then he stops. None of his mature poems is intended to be a final statement, particularly in *Pansies*, where the brief poems throw light on each other. He cannot say all that he means, or all there is to say, so he finishes with an instruction: 'Say no more!' Are those words intended for himself or for the reader, do you think?

Themes

The main theme of the poem is indicated by the title, and has been discussed in the Commentary above. It is also a poem about **belief**, and what Lawrence feels he can commit to believing in, and revere as something **sacred or divine**.

Lawrence lost his faith in Christianity early in his life, but he always insisted he was religious. He wrote about gods a great deal, and believed in the **soul as a divine spark** which would outlive the body, and which he associated with the Holy Ghost. Perhaps that is the idea behind the 'fluttering of pure life', for which he feels a 'tinge of reverence'.

But the second part of the poem feels its way towards a wider belief system – **a mystical sense of the divine** which cannot be understood or defined, but to which he has a **vital connection**, and in which he has faith.

'Say no more!' is a good warning. If Lawrence can't define what he means, or wishes not to, it is better that we don't try. But if you want to find out more about his spiritual ideas, read his poems, novels and essays.

Language and imagery

This is the **purest *pensée*, or thought, among the poems we are studying**. It is a statement, expressed in language that aims at **precision rather than emotional effect**. There is no imagery except in the implied idea of some sort of creature in 'the fluttering of pure life', which might suggest a butterfly or a bird. This is Lawrence's voice, blunt and assertive. Is he addressing an audience, an individual, or talking just to himself?

The free verse is unadorned by rhyme (except for the half-rhyme of 'creative' / 'derivative') or metre or any rich play of sounds, but at moments there is **a pattern of speech** that has a dignity or stateliness that you might find in a prayer book. In line 2 there are two sets of three words that are being negated: 'persons nor things nor ideas, ideals nor religions nor institutions'. The **two sets of three are held in balance by the comma** (creating a **caesura** in the line), and have a heightened, formal rhythm. The three adjectives at the end of line 5 – 'unseen, unknown, creative' – have a similar quality.

Questions

1	What is the difference between 'respect' and 'reverence' as Lawrence sees it in this poem?
2	What do we learn about Lawrence's beliefs from this poem?
3	Comment on the ending of the poem: 'Say no more!' What does Lawrence mean? Is he talking to himself or warning the reader, do you think?
4	Is this really a poem? What, if anything, would be lost if it were written out as prose?
5	What, would you say, is the poem really about? Explain your answer.
6	Does the fact that it was written by a dying man affect your reading of this poem? If so, how?
7	What do you feel absolute reverence for? How about a *tinge* of reverence? Respect? In groups, compare your thoughts, then share them with the class.

What Have They Done to You?

What have they done to you, men of the masses, creeping back and forth to work?

What have they done to you, the saviours of the people, oh what have they saved you from,
    while they pocketed the money?

Alas, they have saved you from yourself, from your own frail dangers
and devoured you with the machine, the vast maw of iron.

They saved you from your squalid cottages and poverty of hand to mouth   5
and embedded you in workmen's dwellings, where your wage is the dole of work,
    and the dole is your wage of nullity.

They took away, oh they took away your man's native instincts and intuitions
and gave you a board-school education, newspapers, and the cinema.

They stole your body from you, and left you an animated carcass
to work with, and nothing else: 10
unless goggling eyes, to goggle at the film
and a board-school brain, stuffed up with the ha'penny press.

Your instincts gone, your intuitions gone, your passions dead
Oh carcass with a board-school mind and a ha'penny newspaper intelligence,
what have they done to you, what have they done to you, Oh what have they done to you?   15

Oh look at my fellow-men, oh look at them
the masses! Oh, what has been done to them?

Glossary

4	*maw*: the jaws and throat of an animal
6	*dole*: something given; the second use of 'dole' in the line refers specifically to the term used for the money given to unemployed workers in the UK
6	*nullity*: lack of importance, nothingness, i.e. when a worker is unemployed
8	*board-school*: state-run elementary school
9	*animated*: brought to life
12	*ha'penny press*: cheap and sensational newspapers; 'ha'penny' (half-penny) is pronounced hayp-nee

Guidelines

'What Have They Done to You?' is one of a group of poems in *More Pansies* in which Lawrence dwells on industrialisation and what it has done to the men who have become part of the 'machine' of industry. Although these poems were probably written while he was in Italy, he is thinking particularly of conditions in England. Perhaps this is because the exhibition of his paintings took place in London about this time, and may have caused him to think about the land of his birth.

Commentary

The poem begins with a reiteration of the question in the title: what have they done to you? He makes it clear who 'you' are: 'men of the masses', the working classes who work to a timetable in factories. In the second line, where the question is repeated, it becomes apparent who 'they' are: the people who 'pocketed the money', the rich factory-owners and industrialists. He may call them 'saviours of the people', and that may have been how many of them saw themselves, but Lawrence is being **ironic**. He asks what 'they' have saved 'you' from.

Most of the rest of the poem is in the form of answers to those questions. They have saved 'you from yourself' but 'devoured you' with the 'vast maw of iron' that is the machine – in other words, mechanical labour in factories and the whole system of which that is a part. Things had not been good for the 'masses' before; they were poor and lived in 'squalid cottages'. But now, in their 'workmen's dwellings', they have become what are now sometimes called 'wage slaves'. They get wages for their work, and 'the dole' when they are unemployed and have no work, which makes of them a 'nullity' or nothingness. It is not accidental that **a secondary, older meaning of 'dole' is pain or grief**.

From line 7 Lawrence explains what 'they took away': 'instincts and intuitions' that come from **a real connection** with the environment and satisfying work, as he makes clear elsewhere. They even stole their bodies to use to run machines, leaving them 'an animated carcass / to work with' (lines 9–10). And what did they give in return? A standardised 'board-school education', sensational newspapers and 'the cinema'.

As the poem goes on, the **emotional temperature rises** and the **language gets more repetitive and disdainful**: 'goggling eyes, to goggle at the film'. The **parallel phrases pile up** like one blow after another – 'Your instincts gone, your intuitions gone, your passions dead' (line 13) – and in the next line Lawrence brings together repeated words from earlier in the poem: 'Oh carcass with a board-school mind and a ha'penny newspaper intelligence'. The tone is scathing, and he is beginning to sound obsessed. There is nowhere to go now but into **an anguish of repetition**: 'what have they done to you, what have they done to you, Oh what have they done to you?'

The final two lines turn towards an imagined audience – presumably his readers – and demand that they 'look' at his 'fellow-men'. The 'Oh's tell you how **exasperated and emotional** Lawrence is. He ends where he began, except that 'you' are now 'them', and there is the added, anguished 'Oh': 'Oh, what has been done to them?' It is a rhetorical device, **aiming to have an effect on an audience**. Perhaps it is also a little hysterical?

Themes

The theme of Lawrence's grief-filled outpourings is the human consequences of the mechanisation of labour and the increasing urbanisation of the working class as the result of industrialisation. Lawrence's father had been a miner, and though the work was physical and brutal it was not mechanical, and the mining village in which the family lived was surrounded by countryside. Mass-production factories required men and women to become, in effect, **part of the machinery**, carrying out repetitive tasks that, Lawrence believed, destroyed the working person's dignity and instinctive life. It was a process that had begun at the end of the eighteenth century, and accelerated through the nineteenth and into the twentieth century. Much of Lawrence's adult life was devoted to travelling the world in order to find a better, more instinctive way of life in other cultures – what he called his **'savage pilgrimage'** (see Biography, p. 246).

But there is a **tension** – perhaps even a contradiction – in Lawrence's attitude in this poem. He is mourning the fate of the working classes, and there is no doubting the strength of his passion. At the same time, he hates what they have become so much that he ends up addressing them like this: 'Oh carcass with a board-school mind and a ha'penny newspaper intelligence'. **He pities them, but he seems to despise them as well.** For Lawrence, they are not individuals but 'the masses'. He calls them his 'fellow-men', but you don't get the feeling that he considers himself one of them. Consequently his pity for them can feel sentimental or patronising.

Imagery

This is not a poem that works through its imagery, except inasmuch as it builds up a picture of the masses, 'creeping back and forth to work', becoming 'an animated carcass' or staring at a film with 'goggling eyes'. The other image that appears once but underpins the whole poem is that of the **machine of industry**, the 'vast maw of iron' (line 4) that is like **a voracious beast that devours** the workers who become part of it.

Form and language

As with the other poems from *More Pansies* which we have looked at, this poem is written in free verse, but here the **long lines suit the outpouring of emotion** in the poem and also help to create the sense of a speaking voice **addressing an audience**. This poem owes something to the American poet Walt Whitman (1819–1892), from whom Lawrence first learned that it was possible to write in this **free, loose way**, and who often poured out his feelings about humanity in his poems in long lines full of repetition:

> 'O you youths, Western youths,
> So impatient, full of action, full of manly pride and friendship,
> Plain I see you Western youths, see you tramping with the foremost,
> Pioneers! O pioneers!'

The rhythms of Lawrence's poem are also reminiscent of the Book of Psalms in the Bible.

The language is rhetorical, **asking questions and stirring up emotions**. The poem builds up a picture of the debased masses through the repetition of key ideas ('board-school', 'ha'penny newspaper', 'carcass') and phrases, primarily 'what have they done to you?'. The rhythms become more **insistent** as the poem goes on, and the 'Oh's express the strength of his feeling. Above all, Lawrence is trying to shake us into seeing what he sees and feeling something ourselves. It makes sense, then, to turn to us, the readers, and say 'look at them' at the end, not letting us ignore the problem, and even implicating us in it. The shorter, terser final two lines help to carry his exasperated anger.

Questions

1	Who is the 'you' Lawrence is addressing in the first fifteen lines of the poem?
2	Who are 'they', and what impression do you get of them?
3	What does Lawrence mean when he says that 'they' have 'devoured you with the machine'?
4	What picture do you get of the 'masses' before they were 'saved'?
5	What does Lawrence think of the cinema? Can you think of any good reasons for his attitude?
6	In what sense did 'they' steal 'your body from you' (line 9)?
7	Who is Lawrence addressing in the final two lines? Why this change of focus?
8	Comment on the use of repetition in the poem.
9	In another poem written at about the same time, Lawrence writes, 'A few are my fellow-men / a few, only a few: / the mass are not.' In your opinion, does this cast any light on 'What Have They Done to You?'?
10	Imagine you are a working man or woman of the time, educated in a state school, with a love of the cinema. Write a letter to Lawrence in response to his poem.
11	Have a class debate on the views about the masses and industrialisation that Lawrence expresses in this poem.

Before you read

What do you know about the Greek myth of Persephone (called Proserpina by the Romans)? Share your knowledge in class.

Bavarian Gentians

Not every man has gentians in his house
in soft September, at slow, sad Michaelmas.
Bavarian gentians, tall and dark, but dark
darkening the daytime torch-like with the smoking blueness of Pluto's gloom,
ribbed hellish flowers erect, with their blaze of darkness spread blue,   5
blown flat into points, by the heavy white draught of the day.

Torch-flowers of the blue-smoking darkness, Pluto's dark-blue blaze
black lamps from the halls of Dis, smoking dark blue
giving off darkness, blue darkness, upon Demeter's yellow-pale day
whom have you come for, here in the white-cast day?   10

Reach me a gentian, give me a torch!
let me guide myself with the blue, forked torch of a flower
down the darker and darker stairs, where blue is darkened on blueness
down the way Persephone goes, just now, in first-frosted September,
to the sightless realm where darkness is married to dark   15
and Persephone herself is but a voice, as a bride,
a gloom invisible enfolded in the deeper dark
of the arms of Pluto as he ravishes her once again
and pierces her once more with his passion of the utter dark
among the splendour of black-blue torches, shedding fathomless darkness on the nuptials.   20

Give me a flower on a tall stem, and three dark flames,
for I will go to the wedding, and be wedding-guest
at the marriage of the living dark.

Glossary

Title	*Bavarian gentians*: blue, trumpet-like flowers from upland areas in Germany (see picture overleaf)
2	*Michaelmas*: the feast of St Michael, 29 September
4	*Pluto*: god of the underworld in Greek mythology; also known as Hades
8	*Dis*: one of the names for the underworld in classical mythology
9	*Demeter*: mother of Persephone; goddess of agriculture
10	*white-cast*: overcast with whiteness
14	*Persephone*: daughter of Demeter
18	*ravishes*: takes by force, fills with rapture
20	*fathomless*: too deep to measure
20	*nuptials*: wedding celebrations

Guidelines

'Bavarian Gentians' is **a poem written by a dying man about his dying**, which he imagines in terms of a myth about the cycle of the seasons, without an ounce of self-pity. In September 1929 Lawrence was staying in Rottach in the Bavarian Alps, Germany, to be near his friend, the doctor and writer Max Mohr. Frieda put by his bed a large bunch of Bavarian gentians, the intensely blue flowers you can see in the picture, and he was struck by the 'dark blue gloom' of the gentians. His imagination worked on them in several versions of the poem, which became more and more focused on the myth of Persephone (see below), and this last version was probably completed in October, when he had returned to Bandol in the south of France.

Persephone and Pluto

The ancient Greek myth of Persephone is concerned with the cycle of the seasons. Persephone was the daughter of Zeus and Demeter, the goddess of agriculture who was responsible for the fertility of the earth. One day Persephone was picking flowers in a meadow when she was seized by Pluto, god of the underworld, and carried off on his chariot. He made her his queen, and goddess of the lower world, for which 'Dis' is one of the names.

Demeter searched all over the world for her and because of her neglect of the earth it became barren. Eventually Zeus helped Demeter to rescue her daughter from the lower world, but because Persephone had eaten six pomegranate seeds while she was there, it was arranged that she would spend six months of each year on earth, the other six in the underworld. The spring and summer is when she is on earth, the autumn and winter when she is in the underworld. At the beginning of autumn, the time of year in which the poem is set, she would descend once more to be with Pluto in Dis. She is often pictured carrying a torch. Each spring she would make the return journey to earth, bringing renewed life.

Commentary

Lines 1–6

The opening statement is **low-key and intimate**, suggesting that the speaker considers himself especially blessed. It is September, summer has ended; the atmosphere is created by the **unassertive adjectives**: 'soft', 'slow', 'sad'. He is looking at the flowers, 'tall and dark', and it is as if they are torches that shed darkness instead of light, 'darkening the daytime'. He associates their 'smoking blueness' with 'Pluto's gloom' in the underworld; 'smoking' might suggest the fires of hell in a Christian context, but this underworld is not primarily a place of punishment, and the smoke here comes from the flower-torches. If he sees them as 'hellish' flowers, it is in the same context.

He is looking closely at the flowers, as you can see from the picture opposite. The flower gains its ribbed appearance from the tight circle of leaves around its base, from which the flowers stand upright, 'erect'. The ends of the petals, however, turn outwards in daylight, 'blown flat' in Lawrence's words, by the 'heavy white draught of the day'. Notice that the day is heavy and white, less alluring than the sensual blue darkness of the flowers.

Lines 7–10

Lawrence keeps looking at the gentians and **working on the image**, repeating and recombining its elements – torch, blueness, darkness, smoke, Pluto – to **mesmerising effect**. If the darkness belongs to Pluto and Dis, the 'yellow-pale' day is Demeter's. That element brings to the fore **the myth** that has been lurking in the background of the poem, and as it is September, it is time for Persephone to be summoned back to the underworld. But perhaps not just her. For Lawrence, the gentian is a sign, **a portent**: 'whom have you come for …?' he asks.

Lines 11–20

He knows the summons is for himself, and does not run or hide. Instead he declares, 'Reach me a gentian, give me a torch!' – if he is going down to the underworld he will need it to light his way. He does not want to be led passively by the hand, but says 'let me guide myself'.

Now he imagines the descent into the underworld down the 'darker and darker' stairs and into the blue darkness, in the footsteps of Persephone into the darkness of 'the sightless realm'. Here 'darkness is married to dark', just as Persephone is a 'gloom invisible' taken into the 'deeper dark' of Pluto's arms. Their marriage union is a **passionate** if not violent one. He is active: he 'ravishes' and 'pierces' her; we know no more about her part than that she is ravished and pierced. The word 'ravish' can mean 'fill with rapture' as well as 'take by force', and Lawrence's language tells you that this is a wedding ('nuptials'), not a rape, but there is horror as well as 'splendour' in the scene.

Lines 21–24

But that is the scene that Lawrence will witness and participate in. He asks for the torch-flower again, announcing that he will follow Persephone and 'go to the wedding'. The implication is that he is going towards his own death; **he too will be 'enfolded' in darkness. But he embraces it**, seeing himself as a 'wedding-guest' and the wedding as a marriage of the '*living* dark'.

Three dark flames

Why 'three dark flames' in line 21? You would expect the flames to be coming from the torch – the gentian – but a Bavarian gentian has five petals, not three. Perhaps it is a reference to the trio he imagines in the underworld: Pluto, Persephone and himself; Lawrence writes elsewhere of human bodies as flames. More likely it relates to theories Lawrence developed in his last months of the individual's journey through the underworld, in which 'the soul, the spirit, and the living "I" are the three divine natures of man', like the three flames here.

Themes

The theme of the poem is, of course, death. But **Lawrence sees death through the lens of mythology** – the journey of Persephone to the underworld. This means that death is understood as part of **a greater cycle of death and rebirth in the endless round of the seasons**. Even the moment of Pluto's violation of Persephone is also the moment of fertilisation that makes possible the coming spring. Though the poem does not state that, the idea is present in the structure of the myth.

It is also a poem about **how to face death**. Understanding death in the mythical context of eternal renewal seems to give Lawrence strength, but this is not grim courage in the face of disaster but something closer to joy, or at least intense anticipation. Lawrence's **vision of the descent into the underworld** is tinged with fear, reverence, horror, sensuality and excitement.

He believed in something beyond himself, as we saw in 'Absolute Reverence', and he knew he was unusual in this attitude to death. Perhaps this awareness of the originality of his attitude lies behind the poem's first line: 'Not every man has gentians in his house'.

Lawrence on death

'Do I fear the strange approach of the creative unknown to my door? I fear it only with pain and with unspeakable joy. And do I fear the invisible dark hand of death plucking me into the darkness, gathering me blossom by blossom from the stem of my life into the unknown of my afterwards? I fear it only in reverence and with strange satisfaction. For this is my final satisfaction, to be gathered blossom by blossom, all my life long, into the finality of the unknown which is my end.'

D. H. Lawrence, 'Life' (1916)

Imagery

The **texture of the poem** – the imagery; the play of words, sounds and rhythms – **works on the reader's feelings** to give substance to the ideas of death and dying that Lawrence is embracing. With 'Bavarian Gentians' it is difficult to separate out the elements, as **they work together to create their powerful effects**, but we will start with the imagery.

The starting point for that, of course, is the gentians, whose blueness suggests **a living darkness**, and whose torch-like shape suggests the myth of Persephone and a descent into the underworld. He imagines this descent as something sensual, even erotic, despite the horror that is lurking. The darkness, rather than being an absence of light, becomes a vivid presence. Reinforcing this paradox, the daylight is 'heavy', 'white-cast', 'yellow-pale'; lifeless in contrast with the rich, fascinating blue darkness. The gentians are still there at the end of the descent, as the 'black-blue torches, shedding fathomless darkness on the nuptials'.

The extraordinary thing about the imagery in this poem is that whole world of Pluto, Persephone, the 'halls of Dis', the torches that light them and the quality of the darkness, together with the mythic story in which they are all involved, grows out of Lawrence's **observation** of the dark blue gentians and their **effect on his imagination**.

Form and language

'Bavarian Gentians' casts **a powerful spell**. The rich sound patterns and rhythmic repetitions, especially in the middle sections of the poem, give it **a hypnotic or trance-like quality**, drawing the reader in to Lawrence's vision just as you feel he is being drawn by his imagination.

Though the poem has no regular metric form, it is interesting that the first line is a perfect iambic pentameter, and indeed all the first three lines could be scanned in that way. The **deeply familiar rhythm of the pentameter helps to create the gentle, intimate atmosphere of the beginning of the poem**, before Lawrence's imagination takes it to very different places.

The **lines become longer as the poem's central images breathe and expand**. The same words or word-roots ('blue', 'blueness'; 'dark', 'darker', 'darkened', 'darkening', 'darkness') occur again and again, in different combinations. **Long vowels combine with chiming consonants**, often in groups of three stressed syllables close together, e.g. 'dark-blue blaze', 'yellow-pale day', 'blue, forked torch', 'first-frosted September'. Alliteration frequently underlines the rhythm, as in line 13: '<u>d</u>own the <u>d</u>arker and <u>d</u>arker stairs, where <u>b</u>lue is <u>d</u>arkened on <u>b</u>lueness'.

In the third verse-paragraph (lines 11–20), **the intensity builds as the descent into darkness takes place** and the climactic moment is reached. It is one complete sentence, led by the phrase 'let me guide myself' (line 12) and followed by phrase after phrase that **thickens the darkness** until Pluto 'pierces' her with his 'passion' (alliteration on the hard 'p' again heightening the rhythm), until we reach the final long line that brings the description of the dark 'nuptials' to a hushed, still conclusion.

In contrast, the shorter three last lines have a determined resolve. The order 'Give me a flower' breaks the spell, and the declaration 'I will go to the wedding' is a plain statement of intent. It is as if, having pictured to himself the journey he is going to go on, he wants now to get on with it.

> **Versions of 'Bavarian Gentians'**
>
> **There are several different versions of 'Bavarian Gentians'. The poem that is printed here grew out of simpler, more descriptive poems about the gentians, starting from Lawrence's intense observation of their blueness and darkness, out of which the imagery of Persephone and the underworld gradually emerged. This version is not the one that was printed in the posthumous *Last Poems*, but it is probably the final one, and the one in which the imagery is most fully developed.**

Questions

1	At what time of the year is the poem set? In what ways is this important to the poem?
2	What qualities of the gentians does Lawrence notice in the first section (lines 1–6)? Name as many as you can.
3	Why does he ask 'whom have you come for …?' in line 10?
4	In your own words, describe the scene Lawrence imagines in the underworld (lines 15–20), and what it means to him.
5	How would you describe the tone of the third section (lines 11–20)? ■ reverential ■ intoxicated ■ ecstatic ■ horrified Or what word would you use? Explain your answer.
6	What does Lawrence mean when he says he wants to be 'wedding-guest / at the marriage of the living dark' (lines 22–23)?
7	What is the significance of the first line: 'Not every man has gentians in his house'?
8	Comment on the role of paradox in the poem.
9	'Lawrence places himself *inside* the myth of Persephone.' Comment on the validity of this remark and its significance to 'Bavarian Gentians'.
10	The sounds that consonants and vowels make are at the heart of this poem. Choose two phrases or lines you find striking and show how Lawrence achieves his effects.
11	The final two lines could have been written as one line. What is the effect of having a line break after 'wedding-guest'?
12	Lawrence has sometimes been accused of misogyny – a dislike of women. Is there anything in this poem that might suggest this attitude? Do you think it is a fair charge? Explain your answer.
13	*Groupwork* Do you think Lawrence's attitude to death in this poem is mad, brave or what? Discuss in pairs or small groups.
14	Imagine you are the writer's sister or brother, and that he has sent you this poem. Write a letter back to him saying what you feel about his attitude to his own death.

SNAPSHOT D. H. LAWRENCE

- Working-class mining background in midlands of England
- Celebrated the body and sexual relations in human life
- Believed in the importance of man's relationship with the natural world
- Wrote about death in a positive way
- Profound spiritual beliefs, but not Christian ones

- A prophet as well as a poet
- Moved away from the conventional poetry he had grown up with
- Used free verse with great variety and musicality
- Free verse gives the sense of someone responding moment-to-moment

Exam-Preparation Questions

1 'Lawrence was a ground-breaking writer, but not a very good poet.' Discuss this statement, supporting your answer with reference to the poetry of Lawrence on your course.

2 'He himself is always so very much there [in the poems], pontific, self-doubtful, humble, raging, letting the free-verse lines rush out ...' Discuss this statement, supporting your answer with reference to the poetry of Lawrence on your course.

3 Lawrence wrote, 'All things are relative, and have their sacredness in their true relation to all other things.' What light does this statement throw on Lawrence's poetry, do you think? Answer with reference to the poems on your course.

4 What do Lawrence's poems tell you about the man who wrote them? Consider in detail at least four poems from those on your course.

5 'We read Lawrence's poetry for what it says, not for how it is said.' Discuss this statement, supporting your answer with reference to the poetry of Lawrence on your course.

6 What do you admire about Lawrence's poems, and what, if anything, do you dislike? Support your answer with reference to the poetry of Lawrence on your course.

7 'Animals, babies, himself, other people, God – all receive the same piercing, honest beam of attention.' Discuss this statement, supporting your answer with reference to the poetry of Lawrence on your course.

8 'Not I, not I, but the wind that blows through me!' This is the first line of Lawrence's poem, 'Song of a Man Who Has Come Through'. Use this line as a starting point for a discussion of Lawrence's poems. You might consider some of the following:
- The subject matter of his poetry
- His use of free verse
- His religious attitudes
- His attitude to death
- His use of language

9 Write an introduction to the poetry of D. H. Lawrence for readers new to his work. In your answer you should discuss:
- The subjects and themes of his poetry
- His use of language and verse forms.

You might also consider some of these subjects:
- The imagery of his poetry
- The development and variety of his poetry
- The impression we get of Lawrence from his poetry
- What you like or dislike about his poetry.

10 Lawrence wrote that 'The essential quality of poetry is that it makes a new effort of attention, and "discovers" a new world within the known world.' Discuss Lawrence's poetry as discovery in the light of this statement, referring to the poetry of Lawrence on your course.

11 'Lawrence wrote poetry on a huge variety of subjects, and in many different styles, but his own voice is always recognisable.' Discuss this statement, supporting your answer with reference to the poetry of Lawrence on your course.

Sample Essay

Lawrence referred to his true, inner self, the artist inside him, as his 'demon'. According to the poet W. H. Auden, Lawrence 'learned quite soon to let his demon speak, but it took him a long time to find the appropriate style for him to speak in'. Discuss this statement, with reference to the poems of Lawrence on your course.

Most of Lawrence's early poetry imitates the styles of the poems he had been read in school as a child, making use of rhyme and regular metre. He rejected some of his own first poems, which he felt were too conventional, because from very early on he had unconventional things he wanted to say in his poems. He realised it was important to let his 'demon' speak, and it was more important to say what he needed to say than to obey the 'rules' of poetry. This created a tension between form and content that is often apparent in his early poems.

Introduction addresses the terms of the question

End of first paragraph indicates what will next be discussed

You can see this in 'Call into Death'. In the first two stanzas there is a lot of rhyme. Stanza 1 rhymes AABA and stanza 2, ACCC. In the third stanza, however, there is no rhyme at all. It is as if Lawrence has given up on the form he had set up at the start. The only reason can be that he couldn't find a way to say what he – or his demon – wanted to say within the constraints of rhyme. The result is sometimes awkward. The first two stanzas contain some startling and memorable images – 'the small sharp stars are quite near, / The white moon going among them like a white bird among snow-berries' – but the next line sounds clumsy: 'And the sound of her gently rustling in heaven like a bird I hear.' The subject and main verb – 'I hear' – have been shifted to the end of the line for the sake of the rhyme. This sort of inversion is common in the Victorian poetry Lawrence grew up with, but the language and voice are not Lawrence's natural ones.

Detailed discussion of first poem

Keeps the terms of the question in mind

In the final stanza of the poem, where there is no rhyme, the phrases flow more naturally and simply. Nothing gets in the way of expressing his desire to 'fall like a breath within the breathing wind / Where you are lost'. It is a striking and tender image, and he does not try to hide the strength of his feeling, although the melancholy mood is unlike what we see in the mature Lawrence.

Quotations incorporated into the sentences

'Piano' is the only poem among those on our course in which the stanza form is fully realised. Each stanza rhymes AABB, and there is a regular underlying metre, though Lawrence takes plenty of liberties with it. Here, though, the theme of nostalgia for the past is appropriate to the old-fashioned form. By the time he wrote the final version of this poem, Lawrence was a different man from the one described in the poem. He was a married man, set on a new course with his wife, Frieda, and in 'Piano' he is writing about an older self. It is an honest and moving depiction of the overwhelming feeling of loss that can arise from a sudden, powerful memory, but the man who wrote it had emerged from the shadow of his mother. He knows that the 'hymns in the cosy parlour' and the 'tinkling piano' are sentimental images, and that his nostalgia is a betrayal of his adult self. He is no longer the man to 'weep like a child for the past', and the rigid stanza form, while giving the poem an attractive gloss, also distances it from the immediate present in a way that Lawrence's mature poems never do.

Second poem introduced

Uses short quotations to make points

Final sentence brings back another of the terms of the question (style)

This poem is a farewell to an older self and an older style of writing poetry.

It is interesting, however, that the earliest of the poems we are studying, 'Trailing Clouds', already contains many of the stylistic elements of Lawrence's mature poetry. Although there is occasional rhyme and poetic inversion ('So clings to me, / My baby'), there is no clear verse form, and the varying line lengths create the sort of hypnotic rhythm we find in some of his later poems. The way that Lawrence takes a word and alters and reuses it to pursue an idea or an image also foreshadows his mature poetic style. Here, for example, the word 'heavy' is taken up in 'storm-heavy', 'heavily' and 'heaviness', and this repetition helps to create the atmosphere of the poem and to give it its particular shape. It is a poem in which Lawrence's 'demon' is finding its voice.

Third poem introduced, referring to the terms of the question

Strong final sentence to end the paragraph

Opening sentence of paragraph sets out what will be discussed next, using the terms of the question

In the collection *Birds, Beasts and Flowers* Lawrence has found his mature style and the true voice – or voices – of his 'demon'. The use of free verse means that the play of his imagination is not held back by the need to rhyme or fit a set rhythm, but there is nevertheless a subtle but powerful music to the poetry. In 'Snake', for example, the long lines, together with the drawn-out syllables, help to create a picture of the snake. The phrase 'trailed his yellow-brown slackness soft-bellied down' gives you a sense of the snake's slow, leisurely movements; and the pattern of consonants – 'l', 'b' and 's' in particular – and the internal rhyme on 'brown'/'down' create a rich sound pattern that suggests the sensuousness and ease of the snake. The longer lines describing the snake contrast with the shorter, more urgent lines that describe the moment of sudden drama in the poem:

Brief but detailed analysis of style using short quotations

> 'I looked round, I put down my pitcher,
> I picked up a clumsy log
> And threw it at the water-trough with a clatter.'

Lawrence is able to evoke not just the movements of the snake, but the movements of the speaker's mind which, unlike the snake, is self-doubting and self-questioning: 'Was it humility, to feel so honoured? / I felt so honoured.' The poem tells a simple story, but Lawrence finds space to suggest the inner life of both man and snake, so that a simple narrative has complex resonances.

Development of argument in brief discussion of several poems

In the shorter poems from *More Pansies*, Lawrence finds a variety of tones and voices within the free verse form. There is wry humour in 'Intimates'. You can hear his matter-of-fact voice in 'Absolute Reverence', the voice of a plain-speaking working-class man who isn't afraid to speak his mind: 'I feel absolute reverence to nobody and to nothing human'. In 'What Have They Done to You?' there is a rhetoric that draws on the repetitions of words and phrasing found in the Bible, particularly in the Book of Psalms, but the anger and pain is Lawrence's own. These are not his finest, most powerful poems, but the loose style he had found could accommodate anything he wanted to say, and Lawrence always had plenty to say.

'Bavarian Gentians' is a wonderful example of what Lawrence's mature style enabled him to do. Because the flexible form lets him follow an ever-changing and developing train of thought, the act of looking at a bunch of deep blue gentians starts him on a profound imaginative journey. He begins by noticing the 'smoking blueness' of the gentians and associating them with Pluto, god of the underworld, thinking of their colour as a 'blaze of darkness'. As in other poems, he repeats key words that take hold of his imagination – 'blue', 'dark', 'darkness', 'Pluto', 'blaze', 'torch' – and he develops the image of the gentians as torches

Introduces final poem to be discussed in detail

that shed darkness instead of light. That leads to the idea of taking one to guide him into the underworld in the footsteps of Persephone: 'Reach me a gentian, give me a torch!' The poem builds in intensity as he imagines the journey down into deeper and deeper darkness, culminating in the savage union of Pluto and Persephone, the 'marriage of the living dark'. As well as repetition, Lawrence uses alliteration and long vowel sounds (e.g. 'dark-blue blaze') to emphasise the strong stresses of the stately rhythm.

There is a freshness and a sense of the unexpected in the way that one idea follows another so that a simple flower leads him into a vision of the underworld, in which his own death takes its place in an ancient myth of seasonal renewal. There is no melancholy at the prospect of death as there had been in 'Call into Death', and no overwhelming desire to escape from the adult world as there was in 'Piano'. Lawrence's 'demon' seems liberated and invigorated, as if finding his poetic style has allowed him to flourish.

Comparison with poems discussed earlier gives shape to the argument

In conclusion, it is true that it took some years for Lawrence to find a style for his 'demon' to speak in, and it involved using a free verse form that was flexible enough to follow changing thoughts and ideas and emotions. It was such a loose form that he could say anything he wanted in it. Sometimes he didn't want to do more than get a thought down on paper, but when his imagination and attention were really engaged he could write intense poems, like 'Snake' and 'Bavarian Gentians', where you can see the process of his mind and instincts at work, and which have a subtle, powerful music of their own.

Final paragraph draws together the discussions of different poems

ESSAY CHECKLIST		Yes √	No ×
Purpose	Has the candidate understood the task?		
	Has the candidate responded to it in a thoughtful manner?		
	Has the candidate answered the question?		
Comment:			
Coherence	Has the candidate made convincing arguments?		
	Has the candidate linked ideas?		
	Does the essay have a sense of unity?		
Comment:			
Language	Is the essay written in an appropriate register?		
	Are ideas expressed in a clear way?		
	Is the writing fluent?		
Comment:			
Mechanics	Is the use of language accurate?		
	Are all words spelled correctly?		
	Does the punctuation help the reader?		
Comment:			

Adrienne Rich

1929–2012

Biography

Early life

Adrienne Cecile Rich was born on 16 May 1929 in Baltimore, Maryland, USA to Doctor Arnold Rich and Helen Gravely Jones Rich. Arnold was an assimilated Austro-Hungarian Jew and Helen was a southern Protestant; their two daughters, Adrienne and Cynthia, were raised as Christians. Rich's Jewish heritage is something she explored in her later poetry and essays.

Rich and her younger sister were educated at home until fourth grade, primarily by their mother, who had been a gifted composer and concert pianist, and also encouraged by their father, who was chairman of pathology at Johns Hopkins Medical University and a renowned expert on tuberculosis. Theirs was a cultured and literary home and Rich was encouraged to read and write poetry from a very young age. She noted that the poets she was reading at this time – Matthew Arnold, William Blake, W. B. Yeats and John Keats – were men. Arnold Rich was determined to raise a 'prodigy' and Adrienne was to excel in her education. She recalls, 'I was supposed to write something every day and show it to him, at some points I hated that. But it was probably a good thing.'

Rich went to high school at Roland Park Country School, a girls' school that she remembered as an institution with teachers described as 'fine role models of single women who were intellectually impassioned'. Rich next attended the prestigious Radcliffe College, from which she graduated Phi Beta Kappa with an excellent degree in 1951. She was nominated by the poet W. H. Auden for the Yale Younger Poets Award for *A Change of World*, her debut collection of poetry, which was very controlled and adhered 'strictly to conventional rhythm and metre'. This was to be the first of many nominations, awards and prizes for her writing. After graduation Rich was awarded a Guggenheim Fellowship, which allowed her to study in Oxford for a year. However, after an Easter holiday in Italy, she decided not to complete her time in England and instead toured Italy, soaking up its culture and composing poems.

Early career and marriage

In 1953 Rich married Harvard economist Alfred Haskell Conrad, whom she met while an undergraduate. She was feeling increasingly stifled at home and consciously decided to marry as 'I knew no better way to disconnect from my first family'. In 1955 she had her first son, David, and also published *The Diamond Cutters and Other Poems*, from which the poem 'Living in Sin' is taken. She later said she wished this collection had never been published. By 1959 the couple had two more sons, Pablo and Jacob, and were living in Cambridge, Massachusetts. Rich found motherhood extremely difficult. Marriage and children was the expected norm for young women at the time, but she felt restricted by both. In her journal in 1960 she wrote:

> It is the suffering of ambivalence: the murderous alternation between bitter resentment and raw-edged nerves, and blissful gratification and tenderness. Sometimes I seem to myself, in my feelings toward these tiny guiltless beings, a monster of selfishness and intolerance.

It was a time when she almost gave up on her craft and found it increasingly difficult to write, 'I was writing very little, partly from fatigue, that female fatigue of supressed anger and loss of contact with my own being.'

The 1960s was a time of radical change in America and Rich became interested and active in the civil rights, feminist and anti-Vietnam movements sweeping the nation at the time, especially when the family moved to New York in 1966 so that Alfred could teach at City College of New York. She was one of many to sign the 'Writers and Editors War Tax Protest', which entailed a refusal to pay tax as long as America was at war with Vietnam. The famous feminist slogan 'the personal is political' was now very much at the heart of her work, which had itself become more radical and freer in terms of form and metre. In 1963 she published *Snapshots of a Daughter-in Law*, from which the poem 'The Roofwalker' is taken. In 1968 her father, who had been so influential on her poetic style and career, died.

Struggling with the demands of marriage and motherhood, Rich wrote, 'I had marriage and a child. If there were doubts, if there were periods of null depression or active despairing, these could only mean that I was ungrateful, insatiable, perhaps a monster.' After the birth of her third son Rich decided to be sterilised, thus preventing further pregnancy. This practice was not freely accepted at the time and when she awoke after the hospital procedure a nurse callously remarked, 'Had yourself spayed, did you?' Rich was reading Mary Wollstonecraft and Simone de Beauvoir and these authors spoke to her about women and their oppression.

Rich and her husband held fundraising parties at their New York apartment for civil rights and anti-war causes, including some events for the Black Panther movement, but within the marriage itself tensions had arisen, perhaps due to Rich's increasing feminism and her becoming more aware of her lesbianism. The couple split, following affairs on both sides, and in mid-1970 Rich moved into her own apartment. That autumn Alfred Conrad drove out to Vermont to the woods and shot himself. This tragic event is something Rich rarely addressed in public, although she did say, 'It was shattering for me and my children. It was a tremendous waste. He was a man of enormous talents and love of life.'

Feminism

Feminism is a belief in the political, social and economic equality of men and women. It is the belief that women and men should have the same rights, opportunities and power.

Later life and career

The poem 'Our Whole Life' was published in the 1971 work entitled *The Will to Change*. In 1973 she published the collection *Diving into the Wreck*, which explores change and relationships and contains the poems 'Trying to Talk With a Man', 'Diving into the Wreck' and 'From a Survivor'. A year later Rich wrote the poem 'Power', which explores the sacrifice of women and their creativity by examining the life and work of Marie Curie. This poem would echo some of Rich's earlier themes as expressed in, for example, 'Aunt Jennifer's Tigers'.

In 1976 Rich published *Twenty-One Love Poems* and a prose exploration of motherhood, *Of Woman Born*. She also came out as a lesbian, beginning a relationship with Michelle Cliff that would endure until Rich's death in 2012. Cliff was a novelist and editor from Jamaica who worked as a copy-editor at Rich's publishers, W. W. Norton. The two had much in common as both were passionate about issues of race, ethnicity and lesbianism. Rich said of this time in her life, 'the suppressed lesbian I had been carrying in me since adolescence began to stretch her limbs'.

In the 1980s Rich taught all over the USA, including spells lecturing at Scripps College, San Jose State University, Stanford University and Cornell University. She also founded and edited the journal *Bridges: A Journal for Jewish Feminists and Our Friends*, which explored Jewish women's rights. In 1981 Rich and Cliff took over the journal *Sinister Wisdom*, which dealt with lesbian issues. In 1984 they moved to Santa Cruz, California and lived there until their respective deaths.

Throughout the 1990s Rich continued to write poetry and prose and to win awards and prizes. For example, in 1992 alone she won the Robert Frost Silver Medal, the William Whitehead Award, the *LA Times* Book Award for poetry and the Lenore Marshall/Nation Award as well as receiving an honorary doctorate from Swarthmore College.

Rich struggled with orthopaedic arthritis for many years and the condition required a number of surgeries and the use of a cane. She was in considerable pain and discomfort towards the end of her life. She died in Santa Cruz on 27 March 2012 from complications of rheumatoid arthritis, aged eighty-two. Her partner of almost forty years, Michelle Cliff, died of liver failure four years later on 12 June 2016.

Rich wrote over two dozen volumes of poetry and more than a half-dozen of prose; the poetry alone has sold nearly 800,000 copies.

Social and Cultural Context

Oppression of women

Growing up in the 1930s, 1940s and 1950s, Adrienne Rich experienced first-hand the oppression of women and their confinement to specific gender roles. 'Aunt Jennifer's Tigers' features a woman who uses embroidery to express herself while controlled by a patriarchal husband. Rich may have had very similar feelings as a daughter. Her father decided she would be an accomplished poet when she was only a young child and groomed her relentlessly for this role. She said, 'His involvement was egotistical, tyrannical, and terribly wearing'. Her 'escape' in the 1950s, through marriage, was 'against her father's vehement opposition' and was to liberate her from 'that most dangerous place, the family home'. However, this proved to be an 'out of the frying pan, into the fire' situation as she had three sons by the age of thirty and felt **overwhelmed by motherhood and marriage**. Many women were feeling the same and feminism was on the rise in 1960s America.

Protest movements

Rich sums up the tumultuous period of radical social change she was a part of in the mid-twentieth century, saying, 'The fifties and sixties were years of rapid revelations: the sit-ins and marches in the South, the Bay of Pigs, the early anti-war movement, raised large questions … I needed to think for myself – about pacifism and dissent and violence, about poetry and society, and about my own relationship to those things'. In fact relationships of various kinds are often at the heart of Rich's poetry. She became a passionate supporter of the **anti-war**, **civil rights** and **feminist movements**. By 1976 she was **openly lesbian** and writing about lesbianism, motherhood, patriarchy and many other **social and cultural issues**. She was often criticised for this and many accused her poetry of being too political, of being 'strident'.

An example of her **strong ethical and political beliefs** can be seen in her treatment of the awards she won. For example, in 1974 Rich was nominated for the National Book Award for *Diving into the Wreck* and co-won with Beat poet Allen Ginsberg. She refused to accept it in her own name alone and instead accepted it on behalf of all women, with fellow nominees Alice Walker and Audre Lorde joining her on stage to do so. But

Rich was more than a feminist lesbian and campaigned against all inequality in society. When President Bill Clinton awarded her the National Medal of Arts, America's highest honour for artists, she declined as a political statement, explaining that she could not accept an award when she could see the 'brutal impact of racial and economic injustice' all around her and added that such honours 'mean nothing if it simply decorates the dinner table of power which holds it hostage'. She continued to use such platforms for protest. In 2003, for example, Rich turned down an invitation from President George W. Bush to a poetry event at the White House in protest against the war in Iraq.

Themes

In her obituary in *The New York Times* Adrienne Rich was described as 'a poet of towering reputation and towering rage, whose work – distinguished by an unswerving progressive vision and a dazzling, empathic ferocity – brought the **oppression of women and lesbians** to the forefront of poetic discourse and kept it there for nearly a half-century'.

Her passionate campaigning for **peace and equality** is reflected in her summary of why she wrote poetry: 'the creation of a society without domination'. Albert Gelpi effectively sums up Rich's themes as '**change and metamorphosis**' and said 'she ponders the dilemma of her **identity** … the **oppression of women by men, of the poor by the privileged**'. We see the theme of **social injustice** highlighted in, for example, 'The Uncle Speaks in the Drawing Room', where the uncle worries about his crystal bowls and chandeliers as an angry mob gathers outside.

A legacy she can be proud of is how **open to interpretation** her work is, how rich her language and imagery are and how her work provokes us to think about ourselves and our place and responsibility in the society we are part of. As Rich wrote, 'instead of poems about experiences I am getting **poems that are experiences** … if I have been a good parent to the poem, something will happen to you who read it'.

Metamorphosis: The term metamorphosis in animals means the process of transformation from an immature form to an adult form in distinct stages. This might mean, for example, changing from a chrysalis to a butterfly as in this image. In humans it means the change of nature from one sort of person to another.

Timeline

1929	Born 16 May in Baltimore, Maryland, USA
1951	Graduates from Radcliffe College; publishes the collection *A Change of World*; chosen by W. H. Auden for the Yale Younger Poets Award
1952	Awarded Guggenheim Fellowship; onset of rheumatoid arthritis
1953	Marries economist Alfred H. Conrad
1955	Publishes *The Diamond Cutters and Other Poems*; first son, David, born
1957	Second son, Paul, born
1959	Third son, Jacob, born
1960	Wins National Institute of Arts and Letters Award for poetry
1962	Lives in Amsterdam, Netherlands for two years; translates Dutch poetry
1963	Publishes *Snapshots of a Daughter-in-Law: Poems 1954–1962*
1966	Publishes *Necessities of Life: Poems 1962–1965*; moves to New York
1968	Father, Arnold, dies; teaches underprivileged children at City College NY
1970	Husband, Alfred, dies
1971	Publishes *The Will to Change: Poems 1968–1970*; writes influential feminist essay 'When We Dead Awaken: Writing as Re-Vision'
1973	Publishes *Diving into the Wreck: Poems 1971–1972*
1974	Wins National Book Award jointly with Allen Ginsberg
1976	Begins relationship with Michelle Cliff
1978	Publishes *The Dream of a Common Language: Poems 1974–1977*
1980; 1982	Undergoes surgery for arthritis
1986	Wins first Ruth Lilly Poetry Prize
1990	Awarded honorary doctorates from City College NY and Harvard University; wins Bill Whitehead Award for Lifetime Achievement (for gay or lesbian writing)
1992	Undergoes spinal surgery; wins Frost Medal
1997	Declines National Medal for the Arts from President Clinton
1999	Publishes the collection *Midnight Salvage*
2003	Refuses to attend poetry function at the White House in protest against Iraq war
2007	Publishes *Telephone Ringing in the Labyrinth: Poems 2004–2006*
2012	Dies from complications of rheumatoid arthritis, 27 March, in Santa Cruz, California

Before you read

Tigers: jot down five or six adjectives that come to mind when you imagine tigers. Compare your list with those of your classmates and note the most popular choices.

Aunt Jennifer's Tigers

Aunt Jennifer's tigers prance across a screen,
Bright topaz denizens of a world of green.
They do not fear the men beneath the tree;
They pace in sleek chivalric certainty.

Aunt Jennifer's fingers fluttering through her wool   5
Find even the ivory needle hard to pull.
The massive weight of Uncle's wedding band
Sits heavily upon Aunt Jennifer's hand.

When Aunt is dead, her terrified hands will lie
Still ringed with ordeals she was mastered by.   10
The tigers in the panel that she made
Will go on prancing, proud and unafraid.

Glossary

1	*prance*: spring forward in a lively and showy manner
2	*topaz*: amber-coloured gemstone
2	*denizens*: inhabitants, permanent residents; also, animals that have become naturalised
4	*sleek*: smooth, fluid, effortless
4	*chivalric*: describes a medieval code of honour, the principles of knighthood and knightly conduct
10	*ordeals*: times of great suffering and difficulty

Guidelines

This poem is from the 1951 collection *A Change of World*, which was Rich's first published collection of poetry. The speaker describes a needlepoint screen or panel depicting 'proud and unafraid' tigers, which Aunt Jennifer is embroidering with 'her terrified hands'. Responding to *A Change of World*, W. H. Auden awarded Rich a place in the Yale Younger Poets series, and praised her 'love for her medium' and her 'determination to ensure that whatever she writes shall, at least, not be shoddily made'. Rich felt that the male poets who dominated her father's library and her college courses were a huge influence on her early style:

I know that my style was first formed by male poets: by the men I was reading as an undergraduate – Frost, Dylan Thomas, Donne, Auden, MacNeice, Stevens, Yeats. What I chiefly learned from them was craft.

Commentary

Stanza 1

The poem makes a contrast between the real woman, Aunt Jennifer, and her embroidered creation of tigers that 'prance' across the tapestry. The verb suggests energy and fun but also perhaps an element of exhibitionism. Are they showing off or merely playful? The tigers are described in imagery that suggests strength and freedom. They move fearlessly and confidently, beautiful in their golden orange colour against a background of green. Significantly, they have no fear of 'the men' under the trees. They inhabit their world as if they have a complete right to be there.

The adjective 'chivalric' is interesting. Chivalry was a medieval code that embodied the qualities of the ideal knight, including bravery, nobility, piety and courtesy towards women. What do you think is implied by the description of the tigers' 'sleek chivalric certainty'? Is the speaker identifying them with the world of male power?

Stanza 2

The creator of these wonderful tigers is a woman whose fingers are 'fluttering' through the wool. The visual imagery cleverly reflects the colours and actions of the tapestry, but the 'ivory' needle pales in comparison with the orange and gold colours of the tigers. She seems powerless, stifled by her role as a traditional woman, married to 'Uncle'. The language used in association with Aunt Jennifer presents her as a woman controlled by others: 'Uncle's wedding band' (Is it significant that it seems to belong to him?) is a 'massive weight' for her. The phrase implies an imbalance of power in the marriage.

Stanza 3

The artistry and success evident in her craft, then, does not translate into personal power for Aunt Jennifer. The picture we are given of her is of a timid woman. Even when she dies, the poem asserts, she will still seem 'terrified'. The hands that made the tigers are those of a fearful victim, as much as they are the hands of an artist. The word 'mastered' reminds us of the source of masculine power in her marriage, while 'ordeals' hints at hidden sufferings. Aunt Jennifer and her life stand in stark contrast to her embroidered tigers, who 'Will go on prancing, proud and unafraid'. They will live on, proof of her creativity and skill, captured forever in their majestic movements.

Themes and imagery

The **contrast between Aunt Jennifer and the tigers she embroiders** is at the heart of this poem. The aunt is a timid, shadowy figure. All we are shown of her is her 'fluttering' fingers and her 'terrified hands', one of which is hampered by the 'massive weight of Uncle's wedding band'. Her needle is 'ivory', the pale colour of bone. The tigers, on the other hand, are 'Bright topaz denizens of a world of green'. They are full of energy, and 'pace in sleek chivalric certainty'. While the tigers show no fear, Aunt Jennifer will remain 'terrified' even in death. Their bright, heroic world makes Aunt Jennifer's seem all the duller.

Is it possible to interpret the poem as a commentary on **how women artists have experienced the restraints put upon them by their traditional roles in society**, seen in relation to other people (Jennifer is someone's aunt, someone's wife) rather than as individuals in themselves? The poem leaves us with a number of questions.

Does Aunt Jennifer realise exactly what she has achieved? Is she quite comfortable with it? Why are her hands, the creators of these magnificent animals, 'terrified'? Is it because she has realised what she has created and cannot face up to its implications, namely that she has repressed her creativity and sacrificed her power as an artist for the restraints of marriage?

Is it significant that the tigers are male, and that the only other people in the poem, the 'men beneath the tree' and the 'Uncle', are male too? Is the poem making a point about **patriarchal power** (that power in society is in the hands of the male sex)? Or is it saying that women like Aunt Jennifer have power too, even if they don't quite realise it yet (the poem was written in the 1950s)? If this is what is indicated, it would fit in with the title of the volume in which it appears, *A Change of World*.

Form and language

Like 'Storm Warnings', the poem has a **formal style**. It is written in **rhyming couplets** ('screen' / 'green') and makes use of **assonance** ('tigers' / 'Bright') and **alliteration** ('fingers fluttering') to create a quiet, pleasant effect. In relation to writing this poem, Rich has said, 'In those days formalism was part of the strategy – like asbestos gloves, it allowed me to handle materials I couldn't pick up barehanded.' The formal structure distances the poet from the subject of the poem.

> **Rich and Aunt Jennifer**
>
> Even though Rich wrote that she 'thought she was creating an imaginary woman … a person as distinct from myself as possible', she acknowledged that in fact Aunt Jennifer resembled her in important ways: 'Looking back at poems I wrote before I was twenty-one, I'm startled because beneath the conscious craft are glimpses of the split I even then experienced between the girl who wrote poems, who defined herself in writing poems, and the girl who was to define herself by her relationships with men.'

The simple, plain sentences and precise, descriptive language add to the effect of distance. Each word is worth pondering for its exact implications. Why 'prance'? Why 'topaz'? Why 'denizens'? What may be implied by the fact that the needle is 'ivory'? **The language is rich with suggestions of meaning but keeps the emotions at a distance.** The relationship between the poem's deliberately controlled expression and the underlying conflict it describes looks forward to some of Rich's most important themes, such as the relationship between the sexes and questions of power.

SNAPSHOT

- Formal structure and rhyming scheme
- Vibrancy of tigers
- Symbolism of wedding ring
- Use of contrast
- Permanence of art
- Use of colour
- Ideas of possession
- Alliteration and rhyme
- Picture of marriage
- Looming presence of the uncle

Exam-Style Questions

Understanding the poem

1	What do we learn about the habitat, appearance and personality of the tigers in the first stanza?
2	Comment on the alliteration of 'z' sounds in the phrase 'Bright topaz denizens' (line 2). What effect is achieved here?
3	The tigers 'do not fear the men beneath the tree' (line 3). What do you imagine is happening here? Who might these men be? Why are they 'beneath the tree'? Why, do you imagine, are the tigers unafraid of them?
4	Comment on the poet's use of colour in the first stanza.
5	What do we learn about Aunt Jennifer's hands in the second stanza? What emotions do you associate with Aunt Jennifer here?
6	The needle Aunt Jennifer uses is made of ivory. What is ivory? Could this be significant or connected to the tigers' world in any way?
7	Why might the wedding band seem to belong to 'Uncle' (line 7)? Also suggest reasons why the poet has not named him.
8	Why, do you think, will Aunt Jennifer's hands remain 'terrified' (line 9) even after she dies?
9	Comment on the use and meaning of the words 'ringed', 'ordeals' and 'mastered' in line 10.
10	The tigers 'Will go on prancing, proud and unafraid' (line 12). Describe the mood of this line. Does the alliteration used enhance this mood? Explain.

Thinking about the poem

1	Rich uses a lot of possible symbolism in the poem. What do the tigers, the needle and the ring represent for you in the poem?
2	Why, do you think, is Aunt Jennifer described in terms of only her hands while the tigers are depicted in more detail?
3	What, do you feel, is the overall theme of the poem? You can choose one of the options here or suggest your own interpretation: ■ The oppression of women ■ The beauty of nature ■ The permanence of art ■ Marriage. ■ Self-expression Justify your answer with close reference to the poem as a whole.
4	Compare the verbs and adjectives attached to the tigers in the poem with those attached to Aunt Jennifer. Perhaps make two lists. What does this comparison tell us about the two worlds depicted in the poem?
5	From your reading of the poem, how does the speaker feel about his or her aunt and uncle?

6	What do you notice about the form and rhyming scheme in this poem? Do these observations in any way reflect the themes and issues dealt with in the poem?
7	Do you like this poem? Give reasons for your answer.
8	'To be a female human being trying to fulfil traditional female functions in a traditional way *is* in direct conflict with the subversive function of the imagination.' Write a response to this poem in light of this statement from Adrienne Rich.

Imagining

1	Add a fourth stanza about the uncle mentioned in the poem, written in the style of the existing three stanzas.
2	Write an epitaph and/or a brief obituary for Aunt Jennifer.
3	If you could choose to draw, embroider, paint or sculpt a scene from nature to reflect your personality, what would it look like and what animal would you choose to feature in the scene? Explain your choices.

Before you read

If your home was somehow threatened, which items would you be most concerned about and why?

The Uncle Speaks in the Drawing Room

I have seen the mob of late
Standing sullen in the square,
Gazing with a sullen stare
At window, balcony and gate.
Some have talked in bitter tones,   5
Some have held and fingered stones.

These are follies that subside.
Let us consider, none the less,
Certain frailties of glass
Which, it cannot be denied,   10
Lead in times like these to fear
For crystal vase and chandelier.

Not that the missiles will be cast;
None as yet dare lift an arm.
But the scene recalls a storm   15
When our grandsire stood aghast
To see his antique ruby bowl
Shivered in a thunder-roll.

Let us only bear in mind
How these treasures handed down   20
From a calmer age passed on
Are in the keeping of our kind.
We stand between the dead glass-blowers
And murmurings of missile-throwers.

Glossary

7	*follies*: mistakes; silly behaviour
16	*grandsire*: grandfather
16	*aghast*: horrified
23	*glass-blowers*: craftspeople who form shapes by blowing through a pipe into melted glass

Guidelines

This poem, like 'Aunt Jennifer's Tigers', is from *A Change of World*, Rich's first collection of poetry published in 1951 when she was twenty-one years old. The poem's title refers to 'The Uncle' whereas the previous poem's title mentioned 'Aunt Jennifer'. An uncle features in both poems; here, the uncle is an authoritative voice, concerned for his home, his heritage and his belongings.

Commentary

Stanza 1
The speaker, the 'Uncle', unlike, say, Aunt Jennifer, is not given a name. (It is tempting to see him as the same persona as 'Uncle' in 'Aunt Jennifer's Tigers'.) The setting of the poem is upper class and rather old-fashioned, as the term 'Drawing Room' in the title suggests; images of a 'balcony' and a 'gate' imply that he keeps his distance, or wishes to, from others. The language in which the uncle speaks indicates that his views are similarly old-fashioned. He expresses a fear and suspicion of 'the mob … Standing sullen in the square', which he sees as a threat to his way of life. His depiction of the crowd reminds us of revolutions of the past: people staring threateningly at the homes of the upper class, talking 'in bitter tones'. Some have even 'held and fingered stones', as if they are about to attack.

Stanza 2
The uncle appears dismissive about the coming revolution: 'These are follies that subside.' Yet he also appears to know that it will happen and that precautions need to be taken. Certain glass objects ('crystal vase and chandelier') need to be preserved at all costs. They seem to represent a whole way of life that he feels it his responsibility to protect. Interestingly, he sets up an opposition between the 'mob', the poor people he fears, and the objects he values.

Stanza 3
Nothing has happened yet, the speaker says: 'None as yet dare lift an arm'. But the scene recalls a storm from the past, when his 'grandsire' (grandfather, or perhaps any ancestor) saw a prized possession, his 'antique ruby bowl', shaken 'in a thunder-roll'. The tone here is ambiguous. Is the speaker referring to a natural storm, or to a storm of protest? Is the tone mocking?

Stanza 4
The speaker takes on a representative voice, speaking of 'us' and 'We' and picking up from the use of 'our' in the previous stanza. He suggests that the precious glass objects ('treasures') represent an artistic legacy passed down to him by his ancestors. He makes, it seems, a conscious differentiation between 'our kind' (the rich and privileged?) and the mob. His duty, he suggests, is to preserve the 'treasures handed down' and keep them safe. He presents himself as standing between the creativity of craftspeople of the past and the destruction of the mob of the present, the unruly 'missile-throwers'. His language is aloof and alienating. 'Our kind' suggests an acceptance of class divisions in society, without any obvious desire to see them disappear.

Themes and imagery

The poem touches on big issues and themes: **inherited wealth**; **power**; **social division and unrest**. Rich allows the uncle to speak in his own voice without revealing her own attitude to what he describes. The uncle's voice is authoritative, formal, perhaps even a bit pompous. He clearly despises 'the mob' and those who threaten his way of life and the precious objects that represent his inherited wealth. Are we to interpret the poem as ironic? Might it be an indication of Rich's dismissal of certain traditional values and structures of wealth and power? Or is it another example of her ambiguous attitude to change at this stage of her life? In 'Storm Warnings' the speaker of the poem takes steps to protect herself from the turmoil of the stormy world. It is worth remembering that both poems are part of the volume called *A Change of World*. However, the two

speakers – the woman in 'Storm Warnings' and the uncle – seem to stand against change. We can also question the implications of the last two lines. Objectively speaking, which image is more deserving of support: creative artists ('glass-blowers') or those who threaten violence ('missile-throwers')?

The 'uncle', like the uncle in 'Aunt Jennifer's Tigers', may be seen as representative of **male dominance in society** at the time of writing (1950s). **Questions of power** – male and class-based – are raised. The poem seems to portray a world in which things of value are the preserve of the upper-class males of society. These political and gender issues became very important in Rich's later poems.

Rich herself did not include 'The Uncle Speaks in the Drawing-Room' in her *Selected Poems*. We could speculate that the ambiguous attitude to change mentioned above may have caused her to revise her opinion of the poem in later years. It is clear that, writing in her own voice, she would be unlikely to have adopted the pompous language and tone of the uncle. But his ominous warnings, however expressed, do relate to questions of traditions and of creative artists, represented by the 'glass-blowers'. Does Rich, despite herself, share in his attitudes? Or is the poem wholly ironic?

Form and language

The poem is written in **a formal, traditional style**. There is a formal division of stanzas (four stanzas of six lines each), which gives a **symmetrical shape** to the poem. As in 'Storm Warnings', each stanza contains a finished thought, signalled by the full stop at the end of each final line. In addition, the poem uses **end-rhyme** ('late' / 'gate'), **alliteration** ('Standing sullen'), **repetition** (the declamatory 'Let us'), **onomatopoeia** ('thunder-roll') and **assonance** ('Lead' / 'fear') to create the **patrician, formal tone** of the speaker. None of the experimentation we see in Rich's later poems is evident here. As her first volume, the poems in *A Change of World* were praised by W. H. Auden as 'neatly and modestly dressed, speak quietly but do not mumble, respect their elders but are not cowed by them, and do not tell fibs: that, for a first volume, is a good deal'.

Exam-Style Questions

Understanding the poem

1	What is the mood of the mob in the square outside the uncle's house? What aspects of the poet's description led you to this conclusion?
2	From the title of the poem and the details given in the first stanza, describe the uncle's house.
3	'These are follies that subside' (line 7). What might the uncle mean here? Is he concerned about the mob?
4	What items in his home is the uncle worried about, according to stanza 2? How does this stanza add to the impression you have formed of his house?
5	In the third stanza, why does the uncle believe that 'missiles' will not 'be cast'?
6	What does his current situation remind the uncle of in stanza 3?
7	What caused the grandsire to stand 'aghast' (line 16)? Is his reaction appropriate? Give reasons for your answer.
8	What must those listening to the uncle 'bear in mind' according to stanza 4?
9	These inherited 'treasures' from 'a calmer age' have been left in 'the keeping of our kind' (stanza 4). Comment on the words used here. What do they tell us about how the uncle sees himself and his class? Be specific and detailed in your answer.
10	What does the uncle feel he must protect, and from whom, according to the final two lines of the poem?

Thinking about the poem

1	What impression do you form of the uncle from the title of the poem? Is this impression reinforced from your reading of the poem as a whole? Explain.
2	Analyse the form and rhyming scheme of this poem. Does its formality suit the subject? Give reasons for your answer.
3	Do you feel the poet is being humorous or serious in this poem or perhaps a combination of both? Give reasons for your answer.
4	Which of the following, do you think, best sums up the main theme of the poem: ■ Protecting one's heritage ■ Wealth ■ Class division ■ Something else? Give reasons for your answer.
5	How are the mob and the storm similar in the poem? What qualities might they have in common? Look carefully at the language describing each.
6	Which images did you find most striking in the poem? Choose two or three and comment on their effectiveness.

7	Which sound effects did you find most striking in the poem? Choose two or three and comment on their effectiveness. For example, you might notice alliteration, assonance and onomatopoeia.
8	What tone of voice do you imagine the uncle uses in the poem? Does the tone (the emotions of the speaker) change as the poem progresses? Trace this through the poem and suggest reasons for how, where and why the tone might change.
9	'Let us only bear in mind' (line 19). Who do you imagine 'us' to be? Give reasons for your answer.
10	Compare and contrast this poem with 'Aunt Jennifer's Tigers'. Look at theme, tone, language, imagery and form. It may be helpful to use a grid to do this.
11	Where do your sympathies lie in the poem – with the mob or with the uncle? Discuss your opinion in pairs first and then as a class. Is there a majority opinion? Do you and your classmates have similar reasons or very different ones?
12	What, do you think, are the main symbols in the poem and what might they be symbolic of?

Imagining

1	Imagine you are a member of the mob outside the uncle's house. With a classmate, write the text of an interview you have with a journalist to explain your reasons for gathering there in a threatening manner.
2	Write a short story based on a treasure handed down in a family.
3	In small groups, turn the poem into a short drama script including stage directions, sound effects, etc. In a brief introductory paragraph describe the set, props, costumes and lighting. If possible, act out the resulting scenes.

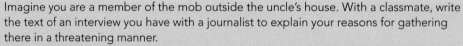

SNAPSHOT

- Formal structure
- Authoritative and dismissive voice of the uncle
- Preserving culture and tradition
- Class division
- Image of storm
- Impending violence contrasts with fragility of glass objects
- Assonance and alliteration
- Objects suggesting wealth
- Nostalgia for a bygone era

Before you read

What are the signs one might notice to suggest a storm is on the way?

Storm Warnings

The glass has been falling all the afternoon,
And knowing better than the instrument
What winds are walking overhead, what zone
Of grey unrest is moving across the land,
I leave the book upon a pillowed chair   5
And walk from window to closed window, watching
Boughs strain against the sky

And think again, as often when the air
Moves inward toward a silent core of waiting,
How with a single purpose time has travelled   10
By secret currents of the undiscerned
Into this polar realm. Weather abroad
And weather in the heart alike come on
Regardless of prediction.

Between foreseeing and averting change   15
Lies all the mastery of elements
Which clocks and weatherglasses cannot alter.
Time in the hand is not control of time,
Nor shattered fragments of an instrument
A proof against the wind; the wind will rise,   20
We can only close the shutters.

I draw the curtains as the sky goes black
And set a match to candles sheathed in glass
Against the keyhole draught, the insistent whine
Of weather through the unsealed aperture.   25
This is our sole defense against the season;
These are the things we have learned to do
Who live in troubled regions.

Glossary

1	*glass*: barometer
11	*undiscerned*: not noticed
25	*aperture*: opening or gap; here, a keyhole

Guidelines

From the 1951 collection *A Change of World*. The glass in the opening line refers to a barometer, which is an instrument used to measure air pressure and predict changes in the weather. This highly metaphorical poem uses weather to mirror the internal world of the speaker.

Commentary

Stanza 1

The speaker describes their reactions to the threatening storm. Safe in their own sheltered room, they watch the signs of the storm: the falling pressure of the barometer, the winds, the 'grey unrest' of the clouds, the trees that they can see straining 'against the sky'. The signs cause them to 'leave the book upon a pillowed chair'. Each image contributes to the atmosphere of impending trouble.

Stanza 2

The speaker reflects on how unpredictable storms are, how they seem to have a purpose of their own that is independent of human beings. At this stage the speaker makes the first link between the storm as a phenomenon of nature and what they term 'weather in the heart', meaning human emotions and situations. Both are unpredictable and neither can be easily contained or avoided. The phrase 'polar realm' is striking and rich in its suggestiveness.

Stanza 3

In the best tradition of literature, the poet gives storms a metaphorical significance. It is not spelled out exactly what this is, but it seems to relate to the idea of human emotions and 'change'. The language in the third stanza suggests the notion of tension that exists between a desire to control change – to foresee it and avoid it – and an inability to withstand its destruction. The instruments that measure time and weather do not control those elements or their consequences: 'Time in the hand is not control of time'. Words such as 'mastery', 'control' and even 'close' express a desire for control and perhaps domination. 'Shattered', on the other hand, suggests destructiveness. All our instruments – clocks, barometers and closed windows – are powerless against the wind that 'will rise'. In the face of storms and change, 'We can only close the shutters'.

Stanza 4

The speaker describes the actions they take to shut out the worst of the storm's destruction: closing the curtains, lighting the candles. These actions are seen as a 'sole defense'. Might this suggest that the speaker is unsure of how effective they are? Even the slightest of openings, the keyhole, seems to allow the storm to enter the room. But these are the only responses that those who 'live in troubled regions' have learned to make. We are not told exactly where these 'troubled regions' are, but it is tempting to read them metaphorically as the society in which the poet finds herself.

Themes and imagery

As the title suggests, the theme of the poem is **impending change and conflict** and **our seeming powerlessness to prevent what we know is coming**: 'Weather abroad / And weather in the heart alike come on / Regardless of prediction.' Although the title of the volume in which the poem first appears is *A Change*

of World, it is ironic that the poet here seems to resist the idea of change. We can sense a feeling of tension at the heart of the poem, despite its calm, controlled tone. The speaker shows no outward fear of the approaching storm and prepares for it, as best they can. In fact, with their book, their 'pillowed chair' and their calm, deliberate actions, they seem to suggest that all is under control, in so far as their limited scope of action allows. The reader wonders if drawing the curtains and lighting the candle will be sufficient preparation for what is approaching. The poem is rich in suggestiveness. The approaching storm can be read as an emotional storm, which opens the poem to a variety of interpretations.

Form and language

The poem is **carefully crafted**, with four stanzas of seven lines each, each of them acting almost as a paragraph containing a specific description or reflection. There is repetition of word patterns such as **half-rhyme** ('afternoon', 'zone'), **assonance** ('black', 'match', 'candles'), **alliteration** ('What winds are walking') and **onomatopoeia** ('whine'). At this stage of her poetic career, Rich was writing in traditional forms, as she had been trained to do by both her father, who encouraged her in her writing, and her education. Later, she rejected these conventional forms as inappropriate for her expression of a changing concept of gender and power. You might like to consider whether the **tight, controlled form** of the poem works well in expressing the themes of change and control.

Questions

1	What details does the speaker use in stanza 1 to establish that a storm is approaching?
2	What had the speaker been doing prior to realising a storm was brewing and what is their first reaction to it?
3	Consider the effect of the phrase 'pillowed chair' in line 5. What does this suggest to you about the physical and mental state of the speaker before the storm's onset?
4	In stanza 2, as the speaker contemplates the inevitability of the storm, they comment that 'Weather abroad / And weather in the heart alike come on / Regardless of prediction' (lines 12–14). How do you interpret these lines? What is being compared?
5	In the light of your answer to the previous question, what might the 'polar realm' (line 12) represent literally and then metaphorically for the speaker?
6	What can't we control, according to stanza 3? Consider the phrasing here carefully in your answer.
7	What has happened to the 'instrument' mentioned in stanza 3? What does this tell you about the progress of the storm?
8	'the wind will rise, / We can only close the shutters' (lines 20–21). What is being conveyed here, in your opinion, about (a) people and nature and (b) people and their inner storms, whatever they may be?
9	'These are the things we have learned to do / Who live in troubled regions' (lines 27–28). What precautions has the speaker taken to protect themself and their home against storm damage? If we take these two lines as metaphorical, what might the speaker be conveying here?
10	What, do you feel, is the theme of this poem? Might it be the power of nature, the powerlessness of people in the face of nature, trying to cope in times of emotional difficulty, or something else? Give reasons for your answer.
11	In your own words, trace as simply as you can the sequence of thought in the poem, commenting as you go on the tone of the speaker as the poem progresses.
12	Write about the poet's use of contrast in this poem.
13	In pairs, discuss the metaphors you identify in the poem and write about the ideas being expressed through each metaphor.
14	Find at least one example each of alliteration, onomatopoeia and assonance in the poem and describe the effect achieved by each.
15	How is the form of this poem similar to or different from the previous three?
16	What is the relationship of the title to the theme and content of the poem?
17	This poem uses weather to mirror mood very effectively. What types of weather would you use to convey the following emotions (choose three): joy, despair, amusement, grief, love, hatred, confusion? Give reasons for your choices.

18 Is the storm here in any way similar to the one alluded to in 'The Uncle Speaks in the Drawing Room'? Explain.

19 Imagine this poem is set to music with accompanying images. In small groups, decide what images you would use and what music would suit best. Perhaps turn your ideas into a short presentation.

20 Write a descriptive passage about a storm, using lots of aesthetic writing. Try to use all five senses in your piece.

Living in Sin

She had thought the studio would keep itself;
no dust upon the furniture of love.
Half heresy, to wish the taps less vocal,
the panes relieved of grime. A plate of pears,
a piano with a Persian shawl, a cat   5
stalking the picturesque amusing mouse
had risen at his urging.
Not that at five each separate stair would writhe
under the milkman's tramp; that morning light
so coldly would delineate the scraps   10
of last night's cheese and three sepulchral bottles;
that on the kitchen shelf among the saucers
a pair of beetle-eyes would fix her own –
envoy from some village in the moldings ...
Meanwhile, he, with a yawn,   15
sounded a dozen notes upon the keyboard,
declared it out of tune, shrugged at the mirror,
rubbed at his beard, went out for cigarettes;
while she, jeered by the minor demons,
pulled back the sheets and made the bed and found   20
a towel to dust the table-top,
and let the coffee-pot boil over on the stove.
By evening she was back in love again,
though not so wholly but throughout the night
she woke sometimes to feel the daylight coming   25
like a relentless milkman up the stairs.

Glossary

1	*studio*: small open-plan flat or apartment
3	*heresy*: belief that disagrees with the official or accepted belief (often of a religion)
6	*picturesque*: beautiful to look at (often used to describe a landscape)
8	*writhe*: wriggle in pain
9	*tramp*: heavy footstep
10	*delineate*: clearly show or describe something
11	*sepulchral*: tomb-like
14	*moldings*: strips of plaster along a wall or ceiling

Guidelines

From *The Diamond Cutters and Other Poems* (1955), this poem looks through the eyes of an unmarried woman who is living with her lover as she wakes one morning in their messy studio flat. Notice how carefully crafted the poem is, its measured pace and the intricate links between words and images.

Commentary

Lines 1–7

Although not written in the first person (I), the poem expresses the thoughts of a woman ('She') who has begun a relationship. The couple are living together and she seems disillusioned at the reality of daily life. Caught up in a romantic dream – there would be 'no dust upon the furniture of love' – she had thought that the apartment would require nothing so mundane as housework. But in reality, there are dripping taps and dirty windows to deal with. The phrase 'Half heresy' suggests that she is aware of how different her view of housework is from the conventional view that it is a woman's job. On the other hand, as an artist (the poem is set in a 'studio' apartment), her partner is free to create beautiful pictures (the 'piano', the 'plate of pears', the 'cat' and 'mouse'). Words such as 'picturesque' and 'amusing' suggest his work is enjoyable and fulfilling.

Lines 8–14

The poem rather wearily lists the reality she faces each day in images that suggest frustration and boredom: the sound of the milkman's step early in the morning, the food to be cleared away, the kitchen to be tidied, even insects to be dealt with. The contrast between the artist's 'amusing mouse' and the real-life insects that invade the kitchen makes the gap between her expectations and her reality clear.

Lines 15–22

Her male partner feels no compulsion to clean and tidy the debris he has helped to create. In fact, he seems oblivious to it. The 'minor demons' urging her to behave like a housewife do not trouble him. The image seems to imply that she is unable to avoid doing the tasks she mentions, while he has the freedom to come and go as he pleases. She is unable to break free of the traditional gendered role of 'housewife'.

Lines 23–26

Will her love last? Although she is 'back in love again' by evening, the final lines suggest that there could be a gradual erosion of that love: she is now 'not so wholly' in love as she was. Might the 'daylight coming' suggest further realisation of the unfairness of the situation? Does it have to go on and on, like the 'relentless' 'milkman's tramp'?

Themes and imagery

A man and a woman living together without being married was deemed 'living in sin' in the 1950s. The phrase expressed disapproval in conventional society. However, it was also considered daring by artistic or progressive people. The **irony** in the poem is that 'living in sin' is not at all exciting for the woman living in this supposedly progressive relationship because she assumes the traditional female role of domestic cleaner.

Interestingly, the imagery of the poem is rooted in **the concrete reality of their lives** rather than the abstract qualities of their love. The woman is conscious of the furniture, the scraps of cheese, the saucers, the sheets and the coffee pot.

This poem reflects some of Rich's major concerns as she evolved into a feminist poet. **Lack of balance in the dynamics of power between the sexes** becomes an important issue, and we see it suggested here. How can it be right that the male artist is free to pursue his craft at the expense of his female partner? The woman's concerns might appear trivial in contrast with his, yet might it be argued that her work frees him to pursue his

artistic endeavours? Or is he simply freer than her? Is the woman's compulsion to clean the house explained by her inability to refuse the domestic role assigned to women in middle-class American society of the 1950s?

The issues raised in the poem are complicated further by an awareness that the male figure is an artist. He is described as unencumbered by any of the domestic problems that concern her. During the 1950s, Rich was struggling to develop as a poet while bringing up her family, so it is likely that these issues were of personal interest to her. This may explain the rather **disappointed tone** of the poem. However, the woman in this poem is not 'terrified' by male power as Aunt Jennifer was in 'Aunt Jennifer's Tigers'. The persona of this poem is questioning the gender roles assigned by society, even if she still feels compelled by 'the minor demons' to adhere to them.

In 'Living in Sin', Rich expresses a **growing feminist consciousness** that was to become extremely important to her and her writing in the 1960s.

Form and language

The poem is written in **free verse**. It is beautifully phrased and paced. Rich uses **punctuation** and **enjambment** to control the flow and movement of the poem. The poem is rich in sounds and sound effects, with runs of **assonance**, **alliteration** and **consonance** creating a dense texture. There is an amusing contrast between ornate vocabulary such as 'heresy', 'Persian', 'picturesque' and 'sepulchral' and the dirt and dinginess of the studio.

Questions

1	What assumption had 'she' made when she first moved in with her lover?
2	In pairs, list the items in their studio (lines 1–14) and say what they suggest to you about the couple's lifestyle and tastes.
3	Describe the attitude and actions of the man in the relationship that morning (lines 15–18).
4	The woman begins to clean up the messy flat, 'jeered by the minor demons' (line 19). What is represented by these 'demons' and why are they 'minor'? What, do you think, makes her feel she is the one who must tidy up?
5	The speaker suggests that 'she' had fallen out of love that day but was 'back in love again' 'By evening' albeit 'not so wholly' as she previously was (lines 23–24). Can you offer an opinion as to why she is going through these changes of emotion?
6	The image of the milkman reappears in the final two lines of the poem in a simile comparing his 'relentless' tread to 'the daylight coming'. What does this simile convey to you?
7	Describe the impression you get of the couple's relationship from your reading of this poem.
8	Comment on the sounds described in the poem and the atmosphere they create.
9	Having studied the poem, how does the reality of 'living in sin' compare with how scandalous or exciting the term sounds?
10	In your opinion, does the poem present a positive, negative or very realistic depiction of a couple living together? Give reasons for your answer.
11	Comment on Rich's descriptive power, selecting at least three examples from the poem to support your comments.
12	Compare the relationship in this poem with the one presented in 'Aunt Jennifer's Tigers'.
13	The poem is about an individual relationship, but how might it be read as a more universal commentary on gender roles and societal expectations of men and women?
14	Imagine the woman writes to or phones a friend to discuss her relationship and to seek advice. In pairs, draught the letter and reply or dialogue that results.
15	Class debate: 'That marriage is an outdated institution in a modern society.'

Before you read

How do you feel about heights? Do you fear them or feel exhilarated by them? List the feelings and thoughts you might have if you were walking on a roof.

The Roofwalker

for Denise Levertov

Over the half-finished houses
night comes. The builders
stand on the roof. It is
quiet after the hammers,
the pulleys hang slack.   5
Giants, the roofwalkers,
on a listing deck, the wave
of darkness about to break
on their heads. The sky
is a torn sail where figures   10
pass magnified, shadows
on a burning deck.

I feel like them up there:
exposed, larger than life,
and due to break my neck.   15

Was it worth while to lay—
with infinite exertion—
a roof I can't live under?
—All those blueprints,
closings of gaps,   20
measurings, calculations?
A life I didn't choose
chose me: even
my tools are the wrong ones
for what I have to do.   25
I'm naked, ignorant,
a naked man fleeing
across the roofs
who could with a shade of difference
be sitting in the lamplight   30
against the cream wallpaper
reading—not with indifferenc e—
about a naked man
fleeing across the roofs.

Glossary

| 7 | *listing*: leaning over to one side (usually refers to a ship with a leak or an ill-balanced cargo) |

Guidelines

This poem is from the collection *Snapshots of a Daughter-in-Law* (1963), which many critics see as a breakthrough volume of Rich's work where she relies less on formal structure, metre and rhyme and allows herself more freedom and experimentation. 'The Roofwalker' is dedicated to Denise Levertov, an English-born poet who moved to New York when she married in 1947 (see page 544). Like Rich, Levertov was an activist and feminist. Also like Rich, her style and her expression in her poetry became more experimental and more open as she grew older.

Commentary

Lines 1–12

The speaker of the poem observes the roofwalkers; builders standing on the roof after their day's work, as night comes. They seem to fascinate her, both literally and metaphorically. She describes them in admiring terms: they are 'Giants' confident in their positions, seemingly unaware of any danger. She sees them as sailors on a precariously leaning ship, oblivious to the potential storm (the 'darkness', the 'burning deck') under the 'torn sail' of the clouds. (We are reminded of a famous poem about a disaster, popular in American schools in the 1950s, 'Casabianca' by Felicia Hemans, which contains the line: 'The boy stood on the burning deck'.)

Lines 13–15

The three lines that make up the second stanza of the poem make the reason for the speaker's fascination clear. She identifies with the roofwalkers, metaphorically seeing her own position as similar. If the speaker of the poem reflects the poet, it may be that Rich has her own situation, as a poet, and as a woman of her time, in mind as she writes. She is thinking of the changes that are about to take place and the risks involved. She expresses mixed emotions: exhilaration in being somehow 'larger than life' and apprehension that she may fall, 'break my neck'.

Lines 16–28

The speaker asks herself a number of questions in the third section of the poem. The impression given is of someone thinking aloud as she looks back at her life. Keeping to the image of the roof, she wonders about the life she has constructed up to now. The images she uses suggest deliberateness, calculation and hard work: 'blueprints, closings of gaps, measurings'. And yet, she states that it was not a life of her own choosing and as such can be of no use to her in the future. She expresses this idea very simply, creating the image of a house: 'a roof I can't live under'.

This seeming contradiction between a life that was planned but was not chosen may be explained by referring to circumstances in Rich's own life. She wrote and spoke extensively about the influence her father had upon her development as a poet. Arnold Rich brought up his daughter with great emphasis on education, overseeing her academic development and encouraging her career. However, she came to recognise that his emphasis on intellectual clarity and detachment, for which he praised her, were not necessarily the only values possible in poetry. There was also room for personal exploration and emotion. Rich came to see that her father's values were representative of the patriarchal aspect of society – perhaps a little like the views expressed by the uncle in 'The Uncle Speaks in the Drawing Room'.

If we identify the speaker of the poem with the poet, it may well be that the poem expresses uncertainty that the craft Rich has cultivated – the 'tools' of her trade as a poet, her use of language – will not serve her in her

future work: 'what I have to do'. What she has to do is not made clear, although we can speculate that even then Rich had a sense that her poetry should take another direction entirely. The image of a naked man fleeing across the rooftops expresses how vulnerable she feels in this new situation as well as the dangerous exhilaration of this flight, of 'what I have to do'.

Underlying the poem is Rich's awareness of the changing roles of women in society, and the changing nature of her own situation. We know from her writings that Rich became actively involved in politics in the 1960s and that her feminist views were beginning to find a focus in her poems. Here the speaker questions her situation and tries to come to terms with it, even if it leads to discomfort and danger.

Lines 29–34

There is a choice, as the last lines make clear. Instead of running across rooftops, metaphorically speaking, the speaker could sit and read about such a feat. This would not in itself necessarily make her indifferent to change, but it does suggest that an alternative attitude, one less disruptive and safer, is possible. It is even attractive: 'sitting in the lamplight' reflected against the restful 'cream wallpaper'. The image leaves us with the sense that the speaker could go either way. Indeed, we could say that the entire poem enacts the drama of choice.

Themes and imagery

'The Roofwalker' is thematically rich and open. It is about **personal change and transformation**; **choice and risk-taking**; **action and passivity**. The builders embody a certain kind of dangerous freedom. In their precarious situation, they represent the speaker's own situation. At this moment in her life, she feels she is 'due to break my neck'. The poem establishes a contrast between the bland domesticity of 'the cream wallpaper' and the startling image of the 'naked man fleeing / across the roofs'. The word 'naked' is used three times. It suggests vulnerability and exposure but also a lack of inhibition, a freedom. The roof itself is a symbol. For the builders who stand on the roof, it provides a platform. For the speaker, it is the roof she 'can't live under', which may suggest constraint and restriction.

'The Roofwalker' is from the volume *Snapshots of a Daughter-in-Law* (1963). The poet herself has referred to this volume as a 're-definition of psychological and poetic perspective'. The critic Albert Gelpi referred to Rich as '**pioneer, witness, prophet**'. 'The Roofwalker' may be said to demonstrate each of these attributes. If we identify the voice in the poem with that of the poet, we may relate the idea of risk-taking to Rich's own life. Rich's vision of how she should proceed as a poet shows her to be a pioneer attempting to chart the unknown for herself. By allowing us into her personal dilemma, she shows herself as a witness to her own journey as a woman and poet. From here on, Rich's poems have a personal honesty about them that was perhaps hidden in her earlier work. There is something of the prophet, too, in her recognition that she cannot and will not live under the particular 'roof' she has built, whether as a poet or even as a woman. In this she looks forward to a time of change in her life.

Form and language

The poem is written in **free verse**. The short lines create a sense of drama and tension. The clever use of **enjambment** and **punctuation** means that the lines slip and slide into one another, reflecting the poem's concern with balance and the danger of falling.

The word choice and phrasing suggest someone **picking each word with great deliberation**, just as the roofwalkers must choose their steps carefully. Read aloud the following lines and note how form and meaning complement each other:

Was it worth while to lay—
with infinite exertion—
a roof I can't live under?

Questions

1	Describe in your own words the setting conveyed in the first twelve lines of the poem.
2	Comment on the effectiveness of the comparison between this setting and an unbalanced ship, how it is created and how the builders are depicted within it.
3	Why does the speaker feel that she is similar to the builders who walk on the roof (lines 13–15)?
4	What planning goes into a home (lines 16–21)? What question is being asked here?
5	'A life I didn't choose / chose me' (lines 22–23). What, do you think, is the speaker referring to here? Have you seen this concept arise in any other poems by Rich? Explain.
6	How does the speaker convey that she feels ill-equipped to deal with the life imposed upon her? What images convey this in the final section of the poem? How do these images relate to the imagery employed in the first section?

7	'who could with a shade of difference / be sitting in the lamplight / against the cream wallpaper / reading' (lines 29–32). How does this image of cosy, if perhaps bland, domesticity contrast with what the speaker is reading in the last two lines of the poem?
8	Could the final two lines be metaphorical? Can you identify any links between them and other parts of the poem? Might the poet be referencing the poem itself here? Give reasons for your answers.
9	Compare the use of the first-person speaker in this poem with the use of a third-person speaker in 'Living in Sin', noting the situation of each speaker.
10	Comment on the idea of nakedness in this poem. What might it represent? Is it an effectively used image? Explain your answers fully.
11	What, do you feel, is the overall tone of the poem? Do you sense fear, resignation, regret or something else? Give reasons for your answer.
12	Look at the placement and use of dashes to punctuate the poem. What is their effect on the form, pace and atmosphere?
13	Examine the symbolism of the roof in the poem. It is above the speaker and below the builders – is this significant in any way? Perhaps think in terms of freedom and support versus oppression and enclosure.
14	Look at how Rich intertwines the ideas of 'difference' (line 29) and 'indifference' (line 32) in the last section of the poem. How is each used and how are they linked by the poet?
15	Do you feel Rich's style is changing or evolving at all in the light of the poems you have studied so far on your course? Explain.
16	In small groups, write a list of words and phrases to describe Rich's treatment of relationships in the poems you have studied so far on your course.
17	Write a stream-of-consciousness piece in which you imagine yourself inside the mind and body of one of the builders on the rooftop.
18	'A life I didn't choose / chose me' (lines 22–23). Write a short story or personal essay inspired by this phrase.

Before you read

Do we lie a lot in life? As a class, discuss the 'white lies' or 'fibs' we often tell on a daily basis and look at the reasons why we might do this.

Our Whole Life

Our whole life a translation
the permissible fibs

and now a knot of lies
eating at itself to get undone

Words bitten thru words   5

meanings burnt-off like paint
under the blowtorch

All those dead letters
rendered into the oppressor's language

Trying to tell the doctor where it hurts   10
like the Algerian
who has walked from his village, burning

his whole body a cloud of pain
and there are no words for this

except himself   15

Glossary

2	*permissible*: allowed

Guidelines

Written in 1969, this poem was published in the collection *The Will to Change* (1971). 'Our Whole Life' is open to a number of interpretations. Some have suggested that this is a woman speaking to her partner about their relationship. Others argue that Rich uses 'Our' to represent a marginalised group in society, pointing out that she was very politically active and campaigned tirelessly against inequality. Of course, both these ideas can exist in the poem at once, along with other interpretations that are open to the reader. It is what the poem seems to say to you that is important.

Commentary

What are the implications of the poem's title? Is Rich suggesting the impossibility of any real communication throughout one's life, or the impossibility of communication for certain individuals, such as the victims of political oppression 'like the Algerian' in the poem? Might 'Our Whole Life' apply to the situation that women have found themselves in, where to communicate what they experience seems futile because 'there are no words for this'? No matter how we interpret the title, the central image in the poem, 'the oppressor's language', becomes a metaphor for failure and frustration rather than communication. In the language of the oppressor, the poem seems to say, it is impossible to communicate the true nature of experience, the true nature of suffering and oppression. The clipped tone of the poem reflects the essential point: the failure of the language of the oppressor to communicate the lived reality of those who are oppressed.

The poem appears to suggest that where there is an imbalance of power, language becomes distorted and communication is impossible. The image of 'Words bitten thru words' suggests uselessness, pointlessness. Trying to articulate what you feel is of no use, as the metaphor of 'dead letters' (undelivered letters) suggests, because you must express yourself in the 'oppressor's language'. The final image of the Algerian with his body 'burning' suggests that for those who suffer, their suffering is the only true way of expressing their reality.

Political activist

'Our Whole Life' is from the collection *The Will to Change*. The mid to late 1960s was a time of great political ferment in the United States. Rich became involved not only in the feminist movement but also in the civil rights movement. Her political commitment included demonstrating in anti-war protests against US involvement in Vietnam as well as teaching in the Open Admissions Program for disadvantaged students at City College, New York. The title of the volume, *The Will to Change*, implies the need and desire for change in the social and political structure of the time. This poem was written during her most politically active period. As her commitment to social justice increased, Rich began to question the type of poems she had hitherto written, seeing the limitations of language to express complex social and political issues.

Themes and imagery

In this short poem Rich touches on the complex themes of **language**, **power**, **oppression**, **suffering** and **alienation**. The poem is open to a wide range of interpretations. Is the first word of the poem, 'Our', intended to identify the speaker with the women's movement, as well as the politically oppressed, of whom the Algerian is a representative? If the poem identifies with the oppressed, who does the 'oppressor' refer to? To what extent is Rich thinking of the language of poetry? Is the poem questioning whether the male-dominated tradition of poetry is valid for the expression of female consciousness? Is the poem born of a view that real communication is impossible between men and women because of the imbalance in power between the sexes? Is the poem more personal and intimate? Is it a woman speaking about her situation?

It is arguable that a sense of **anger and frustration** underlies 'Our Whole Life'. The imagery in the poem ('eating', 'bitten, 'burning') is **emotive** and communicates a sense of suffering and violence. The fact that the images are separate and disjointed adds to the sense of anger and alienation.

Form and language

The poem is written in **short stanzas** of one, two or three lines that run together with **very little punctuation**. Even the final line has no full stop, leaving the reader without any sense of closure. At the time of writing, Rich was fascinated by cinematic and photographic methods of creation. She has acknowledged her debt to the French film director Jean-Luc Godard in some of her poems. This short poem makes its impact as a piece of film might, each image building on another.

Questions

1	According to the first four lines, what has the 'whole life' of this 'Our' couple/group been built on?
2	In pairs, imagine and suggest the white lies or 'fibs' that this 'Our' couple/group may have told and offer reasons why they may have felt lies like these were 'permissible'. Do you think a couple is being described here or does 'Our' represent a group of people?
3	The speaker uses the image of a 'knot' that is 'eating at itself to get undone' (lines 3–4) to describe the form these 'fibs' have taken and the stage the relationship is at. Suggest what the poet might be getting at here. What, do you think, is happening to the relationship in this metaphor?
4	With your first three answers in mind, how, do you think, has their life been a 'translation' (line 1) of these lies? We usually use 'translation' to talk about converting the words of one language into another. Is that what is happening here in any way?
5	In lines 5, 6 and 7 the poet uses imagery of biting and burning. Explain the metaphors here and suggest why such violent imagery is used.
6	What might be meant by the phrase 'dead letters' (line 8)? How do they tie in with the idea of communicating through lies at the start of the poem?
7	'the oppressor's language' (line 9). What, do you think, does Rich mean by this phrase? Who might 'the oppressor' be? Where else have you encountered an 'oppressor' in Rich's poetry?
8	The image of the burning Algerian in the last six lines of the poem is used as a simile. What does this simile represent, in your opinion? What was your reaction to this image? Who or what might the doctor represent here?
9	'A failure to communicate lies at the heart of this poem.' Do you agree with this analysis?
10	How does the form of this poem link to its theme and tone? Consider its brevity, the short lines, the use of single lines and couplets and even the use of the abbreviated word 'thru' (line 5).

11	Burning is used as an image twice in the poem. How is it used each time? What is being communicated to you? Do you find these images effective?
12	Discuss the punctuation in the poem, for example consider the use of capital letters and the lack of full stops even at the end of the poem, and suggest why the poet punctuates the poem as she does.
13	Is 'pain' (line 13) a key idea in this poem? Where can you find references to pain and what kinds of pain do you encounter?
14	Choose two phrases that you found especially striking and justify your choices in each case.
15	What is the relationship of the title to the poem as a whole?
16	Could Rich be commenting on the differences between male and female communication through this poem? Give reasons for your answer.
17	Do you think language is sexist? Is the female secondary in language and how we use it? Look at the word 'history' for instance, and consider the different connotations the words 'spinster' and 'bachelor' have. Discuss this issue in groups and feed your thoughts and ideas back to the class as a whole.
18	Using this poem for inspiration, try to come up with two or three more metaphors to represent the idea of uncovering untruths.

Before you read

What do you know about the atomic bomb? When was it developed and by whom? Do some research on this.

Trying to Talk with a Man

Out in this desert we are testing bombs,

that's why we came here.

Sometimes I feel an underground river
forcing its way between deformed cliffs
an acute angle of understanding   5
moving itself like a locus of the sun
into this condemned scenery.

What we've had to give up to get here –
whole LP collections, films we starred in
playing in the neighborhoods, bakery windows   10
full of dry, chocolate-filled Jewish cookies,
the language of love-letters, of suicide notes,
afternoons on the riverbank
pretending to be children

Coming out to this desert   15
we meant to change the face of
driving among dull green succulents
walking at noon in the ghost town
surrounded by a silence

that sounds like the silence of the place   20
except that it came with us
and is familiar
and everything we were saying until now
was an effort to blot it out –
coming out here we are up against it   25

Out here I feel more helpless
with you than without you
You mention the danger
and list the equipment
we talk of people caring for each other   30
in emergencies – laceration, thirst –
but you look at me like an emergency

Your dry heat feels like power
your eyes are stars of a different magnitude
they reflect lights that spell out: EXIT   35
when you get up and pace the floor

talking of the danger
as if it were not ourselves
as if we were testing anything else.

Glossary

6	*locus*: place; also, in geometry, the shape made by all the points that satisfy certain specified conditions
9	*LP*: long-playing vinyl album of music, known as a record, played on a turntable
17	*succulents*: plants with thick fleshy leaves (usually from very dry areas)
31	*laceration*: cut, wound
34	*magnitude*: large size

Guidelines

Rich wrote this poem in 1971, a short time after the suicide of her husband. It is from the critically acclaimed collection *Diving into the Wreck*. In the opening lines the speaker talks about 'testing bombs'. This refers to the Manhattan Project that led to the development of the atomic bomb, which was first tested in the New Mexico desert in July 1945. Scientists and their families, like the speaker in this poem, moved out to the desert during the project. Characteristically for Rich, the poem is full of metaphors that suggest deeper layers of meaning, both personal and political.

Commentary

Lines 1–7

The poem is set in a desert – a sterile environment – where bombs are being tested. From the beginning there is a link made between the public situation ('testing bombs', presumably nuclear) and the private situation ('trying to talk with a man', testing the extent of the intimacy between a man and a woman). The strange landscape of the desert, with its underground rivers and deformed cliffs, becomes a metaphor for the woman's state of mind. Frustration and despair are suggested by the image of 'condemned scenery'. Nuclear testing obviously caused destruction where it took place, and the woman, too, seems to take on this sense of something being destroyed. However, there is a sense that the female speaker is moving towards some insight, 'an acute angle of understanding'.

Lines 8–14

It becomes clear that the man and the woman have chosen to be in this desert, perhaps both literally and metaphorically, in order to bring about some change in their lives. The poet lists the ordinary, homely things they have left behind with what seems like affection: their music collections, the food they ate, their love letters. The poem suggests that their previous lives were comfortable and companionable, although 'suicide notes' reminds us that the poet's husband, Alfred Conrad, died by suicide in 1970. As the poem was written in 1971, it may be that Rich is remembering the end of their relationship (their marriage had broken down some years earlier). The list may also reflect the trappings of domesticity that the poet, as a radical feminist, tried to leave behind (the sort of concerns referred to in 'Living in Sin', for example).

Lines 15–25

The change that is envisaged clearly has some element of risk attached, just as the activity going on in the desert has. Images of silence in this deserted place echo the silence that exists between the man and woman. Communication appears to have broken down. Confrontation may involve a metaphorical explosion, a rearranging of their relationship: 'coming out here we are up against it'.

Lines 26–39

Being in the desert does not seem to help the couple with their difficulties. In fact, the speaker says it makes them worse. Her admission that she feels 'more helpless / with you than without you' is simply and honestly expressed, emphasising the distance between them. When they actually do manage to 'talk', their concerns are so widely different that there seems little hope of real communication. The male partner speaks of external events – 'danger' and 'emergencies' – in the context of nuclear testing. The implication here is that he is more concerned with public politics (nuclear bomb testing was a controversial issue in the early 1970s).

What she terms his 'dry heat' (perhaps his anger or his energy) seems 'like power' but is not, in the context of the poem, where the real power lies: it lies with the woman, who can sense what is really happening in the world. In contrast to the man, she is aware that the 'danger' comes from themselves, that what is being tested is the strength or otherwise of their commitment to each other as man and woman, and also their concept of what it means to be male and female at that time.

Themes and imagery

The poem touches on a number of related themes: **communication**; **difficult relationships**; **violence and war**; **power and oppression**; **gender differences**.

The feminist slogan '**the personal is political**' is relevant to the themes of this poem. We cannot ignore the political landscape in which Rich has chosen to place the more personal confrontation. Rich herself was deeply committed to resisting violence of all kinds. She saw violence, including the testing of nuclear bombs, as having its origin in the male concept of power. But in this poem she chooses to see the public testing of weapons as

somehow beside the point – what is being tested by the confrontation in the desert is 'ourselves', the private responses of the man and the woman to a changing, and dangerous, world.

Feminist poet

'Trying to Talk with a Man' is from the volume *Diving into the Wreck* (1973). This volume of poems was Rich's first explicitly feminist volume. In it she expresses much of the pent-up anger she felt at what she termed the 'patriarchal' way in which society is organised. In *On Lies, Secrets and Silence*, Rich defined a patriarchal society as 'any kind of group organisation in which males hold dominant power and determine what part females shall and shall not play'. Images of violence, frustration and despair express her rejection of these values, what she called 'the oppressor's language' in the poem 'Our Whole Life'.

Her main theme seems to be **the relationship between men and women**. In the desert, it is the woman who sees more clearly the changes taking place, and who is able to deal with them: 'Out here I feel more helpless / with you than without you'. The **desert imagery** suggests the sterility that has overcome the couple's relationship. The poem has been praised for its honesty in confronting an issue that may have been sidestepped in the past, namely the relations between the sexes.

As in 'Our Whole Life', the issue of **language as a means of communication** (and the difficulties associated with it) is a central idea in the poem. Responding to the pessimism in the poem, Margaret Atwood wrote: 'the desert is already in the past, beyond salvation though not beyond understanding'.

Form and language

It is clear from the title that the speaker of the poem does not hold out much hope for communication between men and women. The implications of the word 'trying' in 'Trying to Talk with a Man' are that it is in the end a futile exercise, and the poem bears this out. The speaker seems frustrated that the male persona cannot or will not meet her halfway in discussing the issues that really should concern them. The metaphors of explosion and testing, and the images of sterility and danger, underline her radical vision of how necessary change in society is. **The tone of the poem is more resigned than angry**, as if the speaker has already moved on in her mind and left the relationship. The opening line, flat and matter of fact, sets this tone: 'Out in this desert we are testing bombs'. The tone continues through lines of **largely unpunctuated verse**, where **successive long-vowel sounds mirror the deadening effect of a break-up**: 'driving among dull green succulents / walking at noon in the ghost town / surrounded by a silence'.

Questions

1	What does the title suggest about talking 'with a man'? Is difficulty implied?
2	Read the first two lines of the poem. What are we told is the reason for this couple being in the desert?
3	What does the speaker compare herself to in lines 3–7? Suggest what she might be trying to convey here.
4	Why, do you think, does the speaker describe the scenery as 'condemned' (line 7) and the cliffs as 'deformed' (line 4)? How do these landscape features interact with the underground river?
5	What word would you use to describe the setting created in the first seven lines of the poem: dramatic, bleak, ugly or something else? Justify the word you choose with reference to this section of the poem.
6	The speaker lists 'What we've had to give up to get here' in lines 8–14. Look at each of the six items in this list and say what they suggest to you about the life this couple had before they went to the desert. What do we learn about their past and their personalities here?
7	The silence of the desert is described in lines 15–19. What do you identify as the mood of this section? Note the use of alliteration and sibilance here. How do these sound effects contribute to the creation of this mood?
8	The speaker tells us that the couple 'meant to change the face of' (line 16) this desert. What does this line suggest about the success or failure of this venture?
9	Lines 20–25 tell us that the couple brought the silence with them. What does this section imply about their relationship and the communication they have had up to this point?
10	'Out here I feel more helpless / with you than without you' (lines 26–27). Comment on what the speaker might mean by this statement. Why might his company make her feel less in control? Have you seen this idea echoed elsewhere in Rich's work?

11	What is the 'danger' mentioned in line 28? Is the danger literal, metaphorical or both? (Think in terms of the bomb test and also the couple's relationship.)
12	How does the man seem to view the speaker in line 32: 'you look at me like an emergency'?
13	What does the man seem to want to do in lines 33–36? Why is he pacing and what does the fact that she sees the word 'EXIT' in his eyes suggest to you? Comment on the effect of the capitalisation of this word.
14	The speaker mentions the word 'danger' again in line 37. Has your understanding of what she might mean by this word changed or developed as the poem has progressed? Explain.
15	In your opinion, is the couple facing up to this 'danger' honestly and openly? Back up your answer with close reference to the poem, particularly the final two lines.
16	What did you notice about the punctuation and form of this poem? How does this affect the theme and mood, if at all?
17	As metaphors, what do you feel the bomb testing, the desert and the silence might represent in the poem?
18	Which of the following best sums up the theme of the poem in your eyes: ■ A troubled relationship ■ Failure to communicate ■ Nuclear war ■ The relationship between oppressor and oppressed ■ Something else? Give reasons for your answer.
19	What impression did you form of the 'I' voice in the poem? Would you agree that this is a woman's voice? Explain.
20	This poem contains vivid imagery; choose the two images that you find most effective or striking in the poem and discuss your choices.
21	Overall, would you say that the atmosphere created in this poem is one of fear, dullness, frustration or something else? Give reasons for your answer.
22	Suggest and justify an alternative title for this poem.
23	Compare the ideas explored here with those in 'Our Whole Life'. Look at theme, tone, imagery and form in your answer.
24	Each section of this poem has a central idea at its heart. Write an analysis of the poem with this in mind. Your answer may take the form of notes or a diagram of some kind for clarity.
25	Imagine you were present at the testing of the first atomic bomb. Write a description of your experience.
26	*Groupwork* Class debate: 'That nuclear weapons are a necessary evil.'

Diving into the Wreck

First having read the book of myths,
and loaded the camera,
and checked the edge of the knife-blade,
I put on
the body-armor of black rubber   5
the absurd flippers
the grave and awkward mask.
I am having to do this
not like Cousteau with his
assiduous team   10
aboard the sun-flooded schooner
but here alone.

There is a ladder.
The ladder is always there
hanging innocently   15
close to the side of the schooner.
We know what it is for,
we who have used it.
Otherwise
it is a piece of maritime floss   20
some sundry equipment.

I go down.
Rung after rung and still
the oxygen immerses me
the blue light   25
the clear atoms
of our human air.
I go down.
My flippers cripple me,
I crawl like an insect down the ladder   30
and there is no one
to tell me when the ocean
will begin.

First the air is blue and then
it is bluer and then green and then   35
black I am blacking out and yet
my mask is powerful
it pumps my blood with power
the sea is another story

Before you read

Groupwork
What does the title 'Diving into the Wreck' lead you to imagine? Using the senses and descriptive language, brainstorm what preparations would be needed and what the actual experience of diving into a wreck might be like.

the sea is not a question of power   40
I have to learn alone
to turn my body without force
in the deep element.

And now: it is easy to forget
what I came for   45
among so many who have always
lived here
swaying their crenellated fans
between the reefs
and besides   50
you breathe differently down here.

I came to explore the wreck.
The words are purposes.
The words are maps.
I came to see the damage that was done   55
and the treasures that prevail.
I stroke the beam of my lamp
slowly along the flank
of something more permanent
than fish or weed   60

the thing I came for:
the wreck and not the story of the wreck
the thing itself and not the myth
the drowned face always staring
toward the sun   65
the evidence of damage
worn by salt and sway into this threadbare beauty
the ribs of the disaster
curving their assertion
among the tentative haunters.   70

This is the place.
And I am here, the mermaid whose dark hair
streams black, the merman in his armored body
We circle silently
about the wreck   75
we dive into the hold.
I am she: I am he

whose drowned face sleeps with open eyes
whose breasts still bear the stress
whose silver, copper, vermeil cargo lies   80

obscurely inside barrels
half-wedged and left to rot
we are the half-destroyed instruments
that once held to a course
the water-eaten log   85
the fouled compass

We are, I am, you are
by cowardice or courage
the one who find our way
back to this scene   90
carrying a knife, a camera
a book of myths
in which
our names do not appear.

Glossary

6	*absurd*: ridiculous
9	*Cousteau*: Jacques Cousteau (1910–1997), French underwater explorer and author
10	*assiduous*: taking great care and attention
11	*schooner*: type of ship with two masts
20	*maritime*: to do with the sea
21	*sundry*: various small things not worth mentioning specifically
48	*crenellated*: of having open spaces at the top of a wall (often a feature on old castles that allowed archers to shoot); irregular-shaped edge
56	*prevail*: continue to exist; have survived
58	*flank*: side
67	*threadbare*: worn away almost completely
69	*assertion*: statement
70	*tentative*: cautious
80	*vermeil*: gilded metal (i.e. a metal that has been covered in a thin layer of gold)

Guidelines

This poem is from the 1973 collection of the same name. The speaker in the poem readies herself and then dives down to explore a shipwreck. The narrative of the poem is full of symbolism with many possible interpretations. It has been suggested by some critics that Rich is talking about society and its inequalities here. Do you agree that this is a possible interpretation or did you see something different when you read the poem?

Commentary

Journeys have often been starting points for myths and legends, and here also there is a heroic figure who braves danger. There is a quest, and insight is achieved. Unlike traditional poems, however, the figure is female.

Stanzas 1 and 2
The poem narrates the diver's descent into the sea in vivid, realistic images, starting with the preparations made and the equipment carried. The objects mentioned are significant. The 'book of myths' highlights the

investigation she wishes to make to see if the 'myths' (the myths of human relationships?) are true. The 'camera' suggests a desire to record what she finds, which the poem itself does. The 'knife-blade' emphasises the dangers of the journey.

She makes a comparison with the diving exploits of a real-life diver, Jacques Cousteau, but unlike Cousteau, who was part of a team, her journey will be carried out alone. This draws attention to the essentially solitary nature of her journey 'into the Wreck'. The speaker describes the ladder, an ordinary object 'hanging innocently' at the side of the ship. For her, it will have significance far beyond 'some sundry equipment': it will provide a gateway to the depths of the sea, where she hopes to find the truth.

Stanza 3

By repeating 'I go down' and 'rung' the speaker emphasises the sensation of someone moving downwards into the depths of the sea, towards an element other than the 'human air' in which she still lives. The image of the flippers and the comparison with an insect prepare us for the strange transformation that Rich describes in later lines. (Many myths have used images of transformation — sometimes animal metamorphosis — as a basis for exploration of human issues.) The speaker makes it clear that this journey has no guide to show her the way. Is it possible to read this as a metaphor for Rich's perception that her personal journey, as a woman and as a poet, is to be undertaken alone?

Stanza 4

You may notice that there is no punctuation in this section, apart from the full stop at the end. This may reflect the sensation of losing consciousness as she dives down further. (We have seen before that Rich makes use of punctuation to create effects.) Vivid visual images re-create the colours of the sea. But the speaker is still in control, protected by the mask, until she learns to abandon herself to the sea itself: to 'turn my body without force / in the deep element'. In this element, the concept of 'power' has no relevance. As in many poems, the sea is a symbol of vastness and mystery and, perhaps, the unconscious.

Stanza 5

The phrase 'And now' seems to signal that the speaker has arrived at her destination. She is amazed at what she sees and almost forgets the reason for her quest. Everything is different at the bottom of the ocean – 'you breathe differently down here' – and so you can see the world from a new perspective. 'Crenellated fans' is a vivid, precise image of sea creatures (scallop-shaped like a fan) as they move to and fro. All these perceptions may be read as metaphors for insights the poem itself achieves.

Stanzas 6 and 7

The speaker describes the wreck, the purpose of her journey. She takes her time to investigate it, to 'stroke the beam of my lamp / slowly' along its side. She wants to discover the 'damage that was done / and the treasures that prevail'.

Exploring the wreck, the diver sees it as 'the thing itself and not the myth'. It is a place where knowledge can be found. She records what the wreck looks like in unusual, almost surreal, images. It is like a corpse with its 'drowned face', but its 'ribs' are still clearly to be seen. Although showing 'evidence of damage', it is not entirely destroyed. Indeed, it still has a 'threadbare beauty'. What is the speaker suggesting here? Is she suggesting that the old myths of patriarchy, which seek to explain human sexuality and the traditional roles of men and women, retain some value, even though they must change at this point in human history?

Stanzas 8 and 9

Diving into the hold, the speaker undergoes a kind of mythic transformation, becoming both male and female: a 'mermaid' with her dark hair that 'streams back' and a 'merman' in her wet suit. It is as if she has magically cast off her old sexual identity and achieved a new androgynous one. She appears to be seeing the world from both male and female perspectives, as if truth or knowledge is not the exclusive preserve of either sex.

The absence of dividing punctuation between Stanzas 8 and 9 indicates that the speaker has fully identified with the mythic creatures she described. In the same mythological vein, she identifies with the 'drowned face' of the wreck, seeing both men and women ('he' and 'she') as 'half-destroyed instruments' who once followed a particular course that can no longer be of value to them. The 'log' and 'compass' of the wreck, the traditional instruments of navigation, are now 'water-eaten' and 'fouled'. They are no longer fit for purpose, which means new instruments will be needed.

Stanza 10

The final stanza, with its different pronouns ('We', 'I', 'you', 'one'), continues the idea of transformation, during which the (female) diver becomes both male and female and takes on a number of identities. The effect is of a loss of personal identity that is almost like a rebirth. (The new 'book of myths', for example, contains no names.) We are not told of the diver's return to land. In fact, it is the image of exploration that is repeated, so that the poem appears to come full circle. Might this suggest the ongoing nature of the quest?

Themes and imagery

The poem is immensely rich in themes and symbols. **The wreck, the journey or quest and the sea are each potent symbols.** Read as a whole, the poem suggests that the diver has undertaken **a journey of transformation in which she explores the old myths of sexuality and achieves a new identity**. However, to summarise 'Diving into the Wreck' in this way does not do justice to the poem's richness or complexity.

'Diving into the Wreck' can be enjoyed on many levels. It works as a simple description of a descent into the ocean: the setting, the actions described, the ocean, the wreck and the experience of losing oneself in one's surroundings – all of which Rich documents vividly in **precise images**, **metaphors** and **similes**. However, it is clear that the dive has a symbolic meaning, as a journey into the unknown, a quest for knowledge. In the mysterious and primal element of the sea, the diver sheds her old identity and undergoes a kind of rebirth as a being who is both female and male. The **symbolism of the wreck** has attracted the attention of many critics. For Judith McDaniel, the wreck is a 'layered image: it is the life of one woman, the source of successes and failures; it is the history of all women submerged in a patriarchal culture; it is that source of myths about male and female sexuality which shape our lives and roles today.' To explore the wreck is to search for knowledge that goes beyond the myths we have inherited.

As we know from this poem and others, Rich was pessimistic about **the relationship between the sexes** at this stage of human history. In this context, the word 'wreck' might signify her perception that these relationships are damaged beyond repair. And yet, as the diver notes, she came to see the 'treasures that prevail' or survive. There may be some hope for the future. Given Rich's interest in male/female roles at this point in her writing career, commentators have suggested that 'Diving into the Wreck' represents a search for an androgynous view of the world, for a new genderless myth to replace the old, sexually based one. In this new world men and women will be equal because they will no longer be limited by their sexuality.

Another possible theme in the poem is Rich's realisation that the 'myths' of the world have been related by men. Like many other female writers, Rich came to see the **dominance of the male perspective** (the patriarchy) in literature, and how that resulted in women's experiences being suppressed. From this point of view, the quest of the diver may be to retrieve the buried treasure, to salvage what she can from the wreck, and in so doing to create a new form of expression or myth.

Many of Rich's poems are concerned with **the theme of power and its opposite, powerlessness**. 'Diving into the Wreck' may offer an imaginative vision of what a quest for power might entail: danger, adventure, a loss of identity, and perhaps finally a sense of hope and achievement.

Form and language

The poem is written in **free verse**. It is divided into ten stanzas of roughly equal length. The breaks between stanzas nearly always indicate a significant shift in the poem, a move from one place to another, or a change in perspective.

Note the changes in **line length**. The opening line of the poem is expansive and leisurely. However, the rhythm changes as the poem proceeds. The short lines of stanzas 2 and 3 suggest the slow, laborious descent of the diver, dressed in her diving suit, into the water. The short phrases that make up each line bring to mind the careful breathing of the diver, as she inhales and exhales, exploring the darkness of the ocean, and reporting back.

Questions

1	What preparations has the diver made, according to the first seven lines? Write a detailed account of the preparations.
2	Assess each component in the preparations you identified above and explain why each might be relevant to or needed for the dive. Is the 'book of myths' (line 1) problematic here at all?
3	How does the speaker differ from 'Cousteau' (line 9) and his undersea explorations? Does this introduce an element of risk to the poem? Explain.
4	How does the ladder appear differently to those who use it and those who don't, according to the second stanza?
5	Lines 22–30 describe the diver's descent of the ladder. How does the speaker convey the length and difficulty of this process? Comment on the simile used here.
6	How is the isolation of the diver further emphasised in lines 31–33?
7	In the fourth stanza, what does the diver notice about the air?
8	After the diver almost passes out she remarks, 'my mask is powerful' (line 37). How is her mask powerful? Is there more than one possible interpretation of this image?
9	How does the mask differ from the sea in stanza 4?
10	In your own words, explain what the diver has to 'learn alone' (line 41).
11	What things threaten to distract the diver from her purpose 'down here' in stanza 5?
12	In the sixth stanza, what does the speaker assert are her reasons for this dive?

13	How is a sense of permanence conveyed in stanza 6 regarding the longevity of the wreck?
14	How does the diver intend to separate the truth or 'the thing itself' from 'the myth' in stanza 7? What has she come here to discover?
15	How has the wreck been personified in stanza 7 and what is the effect of this?
16	Stanza 8 has a surreal quality as the diver morphs into an amalgamation of a mermaid and a merman, becoming both she and he. Show how this is achieved. How did you find this section: confusing, fascinating, disconcerting, or something else? Give reasons for your answer.
17	What has the diver become in stanza 9?
18	Comment on the transition from 'I' to 'she' and 'he' previously in the poem finally to 'we' in this stanza.
19	The shiny, shimmering metals conceal a rotting, decaying structure beneath – do you agree that this is what is communicated in stanza 9? Could this be symbolic in any way? Explain.
20	According to the final stanza, what will bring the diver to revisit the wreck?
21	Why might 'our names' 'not appear' in the 'book of myths' (lines 92–94)?
22	How does the poet create a sense of menace or threat in the poem regarding the diver's descent into the water and the dive itself?
23	This dramatic lyric is highly evocative and descriptive. What emotions and reactions did the poem provoke in you and what were the main images and phrases that provoked those reactions?
24	Consider your answers from the 'Before you read' exercise. Were there any parallels between what you initially imagined and the details in the poem?
25	'The words are purposes. / The words are maps' (lines 53–54). Regarding the poem as a whole, what do you infer from this statement? What are the words for and what might they be maps to? Think about how Rich has talked about communication and language in her other poems you have studied.
26	How does Rich use punctuation to shape her narrative in the poem? Include the division of stanzas in your answer.
27	Comment on Rich's use of repetition in the poem. What effects are achieved?
28	There are myriad possible interpretations for the symbolism in this poem. In groups, divide the following list and suggest what the images here might symbolise in the poem. You may add to the list if you wish: the book of myths, the camera, the knife, the wetsuit, the ladder, the ship, the sea, the mask, the treasure, the reef, the mermaid/man, the shiny metals, the rotting wreck.
29	What possible themes can you identify in this poem? The list below might help guide you but feel free to offer your own interpretation: ■ Appearances versus reality ■ Trying to change tradition and society ■ The importance of exploration and discovery regardless of the dangers ■ Surviving in a difficult environment.
30	Write a descriptive piece about a real or imagined experience of something daring, perhaps a hot-air balloon flight, a bungee jump, a sky dive, a space flight, etc.

Before you read

What connotations does the word 'Survivor' have for you? Jot down four or five words or phrases that spring to mind and explain their relationship to this word.

From a Survivor

The pact that we made was the ordinary pact
of men & women in those days

I don't know who we thought we were
that our personalities
could resist the failures of the race   5

Lucky or unlucky, we didn't know
the race had failures of that order
and that we were going to share them

Like everybody else, we thought of ourselves as special

Your body is as vivid to me   10
as it ever was: even more

since my feeling for it is clearer:
I know what it could and could not do

it is no longer
the body of a god   15
or anything with power over my life

Next year it would have been 20 years
and you are wastefully dead
who might have made the leap
we talked, too late, of making   20

which I live now
not as a leap
but a succession of brief, amazing movements

each one making possible the next

Glossary

| 1 | *pact*: formal agreement (here, marriage contract) |

Guidelines

Written in 1972, this is the third poem on your course from the 1973 collection *Diving into the Wreck*. In it Rich addresses her late husband, Alfred Conrad, who died by suicide in 1970. She moved on to have a close and committed relationship with writer and editor Michelle Cliff until Rich's death in 2012.

Commentary

Lines 1–9

The opening lines are remarkably simple. The speaker remembers how she and her former husband married, full of hope for the future. Marriage, for them, was the 'ordinary pact / of men & women in those days'. For the poet and her late husband, to whom the poem is addressed, as for many of their generation, the 'pact' turned out to be anything but ordinary. The speaker looks back to 'those days', a time when the relations between the sexes had not yet undergone the upheavals they would in the 1960s, particularly with the progress of the women's movement in the Western world. Like most couples entering into marriage, the 'we' of the poem saw no prospect of failure; indeed, they saw themselves as superior to others, as she ruefully suggests in 'I don't know who we thought we were'. With hindsight, the speaker suggests, they were naïve or foolish to think that they could make their marriage work in view of the 'failures of the race'. The phrase suggests that the breakdown of marriage relationships is almost inevitable.

Lines 10–16

In line 10 the poem strikes out in a new direction. The tone is direct and intimate: 'Your body is as vivid to me / as it ever was'. Now that her husband is dead, she remembers him as he was, perhaps even more clearly since, she says, her feeling for him is 'clearer'. She remembers his body and recognises that it was not 'the body of a god'. The reference to a god suggests that, as a young woman, she worshipped her husband and submitted to his power. Line 16 suggests that she has changed, and no man will have 'power over my life'.

Lines 17–24

There is a tone of regret and sadness in 'Next year it would have been 20 years'. The adverb 'wastefully' hints at the speaker's frustration, the sense that the death by suicide might have been avoided. She considers what might have been, 'the leap / we talked, too late, of making'. As the last four lines of the poem make clear, the speaker has made the 'leap' alone. (If we identify the speaker of the poem with the poet, the leap might refer to the enormous changes in Rich's life, including her development as a poet, her feminist views and her sexuality.) The speaker is the 'Survivor' of the title. Her life now, she suggests, has changed and grown and will continue to do so. The final lines have a mood of hope and possibility. They celebrate life as a series of 'brief, amazing movements / each one making possible the next'.

Themes and imagery

Rich wrote very few poems about her husband's death. 'From a Survivor' is one of the few poems in which she addresses the subject.

The words of the poem are **deceptively simple**, but they express a **wide range of emotions**. At first there is a sort of rueful understanding that the sense of superiority that the young couple felt was undeserved and

foolish. There is pessimism, too, in the phrase 'the failures of the race', as if marriage breakdown is almost to be expected. We can sense the speaker's clear-eyed judgement on the power that her husband had over her in their relationship. However, it is impossible to read the poem without sensing the speaker's **regret** at the way things turned out for him. He may have been able to make 'the leap', a metaphor for accepting change in their lives and relationship, as she has done, but his death prevented it. She is the survivor of whatever trauma they have endured, but she is clearly regretful that things have not worked out this way for him. The poem ends on an optimistic, even celebratory, tone. For her, life is now calmer, as the phrase 'not as a leap' indicates; it contains 'brief, amazing movements' that allow her to look forward rather than backwards.

Form and language

The poem is written in **free verse**. It has many of Rich's trademarks: the **rhythms of speech**; the use of **enjambment**; **irregular line and stanza lengths**. The form of the poem follows the voice of the speaker as she addresses her dead husband, the lines following her thoughts and the phrasing of those thoughts. The poem is quiet and conversational, with elements of traditional love poetry, in the direct address of the lover to her beloved, particularly in the beautiful lines, 'Your body is as vivid to me /as it ever was'. The poem is divided into a series of irregular stanzas, varying between one and four lines, reflecting the progress of the speaker's thoughts. Interestingly the poem has **no full stops**. On the face of it, the poem has very little 'poetic' language, but the simplicity and directness of the address make for a moving and affecting poem.

Questions

1	What is the speaker referring to in the first two lines? What 'ordinary pact' did men and women make?
2	With the answer to question 1 in mind, what was the couple's failure and the 'failures of the race' (line 5) in terms of this pact?
3	What were the couple unable to predict and why (lines 6–9)?
4	Would you describe the language of the first nine lines as more positive or more negative in outlook? Explain your answer with close reference to this section and ensuring that you comment on Rich's use of repetition.
5	What did you discover about the expectations this couple had versus the reality of married life in the first nine lines of the poem?
6	Read lines 10 to 15 and say how the speaker's attitude towards and perception of the man's body have changed over time. What might have brought about this change?
7	Rich mentions 'power' in line 16. What sort of power, do you think, is she referring to? What does this tell you about the couple's early relationship? Have you encountered a similar concept of power anywhere else in the poetry by Rich you have studied?
8	'Next year it would have been 20 years' (line 17). Refer to Rich's biography in this book and say what you think she might be talking about here. Keep in mind this poem was written in 1972.
9	Comment on the phrase 'wastefully dead' (line 18) – what is conveyed by this?
10	What 'leap' might he have made, a leap the speaker feels she succeeded in making, 'which I live now' (lines 19–21)?
11	How does the speaker seem to view her life as it is now, according to the last three lines of the poem? Do you think she seems happy with her life now? Explain.
12	Do you agree that Rich uses far less imagery (especially metaphors and symbols) in this poem than she does in the other poems you have studied? If you do agree, suggest why she may have taken a more direct approach here.
13	Trace the tone and mood of the poem as it progresses, noting any change in tone or mood and showing how and where these changes occur.
14	What relationship does the title have to the content of the poem?
15	Suggest why the poet does not put a full stop at the end of the poem. Have you seen Rich use a similar technique elsewhere? Was the effect the same here or different?
16	Do you agree that 'moving on' is the main theme of the poem or did you find a stronger theme in your study of it? Give reasons for your answer.
17	'I hadn't found the courage yet to … use the pronoun "I" – the woman in the poem is always "she".' Compare this poem with two or three other of Rich's poems that feature women in the light of this statement from the poet.

| 18 |  In pairs, examine Rich's biography in this book and perhaps conduct further research into the poet's life. What details from her biography speak to this poem in particular? |

| 19 | Write a series of diary entries where the speaker demonstrates that he or she has survived a harrowing experience of some sort. |

| 20 | The next poem in this collection was entitled 'For the Dead' and in it Rich writes: 'I dreamed I called you on the telephone to say: Be kinder to yourself'. Think of an upsetting or difficult experience you had in the past. Write a letter to your younger self offering comfort and advice. |

Before you read

What do you know about Marie Curie? Discuss this with a partner and if necessary research this famous scientist.

Power

Living   in the earth-deposits   of our history

Today a backhoe divulged   out of a crumbling flank of earth
one bottle   amber   perfect   a hundred-year-old
cure for fever   or melancholy   a tonic
for living on this earth   in the winters of this climate.   5

Today I was reading about Marie Curie:
she must have known she suffered   from radiation sickness
her body bombarded for years   by the element
she had purified
It seems she denied to the end   10
the source of the cataracts on her eyes
the cracked and suppurating skin   of her finger-ends
till she could no longer hold a test-tube or a pencil

She died   a famous woman   denying
her wounds   15
denying
her wounds   came   from the same source as her power.

Glossary

2	*backhoe*: digger, machine for excavating
8	*bombarded*: in medical terms this means to expose a substance to particulate or electromagnetic radiation for the purpose of making it radioactive; it can also mean a sustained attack with missiles
11	*cataracts*: a condition causing the lens of the eye to become clouded, adversely affecting one's vision
12	*suppurating*: to discharge pus from a wound

Marie Curie

Curie (1867–1934) was the first recipient of two Nobel prizes for science, one in physics and the other in chemistry. She coined the term 'radioactivity' and helped to develop the science of X-rays, championing the use of portable X-ray machines on the battlefield. She was the first female professor at the Sorbonne University in Paris and the only woman to be interred in France's famous Panthéon (the resting place of the nation's greatest minds) on her own merits.

Guidelines

From *The Dream of a Common Language: Poems* (1978), this poem begins with a description of a medicine bottle being unearthed by a digger and goes on to ponder the life and work of Marie Curie, the scientist who discovered the chemical elements polonium (named after her native Poland although she became a French citizen) and radium. Her pioneering work, alongside that of her husband, Pierre, exposed her to deadly radiation, which eventually led to the aplastic anaemia that killed her. In this poem we see Rich move away from more rigid and structured forms to experiment with layout and language, much as Curie experimented on radioactive theory.

Commentary

Lines 1–5

The poem begins with a cryptic statement: 'Living   in the earth-deposits   of our history'. The stanza that follows helps us to understand something of the meaning of the opening line. It relates how a mechanical digger threw up a long-buried bottle, which contained a tonic or 'cure for fever' or depression ('melancholy'). Although the speaker sees the historical value of the find, they doubt wryly whether such a cure is possible. Can there really be a cure 'for living on this earth'?

Lines 6–13

The speaker goes on to link the unearthed medicine with Marie Curie, known for her medical research. What interests the speaker is not Curie's success as a woman scientist, it is the nature of the power which it gave her and her attitude to it. Curie was physically affected by overexposure to radium in her scientific and medical research. Curie's physical ailments are described in a series of disturbing images: 'her body bombarded', her skin 'cracked and suppurating'. We can appreciate the deprivation she must have felt by not being able to 'hold a test-tube or pencil', the tools of her trade as a scientist and researcher.

Lines 14–17

The final lines seem to suggest that Curie lived in a state of denial, refusing to recognise that her illness and her wounds came from the same source as her power. Ironically, Curie's life's work – finding a cure for illness – destroyed her in the end. The lack of punctuation in the lines and the spaces placed between words have the effect of making us focus on individual words and phrases; for example, the phrase 'a famous woman' and the words 'denying' and 'wounds'.

The final stanza may leave us slightly puzzled. What is the poem implying here? Is there a suggestion that a successful woman is doomed to destruction unless she recognises the source of her power? Or is the focus solely on Marie Curie? Did she deny the sacrifice of herself in the service of her work? Was her success the source of her failure?

Themes and imagery

Does the poem express **an ambiguous attitude to power and what it implies for women** in particular? Readers may be puzzled that a feminist would seem to undermine the power that Marie Curie had. Rich came to see those women who achieved success in a man's world as extraordinary rather than representative of women in general. Her vision was of a society that would champion the 'common woman'. Increasingly in her writing she identifies with ordinary women, particularly those who lead difficult or obscure lives. Her attitude to power is therefore ambiguous. In her view, a woman such as Marie Curie shares in power, as defined by men. As such, her power may be destructive, literally and metaphorically. In *On Lies, Secrets and Silence*, Rich wrote, 'For us to be "extraordinary" or "uncommon" is to fail'. These views may have influenced this **meditation on power**.

Form and language

The lines of the poem are organised in an unusual way. **The spacing has the effect of isolating individual words and emphasising their significance.** Another feature of this poem is the seemingly disjointed nature of its insights: it is by no means clear why the discovery of a bottle in the earth should lead to a contemplation of Marie Curie and her terrible fate. However, this form mirrors the sometimes illogical movement of actual thought, or **stream of consciousness**.

Marie Curie.

Questions

1	What might the poet mean by 'the earth-deposits of our history' (line 1)?
2	What did the backhoe unearth? Describe this object and mention what it once contained.
3	Does the 'tonic' (line 4) seem authentic? What indication are we given that this may not have been a real or an effective treatment?
4	'Today I was reading about Marie Curie' (line 6). From your reading of the first five lines, what links the beginning of the poem with the mention of this famous scientist?
5	What do we learn about Curie's work and its effects on her health in lines 6–13? What aspects of her character are revealed through this information?
6	How did reading about the physical effects of radiation on Curie's body make you feel?
7	What might the poet mean when they say that Curie died 'denying / her wounds' (lines 14–15)?
8	Where did Curie's wounds come from?
9	What is the source of Curie's power, in your opinion? Do you agree that it has come from the same source as her wounds? Explain.
10	Having studied the poem, what sorts of power does the title suggest? There may be more than one. You may wish to include some of the information you have learned about Marie Curie in your answer.
11	The layout of the poem is visually striking. Why is this? Did you find this unusual format attractive and effective? Explain why or why not. (It might help to write out the poem more traditionally, and to punctuate it, and then compare both versions.)
12	In your opinion, do the first five lines add to or detract from the effect of the poem? Is the speaker giving us any hints as to her own state of mind or emotion in this section?
13	Think about the overall theme and tone of this poem, then pair up with a classmate to share and discuss your ideas.
14	Read the poem aloud, using long pauses where there are gaps. What ideas and phrases did this exercise emphasise for you?
15	What imagery in the poem struck you most? How and why were these images striking for you?
16	Comment on the effectiveness of the title. If you had to suggest an alternative title, what might that be and why?
17	Choose an important figure from history or popular culture who has died and compose a poem about them, inspired by the form, language and imagery in this poem.
18	Suggest possible reasons why Rich chose Marie Curie above other famous scientists as the subject of her poem. Is her gender relevant? Perhaps construct your answer in the form of an imagined interview with the poet. Read Rich's biography in this book and decide if you can find any parallels between the two.
19	Compare this poem to the previous two in terms of the theme of power.
20	Write a short story inspired by the idea of uncovering a mysterious object from the ground.

Marie Curie with her husband, Pierre.

SNAPSHOT ADRIENNE RICH

- Central ideas of power, inequality, communication and change
- Earlier more traditional forms give way to less rigid structures as poems progress (punctuation especially)
- Symbols and metaphors heavily used
- Poems open to multiple interpretations
- Later poems use first-person persona ('I') more often

- Relationships explored and questioned
- Breakthrough political voice in a female poet
- Autobiographical details inform but do not dominate poems; a distance is maintained
- Skilful mastery of language and metre
- Many poems are dramatic lyrics

Exam-Preparation Questions

1	'Adrienne Rich explores the twin themes of power and powerlessness in a variety of interesting ways.' Write a response to the poetry of Adrienne Rich in the light of this statement, supporting your points with suitable reference to the poems on your course.
2	What view of human relationships emerges from your study of the poetry of Adrienne Rich?
3	Explore the themes of inequality and oppression in the poetry of Adrienne Rich.
4	'the desire to be heard, – that is the impulse behind writing poems, for me' (Adrienne Rich). Does the poetry of Adrienne Rich speak to you? Write your personal response, referring to the poems of Adrienne Rich that do/do not speak to you.
5	Charles Altieri stated that Adrienne Rich had an 'obsession with victimhood'. From your experience of studying her poetry, do you agree with his comment? Give reasons for your answer.
6	'Change and the self-discovery which comes with it are central concepts in the poetry of Adrienne Rich'. Evaluate this statement with reference to some of the poems on your course.
7	'Rich employs free verse, dialogue, and the interweaving of several voices. She evolves from a more tightly constructed traditional rhymed poetry to a more open, loose, and flexible poetic line.' Trace the evolution of style and form in Adrienne Rich's work in the light of this statement.
8	'The imagery in the poetry of Adrienne Rich contains a rich array of evocative and interesting symbols and metaphors to express a range of ideas and emotions.' Write a response to the imagery you encountered in the work of this poet and discuss the ideas these images conveyed to you.
9	Imagine your school has invited Adrienne Rich to speak about her poetry. Write the letter of invitation you would send to her, outlining the poems your year group would like her to speak about and the reasons her poetry appealed to you. Your letter should contain close reference to her work.
10	'Rich is able to explore both personal and political matters simultaneously in her poetry.' Agree or disagree with this assessment with suitable reference to the poetry of Adrienne Rich on your course.
11	'Communication and the lack of it is a preoccupation in the poetry of Adrienne Rich.' Discuss this opinion.
12	'Rich's poetry communicates powerful feelings through thought-provoking images and symbols.' Write your response to this statement with reference to the poems by Adrienne Rich on your course.

Sample Essay

'Adrienne Rich explores the twin themes of power and powerlessness in a variety of interesting ways.' Write a response to the poetry of Adrienne Rich in the light of this statement, supporting your points with suitable reference to the poems on your course. (2010 exam)

Question referred to immediately and clear stance taken – student agrees with the statement and clearly understands the task given

Those who have power and those who do not are concepts that dominate the work of American poet Adrienne Rich. She uses vividly evocative imagery and highly descriptive language to explore these ideas in interesting ways. What I noticed most about the theme of power in her poems was how the oppressed, often *Personal response* women, became gradually more powerful as her work progressed; how the oppressed parties allowed the holders of power to have less and less control over them, wrestling with the 'minor demons' that hold sway over their freedom. For me, Rich's poems reflect the patriarchal nature of our society and language, where the holders of power are generally male. She seems to speak for victims of misogyny and inequality everywhere and her brave journey to take control of her own destiny and to speak *The introduction tackles all parts of the question and outlines the shape the answer will take* out about injustice and oppression is an inspiring one. To illustrate these ideas the poems I have chosen to discuss are 'Aunt Jennifer's Tigers', 'Living in Sin', 'The Roofwalker', 'Diving into the Wreck', 'From a Survivor' and 'Power'. In these poems I

Clear engagement with the work of the poet on several levels; student demonstrates a real connection with the poetry and the poet

noted that Rich took us not only on a personal journey but also on a political one. As she once wrote in her notebook: 'I began to feel that politics was not something "out there" but something "in here" and the essence of my condition'. Like Rich, I feel that if we all took more of an interest in equality and justice in our society and not just in our own personal lives, we would live in a fairer, happier place.

'Aunt Jennifer's Tigers' begins with a totally oppressed and repressed woman, the speaker's 'Aunt Jennifer', who is 'terrified' and trapped by the looming presence of her husband, or 'Uncle' as he is called in the poem. 'The massive weight of Uncle's wedding band / Sits heavily upon Aunt Jennifer's hand' – the wedding ring here is a symbol of the ownership and control Uncle wields over this nervous woman. We can see her anxiety in the description of her 'fingers fluttering through her wool', the alliteration emphasising her nervousness as she embroiders a panel depicting tigers. Even in death she fears this powerful man, 'When Aunt is dead, her terrified hands will lie / Still ringed with ordeals she was mastered by.' I feel here that Rich is talking not just about one couple, but about all women who have suffered under the yoke of patriarchy and in marriages that prevented them from having a career and from pursuing their own interests.

Student has researched relevant biographical details

They were expected to sit at home and knit and sew; to be quiet and obedient. It interested me to discover that although Rich's mother was a gifted pianist and composer she gave this up upon marriage to Rich's father. The only release the aunt appears to have is in the art generated by her embroidery skills. She creates a vividly evocative scene of tigers: 'Bright topaz denizens of a world of green'. These colourful and powerful creatures 'do not fear the men' and after her death 'go on prancing, proud and unafraid'. The alliteration

Question fully addressed here and the quotation and explanation support the points made

of the 'z' sounds in the phrase 'topaz denizens' and the exotic nature of the imagery make the theme of power and powerlessness more interesting and has a striking and energetic effect, telling us that Aunt Jennifer had a lively and creative imagination.

However, the problem I found was that her lovely colourful tigers, who seem so confident and fearless, appear to be male, as suggested by the word 'chivalric': 'They pace in sleek chivalric certainty'. It seems Aunt Jennifer cannot give power or fearlessness to female creatures in her tapestry. Obviously the uncle represents power here. His oppressive presence terrifies and subjugates his wife to the point where even in death she is afraid of him. The imagery effectively conveys her lack of power; she is reduced to fingers and hands and we do not hear her voice at all. The language and form of the poem reflect this too as the rigidity of her life, the control exerted over her, is echoed in the tightly controlled structure of the poem. The three four-line stanzas have a measured pace and a tight rhyming scheme of *aabb, ccdd, eeff*. Here we see clearly power and powerlessness, inequality and injustice and in this very early poem from Rich the woman has no real power whatsoever over her own life.

Purpose is clear: the question has been addressed with close reference to this poem and issues raised in the introduction have been analysed

Link to last poem adds to coherence of the essay

A more daring woman appears in the poem 'Living in Sin', or at least one who appears on the surface to be more daring. Unlike Aunt Jennifer the woman in this poem has been brave enough to eschew the societal convention of marriage and live outside wedlock with her lover in a 'studio'. However, we soon see that this woman's life is less liberated than it at first appears. She learns

Language used is in line with higher level expectations; we see an eloquence and clarity of expression

Student appreciates cultural context

quickly that living with her lover in this rebellious and unconventional way (remembering this poem was published in 1955) is not as glamorous as one might first think, 'She had thought the studio would keep itself; / no dust upon the furniture of love.' She feels afraid to say that the disarray and mess in the flat bother her, 'Half heresy, to wish the taps less vocal, / the panes relieved of grime.' The squalid state of the 'studio' becomes ever clearer and more interesting through Rich's vivid imagery, 'a cat / stalking the picturesque amusing mouse', 'last night's cheese', 'a pair of beetle-eyes would fix her own'. The language here also creates interest as Rich uses alliteration, long vowels and sibilance to enhance the effect of the imagery. Her lover rises late and seems completely unaffected by the mess, 'rubbed at his beard, went out for cigarettes'. The woman, however, feels pressure to tidy up the place, 'she, jeered by the minor demons, / pulled back the sheets and made the bed and found / a towel to dust the table-top'. What were these 'minor demons' I wondered, what

Personal engagement and response; lively tone

does this image mean? It seemed to me that she has been unwittingly programmed by the patriarchal society she lives in to be the homemaker. She seems trapped there, horrified by her compulsion to fulfil the role of housewife, while he can disregard the housework and leave the flat at his leisure. She might seem on the surface to be a liberated woman but really he still has the power and she cannot be free of her traditional role even though she longs to be. The 'minor demons' will not let her. She dreads the dawning of the next day when this drudgery will doubtless be repeated, 'she woke sometimes to feel the daylight coming / like a relentless milkman up the stairs'. The measured pace and list-like quality of much of the poem emphasises the inevitability of the life this woman is doomed to live. It is clear she does not have the power here. There seems to be a long way to go before the women in Rich's poetry can be free from oppression and from the confines of the home.

Nod to poet's language in creation of theme of power here but could be expanded upon

Effective linking of paragraphs continues (this is important in terms of Coherence, which accounts for 30% of every question's marks)

Another woman similarly confined to her home while men seem free and far more powerful is described in 'The Roofwalker', a poem Rich dedicated to fellow feminist and poet Denise Levertov. It comes from the collection *Snapshots of a Daughter-in-Law*, a breakthrough work for Rich, where she became less formal in the structure of her work. She was heavily criticised for this and for the political and feminist themes explored. She was accused of being 'strident' and 'too political' for daring to be a woman who wrote about inequality and oppression. In this highly metaphorical poem the builders 'stand on the roof' daringly, they are like 'Giants'. She identifies with them only in terms of the danger they

Imagery is referenced relevantly here

are in, 'I feel like them up there: / exposed, larger than life, / and due to break my neck', but as the metaphor of the roof develops we discover that the speaker is under it. Again we see a woman trapped unhappily in the home, 'Was it worth while to lay –

Effective coherence of ideas and examples as student continues to successfully link the poems together while exploring these themes

/ with infinite exertion – / a roof I can't live under?' At least here there is a hint that this woman cannot take any more and feels compelled to leave when she says 'I can't live under' the roof. She sounds exhausted, 'infinite exertion', and at the end of her tether. Here we see a woman question the status quo and decide not to take her situation lying down. To me, the roof is an interesting, powerful and vivid image, a symbol of oppression for the woman who must live under it and simultaneously a symbol of freedom and power for the men who can dare to walk upon it.

Theme continues to drive the answer forward, relevance and progression of thought and argument maintained

The speaker then says something that I feel also sums up the experience of the women in the two poems discussed above: 'A life I didn't choose / chose me'. The pressure to marry, to be a homemaker was huge and so many women who would have loved more freedom were denied it, rendered powerless by a society that forced women to serve the needs of men. I feel that Rich speaks for all of these women by expressing her own dissatisfaction with domestic life. She has written that initially she felt like a 'monster' for being unfulfilled by marriage and children. But by writing this poetry and addressing these issues Rich breaks out, 'I'm naked, ignorant, / a naked man fleeing / across the roofs', but she so nearly gave in to remaining in a bland and oppressive domesticity: 'who could with a shade of difference / be sitting in the lamplight / against the cream wallpaper / reading'. The speaker is certain she would be reading about danger, about laying oneself bare and breaking out, 'reading—not with indifference— / about a naked man / fleeing across the roofs'. I feel Rich is saying that she would be reading about freedom even if she hadn't dared to reach for it herself. For me, this represents a slight shift in the balance of power. This woman has begun to dare. Unlike Aunt Jennifer and the woman living in sin, she is going to expose herself to being 'larger

Enthusiastic and personal response leading effectively to the concepts to be explored in the following paragraphs – structure of answer is coherent and well planned

than life' and wants to walk naked upon the roof – the roof that symbolises oppression for women who live under it. I also noticed a shift from the speaker being 'she' to the speaker becoming 'I', thus daring, not only in the imagery but also in the language she uses, to own her own narrative, her own voice. This was truly interesting and exciting. I could feel Rich grow braver here and start to take back her power.

In my view the poem richest in imagery pertaining to this theme is 'Diving into the Wreck'. In this poem Rich has grown into the 'I' persona introduced in 'The *Link to previous point* Roofwalker' and is developing her exploration of patriarchy and inequality,

Idea of power changing as poetry progresses was a key point of the introduction – student is ensuring to adhere to the opinions and points raised at the start of the essay

through a metaphorical dive down to a shipwreck. I feel Rich is comparing the wreck to tradition, the tradition of a patriarchal society where women and minorities are subjugated. I found that an interesting concept. This 'wreck' must be explored and indeed revisited; we cannot abandon it completely but must seek to understand it if we are to change and to effect change. For me, this represents a huge leap forward in terms of the theme of power and powerlessness in Rich's poetry as she gives us a poem where 'The words are maps' to guide us in this process. First, to explore the wreck that represents an unequal society we need to carefully prepare ourselves. The diver does this in the first stanza of the poem. She has 'read the book of myths', which might refer to male-dominated books of literature and history that have shaped our past, our language and our traditions. She also needs to record her dive, which the 'loaded' camera will do. She is ready to face the danger of her endeavour, 'checked the edge of the knife-blade / I put on / the body-armor'. This woman is diving into the unfamiliar world without the support of others, unlike men, as implied in her reference to 'Cousteau with his / assiduous team'. This reminded me of the adverse reaction to her collection *Snapshots of a Daughter-in-Law* – Rich realises that if she is to examine and expose and even attack the status quo she must be forearmed. She leaves the safety of the deck and makes the long and difficult journey to the sea, symbolised by the ladder: 'I go down. / My flippers cripple me, / I crawl like an insect down the ladder'. The journey to the wreck is a risky and precarious one, as conveyed by this simile, the word 'cripple' and the alliteration of 'p' sounds that hamper the metre and retard the pace of the line. It is clear one must be completely determined to endure to have any hope of success.

Theme addressed once more

Once in the sea, Rich explores the theme of power immediately, 'I am blacking out and yet / my mask is powerful / it pumps my blood with power'. To me the mask might represent either Rich's use of voices and personae in her work or anything we use to help us survive in a hostile and unfamiliar environment, or both. We all need something to sustain us; Aunt Jennifer's embroidery perhaps did that for her, as did the dream of walking on the roof one day for the speaker in 'The Roofwalker'. She states that 'the sea is another story / the sea is not a question of power'. The ideal environment is one where

Student continues to forge links between different poems and ideas

power is not an issue and we all exist harmoniously and happily. The diver is a woman no longer in a domestic situation, she has entered a new, challenging and exciting world free from the constraints of patriarchy, she is like the roofwalker – outside, looking down, free to explore. The diver wants to examine and understand this wreck, 'I came to see the damage that was done / and the treasures that prevail.' She is determined to discover the truth about our unjust and male-dominated society, 'the thing I came for: / the wreck and not the story of the wreck', and when she finds this, 'This is the place', she is totally transformed by the experience. In a beautifully surreal passage the diver becomes both male and female, both mythical and real, and is no longer alone, 'I am here, the mermaid whose dark hair / streams black, the merman in his armored body … we dive into the hold. I am she: I am he', later stating 'We are, I am, you are'. I like to think that here the speaker has thrown aside issues of gender and race, religion and sexuality, wealth and poverty to imagine someone who is not at the mercy of the 'minor demons' any more but who has been reborn anew through her own efforts, her own struggles, finding her own way. I think this poem, with its interesting and beautiful imagery and its highly descriptive language, reflects the personal, political and professional journey of Rich into new territory. She came out regarding her sexuality and embraced her lesbianism, a brave move for the 1970s, and she found love with her partner, Michelle Cliff. Indeed, the poem celebrates the journey of anyone who has been brave enough to leave their comfort zone and challenge the status quo. It encourages us all to dive into the wreck and be transformed by the experience. Power is in our own hands if only we dare to grasp it.

Imagery supports student's ideas in previous paragraphs of women first being trapped and then slowly escaping enforced domesticity

This quote was used in the introduction and will appear again in the conclusion, providing a link between the beginning, middle and end of the essay

Student has engaged with the poem both in terms of what may have inspired the poet but more importantly regarding his or her own interpretation; again the theme of power is addressed

In 'From a Survivor' Rich takes this theme a step further. Abandoning metaphors and symbolism, she plainly and openly mourns the suicide of her husband now 'wastefully dead' but shows she has moved on and continues to embrace the 'I' in her language. Men do not dominate any more, 'it is no longer / the body of a god / or anything with power over my life'. They say the best revenge is a life well lived. Rich certainly is testimony to this as she seems happy with her life and all that each day may bring. Unlike the diver, she no longer needs to make 'the leap' but can

The exploration of the final two poems is brief but remember that students do not have to analyse every poem equally and some poems may be referred to more briefly than others as long as relevance to the question and coherence are maintained

live life as 'a succession of brief, amazing movements // each one making possible the next'. Like Marie Curie in the poem 'Power', the trials and tribulations of women's struggles or the struggles of anyone who has been oppressed can also make us stronger. Curie became ill and died as a result of her research into radioactive elements, 'she must have known she suffered   from radiation sickness / her body bombarded for years', but she also made huge scientific breakthroughs with her work on radiation and X-rays that has had a transforming effect on medical diagnosis and treatment. Just as the diver dared to explore the wreck, Curie dared to explore the unknown in science. Like Rich in her poetry, knowledge and progress came from suffering, 'her wounds   came from the same source as her power'. What hurts us can also make us stronger.

Bringing the essay back to a statement or idea expressed at the beginning gives closure and a sense of completion to the essay as well as suggesting forethought and planning

As I stated in my introduction, Rich seems to speak for victims of misogyny and inequality everywhere and her brave journey towards taking control of her destiny and speaking out about injustice and oppression is an inspiring one. As Rich's poetry progressed, the women in her work gradually came to overcome their powerlessness and, like Marie Curie, make huge breakthroughs in terms of their power over their own destiny. These women have overcome the 'minor demons' of patriarchy and oppression and are no longer 'terrified' of the 'ordeals' they had once been 'mastered by'. Through her interesting, evocative and vivid language and imagery, Rich has certainly for me explored and made fascinating the themes of power and powerlessness. What a powerful and positive message to give young readers of her poetry!

Clear personal response

ESSAY CHECKLIST		Yes √	No ×
Purpose	Has the candidate understood the task?		
	Has the candidate responded to it in a thoughtful manner?		
	Has the candidate answered the question?		
Comment:			
Coherence	Has the candidate made convincing arguments?		
	Has the candidate linked ideas?		
	Does the essay have a sense of unity?		
Comment:			
Language	Is the essay written in an appropriate register?		
	Are ideas expressed in a clear way?		
	Is the writing fluent?		
Comment:			
Mechanics	Is the use of language accurate?		
	Are all words spelled correctly?		
	Does the punctuation help the reader?		
Comment:			

William Wordsworth

1770–1850

Biography

Early life

William Wordsworth was born into a prosperous family in Cumberland, in the northwest of England, in 1770. His father, John, was a solicitor and land agent for a wealthy landlord and industrialist, Sir John Lowther. His mother, Anne, came from a merchant background. Her family, the Cooksons, ran a successful textile business. William was the second of the five Wordsworth children born into a life of privilege and comfort. His father was a cultured man, who introduced his son to classic literature and encouraged him to learn passages from Shakespeare and Milton by heart.

Of his four siblings, William was closest to his only sister, Dorothy, who was born in 1771. According to his own account, William enjoyed great freedom as a child, roaming the countryside near his home and swimming in the rivers. William was the wild one of the family. He was prone to temper tantrums and was considered a difficult child by his relatives. His mother, a gentle and soft-hearted person, worried about her moody, sensitive son. She sent him to stay with her parents for long periods, hoping that their influence might quieten him.

In 1778, when William was eight, his mother died of pneumonia. She was thirty years of age. Because their father was often away on business, care of the children fell to the Cookson grandparents. The family found William rebellious and defiant, and there were constant clashes between them. Dorothy was sent away to be reared by other relatives and she and William did not see each other for a further nine years. William and his three brothers were sent to a grammar school in Hawkshead in the Lake District, where they boarded with an elderly couple, the Tysons. Mrs Tyson was a kind-hearted woman in her sixties and became a second mother to the children. She afforded them more freedom than might have been expected and allowed William to be fully himself. The nine years he spent with her were among the happiest in his life, and he drew upon these years in the best of his poetry, most notably in *The Prelude*.

Wordsworth's father died in 1783. On paper, he was a wealthy man. In reality, he was owed thousands of pounds by his employer, Sir James Lowther. Lowther refused to settle his debts, so the family was forced to bring him to court and the case dragged on for years.

In 1787, at the age of seventeen, Wordsworth went to study at Cambridge University. His education was funded by his family on his mother's side. The family made sure he understood they were doing him a great favour in paying for him to go to university. They expected him to work hard and to excel. He did neither. After three years, he graduated with a pass BA. He was not happy in Cambridge and looked back on his time there with a mixture of anger and disillusionment. The system was corrupt, and the privileged undergraduates treated the ordinary people of the town with contempt. Many of the lecturers were Anglican clergyman and Wordsworth was disgusted by their behaviour. After Cambridge, Wordsworth knew that he didn't want to be a cleric or a lawyer but had no idea what he did want to do.

Wordsworth had spent the summer of 1789 close to Dorothy and their mutual friend Mary Hutchinson. In 1790 he spent his last summer before graduating on a walking tour of France and Switzerland with his friend Robert Jones. They spent three months on their tour, living on practically nothing, with all their belongings tied up in handkerchiefs, walking twenty miles a day. In many villages in France, the young Englishmen joined in the celebrations to mark the French Revolution, which had begun in 1789. To Wordsworth, it seemed that the 'whole nation was made with joy'. He was excited by the revolution, which engaged his mind and his energies. His family had first-hand experience of the power, corruption and influence of the aristocracy.

Pantisocracy

When Wordsworth met Coleridge and his friend Robert Southey in Bristol in 1795, the two were planning to set up an agricultural commune of twelve young men and twelve young women on the banks of the Susquehanna River on the east coast of America. In their new society, everyone would be equal. All children would be educated together and individuals could hold their own religious and political views. They calculated that each person would need £125 in order to get a boat, sail the Atlantic and start their new life together, free from the corruption and injustice they saw in England. They discussed the plan for two years but the idea was dropped after a cooling off in the relationship between Coleridge and Southey.

Later life and career

After his graduation in 1791 Wordsworth returned to France, ostensibly to learn French but drawn by the revolution, the ideal of equality and the hope of freedom and reform. In Orléans, he took French lessons from a young woman named Annette Vallon. Soon they were lovers and she became pregnant. Shortly before the birth of their child, Wordsworth left for England, promising to return with money for their upkeep. However, it was ten years before he saw Annette again. Their daughter, Caroline, was born in December 1792, and Wordsworth's name was entered on her birth certificate. From letters, it seems that Wordsworth was sincere in his intention to marry Vallon, but then war broke out between England and France and it was not possible for him to go back to Orléans. Wordsworth informed his family and friends about the affair, but the general public knew nothing of it and the story only emerged in the 1920s. Wordsworth's sympathy for the French Revolution waned in the face of mass executions and the Reign of Terror, and due to the war between France and England.

Wordsworth was troubled by guilt, emotional conflicts and intellectual doubts. The three people who helped him recover his balance all recognised his genius and championed him. The first was Raisley Calvert, a school friend who offered to share his income so that his friend could dedicate his life to poetry. Calvert died in 1795 and left Wordsworth a legacy of £900. The second was his spirited and intelligent sister, Dorothy. Although a talented writer herself, she devoted most of her energies to supporting her brother in his writing, and acted for many years as his unpaid secretary and first reader. His regard for her is revealed in both 'Tintern Abbey' and 'To My Sister'. The third was the writer Samuel Taylor Coleridge, whom he met in 1795. Coleridge became his champion, his best friend and his literary collaborator.

Hillwalking

Wordsworth and Coleridge shared a love of walking. Wordsworth often walked twenty miles a day. Coleridge suffered a good deal of ill-health in his life and became addicted to painkilling medication. When his health was good, he did some spectacular hiking and climbing in the Lake District. In 1802 he made the first known ascent of Scafell Peak, writing a poem and a letter on the summit and then rushing wildly and recklessly down again. He was probably the first outsider to climb the mountains of the Lake District for the sheer pleasure of doing so.

With the bequest from Calvert, Wordsworth and Dorothy moved to Dorset, and then to nearby Somerset, where Coleridge was living. The two men sparked off each other and it was a time of great creativity for both. Coleridge was a decisive and perceptive critic and was knowledgeable about philosophy and Greek and Roman mythology.

In Dorset, Wordsworth, Dorothy and Coleridge lived a communal life. Coleridge stayed with his friends for weeks at a time and accompanied them on walking tours, leaving his wife and young child behind. Writing to Mary Hutchinson, Dorothy described

Coleridge as 'a wonderful man' whose 'conversation teems with soul, mind and spirit'. For Coleridge, Wordsworth was a genius and 'a very great man'.

The years 1797 and 1798 were ones of inspired creativity for both Wordsworth and Coleridge, and marked the beginning of a ten-year period during which Wordsworth produced the poetry upon which his fame rests. They jointly published *Lyrical Ballads* in 1798. This was one of the most influential books of poetry in the history of English literature. It is fair to describe the volume as heralding the emergence of modern poetry, with its emphasis on the self as the central subject.

When the book appeared, the friends were in Germany. Both Dorothy and William found Germany dull, unbearably cold and cheerless. Wordsworth wrote about the Lake District and his childhood. He began work on what became *The Prelude* and wrote three of his Lucy poems. Wordsworth determined that he would move back to the Lake District. In 1799 Wordsworth and Dorothy moved to Dove Cottage in Grasmere, the first of the four houses they were to inhabit in the Lake District. Eight happy and productive years followed. *Poems in Two Volumes* was published in 1806; the thirteen-book version of *The Prelude* was finished. Although still in his thirties, Wordsworth had written his best work. He had also married Mary Hutchinson and they had three children between 1803 and 1806. Dorothy continued to live with the couple.

In 1813 the family moved to Rydal Mount, an imposing stately house, and Wordsworth lived there until his death in 1850. By and large, Wordsworth lived a happy life there surrounded by those who loved him: Dorothy, Mary, his sister-in-law Sara and his daughter Dora. However, there were personal losses. He fell out with Coleridge in 1810; his son Thomas and his daughter Catherine died in 1812 and their deaths affected the family for many years; he was also deeply affected by the death of Dora in 1847. Coleridge died in 1834 and Annette Vallon in 1841. Dorothy lived until 1855, but for the last twenty years of her life she was incapacitated by mental illness.

> **Falling out with Coleridge**
>
> Coleridge was living with the Wordsworths but his addiction to opium was affecting his conduct and his physical health. A mutual friend, Basil Montagu, offered Coleridge a room in his house in London, with the hope that his doctor might help Coleridge recover. Wordsworth confided to Montagu that Coleridge had become a drunken nuisance. When Coleridge discovered that Wordsworth had spoken dismissively of him he was deeply hurt. After fifteen years of friendship he felt he deserved better. The two men met in London in 1812 and went for a long walk together. Afterwards Coleridge wrote, 'A reconciliation has taken place – but the feeling can never return.'

It is ironic that honours were heaped upon Wordsworth in the second half of his career, given that the poetry he wrote after 1808 lacked the spark of genius and originality that marked his earlier work. He was industrious and hard-working but the poetry was dull and uninspiring. From the 1820s until his death Wordsworth became something of an institution. Visitors flocked to meet the 'Sage of Rydal'. (So many came that the family began to charge for tea.) The visitors were often rewarded with long, sermon-like speeches explaining his poems or giving his increasingly conservative and moralistic views on the world. The young radical poet had become a spokesman for the establishment. In 1843 he was appointed Poet Laureate. He died, aged eighty, at home.

Wordsworth lived a long life. He was dignified in the face of disappointment and the loss of his poetic vision. He supported a large family and was never entirely free of financial worries. For all his acclaim, he did not own any of the houses where he lived during his lifetime.

Social and Cultural Context

Wordsworth lived through a time of extraordinary change. There was the French Revolution and the Industrial Revolution, and the social revolution brought about by both. Wordsworth himself was an intriguing **mix of the revolutionary and the conservative**.

Political reform

In 1793, after his return from France, Wordsworth, like other young radicals, was filled with revolutionary zeal. His friend Robert Southey described the sense of possibility in the air: 'Old things seemed passing away and nothing was dreamt of it but the regeneration of the human race.' There was talk of the abolition of the monarchy; the reform of the church; the repeal of oppressive laws; and an end to the power of the aristocracy. Wordsworth was in favour of **political reform and the abolition of social injustice**. He was also a very **moral** person and believed in **social order and personal honour**. For this reason, the Reign of Terror that followed the French Revolution, and the murderous excesses of mob rule, alarmed and disappointed him. His feelings were further compromised by the outbreak of war between England and France, which continued from 1793 until 1815. Like many middle-class intellectuals, Wordsworth's patriotism was stirred by the threat of a French invasion. Wordsworth was never a systematic thinker and his **political beliefs were formed by feelings and instinct as much as through reason**.

Social reform

While Wordsworth's poetry celebrated individual characters, his praise for ordinary people was linked to their life in the countryside. He was **horrified by life in the new industrial cities** and wrote of 'pestilential masses of ignorant population'. As a young man, he had resented the aristocratic James Lowther, the Earl of Lonsdale, his father's employer, who had refused to settle his debts to the Wordsworth family after the death of their father. However, when the new earl settled the debt in 1802, Wordsworth saw him as an example of enlightened social responsibility. Wordsworth recognised how the Industrial Revolution affected home life; he saw the abuse of young women and children in the new factories; he witnessed the flight from the land as people flocked to the towns. He was also aware of the activities of political agitators and the rise of religious sects. Wordsworth wanted better education and better living standards for the working classes, but he believed these **reforms should come about under the leadership of the old order**, under the guidance of decent men such as the Earl of Lonsdale. For Wordsworth, the landowning gentry had a stake in the country in a way that the new rich, the manufacturers, had not. Through his friendship with members of the aristocracy he received a government-appointed position and, towards the end of his life, became the Poet Laureate.

Catholic Emancipation

The Daniel O'Connell-led movement in the 1820s called for the removal of laws that discriminated against Catholics. A Catholic, for example, could not take his seat in the House of Commons without denouncing his Catholic beliefs. The younger Wordsworth, filled with ideas of freedom and justice, would probably have supported Catholic Emancipation, but the older Wordsworth opposed it. He did not believe that an Irish Catholic could be loyal to a Protestant monarchy. For him, the granting of emancipation would lead to social division and threaten the stability of English society. Some of the arguments for and against Catholic Emancipation are reminiscent of those made today on the control of immigration into Europe.

Themes

Wordsworth's themes are **his own consciousness** and the **relationship between imagination, moral development and nature**.

For Wordsworth, the natural goodness of humanity was reflected in the ordinary people he met in the Lake District. Wordsworth believed that a close relationship with nature nurtured this natural goodness and helped the individual to grow as a moral human being. This theme dominates *The Prelude*. Contact with nature also stimulates the imagination. Wordsworth's poetic inspiration came from primary experiences stored in the memory and transformed by the imagination. **A successful poem recreates, rather than simply recalls, experience**, as in 'Composed upon Westminster Bridge' or 'Tintern Abbey'. For Wordsworth, encounters with the beauties of nature were spiritual experiences, evidence of a divine presence greater than the individual.

Wordsworth wanted his poetry to reflect the way that people think, feel and speak. For him, poetry had to be renewed and move beyond what he called the 'gaudiness and inane phraseology' of the poetry of his day. For him, the **simple speech of ordinary people living close to nature**, the people he met during his youth in the Lake District, was attuned to 'the essential passions of the heart', passions that were stirred by beautiful scenery. Poetic language was more than a matter of style. 'To My Sister', 'She Dwelt among the Untrodden Ways', 'A Slumber did my Spirit Seal' and 'The Solitary Reaper' are written in the simple language of the heart. On the other hand, it is often pointed out that in such poems as 'Tintern Abbey', Wordsworth employs a more learned diction and a more complex syntax (word order) than one is likely to find in the language of everyday life.

Taken as a whole, Wordsworth's poetry is a remarkable record of his developing self-consciousness and its intimate relationship with the natural world and his own spirituality. **His single great subject is his own spiritual, emotional and intellectual history.** The landscape of his mind is continually reflected, as it is so memorably in 'Tintern Abbey', in the beauty of the natural world. His understanding of the relationship between the inner self and external nature, and of the close bonds between human beings and the natural world, makes him appear a thoroughly modern poet.

Critical reception

Wordsworth's first published works appeared in 1793. There were two reviews, both extremely negative. *Poems in Two Volumes* also met with savage reviews. One influential reviewer dismissed the work as childish, tedious, silly, disgusting and absurd.

Many of his readers **disliked the conversational tone and the subject matter** of his poetry. They believed that his poems lacked the dignity, pomp and artificiality that they associated with poetry. For them, good poetry contained classical allusions and elevated subject matter. Wordsworth wrote about mad and deranged individuals and uneducated people. Moreover, his poetry celebrated the life of the senses and the life of the emotions, which went against the eighteenth-century view that poetry should be informed by reason. For many of his educated readers, Wordsworth's poetry did not meet the standards of the time.

To his credit, Wordsworth put on a brave face, telling friends that both critics and the reading public would have to be educated to appreciate his poetry. And he was right. As Thomas de Quincey put it, 'Up to 1820 the name of Wordsworth was trampled underfoot; from 1820 to 1830 it was militant; from 1830 to 1835 it has been triumphant.'

Timeline

1770	Born in Cumberland in the Lake District
1776–7	Attends Penrith primary school (along with Mary Hutchinson)
1778	Mother dies, aged thirty
1779	Attends Hawkshead School, boarding with the Tysons until 1787
1783	Father dies, aged forty-two
1787	Begins undistinguished academic career at St John's College, Cambridge
1791	Graduates from Cambridge; in France, falls in love with Annette Vallon
1792	Leaves France; Annette Vallon gives birth to their daughter, Caroline
1795	Receives £900 legacy from a school friend; meets Coleridge and Southey
1798	Publishes *Lyrical Ballads* in collaboration with Coleridge; visits Germany; begins work on *The Prelude*, his great autobiographical poem
1799	Settles with Dorothy at Dove Cottage, Grasmere in the Lake District
1802	Visits France and meets Annette Vallon and Caroline; marries Mary Hutchinson
1803	Birth of first son, John; enlists in Volunteers amid fears of a French invasion
1804	Birth of daughter, Dora
1805	Death of his brother John; *The Prelude* expands to thirteen books
1806	Birth of second son, Thomas; *Poems in Two Volumes* published
1808	Moves to Allan Bank in Grasmere; Coleridge comes to visit and stays for two years; birth of daughter, Catherine
1810	Birth of third son, William; falls out with Coleridge; *Guide to the Lakes* published
1812	Partial reconciliation with Coleridge; deaths of Catherine and Thomas
1813	Appointed Stamp Distributor for Westmoreland; settles at Rydal Mount, Grasmere
1819	Meets Annette Vallon and Caroline in Paris
1822	Publishes *A Description of the Scenery of the Lakes*
1831	Last meeting with Coleridge (who dies in 1834)
1835	Dorothy's mind fails
1839	Receives honorary doctorate from Oxford
1841	Death of Annette Vallon
1847	Death of his daughter, Dora, aged forty-two
1843	Appointed Poet Laureate, a token of his acceptance by the establishment
1849	Six-volume *Poetical Works* published
1850	Dies; posthumous publication of *The Prelude*

To My Sister

Before you read

Sunshine: Have a class discussion on the way in which a sunny day spent outdoors affects different people. Having shared your views, read the poem.

It is the first mild day of March:
Each minute sweeter than before,
The redbreast sings from the tall larch
That stands beside our door.

There is a blessing in the air,   5
Which seems a sense of joy to yield
To the bare trees, and mountains bare,
And grass in the green field.

My sister! ('tis a wish of mine)
Now that our morning meal is done,   10
Make haste, your morning task resign;
Come forth and feel the sun.

Edward will come with you; – and, pray,
Put on with speed your woodland dress;
And bring no book: for this one day   15
We'll give to idleness.

No joyless forms shall regulate
Our living calendar:
We from today, my Friend, will date
The opening of the year.   20

Love, now a universal birth,
From heart to heart is stealing,
From earth to man, from man to earth:
– It is the hour of feeling.

One moment now may give us more   25
Than years of toiling reason:
Our minds shall drink at every pore
The spirit of the season.

Some silent laws our hearts will make,
Which they shall long obey: 30
We for the year to come may take
Our temper from to-day.

And from the blessed power that rolls
About, below, above,
We'll frame the measure of our souls: 35
They shall be tuned to love.

Then come, my Sister! Come, I pray,
With speed put on your woodland dress;
And bring no book: for this one day
We'll give to idleness.   40

Glossary

3	*larch*: tree with needle-shaped leaves
6	*yield*: surrender to (the enjoyment of nature)
13	*Edward*: the boy-messenger who carried the poem to Wordsworth's sister, Dorothy. He was really Basil Montagu, the son of Wordsworth's widowed friend. Wordsworth and Dorothy were paid to look after him when they lived in Dorset and Somerset. Wordsworth wrote the poem a little distance from the house and asked Basil to bring it to Dorothy
26	*toiling reason*: studying; thinking long and hard
32	*temper*: mood or humour; in musical terms, tuning
35	*frame the measure*: perhaps, direct the music or melody

Political spies

When they moved to Alfoxden House, the locals were suspicious of them. The couple said they were brother and sister. They said the child they had was the son of a widowed friend. They had no visible means of supporting themselves. They were seen walking the countryside at all hours of the day and night. They had many visitors coming and going. The locals decided they were French spies and reported them to the authorities. A government agent was sent to keep an eye on them.

Guidelines

First published in *Lyrical Ballads*, this poem takes the form of a verse-letter addressed by Wordsworth to his only sister, Dorothy. It was written in 1798 when William and Dorothy lived in Alfoxden House in a picturesque part of the Somerset countryside. In many ways, it is a simple poem. On a bright spring morning, Wordsworth invites his sister to take the day off and enjoy the spring sunshine. The poem also expresses Wordsworth's belief in the power of nature to nurture the heart and open the soul to love.

Commentary

Stanzas 1–4

The first two stanzas describe the weather, 'the first mild day of March' and the sense of 'blessing' that is 'in the air'. In stanzas 3 and 4 the poet encourages his sister to leave her household tasks and come outdoors to enjoy the good weather, to 'feel the sun'. He tells her to dress for the outdoors, and to bring no book, proposing that they give the day over 'to idleness'.

Stanzas 5–6

Stanzas 5 and 6 strike out in a new direction. The poet declares that this day will mark the opening of the year and their lives will not be ruled by 'joyless forms'. Instead they will organise their days according to their own feelings. Traditionally spring is associated with the birth of the year. Here, Wordsworth associates it with the birth of a universal love, a love that passes between nature and humanity. On a beautiful day Wordsworth feels a spirit of love moving through nature.

Stanzas 7–9

Wordsworth seeks to sketch the benefits that will come from surrendering to this beautiful spring day. He distinguishes between the rewards that come from the work of the intellect ('toiling reason') and the greater rewards that come from being in nature. For him, spending the day immersed in nature, in beautiful weather, will help the heart make its own 'silent laws' of love and affection. The mood ('temper') of the year ahead will be fixed by this day. They will set the music of their souls to the powerful rhythms of nature, and their souls, like musical instruments, 'shall be tuned to love'.

> **William and Dorothy**
>
> Dorothy was devoted to her brother. When William later married their mutual friend, Mary Hutchinson, Dorothy was too upset to attend the ceremony. On the night before the wedding, Dorothy wore the wedding ring. When William called to collect it in the morning, he replaced it on Dorothy's finger and blessed her before leaving for the church. Dorothy lived with William and Mary for the rest of her life.

Stanza 10

In the final stanza, Wordsworth once again addresses his sister and urges her to leave what she is doing and to devote 'this one day' 'to idleness'.

Themes and imagery

This poem expresses Wordsworth's **delight in nature** and his belief that a close relationship with nature nurtures natural goodness in the soul. To enjoy a beautiful day, immersed in nature, is to open the heart to love. The mind, the heart and the soul will all be refreshed by the love that is shared between humans and the planet. This theme is explored in greater detail in 'Tintern Abbey'.

'To My Sister' is one of a number of poems in which Wordsworth suggests that the experience of being in **nature nurtures the individual in mind, body and soul**, more than a lifetime of study. He touches on the idea that the instinctual life, the life of feelings, is superior to the life of the intellect. For Wordsworth, nature is the book that deserves reading.

Here, as in many of his poems, Wordsworth takes a **benevolent view of the influence of nature** in all its aspects on human beings. Nature is 'the blessed power that rolls / About, below, above' (lines 33–34). The love and benevolence experienced by people who put themselves into harmony with nature is not a process working in only one direction. **Love is a universal force** moving gently and silently from one person to another, but also moving 'From earth to man, from man to earth' (line 23).

Wordsworth is not advocating that he and his sister live a life of idleness. His proposal is that they spend 'this one day' (lines 15, 39) in 'idleness' (lines 16, 40), convinced of the nurturing and restorative effect that the day will provide. Even on this day of idleness, Wordsworth is composing poetry!

Form and language

The poem is written in ten four-line stanzas, with a rhyme scheme of *abab*. The final stanza repeats much of stanza 4 and emphasises the central idea of the poem. **The language is clear** and simple, with a **conversational** air, and **the tone is joyful** and encouraging. Overall, the poem feels fresh and real. The opening stanzas use **simple images** to evoke the spring day. Wordsworth describes what he hears – 'The redbreast sings' (line 3), how the air feels – 'the first mild day' (line 1), and what he sees – 'grass in the green field' (line 8). Even when the poem deals with big ideas, the language remains clear and simple and words like 'feeling' (line 24), 'spirit' (line 28), 'hearts' (line 29) and 'souls' (line 35) carry the meaning.

Questions

1	What does this poem tell us about the relationship between the poet and his sister?
2	Does the speaker make a good case for giving the day over to idleness?
3	What value does the poet attach to idleness in this context? What benefits does he think will come from a day spent outdoors in nature?
4	In stanza 5 the speaker thinks it a good idea to date 'the opening of the year' to this mild March day. Mention some details in the poem that inspire this idea.
5	What, do you think, does the poet mean by 'toiling reason' in stanza 7?
6	Stanza 8 refers to 'Some silent laws' that the hearts of brother and sister will make and obey. What kind of laws might these be?
7	What is 'the blessed power' mentioned in stanza 9?
8	Select six words that you think capture the mood and tone of the poem. Explain your choices.
9	Which of these statements is closest to your understanding of the poem? ■ The poem is about enjoying good weather when it comes. ■ The poem is about the goodness of nature. ■ The poem is about achieving a balance between work and leisure. ■ The poem is about the close relationship between humans and nature. ■ The poem is about the importance of nurturing our souls through the senses. Explain your choice, considering each statement in your answer.
10	What idea of love is conveyed in the poem?
11	The poem reads like a New Year's resolution. How does the poet look forward to the year ahead?
12	Imagine you are Dorothy. Write a reply to the invitation offered in the poem. OR
13	Write a note to a friend inviting him or her to leave their study and spend a day enjoying the good weather. Your note should outline the benefits you think will come from the day.

Before you read

This poem is a lament for a young woman. Jot down the elements you expect to find in such a poem. When you have read the poem, consider whether your expectations have been fulfilled.

She Dwelt among the Untrodden Ways

She dwelt among the untrodden ways
Beside the springs of Dove,
A Maid whom there were none to praise,
And very few to love.

A violet by a mossy stone   5
Half-hidden from the eye!
Fair as a star, when only one
Is shining in the sky.

She lived unknown, and few could know
When Lucy ceased to be;   10
But she is in her grave, and, oh,
The difference to me!

Glossary

1	*dwelt*: lived
1	*untrodden ways*: little-used or unused roads or paths
2	*springs*: places where a river rises or emerges from the ground
2	*Dove*: three English rivers bear this name although Wordsworth may simply have wanted to associate Lucy with peace, gentleness and purity
3	*Maid*: young unmarried girl or woman

Guidelines

This poem and 'A Slumber did my Spirit Seal' are part of a group of five, traditionally referred to as the 'Lucy poems'. Whether 'Lucy' was a real woman or an invention of the poet's imagination is uncertain. Some critics suggest that 'Lucy' represents a woman whom Wordsworth loved in his youth and who died young. Margaret Hutchinson, younger sister of Mary, the woman Wordsworth married, is often mentioned. Margaret died aged twenty-four. In some of his poems Wordsworth associates the name 'Lucy' with his sister, Dorothy. Coleridge, who believed that Lucy was Dorothy, offered an explanation as to why Wordsworth would represent Lucy as having died: 'Most probably,' Coleridge wrote to a friend, 'in some gloomier moment he had fancied the moment when his sister might die.' Some critics suggest that Lucy represents the poet's inspiration, or Muse, and is an ideal rather than a real woman.

The Lucy poems were written in the German town of Goslar, where Wordsworth and Dorothy spent a miserable few months in the winter of 1798/99. The town was dull and cheerless and the weather was unbearably cold. They could afford only the cheapest lodgings where the food was poor and the hospitality poorer. The severe weather prevented them exploring the countryside. In their cramped lodgings Wordsworth wrote about his childhood memories, as well as completing the Lucy poems. It may well be that the sombre mood of this poem, and of 'A Slumber did my Spirit Seal', is related to the unhappy, confining experience of winter, with its suggestions of the grave and of a kind of living death.

The poem is written in the voice of Lucy's lover. Lucy is presented as a young and beautiful woman who lived her life close to nature and hidden from the world. Her life and her death went almost unnoticed, except for the narrator, who records his distress.

Commentary

Stanza 1

The first stanza provides information about an unnamed 'Maid'. The statements are vague and suggestive rather than clear and precise. The stanza suggests that she lived a hidden life in a remote, rural place, beside fresh springs named 'Dove'. There is a riddling quality to the statements. The past tense suggests that she is dead.

Stanza 2

The second stanza uses two metaphors to describe the 'Maid'. Both are conventional images of beauty, if somewhat paradoxical. The violet represents a delicate, fragile beauty, hidden from view. The single star represents a kind of luminous beauty, like the evening star, visible but unattainable.

Stanza 3

The third stanza contains the most direct statements. In her life, the 'Maid', now named as 'Lucy', was hardly known and her death was known only to a few. Now she is in her grave and, the speaker says, while her death may not have affected many people, it has made a great difference to him.

Themes and imagery

Love, loss and grief are the themes of the poem. Like many of the poems in *Lyrical Ballads*, 'She Dwelt among the Untrodden Ways' is **about an ordinary person**. Lucy is somebody who lived a life hidden from the world, and who possessed great beauty. She is a solitary figure, like the girl portrayed in 'The Solitary Reaper' (see page 401). Her death may not have registered with the world at large but, for the speaker, it made a great difference. The exclamation 'oh' (line 11) hints at the psychological and emotional effect upon the speaker but, as with the rest of the poem, the meaning is implied rather than stated clearly. By the end of the poem, we have no real understanding of the relationship between the speaker and Lucy.

The poem is most direct in stating that Lucy 'is in her grave' (line 11). Lucy's beauty and innocence, her closeness to nature, did not protect her from death. The **bleak, simple ending** of the poem, 'But she is in her grave, and, oh, / The difference to me!', emphasises the **finality of death**. There is no suggestion that, in death, Lucy has been united with nature or with God. It is the blunt fact of death, at the end of the poem, that creates the **elegiac mood**.

Some critics suggest that the poem ends before it begins and that Lucy is dead before we have a chance to hear her speak. For them, Lucy exists merely as an idea of a certain kind of innocent, female beauty rather than as a real woman. Within the poem, Lucy is presented as leading an isolated life, hidden from the view of the human world, and surrounded by nature. We know of her only through the narrator. And we view her from a distance. Like the single star 'shining in the sky' in stanza 2, **Lucy seems distant and unreal**. And it is this distance that causes some readers to feel an emotional detachment in reading the poem. The fact that the narrator emphasises his loss rather than Lucy's death may suggest that, for him, the significance of her life and death is dependent upon his perception of her. Is it a suggestion that without him (the man) Lucy (the girl) is nothing?

Form and language

Shortly before he composed this poem, Wordsworth got a copy of a collection of traditional British folk ballads. His poem follows the rhythm and rhyme scheme of a **folk ballad**. The stanzas rhyme *abab*, with lines 1 and 3 having four beats and lines 2 and 4 having three. As in a ballad, the story of Lucy is told with **great economy**, in the simplest of language, in the voice of her grieving lover. The first stanza tells us where she lived; the second describes her beauty; the third her death. The poem is a lament as it articulates sorrow at someone's death. The **tone and mood is one of loss**, expressed in a quiet undramatic way. The riddling quality of some of the phrases – 'none to praise' (line 3), 'few to love' (line 4), the springs named 'Dove' (line 2), and the use of archaic words such as 'Maid' (line 3) and 'dwelt' (line 1) give a **fairy-tale quality** to the poem.

SNAPSHOT

- Simple poem on the surface; a lament
- Deals with the life, beauty and death of Lucy
- Death presented as final
- Mysterious elements in the poem
- Simple language
- Conventional images
- Ballad style
- Tone is quiet and undramatic
- Emotional distance
- As much about the speaker's feelings as Lucy's death

Exam-Style Questions

Understanding the poem

1	Based on the opening two lines, describe where Lucy lived.
2	What kind of environment is suggested by the phrases 'none to praise' and 'few to love' in the first stanza?
3	Which of the following words best conveys the mood of the opening stanza: loving, bleak, celebratory, sorrowful? Explain your choice.
4	Do you think the flower and star imagery of stanza 2 work? Give reasons for your answer.
5	The speaker uses the phrase 'ceased to be' (line 10) to describe Lucy's death, rather than 'died'. What is the effect of this phrase?
6	The final word of the poem is 'me'. Is this significant?

Thinking about the poem

1	Comment on the language of the poem. In what ways does it suit the theme?
2	What do you learn about the relationship between the speaker and Lucy from the poem?
3	'The poem is less concerned with the death of Lucy than with the effect upon the speaker.' Discuss.
4	'The problem for the reader is that Lucy does not exist as a real human being in the poem. She is a vague presence, bloodless, sexless and voiceless.' Discuss.
5	Which of the following statements is closest to your understanding of the poem? ■ The poem is haunting and mysterious. ■ The poem expresses genuine love and sorrow. ■ The poem is vague and unengaging. Explain your choice.

Imagining

1	Imagine that you are the speaker of the poem. Write a letter to a friend in which you relate the death of Lucy and explain the impact it had on you. Your letter should demonstrate your knowledge of the poem.
2	Imagine you are living in Lucy's neighbourhood. Write your impressions of her and her way of living.

Before you read

With a partner, discuss what you believe to be the deepest human fears. Can sleep protect us from these fears? Share your ideas with the rest of the class.

A Slumber did my Spirit Seal

A slumber did my spirit seal;
I had no human fears:
She seemed a thing that could not feel
The touch of earthly years.

No motion has she now, no force;   5
She neither hears nor sees;
Rolled round in earth's diurnal course,
With rocks, and stones, and trees.

Glossary

1	*slumber*: light sleep
1	*seal*: protect
5	*motion ... force*: terms used in physics
7	*diurnal*: daily

Playing dead

In her journal entry for 29 April 1802, Dorothy wrote: 'William lay, and I lay in the trench under the fence—he with his eyes shut and listening to the waterfalls and the Birds ... William heard me breathing and rustling now and then but we both lay still, and unseen by one another—he thought that it would be as sweet thus to lie so in the grave, to hear the peaceful sounds of the earth and to know that one's dear friends were near.'

Guidelines

'A Slumber did my Spirit Seal' is the only one of the Lucy poems (see the Guidelines on 'She Dwelt among the Untrodden Ways') in which the female subject is not named. The poem explores death and has a sombre, depressing mood that may reflect Wordsworth's unhappiness during his time in Germany, when he wrote it. It presents a more ambiguous attitude to nature than is usual in Wordsworth's poetry.

Commentary

The poem is based on the contrast between the first stanza, with its seeming assurance that the female subject will never die, and the second, which records the cold reality of her death.

Stanza 1

The poem opens with a statement in the past tense. The speaker tells us that a light sleep ('slumber') protected his spirit; while asleep he had no 'human fears'. In this dream-like state, 'She', the unnamed subject of the poem, 'seemed' to exist outside of time ('earthly years') and the effects ('touch') of time and ageing. This stanza raises as many questions as it answers. What human fears does the speaker have in mind? What kind of 'thing' does not feel the 'touch of earthly years'? Beneath the soothing sounds of the stanza, there is an underlying unease.

Stanza 2

The second stanza is written in the present tense. A series of negative statements in the first two lines describe the present state of being (or not-being) of the woman. She has 'No motion', 'no force', and she is unable to hear or see. The phrasing implies a ceasing of the abilities and attributes that 'She' once possessed. The final lines suggest that 'She', unable to act herself, is acted upon. She is 'Rolled round' with 'rocks, and stones, and trees', as the Earth turns on its axis. Unlike the ending of 'She Dwelt among the Untrodden Ways', there is no indication of the speaker's emotional response to the fact that the woman is dead.

Themes and imagery

The poem is **a lyric meditation on the cycle of life and the nature of death**. It is **dark in tone and mood**. Having read the poem we understand that the 'human fears' of line 2 are the **fears relating to the death and loss of a loved one**. In sleep, the speaker loses these fears. His beloved is not subject to the ravages of time and its processes. However, in imagining his beloved beyond time, she loses those qualities that make her human – she becomes a 'thing' (line 3). The word might connote a horror movie, describing a human being who escapes death but is transformed into something monstrous and horrifying, something deathless, in the process.

In the second stanza the speaker confronts his deepest human fear. Awakened from his slumber, he describes what has become of his beloved in death. She has not ceased to be. However, she has lost all agency, 'No motion has she now, no force' (line 5), and all human perception, 'She neither hears nor sees' (line 6). While she cannot act, she is, nonetheless, acted upon, 'Rolled round' (line 7). The phrase conveys the nothingness of the individual in death, in the face of the power of nature, in the face of being itself. The use of the scientific 'diurnal' (line 7) suggests the loss of personal feeling. The existence that survives death is impersonal, an impression emphasised by the geological terms 'rocks' and 'stones' (line 8). The final noun 'trees' softens the effect. They at least are alive, albeit not human.

As described in the poem, death does not take the individual beyond nature but **nature subsumes the individual into a state of being that is impersonal**, and in which the individual loses agency, identity and human perception. It is not a heartening vision of life after death. In 'Tintern Abbey' (see page 417), Wordsworth finds a spiritual presence in nature, which is everywhere in the world, including the human mind. However, the nature that subsumes the female character of this poem is not Mother Nature, a nurturing and

creative presence. On the contrary, it is something impersonal, powerful and relentless. It is one thing to be sealed in restless slumber; it is another to be rolled continuously round 'With rocks, and stones, and trees' (line 8).

Form and language

The poem is distinguished by its **compactness**. In eight short lines, divided into two stanzas, each consisting of one sentence, Wordsworth creates a poem that brims with surprise, tension and energy. As in a ballad, the lines rhyme *abab*, with a four-beat line alternating with a three-beat one. **The tone manages to be both quiet and unsettling.** The alliteration and soft 's' sounds of the first stanza, along with the long vowel sounds, the stressed syllables and the full rhymes, create an atmosphere of hushed quiet, but the use of the adjective 'human' (line 2) and the noun 'thing' (line 3) create a **sense of unease**. A remarkable feature of the poem is the **concentration of complex meanings in simple words**. Take 'touch' (line 4), for example, which suggests all the effects of time and ageing upon the body. In the second stanza the speaker's beloved is dead and is therefore beyond all touch. The verbal phrase 'Rolled round' (line 7) conveys a loss of agency but also the movement of the Earth. The noun 'thing' (line 3) suggests something less than human.

Ambiguities

The interpretation offered here reads the 'She' of line 3 as referring to a woman, probably the 'Lucy' of other poems. However, 'She' could refer back to 'my spirit' in line 1. In this case, the 'She' of the first stanza may not be the same as the 'She' of the second. Of course, the poet may intend 'She' to refer to both his mind and the woman.

Questions

1	What state of mind is described in the first two lines of the poem?
2	Who or what does the narrator describe in lines 3–4 of the poem?
3	What are the common 'human fears' (line 2) in relation to the processes of time?
4	What kind of existence does the speaker imagine after death, as described in stanza 2?
5	Is the poem optimistic or pessimistic in its view of life after death? Explain your answer.
6	Which of the following words best describes the mood in the poem: despairing, unsentimental, reflective, anguished, philosophical? Explain your choices.
7	What, in your view, is the most interesting use of language in the poem?
8	In your view, what does nature mean to the speaker of this poem?
9	Describe a feeling or an emotion you felt in response to this poem.
10	Write a response to this poem, beginning with one of the following phrases: ■ I find the ideas in the poem original and thought-provoking … ■ I find the ideas in the poem challenging and unusual …
11	Imagine you are Wordsworth. Write a letter to Dorothy in which you describe a dream that inspired this poem and the thoughts that followed it.
12	You have been asked to make a short YouTube video to accompany a reading of 'A Slumber did my Spirit Seal'. Describe the key images, text, colours, music, sound effects, etc. that you would use, and explain your choices.

Before you read

Working in pairs, describe a situation in which you encountered a beautiful scene, rural or urban, that made a deep impression on you. Was the experience a spiritual one? Revisit your discussion when you have read the poem.

Composed upon Westminster Bridge

September 3, 1802

Earth has not anything to show more fair:
Dull would he be of soul who could pass by
A sight so touching in its majesty:
This City now doth like a garment wear
The beauty of the morning; silent, bare.   5
Ships, towers, domes, theatres and temples lie
Open unto the fields, and to the sky;
All bright and glittering in the smokeless air.
Never did sun more beautifully steep
In his first splendour valley, rock or hill;   10
Ne'er saw I, never felt, a calm so deep!
The river glideth at his own sweet will
Dear God! The very houses seem asleep,
And all that mighty heart is lying still!

Glossary

5	*bare*: free of the usual smoke and smog in the air
7	*fields*: the southern side of the Thames was largely undeveloped in the early nineteenth century

Guidelines

Wordsworth and Dorothy crossed Westminster Bridge in the early morning of 31 July 1802 on their journey to France to meet his daughter, Caroline, for the first time and her mother, Annette Vallon. The meeting was intended to clear the way for Wordsworth's marriage to Mary Hutchinson. Dorothy made notes of their impressions of the city. Later Wordsworth wrote this poem in which the speaker expresses his response to the beauty of the scene before him.

Commentary

Lines 1–3

The poem begins with a forceful declaration: 'Earth has not anything to show more fair'. It is a dramatic opening, as if the speaker is moved to speech by the beauty of the scene before him and, in his surprise, makes the claim that the scene is so beautiful that nothing can compare with it. Lines 2–3 reinforce this claim by stating that anyone who would pass by such a majestic sight would be 'Dull … of soul'. But what is this incomparable scene?

Lines 4–8

To both the reader's and the speaker's surprise it is 'This City' (London) that is the object of his admiration and not a wild landscape. As the sun rises, the city has taken on the beauty of the morning, and wears it like a garment. The speaker then describes what he sees and the quality of the scene before him. His description lists 'bright and glittering' objects from the city's skyline and their relationship to the natural backdrop ('Open unto the fields, and to the sky') as well as the peace and quiet of the scene and 'the smokeless air'.

Lines 9–14

The speaker now reflects on what he is seeing and the way he is affected by it. He states forcefully that the rising sun has never made any natural landscape seem so splendid. He insists that he has never felt a calm so deep before a scene of beauty. He describes the river gliding gently at its own 'sweet will'. His emotions are touched by what seem to be sleeping houses, and the 'mighty heart' of the city 'lying still'.

Themes and imagery

The theme is **the beauty of the city in the early morning light and the power of this beauty to affect the human heart**. In the poem, the city is as beautiful as anything in nature. It is ironic that one of the most famous poems about London was written by a poet who disliked cities and sought out the beauty of the natural world. Wordsworth surprises himself. What encourages Wordsworth to see the beauty of the city and to reimagine it as a beautiful landscape is the **absence of pollution** and the **absence of human activity**. There are no workers

going to work, no children going to school. There are no stall-holders and vendors; no horses and carts moving goods; no ships loading and unloading. The city that Wordsworth celebrates is the city at a moment when it is most unlike itself.

Wordsworth makes a **subtle argument**. Nowhere does he say that the city itself is beautiful. What he states is that the city has taken on 'The beauty of the morning' (line 5) and wears it 'like a garment' (line 4). This covers what Wordsworth regarded as the usual ugliness of the city. The pleasure and delight that he takes in the scene, which moves him deeply, is related to this precise moment. It is not a beauty that is eternal or that will even survive much beyond the moment of its description.

The imagery in the poem emphasises **brightness, stillness and silence**. It is like **a painting of a city** rather than the city itself. It is this non-city that Wordsworth associates with the power and beauty of nature. The imagery relates the city to its opposite, a rural landscape. The city is bathed in golden light and it is silent. The shapes and forms of the city, 'Ships, towers, domes, theatres and temples' (line 6) are described in terms of the way they sit against the natural backdrop of fields and sky. The phrase 'lie / Open' (lines 6–7) suggests the ruins of an ancient city rather than a modern one, an impression deepened by the choice of buildings and architectural features: 'domes, theatres and temples' (line 6). When Wordsworth reaches for a comparison for the morning's beauty, he turns to 'valley, rock or hill' (line 10). When he speaks of his own deep calm, he immediately refers to how 'The river glideth at his own sweet will' (line 12).

The exclamation 'Dear God!' (line 13) marks the emotional climax of the poem. Wordsworth is moved by the houses that 'seem asleep' (line 13) and the 'mighty heart' of the great city 'lying still' (line 14) before him. By **personifying London**, by giving it a heart, Wordsworth can express his feelings of sympathetic connection to it. The humanised city evokes a tender response in the poet. However, as many critics have pointed out, a heart is still only when it has ceased to operate and when the body it supports has died. When the city comes back to life, it will no longer be the 'silent, bare' (line 5) city, 'All bright and glittering in the smokeless air' (line 8) that Wordsworth celebrates but the noisy, polluted city that will have lost its charm. The London described in the poem, the London of this particular moment, functions in the same way as other places of natural beauty that stimulate powerful feelings. London is beautiful and moves the poet deeply, but only in this **state of suspended animation**, imagined not merely asleep, but lying in heart-stilled death.

Form and language

The poem is written as a **dramatic monologue** in which a speaker records and shares his reaction to the beautiful scene before him. His reactions move from astonished delight to deep emotion. The poem is a **version of a Petrarchan sonnet**, divided into an octet (eight lines) and a sestet (six lines). The first eight lines rhyme *abbaabba*, while the final six lines rhyme *cdcdcd*. Wordsworth does not adhere strictly to the conventions of the sonnet, where eight lines of description are followed by six lines of reflective commentary. Here **description and commentary are mixed**. Nor does he divide his thought into neat units corresponding to the formal arrangement of the sonnet. The octet, the first eight lines, are divided into rhyming groups of four lines (quatrains). However, the thought is divided into three units of one line, two lines and five lines. For the reader, the effect is that of experiencing the speaker's reaction as he does himself.

Wordsworth creates anticipation and surprise in the reader by not revealing the subject of the poem, 'This City', until the fourth line. The opening line 'Earth has not anything to show more fair' is a bold declaration and the succession of stressed syllables gives it an emphatic air. The arrangement of the words (the syntax) makes the declaration sound formal and solemn, as if the speaker wants us to know that what he is claiming is true. The repetition of the word 'never' in lines 9 and 11 serves the same purpose of forcefully making the speaker's case. Alongside the **stately, formal language** of the poem, the **descriptive** passages capture the scene before him. The opening four words of line 4, for example, 'This City now doth … ' slow the rhythm of the poem. The stressed vowels, the 's' sounds and the soft endings of both 'now' and 'doth' reflect the hushed city. In contrast, line 8 is all noisy, joyful consonants, 'bright', 'glittering', 'smokeless', and reflects, in sound, the effects of the refracted light on the buildings and forms of the city, and the delight of the speaker in observing them.

The language is **overwhelmingly positive** and suggests a hymn of praise: bright, glittering, mighty, majesty, splendour, beautifully. Interestingly, the first word of this hymn to the city is 'Earth', and many of the nouns and adjectives suggest the countryside as much as the city: silent, bare, morning, fields, sky, air, sun, valley, rock, hill and river. This is **the city as countryside**.

Questions

1	What is the scene that so moves the speaker of the poem?
2	What claims does the speaker make in the first three lines of the poem? Do you think they are true?
3	Which of the senses are invoked in the description of the city in lines 4–8?
4	Comment on the phrase 'smokeless air' (line 8) and its importance in the poem.
5	What part does the sun play in making the scene beautiful?
6	In line 12 the speaker says, 'The river glideth at his own sweet will'. What is the importance of this detail?
7	What, according to the speaker, is the effect of the scene upon him?
8	In your view, what is the 'mighty heart' (line 14) of any great city? Do you think the speaker understands it in the same way?
9	Examine the poem and pick out the lines that describe the scene and those that comment on it and its effect upon the speaker. Where does the balance lie between description and comment?
10	At line 6 and line 10 the speaker uses lists to communicate his meaning. What do the lists suggest about his view of the city?
11	The poem is written in the present tense. Would it have the same impact if it were written in the past tense?
12	'The language and tone of the poem move between calm serenity and astonished delight.' Discuss.
13	The poem captures a moment in time, when the city is sleeping and all is still. Might the speaker enjoy his experience of London if it were later in the day, do you think? Explain your answer.
14	'This poem suggests that a great city can be as beautiful as any countryside.' Discuss this view of the poem.
15	By personifying the city, the speaker suggests his sympathetic feelings for it. Take a town or city that you know well. Describe it as a person, capturing what you feel are its most notable characteristics, and describe your relationship to it.

Before you read

Groupwork

Have a class discussion on the experience of walking by the sea and the thoughts that are prompted by the ever-present movement of the waves.

It is a beauteous evening, calm and free

It is a beauteous evening, calm and free,
The holy time is as quiet as a Nun
Breathless with adoration; the broad sun
Is sinking down in its tranquillity;
The gentleness of heaven broods o'er the Sea: 5
Listen! The mighty Being is awake,
And doth with his eternal motion make
A sound like thunder – everlastingly.
Dear Child! Dear Girl! that walkest with me here,
If thou appear untouched by solemn thought,   10
Thy nature is not therefore less divine:
Thou liest in Abraham's bosom all the year;
And worshipp'st at the Temple's inner shrine,
God being with thee when we know it not.

Glossary

5	**broods**: hovers or watches over (as a bird watches over her eggs); the image echoes the account of creation in Genesis 1:1–2: 'And the Spirit of God moved upon the face of the waters'
9	**Dear Child!**: Caroline, Wordsworth's daughter with Annette Vallon; she was nine years old when the sonnet was written
12	**Abraham's bosom**: heaven (see Themes and imagery)
13	**inner shrine**: the Holy of Holies, the most sacred part of the Temple in Jerusalem, closest to God

Guidelines

This sonnet may be read as a sequel to 'Composed upon Westminster Bridge'. The coach journey that took Wordsworth and his sister through London was a stage on their trip to Calais, to meet Annette Vallon and, for the first time, Wordsworth's daughter, Caroline. At the time of the visit to Calais, Wordsworth had arranged to marry Mary Hutchinson. In all, Wordsworth and Dorothy spent four weeks in Calais in uncomfortable lodgings. The weather was hot. Dorothy wrote in her journal that the four walked by the shore almost every evening.

Second meeting

After the meeting in August 1802, it was eighteen years before Wordsworth saw his daughter again. In 1820, on their way home from a continental tour, Wordsworth, along with his wife, Mary, and sister, Dorothy, met Annette and the now married Caroline in Paris. The group visited the Louvre together. Afterwards Wordsworth walked in the public gardens with his French granddaughter, one of whose middle names was Dorothy.

This is one of at least five sonnets that Wordsworth wrote in Calais and the only one that gives any hint of his reason for being there. Although it has the usual eight-line, six-line structure, it is divided into three parts. The first five lines are descriptive, evoking the beauty and silence of the evening as the sun sets. Lines 6–8 move from silence to the sound of the waves. For the speaker, the movement of the waves is a sign of the divine energy in nature. The final six lines are addressed to the child who accompanies the speaker and who is not affected by the occasion. The speaker reflects on the difference between her unconscious closeness to the divine and his more intellectual and occasional perception of it.

Commentary

Lines 1–5

The speaker brings the reader into the situation. He describes the evening, emphasising its beauty, and its quiet calmness. For the speaker, the scene has a religious quality, it is a 'holy time' of the day. The scene is dominated by the setting sun and the sea. The emphasis is less on the physical landscape than on the atmosphere and qualities of the evening.

Temple's inner shrine

According to the Old Testament, a thousand years before the birth of Christ, King Solomon built the Temple in Jerusalem to house the Ark of the Covenant, a gold-plated wooden chest containing the tablets of stone inscribed with the Ten Commandments given to Moses by God. The Ark was placed in the inner sanctuary of the Temple, known as the Holy of Holies. For Jews, this most sacred space was the place of God's dwelling on Earth. To worship 'at the Temple's inner shrine' was to be as close to God as was humanly possible on Earth.

Lines 6–8

The dramatic 'Listen!' (line 6) changes the mood and tone of the poem and introduces energy into what has been a description of stillness. The speaker draws attention to the sound of what must be the waves. For him, it is evidence that God ('The mighty Being') is present and active in the world. Because the speaker uses metaphors, the thought is not clear and precise.

Lines 9–14

There is another change of direction in the sestet. The speaker now addresses a child, who is present, though her presence has not been marked until this moment. The use of 'Dear' suggests his closeness to the child. Unlike him, the child does not seem to be affected by the scene. In what amounts to a blessing, he reassures her that she is close to God and God is with her all the time.

Themes and imagery

This sonnet is another poem in which Wordsworth explores **the relationship between the inner self, the external world and the divine**. In this instance, the beauty of the evening is profoundly moving and, for the speaker, reveals the presence of God in the world. He notes, however, that these kinds of spiritual experiences occur in certain moments for an adult, whereas a child's nature is different: children live 'all the year' (line 12) close to God. For some readers, the poem expresses the loving attitude of a father for his daughter.

The opening five lines record the evening. Apart from 'broods' (line 5) there are no active verbs. The present tense of the verb 'to be' is used three times. The concern in these lines is with being in time, **existing in the moment and capturing the quality of this moment**. For the speaker, it is a 'holy time' (line 2), one filled with a sense of the sacred and the divine. It is marked by beauty, quietness, tranquillity, serenity. The adjective 'holy', the image of the nun at prayer, and the reference to the 'gentleness of heaven' (line 5) emphasise the idea of a **sacred moment**.

The image of the heavens brooding over the sea creates an association with the biblical account of creation, where the Holy Spirit hovered over the seas. Whether consciously or not, the poem takes up the idea of a spirit, a 'mighty Being' (line 6), whose energy is heard in the eternal rise and fall of the sea. The dramatic imperative 'Listen!' (line 6) suggests that the sound is not loud but continuous and rumbling, like thunder. The image of thunder and movement contrast with the quiet stillness of the opening lines. As often with Wordsworth, the precise meaning of his words is not clear. What does he mean by 'The gentleness of heaven' (line 5)? Is it a feeling in the air? Is it the light of the setting sun? Are there light clouds in the sky? Is the 'sound like thunder' (line 8) the crashing of the waves? Does the constant ebb and flow of the sea symbolise eternity and, therefore, contrast with the transient moment that the poem celebrates? Because there are no definite answers, the poem is **open to interpretation**.

There is a clear division in the poem between the octet and the sestet. Up to line 9 there is little indication that the speaker has a companion, but then he turns and speaks directly to her. The 'Dear Child' (line 9) appears to be unaffected by the kind of 'solemn thought' (line 10) provoked in the speaker by the beauty of the evening. This may seem that she is lacking in some way, that her nature is not sensitive to the spiritual side of life. The speaker reassures her, telling her that she is close to God 'all the year' (line 12) even 'when we know it not' (line 14). These thoughts and feelings echo Christ's words in Matthew 19:14: 'Let the little children come to me, and do not hinder them, for the kingdom of heaven belongs to such as these.' It is not certain who the speaker has in mind when he uses 'we' in the final line. Does he mean 'you' and 'me', referring to himself and his daughter as a family unit? Or is 'we' a reference to those people who, like him, can be touched by 'solemn thought' (line 10)? It is another instance where the meaning is not clear. It is also not clear how the speaker feels about the little girl being 'untouched by solemn thought' (line 10). Is he disappointed? Does he want to cover his disappointment by giving her reassurances that she has not sought? Does he really believe that she is closer to God than he is? Is he envious of her? It is impossible to say for certain.

Loving or disappointed father?

Not surprisingly, **the final six lines have been interpreted in widely different ways** by critics. For some, the voice of the speaker is that of a loving father giving his blessing to his daughter. It shows his care, affection and appreciation for her. For others, the lines suggest that the speaker is disappointed by the child's lack of appreciation of the moment. His reassurances to her that she is close to God seem lame.

The phrase 'Abraham's bosom' (line 12) has attracted attention. Traditionally this phrase refers to a special place in heaven reserved for faithful servants of God. Abraham was an Old Testament prophet. As he showed himself willing to sacrifice his only child, Isaac, when God asked him to do so, he is said to represent faithfulness. 'Abraham's bosom' is therefore understood as the place where the souls of the faithful go after their death. In Christ's parable of the rich man and the poor man, when the beggar Lazarus dies, he is 'carried by angels into Abraham's bosom' (Luke 16:22), while the rich man is sent to the torments of hell, from where he can see Lazarus but the gulf between them is too great to cross. For the critic Judith Page, 'Wordsworth ... imagines the girl ... dead. Like the celebrated Lucy, she has no motion or force while lying in Abraham's bosom.'

Whatever about the merits of this interpretation, the image is a strange one. We normally associate the image of a child lying in the bosom of a parent with the mother, who nurses and nurtures the child at her breast. It is an interesting choice of phrase when you remember the circumstances. Wordsworth was in Calais to meet his daughter and her mother, before leaving both to return to England to marry Mary Hutchinson. As a parent, he was not going to nurture his child or provide a home for her. Symbolically, he sacrifices her by disassociating from her and her mother and returning home to fulfil the promise he made to his English fiancée. In place of his own care, he imagines his daughter in the bosom of another father, a faithful servant. Oddly, Wordsworth does not address Caroline as 'daughter', but uses the more general and impersonal terms, 'Child' and 'Girl'. Compare this with his manner of address to his sister, Dorothy, in 'To My Sister and 'Tintern Abbey', where the relationship is named for what it is.

The child is given no voice in the poem. The only thing we learn about her is the fact that she is not touched by solemn thoughts as the sun sets over the sea on a beautiful evening. Judith Page suggests that 'the speaker tells the girl who she is and where she lives and what her limitations are'. In the tradition of dramatic monologue, we hear only one voice. But it is impossible not to wonder what Caroline, Wordsworth's daughter, made of the poem when she read it. The poem has something of a **farewell quality** about it. Wordsworth himself is calm and free, ready to return to England and his fiancée.

Form and language

The poem is a **version of a Petrarchan sonnet**. It consists of two sentences, which divide the poem into the traditional octet (eight lines) and sestet (six lines) of the sonnet. However, the octet has two distinct parts, with a clear division occurring at the end of line 5. The rhyme scheme is complex: *abba acca defdfe*. The poem is written in the present tense and creates a sense of the speaker immersed in the scene as it unfolds.

In the first five lines the sounds of the poem reflect the quiet and calm of the evening. The choice of the adjective 'beauteous' in the opening line, rather than the more usual 'beautiful', sets up the soundscape: soft 's' sounds and long vowels. A succession of adjectives in these lines reinforce the sense of hush: 'calm', 'holy', 'quiet', etc. The noun 'gentleness' (line 5) encapsulates the quality of the evening for the speaker. The use of the adjective 'Breathless' (line 3) has been admired by critics. It reflects both the calm stillness of the evening but also the quiet excitement of the nun as she adores God.

A different energy is created by the exclamation marks and the direct address of the speaker, 'Listen!' (line 6), 'Dear Child! Dear Girl!' (line 9). Wordsworth breaks the usual rhyming scheme in a Petrarchan sonnet to rhyme 'awake' and 'make' in lines 6 and 7. The 'k' sounds and the echo in the phrase 'sound like thunder' (line 8) sparkle with electric energy.

Exam-Style Questions

Understanding the poem

1	What time of day is described in the first five lines of the poem?
2	What is it about this time of day that impresses itself upon the speaker?
3	What is it that makes a 'sound like thunder' (line 8)?
4	Who is 'The mighty Being' (line 6)? Has this being more than one identity?
5	Are you surprised that the 'Dear Child' (line 9) is not touched by 'solemn thought' (line 10) on a beach as the sun sets? Do you think the speaker is surprised? Give reasons for your answers.
6	What is your understanding of worshipping 'at the Temple's inner shrine' (line 13)?
7	Identify the words and expressions that give this poem a strongly religious colouring.

Thinking about the poem

1	Comment on the use of the phrase 'Abraham's bosom' (line 12) in the poem.
2	Which of the following is closest to your understanding of the last three lines of the poem? ■ The speaker is reassuring the child. ■ The speaker is reflecting on the child's divine nature. ■ The speaker is dealing with his own disappointment. Explain your answer.
3	How would you describe the mood of the poem: joyful, sad, thoughtful or something else? Give reasons for your choice.
4	Write a reflection on the imagery in this poem, beginning with one of the following phrases: ■ I find the imagery in this poem interesting and easy to understand … ■ I find the imagery in this poem challenging and unusual …
5	Which of the following is closest to your understanding of what the poem is about? ■ The poem considers God's presence in the world. ■ The poem considers the closeness of children to God. ■ The poem considers the effect of natural beauty on the individual. Explain your answer.
6	Based on the evidence of the poem, do you think that Caroline was fortunate to have Wordsworth as her father? Give reasons for your answer.

Imagining

1	Imagine you are Caroline, now aged sixteen. In your diary record your memories of your meeting with your father at Calais. Give your impression of the kind of man you believe him to be. Your entry should demonstrate your knowledge of the poem.
2	'the broad sun / Is sinking down in its tranquillity' (lines 3–4). Write a short descriptive piece on the most beautiful sunset you have ever witnessed.

SNAPSHOT

- Written in the present tense
- Records the speaker's immediate experience
- Captures the beauty of the evening
- Sees a divine being energising nature
- Speaker includes the child in his thoughts
- Speaker reflects on the child's divine nature
- Use of religious imagery
- Richness of language
- Reveals little of the personality of the child

Before you read

Play this game of Dilemma with another classmate. You are on a trekking holiday in a poor country. You come across young woman doing back-breaking work in a field. You see her, but she does not see you. The young woman is singing a song and you have never heard such beautiful singing before. Do you:

(a) go into the field and offer to help the young woman, knowing that your presence will bring her song to an end?

(b) stand and listen to the song and move on when it is finished?

(c) take a photograph of the young woman?

The Solitary Reaper

Behold her, single in the field,
Yon solitary Highland Lass!
Reaping and singing by herself;
Stop here, or gently pass!
Alone she cuts and binds the grain,   5
And sings a melancholy strain;
O listen! for the vale profound
Is overflowing with the sound.

No Nightingale did ever chaunt
More welcome notes to weary bands   10
Of travellers in some shady haunt,
Among Arabian sands:
A voice so thrilling ne'er was heard
In spring-time from the Cuckoo-bird,
Breaking the silence of the seas   15
Among the farthest Hebrides.

Will no one tell me what she sings?
Perhaps the plaintive numbers flow
For old, unhappy, far-off things,
And battles long ago: 20
Or is it some more humble lay,
Familiar matter of to-day?
Some natural sorrow, loss or pain,
That has been, and may be again?

Whate'er the theme, the Maiden sang   25
As if her song could have no ending;
I saw her singing at her work,
And o'er the sickle bending;
I listen'd, motionless and still;
And, as I mounted up the hill,   30
The music in my heart I bore,
Long after it was heard no more.

Glossary

2	*Yon*: in view but at a little distance from the speaker
2	*Highland Lass*: girl or young woman from the mountainous areas of northern and western Scotland
6	*melancholy strain*: sad tune
7	*vale profound*: deep valley
9	*chaunt*: sing (from the French *chanter*)
11–12	*shady … sands*: oasis in the Arabian desert
16	*Hebrides*: Gaelic-speaking islands off the northwest of Scotland, rugged and remote
18	*plaintive numbers*: sad verses
21	*lay*: song

Guidelines

This poem was written in November 1805, inspired by Thomas Wilkinson's 'Tour in Scotland'. Wilkinson wrote: 'Passed … a female who was reaping alone; she sang in Erse as she bended over her sickle: the sweetest human voice I ever heard: her strains were tenderly melancholy, and felt delicious long after they were heard no more.' The last line of the poem is taken directly from Wilkinson's account. Two years earlier, in September 1803, Wordsworth and Dorothy had visited the Scottish Highlands and observed 'small companies of reapers' in the fields. Dorothy remarked that it was not uncommon 'in the more lonely parts of the Highlands to see a single person so employed', as is the case in the poem.

The poem is written in four stanzas. In the first the speaker/traveller invites a fellow traveller/reader to stop and listen to the singing of a 'Highland Lass' as she works in the field. The solitariness of the girl is emphasised. The second describes the profound effect of the song on the hearer. In the third the speaker speculates on the subject of the song (he does not understand the words) and considers different possibilities. In the fourth the speaker returns to the girl's singing and its lasting place in his heart.

When Wordsworth wrote the poem, he was still recovering from the shock of the sudden death of his beloved brother John, drowned when the ship he captained sank with the loss of over three hundred lives. Some of the elegiac quality of the poem may come from his grief.

Wordsworth's legs

Thomas de Quincey made the following humorous observation: Wordsworth's 'legs were pointedly condemned by all female connoisseurs in legs; not that they were bad in any way which would force itself upon your notice—there was no absolute deformity about them; and undoubtedly they had been serviceable legs beyond the average standard of human requisition; for I calculate, upon good data, that with these identical legs Wordsworth must have traversed a distance of 175,000 to 180,000 English miles—a mode of exertion which, to him, stood in the stead of alcohol and other stimulants whatsoever to animal spirits; to which, indeed, he was indebted for a life of unclouded happiness, and we for much of what is most excellent in his writings.'

Commentary

Stanza 1

The poem begins in dramatic fashion with the speaker/traveller pointing out a girl working on her own in a field and filling the valley with her song. He asks his fellow-traveller/reader to stop and listen or pass quietly so as not to disturb the moment. The speaker emphasises the fact that the girl is alone and that her singing has a sad or melancholic quality to it. The word 'profound' suggests the effect of the song on the speaker.

Stanza 2

The speaker uses two comparisons to convey the effect of the girl's song on him. He says that her song was more welcoming than a nightingale's song to a weary group of travellers in the desert. It was more thrilling than the voice of the cuckoo announcing the arrival of spring in the bleak Hebrides.

Stanza 3

Having undertaken an imaginative journey in stanza 2, the speaker returns to the immediacy of the scene and asks if there is a fellow-traveller/reader who can translate the singer's words for him. No answer is given. The speaker asks a series of speculative questions in an attempt to match possible themes to the sound and quality of the song and the singing. The suggestions cover different kinds of traditional song.

Stanza 4

The poem switches to the past tense in the final stanza. The speaker says that whatever the themes of the reaper's song, he carried the music with him in his heart as he climbed up the hill and 'Long after it was heard no more'.

Themes and imagery

One of the major themes of the poem is **the soothing effect of sorrowful songs** upon the listener. Music speaks to the heart and there is comfort and delight to be found in music that expresses human suffering, what Wordsworth called in 'Tintern Abbey' the 'still, sad music of humanity' (line 91, page 419).

The speaker hears a sad song sung, in a language he does not understand, by a young woman engaged in back-breaking work in a field in a remote and inhospitable landscape. How can he convey the impact it has on him? He thinks of the nightingale singing in an oasis in the Arabian desert. The young woman's song is more welcoming. He thinks of the cuckoo announcing the arrival of spring to the inhabitants of the remotest Hebridean islands. The voice of this 'Highland Lass' (line 2) is more thrilling. Like the song of the nightingale and the cuckoo, her song brings hope, and comfort is heard with gratitude and pleasure. Figuratively, her song extends out beyond the vale, spreading towards the cold North Sea and eastwards towards the desert lands. This may suggest that the 'melancholy strain' (line 6) is universal and found in different cultures and climates.

In stanza 3 there is a different kind of expansion, across time rather than space. The speaker speculates on the theme of the song. Its sadness may suggest a song commemorating historical events and sorrows from the history of the Highland Scots, 'old, unhappy, far-off things, / And battles long ago' (lines 19–20). Or perhaps the song refers to more personal events, the 'natural sorrow, loss or pain' (line 23) experienced in everyone's life. From a thematic perspective, the stanza suggests the **centrality of suffering in human existence**, an idea that resounds in the forceful rhyme of the closing couplet of the stanza, 'pain' and 'again'.

However, as is suggested in stanza 4, it does not really matter that the speaker cannot understand the words of the song, it still remains a profound and deeply affecting experience. And the song will go on, 'As if her song could have no ending' (line 26), because there is no end to the still, sad music of humanity and the human suffering that inspires it.

The final stanza is written in the past tense and we lose the immediacy of the first stanza. As the poem concludes, the singer and the song she sings disappear. It is the music that the speaker carries with him in his heart, long after the song ceased to be heard. And the great paradox is that the sad music renews and soothes the spirit.

The imagery in the poem emphasises the reaper's solitariness and her arduous work, and the doubling up of that hard, agricultural work because she is alone. This Highland Lass might be regarded as the solitary **representative of an old Gaelic order**, defeated by the nation and culture of the tourist who observes her. And like a coloniser, he leaves the native girl, the song and her language behind in her impoverished circumstances, but takes comfort from what he heard when he returns to the material comforts of his home in England.

Form and language

This poem is an example of a **lyrical ballad**, combining elements of **personal response and reflection** with the **narrative account of an incident from ordinary life**. The structure and language combine literary and popular forms of poetry. Many ballads and hymns use a four-line stanza form, with alternate four-beat and three-beat lines. Wordsworth uses an eight-line stanza with four-beat lines, except for line 4 in each stanza, which has three beats. This form not only nods at the ballad, but also allows for an interesting effect where the music of the poem seems to swell up from the short fourth line in each stanza. The rhymes add considerably to the **harmonious flow** of the poem and the sweetness of its melody. However, the rhymes are more than sweet-sounding. They draw attention to important themes and connected ideas. For example, the rhyming of 'ending' – 'As if her song could have no ending' (line 26), with 'bending' – 'And o'er the sickle bending' (line 28), links singing and reaping and **suggests that the song will not end because the work itself seems unending**. The rhyming of 'profound' (line 7) with 'sound' (line 8) links the two words so that we understand that the whole surrounding landscape is filled with the singing of the girl, which has the power to move the listener in a profound way. Interestingly, the four unrhymed words in the poem, lines 1 and 3 of the first and final stanza, emphasise the situation of the reaper: 'field', 'herself', 'sang' and 'work'.

Another notable feature of the language is the **use of repetition** and the doubling up of words: 'single', 'solitary', 'by herself', 'Alone' (stanza 1); 'old', 'far-off', 'long ago' (stanza 3); 'sorrow', 'loss', 'pain' (stanza 3); 'motionless', 'still' (stanza 4). The doubling up is evident in: 'Reaping and singing' (line 3); 'cuts and binds' (line 5); 'Stop … pass' (line 4); 'things / And battles' (lines 19–20); 'has been, and may be again' (line 24). Just as the reaper's song is overflowing so **the poem overflows with language**. The sounds of the poem are overwhelmingly comforting. Within this soothing soundscape, Wordsworth creates a sense of immediacy and urgency in his use of direct address, 'Behold her' (line 1), 'Stop here' (line 4), 'listen' (line 7).

For the most part, the poem is written in the simple language of a ballad. However, there are also literary words such as 'melancholy', 'profound' (stanza 1); 'chaunt' (stanza 2); 'plaintive', 'lay' (stanza 3); 'Maiden' (stanza 4). The use of 'Maiden' (line 25) is of particular interest. In the first stanza the singer is referred to as a 'Lass' (line 2), an informal and affectionate term. However, the more literary, formal and distant 'Maiden' is used in stanza 4. It is as if the girl and her song disappear, and what the speaker/traveller carries away is something more abstract and impersonal, 'the music' (line 31).

> **Untrodden ways**
>
> **Wordsworth loved the Lake District for its quiet and isolation. In later life he was involved in a campaign to stop the railway coming into the Lake District. He feared that the uneducated masses would come and spoil the lakes for people of taste and discrimination like him. His stance damaged his reputation.**
>
> **His fears that tourism would ruin the Lake District did not stop him from going on touring holidays. He walked in France, Switzerland, Germany, Belgium and Scotland, as well as visiting Rome and Paris. He did a six-week tour of Ireland in 1829, sailing off Glengarriff and climbing Carrauntoohil. He was impressed particularly by Kerry and Antrim.**

Questions

1	What exactly does the speaker wish to draw attention to in stanza 1 of the poem?
2	'single' (line 1), 'solitary' (line 2), 'Alone' (line 5). Why, in your view, does the speaker emphasise this aspect of the girl's circumstances?
3	Based on the evidence of stanza 1, use three adjectives to describe the song of the 'Highland Lass'.
4	Explain the comparisons used by the speaker in stanza 2 to express the effect of the song upon him.
5	The speaker does not understand the words of the song. Do you think this lessens his enjoyment of it?
6	In stanza 3 the speaker speculates on the theme of the song sung by the girl. What suggestions does he make?
7	What does the speaker take away with him from the experience of hearing the young woman sing?
8	Which of the following statements is closest to your view of the poem? ■ The poem is about the power of music to move the heart. ■ The poem is about the beauty to be found in sad music. ■ The poem is about the joy of travel and tourism. Explain your choice.
9	There is a sense of drama and immediacy about the opening lines of the poem. How does Wordsworth achieve this effect?
10	Comment on two other interesting uses of language in the poem.
11	'As in the Lucy poems, the speaker puts himself at the centre of the experience and the female character remains vague and anonymous.' Do you agree with this statement? Give reasons for your answer.
12	'Although it is a beautiful poem, Wordsworth seems blind to the issues of class, gender and race that it raises.' Discuss this opinion.
13	*Groupwork* Working in groups of three, devise a way of performing the poem that highlights its musical qualities.
14	Write a short monologue prompted by one of the following: ■ 'How typical! The man looks on while the woman does all the work. Then the man writes a poem and gets all the credit and the woman remains nameless!' ■ 'How generous! The poet takes the song of a young girl, working in a field in the middle of nowhere, and immortalises her.'
15	Can you give an example of a song that moves you deeply, even though you do not know or understand the words? Write a short piece describing how that song affects you.

Background to *The Prelude*

Coleridge encouraged Wordsworth to write a masterwork that would provide a statement of his philosophy and act as a moral guide for readers. The proposed work was titled 'The Recluse'. This task worried Wordsworth for the rest of his life. In preparation, he wrote the work that later became known as *The Prelude*, which was **intended to trace his intellectual and emotional development from childhood to early adulthood**. Wordsworth believed that his childhood and youth, spent among the lakes, mountains and rivers of northwest England, had prepared him for his poetic vocation.

The Prelude is addressed to Coleridge, described by Wordsworth as the 'most intense of Nature's worshippers'. It is **marked by narrative accounts, passages of lyrical description and intense self-reflection**. The centre of the poem is the poet's own consciousness, and the relationship between imagination, emotional and intellectual development and nature.

Wordsworth worked on this autobiographical poem from 1798 until 1805, when he produced the first full-length version in thirteen books. Over the years, right up to his death, he continued to revise and tinker with the work. Wordsworth never intended that it would be published separately from 'The Recluse', realising that it would appear a self-centred exercise. He did not give the work a title, thinking of it as **an extended letter-poem to his friend Coleridge**. It was his widow, Mary, who suggested the term 'prelude' as a suitable title for the first published version of the poem in 1850.

The most impressive passages in *The Prelude* occur in the first two books, which deal with the poet's childhood and schooldays. **The impressions of his early years formed the deepest part of Wordsworth's relationship with nature.** In a key passage he refers to certain events in people's lives, which he calls 'spots of time', that have a decisive influence on the heart and mind of those who experience them. These events (feelings, sights or impressions) can leave indelible marks on the mind and can have healing or morally enhancing effects. By means of such experiences, Wordsworth believed that 'our minds are nourished / And invisibly repaired'. When he himself looked back on some particularly vivid **'spots of time'**, such as the skating or boating episodes that feature in the poems that follow, he was **able to restore his spirits when he felt depressed**.

Dove cottage, the home of William Wordsworth.

Before you read

With a partner, describe the best and most thrilling experience you ever had as a child. As clearly as you can, identify what made it so memorable.

from The Prelude: **Skating**

And in the frosty season, when the sun
Was set, and visible for many a mile
The cottage windows blazed through twilight gloom,
I heeded not their summons: happy time
It was indeed for all of us – for me   5
It was a time of rapture! Clear and loud
The village clock tolled six, – I wheeled about,
Proud and exulting like an untired horse
That cares not for his home. All shod with steel,
We hissed along the polished ice in games   10
Confederate, imitative of the chase
And woodland pleasures – the resounding horn,
The pack loud chiming, and the hunted hare.
So through the darkness and the cold we flew,
And not a voice was idle; with the din   15
Smitten, the precipices rang aloud;
The leafless trees and every icy crag
Tinkled like iron; while far distant hills
Into the tumult sent an alien sound
Of melancholy not unnoticed, while the stars   20
Eastward were sparkling clear, and in the west
The orange sky of evening died away.
Not seldom from the uproar I retired
Into a silent bay, or sportively
Glanced sideway, leaving the tumultuous throng,   25
To cut across the reflex of a star
That fled, and, flying still before me, gleamed
Upon the glassy plain; and oftentimes,
When we had given our bodies to the wind,
And all the shadowy banks on either side   30
Came sweeping through the darkness, spinning still
The rapid line of motion, then at once
Have I, reclining back upon my heels,
Stopped short; yet still the solitary cliffs
Wheeled by me – even as if the earth had rolled   35
With visible motion her diurnal round!
Behind me did they stretch in solemn train,
Feebler and feebler, and I stood and watched
Till all was tranquil as a dreamless sleep.

Glossary

6	*rapture*: great delight, ecstasy
8	*exulting*: intensely joyful
9	*shod with steel*: wearing skates
10–11	*games/Confederate*: games in which all joined
15	*din*: continuous loud noise
16	*Smitten*: struck (by the noise of the children)
16	*precipices*: cliffs
19	*tumult*: uproar (excited noise made by the crowd of children)
20	*melancholy*: sadness
24	*sportively*: playfully
25	*throng*: crowd
26	*reflex*: reflection (in the ice)
28	*glassy plain*: frozen stretch of water
36	*diurnal round*: daily movement (orbit of the sun)

Guidelines

In this passage from *The Prelude* Wordsworth recalls skating in winter with friends after the sun had set. He paints a scene of children skating at speed under a dark, starry sky on a plain of ice in a valley. The writing brings the memory to life with dramatic intensity.

Commentary

Lines 1–13

The opening lines establish the setting of the poem – winter in the village at evening time. The lights blazed in the cottage windows and the village clock struck six o'clock. But the speaker was not ruled by time. Like a horse who is not tired, he turned away from home. Together, the children of the village sped across the ice on their skates, like a pack of hounds in pursuit of a hare.

Lines 14–22

The children skated through the darkness and there was much noise and excitement. The noise echoed back from the cliffs, the trees and the rocks and from the far distant hills. In the east the stars shone. In the west the last light of the sun died away.

Lines 23–36

The speaker often separated himself from the noisy group. He went into 'a silent bay' or cut across the reflection of a star that gleamed on the ice. Often when the children skated at dizzying full speed it seemed that the shadowy banks of the hills raced past him. And even as he slowed, the cliffs seemed to wheel by him, as if he could see the world turn slowly in its daily rotation.

Lines 37–39

As he came to a halt and the dizzying effect of speed left him, the Earth's motion lessened. The boy stood and watched until a calm descended that was as 'tranquil as a dreamless sleep'.

Themes and imagery

The passage works on a number of different levels. **It celebrates speed and motion** and **the sheer joy of physical well-being** and play. It celebrates the boy's **sense of freedom**, his turning away from the 'summons' (line 4) of the 'cottage windows' (line 3) and tolling of the clock. As part of the speaker's poetic autobiography, it marks him as separate from the other children. For them, the 'frosty season' (line 1) was a 'happy time' (line 4). For him, 'It was a time of rapture!' (line 6). The poem marks the threshold in the boy's experience of nature. His physical motion through the space, on a line through a valley, is gradually transformed into a vision of the spinning world, which hints at the visionary nature of the poetry he will later write.

The imagery moves between sight, sound and motion. Wordsworth **constantly draws comparisons and contrasts between the human world and the natural world**. The noisy tumult of the young skaters, not an idle voice among them, is evoked in terms of a woodland hunt: 'the resounding horn, / The pack loud chiming, and the hunted hare' (lines 12–13). By contrast with this uproar, there is the restrained response of the far distant hills, which 'Into the tumult sent an alien sound / Of melancholy not unnoticed' (lines 19–20).

Interestingly, this note of sadness is echoed elsewhere in the poem, in the 'twilight gloom' (line 3), the tolling of the 'village clock' (line 7), 'The orange sky of evening' dying away (line 22), the 'dreamless sleep' (line 39). The imagery **gives an agency to nature**. The hills send a sound into the tumult. The 'shadowy banks' (line 30) sweep through the darkness. In lines 7–8 it is the boy who 'wheeled about', 'Proud and exulting like an untired horse', but by lines 34–35, it is the 'solitary cliffs' that wheel by him.

The final twelve lines are crucial in understanding why Wordsworth writes about this experience as **an important moment in forming his poetic vision**. All the skaters give their 'bodies to the wind' (line 29). However, the final part of the description is unique to him. He is now skating so fast that everything seems to spin off his 'rapid line of motion' (line 32). Even after he stops propelling himself forward, and leans back upon his heels, he continues to feel the dizzying effects of the violent movement he has been engaged in: 'yet still the solitary cliffs / Wheeled by me' (lines 34–35). In this dizzy state he moves from perception and sensation (what he feels and sees) to something that he imagines, something that has a visionary quality. When he comes to a stop, it is as if he sees the world's daily revolution on its axis: 'as if the earth had rolled / With visible motion her diurnal round!' (lines 35–36). From a still point, he stands and observes until 'all was tranquil as a dreamless sleep' (line 39). The use of 'all' suggests that both nature and the watching boy share in the sense of calm. This is not a mystical vision, but it points towards moments of vision that the poet will experience in later life.

Form and language

The Prelude is written **in blank verse**, that is unrhymed lines of mostly ten syllables, with an underlying pattern of iambic pentameter. The iambic foot, with its unstressed syllable followed by a stressed syllable, has a natural connection with the beat of the heart or the rhythm of walking. In Wordsworth's hands, it sounds **natural and conversational**. The absence of rhyme and the use of run-on lines and punctuation ensure that the rhythm never becomes monotonous.

The conversational 'And' that opens the poem invites the reader in, as if the speaker is continuing an ongoing conversation. Wordsworth is particularly successful in his description of the ice-bound landscape. His use of hard, sharp consonant sounds and hissing 's' and 'c' sounds imitate the clear metallic hardness of the children skating on ice in a space surrounded by cliffs and rocks and leafless trees.

The poem brilliantly **conveys a sense of movement and energy** in its strong, surging rhythms. Note how the run-on lines and the choice of verbs aid the feeling of a headlong rush. For example: '... leaving the tumultuous throng, / To cut across the reflex of a star / That fled, and flying still before me, gleamed / Upon the glassy plain ... ' (lines 25–28).

SNAPSHOT

- A memory poem
- Recalls the joy of skating
- Vivid piece of description
- Language is clear and simple
- Wintry atmosphere
- Hints of sadness
- Nature is active

- Portrait of a young imaginative mind
- Rhythm reflects the rapid movement of the skaters
- Movement from the senses to the imagination
- Presentation of the young Wordsworth as a poet in the making

Exam-Style Questions

Understanding the poem

1	How does the speaker react to the summons of the cottage windows and the tolling bell?
2	The speaker distinguishes himself from the other children (lines 5–6). How does he do this?
3	Explain the hunting imagery in lines 11–13.
4	What aspects of the landscape are described in lines 14–22?
5	Describe the difference between the sky in the east and the sky in the west (lines 21–22).
6	Describe three ways in which the speaker seems different from his friends from line 23 to the end of the poem.
7	Although it is clearly a poem about joy, indicate anywhere you think there are hints of sadness.
8	The imagery captures the sights, sounds and movement of the scene. Pick your favourite example of each of these. Explain your choices.

Thinking about the poem

1	Identify two examples from the poem where the sounds of the words echo the meaning.
2	Discuss the role of rhythm, the sense of movement and the choice of words in conveying the atmosphere of the poem. Pick out some lines that particularly suggest the rapid motion of the skaters.
3	Where, do you think, is the idea of freedom most evident in the poem?
4	Show where nature is given human-like qualities in the poem.
5	Based on this passage, what kind of boy do you imagine the young Wordsworth to have been? Give reasons for your answer.
6	Why, do you think, did Wordsworth decide to record this episode in his poetic autobiography?
7	Which of the following statements is closest to your understanding of the poem? ■ The poem is about the joy of skating.　　■ The poem is about the vision of the young poet. ■ The poem is about the wonder of nature. Explain your choice.

Imagining

1	Can you identify with the boy's experience? Based on a real or imagined memory, write a descriptive passage that captures a thrilling experience from childhood. Use rhythm, repetition, onomatopoeic sounds and word choice to convey the excitement of the occasion.
2	You have been asked to organise a performance of this poem by one or more performers. Describe the set you would create, the costume(s), make-up and music you would use and any other sound or special effects that you think would enhance the performance. Support your proposal with reference to the poem.

Before you read

Have you had the experience of seeing something that did not make logical sense but that troubled your imagination for days afterwards? If so, describe the experience and its effect.

from The Prelude: **The Stolen Boat**

One summer evening (led by her) I found
A little boat tied to a willow tree
Within a rocky cave, its usual home.
Straight I unloosed her chain, and stepping in,
Pushed from the shore. It was an act of stealth   5
And troubled pleasure; nor without the voice
Of mountain-echoes did my boat move on,
Leaving behind her still, on either side,
Small circles glittering idly in the moon,
Until they melted all into one track   10
Of sparkling light. But now, like one who rows
Proud of his skill, to reach a chosen point
With an unswerving line, I fixed my view
Upon the summit of a craggy ridge,
The horizon's utmost boundary; far above   15
Was nothing but the stars and the grey sky.
She was an elfin pinnace; lustily
I dipped my oars into the silent lake,
And, as I rose upon the stroke, my boat
Went heaving through the water like a swan,   20
When, from behind that craggy steep till then
The horizon's bound, a huge peak, black and huge,
As if with voluntary power instinct
Upreared its head. I struck and struck again,
And growing still in stature the grim shape   25
Towered up between me and the stars, and still
For so it seemed, with purpose of its own
With measured motion like a living thing,
Strode after me. With trembling oars I turned,
And through the silent water stole my way   30
Back to the covert of the willow tree;
There in her mooring-place I left my bark,
And through the meadows homeward went, in grave
And serious mood; and after I had seen
That spectacle, for many days my brain   35
Worked with a dim and undetermined sense
Of unknown modes of being; o'er my thoughts
There hung a darkness, call it solitude
Or blank desertion. No familiar shapes
Remained, no pleasant images of trees,   40
Of sea or sky, no colours of green fields;
But huge and mighty forms that do not live,
Like living men moved slowly through the mind
By day, and were a trouble to my dreams.

Glossary

1	*her*: nature
4	*Straight*: straightaway
5	*stealth*: theft
13	*unswerving*: straight
14	*craggy*: rocky
17	*elfin pinnace*: little boat that might have belonged in a fairy tale
17	*lustily*: vigorously
22	*bound*: limit, boundary
23	*with ... instinct*: possessed with a power of its own
31	*covert*: shelter
32	*bark*: boat
36	*undetermined*: vague, unsettled

Guidelines

In a celebrated passage, the poet describes how as a young boy he took a small boat and rowed across Ullswater Lake at night. Out of the darkness a huge mountain peak seemed to rear its head and follow him. In a panic, he fled. For days and nights afterwards, his mind was troubled. In *The Prelude* Wordsworth names the two forces that influenced his early years: beauty and fear: 'Fair seed-time had my soul, and I grew up / Fostered alike by beauty and by fear'. The controlling influence in the skating episode is beauty, and the feelings associated with it are those of joy and pleasure. In 'The Stolen Boat', on the other hand, he describes an evening dominated by fear, and the associated feelings of guilt and loneliness. In 'Tintern Abbey' Wordsworth describes nature as: 'The anchor of my purest thoughts, the nurse, / The guide, the guardian of my heart, and soul / Of all my moral being' (lines 109–111, page 419). This passage shows this idea in practice.

Commentary

Lines 1–11
The narrator explains how he found a boat, untied it and rowed away from the shore. He describes his action as one of stealth, which troubled him and seemed to cause the mountains to voice their concerns. As the boat moved across the lake, the water disturbed by the oars sparkled in the moonlight in a magical way.

Lines 11–24
The rower fixed his gaze on a rocky ridge on the horizon and rowed, enjoying his skill. Under the starry sky his boat was like one from a fairy tale and moved through the water like a swan. Then, from behind the rocky ridge, a huge mountain peak seemed to rear its head.

Lines 24–34
Panicked, the boy rowed and rowed. But the mountain grew bigger and blocked the stars. And then, like a living thing, the mountain strode after the boy. Frightened, the boy made his way back and left the boat in its mooring place. He went home in a serious mood.

Lines 34–44
For days afterwards the boy's brain worked to understand what had happened. He felt lonely and depressed. His thoughts were haunted by day and his dreams were troubled at night.

Themes and imagery

The poem illustrates the most important themes in Wordsworth's poetry: **the relationship between nature, imagination and emotional and intellectual development**. The passage is a **vivid presentation of a childhood memory**. For Wordsworth, poetic inspiration came from primary experiences stored in the memory and transformed by the imagination. The passage shows **one of the young poet's first inklings of a presence in nature that was greater than any human being**.

There are **many different interpretations** of the passage. One reads the passage as showing **a stern nature enforcing a moral lesson on the young boy**. According to this reading, the phrase in parenthesis, '(led by

her)', in line 1 suggests that nature has prompted him to break the moral law by taking someone's boat without permission in order to teach him the consequences of such acts. Even as he takes the boat, his conscience is not entirely clear: he recognises the theft as 'an act of stealth / And troubled pleasure' (lines 5–6), but nevertheless enjoys his trip on the lake, in much the same way as he enjoys the more innocent sport of skating. He is 'Proud of his skill' (line 12) as an oarsman, his ability to make his boat go 'heaving through the water like a swan' (line 20). At the height of his enjoyment, however, nature intervenes to trouble his imagination and arouse his moral sense. The effect of the experience is profound, haunting his mind by day and troubling his dreams. The 'huge and mighty forms' (line 42) that disturb his peace of mind have an important function in the scheme of Wordsworth's beliefs. The passage underlines his conviction that there is **a close relationship between breaches of the moral law (theft, for example) and the harmony of nature**. Disruption in one sphere involves disharmony in the other: a person's activity cannot be isolated from the natural world of which he or she is a part.

Other critics stress the link between this vivid spot of time in the poet's childhood and the **development of his imagination**. For these critics, the interest is not in the moral lesson, if that is what it was, but in the lesson that the mind is its own place, capable of creating what Wordsworth himself said elsewhere were 'impressive effects out of simple elements'. The simple episode of taking a boat has now been linked to something vast, which the young boy could not name, that replaces the familiar world of 'shapes' (line 39), 'images' (line 40) and 'colours' (line 41). In their place, 'huge and mighty forms' (line 42) fill his waking and his sleeping mind. For these critics, Wordsworth is not looking back and saying he was punished for stealing a boat. Rather he is suggesting that **the experience provided the means by which he learned how to turn the emotion of fear into a poetry of wonder**. The young Wordsworth is troubled at the end of the passage, not by guilt but by the limitations of his own understanding, by his inability to name the mighty forms and to understand the 'unknown modes of being' (line 37). In effect, the passage reveals his poetic task: the naming of the mysteries he senses in nature.

Other critics read the passage as **unconsciously dramatising a stage in Wordsworth's psychological development**. For them, the passage is **full of hidden emotional meaning**. According to this reading, the young boy is 'led' (line 1) by a permissive mother figure. The huge cliff that towers over the boy, and from which he flees in terror, is a projection of a stern father figure. The boy's pride in his skill and physical strength, 'lustily / I dipped my oars' (lines 17–18), is reduced to nothing. 'I struck and struck again' (line 24) suggests the boy's aggressive frustration with the intervention of the father figure. But the boy is powerless in the face of the towering figure. Confronted by it, his language is childlike. He describes it as 'black and huge' (line 22). The description of the 'trembling oars' (line 29) suggests what one critic called 'the boy's obscure sense of impending punishment'. In the **psychic drama of growing up**, the boy is not yet ready to challenge the power of the father. These critics often relate the passage to Wordsworth's biography, to the deaths of his mother when he was eight, and of his father when he was thirteen. **The mother and father figures that the poet finds in nature are substitutes for the parents he lost in childhood.**

However you interpret 'The Stolen Boat', you are likely to be struck by how **the boy's imagination transforms the lakeland scene into a fairy-tale world**. The small boat becomes an 'elfin pinnace' (line 17) 'heaving through the water like a swan' (line 20). The boat leaves a trail of 'sparkling light' (line 11) across the lake. The huge shape, when it appears, is like a giant or an ogre pursuing him to where he returns the boat. But what did the young boy see? What was it that his imagination turned into a 'grim shape' (line 25) that terrified him? The rising mountain was an optical illusion, **a trick of perspective**. The shadowy light increased the effect. As he rowed, the angle of vision increased and he could see beyond the ridge, where he had fixed his view to give himself a straight line. As the black shape of the mountain loomed in the darkness, he rowed more quickly, getting further away from it. However, because he was rowing facing backwards, the further away he got the more he could see the mountain rising higher and higher. This filled him with panic, because it seemed that the peak was coming after him. **The older Wordsworth was interested in the laws of physics and the way we perceive and understand the world.**

Form and language

This passage, like all of *The Prelude*, is written in blank verse, with an underlying pattern of iambic pentameter. The opening is **conversational** and the whole passage has a **confessional tone**, as if Wordsworth is sharing the experience with a good friend. If 'Skating' expressed a sense of movement and energy, 'Boating' conveys the heavy burden upon the boy as he tries to understand what happened.

The final ten lines move slowly, with a succession of stressed syllables, reflecting the images that 'moved slowly through the mind' (line 43). There are some brilliant choices of words. Take the choice of 'stole' (line 30), for example, to describe the boy's return of the boat to its shelter. It combines the idea of hiding with that of stealing. It hovers between describing an action and conveying the feelings of the person doing the action. The young boy only dimly understands what has happened and the language reflects this. The 'huge and mighty forms' (line 42) that fill his imagination are clouded in mystery and uncertainty and neither the narrator nor the reader knows who or what these beings are or what they represent. They remain 'undetermined' (line 36). Is this a failure of language or a successful presentation of the boy's confusion?

Questions

1	What, if any, is the significance of 'led by her' in the first line?
2	The boy has mixed feelings as he takes the boat. What are these?
3	As the boy begins his journey, he hears 'the voice / Of mountain-echoes' (lines 6–7). Why is this detail important?
4	What fairy-tale elements are present in the description of the scene?
5	What words and phrases suggest the boy's pride and pleasure in his rowing?
6	Describe the change of mood that overcomes the boy from line 22 on. As clearly as you can, explain what causes this change.
7	What makes the boy think of the black peak as 'a living thing' (line 28)?
8	What causes the boy to steal his way back to the mooring place?
9	Why is the boy 'in grave / And serious mood' (lines 33–34) as he makes his way home?
10	What, in your opinion, are the 'unknown modes of being' (line 37)?
11	How do you visualise the 'huge and mighty forms' mentioned in line 42?
12	In your view, are the last ten lines of the poem a brilliant account of the boy's confusion, or a failure on Wordsworth's part to clarify the boy's thoughts and feelings for the reader? Explain your answer.
13	Which of the following statements is closest to your understanding of the poem? ■ The poem is about guilt. ■ The poem is about the power of the imagination. ■ The poem is about facing up to your fears. ■ The poem is about being punished for doing wrong. Explain your answer.
14	'This is a simple poem. Nature, offended by the theft of the boat, intimidates the young thief and punishes him with bad dreams and unhappy feelings.' Discuss.
15	Using 'The Stolen Boat' as inspiration, write a descriptive piece that begins, 'I am haunted …'.

Lines composed a few miles above Tintern Abbey

Before you read

Nominate a place that has a special meaning for you and where you love to visit. Describe the effect that this place has on you. Share your experience with a partner.

Five years have passed; five summers, with the length
Of five long winters! and again I hear
These waters, rolling from their mountain-springs
With a soft inland murmur. – Once again
Do I behold these steep and lofty cliffs,   5
That on a wild secluded scene impress
Thoughts of more deep seclusion; and connect
The landscape with the quiet of the sky.
The day is come when I again repose
Here, under this dark sycamore, and view   10
These plots of cottage-ground, these orchard-tufts,
Which at this season, with their unripe fruits,
Are clad in one green hue, and lose themselves
'Mid groves and copses. Once again I see
These hedge-rows, hardly hedge-rows, little lines   15
Of sportive wood run wild: these pastoral farms,
Green to the very door; and wreaths of smoke
Sent up, in silence, from among the trees!
With some uncertain notice, as might seem
Of vagrant dwellers in the houseless woods,   20
Or of some Hermit's cave, where by his fire
The Hermit sits alone.
                    These beauteous forms,
Through a long absence, have not been to me
As is a landscape to a blind man's eye:
But oft, in lonely rooms, and 'mid the din   25
Of towns and cities, I have owed to them,
In hours of weariness, sensations sweet,
Felt in the blood, and felt along the heart;
And passing even into my purer mind,
With tranquil restoration – feelings too   30
Of unremembered pleasure: such, perhaps,
As have no slight or trivial influence
On that best portion of a good man's life,
His little, nameless, unremembered, acts
Of kindness and of love. Nor less, I trust,   35
To them I may have owed another gift,
Of aspect more sublime; that blessed mood,
In which the burthen of the mystery,
In which the heavy and the weary weight

Of all this unintelligible world,   40
Is lightened: – that serene and blessed mood,
In which the affections gently lead us on, –
Until, the breath of this corporeal frame
And even the motion of our human blood
Almost suspended, we are laid asleep   45
In body, and become a living soul:
While with an eye made quiet by the power
Of harmony, and the deep power of joy,
We see into the life of things.
                     If this
Be but a vain belief, yet oh! how oft –   50
In darkness and amid the many shapes
Of joyless daylight; when the fretful stir
Unprofitable, and the fever of the world,
Have hung upon the beating of my heart –
How oft, in spirit, have I turned to thee,   55
O sylvan Wye! thou wanderer thro' the woods,
How often has my spirit turned to thee!

And now, with gleams of half-extinguished thought,
With many recognitions dim and faint,
And somewhat of a sad perplexity,   60
The picture of the mind revives again:
While here I stand, not only with the sense
Of present pleasure, but with pleasing thoughts
That in this moment there is life and food
For future years. And so I dare to hope,   65
Though changed, no doubt, from what I was when first
I came among these hills; when like a roe
I bounded o'er the mountains, by the sides
Of the deep rivers, and the lonely streams,
Wherever nature led: more like a man   70
Flying from something that he dreads than one
Who sought the thing he loved. For nature then
(The coarser pleasures of my boyish days,
And their glad animal movements all gone by)
To me was all in all. – I cannot paint   75
What then I was. The sounding cataract
Haunted me like a passion: the tall rock,
The mountain, and the deep and gloomy wood,
Their colours and their forms, were then to me
An appetite, a feeling and a love,   80
That had no need to a remoter charm,
By thought supplied, nor any interest
Unborrowed from the eye. – That time is past,

And all its aching joys are now no more,
And all its dizzy raptures. Not for this   85
Faint I, nor mourn nor murmur; other gifts
Have followed; for such loss, I would believe,
Abundant recompense. For I have learned
To look on nature, not as in the hour
Of thoughtless youth; but hearing oftentimes   90
The still, sad music of humanity,
Nor harsh nor grating, though of ample power
To chasten and subdue. And I have felt
A presence that disturbs me with the joy
Of elevated thoughts; a sense sublime   95
Of something far more deeply interfused,
Whose dwelling is the light of setting suns,
And the round ocean and the living air,
And the blue sky, and in the mind of man –
A motion and a spirit, that impels   100
All thinking things, all objects of all thought,
And rolls through all things. Therefore am I still
A lover of the meadows and the woods,
And mountains; and of all that we behold
From this green earth; of all the mighty world   105
Of eye, and ear, – both what they half-create,
And what perceive; well pleased to recognise
In nature and the language of the sense
The anchor of my purest thoughts, the nurse,
The guide, the guardian of my heart, and soul   110
Of all my moral being.
                  Nor perchance,
If I were not thus taught, should I the more
Suffer my genial spirits to decay:
For thou art with me here upon the banks
Of this fair river; thou my dearest Friend,   115
My dear, dear Friend; and in thy voice I catch
The language of my former heart, and read
My former pleasures in the shooting lights
Of thy wild eyes. Oh! yet a little while
May I behold in thee what I was once,   120
My dear, dear Sister! and this prayer I make,
Knowing that Nature never did betray
The heart that loved her; 'tis her privilege,
Through all the years of this our life, to lead
From joy to joy: for she can so inform   125
The mind that is within us, so impress
With quietness and beauty, and so feed
With lofty thoughts, that neither evil tongues,

Rash judgments, nor the sneers of selfish men,
Nor greetings where no kindness is, nor all   130
The dreary intercourse of daily life,
Shall e'er prevail against us, or disturb
Our cheerful faith, that all which we behold
Is full of blessings. Therefore let the moon
Shine on thee in thy solitary walk;   135
And let the misty mountain-winds be free
To blow against thee: and, in after years,
When these wild ecstasies shall be matured
Into a sober pleasure; when thy mind
Shall be a mansion for all lovely forms,   140
Thy memory be as a dwelling-place
For all sweet sounds and harmonies; oh! then,
If solitude, or fear, or pain, or grief,
Should be thy portion, with what healing thoughts
Of tender joy wilt thou remember me,   145
And these my exhortations! Nor, perchance –
If I should be where I no more can hear
Thy voice, nor catch from thy wild eyes these gleams
Of past existence – wilt thou then forget
That on the banks of this delightful stream   150
We stood together; and that I, so long
A worshipper of Nature, hither came
Unwearied in that service: rather say
With warmer love – oh! with far deeper zeal
Of holier love. Nor wilt thou then forget   155
That after many wanderings, many years
Of absence, these steep woods and lofty cliffs,
And this green pastoral landscape, were to me
More dear, both for themselves and for thy sake!

Glossary

Title	
	Tintern Abbey: ruined Cistercian monastery on the banks of the River Wye, south Wales
7	*seclusion*: peacefulness; privacy
9	*repose*: rest
14	*groves and copses*: trees and woodlands
16	*sportive*: playful
37	*sublime*: noble
38	*burthen*: burden
43	*corporeal frame*: body
56	*sylvan*: of the woodlands
76	*cataract*: waterfall
88	*recompense*: reward
93	*chasten*: punish
96	*interfused*: joined together
113	*genial*: cheerful
115	*dearest Friend*: Dorothy (the poet's sister)
146	*exhortations*: strong encouragements
154	*zeal*: warm enthusiasm

Guidelines

This poem was written in 1798 and is the last poem in the collection *Lyrical Ballads*. It was written after Wordsworth had sent the rest of the book to the printers. Having finished the book (as he thought), Wordsworth and Dorothy went on a walking tour of the Wye Valley. On the way back from Tintern Abbey, he was inspired to write a poem and composed it over the next three days. When it was finished he rushed it to the printers, without making any alterations, and asked them to include it in the collection. Later he said that 'No poem of mine was composed under circumstances more pleasant to me than this.' Like *The Prelude*, 'Lines composed a few miles above Tintern Abbey' is a record of Wordsworth's developing imagination, his relationship with nature and the changing character of that relationship. Coming back to a landscape that he loves, the poet reviews the changes that have taken place in his feelings and outlook since his previous visit.

> **Religious belief**
>
> **Wordsworth was neither a philosopher nor a systematic thinker. He had a strong sense of encountering the divine in nature. At times, it seems as if nature is God, as here in 'Tintern Abbey'. In the sonnet 'It is a beauteous evening', the ideas appear more like orthodox Christianity, an impression reinforced by the biblical references.**

Commentary

Lines 1–22

The opening section establishes the setting of the poem, the Wye Valley, and the fact that the poet is revisiting it after an absence of five years. The speaker's joy in returning to this secluded spot is evident. Interestingly, the speaker refers to 'vagrant dwellers in the houseless woods' (line 20) and the poverty suggested by them but does not mention them again in the poem. Instead, the poem concentrates on the 'beauteous forms' of nature (line 22).

Lines 22–49

In the intervening years the speaker has remembered the Wye Valley with pleasure. The memories have given him comfort in times of depression. They may even have influenced him to act with kindness and love towards others. He believes these memories have allowed him, on occasions, to enter into a mood of trance-like contemplation, in which, filled with a sense of harmony and joy, he could look deeply 'into the life of things' (line 50) and be blessed with understanding.

Lines 49–57

The speaker wonders if his belief in nature and the power of memory is false and conceited. But he quickly reassures himself and, personifying the River Wye and speaking directly to her, says how often he has turned to her for comfort when he has felt depressed.

Lines 58–67

Surveying the scene, the speaker experiences a sad confusion in the difference between what he remembered and the actual place he encounters. However, as he takes in the landscape he realises that he is creating new memories that will offer sustenance in future years. This is what he hopes, although he knows that he has changed from when he first saw these hills.

Lines 67–111

When he first came to the Wye, nature was everything to him and he loved it with a passion that needed no justification or explanation supplied by the intellect. He recognises now that the joys and raptures of that time are gone, but he does not mourn them because other gifts have followed. One of these is a sympathetic understanding of human sadness. The second is an awareness of a presence of a spirt that is everywhere in the world and in the human mind and which provides the energy for 'all things' (line 102). For this reason, he still loves nature and all that his senses perceive and half-create. And he recognises that nature, and the senses through which he perceives it, is the foundation of his purest thoughts, his guide and the guardian of his heart, his soul and his moral being.

Lines 111–146

Even if he had not been taught by nature, he would not lose heart because his dearest friend is with him. And he sees his former self in his sister. In looking at Dorothy, he relives his past and hopes he may do so for a little while yet. And he prays, confident that nature never betrays those who love her, that his sister will be blessed. And he hopes that in years to come, when her 'wild ecstasies' (line 138) have given way to 'sober pleasure' (line 139), she will remember him and his prayers and this day and these memories might serve to heal any sorrow that overcomes her.

Lines 146–159

The speaker thinks of his own death and asks his sister not to forget that they stood here on the banks of this river together, and that he came as a worshipper of nature. And he asks her not to forget that, after many years away, this landscape was more precious to him, both for itself and for the fact that she was with him.

Themes and imagery

The opening lines describe what the speaker surveys: the 'steep and lofty cliffs' (line 5), the 'dark sycamore' (line 10) and the 'orchard-tufts' (line 11). However, once the setting has been established, for a poem that **celebrates nature**, there is little description of the landscape of the Wye Valley. What is more evident in the poem is the **landscape of the mind**. The poem lists the speaker's mood, feelings, ideas, memories, hopes, and fears.

This poem is **personal, autobiographical and philosophical**. It offers **a summary history of the development of the poet's imagination** and explores **the relationship between the poet's mind and nature**. The poem expresses Wordsworth's belief in the therapeutic power of memory. In revisiting the much-loved and remembered landscape of the Wye Valley, the poet hopes he will give himself emotional and intellectual comfort for the years to come. Coming back to the Wye Valley is a kind of renewal for him. It brings out the best in him and fills his heart with a feeling of generosity, not just for the natural world but also for his fellow human beings.

For Wordsworth, **the relationship between nature, in all its forms and meanings, and the heart and mind of the person who contemplates it, is benevolent**. As he tells his sister, 'all which we behold / Is full of blessings' (lines 133–134). These blessings, accessed through memory, are described in the passage between lines 25 and 49. One blessing is the 'tranquil restoration' (line 30) of his body and his mind after weariness. Wordsworth suggests that the blessings he receives may work in unconscious ways, influencing him to perform 'little, nameless, unremembered, acts / Of kindness and of love' (lines 34–35). The most important gift that

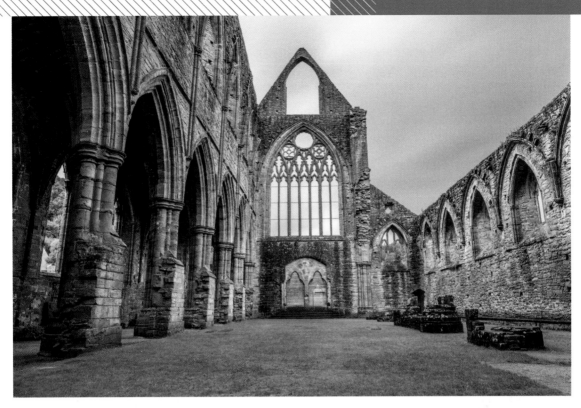

Wordsworth owes to the 'beauteous forms' (line 22) imprinted on his mind is the deepest of all his experiences – a trance-like state of calm serenity when, with a feeling of joy and harmony, he acquires the visionary power to 'see into the life of things' (line 49). Wordsworth immediately questions whether this is a 'vain belief' (line 50), something foolish and conceited. In one of the most celebrated passages of the poem (lines 93–102), Wordsworth expresses his belief in the presence of a life force that exists in both the human mind and in nature and which unites them. For him, this energy, this spirit (which in later life he referred to as God), pervades and sustains everything in the world. Interestingly, the use of the phrase 'A worshipper of Nature' (line 152) was one the poet later regretted. In a letter written sixteen years after he wrote 'Tintern Abbey' he claimed that this was 'a passionate expression used incautiously', and that he had not intended to make a god of nature.

An interesting idea occurs in the passage between lines 102 and 111. Wordsworth says that he is a lover of 'all the mighty world / Of eye, and ear, – both what they half-create, / And what perceive'. This suggests that the world we internalise in our minds is not simply the product of perception, of our sense, but is, in part, a creation, a product of imagination and perception combined.

A key component in the poem is the question of time. In returning to the Wye Valley, Wordsworth is aware that he is growing older. In one sense, the poem is a way of **rationalising the effects of time and the losses he suffers as time marches on**. The presence of Dorothy is a living reminder of what he once was but also of what he has lost. The **role of Dorothy** in the poem is interesting. She is the unspeaking companion of the poet. She is also a point of reference for some of the main concerns of the poem, helping Wordsworth to identify more precisely some of his earlier attitudes, 'in thy voice I catch / The language of my former heart' (lines 116–117). Dorothy takes the same instinctive pleasure in natural things that he once felt: a delight that has nothing to do with thought, but is formed of pure joy and affection. There is no doubt that the Dorothy of the poem is in part a self-projection of the poet. However, equally, there can be no doubting the genuine affection he has for his sister. His hopes for her are what he hopes for himself, that memory will be 'as a dwelling-place / For all sweet sounds and harmonies' (lines 141–142) that will sustain and comfort her. His fears for her are the same as his fears for himself: loss of youth and memory. Some critics do not read the final section of the poem in this sympathetic way. For them, the poem is another example of Wordsworth's unwillingness or failure to create a substantial and credible female presence in his poetry.

Form and language

Wordsworth's method

Dorothy described her brother's way of composing a poem: 'At present he is walking, and has been out of doors these two hours though it has rained heavily all the morning. In wet weather he takes out an umbrella, chooses the most sheltered spot, and there walks backwards and forwards, and though the length of his walk may be sometimes a quarter or half a mile, he is as fast bound within the chosen limits as if by prison walls. He generally composes his verses out of doors, and while he is so engaged he seldom knows how the time slips away, or hardly whether it is rain or fair.'

'Tintern Abbey' is **a dramatic lyric in which the speaker addresses his own mind**. In one passage, as in a classical ode, he addresses the River Wye as a spirit in nature. Towards the end of the poem, the poet addresses Dorothy, his sister and companion. The poem is written in unrhymed iambic pentameter, considered the most suitable form of verse for a long, philosophical work. The great benefit of blank verse is that it is fluid and flexible and allows ideas to develop without being forced into a rhyming scheme or shaped into the form of a stanza. The voiced thoughts of the poet sound **natural and conversational, though heightened and carefully constructed**. For the most part, the language is plain and unadorned and from the heart. This is not to say that the thoughts of the speaker are simple or easy to follow. They are not. But neither are they expressed in language that is complex or convoluted.

What is most striking is the **beauty of the language when the poem is read aloud**. See, for example, lines 93–102, a hymn to the unity of nature with humanity, and the internal mind with the external world. These ten lines form one sentence, where the thought expands and develops across and within lines. Like a piece of symphonic music, the **sounds swell up and out**, in sweet and full phrases. Sounds echo and repeat. There is a succession of beautiful-sounding noun phrases: 'the light of setting suns', 'the round ocean', 'the living air', 'the blue sky', 'the mind of man'. These are the places where the 'presence' (line 94) is found. The brilliant placing of the verb 'impels' at the end of line 100 pushes the rhythm forward and mirrors the energy, the spirit and the motion that he is describing. And then there is the **impressive phrasing** and the **choice of simple words to convey complex ideas**. Look, for example, at the movement from physical feeling to thought, and the interesting association of 'joy' with 'disturbs' in 'I have felt / A presence that disturbs me with the joy / Of elevated thoughts' (lines 93–95). It is a rich and stimulating use of language.

Throughout the poem there are **changes in tone and mood**. The speaker is lyrical and expressive. His voice is earnest and thoughtful. On occasions, the language conveys an underlying sadness in phrases such as 'in lonely rooms' (line 25), 'hours of weariness' (line 27) and 'joyless daylight' (line 52). Towards the end there is a note of urgency that borders on desperation, 'and this prayer I make, / Knowing that Nature never did betray / The heart that loved her' (lines 121–123). As the poem moves towards its conclusion, the language borrows from the phrasing and vocabulary of Christian prayer: 'evil tongues' (line 128), 'Rash judgments' (line 129), 'Shall e'er prevail against us' (line 132), 'dwelling-place' (line 141), 'deeper zeal / Of holier love' (lines 154–155).

Questions

1	Suggest why the 'vagrant dwellers in the houseless woods' (line 20) mentioned by the speaker in the opening section of the poem are not referred to again.
2	What does Wordsworth claim he owes to the memory of the beautiful landscape of the Wye Valley in lines 22–49?
3	As clearly as you can, explain the 'blessed mood' (line 37) of which Wordsworth speaks.
4	Does Wordsworth fully believe in the power of nature and memory to restore and sustain an individual's physical, emotional, intellectual and spiritual well-being, do you think? Explain your answer.
5	What is the 'sad perplexity' that the speaker experiences (line 60)?
6	Comment on the phrase 'The still, sad music of humanity' (line 91) and what it suggests about Wordsworth's attitude to life.
7	What difference is there between the youthful Wordsworth's relationship with nature and the relationship of his more mature self?
8	What do you understand by the term 'presence' in the passage beginning, 'And I have felt / A presence …' (lines 93–102)?
9	Would you say that the end of the poem is an honest tribute to the poet's sister, or is it a failure to bring her to life in her own right? Explain your answer.
10	Why, do you think, does Wordsworth call himself 'A worshipper of Nature' (line 152)?
11	Which of the following statements is closest to your understanding of the poem? ■ It is a poem about the beauty of nature. ■ It is a poem about memory. ■ It is a poem about the divine in nature. ■ It is a poem about unity in all things. Explain your choice, discussing each statement in turn.
12	'In "Tintern Abbey" Wordsworth creates a world which is a reflection of his own mind.' Discuss this view of the poem.
13	Nature is presented in the poem in many different guises (as comforter, source of visual delight, mystical presence …). Identify as many of these as you can.
14	Discuss 'Tintern Abbey' under the title 'Loss and Gain'.
15	Might Wordsworth fairly be described as a prophet of modern environmentalism? Why?
16	How old, do you think, was Wordsworth when he wrote this poem: 28, 48, 68? Give a reason for your answer. Then check the biography to establish his age.
17	Would you have enjoyed going on a walking tour with Wordsworth? Explain.
18	'This is where I long to be.' Using this line as your inspiration, write a description of a favourite place (real or imagined) that is an escape from the worries and frustrations of daily life.

Exam-Preparation Questions

1	Discuss the view that William Wordsworth's poetry is largely the history of his own mind and displays a concentrated self-absorption.
2	'Wordsworth is fascinated by the power of nature to affect his thoughts and feelings.' Discuss the meaning and significance of nature in the poems by William Wordsworth on your course.
3	'We admire Wordsworth's poetry for its honesty, its seriousness and its hopefulness in the face of fear and loneliness.' Discuss this statement, supporting your answer with reference to the poetry of William Wordsworth on your course.
4	'Wordsworth creates memorable and dramatic scenes to convey his ideas on the relationship between nature and the individual mind.' To what extent do you agree or disagree with this statement? Support your answer with reference to the poetry of William Wordsworth on your course.
5	'We read Wordsworth's poems as much for the beauty of the language as for the ideas they explore.' Discuss this view of William Wordsworth. Support your answer with reference to the poems on your course.
6	Trace William Wordsworth's belief in the power of nature to nurture the human heart and influence moral development in both 'Tintern Abbey' and the two passages from *The Prelude* on your course.
7	William Wordsworth is often described as a decidedly 'modern' poet. Consider some features of his poetry that you think might justify this description.
8	Do his poems suggest that William Wordsworth had a generally optimistic outlook? Support your answer with references to the poems on your course.
9	Wordsworth said that the praise he wanted most was from readers whose suffering he had helped to lighten. To what extent do you believe that William Wordsworth's poetry has the power to heal and is still relevant to readers today? Support your answer with reference to the poems on your course.
10	Write an essay in which you give your reasons for liking and/or not liking the poetry of William Wordsworth. Support your answer with reference to the poems on your course. Here are some reasons you might give for liking Wordsworth's poetry: ■ His poems are wonderfully written ■ His poems convey a deep feeling for the natural world ■ His poems make the beauty of the world alive for the reader ■ His poems give a vivid impression of his personality and ideas ■ He conveys complex meanings in a language that is clear and simple. Here are some reasons you might give for not liking Wordsworth's poetry: ■ His poems have little appeal for modern readers living in towns and cities ■ His poems are too focused on himself ■ His poems lack either wit or humour and are too solemn and serious ■ His ideas on nature are confused and confusing.

11 Using the word cloud as a guide, write an essay giving your personal response to the poetry of William Wordsworth on your course.

SNAPSHOT WILLIAM WORDSWORTH

- Autobiographical poet
- Poems often based on real incidents and feature real people
- Importance of childhood experiences of nature
- His sister, Dorothy, is a presence in his poetry
- Dramatic quality to his writing
- Poems trace his emotional, intellectual and spiritual growth
- Philosophical poet
- Elevated thoughts are expressed in plain language

- Unashamed love of and delight in nature
- Beautiful landscapes and memories are central to his poetry
- Poems record his changing relationship with nature
- Belief in the power of nature to nurture human goodness
- Sees nature in divine terms
- Beauty and harmony in the language of the poetry

Sample Essay

'The bond between the poet and Nature is at the heart of Wordsworth's poetry.' Discuss this statement, supporting your answer with reference to the poetry of William Wordsworth on your course.

Addresses question in first line

Clarifies key term in the question

It is almost impossible to disagree with this statement. However, the definition of 'Nature' lies at the heart of the discussion. We cannot speak of a bond between the poet and Nature if we think of Nature simply as trees, flowers, streams, waterfalls and mountains, as 'all which we behold', as Wordsworth puts it in 'Lines composed a few miles above Tintern Abbey' (hereafter 'Tintern Abbey'). For Wordsworth, Nature is a larger and more universal force than a collection of beautiful sights.

Strikes appropriate tone

'Tintern Abbey' is a good place to start examining the bond between Wordsworth and Nature. In this dramatic lyric he claims that the 'mighty world / Of eye, and ear' is sustained by a force capable of restoring his distracted mind to tranquillity and harmony, of making him feel at one with the whole universe, uniting 'All thinking things' and 'all objects of all thought'. For Wordsworth, it is Nature that puts him in tune with the 'still, sad music of humanity'. As he describes it, Nature is both an energy and a presence that 'rolls through all things'. Wordsworth insists that he recognises Nature as his moral guardian, a positive influence on him and on all good people who love her as he does. For him, Nature is: 'The anchor of my purest thoughts, the nurse, / The guide, the guardian of my heart, and soul / Of all my moral being'. According to his argument, Nature influences conduct in a fundamental way, acting on that 'best portion of a good man's life' to bring forth 'His little, nameless, unremembered, acts / Of kindness and of love'.

Good distribution of quotations through the answer

Does the student need to offer more of his/her personal views?

In 'Tintern Abbey Wordsworth argues that all the benign effects that he identifies are brought about by the contemplation of the 'beauteous forms' of external Nature, as found in the landscape surrounding the River Wye, and the recollection of these years later 'in lonely rooms', and 'mid the din / Of towns and cities'. It is a big claim to make and Wordsworth has some moments of doubt about its validity. But he keeps his faith with Nature.

Avoids giving summaries

In an important sense, the bond between Wordsworth and Nature is similar to that between a religious worshipper and the god he or she worships. In 'Tintern Abbey' he declares himself 'A worshipper of Nature' and he uses religious terms to express his faith. The language in the final section of the poem borrows terms from Christianity: 'this prayer I make', 'Our cheerful faith', 'all which we behold / Is full of blessings', 'Unwearied in that service', 'with far deeper zeal / Of holier love'. As in Christianity, Wordsworth believes that the spirit of his god is present in him. This spirit unites Wordsworth with all of creation. Its dwelling is 'the light of setting suns, / And the round ocean and the living air, / And the blue sky'. Above all, it lives 'in mind of man'. The spirit that unites Wordsworth, and humankind in general, with all the rest of Nature, which 'rolls through all things', is like a god who cannot be separated from any part of her creation, who is everywhere and who cannot be thought of as distinct.

Takes on the ideas in the poem

Tone and register is appropriate

Returns to theme of the question → 'Tintern Abbey' is the finest expression of the bond that exists between the poet and Nature. However, this bond is also at the heart of 'The Stolen Boat' episode of *The Prelude*. Here Wordsworth develops the idea that even in youth he could not break the bond uniting him to Nature. *← Introduces second poem into the discussion*

Distinguishes between the poems → The aspect of Nature considered in this context is its powerful moral influence, its role as the conscience of the individual. The incident recalled in the episode is simple, even commonplace. The young Wordsworth steals a boat in a mood of 'troubled pleasure'. It is not long before Nature asserts its influence as his guide and conscience. The point made by the episode is that to break the moral law, in this case by stealing a boat, is to break the bond with Nature. This point is dramatically enforced when Nature impresses on his mind, emotions and imagination *← Careful phrasing* a sense of the wrong he has done. As he rows along, 'A huge peak, black and huge, / As if with voluntary power instinct / Upreared its head'. His fear intensifies as the *← Uses quotations throughout answer* peak, 'With measured motion like a living thing', seems to follow him. In 'Tintern Abbey' Nature operates to inspire people to perform deeds 'Of kindness and of love'. In 'The

Contrasts one poem with another → Stolen Boat' its function is sterner. Here the spirit of Nature chastises the boy for the theft of the boat and deepens his sense of right and wrong. The bond between the young Wordsworth and Nature in this poem is like that between a teacher and an erring pupil who is forced to learn a lesson. His experience of the sinister peak leaves a deep impression on his mind and imagination, as 'huge and mighty forms' 'Like living men moved slowly through the mind / By day, and were a trouble to my dreams.'

Wordsworth's sense of his intimate bond with Nature convinces him that what happened as he rowed the stolen boat had a meaning for him: whether as a message, a revelation or a warning.

Is there enough discussion? → In the 'Skating' episode from *The Prelude* Wordsworth describes a parallel experience: a sense that the solitary cliffs wheeled by him, as if the earth had rolled 'With visible motion her diurnal round'. Again, he experiences a living connection with Nature. The Earth was not a ball of matter moving mechanically through space, but a living being with feeling and sense, a mysterious presence to whom he felt himself bound.

Wordsworth's sense of an intimate relationship with the natural world is conveyed in one of his brightest and most optimistic poems, 'To My Sister'. Wordsworth invites his sister to abandon the indoors and spend the day with him in the open air. In this, as in his other Nature poems, he sees

Keeps to the theme but broadens the idea → his bond with Nature as if it were one between two living beings, with Nature as the giver of gifts and he as the grateful recipient. He experiences the 'blessing in the air' that also gives joy to 'the bare trees, and mountains bare'. The bond between Nature and himself, the lover of Nature, is best described in terms of a universal relationship of love:

> Love, now a universal birth,
> From heart to heart is stealing,
> From earth to man, from man to earth:
> – It is the hour of feeling.

The bond Wordsworth has in mind is a happy one for the poet, and a beneficial one. It enables his sister and himself to 'drink at every pore / The spirit of the season'. Those in communion with Nature are in tune with 'the blessed power that rolls / About, below, above'. The bond between

The idea of a cheerful faith is interesting. Is it sufficiently developed?

such people and Nature, as Wordsworth recognises, is one of love. It impresses on his mind feelings of quietness and beauty, and, as he puts it in 'Tintern Abbey', is the foundation of a 'cheerful faith, that all which we behold / Is full of blessings'.

Shows relevant background knowledge

In the sonnet written on Calais beach ('It is a beauteous evening …') the sense of the bond between the poet and Nature is particularly strong. Again, as in 'Tintern Abbey', the bond has a strong religious character. The beauty and tranquillity of the scene fills Wordsworth with a sense that Nature, 'the mighty Being', is to be worshipped. This idea is conveyed in the image of a praying nun: 'The holy time is as quiet as a Nun / Breathless with adoration'. Wordsworth believes himself to be in communication with a kindly being as

Is this the best choice of quotation to close the essay?

he contemplates Nature, which in this poem, as the final line suggests ('God being with thee'), is a reflection of a divine power whose essence is everlasting beauty: 'The gentleness of heaven broods o'er the Sea.'

Is the conclusion too brief?

In conclusion, as this brief survey of a selection of Wordsworth's poems demonstrates, there can be no doubt that the bond between the poet and Nature is at the heart of Wordsworth's poetry.

ESSAY CHECKLIST		Yes √	No ×
Purpose	Has the candidate understood the task?		
	Has the candidate responded to it in a thoughtful manner?		
	Has the candidate answered the question?		
Comment:			
Coherence	Has the candidate made convincing arguments?		
	Has the candidate linked ideas?		
	Does the essay have a sense of unity?		
Comment:			
Language	Is the essay written in an appropriate register?		
	Are ideas expressed in a clear way?		
	Is the writing fluent?		
Comment:			
Mechanics	Is the use of language accurate?		
	Are all words spelled correctly?		
	Does the punctuation help the reader?		
Comment:			

W. B. Yeats

1865–1939

Biography

Family and childhood

William Butler Yeats was born on 13 June 1865 in Sandymount, Dublin. His father, John Butler Yeats, was an artist from an Anglo-Irish Protestant family that had come to Ireland from the north of England in the seventeenth century. He was sociable, free-thinking, a great reader and talker, and encouraged his children's creativity. W. B.'s mother, Susan, came from the wealthy Pollexfen family who were merchants in Sligo. They were practical, hard-headed people, not given to showing emotion. Yeats always believed that the contradictions he saw in his own nature came from the conflict of those two very different family influences.

Much of Yeats's childhood was spent in London, where his father was trying to make a career as an artist. He had no great success as he found it hard to bring himself to finish a painting, so the family was always short of money. They spent holidays – and the children often longer periods – with the Pollexfens in Co. Sligo. Though Yeats was not always happy there, he came to love the place. The family left London for Dublin in 1881, and it was here that Yeats attended first High School and then the Metropolitan School of Art.

Becoming a poet

Yeats was writing poetry and plays from his teenage years, with his father's encouragement. As a young man he became deeply involved in two areas that were to be constant throughout his life.

The first was mysticism and the occult. His father's atheism had undermined any Christian faith in him, but Yeats always felt a strong hunger for the spiritual, and he joined mystical orders and spiritualist groups, in Dublin and in London. Eventually he developed his own occult philosophy and mythology, discussed below (page 436).

Maud Gonne.

The second was Irish nationalism. Yeats was in his twenties at an exciting time in Ireland. Parnell had helped to make Home Rule for Ireland the dominant political issue in Britain and Ireland. Yeats's main influence here was John O'Leary, the Fenian leader, whom he met in 1886. Yeats joined the Irish Republican Brotherhood, of which O'Leary had been an influential member, and O'Leary encouraged Yeats to understand **the importance of Ireland's cultural heritage of myth, poetry and folktales in helping forge a new Irish identity**. Throughout his life, as poet, theatre manager and senator, Yeats was always concerned with the ways in which art and literature could help to shape modern Ireland.

The Yeats family moved back to London in 1887, and it was there in 1889 that he met Maud Gonne. It was the moment when, as he said, 'the troubling of my life began'. She was tall, strikingly beautiful and he fell utterly in love with her. They became close friends, but she didn't want the relationship to go any further. He proposed marriage several times but she always turned him down.

Her passionate Irish nationalism spurred his own political interests, although they often disagreed. She inspired his poetry and he wrote the play *The Countess Cathleen* for her to star in.

The poetry he wrote in these early years is dominated by **Celtic myths, melancholy and unrequited love**. There is **a rich play of sounds and hypnotic rhythms**, and the poems make use of striking, sometimes mysterious, adjectives. 'The Lake Isle of Innisfree' is the only poem of this period included in the selection we are studying.

Maturity

Yeats continued to spend periods of time in London, but it was back in Ireland in 1896 that he met Lady Augusta Gregory, whose Coole Park estate in Co. Galway was to become a refuge and an inspiration to him over many years. She encouraged his interest in Irish folktales, and he wrote many of his finest poems while he was a guest in her house, where he often stayed for long periods. They also collaborated in setting up the Abbey Theatre in Dublin in 1905, for which Yeats wrote many plays. In 1917 Yeats bought Thoor Ballylee, an old Norman tower close to Lady Gregory's estate.

> **Yeats on rhythm**
>
> 'The purpose of rhythm, it has always seemed to me, is to prolong the moment of contemplation, the moment when we are both asleep and awake, which is the one moment of creation, by hushing us with an alluring monotony, while it holds us waking by variety, to keep us in that state of perhaps real trance, in which the mind liberated from the pressure of the will is unfolded in symbols.'
>
> **Yeats, 'The Symbolism of Poetry' (1900)**

The publication of the collection *Responsibilities* in 1916 was a landmark. The poems in it (including 'September 1913') were less elaborate than his early work and **more engaged with public life**. The title of the volume hints at Yeats's new sense of what he felt a poet should be. But although he was now an established writer, he was in his fifties and still single. The poem 'Wild Swans at Coole' is full of the loneliness he felt. He was determined to marry.

Yeats again proposed to Maud Gonne, whose estranged husband, Major John McBride, had been executed for his part in the Easter Rising of 1916. When he was turned down, he proposed to her daughter, Iseult, and was refused by her also. In September 1917 he proposed to Georgie Hyde-Lees, who was twenty-five. She accepted him and they were married the next month. They had two children: Anne, born in 1919, and Michael, born in 1921.

Settling into old age

These were years when **Yeats came into his power**. Following the establishment of the Irish Free State in 1922, he was made a senator and bought a house in Dublin's Merrion Square. In 1923 he was awarded the Nobel Prize for Literature. 'I feel I have become a personage,' he remarked.

He was also writing his finest poetry. His marriage gave him renewed energy, and although his body was getting weaker, his mind and his passions were unflagging. His poetry became **more vigorous and assured**, stripped of the adjectives and rich sound patterns that marked his earlier work. The collections *The Tower* (1928) and *The Winding Stair* (1933) are generally considered his greatest achievements. He said himself, reflecting on the melancholy and weariness felt in his early poems, that when he was young his Muse was old, **but as he grew older, his Muse grew younger**.

Yeats's bones

In accordance with local French custom, a few years after Yeats was buried, his remains were taken from the ground and his bones put in an ossuary (bone house) along with those of many others. It has recently been revealed that the French diplomat who was sent to collect Yeats's bones on behalf of the Irish government declared that it was impossible to know for certain which bones belonged to the poet, but a skeleton was assembled and the coffin sealed shut to be taken to Ireland.

During the 1930s he spent more time abroad, in Italy and France especially, for the sake of his health. In 1934 he had what was known as a Steinach operation – a partial vasectomy that was meant to increase the patient's energy. Yeats certainly believed that it worked for him. He kept on writing to the end of his life. His final, posthumous *Last Poems* (1940) are full of passion and rage – which he calls in 'An Acre of Grass' 'an old man's frenzy'. They are also more frankly sexual than anything he had written before.

Yeats became ill in the south of France and died on 28 January 1939. He was buried in France, but after the Second World War his remains were taken back to Ireland and buried, as he had wished, in Drumcliff churchyard, Co. Sligo.

Social and Cultural Context

The Irish Literary Revival

Irish language revival

The Irish Literary Revival with which Yeats was involved was an English-language movement. It ran in parallel with other movements aimed at reviving the Irish language and culture, such as the Gaelic League and the Gaelic Athletic Association. There was often hostility between the two camps. Patrick Pearse said the Irish Literary Theatre should be 'strangled at birth'.

Yeats was at the centre of a movement in the late nineteenth and early twentieth centuries to revive interest in Ireland's heritage of myth, folklore and fairy tale, and to **renew the sense of a culture that was specifically Irish**. As a young man, he helped to set up Irish literary societies in both Dublin and London. John O'Leary was an inspiration, and in 1893 Yeats published *The Celtic Twilight*, a collection of folklore and fairy tales from the west of Ireland, which gave the movement the nickname by which it was often known. It was the same impulse to create a specifically Irish culture that was behind the establishment of the Irish Literary Theatre, which led to the founding of the Abbey Theatre.

Irish history

Yeats came to manhood and lived most of his adult life in exciting but turbulent times for Ireland. As noted above, the question of Home Rule and Irish independence dominated politics until he was well into his fifties. He was **a committed nationalist**, but **distrusted the use of violence** and the idea of 'blood sacrifice' that lay behind the Easter Rising of 1916. He **distanced himself from organised politics**, and was saddened when Maud Gonne and other friends threw their energies into it so completely. When the First World War ended in 1918, the violence of the War of Independence (1919–21) was followed by that of the Civil War (1922–23). These events all had a profound effect upon Yeats's mind and his poetry. Some of his finest poems were written in response to the upheavals of these years, and he found a way of writing about public events that didn't put his poetry at the service of any political grouping. Instead, **he wove these events**, and those that took part in them, **into a new mythology of Ireland**. As a renowned Irish poet, and as someone who had always looked to explore and encourage a specifically Irish culture, he believed he had a responsibility as a shaper of modern Ireland. His verdict on the Easter Rising in 'Easter 1916' – 'A terrible beauty is born' – did much to determine how that event was understood.

Ben Bulben – Yeats spent his childhood summers in Co. Sligo.

Anglo-Irish heritage

Yeats's reactions to political events in Ireland were complicated by the fact that, although he was a nationalist himself, he was the product of a Protestant Anglo-Irish culture whose values, and even existence, were threatened by the nationalist tide.

As a young man his Anglo-Irish roots had not been of particular interest to him. Although the Yeatses claimed distant relationship with the Dukes of Ormonde, they were not part of the wealthy land-owning elite. However, Yeats got a glimpse of that life as a young man at Lissadell in Co. Sligo (see 'In Memory of Eva Gore-Booth and Con Markiewicz'), and as a guest and close friend of Lady Gregory at Coole Park he experienced the country-house life, and came to cherish the values it stood for and the culture of which it was part.

He was proud of the part that the Anglo-Irish had played in Irish history: not only Wolfe Tone, Robert Emmett and Edward Fitzgerald (see 'September 1913'), but also Parnell, as well as Maud Gonne and Con Markiewicz, came from that stock. He felt that the Anglo-Irish had contributed a great deal to Irish culture, and that that contribution should be acknowledged and respected, rather than swept away in the new, post-independence Ireland. In his later years he came especially to value the contribution of eighteenth-century Anglo-Irish writers and thinkers, Jonathan Swift in particular. He believed they were the founders of Irish thought, and that modern Ireland needed some of Swift's clear thinking and sense of right and wrong.

Personal mythology

'Gyres'

Yeats saw individual lives, human character and human history as being subject to cycles. The image he used to explain this was the 'gyre', which is an expanding spiral in the shape of a cone. He imagined opposite forces at work in the world in terms of interlocking gyres.

Yeats's interest in mysticism and 'esoteric' philosophy (one that is meant to be shared and understood only by a small group) continued throughout his adult life, and he spent a lot of time writing and reworking a book in which he set out his personal system of beliefs, which he called *A Vision*. In it Yeats describes theories of cyclical human history based on periods of two thousand years. Those periods are further subdivided into twenty-eight eras based on the phases of the moon. Human personalities, he believed, could also be categorised according to the phases of the moon. **His poems are full of images that derive from his system of beliefs**, but it would be impossible to try to explain all Yeats's theories here – nor is it necessary. His poems can be understood and enjoyed without this knowledge.

Yeats uses many symbols in his poetry. He believed that there exists a **universal store of symbols** developed through human history; he calls this 'Spiritus Mundi' (the spirit of the world) in 'The Second Coming' (see page 461). But he also has his own system of personal symbols or **'emblems'**, built up and often explained in the course of his mature poetry.

Themes

Many of Yeats's poems, especially his earlier ones, are love poems, and **love in its different forms** is a theme that runs throughout his work, although none of the poems in this anthology is a simple love poem. **Celtic myth and legend** is the other major theme of his early poems. In his middle period (from about 1909), **public events in Ireland** become a more important subject, and the upheavals that followed the 1916 Rising, including the War of Independence and the Civil War, are reflected and considered in his poetry. He was also interested in the **relationship between the private individual and public life**, and the distance that always exists between them. Different aspects of that theme are explored in 'An Irish Airman Foresees His Death', 'Easter 1916', 'Meditations in Time of Civil War' and 'Politics'.

The tension between private and the public is one of the driving forces in Yeats's poetry. There are many other pairs of opposing forces active in his work: nature and art, the body and the soul, youth and age, passion and detachment. He saw the world in terms of these conflicting opposites, as is clear from his personal mythology in *A Vision*. Many of his poems are written in the form of **dialogues** between characters or abstractions that represent opposing viewpoints or forces.

In his later poetry, especially from *The Tower* (1928) onwards, Yeats develops a **network of symbols**, many of which are derived from the philosophy he describes in *A Vision*, and the world view he sets out there is also a subject of his poetry, notably in 'The Second Coming'. But the **details of his own life also become part of that network**. Thoor Ballylee, with its winding stair, the river running by it, even the starling's nest by his window, are woven into the mythology that his poems create. His friends too become part of that mythology. Con Markiewicz and Eva Gore-Booth, John O'Leary, Lady Gregory and her son Richard, and especially Maud Gonne, all feature in his poems and are given their place in his personal mythology.

Timeline

1865	Born on 13 June in Sandymount, Dublin
1867	Yeats family moves to London
1881	Family moves to Dublin
1884–5	Attends Metropolitan School of Art, Dublin
1886	Meets John O'Leary
1889	Publishes *The Wanderings of Oisín and Other Poems*; meets Maud Gonne
1896	Meets Lady Gregory
1904	Abbey Theatre founded, with Yeats and Lady Gregory as founder members
1916	*Responsibilities* published
1917	Publishes *The Wild Swans at Coole*; buys Thoor Ballylee; marries Georgie Hyde-Lees
1919	Birth of daughter Anne; revised version of *The Wild Swans at Coole*, including 'An Irish Airman Foresees His Death'
1921	Birth of son, Michael; publishes *Michael Robartes and the Dancer*
1922	Made a senator
1923	Awarded the Nobel Prize for Literature
1926	The first version of *A Vision* published
1928	Publishes *The Tower*
1933	Publishes *The Winding Stair*
1934	Undergoes the Steinach operation
1939	Dies in the south of France
1940	*Last Poems* published
1948	Body reburied in Drumcliff, Co. Sligo

Before you read

Do you ever want to 'get away from it all'? Where would you go? What do you imagine yourself doing? Discuss in pairs or small groups.

The Lake Isle of Innisfree

I will arise and go now, and go to Innisfree,
And a small cabin build there, of clay and wattles made:
Nine bean-rows will I have there, a hive for the honey-bee,
And live alone in the bee-loud glade.

And I shall have some peace there, for peace comes dropping slow,   5
Dropping from the veils of the morning to where the cricket sings;
There midnight's all a glimmer, and noon a purple glow,
And evening full of the linnet's wings.

I will arise and go now, for always night and day
I hear lake water lapping with low sounds by the shore;   10
While I stand on the roadway, or on the pavements grey,
I hear it in the deep heart's core.

Glossary

Title	*Innisfree*: an island in Lough Gill, Co. Sligo
2	*wattles*: woven strips of wood
4	*glade*: open area in a wood
8	*linnet*: small bird known for its trilling song

Guidelines

Yeats wrote the first version of 'The Lake Isle of Innisfree' at the age of twenty-three when he was living in London. The impulse for the poem came when he was walking down a busy shopping street and heard the sound of water from a fountain in a shop window. The sound suggested the lapping lake water described in the poem, and woke in him an urge to escape the city for a simple life in a place he knew and loved from his Sligo childhood. The poem was altered and first published two years later in the *National Observer*. It has always been one of Yeats's most popular poems.

Commentary

The prose meaning of the poem is easy to summarise. The poet is in the city – 'on the pavements grey' – and declares that he will leave it and go and live a simple life alone in a cabin on the isle of Innisfree. He describes the peaceful life he imagines for himself there, and tells us, in stanza 3, that he is always drawn to the idea of this place. The fact that the poem can be so simply summarised is a good indication that the lasting appeal of this poem is due less to what it says than the way in which it is said.

Themes and imagery

The main theme of the poem is **the desire to escape to an idealised pastoral world**. This desire is a reaction to the poet's circumstances in London, and expresses a longing rather than a concrete plan or even possibility. Innisfree is a real place, and one that Yeats knew and loved, but the rural haven that the poet dreams of is a romantic Ireland of the imagination.

The poem belongs in a long literary tradition with the theme of retreating to a simpler country life, which is described in traditional pastoral terms with its 'small' cabin made of 'clay and wattles', the rows of beans, the bees, birds and crickets. There is a **dreamlike** quality to the description. We are given **impressions** rather than clear images: 'midnight's all a glimmer, and noon a purple glow'. Sounds are important too: the 'bee-loud glade', the cricket singing, and above all the 'low sounds' of the lapping water. The peace and beauty of Innisfree is a bewitching alternative to the roadways and grey pavements of London. The very name of the island, which contains the word 'free', adds to the meaning of the poem.

Form

The poem is written in four-line stanzas, rhyming *abab*. The first three lines in each stanza are longer, with a distinct **caesura** (mid-line break) in each one, while the fourth is shorter and slower. It is hard to pin down the metre of the poem, though it is largely iambic, but Yeats called it 'my first lyric with anything in its rhythm of my own music'.

Notice how the long lines with the caesura have a **relaxed back-and-forth rhythm**. Does it remind you of breathing in and out? Or the swash and backwash of waves, like the 'lake water lapping' described in line 10?

Pastoral

Pastoral: To do with the countryside, particularly animals that graze in fields (pasture). In literature, it is the name given to a tradition that portrays an idealised version of country life.

Walden

Yeats was influenced by a book by the American writer Henry Thoreau called *Walden*, first published in 1854. In it Thoreau describes the life he led for more than two years alone in a cabin he had built in the woods. He was looking for a simpler life, closer to nature, so that he could understand the world and his own self more clearly. As a teenager, Yeats dreamed of imitating Thoreau, and imagined Innisfree in Sligo, which he had known as a boy, as the place he would retreat to. It never became more than a dream.

Speaking poetry

As a young man, Yeats composed by reciting his poetry out loud. At home his sisters would always know when he was working on a poem because they would hear Willy murmuring, then, as he grew more excited, chanting his lines, until they had to ask him to 'stop composing!' The spoken word rather than the written was always uppermost in his mind.

You can hear Yeats himself reading 'The Lake Isle of Innisfree' on various sites on the internet – search for "Yeats reading The Lake Isle of Innisfree". Listen to the recording in class, and discuss what we can learn about the poem from the poet's manner of reading it.

Notice too how the **shorter final lines of each stanza slow down the movement and bring it to stillness**. The three stressed long vowels that end the first and third stanzas ('bee-loud glade' and 'deep heart's core') are particularly striking, and characteristic of this poem's special music.

Language

The language of the poem has a somewhat **heightened tone** that **is in part borrowed from the Bible**. Its opening declaration, 'I will arise and go now', carries an echo of the story of the prodigal son in Luke's gospel (chapter 15, verse 18): 'I will arise and go to my father'. The solemnity is reinforced by the repetition of 'go' (line 1), 'peace' (line 5) and 'dropping' (lines 5–6), and the inversion of words in 'will I have' (line 3) instead of 'I will have'. The 'I' of the poem is **conscious of its own dignity**.

What drives the language of the poem, though, is **the sounds the words make**. The calm and beauty that Yeats imagines is conjured by the **lapping rhythms** and **the patterns of sound** – not just alliteration and assonance, but **a seductive mixture of light, short sounds and long, slow ones**. Look, for instance, at the pattern of 'n', 'b', 'h', and then 'l' and 'd' sounds, together with the long vowels which almost rhyme in lines 3–4: 'Nine bean-rows will I have there, a hive for the honey-bee, / And live alone in the bee-loud glade.'

SNAPSHOT

- The desire to escape to a simpler world
- Draws on a tradition of pastoral poetry
- Images drawn from the natural world
- Rich pattern of sounds
- Heightened language and dignified tone
- Written when Yeats was living in London

Exam-Style Questions

Understanding the poem

1. What, in your own words, does the poet say he wants to do in the first stanza?

2. Why, do you think, does Yeats specify 'nine' bean-rows, rather than eight or ten or some other number?

3. What positive qualities does he imagine life in Innisfree will have? Mention three.

4. What does the third stanza add to your understanding of Yeats's desire to go to Innisfree?

Thinking about the poem

1. What is the effect of writing 'arise' in line 1? How would the poem be different if Yeats had written 'get up'?

2. Why, do you think, does Yeats mention linnets in line 8? How would the poem be different if the wings had been the sparrow's wings, for instance?

3. Did Yeats think of going to Innisfree as a real possibility, do you imagine? What in the poem leads you to this belief?

4. Why, do you think, has this poem been so popular ever since it was written?

5. Comment on the use of repetition in the poem.

6. 'Sound is more important than sense in this poem.' Do you agree with this point of view? Why or why not?

7. Below is the first version of 'The Lake Isle of Innisfree' (with Yeats's spelling).

> I will arise and go now and go to the island of Innis free
> And live in a dwelling of wattles – of woven wattles and wood work made,
> Nine been rows will I have there, a yellow hive for the honey bee
> And this old care shall fade
>
> There from the dawn above me peace will come down dropping slow
> Dropping from the veils of the morning to where the household cricket sings.
> And noontide there be all a glimmer, midnight be a purple glow,
> And evening full of the linnets wings.

In what ways is the final version an improvement on the first one? Choose three points of difference and explain what the changes do for the poem. You might consider rhythm, sound, diction, phrasing and tone.

Imagining

1. Do you think this poem is relevant in a world where farming is big business and efficiency and profit are everything? Does this model of self-sufficiency appeal to you? Discuss in small groups.

2. Where would you like to escape to? Write a piece of prose or poetry about your ideal refuge, how you imagine it would be and what you imagine you would do.

September 1913

What need you, being come to sense,
But fumble in a greasy till
And add the halfpence to the pence
And prayer to shivering prayer, until
You have dried the marrow from the bone?   5
For men were born to pray and save:
Romantic Ireland's dead and gone,
It's with O'Leary in the grave.

Yet they were of a different kind,
The names that stilled your childish play,   10
They have gone about the world like wind,
But little time had they to pray
For whom the hangman's rope was spun,
And what, God help us, could they save?
Romantic Ireland's dead and gone,   15
It's with O'Leary in the grave.

Was it for this the wild geese spread
The grey wing upon every tide;
For this that all that blood was shed,
For this Edward Fitzgerald died,   20
And Robert Emmet and Wolf Tone,
All that delirium of the brave?
Romantic Ireland's dead and gone,
It's with O'Leary in the grave.

Yet could we turn the years again,   25
And call those exiles as they were
In all their loneliness and pain,
You'd cry, 'Some woman's yellow hair
Has maddened every mother's son':
They weighed so lightly what they gave.   30
But let them be, they're dead and gone,
They're with O'Leary in the grave.

Glossary

5	*dried... bone*: allowed life to dry up; lost all human feeling
8	*O'Leary*: John O'Leary (1830–1907); see page 443
17	*wild geese*: Irish soldiers who served in foreign armies in the seventeenth and eighteenth centuries
20	*Edward Fitzgerald*: Lord Edward Fitzgerald (1763–98) was one of the leaders of the 1798 Rebellion, and died of wounds sustained while he was being arrested
21	*Robert Emmet*: Robert Emmet (1778–1803) Irish revolutionary leader hanged in September 1803 following the failure of the rising he led
21	*Wolf Tone*: Theobald Wolfe Tone (1763–98) organised a French military expedition to Ireland in support of a planned revolution; he was condemned to death as a traitor but committed suicide in prison while waiting to be hanged

Guidelines

The writing of 'September 1913' was sparked by the debate about a collection of paintings owned by Sir Hugh Lane. Its publication in the *Irish Times* on 8 September 1913 meant that it became part of that debate. It was collected in *Responsibilities* (1916).

The Hugh Lane bequest

Hugh Lane, nephew of Yeats's friend Lady Gregory, was an art collector who offered his collection of Impressionist paintings to Dublin on the condition that a suitable gallery was built to house them. There was a good deal of resistance to his plans from the Dublin Corporation, which was expected to come up with much of the money, and from the public, many of whom considered some of the paintings obscene. Yeats was angered by what he saw as the ignorance of those who would not seize the chance to have a great collection of modern art in Dublin.

The controversy surrounding the paintings went on long after Hugh Lane's death in 1915, but most of the collection can now be visited for free in the Dublin City Art Gallery on Parnell Square.

Commentary

Stanza 1

The first question to ask is who is the 'you' of the first line: **who is the poem addressed to**? It is clear that, although the poem was first published in the *Irish Times*, whose readers were largely Protestant and unionist, they are not the 'you' of the poem. Rather, Yeats is addressing the Catholic middle classes, whose main concerns are money and religion – 'pence' and 'prayer'. Their attitude is seen as petty and small-minded: the till is 'greasy', the coins are small and the prayers are 'shivering'.

Against this the speaker sets 'Romantic Ireland', represented by the Fenian John O'Leary. As the speaker tells it, the people have 'come to sense' by rejecting the heroic ideals of 'Romantic Ireland', but **the tone is bitterly ironic**.

Stanza 2

In contrast with the 'you' described in the first stanza, the speaker now presents 'they' (line 9) – the heroes who fought and died for the cause of Irish independence, whose names 'stilled your childish play'. In other words, when they were children, those who now dominate Ireland would have heard those names with awe. But now, as the speaker asks, what is there left to save? The tone of the refrain carries an added bitterness after this question.

> **John O'Leary**
>
> O'Leary was a passionate nationalist who was imprisoned and exiled for his involvement with the Irish Republican Brotherhood. He was a strong believer in the importance of Irish culture as an essential part of Irish nationalism. He was a powerful influence on the young Yeats, who came to know him well in the 1880s. His ideas shaped Yeats's thinking about Irish politics and culture. He died in 1907.

Stanza 3

The speaker goes on to specify some of the names he referred to in the previous stanza: Fitzgerald, Emmet and Wolfe Tone. He sums up their acts as the 'delirium of the brave'; 'delirium' is not meant to imply that they were mad, but that their actions were emotional rather than rational. They were idealists and dreamers, rather than merchants. The whole stanza is governed by the despairing question with which it starts: 'Was it for this…?' Was their sacrifice worthwhile if all it produced was the petty modern Ireland described in the first stanza?

Stanza 4

In the final stanza the speaker asks us ('we', not 'you', in line 25) to make a personal connection with those 'exiles' and imagine that we could see them in life, 'In all their loneliness and pain' (line 27). He declares that the modern Irish 'you' would think that what those exiles did was motivated by a mad passion such as one would have for a woman, not understanding the true motive of their heroism.

What is the tone of the refrain now? Resigned? Scornful? What do you think?

Themes

The main theme of this poem is **an argument over Irish identity** – what it means to be Irish and what it could and should mean. The central contrast is between the petty, penny-pinching modern Irish middle classes who are dominated by a small-minded religion, and the nationalist heroes of the past.

By publishing this poem in the *Irish Times* Yeats was **deliberately entering a national debate** concerning the Hugh Lane bequest, which was in essence about the nature of Ireland's past, present and possible future. Yeats saw that he was living at a key moment in Irish history, 'when it is plastic, when it is like wax, when it is ready to hold for generations the shape that is given to it', as he said in a speech at that time.

Although Yeats famously wrote that 'We make out of the quarrel with others, rhetoric, but of the quarrel with ourselves, poetry', there is no doubt that this is **a powerfully rhetorical poem** with a point to make. The scornful dismissal of 'Romantic Ireland' as 'dead and gone' is ironic. It is meant to **goad the reader** into considering what has apparently been lost, and so what might be needed in the coming times.

Who was Yeats addressing?

As noted above, 'September 1913' was first published in the largely unionist and Protestant newspaper, the *Irish Times*, but primarily addressed to Catholics. It is noticeable, too, that all the heroes named in the poem were Protestants from the Anglo-Irish 'Ascendancy' classes.

What is the significance of this? You could argue that Yeats was inviting his (Protestant) readers to share his scorn of the Catholic merchant classes. But Yeats was no unionist; he was a dedicated nationalist and had been a member of the IRB. Is the poem, then, also a reminder to its Protestant readership of the heroic acts of eighteenth-century Protestants in the cause of Irish independence, and perhaps a spur for future ones? Certainly, whatever Ireland was to be forged in the future, Yeats wanted to stake the claim of the Anglo-Irish for a share of that Irishness.

Form and language

The poem is written in eight-line stanzas of iambic **tetrameters** (four beats in a line), rhyming *ababcdcd*. The language is generally plain, sometimes very **colloquial** ('God help us', line 14), with some poetic phrase-making: 'All that delirium of the brave' (line 22). But above all, **the language is driven by rhetoric. It asks questions** – 'What need you …?'; 'what … could they save?'; 'Was it for this …?' – and answers them with a bitter dismissal of the hopes of 'Romantic Ireland'. That dismissal is **ironic**, however – **another rhetorical device**. The repetition of the refrain makes the reader question the absence of 'Romantic Ireland' and all that the phrase implies.

Notice, too, how the sounds of the words help to channel the emotion of the poem. The **hard consonants** (*p*, *b*, *d*, *g*) in the first stanza ('pence', 'prayer', 'bone', 'born') and again in the refrain ('dead and gone') **carry anger and bitterness**. Contrast those effects with the **slow, long monosyllables** of 'wild geese spread / The grey wing' (lines 17–18) which help to **suggest the sense of freedom and exhilaration** associated with the heroic acts being described.

> **Yeats on the middle class**
>
> In a note he added to 'September 1913' Yeats wrote: 'we have but a few educated men and the remnants of an old traditional culture among the poor. Both were stronger forty years ago, before the rise of our new middle class.'

Imagery

'September 1913' is not rich in poetic images, but the central conflict of the poem is captured in the contrast between the **close-up, sordid physical imagery in the first stanza** of those who 'fumble in a greasy till' and add 'prayer to shivering prayer', and the **wild, natural forces through which the self-sacrificing heroes are depicted**: those who 'have gone about the world like wind' (line 11), the 'wild geese' with their brave 'delirium'.

Questions

1	Who is the 'you' in line 1?
2	How does Yeats convey in the first stanza what he sees as the absence of human feelings and idealism in Ireland in 1913?
3	Who are the 'they' in line 9?
4	What impression do we get of the heroes of the past in stanzas 2 and 3? How does Yeats create that impression?
5	'Was it for this …' (line 17). What does Yeats mean by 'this'?
6	Yeats lists a number of patriots in the poem. What did they have in common?
7	In stanza 4 Yeats imagines being able to bring those 'exiles' back to life. How does he imagine they will be? And what does he believe a modern Irish person would think of them?
8	Irony plays a significant part in the poem, with one thing being said but another meant. Give examples of this feature. Is it an effective device?
9	How would you describe the tone of this poem?
10	What is the central contrast in this poem? Show how Yeats manages this contrast.
11	This is a poem of protest and complaint. What exactly is Yeats complaining about?
12	Does Yeats present an ideal for his readers' approval? If so, how can it be described?
13	What does 'Romantic Ireland' mean in the context of this poem?
14	What in modern Ireland makes you angry? Discuss in pairs or small groups.
15	Write a letter – or a poem – protesting about what makes you angry. Use irony if you can.

The Wild Swans at Coole

Before you read

What do you think of when you think of swans? What qualities do you associate with them? What might a swan be a symbol for? Discuss in pairs.

The trees are in their autumn beauty,
The woodland paths are dry,
Under the October twilight the water
Mirrors a still sky;
Upon the brimming water among the stones   5
Are nine-and-fifty swans.

The nineteenth autumn has come upon me
Since I first made my count;
I saw, before I had well finished,
All suddenly mount   10
And scatter wheeling in great broken rings
Upon their clamorous wings.

I have looked upon those brilliant creatures,
And now my heart is sore.
All's changed since I, hearing at twilight,   15
The first time on this shore,
The bell-beat of their wings above my head,
Trod with a lighter tread.

Unwearied still, lover by lover,
They paddle in the cold   20
Companionable streams or climb the air;
Their hearts have not grown old;
Passion or conquest, wander where they will,
Attend upon them still.

But now they drift on the still water,   25
Mysterious, beautiful;
Among what rushes will they build,
By what lake's edge or pool
Delight men's eyes when I awake some day
To find they have flown away?   30

Glossary

Title	*Coole*: Coole Park was the country home of Lady Gregory
5	*brimming*: filled to the brim
12	*clamorous*: noisy
13	*brilliant*: bright, shining (because they are white)
21	*Companionable*: friendly; where the swans can enjoy each other's company

Guidelines

Yeats completed the first version of this poem in early 1917. It became the title poem of the collection first published in November that year. Its setting is Coole Park, Co. Galway, the home of his great friend and patron Lady Augusta Gregory, where he had often been a guest for almost twenty years. It was written at a time when Yeats was fifty-one, still unmarried, and concerned about the effects of old age on his creative powers.

Commentary

'The Wild Swans at Coole' is a **deceptively simple** poem, and it is not hard to follow its surface meaning. Its power and beauty come from **the images of the swans and all they suggest or symbolise, and from their relationship to the speaker.**

Stanzas 1 and 2

In the first stanza, Yeats sets the scene in simple descriptive phrases: it is autumn, evening (twilight); there is the wood, the lake, and on the lake, fifty-nine swans. As the title tells us, the setting is Coole Park, and in the second stanza the poet remembers the first time he visited the place and counted the swans, nineteen years before. Then, while he was still counting ('before I had well finished'), they took to the air and circled, 'wheeling in great broken rings'.

> **Lady Gregory and Coole**
>
> **Lady Gregory took an important role in the Irish Literary Revival, both as a collector and publisher of folktales and as one of the moving spirits behind the Irish National Theatre Society, which eventually founded the Abbey Theatre. Her great house at Coole Park played an important role in everything she did. With its large library and significant art collection, it became a place where many of the leading literary and artistic figures of the era would gather at Lady Gregory's invitation to share ideas, write, paint or just relax. For Yeats it was a refuge and an inspiration for much of his life.**

Stanza 3

In the third stanza he thinks about the differences in himself between when he first saw and heard the swans, when he was younger and happier and 'Trod with a lighter tread', and the present: 'now my heart is sore'. The fact of seeing 'those brilliant creatures' again has brought home to him how much he has changed.

Stanza 4

In the fourth stanza he **contemplates** the apparently unchanging nature of the swans. They are 'Unwearied' and apparently youthful: 'Their hearts have not grown old'. They are associated with 'Passion or conquest' and have the freedom to 'wander where they will'. In contrast with the unmarried poet, they are in loving pairs, 'lover by lover'; even the streams they paddle in are 'Companionable'.

Stanza 5

The final stanza returns to 'now', and ends with a question that looks to the future: where will the swans go when the poet wakes up one day 'To find they have flown away'? The tone is hard to pin down. Yeats imagines – and expects – a day when the swans will have left him. There is a sense of loss, but at the same time the swans will not vanish completely; they will still 'Delight men's eyes' – other men in another place.

Themes

The passing of time

Perhaps the primary theme of the poem is the **passing of time. The central contrast is between the ageing poet and the apparently ageless swans.** Where the speaker is alone and lonely ('sore' of heart), the swans are in pairs, 'lover by lover', and 'Their hearts have not grown old'. The poet is subject to time and change, whereas the swans are the same 'brilliant creatures' still.

A still moment of clarity

But the beauty of this poem is that it cannot be reduced to a single straightforward meaning. Rather, it focuses on a **vivid image** and a **moment of vision**, evoked with simple clarity in the first stanza. It is **a moment that seems held in time.** The sky is 'still'; in fact, the word 'still' is used four times in the poem. The water is 'brimming', as if the lake is as full as it can possibly be, just as the moment seems **full of meaning.**

Imagery

The meaning – or rather, **the complex of meanings** – of the poem **is carried above all in the images**. The **autumn evening setting** is important, not least because the poet has arrived at the autumn of his own life. But it is the **swans** that stay in the memory. There is no doubt that the swans were real, but in Yeats's description of them **they take on symbolic significance**. We have already noted their apparent agelessness and vitality; **their wheeling flight also suggests the circle that for Yeats represented eternity**. They belong both to the water where they swim and the air where they fly. To the poet they represent **youth, vigour, passion, freedom** – things he desires for himself. They are, as the poem's title tells us, wild. It is an easy step to see them as **symbolising the poet's creative energies**, and perhaps that is what is uppermost in his mind in the final stanza when he considers the time 'when I awake some day / To find they have flown away'. Is he thinking of the loss of his poetic inspiration? Or of his death – awaking to an afterlife? Or both? It is one of the great achievements of the poem that all these possibilities are gathered and held and contribute to its effect.

Form and language

The poem is written in six-line stanzas rhyming *abcbdd*. **The final couplet at the end of each stanza helps to create the sense of stillness and balance that pervades the poem.** Longer **tetrameters** (four beats in a line) alternate with shorter **trimeters** (three beats).

The language of the poem is mostly spare and simple. The image of the first stanza, for example, is built out of **short, plain, descriptive phrases**. There are moments when Yeats uses the sounds of the words to add a dimension to the description, such as the long vowel of 'wheeling' (line 11) to suggest the big circles in which the swans fly, or the alliteration of 'The bell-beat of their wings'. But in general Yeats trusts that clear images and carefully chosen words will have the resonance he wants them to have without the poetical fireworks of, for example, 'The Lake Isle of Innisfree'.

Exam-Style Questions

Understanding the poem

1	The poem is set in autumn. Why, do you think, is that important?
2	What meaning or meanings do the swans have for the poet? Mention as many as you can.
3	The poem centres on a contrast between the poet and the swans. In what ways do they contrast?
4	Why is the poet troubled as he contemplates the swans?
5	How do you respond to the ending of the poem? Is it entirely sad or is there some optimism in it?

Thinking about the poem

1	How does the language of this poem differ from that in 'The Lake Isle of Innisfree'?
2	Is the number of the swans significant, do you think? If so, in what way?
3	Choose your favourite image from the poem, and explain why you have chosen it.
4	The word 'still' is used four times in this poem, and in two different senses. Can you explain the two meanings, and say why they are both so central to the poem?

Imagining

1	You have been asked to make a short film to accompany a reading of this poem. Say how you would use music, sound effects, images and colour to convey the atmosphere of the poem.
2	Write about a moment when you became aware that something important in your life had changed.

SNAPSHOT

- Autumn evening setting
- Sense of sadness and loneliness in the poem
- Poem about the passing of time
- Swans give the illusion of immortality
- Contrasts between the poet and the swans
- Swans represent freedom, passion, youth, creative vitality
- Hope or despair in the ending?

Easter 1916

Before you read

In pairs or groups discuss what you know about the Easter Rising and its leaders. What would you expect to find in a poem called 'Easter 1916'?

I have met them at close of day
Coming with vivid faces
From counter or desk among grey
Eighteenth-century houses.
I have passed with a nod of the head   5
Or polite meaningless words,
Or have lingered awhile and said
Polite meaningless words,
And thought before I had done
Of a mocking tale or a gibe   10
To please a companion
Around the fire at the club,
Being certain that they and I
But lived where motley is worn:
All changed, changed utterly: 15
A terrible beauty is born.

That woman's days were spent
In ignorant good-will,
Her nights in argument
Until her voice grew shrill.   20
What voice more sweet than hers
When, young and beautiful,
She rode to harriers?
This man had kept a school
And rode our wingèd horse;   25
This other his helper and friend
Was coming into his force;
He might have won fame in the end,
So sensitive his nature seemed,
So daring and sweet his thought.   30
This other man I had dreamed
A drunken, vainglorious lout.
He had done most bitter wrong
To some who are near my heart,
Yet I number him in the song;   35
He, too, has resigned his part
In the casual comedy;
He, too, has been changed in his turn,
Transformed utterly:
A terrible beauty is born.   40

Hearts with one purpose alone
Through summer and winter seem
Enchanted to a stone
To trouble the living stream.
The horse that comes from the road,   45
The rider, the birds that range
From cloud to tumbling cloud,
Minute by minute they change;
A shadow of cloud on the stream
Changes minute by minute;   50
A horse-hoof slides on the brim,
And a horse plashes within it;
The long-legged moor-hens dive,
And hens to moor-cocks call;
Minute by minute they live;   55
The stone's in the midst of all.

Too long a sacrifice
Can make a stone of the heart.
O when may it suffice?
That is Heaven's part, our part   60
To murmur name upon name,
As a mother names her child
When sleep at last has come
On limbs that had run wild.
What is it but nightfall?   65
No, no, not night but death;
Was it needless death after all?
For England may keep faith
For all that is done and said.
We know their dream; enough   70
To know they dreamed and are dead;
And what if excess of love
Bewildered them till they died?
I write it out in a verse —
MacDonagh and MacBride   75
And Connolly and Pearse
Now and in time to be,
Wherever green is worn,
Are changed, changed utterly:
A terrible beauty is born.   80

September 25, 1916

Glossary

2	*vivid*: bright-coloured; full of life
4	*Eighteenth-century houses*: much of central Dublin was built in the Georgian period (1714–1830)
10	*gibe*: insulting comment
14	*motley*: multi-coloured costume worn by a fool in a play
17	*That woman*: Constance Markiewicz (1868–1927), a Volunteer officer in the Rising, who was condemned to death by the British but not executed because she was a woman; see also 'In Memory of Eva Gore-Booth and Con Markiewicz'
23	*harriers*: hunting dogs
24	*This man... school*: Patrick Pearse (1879–1916), one of the leaders of the Rising, who was executed for his part in it
25	*wingèd horse*: Pegasus, associated with poetic inspiration; Pearse was also a poet
26	*This other*: Thomas MacDonagh (1878–1916), writer and teacher, who was also executed for his part in the Rising
31	*This other man*: Major John MacBride (1868–1916) was the husband of Maud Gonne, though they had separated; he was executed for his part in the Rising
32	*vainglorious*: proud and boastful
52	*plashes*: splashes
53–4	*moor-hens ... moor-cocks*: females and males of a black bird that lives in rivers and lakes
68	*England may keep faith*: the British government had agreed to grant Home Rule, which would have satisfied many Irish nationalists; the outbreak of the First World War meant that it was postponed
73	*Bewildered*: confused
76	*Connolly*: James Connolly (1868–1916) was a socialist leader whose Citizen Army took part in the Rising; he was severely wounded, and was executed despite being in a wheelchair
78	*Wherever green is worn*: green is the colour most associated with Ireland, as in patriotic songs like 'The Wearing of the Green'

Guidelines

This poem was written in response to one of the central events of Irish history, the Easter Rising of 1916. Yeats was in England when the Rising happened, and he was both shocked by the news and disapproving at first of what had happened. Though he was an Irish nationalist, he did not believe in using violence for political ends. He had known many leaders of the Rising, and did not have a high opinion of some of them, but when the British started to execute them public opinion shifted and they were seen as martyrs and heroes. Yeats's feelings changed too. As he said at the time, 'I had no idea that any public event could so deeply move me'. 'Easter 1916' is the poet's attempt to understand the impact the events of the Rising had on him, and to understand its place in the history of Ireland.

Yeats wrote the poem in 1916 and circulated it among his friends, but it was not published until 1920, and appeared in the collection *Michael Robartes and the Dancer* (1921).

Commentary

Stanza 1

Yeats starts by giving his impressions of the rebel leaders ('them' in line 1). He knew them enough to exchange 'polite meaningless words' with them, but for him they were not really serious, but figures of fun – people to make jokes about ('a mocking tale or a gibe') with his friends. He believed, as he wrote in 'September 1913', that 'Romantic Ireland' – the patriotic heroism of the old Fenians – was 'dead and gone'. He thought that all the plans of the new generation of rebels would come to nothing, just as he didn't expect his own engagement with Irish culture to change the political system. He was 'certain that they and I / But lived where motley is worn'. In other words, they were like characters in a comic play, not tragic or heroic figures.

The **final two lines** of the stanza not only declare that everything has changed, but also **change the tone** of the poem: 'All changed, changed utterly: / A terrible beauty is born.' The phrase 'terrible beauty' resonates through the poem. It contains in itself the **central tension** of the poem: the Easter Rising, as far as Yeats is concerned, was **both beautiful and 'terrible'** – not in its usual modern meaning of something bad, but in its original sense: something frightening; something that causes terror.

Stanza 2

Yeats now considers some of the rebel leaders he knew.

The first is Constance Markiewicz, a friend whose fierce republican politics had spoiled her, as far as the poet was concerned. This is described in terms of her voice, which had been 'sweet' when she was a beautiful young woman, but which has grown 'shrill' from arguing her political convictions.

The next two are Pearse and MacDonagh, both teachers and poets and both associated with Pearse's school St Enda's. There is a sense of regret in Yeats's description of MacDonagh's 'sensitive' nature and 'daring and sweet' thought that is absent from the mention of Pearse. Yeats did not like Pearse and his ideas of 'blood sacrifice'.

The fourth rebel leader is John MacBride, Maud Gonne's estranged husband. It is clear that Yeats had, for personal reasons, a very low opinion of the man he had believed to be a 'drunken, vainglorious lout'. But, like the others, he can no longer be seen as an ordinary figure; he 'has resigned his part / In the casual comedy' and been 'Transformed utterly'.

Stanza 3

In this stanza Yeats contemplates the contrast between the stone-like nature of 'Hearts with one purpose alone' and the ever-changing life of the world around them – the 'living stream' where horses and riders, birds and clouds are always moving and changing.

It is not, however, a simple antithesis between the living and the lifeless. The 'stone' may 'trouble' the stream, but the final line of the stanza suggests that the stone is also an essential part of this world: 'The stone's in the midst of all.'

This stanza has been seen as part of an ongoing argument with Yeats's great love, Maud Gonne. He felt she had given too much of her energy to politics, and lost a precious part of herself by doing so.

Stanza 4

Yeats's **conflicted feelings** about the Rising are felt most strongly in the final stanza.

He starts by throwing light on his own image of the stone in the previous stanza: 'Too long a sacrifice / Can make a stone of the heart.' It is those who have sacrificed their lives – not only through execution but in their long-term dedication to their cause – whose hearts have turned to stone. The poet's agonised question, 'O when may it suffice?', has no answer that he can give. Yeats grapples with the gap between his doubts about the Easter Rising and the historical and symbolic meaning of it. 'Was it needless death after all?' he asks. He can't be sure that what the rebels did was worthwhile because 'England may keep faith' and bring in Home Rule, as had been promised. He wonders, too, whether he had judged the rebels correctly. He questions whether it was a matter of dedication turning their hearts to stone, or an extreme form of love that 'Bewildered' them. He does not try to answer his own question. The doubts are left **unresolved**. In the end, he can only do what he indicated earlier in the stanza: 'murmur name upon name'.

This final part of the poem carries great power, whatever Yeats's private doubts. The names of some of the rebel leaders are written out, along with a statement of faith – that 'Wherever green is worn', they are 'changed utterly'. Though he hated MacBride and despised Pearse, he saw that something had happened that was more important than his personal feelings or even his views on the rights and wrongs of the rebellion. In fact, in writing 'Easter 1916' Yeats helped to create the national significance of the event whose importance he had recognised, captured above all in the repeated line that ends the poem: 'A terrible beauty is born'.

Themes

The primary theme of the poem is, of course, the 1916 Easter Rising and the contrast between the ordinary, flawed men and women involved in it and the symbolic meaning of what they achieved. Notice, though, that Yeats makes use of the **Christian symbolism of Easter** to underpin contemporary events. The sacrifice and death of the rebel leaders parallels Christ's crucifixion, and the 'terrible beauty' that is born from those deaths hints at the resurrection of Christ. Perhaps Yeats is also suggesting that just as the crucifixion brought about a new world order, the events of Easter 1916 had produced a new Ireland where all is 'changed utterly'.

Imagery

There is a **theatrical metaphor** in the first stanza of the poem, where the poet thinks of the rebels and himself as wearing 'motley' – the dress of a fool in a comic play. The image is taken up in the second stanza, when Yeats says that MacBride 'has resigned his part / In the casual comedy', as if he had been acting a role.

The central image of stanza 3 is **the stone in the living, changing stream**, which Yeats uses as a metaphor for the sacrifices made out of political commitment, creating an association with the **hardening of intent** of the revolutionaries.

In the final stanza the main image is of a **mother** soothing her tired child by murmuring its name. Do you think the image carries a suggestion of the traditional figure of Mother Ireland?

Form and language

'Easter 1916' is written in short lines with three stresses (trimeters), rhyming *ababcdcd* etc. The short lines have a somewhat **troubled nervous energy**, but Yeats can also use the strong accents to create an impressive, stately power. This is particularly true of the refrain – 'All changed, changed utterly: / A terrible beauty is born.' – where the stresses are reinforced with alliteration on 'ch', 't' and 'b'.

> **Numerology**
>
> Yeats has moulded the form of this poem to its subject with unusual care in one respect. The Rising took place on 24 April 1916. The stanzas have either 24 or 16 lines, and there are four of them. April is the fourth month, so the short form of the date (24/4/16) is embedded in the poem. Yeats was fascinated by numerology – the power of numbers.

Tone and mood

In 'Easter 1916' Yeats is aware that he is writing about an important historical event. Although he expresses personal doubts and reservations, **he strives for a tone which creates an impersonal detachment from events** rather than an individual's emotional reaction to them. For example, there is a distance in describing the rebel leaders he mentions as 'That woman', 'This man', 'This other man'. He is trying to find the proper role of the poet faced with such dramatic events. In the troubled questioning of the fourth stanza, he falls back on the idea of what is **'our part' – the response of a group rather than an individual**. Who, do you think, is he thinking of when he writes 'our'? The Irish people? Poets? Certainly, he is conscious of his role as poet when he writes of himself writing: 'I write it out in a verse.'

The poem draws to an end by naming some of the executed leaders, and makes a statement about their place in Irish history. Here, the **steady, simple beat of the rhythm helps to create a solemn atmosphere**. It is like an **incantation** (magic spell) or a **prayer**, or perhaps like someone telling rosary beads. The final restatement of the poem's crucial phrase – 'A terrible beauty is born' – is a plain declaration which rises above any purely personal response and seems to carry authority. But the opposing meanings of the oxymoron 'terrible beauty' are **held in balance, unresolved**. It is up to the reader to imagine exactly what that terrible beauty might be, and what sort of future might be contained within it.

Questions

1. What is Yeats's attitude to 'them' (line 1) – the rebel leaders? What do we learn about them in the first stanza?

2. What impression do you get of the speaker, 'I', in the first stanza?

3. Discuss the ways in which Yeats's attitude to the leaders of the 1916 Rising changes in the course of the poem.

4. What, do you think, is the purpose of stanza 3, which does not mention Easter 1916 and its participants at all?

5. Why does Yeats repeat the line 'A terrible beauty is born'? What does this beauty consist of? In what way is it terrible?

6. Does 'Easter 1916' achieve a resolution of the conflicts and doubts it contains?

7. What is the effect of the final seven lines of the poem where the leaders are named? How would you describe the tone?

8. What is the effect of Yeats's use of the word 'vivid' in line 2?

9. Comment on Yeats's use of active verbs in stanza 3.

10. What is the effect of the image of the mother and her child in stanza 4?

11. In the last stanza the poet asks a number of questions. List these questions. What do they suggest about his attitude to his theme?

12. Imagine you had been involved in the Rising yourself. Write a letter to Yeats to tell him what your feelings were when you read this poem.

Before you read

This poem is about an Irishman who volunteered to fight with the British in the First World War. He was one of more than a hundred thousand Irishmen who joined the British forces in the course of the war. Find out what you can about why so many joined, and about the people who encouraged them to do so.

An Irish Airman Foresees His Death

I know that I shall meet my fate
Somewhere among the clouds above;
Those that I fight I do not hate,
Those that I guard I do not love;
My country is Kiltartan Cross,   5
My countrymen Kiltartan's poor,
No likely end could bring them loss
Or leave them happier than before.
Nor law, nor duty bade me fight,
Nor public men, nor cheering crowds,   10
A lonely impulse of delight
Drove to this tumult in the clouds;
I balanced all, brought all to mind,
The years to come seemed waste of breath,
A waste of breath the years behind   15
In balance with this life, this death.

Glossary

5	*Kiltartan Cross*: place in Co. Galway near Coole Park, where the Gregory family lived
12	*tumult*: a state of chaos and uproar; here, presumably the speaker's death in an aeroplane

Guidelines

This poem, first published in the second version of the collection *The Wild Swans at Coole* (1919), was written in 1918 as a response to the death of Robert Gregory, son of Lady Gregory, who fought for the British army in the First World War. He later joined the Royal Flying Corps, and was mistakenly shot down by an Italian pilot in January 1918.

Commentary

Lines 1–8

The speaker has a premonition of his own death – his 'fate' – in the air, and considers how he stands in relation to the war in which he is fighting. He doesn't hate the enemy, nor love the country he is fighting for. His loyalty is to Kiltartan Cross – the place he comes from – and the people there. The result of the war (the 'end', line 7) isn't going to make any difference to them. Personal and local loyalties are more important to him and them than national or political ones.

Lines 9–16

The speaker goes on to consider his reasons for fighting. He is not fighting because he has been forced to do so by law (conscription was brought in during the First World War, though it wasn't imposed in Ireland). It was not a sense of duty to his country that led him to enlist, nor was it the rhetoric of politicians stirring up crowds to persuade men to join the army. Instead, he was driven by a 'lonely impulse of delight' to his fate – the 'tumult in the clouds'. **The motivation is personal and internal, emotional rather than rational, and, in some sense, joyful.**

In the final four lines the speaker explains his thinking. It is all about **balancing opposites**. Both the future and the past seem a 'waste of breath'. The death he foresees seems to balance his life, and is therefore appropriate. Rather than horror or fear, there is **calm acceptance**.

Themes

This poem is sometimes described as an elegy for Robert Gregory. A traditional elegy, however, celebrates the virtues of the dead person and laments their death. Yeats wrote another poem 'In Memory of Major Robert Gregory', in this form. 'An Irish Airman Foresees His Death' does something different. In it Yeats imagines being in the position of Robert Gregory in order to write a **poem about** (among other things) **the individual and society, and the nature of heroism.**

Although it is generally accepted that this poem is 'about' Robert Gregory, the speaker identified in the title is something else: 'An Irish Airman'. This means that the speaker is not a particular individual, however remarkable, but **an anonymous voice** that **expresses a state of mind (and a dilemma)** that Yeats wanted to explore. By using a voice that is not his own Yeats gives himself the freedom to write about an attitude without committing himself to that attitude.

What, then, is Yeats interested in here? The poem presents **the inner workings of the mind of an individual in the face of a great public event** – the Great War. The poem was written at a time when the war was still raging, and Ireland was bitterly divided in its attitude to it. To go back to the title, note that the speaker is an

Irish airman. The poem is intensely personal, but it is not simply an account of an individual's detachment from the war; it also **reflects on the relationship of Ireland to a war fought by the United Kingdom**.

The speaker is not impressed by the 'public men' who might have urged him to fight. His loyalty is to his townland, not some notion of nationality, either British or even Irish. Like Yeats, Gregory was from an Anglo-Irish family – a group often regarded by Irish nationalists as not 'properly' Irish. In light of that, the speaker's isolation, and **his attachment to the local area** rather than the nation, might suggest another aspect of the underlying debate about nationality and identity. In that view, the speaker's isolation and uneasy relationship to his 'country' reflects that of the Anglo-Irish community.

A related theme of the poem is the **nature of heroism and self-sacrifice**. The speaker exhibits a combination of two opposed attitudes: the **detachment** shown in his distance from the demands of society on him, and the **passion** shown in his motive to action – the 'lonely impulse of delight'. The phrase – and the attitude – calls to mind the nationalist heroes of 'September 1913', who 'weighed so lightly what they gave'. That balance of detachment and passion was also regarded by Yeats as the **mark of a true artist**, so the fact that Robert Gregory was himself an artist can be no coincidence.

Language and form

The language of the poem is plain, made of **direct statements rather than poetic images**. The overwhelming impression is of **poise and balance**, and the form of words always reinforces this. To take one small example, in line 9, instead of 'Neither law nor duty', which would be the normal informal phrasing, the more formal 'Nor law, nor duty' creates a verbal parallel which adds to the sense of careful balancing that runs through the poem. The comma between the two parts of the phrase, which is not grammatically necessary, adds to that poise.

The poem is written in iambic tetrameters (four stresses per line) that have a **simplicity and regularity** that matches the direct language that is used. Although it is not separated into stanzas on the page, the poem can be divided into quatrains (four-line units), rhyming *abab*. The argument of the poem follows these divisions precisely. The **poem consists of two sentences, each exactly eight lines long**; within the two halves a semi-colon separates the quatrains.

Technically, this is an extremely accomplished poem. The form of it mirrors in detail what it describes – the act of balancing one thing against another and finding an equilibrium. Lines 3 and 4, for instance, work in parallel to summarise the speaker's attitude to the two sides in the war. He uses the caesura (mid-line break) to create a similar balance within a single line, as in 'Nor public men, nor cheering crowds', where the comma divides the line into two parallel phrases. The lines are mostly end-stopped, and it is significant that **the only real enjambment** (where the statement runs over the end of the line) comes between lines 11 and 12, which describe **the one moment** – the 'lonely impulse of delight' – **that breaks through the careful, detached poise of the rest of the poem**.

The final four lines demonstrate Yeats's mastery of his art. Line 13 describes **the act of balancing**, and is itself balanced by the caesura at the comma; the repetition of 'all' reinforces this balance. Lines 14–15 are a good example of **antithesis**, precisely mirrored across the line break, with 'The years to come' at the beginning, 'the years behind' at the end, and 'waste of breath' repeated in between. The final line expresses **the poem's central balancing act, between life and death**, held in equilibrium by the parallel phrasing: 'this life, this death'.

Imagery

This poem works by means of its balanced phrasing and plain language rather than its images. Even the 'impulse of delight' that drives to the 'tumult in the clouds', which is the central active moment of the poem, is something that can't be clearly pictured. It is **both vivid and open to the reader's imagination at the same time**.

Exam-Style Questions

Understanding the poem

1	What do we learn from the poem about who the speaker is and what motivates him?
2	What is the speaker's attitude to the war?
3	What impression do you get of the sort of man the speaker is? Does he come across as self-centred or even selfish? Give reasons for your answer.
4	How would you describe the tone of the poem? ■ defeatist ■ heroic ■ joyful Can you suggest another word to use?
5	How would you describe the language of the poem?

Thinking about the poem

1	What do you understand by the phrase 'A lonely impulse of delight'?
2	Is this a political poem? In what ways? Give reasons for your answer.
3	This poem has been described as a work of 'pure joy'. Would you agree with this description? Explain your answer.
4	The idea of balance is central to the poem. Discuss some of the ways in which Yeats creates a sense of poise and balance.

Imagining

| 1 | Write your own epitaph for the Irish airman of the poem. |
| 2 | Does the speaker of the poem remind you in any way of a modern 'suicide bomber'? How is he similar or different? Discuss in pairs or small groups. |

> ### SNAPSHOT
> ■ Speaker takes a balanced view of the war
> ■ Balance is reflected in the poem's form
> ■ Speaker not motivated by patriotism
> ■ Poem reflects on the nature of patriotism and nationality
> ■ Theme of heroism and self-sacrifice

Before you read

Does the phrase 'the second coming' have any associations for you? If so, what does it suggest? Discuss in pairs.

The Second Coming

Turning and turning in the widening gyre
The falcon cannot hear the falconer;
Things fall apart; the centre cannot hold;
Mere anarchy is loosed upon the world,
The blood-dimmed tide is loosed, and everywhere   5
The ceremony of innocence is drowned;
The best lack all conviction, while the worst
Are full of passionate intensity.

Surely some revelation is at hand;
Surely the Second Coming is at hand.   10
The Second Coming! Hardly are those words out
When a vast image out of *Spiritus Mundi*
Troubles my sight: somewhere in sands of the desert
A shape with lion body and the head of a man,
A gaze blank and pitiless as the sun,   15
Is moving its slow thighs, while all about it
Reel shadows of the indignant desert birds.
The darkness drops again; but now I know
That twenty centuries of stony sleep
Were vexed to nightmare by a rocking cradle,   20
And what rough beast, its hour come round at last,
Slouches towards Bethlehem to be born?

Glossary

Title	*Second Coming*: the phrase is usually associated with the Second Coming of Christ to judge humankind, as predicted in the Book of Revelation
1	*gyre*: a spiral that expands as it goes up; see also 'Personal mythology', page 436
4	*Mere*: here, pure or total
4	*loosed*: let free
12	Spiritus Mundi: literally, the spirit of the world; a store of images and symbols built up in the course of human history that are the shared inheritance of all humans
17	*Reel*: fall back and away, with a spinning motion

Guidelines

'The Second Coming' was written in early 1919, soon after the end of the bloody conflict we now know as the First World War, and at the point where a war for independence from Britain was starting in Ireland. Yeats had been shocked too by the Russian Revolution of 1917. He was not the only writer to feel that Western civilisation was in **crisis**, but his expression of that feeling evokes a particular horror and fascination, and has held a grip on the world's imagination throughout the hundred years since it was written.

Commentary

Lines 1–8

The first eight lines of the poem describe in **plain, declarative sentences** the current state of the world as it appears to the speaker. The first image is taken from falconry: instead of returning to the falconer who should be controlling the bird, the falcon is circling ever further away in a 'widening gyre'. Then, in a bold, bare statement which seems unremarkable, but which is the poem's most famous line, the speaker declares, 'Things fall apart; the centre cannot hold'. The image of the falcon is still there, but the **implications** are much wider. As the fourth line makes clear, the whole world is caught up in what is happening – the outbreak of 'Mere anarchy'. Lines 5–6 introduce the **half-hidden metaphor of a flood**: the 'blood-dimmed tide' could be thought of as a tsunami, full of the blood of war, overwhelming and drowning the ordered life – the 'ceremony of innocence' – that had previously existed. The next two lines declare that the 'best' (best in what way, we might ask) have no strong beliefs, whereas the 'worst' are 'full of passionate intensity'. In a world where people are killing themselves and others almost every day out of a passionate belief in a cause, it is not hard to understand the dangers of 'passionate intensity'.

Lines 9–22

The tone changes in the second part of the poem. If the first part is a plain description of the state of the world, the second part is an attempt to **understand and interpret** this state. A different, more excited, more emotionally involved voice is heard. Instead of the impersonal, descriptive statements of the first part, there is now **an uncertain 'I'** struggling to come to terms with what he has observed, and the 'vast image' that 'Troubles my sight'.

The mentions of 'revelation' and the 'Second Coming' at first suggest a Christian context. The Book of Revelation in the Bible tells of the Second Coming of Christ to judge the world at a time of terrible devastation. But there is no sign of Christ arriving in this poem. Instead the speaker is granted a vision, an image 'out of *Spiritus Mundi*'. Notice that the vision is something that happens *to* the speaker, not something that he conjures up: it 'Troubles my sight'.

What is this vision? It seems to come from far away – 'somewhere in sands of the desert' – and long ago: the 'shape with lion body and the head of a man' suggests the Sphinx, known from ancient Greek and Egyptian mythologies. **The vision is indistinct.** We see certain attributes – the blank gaze, the slow thighs – rather than a clear image of the whole. Even the desert birds are known by their shadows, which 'Reel', implying a spinning motion like that of the falcon in the first two lines. And what birds are they? Vultures perhaps? And why are they 'indignant'? The vision is as full of **mystery** as it is of horror.

> **Book of Revelation**
>
> This book in the New Testament predicts and depicts the Apocalypse – the end of the world as we know it. It describes signs or portents of the end, including Seven Seals and Four Horsemen, and also the appearance of a number of 'beasts', one with seven heads and ten horns, and one with two horns, a lamb's head, a sheep's body, a tail like a wolf, feet like a goat, and a speaking voice like a dragon. The culmination is the Second Coming of Christ.

It is only a glimpse before 'The darkness drops again', but the speaker regards it as a true and reliable vision, not a delusion. It has told him something: 'now I know …'. What has it told him?

> 'That twenty centuries of stony sleep
> Were vexed to nightmare by a rocking cradle'

Yeats believed that history worked in 2000-year cycles, and that the change from one cycle to the next would always be violent and chaotic. The 'twenty centuries of stony sleep' are usually interpreted as the 2000 years since the birth of Christ, but they can also be understood as the 2000 years *before* the birth of Christ, in which case the 'rocking cradle' is the manger where the baby Jesus was laid. His birth – and violent crucifixion – ushered in a new era. Now, in 1919, another 2000 years have almost passed and another era is about to begin. The final two lines ask what sort of era it will be, and suggest answers. It is not a 'Second Coming' of Christ that he expects, but the birth of a 'rough beast'. The verb 'Slouches' tells us a great deal about the beast that is preparing to be born. What does that word suggest to you?

Themes

'The Second Coming' presents **a vision** of the collapse of civilisation and the approach of an ominous new world order. It is, in part, a response to the violence and upheavals of the First World War and the Russian Revolution. It uses Christian terminology to suggest a world view which is far from the traditional Christian one.

Yeats lost any active belief in Christianity early in his life, but his understanding of the world was always, as he insisted himself, a religious one. Indeed, he developed his own religious philosophy, set out in *A Vision* (see 'Personal mythology' page 436), which involved the 2000-year cycles of history, the image of the gyres, and theories of personality according to the phases of the moon.

He was, however, careful to ensure that his poems could stand on their own. Although his theories underpin the vision in this poem, and knowledge of them adds to an understanding of it, it is not necessary to study those theories in order to experience the power and meaning of this poem.

Form and language

The poem is written in iambic pentameters with no rhyme scheme, though with occasional use of half-rhyme. **Yeats uses the metre with great flexibility and much variation.** The first syllable of a line or phrase is often stressed, against the basic metre, as in the first line of the poem: 'Túrning …'. Sometimes there are extra unstressed syllables in a line (e.g. line 13), and sometimes extra stresses, most notably in line 5, where we cannot help stressing all three monosyllables of 'blood-dimmed tide', which gives **a slow weight** to the phrase that is heightened by the repetition of the 'd' sounds. The metre is not obtrusive, but is always present, **underpinning and giving power to the images**.

The **language is blunt**, but the words are very carefully chosen. The poem works by plain, bold statement, especially in the first section: 'Things fall apart; the centre cannot hold'. We have already touched on the resonances of the verb 'Slouches' (line 22). Consider, too, the effect of the choice of apparently unobtrusive adjectives: 'Mere' (line 4), 'blank' (line 15), 'slow' (line 16), 'indignant' (line 17).

Imagery

We have looked at the individual images Yeats uses in the course of the Commentary above. They are multiple, powerful and often horrific. They come from very different sources: the Bible (Second Coming, Bethlehem, the 'blood-dimmed tide', and the beast perhaps from the Book of Revelation); ancient mythology (the Sphinx); falconry; Yeats's own private mythology (the gyres, *Spiritus Mundi*). They are images that have the power to **trouble the reader's imagination**, just as they trouble the speaker's sight (line 13).

Quotations as titles

The great Nigerian novelist Chinua Achebe called his first novel *Things Fall Apart* (1958); the American writer Joan Didion wrote a book of essays called *Slouching Towards Bethlehem* (1968), which is also the title of a song by Joni Mitchell; Robert B. Parker wrote a detective story called *The Widening Gyre* (1983); Woody Allen published a collection of his comic essays called *Mere Anarchy* in 2007; and a 2013 album by the metal band Whelm is titled *A Gaze Blank and Pitiless as the Sun*. You can find many other 'Second Coming' titles online. The poem certainly makes an impression on people!

The impact of the poem

Why is this poem so powerful? Why is it so well known that many other writers have taken phrases from it as titles for their own books? Is this popularity proof of the power of Yeats's prophecy?

One answer might lie in Yeats's mastery of his craft – the rhythms and sound choices of words that pack a punch and stay in the memory.

Another might be found in the voice of the speaker of the poem. The pronouncements of the first part carry conviction – they are plain and bald and sure of themselves. The certainty of 'now I know' in the second part of the poem is also **compelling**. Yeats speaks to us as a prophet as well as a poet, and he was not (in this poem, at least) afraid of the idea that a poet could and should have access to a special truth and knowledge. To tell the truth as he saw it, like a prophet, was, for Yeats, a proper function of a poet.

Beyond that, though closely connected to it, Yeats believed in the *Spiritus Mundi* – the store of shared images common to all humanity. His revelation, he declares, comes from that common store. It is easy to dismiss the image as a piece of old-fashioned nonsense. A lion's body with a man's head? But perhaps Yeats was right. **Is it possible that the power of the image does come from a source that is deep in the unconscious of all of us?** Certainly the fear – even the premonition – of an apocalypse, of the end of the world, is something that has been evident again and again in human history, and has often been seen as something to be desired as much as feared. 'The Second Coming' taps into these fears and desires in all of us.

Questions

1	In your own words, explain the image of the falcon in the first two lines of the poem.
2	What is the effect of the repetition of 'loosed' in lines 4 and 5?
3	Comment on the contrasts in sound and meaning of the phrases 'blood-dimmed tide' and 'ceremony of innocence' (lines 5 and 6).
4	Why, do you think, do the 'best' 'lack all conviction'?
5	Why, in your opinion, might 'passionate intensity' be a negative thing?
6	Is there a difference in the speaking voice between the first stanza and the second? If so, can you describe that difference?
7	Comment on the description of the desert birds as 'indignant' (line 17).
8	What has changed in the speaker after 'The darkness drops again' in line 18?
9	'What rough beast'. How do you imagine this beast? Or does the poet wish us to imagine it at all?
10	Why, do you think, does Yeats refer to Bethlehem in the final line of the poem?
11	In 'The Second Coming', Yeats presents his ideas in terms of images. Describe the kinds of images that dominate the poem and discuss their effect on the reader's imagination.
12	It has been said that 'The Second Coming' has elements of a horror film. Can you identify any such elements?
13	How does Yeats's vision of a world heading towards chaos strike you now, nearly a hundred years after it was written? Is it relevant today? Discuss in small groups.
14	Why, do you think, is this one of Yeats's best-known poems?

Before you read

Go online or find a good book on art history to find images of the wonderful works of art that came from the Byzantine civilisation. Look especially for the mosaics. This will give you an idea of what Yeats was thinking of when he wrote the poem.

Sailing to Byzantium 🔊

I

That is no country for old men. The young
In one another's arms, birds in the trees
– Those dying generations – at their song,
The salmon-falls, the mackerel-crowded seas,
Fish, flesh, or fowl, commend all summer long   5
Whatever is begotten, born, and dies.
Caught in that sensual music all neglect
Monuments of unageing intellect.

II

An aged man is but a paltry thing,
A tattered coat upon a stick, unless   10
Soul clap its hands and sing, and louder sing
For every tatter in its mortal dress,
Nor is there singing school but studying
Monuments of its own magnificence;
And therefore I have sailed the seas and come   15
To the holy city of Byzantium.

III

O sages standing in God's holy fire
As in the gold mosaic of a wall,
Come from the holy fire, perne in a gyre,
And be the singing-masters of my soul.   20
Consume my heart away; sick with desire
And fastened to a dying animal
It knows not what it is; and gather me
Into the artifice of eternity.

IV

Once out of nature I shall never take   25
My bodily form from any natural thing,
But such a form as Grecian goldsmiths make
Of hammered gold and gold enamelling
To keep a drowsy Emperor awake;
Or set upon a golden bough to sing   30
To lords and ladies of Byzantium
Of what is past, or passing, or to come.

Title	**Byzantium**: ancient city which had been part of the Greek and then the Roman empires; later known as Constantinople, now as Istanbul, in Turkey
5	**commend**: recommend as good
6	**begotten**: brought into existence by means of sexual reproduction
7	**sensual**: to do with physical pleasures
9	**paltry**: pathetic; insignificant
12	**mortal dress**: the body (which here is old and tattered)
17	**sages**: wise or holy men
19	**perne in a gyre**: to spin within a spiral
24	**artifice**: something made by craft or art

Guidelines

'Sailing to Byzantium' is the first poem in what many regard as Yeats's greatest volume of poetry, *The Tower*, first published in 1928. It sets the tone for the volume, in which Yeats both responds to the events of his day (including the Civil War in Ireland) and looks back over his own past and contemplates the future.

The 'I' of the poem

The speaker of the poem is **a man grown old**, a man **who yearns for purity and eternity**. It is easy to imagine that that man is simply Yeats, and that the voyage to Byzantium is therefore an imaginary or purely symbolic one. It is certainly true that Yeats projected many of his fears and desires on to the 'I' of the poem, and that the poem tells us a lot about him, but Yeats liked to try out different voices and personas in his poems. Here it is worth taking note of the fact that when he went away to Killarney to compose this poem, he wrote to a friend, 'I came here to write a poem about a medieval Irishman longing for Byzantium'.

Thoor Ballylee

In 1917 Yeats bought this fifteenth-century tower, part of the Coole estate, for £35, and restored and refurbished it with the help of an architect. It was for many years a rural retreat and a summer home for all his family, including two small children. It was also a source of inspiration and symbolism. The tower and the 'winding stair' within it provided names for two of Yeats's finest volumes of poetry, and the river beside it and the bridge over the river were given their own symbolic value in his private mythology. The poet Ezra Pound, however, referred to it as Yeats's 'phallic symbol on the bogs'. In 1929, the Yeats family moved out and Ballylee fell into disuse and ruin.

The Byzantine Empire and culture were powerful for more than a thousand years, from the end of the Roman Empire to the late Middle Ages, roughly 330–1450 AD. Yeats believed that Byzantium was the holy centre of European civilisation – the meeting point of east and west. He also believed that Byzantine art had influenced Celtic art, especially in the highly intricate and brightly decorated religious artwork found, for example, in the Book of Kells. So a journey from Ireland to Byzantium around 800–1000 was not a fantasy, but a real possibility.

If we keep this in mind, we can see the extreme desires of the poem's speaker as something other than Yeats expressing his own personal wishes. In fact, by **adopting a persona**, Yeats is able to explore an extreme state of mind fully without completely identifying himself with the views expressed. This is similar to his method in 'An Irish Airman Foresees His Death'.

Commentary

Stanza I

The country that is not 'for old men' is not named, but can be thought of as Ireland, with its 'salmon-falls' and 'mackerel-crowded seas'. One might even see it as Tír na nÓg, the mythical land of eternal youth, with 'The young / In one another's arms'. But here, life, however vibrant and teeming, also involves death: 'Whatever is begotten, born, and dies.' Both birds and humans are 'Those dying generations'. **The life of the body implies death.** But what all ignore, because they are so involved with ('caught in') the 'sensual music', is the timeless ('unageing') and the spiritual or intellectual side of existence.

Stanza II

The speaker turns to consider himself – an 'aged man', a 'paltry', useless thing. He feels he is like a scarecrow – 'A tattered coat upon a stick'. But the final word of that line, **'unless'**, isolated by the comma before it and the line break after it, brings **a moment of suspense and possibility**. What can compensate for physical frailty? The answer he gives, the first word of the next line, is 'Soul'. **The soul must be active.** It must 'clap its hands and sing, and louder sing'. Notice **the work that the verbs do here**, the **repetition of 'sing' indicating the urgency** of what is needed. And how does a soul learn to sing? In 'singing school', of course, and that means studying 'Monuments of its own magnificence'. What are those monuments? It is not clear, but they are something to do with the highest achievements of a culture and a civilisation, and they are to be found, he believes, in Byzantium: 'therefore I have sailed the seas and come / To the holy city of Byzantium.'

Stanza III

The speaker is now in Byzantium. One might imagine him looking at the golden mosaics, like those Yeats had seen with Lady Gregory in Ravenna in 1907 or with his wife in Sicily in 1925. He speaks to the 'sages' – perhaps those pictured in the mosaic – and asks for their help. It is like a prayer. To him, they are 'standing in God's holy fire'. He asks them to come from that fire to be 'the singing-masters of my soul'. He imagines them coming 'perne in a gyre', spinning within a spiral. There is a real **urgency** to the speaker's **plea**: 'Consume my heart away', he cries. He wants to be rid of his decaying body and the passions that come with it and the death it will face. Instead, **he wants to be part of the 'artifice of eternity'** – not a human or an animal, but something artificial, something that will last forever. He pleads the sages to 'gather me', as if he is entirely passive, like a crop to be harvested.

Stanza IV

Yeats believed that the soul after death could choose its own shape. In this stanza the speaker describes what he wants to become when he has passed on from this life – 'out of nature'. He doesn't want to take his shape (his 'bodily form') from any living creature, but an artificial, man-made one. He wants to become **a work of art**. He imagines something made of **gold** – the metal that does not tarnish; the word 'gold' occurs four times in four lines (27–30). He imagines himself as a golden bird singing on a golden bough. The 'drowsy' emperor, the lords and ladies seem almost oblivious of this miracle, and yet the bird has a very special power. What it sings is not ordinary birdsong or the 'sensual music' of stanza I; it sings of 'what is past, or passing, or to come' – the past, the present, and, most remarkably, of the future. **The bird is also a prophet.**

Themes and imagery

Both themes and imagery in the poem are organised around **pairs of opposites**: age is set against youth, the body against the soul, time against eternity, sensual life against artifice and works of art. The country of stanza I, with its teeming creatures and carefree people, represents one pole. It stands for youth, the cycle of life and death, and sensuality. Against that is set the old man with his decaying body who wants to nourish his eternal soul and escape from the cycle of life and death. The other pole is Byzantium, which stands for the spirit, the intellect, art and artifice, and which seems to hold out the possibility of a kind of immortality. **The movement of the poem is from one to the other**, away from the cycle of life and death towards art and eternity. At its simplest, this is an expression of the old man's **wish to escape**: to escape from his ageing body, and the humiliation he feels in being identified with it, **towards an idea of perfection** which can rise above death. It is no coincidence that Yeats was over sixty when he wrote the poem, and becoming increasingly aware of his age and his dwindling energy.

The **nature and value of art – and song in particular** – is another thread that runs through this poem, and a central image in it. Singing is mentioned in the first stanza. The 'dying generations' are 'at their song', which must be related to the 'sensual music' they are caught up in. In stanza II the speaker urges his soul to 'sing, and louder sing'. That might be interpreted as the soul learning to be alive, but 'song' is also another term for poetry – **Yeats called many of his poems 'songs'**; thus, becoming a better poet by putting all his efforts into singing is one of the things on Yeats's mind, if not the speaker's. The 'Monuments of its own magnificence' he would study in 'singing school' might be thought of as the great poetry (and other works of art) of the past. The sages in stanza III that he asks to be the 'singing-masters of my soul' would then be seen as poets and artists as well as wise men.

The final image of becoming a golden bird singing is what the speaker says he desires most. He wants to be a work of art (the golden bird) which in turn creates works of art (the songs). Moreover, his songs can speak of the future. Yeats believed a poet could and should also be a prophet. The final image of 'Sailing to Byzantium' can be seen as presenting a vision of that possibility. Yeats is not ashamed of his ambition. By making this the first poem in *The Tower*, the poet is suggesting something about what he is setting out to accomplish in the rest of the book: **singing about past, present and even future**.

Form and language

This poem is written in eight-line stanzas rhyming *abababcc*, **a tight form** that perhaps reflects the intricate craftsmanship of Byzantium. Notice that **every stanza ends with a rhyming couplet**, which gives it the sense of something being neatly tied up. Yeats uses the iambic pentameter (five stresses to a line) with his accustomed flexibility and skill. **He often uses the caesura and enjambment to carry the energy through to the following line.** We looked at one example in lines 10–11: 'A tattered coat upon a stick, unless / Soul clap its hands and sing'. Can you identify others?

This is in many ways a difficult poem, and the language can be mystifying: 'perne in a gyre'; 'the artifice of eternity'. There is something abstract and hard to grasp in some of the vocabulary. Nevertheless, Yeats makes the words work hard for him. The 'sensual music' mentioned in the first stanza can be felt in the **rich, hyphenated phrases Yeats has invented** – 'The salmon-falls, the mackerel-crowded seas' – and in the alliteration of 'Fish, flesh, or fowl' and 'begotten, born'.

In the second stanza Yeats uses the sounds of the words to carry the bitter resentment of old age that the speaker expresses. **The burst of energy that comes with the initial 'p' of 'paltry'** (line 9), which is **almost like spitting**, is carried over into the next line, where the hard consonants ('t' and 'c') of 'A tattered coat upon a stick' tell us all we need to know about how he feels about what old age has done to him. In contrast with that, the **alliteration of 'm' sounds** and the **half-rhyme of '–ents' / '–ence'** in 'Monuments of its own magnificence' **suggest a delighted relish** at the prospect of encountering these monuments in Byzantium.

Interpreting the poem

Some readers are disappointed by the poem's ending: the fact that all the speaker aspires to, in the end, is to be an artificial bird. It lacks life compared with the 'sensual music' of the first stanza. Did you have that feeling when you read it? It is a fair reaction.

It is worth bearing in mind, though, as discussed above, that although the speaker dwells on matters that preoccupied the poet, he is not simply Yeats. The poem is an expression of a state of mind taken to an extreme, and the poem follows the logic it sets up to this rather bizarre destination. But a poem does not have to express its author's final conclusions. In other poems Yeats (or the speaker) expresses quite different views, some of which we shall be examining.

Questions

1. In your own words, describe the country depicted in stanza I.

2. Why are its inhabitants described as 'Those dying generations'?

3. What does the country lack, in the view of the speaker?

4. According to stanza II, what is the only thing an old man can do to rise above his physical decay? Use your own words.

5. Stanza III is like a prayer. Who is the speaker praying to and what, in your own words, does he want?

6. In stanza IV the speaker imagines being free to choose his shape. What shape does he choose, and why?

7. This poem could be seen as an expression of escapism. Can you see any parallels with 'The Lake Isle of Innisfree'? Explain.

8. This poem could be seen as being about poetry. Does this interpretation make sense to you? Explain.

9. Choose two lines or phrases that you particularly like, and explain why you like them.

10. Comment on the repetition of 'gold' in stanza IV.

11. Yeats wrote this poem when he was sixty-one. Might this account for the attitude to life expressed in it? Support your comments by reference to the text.

12. One of the themes of the poem is the relationship between art and life. Develop this idea.

13. Which do you find more appealing – the country depicted in stanza I or Byzantium? Discuss in pairs or groups.

14. Imagine you are a mechanical bird which had once been human and now can only sing. What would you sing? Write in verse or prose, as you wish.

Before you read

The next poem is taken from a sequence of poems called 'Meditations in Time of Civil War'. In class or in groups, discuss what you know about the Irish Civil War (1922–23).

from Meditations in Time of Civil War:
VI The Stare's Nest by My Window

The bees build in the crevices
Of loosening masonry, and there
The mother birds bring grubs and flies.
My wall is loosening; honey-bees,
Come build in the empty house of the stare.   5

We are closed in, and the key is turned
On our uncertainty; somewhere
A man is killed, or a house burned,
Yet no clear fact to be discerned:
Come build in the empty house of the stare.   10

A barricade of stone or of wood;
Some fourteen days of civil war;
Last night they trundled down the road
That dead young soldier in his blood:
Come build in the empty house of the stare.   15

We had fed the heart on fantasies,
The heart's grown brutal from the fare;
More substance in our enmities
Than in our love; O honey-bees,
Come build in the empty house of the stare.   20

Glossary

Title	*Stare*: starling
1	*crevices*: cracks, narrow openings
2	*masonry*: stonework
9	*discerned*: discovered, made out
11	*barricade*: barrier, usually constructed in a conflict to block opposing forces
12	*civil war*: the Irish Civil War (June 1922 – May 1923)
17	*brutal*: violent, savage, lacking compassion
17	*fare*: diet (in this case, what the heart has been fed on)
18	*substance*: weight, significance
18	*our enmities*: our hatreds; the things that divide us

Guidelines

This poem comes from a sequence of seven poems called 'Meditations in Time of Civil War', in which Yeats contemplates the terrible events of the world around him from his tower in Co. Galway, Thoor Ballylee. It was published in *The Tower* (1928). In that sequence Yeats uses his immediate surroundings – the tower and certain items in it – to make **symbols** (or, to use his term, '**emblems**') that stand for different aspects of the wider world. In 'The Stare's Nest by My Window' he looks from the window of his study at the signs of civil war, but also at the wildlife around him.

The speaker of the poem

In discussing this poem it feels natural to say 'Yeats' rather than 'the speaker', as Yeats puts himself and his tower at the centre of this sequence of poems. This poem is called 'The Stare's Nest by *My* Window'; others in the sequence are called '*My* House', '*My* Table', '*My* Descendants', 'The Road at *My* Door'.

Commentary

Stanza 1

Yeats starts by observing the wildlife – the birds and the bees that fly around his tower, the nurturing of the young. The starling's nest by his window is empty now, and he asks the honey-bees to build their own nest in it. At this stage all seems calm and peaceful; the focus is on the harmony of nature. Only the repetition of 'loosening' in the phrase 'My wall is loosening' alerts the reader to the sense that all is not well.

Stanza 2

The opening of stanza 2 takes a sinister turn: 'We are closed in, and the key is turned'. The image is of being locked up, as if in prison, but Yeats does not write 'We are locked in'. Presumably they (he and his family there) locked the door to protect themselves from what was going on around them, but once the door is locked the outside world becomes separate and hard to know, so it is their 'uncertainty' that is locked in place by the turning of the key. Only rumours are heard – a man killed, a house burned – but there is always that uncertainty to bear: 'no clear fact to be discerned'.

Stanza 3

The third stanza offers glimpses of what Yeats can discern from his tower. 'A barricade of stone or of wood' might refer to the barricades constructed by the warring factions, but it may also refer to the tower, with its stone walls and wooden door, which is his own barricade against the threats from outside. Line 12 makes clear what is going on: 'civil war'. Then we get an image of something horrifying glimpsed from his window – the 'dead young soldier in his blood' being dragged down the road by a nameless 'they'. The soldier was, presumably, a member of the Free State army. The refrain of the final line now seems very detached from the action – a plea that some small thing may be made right.

Stanza 4

Yeats now gives his **diagnosis** of events. The 'fantasies' 'We' (the Irish people) had 'fed the heart on' are presumably the republican notions of 'blood sacrifice' and the need for violence to create a free and independent Ireland. Yeats's views of those ideas have been discussed in relation to 'Easter 1916'. Now he sees what he regards as the consequences of those views – the heart grown 'brutal' and ready for further violence. Hatred ('our enmities') is proving stronger than love.

The final repetition of the refrain is a desperate prayer. The 'O' before 'honey-bees' (line 19) adds an intensity to the **plea** to 'build in the empty house of the stare', and its symbolic meaning is now inescapable.

Themes and imagery

This poem **sets the destruction and brutality of civil war**, seen most vividly in stanza 3, **against the beauty and productivity of nature** seen in stanza 1. The **central image**, which seems to become more intense as the counter-images of brutality build up, is that of **the honey-bees building a nest**. With this image the poet clings to a hope for the future. It is easy to see the **bees as symbolic of a productive society** and their **honey as peace and harmony**. There is even hope in the fact that because the masonry is 'loosening', it allows them to build 'in the crevices' there (lines 1–2). Now that the stare's nest is empty **there is a space to fill**. The speaker pleads for the honey-bees to fill that space and 'build' for a sweeter future. For all the brutality and fear in the poem, the refrain always takes the reader back to **hope**.

> **The origin of the poem**
>
> In his volume of *Autobiographies*, Yeats says this poem came from 'an overmastering desire not to grow unhappy or embittered, not to lose all sense of the beauty of nature'.

Form and language

The poem is written in five-line stanzas rhyming *abaab*, with the **repeated final line like a prayer or incantation** running through it. It is written in iambic tetrameters (four stresses per line), with the refrain given a lulling rhythm by the extra unstressed syllables.

The language varies from the plain description of the first stanza to the authoritative, assured diagnosis of the country's ills in stanza 4, but **simple, blunt statements**, **often lacking a verb** (lines 11–12 and 18–19) are used throughout. **Against these is set the insistent incantation of the refrain.**

As ever, Yeats enriches the poem with textures of sound and rhythm. Notice, for example, how the patterning of 'b', 'm' and 's' sounds in the first stanza helps to create a harmonious image.

Questions

1	Describe, in your own words, the activity Yeats describes in stanza 1.
2	How would you describe the atmosphere indicated in stanza 2?
3	What, according to stanza 3, can be 'discerned' of the civil war?
4	What, do you think, were the 'fantasies' Yeats mentions in line 16, and why did they make the heart 'brutal'?
5	What do the honey-bees represent? And what are the implications of asking them to 'build in the empty house of the stare'?
6	What is the atmosphere of the first stanza? How does Yeats create this?
7	Comment on the use of the word 'trundled' in line 13. What does it tell us about Yeats's viewpoint on what was happening outside his window?
8	Which is uppermost in your reading of the poem – hope or despair? Explain your answer.
9	The poem raises questions about the nature of nationalism, particularly in its extreme forms. What are those questions? Are they still relevant today, in Ireland or elsewhere?
10	*Groupwork* How do you see Ireland at the present time, and what would you wish for its future? Discuss in pairs or small groups.

In Memory of Eva Gore-Booth and Con Markiewicz

The light of evening, Lissadell,
Great windows open to the south,
Two girls in silk kimonos, both
Beautiful, one a gazelle.
But a raving autumn shears   5
Blossom from the summer's wreath;
The older is condemned to death,
Pardoned, drags out lonely years
Conspiring among the ignorant.
I know not what the younger dreams –   10
Some vague Utopia – and she seems,
When withered old and skeleton-gaunt,
An image of such politics.
Many a time I think to seek
One or the other out and speak   15
Of that old Georgian mansion, mix
Pictures of the mind, recall
That table and the talk of youth,
Two girls in silk kimonos, both
Beautiful, one a gazelle.   20

Dear shadows, now you know it all,
All the folly of a fight
With a common wrong or right.
The innocent and the beautiful
Have no enemy but time;   25
Arise and bid me strike a match
And strike another till time catch;
Should the conflagration climb,
Run till all the sages know.
We the great gazebo built,   30
They convicted us of guilt;
Bid me strike a match and blow.

Glossary

1	**Lissadell**: early nineteenth-century country house near Sligo, home of the Gore-Booth sisters; Yeats visited the house as a young man
3	**kimonos**: Japanese robes
5	**raving**: savage, mad
5	**shears**: cuts off
6	**wreath**: arrangement of flowers and leaves in a ring, often associated with funerals
11	**Utopia**: ideal world
12	**gaunt**: thin
16	**Georgian mansion**: big eighteenth- or nineteenth-century house; here, Lissadell
27	**catch**: catch fire
28	**conflagration**: huge fire
30	**gazebo**: a building with a commanding view and open sides usually built in the grounds of a large house

Guidelines

The subjects of this poem are the Gore-Booth sisters, in whose splendid house, Lissadell, Yeats had stayed in the winter of 1894–5.

The elder, Constance, became a painter, married a Polish count called Casimir Markiewicz, and settled in Dublin. She fought in the 1916 Easter Rising (see 'Easter 1916'), and was condemned to death for her part in it, though the sentence was reduced to life imprisonment because she was a woman. She was released in 1917 and resumed her political activity. She was the first woman elected to the British parliament, though she did not take her seat, and later became Minister for Labour in the first Dáil Éireann cabinet. She supported the republican cause in the Civil War.

> **Lissadell House**
>
> Built in the 1830s for the Gore-Booth family in a neo-classical style, it is an imposing building, austere rather than elegant. On the south shore of Magherow peninsula in northern Co. Sligo, it remained in the Gore-Booth family until 2004. See picture overleaf.

Yeats was closer as a young man to the younger, Eva – the 'gazelle' of line 4 – who was, he thought, a promising poet. She moved to England in 1897, but instead of pursuing her poetry she devoted herself to the poor, becoming involved with the trade union movement and the struggle for women's rights.

Both sisters, then, rejected their privileged Anglo-Irish background out of political conviction. Eva died in 1926, Con in July 1927. This poem was completed in October 1927. It was published as the first poem in Yeats's collection *The Winding Stair* (1933).

Commentary

Stanza 1

The poem begins by conjuring a beautiful image of the past out of a few elements: the big house, the light, the windows, the girls in silk kimonos. The sentence, which lasts four lines, has no verb, **as if the image exists outside time**. The first verb comes at the end of the fifth line, and it is a brutal one: 'a raving autumn *shears* / Blossom from the summer's wreath'. In other words, the passing of time destroys beauty, just as autumn destroys summer's flowers.

Lissadell House, Co. Sligo.

Yeats goes on to describe the ways in which the sisters' beauty has been destroyed by their political convictions. Con's achievements are dismissed as 'Conspiring among the ignorant'; Eva in 'withered' old age is described as 'An image of such politics', as if that is what her strong socialist views deserved. Yeats goes on to imagine looking one of the sisters up to reminisce about that distant time. Notice that he writes as if it is still possible: 'Many a time I think to seek / One or the other out'. It is as if the sisters were still alive. The stanza ends with a restatement of the first image, as if it has not changed: 'Two girls in silk kimonos, both / Beautiful, one a gazelle.'

Stanza 2

Now Yeats addresses the 'shadows' or ghosts of the two dead sisters. He imagines, confidently, that now they are dead they understand the 'folly' of pursuing a political cause, fighting with 'a common wrong or right'.

The 'innocent and the beautiful', as they were when they were young, have, he says, 'no enemy but time'. One of the implications of this statement is that they both made enemies as a result of their political actions. Another implication is that if **you could defeat time** you could restore innocence and beauty – the moment in Lissadell Yeats contemplates at the beginning of the poem. This thought is behind the following two lines: Yeats summons the sisters to 'Arise and bid me strike a match / And strike another till time catch'. The idea is that time itself could be burned up and destroyed, and the past restored.

But the image goes beyond that idea. Yeats imagines the 'conflagration' climbing, as if it destroyed more than it was meant to. It is hard to say who the 'sages' in line 29 are – perhaps the same ones as were standing in 'God's holy fire' in 'Sailing to Byzantium'. It is as if heaven itself were ablaze.

The last three lines have been interpreted in many different ways. It is not clear who 'We' are, or what the 'great gazebo' represents. A gazebo is the sort of thing a big house like Lissadell might have had: a place to sit and gaze at the countryside. It could stand for the Anglo-Irish 'Ascendancy' culture, of which the Gore-Booth sisters were part. It could represent the cultural nationalism of 'Romantic Ireland', which Yeats's poetry did much to shape. What is certain is that by the poem's final line, the instruction to 'Bid me strike a match and blow', **what is at stake has shifted and grown**. There are resonances here of the burning down of big Anglo-Irish houses that happened during the Civil War. What is it that the speaker is now suggesting might be set fire to? Time, certainly. A whole culture, possibly. It is hard to know whether he would destroy time in order to restore innocence and beauty and the culture they emerged from, or destroy that innocence and beauty.

Themes and imagery

Time is one of the main themes of this poem. Thinking about two dead sisters and an image of them from decades before, 'both / Beautiful, one a gazelle', leads Yeats to **contemplate the mysteries of time**, as we have discussed above. Yeats believed that time was merely **a construction of the human mind**, and in the central image of the second stanza he writes of striking matches to set fire to time, as if it could be destroyed by human action. He considers the possibility that the 'conflagration' could get out of control. At the end he is ready to commit arson, to strike the match, and 'blow' to get the flames going.

The poem is also concerned with the **legacy of the Anglo-Irish 'Ascendancy' classes**. Yeats was proud of that heritage, and he must have felt special pride and privilege in the surroundings of Lissadell, as it is presented in the opening lines of the poem. It was a civilisation of which Yeats felt himself not only to be part, but also, as a poet, one of the creators of its culture and values: 'We the great gazebo built'. It is this culture that the sisters represent at the beginning in their youth and beauty, but rejected through their political activism, which Yeats felt had diminished them. If 'We' who built the 'great gazebo' (such as the one below) are Yeats and men such as the Anglo-Irish patriots he celebrated in 'September 1913' – Fitzgerald, Emmet and Tone – it is possible to read 'They' in line 31 as the sisters, whose rejection of the values of the society from which they came throws blame on that society. The poem is filled with **nostalgia for that civilisation**, and can be viewed as **marking its disappearance**.

Form and language

The poem is written in iambic tetrameters (four stresses per line) with a rhyming pattern of *abbacddc* etc. It is divided into two parts, the second part of which develops the ideas of the first part. In this it is like a sonnet, and although it is more than twice the length of a sonnet, **its proportions are roughly similar**.

There is a **directness and simplicity to the language which masks the obscurity of meaning in places**. Nevertheless, Yeats creates some subtle and telling effects with the words he chooses. The delicate, harmonious atmosphere of the first four lines is conjured with a pattern of light, delicate consonants, especially 'l', 'k', 's' and 'n' sounds (e.g. 'silk kimonos'); the name of the house, with its double 'l' sounds, is a gift in this respect: 'Lissadell'. In contrast with that, the long vowel in the active verb 'shears' in line 5 brings that delicate beauty to an abrupt and tangible end.

It is worth noting, too, that Yeats's handling of the language, and of **verbs** in particular, is central to his development of the theme of time. We have already looked at the way in which the lack of verbs in the image of the sisters in Lissadell in the first four lines means that that image seems suspended in time. In the rest of that stanza Yeats **uses the present tense** – 'is condemned', 'drags out', 'dreams', 'seems' – **although he is**

Con Markiewicz

talking about past events in the lives of women who are dead. Then he declares that 'Many a time I *think* to seek / One or the other out', not '*thought* to seek', as if it is still possible to meet up and talk. He imagines he can 'recall' that scene, not only in the sense of 'remember' it, but also actively 'call it back to life'. Similarly, in the second stanza he addresses the 'shadows' directly, as if they are still present despite being dead, and could order him to bring them back to life: 'Arise and bid me strike a match'. They remain, in his and our imaginations, not the old women they became but 'The innocent and the beautiful'. **The ordinary workings of time are suspended by Yeats's subtle use of grammar.**

Questions

1	Explain the image in lines 5–6. What is its meaning in the context of the poem?
2	How does Yeats view the later lives of the two sisters? What words and phrases indicate how he feels?
3	Why, do you think, does Yeats repeat lines 3–4 at the end of the first stanza?
4	What is Yeats asking the 'shadows' to 'bid' him to do in lines 26–27, and why?
5	In your view, what does the 'great gazebo' (line 30) represent?
6	Is this an optimistic or a pessimistic poem? Give reasons for your answer.
7	The passing of time and its effects are at the heart of the poem. Show how Yeats treats this idea.
8	The poem betrays Yeats's social and political attitudes. How would you describe them, on the evidence it provides?
9	Comment on Yeats's handling of sounds and images to create atmosphere and emotion in this poem.
10	If Eva Gore-Booth and Con Markiewicz could be conjured back to life and were shown Yeats's poem, what might they say? Discuss in pairs.
11	Imagine you are Con or Eva. Write about what you remember of the young poet Yeats when he came to visit you in Lissadell, and about what you think of what he has since become.
12	Think of a vivid memory of a happy or treasured day. Try to find one image that sums up the day and what it meant to you. Write it down in as few words as possible.

Swift's Epitaph

Swift has sailed into his rest;
Savage indignation there
Cannot lacerate his breast.
Imitate him if you dare,
World-besotted traveller; he   5
Served human liberty.

Glossary

Title	*Epitaph*: an inscription on a gravestone or plaque in memory of a person who has died
1	*Swift*: Jonathan Swift (1667–1745), Dean of St Patrick's Cathedral, Dublin; best known as the author of *Gulliver's Travels*
2	*indignation*: righteous anger
3	*lacerate*: tear and wound
5	*World-besotted*: too attached to worldly things

Guidelines

This short poem is a loose translation of the Latin epitaph that Swift wrote for himself, which can be found carved in St Patrick's Cathedral, Dublin, where Swift was Dean. Swift was also a writer of poetry and satire, in which he used his wit and his anger to attack cruelty, hypocrisy, vanity and stupidity.

Swift had a strong hold on Yeats's imagination, especially at this point in his life. Yeats wrote about him and other eighteenth-century Anglo-Irish authors in several poems in *The Winding Stair* (1933), from which this poem comes.

Commentary

The first line tells us Swift has died; he has gone to his 'rest' because he can no longer be torn apart by his 'savage indignation' at the injustices of the world, and so he is at peace. In the final three lines the poem turns to address its reader. This idea is clearer if you think of a visitor – a tourist, perhaps – finding and reading the epitaph carved in stone in St Patrick's Cathedral. He or she is the 'World-besotted traveller', too attached to things of the material world. The poem/epitaph issues **a challenge**: 'Imitate him if you dare' because he served the cause of 'human liberty'.

One possible way of understanding the poem is to **think of Yeats as the traveller**, which makes sense because he liked to sit beside Swift's monument in the cathedral where the epitaph is carved. In this reading, Yeats is, in effect, **challenging himself** to live up to the example of one of his literary heroes.

Themes

What sort of liberty did Swift serve and Yeats aspire to? In 1930 Yeats considered Swift's epitaph in his diary, and wrote, **'the liberty he served was that of intellect**, not liberty for the masses but **for those who could make liberty visible'**. Swift often found himself at odds with the 'masses', but he had the **courage to think for himself**, to **trust his own reason and moral sense**, and to **speak and write what he thought**.

Yeats, too, was no lover of mass thinking, and although he was involved with the Irish Republican Brotherhood in his early years and worked for the independence of Ireland, he valued his independence of thought just as much, and **championed freedom of artistic expression**. As one of the founders of the Abbey Theatre, he defended works that had caused public outrage, notably Synge's *The Playboy of the Western World* and O'Casey's great play, *The Plough and the Stars*, putting artistic freedom above mass indignation. In both cases he was able to help sway public opinion rather than give way before it.

Jonathan Swift.

Yeats felt strong affinities with Swift and other eighteenth-century Anglo-Irish writers and thinkers. He, like they, was part of a significant minority in Ireland who considered themselves Irish but, being of Protestant stock and from privileged backgrounds, were not always regarded as truly Irish by the Catholic majority.

For Yeats, the loyalty to his roots and his sense of what liberty meant came to a head in a famous speech to the Senate in 1925. He was speaking in a debate on divorce, which was being made illegal in the strongly Catholic post-independence Ireland, a move which he believed was 'grossly oppressive' to the significant minority of Protestants who didn't share the religious beliefs upon which the law was based. Speaking as part of that minority, he said:

> 'We against whom you have done this thing, are no petty people. We [Irish Protestants] are one of the great stocks of Europe. We are the people of Burke; we are the people of Grattan; we are the people of Swift, the people of Emmet, the people of Parnell. We have created the most of the modern literature of this country. We have created the best of its political intelligence.'

These sentiments are reflected in many of Yeats's poems, including 'September 1913' and 'In Memory of Eva Gore-Booth and Con Markiewicz'.

Imagery, form and language

This poem consists of six short lines rhyming *ababcc*. **The rhythm is interesting.** It has a solemn weight that is appropriate to an epitaph, given to it by starting each line with a single stress rather than an iambic foot (unstressed–stressed: ˘ ´), e.g. 'Swíft hăs sáiled ĭntó hĭs rést'. Notice too how **placing 'he' at the end of line 5**

creates a moment of suspense before the final line, which tells us the **most important thing the poem has to say**.

The language is **dignified**, and has a **somewhat haughty tone** as it addresses, a little scornfully, the 'World-besotted traveller' and issues its challenge to 'Imitate him if you dare'. There is a suggestion of personification in the idea of 'savage indignation' being able to 'lacerate' Swift's breast. The only image is that of death being like a journey which Swift has 'sailed' towards his 'rest'.

Swift on government

'all government without the consent of the governed is the very definition of slavery'.
Jonathan Swift

Questions

1	On the evidence of this epitaph, what kind of man was Swift?
2	Who, do you imagine, is the 'World-besotted traveller' addressed in the poem?
3	Why do you think Yeats included this translation among his own poems in *The Winding Stair*?
4	Comment on the rhythm of the poem. Why is it appropriate for an epitaph?
5	What is the effect of the line break after 'he' (line 5)?
6	In pairs, compare this epitaph with the one Yeats wrote for himself in 'Under Ben Bulben' (page 489).
7	Write a short epitaph for a well-known person who died during the last twenty years.

An Acre of Grass

Picture and book remain,
An acre of green grass
For air and exercise,
Now strength of body goes;
Midnight, an old house   5
Where nothing stirs but a mouse.

My temptation is quiet.
Here at life's end
Neither loose imagination,
Nor the mill of the mind   10
Consuming its rag and bone,
Can make the truth known.

Grant me an old man's frenzy,
Myself must I remake
Till I am Timon and Lear   15
Or that William Blake
Who beat upon the wall
Till Truth obeyed his call;

A mind Michael Angelo knew
That can pierce the clouds,   20
Or inspired by frenzy
Shake the dead in their shrouds;
Forgotten else by mankind,
An old man's eagle mind.

Glossary

15	*Timon and Lear*: central characters from two of Shakespeare's tragedies, both old and, at times, full of rage
16	*William Blake*: William Blake (1757–1827) poet, artist and mystic; as a young man, Yeats edited an edition of his poetry
19	*Michael Angelo*: Michelangelo Buonarroti (1475–1564), one of the greatest artists of the Renaissance; best known for his statue of David and for his paintings on the ceiling of the Sistine Chapel in Rome
22	*shrouds*: cloths in which a dead person is wrapped for burial

Guidelines

'An Acre of Grass' was written in November 1936, when Yeats was seventy-one. It was first published in *Last Poems*, after the poet's death. Its setting is Riversdale, the old farmhouse in Rathfarnham in which Yeats lived from 1932 until his death in 1939.

Commentary

Stanza 1

Yeats **takes stock** of his situation, as an old man in a house he knows will be his last. His 'strength of body' is going, and though he has what he needs – books, pictures, his garden – it feels like a reduced life compared with what has gone before. The singular form of 'Picture and book' and the single acre of grass all suggest this. You can imagine him contemplating all this, alone, in his study (Yeats had taken the biggest room in the house in Rathfarnham for his study), listening to the quiet of the night, as lines 5–6 suggest. The atmosphere is calm, but is he happy?

Stanza 2

He could easily relax and take it easy: 'My temptation is quiet'. But he knows that it would be a mistake because neither 'loose' (undirected, unfocused) imagination, nor the 'mill of the mind' working on its random thoughts and emotions – 'its rag and bone' – can achieve what he wants: to 'make the truth known'. In other words, taking things easy isn't going to get any poems written.

Stanzas 3 and 4

Now he prays for the '**frenzy**' he needs to continue to create and write true poetry. **The word is used twice** (lines 13 and 21). It **implies passion** and **inspiration** and **a bit of madness**, and brings to mind the 'delirium of the brave' from 'September 1913'. He says he must 'remake' himself and become like the figures he names from Shakespeare or from life. Timon and Lear were passionate old men; both raged against injustice and human vice; Lear goes mad. The artists he names both kept their creative energy into old age: Blake, a poet, artist and mystic, died at seventy; the great Renaissance artist Michelangelo lived to nearly ninety. He asks for a mind like Michelangelo's, with the ability to excite the world – to 'Shake the dead in their shrouds'. He may be forgotten by most of mankind in his quiet farmhouse, but he still has – or aspires to – 'An old man's eagle mind'. The image suggests **a mind that is far-seeing, sharp-thinking and also, perhaps, savage**.

Themes

The primary theme of this poem is one that we have encountered in 'Sailing to Byzantium': the sense of being diminished physically by old age and the urgent need not to give in to it, but to live all the more fully, with a passionate soul and an inspired mind. The speaker here desires 'frenzy': passion, energy and even a little madness. This is a theme that runs through many of Yeats's later poems, and forms a stark contrast with the dreamy, twilit atmosphere of many of his early poems, notably 'The Lake Isle of Innisfree'.

Imagery

The first half of the poem focuses on the quiet scene in the 'old house'. The only metaphor is of the mind consuming its 'rag and bone' – a phrase Yeats uses, here and elsewhere, to refer to the disordered mess of thought and emotion we all have inside us. In the second half of the poem he uses vivid, physical images to express his impassioned need to 'remake' himself: Blake who 'beat upon the wall' until he got the answer he wanted; the 'mind Michael Angelo knew' which can 'pierce the clouds' or 'Shake the dead in their shrouds'. Notice the **active, physical verbs** he uses: 'beat', 'pierce', 'Shake'.

Form and language

The poem is written in six-line stanzas which rhyme *abcbdd*. In fact, in **the first two stanzas the *b* rhymes are only half-rhymes**: 'grass'/'goes'; 'end'/'mind'. The **urgent energy of the third and fourth stanzas** is felt all the more strongly thanks to the **full rhymes** that are used there: 'remake'/'Blake'; 'clouds' / 'shrouds'.

The **spare descriptive language of the opening**, which conjures a daily life and a state of mind in a **few simple images**, gives way in stanza 3 to a plea or a prayer: 'Grant me an old man's frenzy…'. The **physical passion of the imagery is reinforced by alliteration** in, for example, 'Myself must I remake'; 'Blake / Who beat'; 'Till Truth'; 'Shake the dead in their shrouds'.

Questions

1	What impression do you get of the speaker in the first stanza? How would you describe the mood of this stanza?
2	Explain, in your own words, why 'quiet' (line 7) is a 'temptation'. Why would it be a dangerous thing for the speaker?
3	What do you learn about what the speaker desires from the real and fictional men he names in the poem?
4	What do you understand by 'frenzy' (lines 13 and 21)? Is it a good thing, in the speaker's view? Explain.
5	'An old man's eagle mind.' What qualities are suggested by this image, do you think?
6	In stanza 3 the speaker declares 'Myself must I remake'. For what purpose must he 'remake' himself?
7	Explain the significance of the title. Can you suggest another title?
8	Choose two images from the poem that strike you as particularly effective. Explain your choice.
9	Do you think the speaker deserves our admiration? In pairs or groups share your thoughts.
10	How do you imagine yourself when you are old? How would you like to be? Write your thoughts as a poem or in prose.

Politics

Before you read

What is your own attitude to politics and politicians? In class or groups, share why you feel this way.

How can I, that girl standing there,	
My attention fix	
On Roman or on Russian	
Or on Spanish politics?	
Yet here's a travelled man that knows	5
What he talks about,	
And there's a politician	
That has read and thought,	
And maybe what they say is true	
Of war and war's alarms,	10
But O that I were young again	
And held her in my arms!	

Glossary

Epigraph **Thomas Mann**: (1875–1955), German writer

Guidelines

The first draft of this poem was written in May 1938. This was a time of crisis in Europe. There was civil war in Spain, a fascist government in Italy, Stalin's communist dictatorship in Russia, and although Germany is not mentioned in the poem, Adolf Hitler was in power. It was not hard to imagine that the continent was heading towards war, which eventually broke out in September 1939. Politics, therefore, were hard to ignore.

'Politics' was written in response to an article by the poet Archibald MacLeish in an American journal, the *Yale Review*. MacLeish had praised Yeats's 'public' language, but regretted the fact that he did not devote more attention to political subjects, quoting the words of Thomas Mann that Yeats uses in the epigraph to the poem.

Commentary

The question the speaker asks in the first four lines is simple: How can he 'fix' his 'attention' on politics when there's a beautiful girl standing near him? He allows some self-doubt to enter in lines 5–10, admitting that there are things worth knowing in politics and that there may be truth in what politicians say 'Of war and war's alarms'. But the poem's ending sweeps all that aside with a passionate exclamation:

'But O that I were young again
And held her in my arms!'

Politics pales to insignificance compared with that prospect.

Themes

The poem's title proclaims its main theme – or at least half of it. Yeats had long considered politics fundamentally dishonest, defining the job of the professional politician as 'the manipulation of popular enthusiasm by false news'. It is clear he has his doubts when he says, 'And maybe what they [the politicians] say is true' (line 9). Nevertheless, as we have seen in other poems, Yeats often dealt with politics in his poetry, and he engaged, both as poet and later as senator, in the great public debates of his day.

'Politics' is best seen not as a considered statement of Yeats's priorities, but as **a spirited retort** to MacLeish's article in the *Yale Review*. He does not want to be told what to write, and is not going to put his poetry at the disposal of professional politicians, but **he makes his point with a light and humorous touch**. He makes no great claims for his insight that he'd rather be in the embrace of a young woman than talking about politics. Nevertheless he is making a real point about the importance of passionate human relationships as opposed to political abstractions – the other half of the theme. This was **the last lyric poem** Yeats wrote, so it is not surprising that his **age is always present in his mind** – 'O that I were young again'. The recognition that he would have to be much younger before the girl would be likely to take him in her arms gives the ending a wistful note of regret to balance the delight he clearly feels at the prospect.

There is no poetic imagery in the poem, but there is **an essential contrast between the talk of politics**, which is all abstract and generalised, and **the physical presence of the girl**, and especially the imagined image of her in the speaker's arms.

Form and language

The twelve lines of the poem **divide naturally into three quatrains** rhyming *abcb*, though they are not divided this way on the page. For most of the poem it is hard to make out any regular metre, but lines with seven or eight syllables alternate with shorter lines of five or six. In lines 5–8 the language is casual and conversational, and there is hardly any hint of metre, but in **the final four lines of the poem the underlying iambic beat comes strongly through**. The thought in the final two lines is expressed in conventional poetic terms, as an exclamation with 'O', and with clear accents: 'But Ó that Í were yoúng agaín'. This adds zest to a thought that is already full of relish, and the delight in the idea is clinched by the **final strong rhyme** on 'arms', bringing the poem to a satisfying close.

Questions

1	What does the young girl in this poem represent, or is she just a young girl?
2	Is the speaker in this poem impressed by world affairs and by what people say about them?
3	How would you describe the tone of this poem? ■ Angry ■ Regretful ■ Light-hearted ■ Joyful Or what other term would you use?
4	What, if anything, does this poem have in common with Yeats's other 'political' poems?
5	Did you enjoy reading this poem? Discuss in groups or pairs.

from Under Ben Bulben: V and VI

V

Irish poets, learn your trade,
Sing whatever is well made,
Scorn the sort now growing up
All out of shape from toe to top,
Their unremembering hearts and heads   5
Base-born products of base beds.
Sing the peasantry, and then
Hard-riding country gentlemen,
The holiness of monks, and after
Porter-drinkers' randy laughter;   10
Sing the lords and ladies gay
That were beaten into the clay
Through seven heroic centuries;
Cast your mind on other days
That we in coming days may be   15
Still the indomitable Irishry.

VI

Under bare Ben Bulben's head
In Drumcliff churchyard Yeats is laid.
An ancestor was rector there
Long years ago; a church stands near,   20
By the road an ancient cross.
No marble, no conventional phrase;
On limestone quarried near the spot
By his command these words are cut:
    Cast a cold eye   25
    On life, on death.
    Horseman, pass by!

Glossary

6	***Base-born products of base beds***: of low descent; illegitimate
16	***indomitable***: stubborn; impossible to defeat
17	***Ben Bulben***: mountain that dominates the landscape around Drumcliff, Co. Sligo, where Yeats is buried

Guidelines

'Under Ben Bulben' is often regarded as Yeats's **poetic last will and testament**. In it he **reviews his beliefs and artistic principles**. He wrote many elegies for other people; this is **his own elegy**, and includes an epitaph for his gravestone.

Yeats intended the poem to be the opening one of his final book, to be published after his death. In fact it has often been printed as the last of his *Last Poems*.

Commentary

V

This section presents Yeats's **assessment of contemporary poetry** and **his advice to current and future poets**. He tells them to 'learn your trade', and to 'Sing' – in other words, write in verse – 'whatever is well made'. They should be **good craftsmen**, and avoid the poetry 'now growing up' that he describes as 'out of shape'. Who he was thinking of is open to debate: perhaps the modernist British and American poets; probably the lesser post-independence Irish poets. He accuses them of being 'unremembering' in head and heart, ignoring national history and poetic tradition. Then, in a somewhat shocking phrase, he calls them 'Base-born products of base beds' – the 'wrong' sort of people, you might say. This line alerts us to Yeats's controversial ideas and fears about the decline of the Irish stock (see sidebar).

The instructions he gives in the remainder of this section are straightforward, if rather old-fashioned. He tells Irish poets to 'Sing' of the peasants and the gentry, the holy (monks) and the profane (porter-drinkers), and the 'lords and ladies gay' that have come and gone 'Through seven heroic centuries' – in other words, the aristocracy of Ireland since the Norman invasion of 1169. He tells them to think of the past ('Cast your mind on other days') so that in the future ('coming days'), Irish poets can help to maintain the 'indomitable' Irish traditions. It is noticeable that the modern middle classes are not part of the heritage Yeats wants the poets to celebrate.

Eugenics: the indomitable Irishry

Yeats was interested in theories of eugenics, the science of breeding selectively to produce desirable qualities in a population. He believed, for example, in limiting the size of families among the poor. The science has been tainted by its association with Hitler and Nazi Germany, where it was used to justify the extermination of the Jewish people, but Yeats was not anti-Semitic or pro-Nazi. His concern was that the Irish culture and the Irish people were becoming degenerate, owing to the bad influences of English materialism and the small-mindedness of the Irish middle class. This, he thought, was not just a matter of mind and soul, but of body too. He complained in a letter, at the same time that this poem was written, that the new, young actors at the Abbey Theatre in Dublin were coming out of school with 'misshapen bodies'. Yeats believed in the virtues of aristocracy, 'the best born of the best'.

VI

In the sixth and final part of 'Under Ben Bulben', Yeats speaks as if he is already dead, describing his grave and the epitaph on the gravestone. He gives no instructions but states bare facts. The location in Sligo, 'Under bare Ben Bulben's head', was where he felt he belonged, a place he had known as a child, and in Drumcliff he had family roots, as he tells us: 'An ancestor was rector there / Long years ago'. Yeats emphasises **the depth of history and local connection**: the ancient cross, the local limestone. It is a **scene that is fitting, complete, almost self-contained**.

The epitaph that concludes the poem helps to make this a self-contained scene. Instead of the conventional instruction for the passer-by to stop and consider the dead person or his/her own mortality, Yeats tells the 'Horseman' to 'pass by'; not linger but keep going. The instruction to '**Cast a cold eye / On life, on death**' is reminiscent of the 'Irish Airman' who sees his fate in the same cold light: 'In balance with this life, this death.'

Themes and imagery

These two sections of 'Under Ben Bulben' share **a concern with Irish heritage** – in V, **historic and cultural**; in VI, of **family and place**. These might be seen as what Yeats calls, in section II of the poem, man's 'two eternities, / That of race and that of soul'.

In section V Yeats gives instructions meant to help poets shape Irish culture and the Irish people, a theme that runs through his poetry from the beginning. The imagery is of the different Irish people Yeats wants to celebrate in song. Notice that the 'lords and ladies' are 'beaten into the clay' over the centuries, implying not just that they are dead but that they have become part of Irish soil – of Ireland itself.

In section VI the imagery is simply that of the scene described, and the main impression given is of the rightness of this burial, rooted in family history and a connection with the place. The death is seen as a proper end to the life, just as in the epitaph the reader is told to 'Cast a cold eye' equally on life and death.

Drumcliff Churchyard

If you visit Drumcliff today you can see it all as Yeats describes: churchyard, simple grave, church, cross, the stone with Yeats's epitaph, with the bare steep slopes of Ben Bulben in the background. Yeats commented in a letter that his description of his grave in a remote Irish village 'will bind my heirs thank God. I write my poems for the Irish people but I am damned if I will have them at my funeral'. He didn't want a big funeral in Dublin, and knew that his poem would act as a set of instructions. Although he died in the south of France in 1939, his bones were reburied in Drumcliff churchyard after the Second World War.

Form and language

The poem is written in **rhyming couplets**, in a metre which is basically iambic but which is often missing the first, unstressed syllable, so that there are seven syllables rather than eight: 'Írish póets, léarn your tráde' This is the metre in which 'Swift's Epitaph' is written. It creates an **insistent, quite heavy rhythm**. Yeats uses this to lay down his law in section V, using the self-assured style of confident statement that we have seen in, for example, 'The Second Coming'.

At the start of the final section, Yeats uses the insistent rhythm along with alliteration to create a drum-like beat: 'Únder báre Ben Búlben's héad'. The fact that the churchyard is called 'Drumcliff' underlines the effect.

The epitaph that ends the poem consists of three lines with four syllables in each. Apart from 'Horseman', every word is a single syllable. The effect is weighty and considered.

Yeats is buried in Drumcliff churchyard, Co. Sligo.

Questions

1	What attitude does Yeats show to contemporary poets here?
2	What kind of Irish poetry would he like to see in the future?
3	From what we see in section V, what elements of Irish life and culture does Yeats value?
4	Does Yeats see himself as an Irish patriot?
5	How would you describe the tone of section V?
6	In section VI Yeats describes the setting in which he wants to be buried. What elements of it are important to him, and why?
7	What does the three-line epitaph at the end tell us about Yeats?
8	Comment on some of the poetic effects Yeats achieves in this poem through rhythm, rhyme, alliteration, assonance, etc.
9	Yeats originally included another line at the start of the epitaph: 'Draw rein, draw breath'. This would have completed the quatrain and added another rhyme. Can you suggest any reasons why he decided to leave it out of the final version?
10	*Groupwork* Do you like Yeats's plan for his burial? In groups, imagine a better one, for him or for an important public figure of your choosing.

SNAPSHOT W. B. YEATS

- Balances opposing ideas in his poetry
- Balance of passion and detachment
- Balance of the personal and political in his poetry
- Opposition between the body and the spirit
- Opposition and conflict are central to his vision
- Increasingly valued his heritage as a member of the Anglo-Irish community
- Conscious of his role as a poet in shaping modern Ireland

- Early poetry rich in adjectives and word music
- Poetic style and language become more direct and simple
- Creates his own symbolism and mythology
- Best work as a poet came relatively late
- Wrote with sustained vigour into old age

Exam-Preparation Questions

1. 'Yeats uses evocative language to create poetry that includes both personal reflection and public commentary.' Discuss this statement, supporting your answer with reference to both the themes and language found in the poetry of W. B. Yeats on your course.

2. 'Yeats conveys his meanings through images and symbols to a greater extent than through statement and argument.' Would you agree? Give reasons for your answer.

3. What do Yeats's poems, taken as a whole, tell you about the man who wrote them?

4. Outline the qualities of Yeats's poetry you admire or dislike. You might discuss Yeats's ideas, his images, his descriptive power, his rhetoric, his patriotism, his use of language and his mastery of poetic technique.

5. 'Yeats's poems attempt to recreate Ireland and Irishness in a changing world.' Discuss the ways in which Yeats's poetry responds to and tries to shape the political events of his time.

6. 'Yeats was given the Nobel Prize in 1923 for the poetry he had then written, but his best poetry was written after he won the prize.' Do you agree with this assessment of Yeats's work? Give reasons for your answer.

7. 'Much of the poetry of W. B. Yeats is based on contrast.' Discuss this comment with reference to, and quotation from, some of the poems by Yeats on your course.

8. 'The past, in one form or another, is often central to Yeats's poems.' Does Yeats often make the past seem better than the present? If so, why is this, and what does it tell you about Yeats as man and poet? Answer with close reference to the poems of Yeats on your course.

9. Write an introduction to the poetry of W. B. Yeats for someone new to his verse. In your answer you should discuss:
   - The themes of his poetry
   - His use of language and your response to it
   - His use of form and poetic technique.

   You might also consider some of these subjects:
   - His use of symbols
   - The way in which he uses his personal life in his poems
   - His response to public events
   - The development and variety of his poetry.

10. Yeats is often considered the greatest of all Irish poets. Why is this, do you think? Is it a fair judgement? You might consider:
    - The way in which his poetry is both very personal and very public
    - His skilful use of the sounds and rhythms of language
    - His use of symbols
    - The variety of subjects with which he deals
    - The obscurity of some of his poetry
    - The development of his poetry over many decades.

Sample Essay

'Yeats's poetry is driven by a tension between the real world in which he lives and an ideal world that he imagines.'

Write a response to the poetry of W. B. Yeats in the light of this statement, supporting your points with suitable reference to the poems on your course.

Answer addresses the question immediately

It is certainly true that Yeats's poetry sometimes imagines worlds that contrast with the everyday world, and that the emotional power of the poems often results from the tension between those worlds. As a poet, Yeats lived and worked through his imagination, but the worlds his imagination drew him to changed over the course of his life as a poet. I will start with his early poetry.

Introduces the first poem to be discussed, using the terms of the question

'The Lake Isle of Innisfree' is the earliest of the poems we have studied, and is the clearest and simplest example of Yeats imagining an ideal world. The tension here is between the 'pavements grey' of London, where Yeats was living when he wrote the poem, and the imagined life on an island in a lake in County

Short quotations used throughout the essay

Sligo. He declares that he 'will arise and go now', but it is the expression of a strong urge rather than a firm intention. The ideal world that Yeats imagines here is a hermit's solitary retreat – a simple, pastoral life in harmony with nature and self-sufficient: 'Nine

Keeps the terms of the question in mind, and defines them as they apply to this poem

bean-rows will I have there, a hive for the honey-bee'. The ideal world is, above all, a place of escape from the big city, a place of rest where 'peace comes dropping slow'. Though the island exists, this is really an imagined place, but Yeats's poem pictures it so vividly, with its glimmering light and the sounds of bees ('bee-loud glade'), crickets and the 'lake water lapping with low sounds by the shore', that it seems more real than London. The rich patterns of word music – alliteration, assonance, rhyme and rhythm – all combine to conjure up

Paragraph concludes with a strong image

the peace and beauty of this world for which the poet yearns, so that the reader, like the poet, hears its sounds 'in the deep heart's core'. Nowhere else in the poems we have studied do we find such a straightforward urge to escape to an idealised world.

Introduces second poem using the terms of the question

In 'Sailing to Byzantium' there is a more complex yearning for a different sort of ideal world. Like Innisfree, the Byzantium Yeats depicts is an idealised place based on a real one. Innisfree is rural and close to nature, whereas Byzantium is urban and highly artificial. In this poem the tension is between the 'country' of the first stanza, which is caught up in the cycle of life and death, and Byzantium of the latter part of the poem, which is a place of art and artifice, the soul rather than the body.

Continues to use short quotations

In this poem, however, the reality which the speaker wants to escape has less to do with the teeming life of the first stanza than with the fact that he is old – 'a dying animal'. Driven by old age and impending death, he yearns for a kind of immortality that he believes can be found in Byzantium. That immortality is the permanence of art, the 'artifice of eternity', and his image for it is the artificial bird made of 'hammered gold and gold enamelling' that is 'set upon a golden bough to sing'. It is a strange sort of ideal world, and in many ways the

Discussion of second poem ends with a return to the terms of the question

'sensual music' of the first stanza is much more attractive, but the power of the poem certainly comes from the tension between the two worlds.

Other poems also contain a tension between the poet's current reality and an idealised element of some kind. In 'Wild Swans at Coole', the poet's awareness of his age and the passing of time is the emotional reality that drives his imagination to see the swans as symbols not just of vigour and passion, but of eternal youth: 'Their hearts have not grown old'. The central contrast is between the speaker's sadness and loneliness – 'my heart is sore' – and the swans' beauty, strength and loving companionship – 'lover by lover'. In this poem, however, although the speaker idealised the swans, he does not really imagine an 'ideal world'.

A further poem is introduced mentioning a theme that links it to the previous paragraph

Discussion of third poem concludes by addressing the terms of the question, and introduces a qualification

The passing of time is also a central theme of 'In Memory of Eva Gore-Booth and Con Markiewicz'. There, the ideal world is in the past, merely a memory. That memory is of the two sisters at Lissadell, 'both / Beautiful, one a gazelle', who stand for a whole Anglo-Irish culture whose values Yeats admired. The real world is the one in which the sisters grew old and lonely and died. The past cannot be brought back to life, of course, but the daring power of the poem comes from the idea that such a thing might happen. It might be possible to destroy time by setting fire to it: 'bid me strike a match / And strike another till time catch'. Yeats's yearning for the 'innocent and the beautiful' is channelled into this wish to abolish time and restore the past. In one sense, Yeats succeeds. The image with which the poem opens contains no verbs, and therefore seems to hang outside time. Yeats writes as if it is still possible to see the sisters again: 'Many a time I think to seek / One or the other out'. The recurrence of the opening image at the end of the first stanza consequently prepares the reader for the idea of destroying time which dominates the second stanza. At the end of the poem Yeats is ready to begin the 'conflagration': 'Bid me strike a match and blow'. It is as if the power of his imagination and his desire were able to change reality.

Discussion of theme leads into discussion of Yeats's technique

Striking phrase to end the paragraph

The tension between an idealised past and the realities of the present is also central to 'September 1913', but here the context is public and political. The present small-minded middle classes who 'fumble in a greasy till' are set against the self-sacrificing heroes of the past. The poem is full of bitterness and irony, and though Yeats proclaims that 'Romantic Ireland's dead and gone', as if that was a good thing, the poem calls our attention to what is missing in the modern world, and hence for the need for the idealism of the past.

While continuing to address the question, the particular focus of this paragraph is defined

Discussion of poem which suggests a challenge to the terms of the question

The imagined ideal world features much less in Yeats's later poetry. In 'An Acre of Grass', for example, the 'real world in which he lives', in a smaller house as an old man, is set against his hopes for the future: 'Grant me an old man's frenzy'. He is not imagining an ideal world or an idealised past, but expressing a desire to fight against the limitations that his real-world existence imposes on him. His mind and imagination are still in tension with his everyday reality, but they are not drawn to a dreamy idealism but to an urgent need to reinvent and reinvigorate himself: 'Myself must I remake'.

Final paragraph summarises the arguments and suggests a qualification to the statement in the question

In conclusion, although the pull of an ideal world is particularly strong in his earlier poems, there is no single ideal world that features throughout Yeats's poetry. What can be said is that the possibilities created by his imagination are always in tension with the real world in which he lives. Yeats was always striving to make a reality rather than just describe one. It is one of the most remarkable things about Yeats that his poetic imagination fought on with such passion until the end of his life.

ESSAY CHECKLIST		Yes √	No ×
Purpose	Has the candidate understood the task?		
	Has the candidate responded to it in a thoughtful manner?		
	Has the candidate answered the question?		
Comment:			
Coherence	Has the candidate made convincing arguments?		
	Has the candidate linked ideas?		
	Does the essay have a sense of unity?		
Comment:			
Language	Is the essay written in an appropriate register?		
	Are ideas expressed in a clear way?		
	Is the writing fluent?		
Comment:			
Mechanics	Is the use of language accurate?		
	Are all words spelled correctly?		
	Does the punctuation help the reader?		
Comment:			

Colette Bryce

b. 1970

Self-Portrait in the Dark (with Cigarette) 498

Biography

Colette Bryce was born in Derry in 1970. She moved to England as a teenager and has lived in London, Spain and Scotland. From 2002 to 2005 she taught creative writing at the University of Dundee.

In 2003 Bryce was appointed to the North East Literary Fellowship and moved to Newcastle upon Tyne, where she now lives. She teaches for various creative writing organisations, including the Arvon Foundation, the Poetry School and the University of Newcastle. She was the editor of Britain's poetry magazine, *Poetry London*, from 2009 to 2012.

Her poetry collections are: *The Heel of Bernadette* (2000), *The Full Indian Rope Trick* (2004), *Self-Portrait in the Dark* (2008) and *The Whole & Rain-domed Universe* (2014). Her *Selected Poems* was published in 2017.

Bryce has received several awards for her books, including the Aldeburgh Prize, the Pigott Poetry Prize and the Strong Award. For individual poems, she has won both the National Poetry Competition (2003) and the Academi Cardiff International Poetry Competition (2007). She received the Cholmondeley Award in 2010.

Before you read

If you have access to the Internet, search it for works of art (mainly paintings) that are known as self-portraits.

In small groups, discuss the idea of a self-portrait. What does it suggest to you? Would it suggest someone vain enough to paint themselves in a flattering way, or someone who is trying to be honest? Keep these ideas in mind when you read Bryce's poem.

Self-Portrait in the Dark (with Cigarette)

To sleep, perchance
to dream? No chance:
it's 4 a.m. and I'm wakeful
as an animal,
caught between your presence and the lack.   5
This is the realm insomniac.
On the window seat, I light a cigarette
from a slim flame and monitor the street –
a stilled film, bathed in amber,
softened now in the wake of a downpour.   10

Beyond the daffodils
on Magdalen Green, there's one slow vehicle
pushing its beam along Riverside Drive,
a sign of life;
and two months on   15
from 'moving on'
your car, that you haven't yet picked up,
waits, spattered in raindrops like bubble wrap.
Here, I could easily go off
on a riff   20

on how cars, like pets, look a little like their owners
but I won't 'go there',
as they say in America,
given it's a clapped-out Nissan Micra ...
And you don't need to know that   25
I've been driving it illegally at night
in the lamp-lit silence of this city
– you'd only worry –
or, worse, that Morrissey
is jammed in the tape deck now and for eternity;   30

no. It's fine, all gleaming hubcaps,
seats like an upright, silhouetted couple;
from the dashboard, the wink
of that small red light I think
is a built-in security system. 35
In a poem
it could represent a heartbeat or a pulse.
Or loneliness: its vigilance.
Or simply the lighthouse-regular spark
of someone, somewhere, smoking in the dark. 40

Glossary

1	*perchance*: perhaps
6	*realm*: kingdom, country
6	*insomniac*: inability to sleep
9	*amber*: brownish-yellow/orange colour
10	*in the wake of*: as a result of; a wake is the wave made by a ship moving on the water
20	*riff*: quick-fire, off-the-cuff speech
24	*clapped-out*: useless, worn out
29	*Morrissey*: singer-songwriter, lead vocalist with The Smiths in the 1980s
32	*silhouetted*: outlined in shadow
38	*vigilance*: watchfulness

Guidelines

This is the title poem in the collection *Self-Portrait in the Dark*, published in 2008. It is set in the Scottish city of Dundee, where Bryce lived for a time: she mentions real places (Magdalen Green and Riverside Drive) in the second stanza.

Commentary

Stanza 1

The poem opens with a quotation from Shakespeare's *Hamlet*: 'To sleep, perchance / to dream?'. It is from the well-known soliloquy that starts 'To be, or not to be', in which Hamlet imagines what death might be like. Here, it is the idea of sleeping that seems to be more important; the possibility of the speaker doing that is brushed away with the colloquial 'No chance'.

The scene is then briefly set: it's four in the morning and the speaker cannot sleep. The reason for her sleeplessness is explained: she is 'caught between your presence and the lack'. This suggests that the poem is about **a love relationship that has ended**. She is thinking of her lover, who is no longer present, and yet not really absent. The whole poem is addressed to that **semi-absent figure**, the 'you' of the poem.

To be, or not to be: that is the question:
Whether 'tis nobler in the mind to suffer
The slings and arrows of outrageous
    fortune,
Or to take arms against a sea of troubles,
And by opposing end them? To die: to
    sleep;
No more; and by a sleep to say we end
The heart-ache and the thousand natural
    shocks
That flesh is heir to, 'tis a consummation
Devoutly to be wish'd. To die, to sleep;
To sleep: perchance to dream: ay, there's
    the rub;
For in that sleep of death what dreams may
    come
When we have shuffled off this mortal coil,
Must give us pause ...
    Hamlet, Act III, Scene 1

The speaker goes on to describe the scene in more detail, with herself at the centre of it in the window seat, watching the street and smoking a cigarette. The outline of the 'Self-Portrait' of the title has been drawn. The outside world is depicted like an image from a film: the amber light, presumably from street lamps, and the rain-washed street. The fact that the 'downpour' has passed and everything seems softened now might suggest something about the state of her feelings. What exactly does it suggest, do you think?

Stanza 2
The second stanza starts with a 'sign of life' outside after the stillness of the first stanza: a slow-moving car 'pushing its beam' along the road. The sight of something moving seems to spark the idea of 'moving on', which is apparently what her former lover has done.

In contrast, her ex's car is still there on the street, waiting to be picked up – a reminder of something that has ended. The raindrops on it look like 'bubble wrap', which is often used to package delicate things, perhaps for sending them away. The choice of comparison may say something about how she sees their relationship now.

At this point **the car becomes the centre of attention**. The speaker says she could go off on a 'riff' – a long, inventive speech – and although she says she won't, she has already planted in the reader's mind the idea of the car as a metaphor for her lover or their relationship.

Stanza 3
The 'riff' jumps, unpunctuated, into the third stanza, where the speaker tells us that the car is small (a Nissan Micra) and 'clapped-out'. As readers, we can't help wondering if this is a comment on her ex or their relationship. What does it suggest? And what should we make of the fact that she has been 'driving it illegally at night'? She says she won't tell her former lover because 'you'd only worry'. Does she want to spare their feelings? Is she implying that there are still strong feelings between them? Or is it a dig at her ex, who would only be concerned about the car, not her? **The playfulness of the poem means that all these possibilities are there.**

The speaker goes on to tell her ex something 'worse' – that a Morrissey tape is jammed in the car's tape deck 'now and for eternity'. Morrissey is best known, as Wikipedia says, for his songs of 'emotional isolation and sexual longing', so the particular tape is significant. Is it a dark joke or a bitter irony that the tape is stuck there? And what does it suggest about the speaker that she was playing it, presumably as she drove around alone in the silence of the night? These are questions that individual readers can find their own answers to.

Stanza 4
The fourth stanza begins by rejecting all the dark thoughts with one word: 'no' – but **the ironic humour continues**. The speaker decides to pretend to the imagined former lover that the car is 'fine', and even that the seats are 'like an upright, silhouetted couple', even though they are no longer a couple themselves.

The final eight lines of the poem focus on the winking red light of the security system on the car's dashboard, and what it might symbolise. The speaker distances herself from the possible meanings and the emotions connected with them by pretending she is only speaking **hypothetically** (in theory): 'In a poem / it could represent …' In fact, the idea of 'loneliness: its vigilance' inevitably takes us back to the first image of the poem, as the speaker monitors the empty street, alone and all too wide awake.

The last two lines seem to reinforce that image, connecting the flashing red light to 'the lighthouse-regular spark / of someone, somewhere, smoking in the dark', just as the speaker was at the beginning. But although she says 'simply', as if the image has no deeper meaning, it is far from simple. As readers, we can't ignore all the meanings that have already been suggested. And these lines also suggest another possibility: Is there, perhaps, somebody else, somewhere else, also smoking in the dark and thinking similar thoughts about the speaker?

Themes and imagery

This is a poem about the aftermath of a break-up and the complex, many-layered feelings that such an experience can leave you with. **Its mood is dark, but the poem's playful humour keeps the feelings at bay** and avoids sentimentality, so that we are not quite sure how hurt or bitter or lonely or devastated (or otherwise) the speaker is. The fact that the speaker is able to be humorous might suggest a certain **toughness as well as vulnerability**.

The **night-time setting** is important. It is not just that the speaker is sleepless; the world seems transformed by her sleeplessness, so that she inhabits a strange land: 'the realm insomniac' (line 6). She is 'wakeful / as an animal', and her senses seem heightened, particularly her visual sense, as she 'monitor[s]' the street. The imagery is largely visual. Each element of it – the street scene, the clapped-out car, the red light – has its suggestive power, and together they create **an atmosphere of loneliness and melancholy**.

There are many **images of light** – the car headlights, the street lamps, the gleaming hubcaps, the winking red light on the car's dashboard, and of course the spark of the cigarette. Every one is an artificial light, and they all depend on the darkness that surrounds them.

Missing a former lover is a subject that many poets have tackled, as this poem recognises. In some ways, it can be read as **a poem about writing a poem**. We are always aware of the poet at the centre of the poem – not only in the description in the first stanza but also in the way she keeps bringing the reader's attention to the process of writing – 'I could easily go off / on a riff' (lines 19–20); 'In a poem / it could represent ...' (lines 36–37).

It is a self-aware and knowing poem. The speaker-poet knows the difficulty of avoiding clichés. She is aware of how images can conjure emotion, and how they connect with each other and can be assembled and organised in a poem. As the poem's title declares, it is a self-portrait, and the speaker knows that **all self-portraits are works of art** – they can be honest, but they always contain an element of artificiality.

Language and form

The poem uses **a blend of colloquial and heightened, poetic language**. The first sentence, a quotation from Shakespeare and clearly not written in everyday speech, is followed by the more everyday 'No chance' as the speaker accepts her insomnia. Self-consciously poetic language, such as 'the realm insomniac' (line 6), and metaphors, such as the description of the street as 'a stilled film, bathed in amber' (line 9), are set beside colloquial expressions: 'I could easily go off / on a riff' (lines 19–20), the Americanism 'I won't "go there"' (line 22) and 'clapped-out Nissan Micra' (line 24).

The contrast of the casual and the poetic also prevents the tone of the poem becoming too solemn or gloomy. It is part of the playful humour that keeps the strong emotions underlying the poem at arm's length. **The poet may be very present in her poem, but she is elusive too**; her emotions are expressed through images and metaphors from which she is always distancing herself: 'In a poem / it could represent ...' (lines 36–37).

Although the poem reads as if the speaker is simply putting into words what she is thinking, it is more tightly organised than it might at first appear. It is divided quite formally into four stanzas, each of ten lines. The line lengths vary to reflect the speaking voice. You might not notice it at first, but the poem is written **in rhyming couplets**, although most of the rhymes are only half-rhymes: 'up' and 'wrap', 'off' and 'riff', 'America' and 'Micra'. There are also examples of assonance: 'slim' and 'stilled film', 'spattered' and 'wrap'; and alliteration: 'someone, somewhere, smoking'. The pattern of the rhymes and sounds helps maintain a lightness, even a playfulness, in a poem whose subject could easily become sentimental. The full rhyme in the last two lines ('spark' and 'dark') gives a **sense of closure**.

Exam-Style Questions

Understanding the poem

1	What is the speaker's situation, as described in the first few lines?
2	Why, according to herself, is she unable to sleep?
3	What does she see from her window? How does the scene she sees add to the atmosphere she creates in the poem?
4	What does she tell us about her relationship with her former lover?
5	Do the lines about the Nissan Micra reveal anything further about the relationship between the speaker and her lover?
6	What does the speaker suggest the flashing red light on the car's dashboard could 'represent' (line 37)? Name all the possibilities.

Thinking about the poem

1. How would you describe the mood in the first stanza? How does the poet create that mood?

2. Why, do you think, does the poet use the word 'pushing' about the beam of the car headlights (line 13)? What does the word suggest about the atmosphere of the poem?

3. 'no. It's fine, all gleaming hubcaps, / seats like an upright, silhouetted couple' (lines 31–32). Why, in your opinion, does the poet pretend to her lover that the car is 'fine'? What does this suggest about her feelings about the end of the relationship?

4. What would you say is the main feeling expressed in the last five lines of the poem?

5. Give possible reasons for the poet's inclusion of real names of places (Magdalen Green and Riverside Drive) and of a model of car (Nissan Micra) in her poem.

6. Which of these statements most closely represents your opinion?

   - The speaker expresses a great sense of loneliness and regret.
   - The speaker would like to hide her true feelings, even from herself.

   Explain your choice.

7. Comment on the use of quotation and quotation marks in the poem.

Imagining

1. Imagine you are the poet's former lover. Perhaps you too are awake in the night and thinking about her. Perhaps you have 'moved on' and forgotten about her. Write your response to this poem, in prose or verse, and in whatever style you like. (Feel free to give those involved whatever genders your imagination dictates.)

2. Your group is making a video to accompany a reading of this poem. How would you use sound and visual images to create the atmosphere you think it needs?

SNAPSHOT

- End of a relationship
- Atmosphere of loneliness and melancholy
- Playful humour avoids sentimentality
- Extended image of car as metaphor for relationship
- Strong visual imagery
- Blend of everyday and poetic language
- Four stanzas of ten lines with varying line lengths
- Rhyme and half-rhyme

Moya Cannon

b. 1956

Biography

Moya Cannon was born in Donegal and grew up in a small village by the sea, surrounded by natural beauty. As a child she spent hours on the beaches beside her house. From her mother she inherited a love of poetry; from her father she inherited an interest in legends and the folklore associated with place names. She studied History and Politics at University College Dublin and later at Cambridge University. She lived most of her adult life in Galway and now lives in Dublin. Moya Cannon has published five collections of poetry. She is a member of Aosdána, the artists' organisation which recognises outstanding contributions to the arts in Ireland.

Shrines

 Moya Cannon reads an earlier draft of her poem 'Shrines'.

Before you read

 In pairs, share your views on roadside memorials and shrines.

You will find them easily,
there are so many –
near roundabouts, by canal locks,
by quaysides –
haphazard, passionate, weathered,   5
like something a bird might build,
a demented magpie
bringing blue silk flowers,
real red roses,
an iron sunflower,   10
a Christmas wreath,
wind chimes,
photographs in cellophane,
angels, angels, angels
and hearts, hearts, hearts   15
and we know
that this is the very place
the police fenced off with tape,
that a church was jammed
with black-clad young people,   20
that under the flowers and chimes
is a great boulder of shock
with no-one to shoulder it away
to let grief flow
like dense tresses of water   25
over a weir.

Glossary

Title   **Shrines: objects or constructions which mark a sacred place;
objects marking the place where a person died, and dedicated to
their memory**

Guidelines

'Shrines' comes from Moya Cannon's fifth collection, *Keats Lives*, published in 2015. Many of the poems are meditations on simple objects and explore the theme of grief.

Commentary

The poem is a **meditation** prompted by the number of makeshift shrines around the country marking the places where young people have lost or taken their lives. **The first half describes** the shrines. **The second part meditates on their significance.**

The poem opens in **a quiet, conversational way**, as if we are entering into a conversation which has already begun. The speaker informs the 'you' that the shrines of the title are both numerous and easy to find, and then lists the locations 'near roundabouts, by canal locks, / by quaysides –' (lines 3–4). When we have read to the end, we will realise that these are the sites where young people have lost their lives.

In line 5, the speaker uses three adjectives to describe the shrines: 'haphazard' suggests that the shrines are **makeshift**, unplanned, accidental; but they are 'passionate', too, reflecting the **deep emotion** which inspired their construction; 'weathered' suggests that these structures have been there for some time. The **nature of the shrines reflects the struggle of those left behind to find a response adequate to the circumstances**. The shrines are compared to something 'a demented magpie' might build (line 7). The comparison captures the haphazard nature of the shrines and the distress and confusion of those who constructed them. The flowers (lines 8–10) are symbols of love; the Christmas wreath and the wind chimes (lines 11–12) hint at the beliefs that people have about death and the afterlife. The photographs wrapped in cellophane (line 13) testify to the desire to hold on to the memories of loved ones and the **flimsiness of our gestures in the face of death**.

The **repetition of the words 'angels' and 'heart'** is heart-breaking. It testifies to our deepest human emotions: love and the hope that our loved ones will live forever. The poet suggests that 'the flowers and chimes' hide what the poet calls a 'great boulder of shock' (line 22), something weighty and immovable that prevents the mourners from expressing their grief, from letting their tears flow and their lives move forward. The **final image of the poem is one of grief, imagined as water flowing over a weir**. The water is compared to tresses of hair.

Themes and imagery

The poem is a meditation on grief and what it means to be **grief-struck**. The use of the word 'shrines' associates the making of these makeshift monuments with **the sacred and the holy**. The young people to whom the shrines are dedicated are commemorated in ways once associated with saints. It is as if those who erect the shrines want **to make holy the places where their loved ones died**. The shrines mark the place where an individual lost or took his or her life. They mark it and hold it as **somewhere sacred**. The shrines speak of love and of death and of eternal life. The **flimsiness of the shrines adds to their poignancy**.

The **image of the demented magpie** is powerful, and links the shrines to the **idea of nests**, which are safe places, family places. It captures the unpreparedness of the mourners; the natural tendency to reach immediately for the things at hand to mark the death of their loved one. The objects assembled are incongruous, maybe even gaudy, but the poem understands and respects the emotions which inspired these shrines and the human need to which they testify: the **need to mark the lives of those who died too soon**, in tragic circumstances, and the plight of those left behind, as they struggle to come to terms with their loss. The flowers are a confusing mixture of the real and the artificial, of soft silk and hard iron, of red and blue and yellow, a rainbow of colours and emotions which **contrast** with the blackness of death.

The **image of the 'great boulder of shock'** succeeds in suggesting the **numbness of the mourners which prevents their sorrow from flowing**. Their grief is frozen. The image of the water flowing in abundance over the weir represents the tears of grief that the mourners cannot shed because the deaths they are mourning are too shocking. The image suggests that the waters of grief are a **powerful, flowing force** and a healing one, too. The dense tresses of water suggest a feminine force, the tears of young women, the tears which cannot be shed for the young lives which have been lost.

Language and form

The poem consists of **a single sentence spread over twenty-six short lines**. There are no formal rhymes, but many of the lines form couplets where the **end words echo each other**: 'easily' / 'many'; 'locks' / 'quaysides'; 'weathered' / 'build'; 'water' / 'weir'; 'place' / 'tape'. The use of long vowel sounds, alliteration, repetition and an 's' sound that whispers through the poem; 'like dense tresses of water / over a weir', creates a **sense of hush and reverence**. There is music in the poem but it is sad music. The effect of the **sound patterns** in the poem is to create **a quiet song of grief**.

Exam-Style Questions

Understanding the poem

1	In what places might the shrines be found?
2	Comment on each of the adjectives used to describe the shrines.
3	What, if anything, might Christmas wreaths and wind chimes have in common?
4	Why are the photographs wrapped in cellophane?
5	Why are the words 'angels' and 'hearts' repeated?
6	What is the effect of the phrase 'a great boulder of shock' in line 22?
7	What, do you think, does the poet mean when she says there is 'no-one to shoulder it away' (line 23)?
8	What comparison does the poet use to describe the water flowing over the weir?

Thinking about the poem

1	'The poem is about the confusion and numbness of grief.' Discuss this statement. Support your answer with reference to the poem.
2	The poem focuses on the objects, the shrines, rather than individual people. Do you think this strategy works in exploring the theme of grief?

Imagining

1	'The shrines are useless but essential.' Write a short piece (poetry or prose) in response to this statement.

SNAPSHOT

- Shrines commemorate deaths of young people
- Meditation on grief
- Simple language and lyrical expression
- Tone is quiet and respectful
- Vivid images
- Music of sadness
- Mood is poignant

Kate Clanchy

b. 1965

Biography

Kate Clanchy was born in Glasgow, Scotland in 1965. She is a poet, print and broadcast journalist, teacher, playwright and novelist. After completing her education in Edinburgh and Oxford, Clanchy moved to London for a few years before settling in Oxfordshire, where she now lives.

She has won numerous awards, including the Somerset Maugham Award for her 1995 collection *Slattern* and the Scottish Arts Council Book Award for *Samarkand* (1999). She was awarded an MBE and was poet-in-residence for the UK Red Cross.

The poet Carol Ann Duffy taught her at Arvon (a charitable organisation in the UK that promotes creative writing) and was a major influence on Clanchy, whose poetry regularly tackles social and cultural issues, but often with a very personal slant. She has been criticised for describing the lives of women in overly traditional terms, but others see her differently. Jules Smith wrote that Clanchy is 'a sympathetic chronicler of female lives and experiences – her own and those of other women'.

She is married to Oxford academic Matthew Reynolds, and this poem details the journey to the hospital for the birth of their first son, Michael.

Driving to the Hospital

Before you read

When you hear the phrase 'driving to the hospital', what thoughts come to mind? Do you have a specific experience relating to this? Does this phrase have positive or negative connotations for you?

We were low on petrol
so I said let's freewheel
when we get to the hill.
It was dawn and the city
Was nursing its quiet   5
And I liked the idea
Of arriving with barely
A crunch on the gravel.
You smiled kindly and
eased the clutch gently   10
and backed us out of
the driveway and patted
my knee with exactly
the gesture you used
when we were courting,   15
remember, on the way
to your brother's: I like
driving with my baby,
that's what you said. And
at the time I wondered   20
why my heart leapt and leapt.

Glossary

2	*freewheel*: using the slope of a hill to propel a vehicle rather than using the power of the engine
5	*nursing*: tending to, breast-feeding, looking after someone who is ill
15	*courting*: an old-fashioned term for dating

Guidelines

This poem comes from the collection *Newborn*, published in 2004, the same year in which Clanchy also edited *The Picador Book of Birth Poems*. *Newborn* chronicles pregnancy and birth in a sequence of poems. 'Driving to the Hospital' mixes the present with memories from the past to create a simple yet evocative poem full of love, hope and possibility, and it is one of a pair of poems from the collection that describe this momentous journey in the life of a couple.

Commentary

Lines 1–8

The couple in the car seem either to be lacking funds or ill-prepared for this important journey, 'we were low on petrol', but the speaker seems unruffled by this and calmly suggests 'let's freewheel / when we get to the hill'.

The setting is dawn, approaching a sleeping city. The idea that this couple are on their way to have a baby is reinforced by the image of the city 'nursing its quiet' like a mother nurses her infant. The speaker appreciates this tranquillity and hopes to arrive at the hospital with little fuss, 'with barely / A crunch on the gravel'. She seems to savour this calm and quiet, as these first lines show.

Lines 9–21

The attention now shifts to the speaker's partner, who is similarly calm and reassuring. He is driving the car and eager to show his partner affection and consideration. Words like 'kindly' and 'gently' demonstrate this. His loving pat on her knee evokes a memory from when they first dated, 'when we were courting'. She recalls a specific journey to his brother's when he had said to her 'I like / driving with my baby'. Recalling this moment now of course takes on a whole new significance. 'My baby' is no longer just a term of endearment for her; it has become literal.

As they carry on their journey to experience the birth of their child she recalls the passion she felt in the early stages of their relationship and how this had taken her by surprise, 'at the time I wondered / why my heart leapt and leapt'.

Themes and imagery

The dawn setting is a fitting one. Dawn is often an image of new beginnings, of **birth and hope**. The unusual personification of the city as a nursing mother adds to this idea. The city is 'nursing its quiet' much like a new mother breastfeeds her baby. The theme of **birth** combines with the theme of **love** and this union can be seen clearly in the remembered phrase 'I like / driving with my baby'. The word 'baby' now has a twofold meaning; it was an affectionate term for the partner's girlfriend in the past, but now takes on a new significance as it refers to the child about to be born to the couple.

An underlying theme and image in the poem is also of a **journey**, both the physical journey the couple are taking to the hospital and also the metaphorical journey they embarked upon many years before as a couple in love. Becoming a family is the next stage of this journey and it is one they are now approaching. Time becomes fluid, a mixture of memories of the past; the now – their current situation; and also the future, when they will become parents.

The overall atmosphere is one of **calm affection** embodied by the partner's gentle pat on the woman's knee and how he always seemed to call her 'my baby'. Not having enough fuel for their journey doesn't mean they aren't prepared and ready to share their deep love, trust and affection with their new child.

Form and language

'Driving to the Hospital' is a **lyric of twenty-one lines** using simple and straightforward language. The tone is calm and conversational: 'I said let's freewheel'. The speaker addresses her partner directly: 'You smiled kindly'. Calmness is conveyed though images and sounds relating to peace and quiet; the city nurses its quiet and the couple hope to arrive soundlessly, 'with barely / A crunch on the gravel'.

The couple's affection for one another is demonstrated repeatedly through the language using verb and adjective phrases like 'smiled kindly' and 'eased … gently'. Clanchy's use of the word 'courting' is an old-fashioned one and adds **a quaintness and sense of nostalgia** to the poem, while specifying that a past journey they took was 'to your brother's' lends authenticity to the account.

The repetition of 'leapt and leapt' at the end of the poem lifts this lyric from its calmness and quiet affection by introducing **a note of passion**; at once nostalgically recalling falling in love but simultaneously perhaps relating to the excitement and nervousness an expectant mother feels on this journey.

SNAPSHOT

- Journey to hospital to give birth
- Personification
- Affection between couple
- Calm and peaceful tone
- Repetition in last line
- Mix of past and present
- Love poem
- Birth
- Literal and metaphorical journey

Exam-Style Questions

Understanding the poem

1	What does the information that the car was 'low on petrol' suggest to you about this couple? How do they deal with this potentially worrying situation?
2	Describe the setting of the poem – time and place.
3	What sort of arrival does the speaker wish to make at the hospital (lines 6–8)? Why, do you think, is this so?
4	Read lines 9–15 again. How is the care and affection the couple share conveyed in this section?
5	In lines 17 and 18 the speaker recalls her partner saying 'I like / driving with my baby'. What, do you think, did this originally mean to the couple? Might the meaning of 'baby' have changed in their current situation? Explain. In your answer identify the physical gesture made by the poet's partner that triggered this memory.
6	In the last sentence of the poem the speaker recalls the reaction she had all those years ago to her partner saying, 'I like / driving with my baby'. Re-read this last sentence. Did she seem to fully understand why her 'heart leapt and leapt' at the time? Do you think she understands now? Explain.

Thinking about the poem

1	How is the city personified in lines 4 and 5: 'It was dawn and the city / was nursing its quiet'? How does this image relate to the theme of birth in the poem?
2	The poem has a calm and gentle tone. Show how Clanchy creates this through her language and imagery.
3	How would you describe the relationship between the couple? Use details in the poem as you answer.
4	Past, present and future shift and merge as the poem progresses. Trace and describe this.
5	Which of the following best describes what you feel to be the main theme of the poem: falling in love, birth, memory? Justify your choice through specific quotation and reference.

Imagining

1	Write about the same journey from the driver's point of view in any format you like – a diary entry, poem, descriptive passage, etc.
2	Clanchy said: 'People think, oh, that's about mothers and babies, that's very nice, then put the poem away. People do that to women poets – they minorise them.' Do you agree that poems about birth and motherhood seem less important than poems dealing with other themes? Discuss in pairs or groups, perhaps referring to other poems you have studied.
3	Write a descriptive piece about a real or imagined important journey.

Carol Ann Duffy

b. 1955

Biography

Carol Ann Duffy was born in Glasgow in 1955 and grew up in the English Midlands. She studied philosophy at university and started work as a writer for television. She has published many books of poetry and won most of the major poetry prizes. Dramatic monologues, memorable characters and social concerns are evident in her early work. Recent collections explore the many sides of love. She was appointed Britain's Poet Laureate in 2009 – the first woman to hold the position since it was established in 1668 and also the first openly gay laureate. Duffy said she would not feel bound by tradition and would ignore royal events if they did not inspire her. By common consent, she is the most popular living British poet. She is the Professor of Contemporary Poetry at Manchester Metropolitan University.

Before you read

Have you ever given or received a Valentine card? Is Valentine's day an important or a trivial event? Share your views with a partner. Revisit your discussion when you have read the poem.

Valentine

Not a red rose or a satin heart.

I give you an onion.
It is a moon wrapped in brown paper.
It promises light
like the careful undressing of love.   5

Here.
It will blind you with tears
like a lover.
It will make your reflection
a wobbling photo of grief.   10

I am trying to be truthful.

Not a cute card or a kissogram.

I give you an onion.
Its fierce kiss will stay on your lips,
possessive and faithful   15
as we are,
for as long as we are.

Take it.
Its platinum loops shrink to a wedding-ring,
if you like.   20
Lethal.
Its scent will cling to your fingers,
cling to your knife.

Glossary

Title	**Valentine**: person chosen on St Valentine's day, 14 February, to be one's sweetheart; card or gift sent on Valentine's day (often anonymously) as a mark of love or affection
1	**satin**: silk with a smooth, shiny finish and a soft, luxurious texture
12	**kissogram**: novelty message for a special occasion delivered with a kiss (usually by someone in fancy dress)
19	**platinum**: silvery-white precious metal used in making jewellery
21	**Lethal**: causing death; deadly, vicious

Guidelines

'Valentine' is from the collection *Mean Time* (1993), which features poems on failed and broken relationships and explores issues of power, desire and obsession between lovers. The view of life (and love) that emerges from the collection is not very optimistic. This poem was written in response to a request from a BBC producer for a Valentine's day poem. It rejects the conventional representation of love associated with Valentine's day. What is presented in its place, however, is unclear.

> **Duffy on the relationship between love and poetry**
>
> 'Poetry is what love speaks in. Longing, desire, delirium, fulfilment, fidelity, betrayal, absence, estrangement, regret, loss, despair, remembrance – every aspect of love has been celebrated or mourned, praised and preserved in poetry.'

Commentary

Lines 1–2

The poem begins with a negative statement. The speaker tells the addressee, the 'you' in the poem, what is 'Not' being offered. Instead of the popular symbols of romance on Valentine's day, 'a red rose or a satin heart', the speaker offers an onion to her lover. **The rest of the poem explains the logic of this choice**, as the speaker perceives it.

Lines 3–5

The speaker compares the onion to 'a moon wrapped in brown paper' and extends this comparison in the stanza (see Themes and imagery). **The language of the poem is ambiguous.** This can be seen in the use of the pronoun 'it' throughout. Does it refer to the onion or to love?

Lines 6–10

The speaker offers the onion a second time. She compares the blinding tears caused by onions to the tears caused by a lover (see Themes and imagery). Again the language is **open to more than one interpretation**, particularly 'you' and 'your' in lines 7 and 9. Is the speaker suggesting that it is only the lover, the 'you' of the poem, who will be blinded by the tears of love? (Does this turn the offer of the onion into some kind of threat, or a prediction of unhappiness?) Or is it a more generalised use of 'you'? Is the speaker suggesting that she, too, will be hurt by love? Is love always accompanied by grief?

Line 11

Declarations are common on Valentine's day. However, the speaker's declaration here is not the usual declaration of undying love associated with the feast of Valentine. Instead, the speaker insists she is 'trying to be truthful'. The implication may be that others are not truthful on Valentine's day, but it is an interesting choice of phrasing. Has the speaker not always been truthful? Is truthfulness difficult for her? **Depending on the tone, this line may express cruelty or indifference as much as truthfulness.**

Lines 12–13

As in line 1, the speaker states what is not being offered, again referring to some of the popular gifts on Valentine's day, and repeats that she is instead giving her lover an onion. It seems that, in the dramatic situation which the poem portrays, the 'you' of the poem has not yet taken the onion. This creates another layer of ambiguity. Is the 'you' moved by the token of love? Amused? Offended? Or is the tone of the speaker such that the lover is nervous, or even frightened?

Lines 14–17

The speaker compares the strong taste of an onion to a 'fierce kiss' and the way it lingers on the mouth, and she describes the relationship between the two lovers as 'possessive and faithful'. **These three adjectives, 'fierce', 'possessive' and 'faithful', seem to characterise their relationship.** The first two do not suggest a gentle or tender relationship. On the contrary, they hint at violence and possessiveness. The last line of the stanza, 'for as long as we are', gestures towards the common theme of Valentine messages that love is eternal. The speaker seems to reject this idea, limiting their love to 'as long as we are'. This phrase may suggest love until death or, more simply, 'until we are no longer lovers' or, more literally, 'until we are no longer faithful and possessive'.

Lines 18–23

Once again, the speaker urges her lover to take the onion. She notes that one of the loops of peeled onion may be the size of a wedding ring. The 'you' can take it (as a wedding ring), 'if you like'. Is this a proposal of marriage? **The one-word line 'Lethal' continues the deliberately confusing ambiguity of the poem.** What is lethal? The onion? Marriage? Love? Does the description look forward to 'scent' in line 22? Is it the perfume of the onion that is lethal, in the way it clings to 'your fingers' and 'to your knife'? Notably, this **unconventional Valentine's poem** ends on the word 'knife'.

Themes and imagery

'Valentine' is generally read as a critique of romantic and popular representations of love, particularly as lines 1 and 12 clearly dismiss conventional love tokens. However, **the poem is nuanced and ambiguous and open to a wider range of interpretations than is apparent at first reading.**

Some readers suggest that the onion is an extended metaphor for love. It might be more accurate to say that **the onion represents the many aspects of love.** In the second stanza, for example, the onion is compared to the 'moon wrapped in brown paper' (line 3). Here the onion is not compared to love itself, but instead to a symbol (i.e. the parcelled-up moon) used to depict love. Just as the moon offers a suitable light for love, so, the speaker suggests, **the onion promises light.** The line break at line 4 releases the simile 'the careful undressing of love' in line 5. But what is being compared? Is the speaker suggesting that the promise of the onion is like the promise in the undressing that precedes a sexual encounter? Or does the phrase 'the careful undressing of love' relate to the noun 'light', rather than the verb 'promises'? Is the suggestion that love brings light, and all that it symbolises, into a lover's life? Is 'light' intended to signify knowledge, to suggest that lovers come to know each other thoroughly when all the outer layers of personality are stripped away?

In the third stanza, **the blinding effect of an onion**, the way in which it causes the person chopping it to cry, is compared to the way in which a lover can cause a beloved to cry. The word 'blind' (line 7) brings to mind Cupid, whose arrows wounded lovers' hearts – in classical mythology, love is an ordeal that causes suffering. Lines 9–10 suggest that the tearful lover will see her/his reflection as a **quivering image of grief**. Here the tearful effect of the onion is compared to the grief caused by love.

The **image of the onion is developed further in the poem by considering its strong taste, pungent smell and its circular shape** when peeled and sliced. The speaker picks up on the association of Valentine's day with proposals of **marriage** by suggesting that the 'platinum loops' (line 19) of sliced onion shrink to the size of a wedding ring. Does the use of the word 'shrink' (line 19) imply that marriage is a diminution of love? Does it mock marriage? Or is this proposal of marriage a playful one? The phrase 'if you like' (line 20) is ambiguous. Is it coy? Is it indifferent? What response would the speaker like?

The poem raises a seemingly endless list of questions. Is love, like the onion, something to be consumed, sliced and devoured? Is love, like the onion, something that leaves a clinging, unpleasant perfume? And what is the addressee (and the reader) to make of **the knife** at the end of the poem? Does the presence of the word 'knife' in a poem about love suggest the potential for lovers to harm each other? Does it simply indicate that the scent of love clings to everything?

It seems clear that the speaker wants to offer a more considered alternative to the popular and superficial symbols of romantic love (roses, hearts, kisses, etc.). It is not clear, however, that the speaker is offering a more authentic version of love or even presenting a truthful and honest account of love. Is the speaker perhaps describing a love and a relationship that is damaged and broken? Is the love token (the onion) offered at a moment of crisis? Is the poet's intention to suggest that romantic relationships are as much dark and troubled as they are light-filled and happy? Certainly, **there is little tenderness in the poem.** The love depicted seems somewhat intense and controlling. The forceful presentation of this gift and the offhand manner of the speaker could suggest a domineering and menacing attitude. And maybe this is the real theme of the poem: **love takes on many and varied guises and is more complex than Valentine tokens allow.**

Form and language

The poem is written as a **dramatic monologue**. The present tense gives a **sense of immediacy** to the words. It is as if the reader is the one addressed. Although there are no clues about the circumstances of the speaker, we sense that she speaks to her experience. She makes a virtue of being truthful, but at times seems **bitter as much as honest**. The voice seems adult, and the tone is ambiguous, possibly hurt and, arguably, cruel.

The speaker offers the onion to her lover on four occasions in the poem: 'I give you an onion' (line 2); 'Here' (line 6); 'I give you an onion' (line 13); 'Take it' (line 18). **Interpretations of the poem vary depending on how the reader understands or imagines the tone used by the speaker in these key lines.** How are these lines uttered? Does the tone change? Is the speaker insistent? Is the speaker pleading, offhand … ? Is the speaker confident, weak … ? Try reading the poem in a variety of ways and see which one works best.

The language is simple. However, **many of the words carry darker meanings and associations**: 'fierce' (line 14), 'shrink' (line 19), 'knife' (line 23). In the case of 'cling' (lines 22 and 23), the speaker might have used 'linger' to describe the scent of the onion. 'Cling' has more negative connotations. It suggests stubborn persistence, an unwelcome holding on, a refusal to separate, and an emotional dependency. These are not qualities normally associated with Valentine's day declarations.

The poem is written in free verse. It displays Duffy's talent for what one reviewer called **'razor-edge line-breaks'** (see, for example, lines 4–5, 7–8 and 15–16). Unlike popular Valentine verses, there is no rhyme in the poem and no regular metre. The only examples of alliteration, 'red rose' (line 1) and 'cute card' (line 12), refer to love tokens rejected by the speaker. Tellingly, there is no sweet note at the end of the poem. Instead the poem ends on the word 'knife'.

Exam-Style Questions

Understanding the poem

1	What popular tokens of love are rejected by the speaker in the poem?
2	In your view, does the onion work as a love token?
3	What view of love does the speaker hold, in your opinion?
4	Do you think the speaker offers the onion with warmth or with coldness? Explain your thinking.
5	Explain what you think the speaker means by the phrase 'the careful undressing of love' (line 5)?
6	Where, in your view, is the poem most ambiguous?
7	Which (if any) of these statements describes your experience of reading the poem: ■ The poem is uncomfortable to read. ■ The poem is amusing to read. ■ The poem is thought-provoking to read. Explain your answer.

Thinking about the poem

1	There is an 'I' and a 'you' in the poem. Does it make any difference if you imagine each in turn as a man or a woman? Explain your answer.
2	The speaker claims to be truthful. Suggest three other adjectives to describe the speaker of the poem.
3	'The imagery of the poem suggests danger.' Discuss this view.
4	Carol Ann Duffy has said, 'I like to use simple words, but in a complicated way.' Select two words from this poem to illustrate Duffy's complicated use of apparently simple words.
5	Which of the following statements is closest to your understanding of the poem? ■ The poem presents love as something complicated but rewarding. ■ The poem presents love as something stifling and hurtful. ■ The poem presents love as something tough and unromantic. ■ The poem presents love as something nourishing and long-lasting. Explain your answer.
6	If you were the person addressed, the 'you' of the poem, would you be reluctant or eager to accept the onion? Explain your answer.
7	'Unlike the Valentine tokens that the speaker rejects, the poem lacks warmth and humour.' Discuss this view of the poem.

Imagining

1 The poem is spoken by a character in a dramatic situation. You are directing a staging of the poem. Write a short biographical note for the actor playing the character, explaining the circumstances of the speaker and identifying the person to whom she/he is speaking.

2 You are the person to whom the onion is offered. Write a dramatic monologue in which you answer the speaker.

3 Select a common object that you think works as symbol of love. Explain your choice.

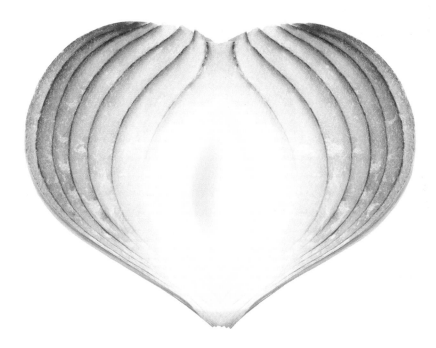

SNAPSHOT

- Dramatic monologue
- Rejects conventional symbols of love
- Rejects the conventional language of love
- Written in free verse
- Onion as an extended metaphor of love
- Ambiguous
- Variety of tones
- Unusual similes
- Complex view of love

Linda France

b. 1958

Biography

Linda France was born in 1958 in Newcastle upon Tyne in the north-east of England. After living in other places she returned in 1981 to live in Northumberland, near Hadrian's Wall. In 1992 she published her first volume of poetry, *Red*, from which 'If Love Was Jazz' is taken. She edited the influential anthology *Sixty Women Poets* (1993), and her eighth, and most recent, poetry collection is *Reading the Flowers* (2016). She has often collaborated with visual artists and musicians, and her love for jazz is expressed and explored in many of her poems. She is a practising Buddhist.

If Love Was Jazz

Before you read

Do you know much jazz music? Do you like it? Listen to some in class. If you're not sure where to start, try 'So What' by Miles Davis or John Coltrane's 'My Favorite Things'. What characteristics can you identify?

If love was jazz,
I'd be dazzled
By its razzmatazz.

If love was a sax,
I'd melt in its brassy flame   5
Like wax.

If love was a guitar,
I'd pluck its six strings,
Eight to the bar.

If love was a trombone,   10
I'd feel its slow
Slide, right down my backbone.

If love was a drum,
I'd be caught in its snare,
Kept under its thumb.   15

If love was a trumpet,
I'd blow it.

If love was jazz,
I'd sing its praises,
Like Larkin has.   20

But love isn't jazz.
It's an organ recital.
Eminently worthy,
Not nearly as vital.

If love was jazz,   25
I'd always want more.
I'd be a regular
On that smoky dance-floor.

Glossary

3	*razzmatazz*: noisy, showy, exciting activity designed to impress
4	*sax*: saxophone; a brass instrument much used in jazz music
9	*Eight to the bar*: eight beats in a bar of music; suggests double speed since four beats is more usual
14	*snare*: trap; also a type of drum
20	*Larkin*: the poet Philip Larkin, who loved and wrote about jazz
23	*Eminently worthy*: very respectable, well-intentioned (but probably dull)

Guidelines

In this poem from *Red* (1992), France explores love in terms of jazz, looking for resemblances between them but aware of the differences. She has written and spoken widely of her love for jazz, of which she says:

> Like poetry, jazz is essentially a way of talking about life. They are both powerful agents of transformation. In working on experience – in words or musical notes – they articulate reality, make it more visible. And the effect of it, reading or listening, is to leave you changed, more fully engaged with the world inside you and around you.

Commentary

Stanza 1

The title and first line set up the idea on which the poem is based: 'If love was jazz'. The first stanza finishes this thought: 'I'd be dazzled / By its razzmatazz'. The rhyming and repetition of 'azz' sounds gives the verse its own showy razzmatazz.

Stanzas 2–6

France plays with the idea of love being a series of instruments used in jazz music. The first is the **saxophone** ('sax'), a brass instrument that has a special affiliation with jazz music. Its sound is described here as a 'brassy flame' in which the speaker will 'melt … / Like wax'. The sensuousness of the image and the rasping sound of 'brassy' are beautifully suggestive of the sax's rich, raunchy sound.

Next is the **guitar**, which the speaker imagines plucking 'Eight to the bar', implying a pacy rhythm that might suggest the energy that love can bring. The numbers 'six' (strings) and 'Eight' (beats) so close together might also suggest the **syncopated rhythm of jazz**, where the weak beats are stressed instead of the strong ones. Emphasising the 'wrong' note in a bar, in terms of the norms of classical music, is what makes jazz 'swing'.

Stanza 4 turns to the **trombone**, another brass instrument. Here France has some fun with the way the trombone is played, by moving a 'slide' in and out to change the note. 'If love was a trombone' that slide would be felt like a caress 'right down my backbone', the speaker says. Notice how the long vowels of 'slow / Slide, right down' slow down the pace of the verse and imitate that slide. The alliteration of 'slow / Slide' adds an extra sensuality.

There is more wordplay in the next stanza, where the idea of being 'caught in its snare' depends on the double meaning of 'snare' as a trap and as a type of **drum**. The snare leads to the idea of love being a thing that can dominate you – catch you and keep you 'under its thumb'.

Stanza 6 plays with the reader's expectations rather than with the words. Instead of the three-line stanza we've grown used to, this stanza comes to an abrupt end after a short second line, like a blast on a **trumpet**. It is bold, witty and provocative.

Stanzas 7–9

Now the poem returns to the original idea, 'If love was jazz'. If that were so, then the speaker would 'sing its praises', just as the poet Philip Larkin did over many years of writing about jazz. But now **the word 'If' that**

has been repeated throughout the poem becomes important in a new way, not just as a convenient device to introduce a metaphor but as a real doubt. Stanza 8 throws cold water on the whole idea: 'But love isn't jazz.' Rather, love is good but dull ('Eminently worthy'), lacking vitality, and also, perhaps, a less 'vital' part of the speaker's life.

The poem ends with the image of the 'smoky dance-floor' of a jazz club. That's not what love is like, the poet says. There is regret here, perhaps, that love is disappointing, but the speaker is also telling you about the real, reliable, sensuous pleasures of jazz.

Themes and imagery

This is a poem about **love and jazz**. It is a celebration of the sensual pleasures that jazz can give and that are often associated with love. For much of the poem there is no apparent disharmony between the two, and we enjoy a series of images that explore the energies they share. **Each image, each instrument, conjures up a different aspect of what jazz is and what love might be.** Notice how each image centres on a vivid, often sexual, verb: 'be dazzled' (line 2), 'melt' (line 5), 'pluck' (line 8), 'feel' (line 11), 'be caught' (line 14), 'blow' (line 17), 'sing' (line 19).

The ending, however, unsettles the reader's expectations. These were not straightforward comparisons, they were **romantic notions**. In reality, according to the speaker, love is not jazz but 'an organ recital' (line 22). The 'smoky dance-floor' (line 28) may not be a true image for love, but that does not diminish the jazz-related joy that the poem has expressed.

> **Linda France on jazz**
>
> **'The best thing about jazz is the same thing as the best thing about being alive – the terrible beauty of every single second. It takes life by the hips and isn't satisfied until it finds some friends to shimmy through the night with. It sparks like a firework, crazy, enchanting, elusive. In the morning the light hurts its eyes and it knows it's alone and this is the way it is. Like an achingly gorgeous melody, jazz haunts us with our own longing to be free. Go listen to some. Live a little.'**

Form and language

Jazz is more than a subject of this poem. **The poem's form and language have absorbed some of the character and techniques of jazz.** Jazz music usually works by taking a tune and playing with it, by creating variations on it and on its basic musical structure. Jazz also uses syncopation, stressing the weak, unexpected beat in a bar of music to create a rhythm that is jumpy, irregular and unpredictable.

In this poem France establishes a basic form in the first half – a three-line stanza whose first and third lines rhyme (*aba*). The line lengths are variable but quite short. There is no regular metre, although there are **strong stresses**, and most lines have two of them. France keeps varying the patterns, however. The drum stanza (lines 13–15) is the most regular of these, as is appropriate to the instrument that keeps the beat in a jazz band. The trombone stanza (lines 10–12) slows down the rhythm like a trombone slowly sliding from one note to another by way of many others. Sometimes there are missed or transferred beats, as in the saxophone stanza (lines 4–6), where the second line has three stresses and the third just one: 'I'd mélt in its brássy fláme / Like wáx'. It is a sort of syncopation.

The two-line sixth stanza, however, goes straight for the rhyme in the second line. It is another sort of variation, playing with our expectations as jazz does.

After a return to the basic form in lines 18–20, the final two stanzas have a different shape. They are both four lines long, rhyming *abcb*. This is a much more conventional shape than the three-line stanzas at the start. The rhythm is also more even, with a regular two beats a line in lines 21–24. **It is conventional – not jazzy – and more like the organ recital the stanza describes.** Perhaps, though, a hint of jazz returns in the final line, with the three stresses in 'smoky dance-floor'.

Exam-Style Questions

Understanding the poem

1   What different aspects or moods of love and jazz are evoked in the first five stanzas? Consider each stanza in turn.

2   What is the speaker's actual experience of love, to judge by the last two stanzas?

3   What is the speaker's experience of jazz, to judge by the whole poem?

Thinking about the poem

1   Is this a poem that celebrates love or jazz, or both, or neither? Give reasons for your answer.

2   Which is your favourite comparison in the poem? Explain why you like it and what it suggests to you.

3   Do you find the ending disappointing? Give reasons for your answer.

4   Describe the tone of this poem. Is it joyful, regretful, playful, disillusioned? Or would you choose a different word? Give reasons for your answer.

5   What do you like (or dislike) about the rhythms and sounds of this poem? Comment on any aspect that strikes you.

Imagining

1   Write your own verses, as many as you like, beginning 'If love was … ', and using Linda France's poem as a model.

2   In small groups, listen to some jazz tracks to find suitable music to accompany this poem. Try looking for music by Miles Davis, Charlie Parker, Louis Armstrong, Duke Ellington, Lester Young, John Coltrane, Django Reinhardt and Thelonious Monk.

SNAPSHOT

- Comparison of love and jazz
- Form and rhythm influenced by jazz
- Playful use of rhyme and word music
- Sensual imagery
- Disillusioned about love
- Celebration of jazz

Randolph Healy

b. 1956

Biography

Randolph Healy is an Irish poet, publisher and teacher who was born in Irvine, Scotland in 1956 and moved with his family to Dublin aged eighteen months. His father was a postman who wrote ballads; his mother was 'well read' and 'had a store of folk songs'. He left school at fourteen and worked in many different jobs before returning to education, attending Trinity College, Dublin, where he studied maths and science before graduating and becoming a secondary-level teacher in these subjects.

Healy has become part of the modern poetry movement Another Ireland, a group that rejects being defined as 'Irish poets', as this so often means referencing history, colonisation, etc. Peter Riley says of Healy, 'he doesn't trade in that substance: nationality'. Healy prefers to use scientific data and logic rather than 'tribal memory'. His style is experimental and innovative, for example 'writing a computer program that will write itself part of your poem'.

He married Louise McMahon in 1983 and they have two daughters, one of whom is deaf, which inspires him to examine issues around language, exploring deafness and sign language. He lives in Co. Wicklow.

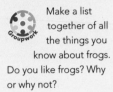

Before you read

Make a list together of all the things you know about frogs. Do you like frogs? Why or why not?

Frogs

On a grassy hill, in a luxury seminary in Glenart,
I found, screened by trees,
a large stone pond.
The waters of solitude.
Friends.   5

Patriarchs,
ten thousand times older than humanity,
the galaxy has rotated almost twice
since they first appeared.

They get two grudging notices in the Bible: 10
Tsephardea in Exodus,
Batrachos in the Apocalypse.
I will smite all thy borders with frogs.
I saw three unclean spirits, like frogs.

Their numbers have been hugely depleted,   15
principally by students.

Sever its brain.
The frog continues to live.
It ceases to breathe, swallow or sit up
and lies quietly if thrown on its back.   20
Locomotion and voice are absent.
Suspend it by the nose,
irritate the breast, elbow and knee with acid.
Sever the foot that wipes the acid away.

It will grasp and hang from your finger.   25

There is evidence that they navigate
by the sun and the stars.

This year, thirty-two, I said
'I'll be damned if Maureen has frogs'
and dug a pond.   30
Over eighty hatched, propped up with cat food.
Until the cats ate them.
It was only weeks later we discovered
six shy survivors.

The hieroglyph   35
for the number one hundred thousand
is a tadpole.

Light ripples down a smooth back.
La grenouille.
Gone.   40

Glossary

1	*seminary*: institution for training priests
1	*Glenart*: place in County Wicklow, location of seminary
6	*Patriarchs*: male heads of a family or tribe; in the Bible a patriarch is a figure regarded as a father of the human race, such as Adam, Noah and Abraham
11	*Tsephardea in Exodus*: Tsephardea is the Hebrew word for frogs (literally meaning 'marsh-jumper'); it appears in the Old Testament Book of Exodus (8:12–24)
12	*Batrachos in the Apocalypse*: Batrachos is the Greek word for frogs from the New Testament Book of Revelations, which describes the end of the world, which we know now as the Apocalypse (16:13)
13	*smite*: to strike with a violent blow
21	*Locomotion*: movement
35	*hieroglyph*: Egyptian symbol
39	*La grenouille*: French word for frog

Guidelines

From the collection *Green 352. Selected Poems 1983–2000*. Randolph Healy is an innovative modern poet who uses science, data and logic in his work. He has spoken of how evolution fascinates him, how patterns arise, yet he comments that evolution is 'by no means green', referring to the waste and death that occurs in the natural world. 'Frogs' explores this idea and looks at the human contribution to the decline of the frog population in Ireland, as well as **exploring the existence of frogs through the ages, and mankind's changing attitude towards them**.

Commentary

Lines 1–9

The speaker describes the setting: 'Glenart' is a 'luxury' training college for priests in Co. Wicklow and in its grounds on a 'grassy hill' there is a secluded pond, 'screened by trees'. In its 'waters of solitude' the speaker finds 'Friends'. The first description of frogs here is a **positive** one, they are the 'Friends' of line 5 and seem shy creatures who live in 'solitude', peacefully.

In keeping with the **religious allusion** in the first line, the speaker then calls the frogs 'Patriarchs'. In biblical terms this refers to the founders of the first tribes of mankind (see Glossary, above). He sees the **frogs as our**

forebears, perhaps because of how long they have been in existence compared to us – 'ten thousand times older than humanity'. The speaker then measures this time in another way, astronomically; our galaxy, the Milky Way, has 'rotated almost twice / since they first appeared'.

Lines 10–14

In **contrast** with this respectful and positive view of frogs, the speaker goes on to describe how the two mentions of frogs in the Bible express something quite different. He uses one example each from the Old Testament and the New Testament – 'They get two grudging notices in the Bible'. In the first, from the Book of Exodus, a plague of frogs is sent to punish Egypt for its enslavement of the Jews: 'I will smite all thy borders with frogs'; *tsephardea* is the Hebrew word for frog (this is the language the Bible was originally written in). The New Testament reference comes from the Book of Revelation: 'I saw three unclean spirits, like frogs'. **In the Bible, frogs symbolise spiritual impurity.** In this instance the three spirits emanate from the mouth of a dragon during the apocalypse, the end of the world. *Batrachos* is the Greek word for frog (Greek was the first language the Bible was translated into). Frogs are therefore seen in religion as something malign, **a curse or punishment**.

Lines 15–25

The huge decline in the frog population in Ireland is the next subject on the speaker's 'list'. He accuses science students of being 'principally' at fault for this, and goes on to describe in vivid detail how the dissection of a frog is carried out. The speaker seems very familiar with this procedure and the description **sounds like a set of instructions**. We are told that even if its brain is severed, the frog will still be alive. He notes that even though it stops breathing and ceases moving, if it is hung 'by the nose' and acid is rubbed onto its 'breast, elbow and knee', once its foot is cut off it will 'grasp and hang from your finger'. The reaction expected from us is unclear at this point, **the tone of the speaker is so matter-of-fact that it's difficult to know whether we are supposed to be horrified, fascinated or merely informed** by this.

Lines 26–27

The next two lines suggest that frogs have **an innate wisdom and a harmony with the universe**. The lines 'There is evidence that they navigate / by the sun and the stars' remind us of lines 7 and 8, where the speaker commented on how long frogs have been on Earth, using the age of our galaxy to explain this. Placed just after the description of a frog being scientifically dissected, this account of frogs (as in tune with the universe) suggests that these wise creatures don't deserve to be treated so callously. Just like the first sailors and explorers, frogs use the heavens to find their way and were doing this long before we were.

Lines 28–40

The speaker now brings the poem back to his **personal experience** of frogs. He describes how, at age 'thirty-two', having found that 'Maureen has frogs', he undertook to dig a pond to encourage their numbers, feeding with cat food the 'Over eighty' which subsequently hatched. This unfortunately led to the cats eating all but six of the frogs. Like the frogs in stanza 1, these were 'shy' and had evaded discovery for weeks. His misguided efforts to help them had been almost in vain. **Perhaps this is a commentary on the damage we frequently do to the natural world, often despite our best efforts and intentions.**

Juxtaposed with this tiny number of just six surviving frogs, the speaker notes that the signifier for the number one hundred thousand in ancient Egypt 'is a tadpole'. Something that once symbolised a teeming multitude, an abundance, now exists in a tiny number. Frogs were once an ancient symbol of fertility due to their **vast numbers**, particularly when depicted as spawn and tadpoles.

The final stanza **focuses on the beauty of the frog and its looming extinction**. 'Light ripples down a smooth back' – the light acts like the watery conditions the frog lives in and the frog is not slimy but smooth. The French word for frog is used here: *'La grenouille.'* Could this be a reference to the French delicacy of frogs' legs? The last word is simple yet startling – 'Gone'. All of this history, these fascinating snippets of information about this shy, mysterious ancient species culminates in the terrible possibility of their extinction.

Themes

Man's fickle attitude to these gentle creatures is explored by the poet here and, in a wider sense, perhaps **our attitude to nature** is under scrutiny too. This relationship is one-sided; frogs are depicted as shy, solitude loving creatures and 'Friends'. They are far older than us and in an evolutionary sense are our forebears – 'Patriarchs'. All life began in a primordial swamp, therefore amphibious creatures like frogs were near the very beginning of life on Earth. **Mathematical and scientific ideas** feature in Healy's poetry and they are prominent in this poem, from **measurements** of time and astronomy to **scientific experimentation**. Religion is a theme also: the poem opens in the grounds of 'a luxury seminary in Glenart' and references to the Bible fill the third stanza. The **depiction of religion** is ultimately a negative one in terms of how it views this ancient species as a curse, impure and unclean.

Humanity is depicted as a callous, invasive and ultimately destructive presence in the world of frogs. We dissect them, use them to symbolise evil and impurity (as the Bible references show), and even when we try to help them we often do more harm than good, as shown in the comical effort to build a pond and feed the frogs.

Language and imagery

The form of the poem seems at first to be a **lyric**. There is **a list-like accumulation of facts, figures and anecdotal stories about frogs** in unrhymed stanzas which vary in length from one to eight lines. In fact the poem is much more than a list of interesting snippets about these creatures. It **builds steadily** to the final stark prediction 'Gone'. Frogs through the ages, and our changing relationship with them, is **explored in a series of scientific, mathematical, religious and anecdotal ways**.

Religion

The first image shows the secluded pond in the seminary grounds. 'Luxury' is an interesting adjective here – why would an institution for training priests be luxurious? Is this sarcasm? This suggests an already antagonistic attitude towards religion which the speaker elaborates on in stanza 3. The references to frogs in the Old and New Testament both depict them negatively: first as a punishing plague on Egypt; second, used in a simile comparing them to 'unclean spirits'.

Language

Healy's interest in language is evident in the biblical references; he is known as **a poet who explores language in various ways**. This poem uses the words for frogs in **three different languages besides English**: Hebrew, Greek and French. Healy also recognises that language can be more than words. **Hieroglyphs** also convey meaning. The form of a tadpole is the signifier, as the symbol for a vast number (one hundred thousand). The mention of hieroglyphs connects us back to the reference in stanza 3 to the biblical story of the plague of frogs in Egypt.

Number

Data like **numbers and measurements** feature in the language of this poem. Frogs are: '**ten thousand** times older than humanity'; 'the galaxy has rotated almost **twice** / since they first appeared'; they get '**two** grudging notices in the Bible'; they are compared to '**three** unclean spirits'; '**thirty-two**' may be the age of the speaker when he dug them a pond; 'Over **eighty** hatched' but only **six** survived; the 'hieroglyph / for the number **one hundred thousand** / is a tadpole.' All of these numbers lead the reader to the final word – 'Gone'.

Dissection

One of the most **vivid series of images** in the poem concerns the dissection of a frog. The poet is a science teacher and clearly knows this process intimately. The instructions given are related dispassionately like **instructions in a manual**, but at the same time seem cruel: 'Sever its brain'; 'Suspend it by the nose, / irritate the breast, elbow and knee with acid. / Sever the foot'. The **sibilance here creates an uneasy, sinister effect**. The image of the frog's foot trying to wipe the acid away during this process is disconcerting to say the least. There is a clear sense of the animal being tortured. The astronomical reference that directly follows this: 'they navigate / by the sun and the stars' – suggests an ancient wisdom in these creatures which puts them in harmony with a universe where they have existed for millennia. This makes their dissection all the more uncomfortable to dwell on, making us **question whether we have the right** to do this to these animals.

Mystery and beauty

The overall image of the frogs is of ancient, shy creatures who just want to be left alone. They live in 'The waters of solitude', they are 'Friends' and 'Patriarchs' who have amazing physical mysteries, as explored in stanzas 5, 6 and 7. The 'six shy survivors' in the speaker's homemade pond represent the few frogs that remain, largely due to our variously bungling, unkind and callous treatment of these gentle amphibians. The **image of light rippling** down the smooth back of the frog is a final testament to their **beauty** and innate right to survive in nature, but then quick as a flash that pleasant image is snatched from us as the speaker predicts their extinction – 'Gone'.

Exam-Style Questions

Understanding the poem

1	What details do you learn about the frogs in the first two stanzas?
2	According to stanza 3, how does the Bible depict frogs?
3	Why might students be responsible for the huge depletion in the numbers of frogs?
4	Explain in your own words the process of dissection outlined by the speaker. How did you feel reading this?

5 What happened when the speaker tried to encourage frogs to breed (lines 28-34)? What might this anecdote say about man's attempts to preserve nature?

6 'Gone.' Has the frog here simply hopped away out of sight or is a larger point being made?

Thinking about the poem

1 What picture of frogs emerges from the poem as a whole? What details in the poem help to create this picture?

2 Examine and comment on the religious references in the poem.

3 How is humanity's relationship with frogs through the ages depicted by the poet?

4 Examine the references to science and maths. What do these bring to the poem as a whole?

5 'I'll be damned'. Why might the poet have chosen this phrase? Could it link back to the religious references in the poem as well as having a more colloquial meaning?

6 Which of the following is closest to what you think the main theme of this poem is?
- Frogs are fascinating creatures.
- People have been very cruel to frogs.
- The complex relationship between humanity and nature.

Discuss with reference to the poem.

Imagining

1 Make two lists, one cataloguing the positive references to frogs in the poem and the other listing the negative references. Which list is longer? Does this reflect the poet's opinion in your view? Does it reflect your own?

2 Write up the dissection section of the poem as a scientific experiment; list the equipment you will need, the reason for the experiment and the process. What are your findings at the end?

3 Write three diary entries describing and expanding on the 'cat massacre' anecdote (lines 28–34). You might add details from elsewhere in the poem to your account.

SNAPSHOT
- Shy, solitude-loving nature of frogs
- Scientific, astronomical and mathematical data
- Anecdote
- Religion's attitude towards frogs
- Different translations of word for 'frog'
- Varying styles of language including religious to scientific and everyday speech
- Alliteration and sibilance
- Humanity's complex relationship with these creatures
- Decline in frog population and their possible extinction

Andrew Hudgins

b. 1951

Biography

Andrew Hudgins was born in 1951 in Killeen, Texas, USA. His strict father was a soldier, so his childhood was spent moving between different military bases in the southern states of America. His first collection of poetry, *Saints and Strangers*, was published in 1986 and shortlisted for the Pulitzer Prize. He has said that he tries to write poems he'd like to read. His poems tend to have a strong narrative voice and are often quirky and amusing; his style has been described as modern American Gothic. He admits to exaggerating autobiographical events in his poetry to add impact and interest to his work. He has completed several residencies, been awarded a Guggenheim Fellowship, and taught at universities such as Baylor, Cincinnati and Ohio State.

Before you read

What is meant by the term 'urban legend' or 'urban myth'? Do you know of any?

The Cadillac in the Attic

After the tenant moved out, died, disappeared
—the stories vary—the landlord
walked downstairs, bemused, and told his wife,
'There's a Cadillac in the attic,'

and there was. An old one, sure, and one   5
with sloppy paint, bald tires,
and orange rust chewing at the rocker panels,
but still and all, a Cadillac in the attic.

He'd battled transmission, chassis, engine block,
even the huge bench seats,   10
up the folding stairs, heaved them through the trapdoor,
and rebuilt a Cadillac in the attic.

Why'd he do it? we asked. But we know why.
For the reasons we would do it: for the looks
of astonishment he'd never see but could imagine.   15
For the joke. A Cadillac in the attic!

And for the meaning, though we aren't sure what it means.
And of course he did it for pleasure,
the pleasure on his lips of all those short vowels
and three hard clicks: the Cadillac in the attic.   20

Glossary

Title	*Cadillac*: American car brand
1	*tenant*: person who rents accommodation
3	*bemused*: bewildered; confused
9	*transmission*: mechanism by which power is transmitted from an engine to the axle in a motor vehicle
9	*chassis*: frame upon which the main parts of a motor vehicle are built
9	*engine block*: cast metal block that houses the cylinders of a car's engine

Guidelines

This poem is taken from the 2003 collection *Ecstatic in the Poison*. **Hudgins was inspired to write the poem after reading about someone who mentioned a similar practical joke.** The poet was entertained by the idea of a tenant disassembling and rebuilding this huge car in his rented attic. On the surface this poem is about an elaborate practical joke, but it also has a deeper meaning.

Commentary

Stanzas 1–3

Right away the speaker lets us know that the tale he is about to tell is far from concrete fact. He is unsure of the exact circumstances, as revealed by the trio of possibilities given for the tenant's leaving, 'After the tenant moved out, died, disappeared', and also by the phrase 'the stories vary'. The story goes that the landlord comes downstairs and, 'bemused', tells his wife, 'There's a Cadillac in the attic'. **The deadpan delivery of such a seemingly impossible and ludicrous assertion creates great humour while also underlining the incredulity and shock of the landlord and the speaker.** We get the sense that we are being regaled with an oft-spun anecdote, an urban myth, and the effect is intimate and friendly as if a pal is telling us an entertaining story.

The **poet uses enjambment** to continue the tale into stanza 2, 'and there was', giving a natural flow to the account. We are then brought through a detailed description of this iconic American car and left in no doubt as to the Herculean nature of the effort taken to complete this unlikely task. The Cadillac has seen better days, 'An old one, sure'. It is not the pristine, gleaming behemoth of chrome and shiny paint we might first imagine. It has 'sloppy paint, bald tyres, / and orange rust', but despite its state of disrepair we must still wonder at the fact that 'still and all' there was a 'Cadillac in the attic'. This phrase is in the title of the poem and **the refrain ending each stanza**.

The verbs 'battled' and 'heaved' indicate the near impossibility of the task achieved and the size and weight of the items that had to be dragged 'through the trapdoor', involving climbing 'the folding stairs' (these don't sound very sturdy!), and 'rebuilt' in the attic. The speaker clearly knows about cars as he lists the larger parts of the vehicle that had to be hauled into the attic by the tenant: 'transmission, chassis, engine block, / even the huge bench seats'. Cadillacs were particularly famous for their full-width front seats, which would be incredibly unwieldy to manage.

Stanzas 4–5

Having told the story, the speaker now meditates on the motivation and meaning of undertaking this bizarre effort, 'Why'd he do it? we asked'. Clearly the reasons for this have puzzled many. Yet it seems the answer is simple: 'But we know why.' He obviously did it for the reaction it would provoke, as we might say in Ireland 'for the craic'! He pictured with pleasure 'the looks / of astonishment he'd never see but could imagine. / For the joke.' Even though the joker has long gone, his joke will continue to entertain and inspire wonder in others. The refrain is repeated here, but this time with an exclamation mark, 'A Cadillac in the attic!', serving to highlight our incredulity, our realisation of his motivation and perhaps also to mimic how the punchline to a joke might be written.

Less certain than the why he did it **is the meaning** of why he did it, 'though we aren't sure what it means'. What is certain is that it brought the tenant 'pleasure'; however, the pleasure here is not what we might first assume. It is **the pleasure of the sound** the phrase has, 'the pleasure on his lips of all those short vowels / and three hard clicks: the Cadillac in the attic'. Here the poem is suddenly transformed from an entertaining anecdote, an item of interest, into something much deeper and more meaningful.

Themes and imagery

Hudgins identified the main themes in the poem when he said: 'it seemed almost like a parable of creating art. Yet you ultimately do it for the pleasure, and then you do it so you can tell people you did it. … So it was one of those things where there was pleasure and something serious also going on at the same time, underneath what just seemed like a good practical joke.' On one level, therefore, the theme is **the reason someone would play a practical joke** – for the pleasure it brings to imagine the reaction of the person on the receiving end. And on a deeper level, building the Cadillac in the attic is **an analogy for 'creating art'**. The poet will not get to see his readers' reaction to his poems but takes pleasure in imagining them and pleasure in the act of creating 'those short vowels / and three hard clicks' (lines 19–20). **Here is a poet enjoying the sounds created in his arrangement of the words in his poem.**

The poem takes this metaphor further by suggesting that disassembling and reassembling the car is like writing a poem. One takes words and phrases, stories and experiences and rearranges them in one's mind, the attic possibly becoming an image for this. We see that this is a difficult process, 'He'd battled transmission, chassis, engine block' (line 9); we might here think of the building blocks of a poem: language, imagery, metre, form and so on. It is a challenging process to bring these together effectively in the mind, 'heaved them through the trapdoor' (line 11), and to make them into something functional and meaningful,

> The *symbolism of the Cadillac* is interesting, as apart from being part of the poet's metaphor for the creative process the Cadillac is an iconic piece of Americana. It is a symbol for the American dream, embodying the idea that bigger is better. This is a huge luxury car with a massive engine, lots of chrome, famous especially for its tail fins and bench seats and for being a guzzler of fuel. It yells power, wealth and ostentation.

to puzzle and delight people he will never meet. With some humility, Hudgins does not claim that his work is totally original or even superbly crafted, it has 'sloppy paint, bald tyres, / and orange rust chewing at the rocker panels' (lines 6–7), yet it is a poem, a composition, art – 'but still and all, a Cadillac in the attic' (line 8).

Form and language

'D' sounds pepper the first stanza, creating a **staccato effect**; 'move**d** … **d**ied, **d**isappeared … lan**d**lord … walke**d** **d**ownstairs, bemuse**d** … tol**d** … Ca**d**illac'. Think about the reason the poet might have done this. The language is very relaxed and conversational and lets us know that the tale we are about to be told is based on hearsay, 'the stories vary' (line 2). The speaker seems **relaxed and the accessible language is colloquially American**, with phrases such as, 'An old one, **sure**' (line 5) and '**Why'd** he do it?' (line 13). However, **the use of technical language specific to cars lends authenticity to the account**, nouns such as 'chassis, engine block' (line 9) tell us the speaker knows about cars. The verbs 'battled' (line 9) and 'heaved' (line 11) convey the massive undertaking of this prankster to shift these huge car parts up into the attic. The technical and methodical process undertaken by the tenant is mirrored in the **careful structure of the poem**, five four-line stanzas all ending with the same phrase, conveying care and planning. Just as the tenant must know what he is doing to rebuild the car, so the poet must have skill and the requisite expertise to create his art.

In stanza 4 the speaker **uses inclusive language**, '**we** asked. But **we** know why' (line 13). 'We' here suggests that many people have pondered this question, perhaps those the speaker has told the story to or heard it from. These people may include the landlord and his wife and probably at this stage the reader of the poem also. This makes the reader feel included and adds to the **intimacy of tone** in the poem. Love of language is clear. The **repetition of the refrain** ending each stanza is explained in the final stanza, where the poet tells us he loves the sounds that echo and ricochet off each other in the phrase 'Cadillac in the attic': 'the pleasure on his lips of all those short vowels / and three hard clicks' (lines 19–20). The ending of the poem introduces the theme of artistic creativity and the process of creating poetry, which depends so much on sound. It is as if Hudgins is explaining to us why he is a poet, why poets love what they do, and his **enthusiasm** is palpable. **He said of writing this poem, 'It just seemed like a terrific thing to think about, and the more I thought about it the more I kind of fell in love with that phrase, the Cadillac in the attic, and how cool it sounded.'**

SNAPSHOT

- Story of an extreme practical joke
- Anecdotal, colloquial style
- Friendly, conversational tone
- Narrative voice
- Use of refrain
- Symbolism of the Cadillac
- Theme of creating poetry
- Humour
- Description becomes a meditation
- Alliteration and long vowels

Exam-Style Questions

Understanding the poem

1	How does the speaker make it clear that this story is not a reliable one?
2	What is the landlord's initial reaction to what he finds in the attic? Do you think the speaker shares this reaction? Did you?
3	How is the Cadillac described in stanzas 2 and 3? Comment on the effect of the subject-specific language here.
4	What did you learn in the third stanza about the effort it took to move the car?
5	There is a change of focus in the fourth stanza. Show how this is so. Where has the focus shifted to?
6	Why did the tenant undertake this strange task, according to stanza 4?
7	What are 'we' not sure of in stanza 5? Comment on the effect of the inclusive language here. Who, do you think, is being addressed here?
8	How does the pleasure of the tenant transfer to the pleasure of the poet in the last stanza?
9	What is it about the phrase 'the Cadillac in the attic' that pleases the speaker so much? Do you agree with this?

Thinking about the poem

1	Examine the alliteration used in the first stanza and comment on its effect.
2	In your opinion, what is the role in the poem of the landlord and his wife?
3	What is the effect of the repetition in the poem, including the refrain?
4	How is the refrain in stanza 4 slightly different from the refrain in the other stanzas? Why, do you think, has the poet done this?
5	What are the main metaphors and symbols in the poem and what do they represent to you? Give reasons for your answers and refer closely to the poem.
6	What, do you feel, is the main theme of the poem? You may suggest your own or choose from these options: ■ Playing a practical joke ■ Urban legends ■ A love of cars ■ A love of words and sounds ■ The creative process. Give reasons for your answer.
7	What are your favourite phrases and sounds in the poem and why?
8	Comment on the tone and effect of the narrative voice in this poem and consider how this is created by the poet.

Imagining

1	Hudgins has said that the Johnny Cash song 'One Piece at a Time', although it did not directly inspire the poem, 'flitted through [his] mind' as he wrote it. Listen to the song and note its similarities to the poem.
2	Imagine you are the landlord and you have discovered the Cadillac that day. Write your diary entry for that evening.
3	Compose a tabloid newspaper article based on the events in the poem accompanied by a suitably sensational headline.

Ted Hughes

1930 – 1998

Biography

Ted Hughes was born in West Yorkshire, England. A bright student, he won a scholarship to Pembroke College, Cambridge, where he published poems in university magazines. His first collection was published in 1957 to much critical acclaim.

In 1956, Hughes met and married Sylvia Plath, the American poet. Theirs was an intense relationship, and although they supported each other's work as poets and had two children together, they separated in 1962 as a result of his affair with Assia Wevill. A lifelong sufferer of mental health issues, Plath took her own life soon afterwards. Wevill also developed serious depression. In 1969 she killed herself and their four-year-old daughter. In 1970 Hughes married Carol Orchard and they remained together until his death. He was made Britain's Poet Laureate in 1984.

Hawk Roosting 🔊

Before you read

What do you know about hawks, their habitats, the kind of life they lead, their physical characteristics, and how they differ from other wild birds?

I sit in the top of the wood, my eyes closed.
Inaction, no falsifying dream
Between my hooked head and hooked feet:
Or in sleep rehearse perfect kills and eat.

The convenience of the high trees!   5
The air's buoyancy and the sun's ray
Are of advantage to me;
And the earth's face upward for my inspection.

My feet are locked upon the rough bark.
It took the whole of Creation   10
To produce my foot, my each feather:
Now I hold Creation in my foot

Or fly up, and revolve it all slowly –
I kill where I please because it is all mine.
There is no sophistry in my body: 15
My manners are tearing off heads –

The allotment of death.
For the one path of my flight is direct
Through the bones of the living.
No arguments assert my right: 20

The sun is behind me.
Nothing has changed since I began.
My eye has permitted no change.
I am going to keep things like this.

Glossary

Title	*Roosting*: perching, ready to sleep or rest
2	*Inaction*: the state of not being active
6	*The air's buoyancy*: the ability of the air to support the hawk in flight
11	*my each feather*: each of my feathers
15	*sophistry*: dishonest argument
17	*allotment*: allocating; giving out to particular individuals their due
20	*assert*: declare, insist upon

Guidelines

This poem, from the collection *Lupercal* (1960), is one of Hughes's many poems about animals. Hughes's love of the natural world stemmed from his Yorkshire boyhood, and his poetry, like that of D. H. Lawrence, is full of animals that are both **vividly pictured and symbolic at the same time**. He respected the brutal instincts that enable animals to survive in a world that has no pity for weakness.

Commentary

Stanza 1

'Hawk Roosting' takes the form of a **monologue**. The **speaker of this poem is a hawk** roosting on a branch of a tree high above the ground and talking to itself. Its eyes are closed; the bird does not move, but unlike a sleeping human being it is not caught up in a 'falsifying dream'. Even its sleep is purposeful, as it 'rehearse[s] perfect kills'.

Stanza 2

In the second stanza it **considers its situation and counts its blessings** in a self-centred yet apparently impersonal way. Trees, air and sun are perfectly arranged for the 'convenience' of the hawk. Even 'the earth's face' is presented 'for my inspection'.

Stanza 3

The third stanza develops the **idea of the hawk as the centre of the universe**. Not only did it take 'the whole of Creation' to produce its every feature, but, as far as the hawk is concerned, 'Now I hold Creation in my foot'.

Stanza 4

The fourth stanza starts with the idea of the hawk flying to hunt. It is as if, with the beginning of the stanza, it has taken off to scan the earth for its prey. This line develops the idea expressed in line 8 that the surface of the earth (its face) presents itself for the hawk's inspection. In line 13 the hawk sees itself as being able to turn the earth beneath it ('revolve it') as it flies. **Its purpose is simple**: 'I kill where I please'. Its **focus is absolute**: 'There is no sophistry in my body'. In other words, the hawk goes straight to his work of killing without debating within itself whether what it does ('tearing off heads') is good or bad, right or wrong.

Stanza 5

What the hawk does – its function – is stated at the start of the next stanza: 'The allotment of death'. Deciding what is going to die, in other words. The next two lines describe the **directness with which it kills** on the 'one path' of its flight. Again, the focus is absolute. It **does not have to argue its right**, as a human might.

Stanza 6

The final stanza takes even further the idea that the hawk is at **the centre of the world**, as far as it is concerned. Arguments are unnecessary because 'The sun is behind me'. Nothing has changed since the hawk 'began' because it has allowed nothing to change. The final statement is a claim to power over time as well as space: 'I am going to keep things like this.'

Themes

On one level, this is **a poem about the hawk and its nature**. The poet is contemplating the long evolutionary process that has gone into the making of the hawk's feet, beak and feathers. It has been designed by evolution to be a killing machine, and does what it has to do, 'tearing off heads', because nature gives the hawk no choice but to be as violent as it is. **There is no issue of morality or judgement.** At this level, 'Hawk Roosting' is an unsentimental, even admiring look at the hawk and the world as seen from the hawk's point of view.

At the same time, the poem cannot help reflecting on the human world too. As readers, we are well aware that the words are not the hawk's, but a human's: **an imagined vision** of what it is to be a hawk. It might make us think about the utterly, shamelessly self-centred view of the world that a hawk has, and both the similarities and differences between that view and our own. All the time there is **an implied comparison between the hawk's directness and human hypocrisy and dishonesty**.

The words Hughes uses – 'sophistry', 'manners', 'argument' – imply the comparison between human ways and animal ones. The hawk kills. Human beings kill each other too. But when humans kill they find justifications and arguments. For example, the commonest 'falsifying dream' to justify the mass killing of enemies in wartime is based on seeing the enemy as people fighting for an evil cause, and seeing one's own side as patriots defending their country. In contrast to this dishonesty, the hawk's account of its own violent acts is honest and straightforward and free from excuse-making.

Imagery

The main image of the poem is, of course, the hawk roosting, its feet gripping a tree branch. Line 21, 'The sun is behind me', adds to the imposing, dramatic quality of that image. In the poem, **both the world and the hawk itself are seen from the hawk's point of view**, with the hawk in control at the centre and the world arranged for its 'convenience' (line 5). The power and violence of the hawk is conveyed through details: the 'hooked head and hooked feet'; 'tearing off heads'; its flight 'Through the bones of the living'.

Form and language

'Hawk Roosting' is written in quatrains which are mostly unrhymed and have no regular metre. The language is plain, governed by the fact that most of the poem consists of statements made by the hawk about the hawk, using the personal pronouns 'I', 'me' and 'my'. The **bold bluntness** of the assertions is strengthened by the **use of words that are monosyllabic** (consisting of one syllable) and by the fact that most of the lines are end-stopped. That is, the meaning stops at the end of the line, often with the use of a comma or full stop. This is most apparent in the final stanza, which consists of four complete sentences, each one an assertion of the hawk's power and status, and each one taking exactly one line:

'The sun is behind me.
Nothing has changed since I began.
My eye has permitted no change.
I am going to keep things like this.'

The **combination of personal pronouns in the first person ('I', 'me', 'my') with plain assertions** communicates a quality that in a human being you would think of as arrogance, but which in this poem comes across as an honest statement of fact.

> ## SNAPSHOT
> ■ Portrait of a hawk's world view
> ■ Implied comparison with human beings
> ■ Free from moral judgement
> ■ Use of first person pronouns
> ■ End-stopped lines
> ■ Language of statement and assertion

Exam-Style Questions

Understanding the poem

1	What image of the hawk do you get from the first stanza of the poem?
2	Do you think the poem shows the hawk as having no interest in anything outside itself? Refer to the text of the poem in support of your answer.
3	The hawk says: 'I kill where I please because it is all mine' (line 14). What does this line tell you about the hawk? Quote two other lines from the poem in which the hawk expresses similar ideas.
4	Does the poem tell you that the hawk enjoys killing and eating other creatures. If not, what is the hawk's attitude? Refer to the poem in support of your answer.
5	The poem hints at the difference between the human attitude to the violent killing of others, and the hawk's attitude to its violent killing ('tearing off heads' and breaking bones) of its victims. Where in the poem is this difference suggested?
6	Is this poem about nature as well as being about the hawk? What does it tell you about the natural world?
7	'What the hawk does is neither good nor evil.' Give your own view of this comment, referring to the text in support of your answer.
8	'The hawk has a strong sense of entitlement.' How is this expressed in the poem?
9	Do you find what you learn from this poem disturbing or reassuring?

Thinking about the poem

1	What, do you think, is meant by 'falsifying dream' in line 2? What is the difference between that and 'inaction'?
2	Comment on the line, 'There is no sophistry in my body'. Look up 'sophistry' in a dictionary to help you.
3	Choose one sentence from the poem which, for you, sums up the hawk's sense of its own importance. Try to explain why and how the sentence works.

Imagining

1	Describe your feelings about the hawk's victims, whose heads are torn off and bones are broken.
2	Should you feel guilty about eating parts of an animal that has been killed for your benefit? Discuss in groups or pairs.
3	Write your own poem from the point of view of an animal of your choosing, trying to imagine how it might see the world.

Denise Levertov

1923–1997

An Arrival (North Wales, 1897)   545

Biography

Denise Levertov was born in Essex, in England. Her father, who taught at the University of Leipzig in Germany, was a Russian Jew. After the First World War, he converted to Christianity and came to England. Her mother, Beatrice Adelaide Spooner-Jones, was Welsh and traced her ancestry back to a Welsh mystic. Levertov's poetry often has a spiritual, mystical quality that celebrates the sacredness of all living things.

Denise Levertov was educated at home by her mother and was writing poetry from an early age. She also studied ballet, art, piano and French. She said that growing up part Jewish, German, Welsh and English made her feel special. From an early age, she wanted to write and sent some of her poems to T. S. Eliot, who replied with an encouraging letter.

Levertov was involved in many civil rights struggles throughout her life. Her first book of poetry was published immediately after the Second World War, to wide acclaim. In 1947, she married the American writer Mitchell Goodman and moved to the United States. The couple had one son, Nikolai, and lived in New York.

Levertov's poems brought recognition from critics and writers alike. During the 1960s, the Vietnam War and feminism became central concerns in her work. Her 1967 collection *The Sorrow Dance* brings together the political and the personal. In the 1970s and 1980s, she taught at a number of American universities.

Denise Levertov continued to write and publish poetry, translations and essays up to her death in 1997.

An Arrival (North Wales, 1897)

Before you read

 Have you ever arrived in a new place that was utterly different from your familiar surroundings? Relate the experience to a partner and describe your feelings.

The orphan arrived in outlandish hat,
proud pain of new button boots.
Her moss-agate eyes
photographed views of the noonday sleepy town
no one had noticed. Nostrils flaring,   5
she sniffed odours of hay and stone,
      absence of Glamorgan coaldust,
and pasted her observations quickly
into the huge album of her mind.
Cousins, ready to back off like heifers   10
were staring:
     amazed, they received
the gold funeral sovereigns she dispensed
along with talk strange to them as a sailor's parrot.

Auntie confiscated the gold;   15
the mourning finery, agleam with jet,
was put by to be altered. It had been chosen
by the child herself and was thought
unsuitable. She was to be
the minister's niece, now,   20
not her father's daughter.
      Alone,
she would cut her way through a new world's
graystone chapels, the steep and sideways
rockface cottages climbing   25
mountain streets,

enquiring, turning things over
in her heart,
     weeping only in rage or when
the choirs in their great and dark and   30
golden glory broke forth and the hills
skipped like lambs.

Glossary

1	*orphan*: the poem is based on the experience of the poet's mother, Beatrice Adelaide Spooner-Jones, who was orphaned at the age of twelve and sent to North Wales to live with the family of her maternal aunt
3	*moss-agate eyes*: moss agate is a semi-precious gem, which is often used in rings. The stone is white with green markings, which give it a moss-like appearance
7	*Glamorgan coaldust*: Glamorgan is a region in South Wales formerly known for its coalmines
13	*funeral sovereigns*: there is a tradition of mourners handing out coins at a funeral. What is unusual here is that the coins are gold sovereigns, and the chief mourner is a little girl. A sovereign was worth one pound
16	*agleam with jet*: the girl's clothes are decorated with shiny black beads or buttons. Jet is a polished black stone used in jewellery
20	*minister's niece*: David Oliver, a well-known Protestant minister. In the parish records he is described as 'Minister of the Gospel in the Congregational Dissenters Chapel'
21	*father's daughter*: Beatrice Adelaide was an only child, doted on by her father
24	*chapels*: in Wales, churches were associated with the Anglican Church, whose priests were often English, and chapels with a wide range of non-Anglican congregations – Methodists, Presbyterians, Baptists, Congregational Dissenters. There is a great tradition of choral singing in Welsh chapels
31–32	*the hills / skipped like lambs*: the lines come from Psalm 114, 'When Israel went out of Egypt'. In the psalm, the mountains and the hills seem to celebrate God's power in rescuing His chosen people. As a minister's daughter, Levertov would have been familiar with hearing the Psalms sung during services

Guidelines

The poem recreates the arrival of a young girl into a farming community in North Wales. The child is an orphan and is dressed in her mourning clothes. She has come from a mining area in Glamorgan, South Wales. The poem captures the strangeness of the experience and the loneliness the girl feels as she comes to live among cousins whom she scarcely knows. The poem is **based on the experience of Levertov's mother**, Beatrice Adelaide Spooner-Jones.

Commentary

Stanza 1

The orphan girl makes quite an impression when she arrives in her 'outlandish hat' and 'new button boots'. Not only does her dress make her stand out, but also her eyes are the colour of 'moss-agate' (line 3). She is alert, like a nervous pony, nostrils flaring, eyes on the move, taking in everything. She is quick and observant, noting the absence of the coaldust, which was such a feature of her former life. She takes everything in and pastes her observations 'into the huge album of her mind'.

The **first nine lines focus on the girl** and her impression of her new surroundings. In the last five lines of the stanza, **the focus shifts to the cousins** who meet her. If the orphan is like a pony in stanza 1, all nervous energy and alertness, they are compared to heifers, staring in amazement at this young girl who gives them 'funeral sovereigns'. Her talk is as strange to them as a 'sailor's parrot' (line 14). Is there a hint of mockery directed towards the cousins in this stanza?

Stanza 2

The first seven lines of stanza two (lines 15–21) **shift the perspective to that of the aunt**, who confiscates the gold coins. She puts the 'mourning finery' aside so that it can be altered. Levertov manages to suggest the aunt's disapproval of the child and the child's father by **implication rather than direct statement**. Although written in the third person, we can almost hear the aunt saying the words of the stanza: 'She was to be / the minister's niece, now, / not her father's daughter.' We sense that the child will be subject to a strict regime with less freedom than she has been used to. The word 'Alone', standing alone in line 22, emphasises the child's **isolation**. The child is determined, independent and resilient. Just like the villages cut into rock, she cuts her way through her new world, investigating it.

Stanza 3

The suggestion in this stanza is that the girl's exploration of the world of her new surroundings is a solitary one. She turns things over 'in her heart' (line 28). The break in the line after 'heart' mirrors the child turning things over. The word 'heart' is followed, in the next line, by 'weeping', though we are told that the child 'only' wept in rage or when she was moved by the beauty of the choirs singing in the chapels.

Themes and imagery

The poem is a **character study** of the poet's mother as a young child. The young girl has been orphaned and is sent to begin a new life with relatives she scarcely knows, moving from an industrial coalmining town in South Wales to a farming community in North Wales. As presented in the poem, the young girl achieves a kind of magnificence in her 'outlandish hat' (line 1) and 'new button boots' (line 2). She is presented as a spirited child who is **alert and observant**. Although she is 'alone', she explores her new world with an enquiring mind and considers all she observes and experiences, 'turning things over / in her heart' (lines 27–28). The young girl is **adventurous and sensitive**. She is moved by the beauty of music she hears in the chapels and the natural beauty around her. The description of the choirs, 'in their great and dark and / golden glory' (lines 30–31) is magnificent, the phrasing capturing the richness of choral singing, even when some of the hymns refer to dark and gloomy subjects. It is not hard to imagine how the beauty of the words of the psalm, as captured in the last line, would have moved the soul of a sensitive and artistic child. The final line of the poem gives a sense of joy and optimism that is, in many ways, at odds with the rest of the poem and the circumstances of the young girl who is grieving for her father.

The **animal imagery** of nervous pony and staring heifers in stanza 1 brilliantly and humorously captures the difference between the young girl and her cousins. The image of the 'huge album of her mind' (line 9) hints at the child's intelligence and her capacity to observe and make sense of her world. The quality of her sharp intelligence is also suggested in the imagery of cutting her way through her new world (lines 23–26).

Form and language

The poem is written in **three irregular stanzas** and is carefully phrased. The phrases are full sounding. Note, for example, in the first stanza, the long vowel sounds; the alliteration of 'p' and 'b' in line 2. Note the number of words which end in 't' or 'd', which give a definite ending to the sound of the words. Note the number of times the sounds 'l', 'r' and 's' appear. These are among the most musical sounds in the language.

The tone of the poem is influenced by its careful observation. For the most part, it is detached, though we can sense the poet's sympathy and admiration for the young girl. **The final three lines of the poem suggest the emotional energy contained within the child.**

Exam-Style Questions

Understanding the poem

1	Relate in your own words the story the poem tells.
2	Describe how the orphan girl was dressed when she arrived in her new town.
3	In whose eyes was the orphan's hat outlandish? Explain your answer.
4	In what way is the girl like a nervous pony?
5	What difference does the young girl notice between the air in her new town and the air in the place she left behind?
6	What, according to the poem, does the young girl do with her observations of the new town in which she has arrived?
7	Comment on the impact of the phrase 'moss-agate eyes'. Refer to both the sound and the sense of the phrase.
8	How is the difference between the girl and her cousins suggested in the first stanza?
9	Comment on the effectiveness of the phrase 'a sailor's parrot' (line 14).
10	What is your view of the cousins, based on the evidence of the poem?
11	What impression of the young orphan do you form from stanza one? Is she: ■ Curious ■ Observant ■ Cheeky ■ Shy ■ Spoiled? Explain your answer.
12	(a) What words in stanza 2 suggest the aunt's attitude to her orphaned niece? (b) On the basis of this stanza, what kind of relationship, do you think, will develop between the aunt and her niece from Glamorgan?
13	'Auntie confiscated the gold' (line 15). Comment on the impact of the verb 'confiscated' in this line. Explain your thinking.
14	'turning things over / in her heart' (lines 27–28). Comment on these lines from the poem. What do they tell us about the orphan girl?
15	Working in pairs, take one stanza and read it aloud, paying attention to every word. Note as many sound repetitions as you can and discuss their effect in the poem.

Thinking about the poem

1	Which of these three statements is closest to your interpretation of the poem? ■ It is a poem about the inner life of a child. ■ It is a poem about loss. ■ It is a poem about arriving in a new place. Explain your choice.
2	Think about the use of the word 'Alone' (line 22). What are the implications of this word?

3	'The choirs in the poem can shake the heart and soul of the child.' Give your response to this reading of the poem.
4	Based on lines 22–32, what combination of words best describes the girl's life in North Wales? ■ Lonely ■ Exciting ■ Solitary ■ Adventurous ■ Sad ■ Frustrating ■ Joyous Explain your choice.
5	'The child in the poem is like an exile, taking photographs of a strange land, as she waits to return home.' Give your response to this reading of the poem.
6	The poem is about the poet's mother. Based on the poem, how does the poet view her mother's experience?

Imagining

1	What did the townspeople in North Wales think about the orphan girl? Working in pairs, write a dialogue between the girl's aunt and a neighbour in which they discuss the new arrival.
2	You are the child in the poem. You are now an adult with children of your own. Tell your children about any **three** of the following: ■ Your arrival in North Wales ■ Losing your 'mourning finery' ■ Being the minister's niece and not your father's daughter ■ Turning things over in your heart ■ Weeping in rage ■ The choirs and their music.
3	Suggest a piece of music or a set of images to accompany a reading of the poem. Explain your choice.

SNAPSHOT

- Story poem
- Based on the life of the poet's mother
- Careful descriptions
- Different perspectives
- Sense of isolation
- Sense of independence
- Emotional impact of the choirs
- Carefully phrased
- Musical language
- Emotional ending

Paula Meehan

b. 1955

The Russian Doll   551

Biography

Paula Meehan was born in 1955 in Dublin, where she still lives. She grew up in Finglas and recalls her grandfather keeping a book of Emily Dickinson's poems – given to Meehan's aunt by an American boyfriend – in his writing cabinet. She was drawn to the book and still has it today. Meehan went on to study English, Classical Studies and History at Trinity College, Dublin and at Eastern Washington University in America. She has received many awards, including the Marten Toonder Award for Literature, the Butler Literary Award for Poetry, the Denis Devlin Memorial Award and the PPI Award for Radio Drama. She has published several collections of poetry, including *Pillow Talk* (1994), from which this poem is taken. Her writing for stage includes the plays *Mrs Sweeney* (1997), *Cell* (1999) and, for children, *Kirkle* (1995) and *The Wolf of Winter* (2003/2004). She has collaborated throughout her working life with dancers, visual artists and film makers. Paula Meehan is a member of Aosdána, the Irish group of writers and artists. She is also an activist who campaigns on many issues including drugs, women's issues and, more recently, the homelessness crisis in Ireland.

Before you read

Share what you know about or research matryoshka dolls, more commonly known as Russian dolls.

The Russian Doll

Her colours caught my eye.
Mixed by the light of a far off sun:
carmine, turmeric, indigo, purple –
they promised to spell us dry weather.

I'd a fiver in my pocket; that's   5
all they asked for. And gift wrapped her.
It had been grey all month and damp.
We felt every year in our bones

and our dead had been too much with us.
January almost over. Bitter.   10
I carried her home like a Holy Fire
the seven miles from the town,

my face to a wind from the north. Saw
the first primroses in the maw of a fallen oak.
There was smoke from the chimney   15
When I came through the woods

and, though I had spent the dinner,
I knew you'd love your gaudy doll,
you'd love what's in her
at the end of your seventh winter   20

Glossary

3	*carmine*: also called cochineal, a bright red colour
3	*turmeric*: an Asian spice which is a deep yellow colour
3	*indigo*: a deep rich blue colour
14	*maw*: the inside of the mouth, throat or stomach
18	*gaudy*: brightly coloured in a clashing or tasteless way

Guidelines

This poem comes from the 1994 collection *Pillow Talk*. In it a parent gives their daughter a brightly coloured Russian doll which seems to have a magical quality, bringing cheer after a cold winter of hardship and loss.

Commentary

Stanza 1

It is the exotic bright colours of the doll that attract the speaker to it. After a wet and grey winter, its colours, 'carmine, turmeric, indigo, purple', suggest sun-soaked faraway places – 'far off sun' – and it 'promised' to lift the gloom and 'bring dry weather'.

Stanzas 2 and 3

After the exotic language in stanza 1 the speaker becomes more colloquial and low-key in stanza 2, 'I'd a fiver in my pocket'. She is relieved that this is all the doll cost and seems delighted at the bonus of the doll being 'gift wrapped'. Poverty is implied here, yet great affection too.

The Holy Fire is a phenomenon celebrated by Orthodox Christians everywhere. It is believed to be a miracle that occurs every Easter Saturday, in which a blue fire comes from the tomb of Jesus in the church of the Holy Sepulchre in Jerusalem. A priest brings two candles containing the flame out of the tomb and this is used to light many more flames, even being flown on special flights to Orthodox Christian countries, including Russia.

The next four lines convey that a cold and difficult winter, full of loss and hardship, has been endured. It has been 'grey' and 'damp' and everyone has felt their age through the cold 'in their bones'. Great loss and grief has been endured, 'our dead had been too much with us'. All this **suffering can be summed up in the word 'Bitter'**, which ends this description but is quickly followed by hope, warmth and light, 'I carried her home like a Holy Fire'. The doll seems to represent a better future and is worth the 'seven miles' trek to bring her home.

Stanzas 4 and 5

Like a heroine in a myth or fairy tale, the speaker seems to be on a quest, travelling miles through the woods in the face of a biting north wind. The doll is the object of this quest and the hope it represents is echoed by other signs of hope: the primroses – one of the first flowers of spring – and the fire burning that greets her return, 'smoke from the chimney'.

Although the speaker has 'spent the dinner' money buying the doll there is no regret and she seems sure the sacrifices made were worth it, 'I knew you'd love your gaudy doll'. She knows this seven-year-old child will have even more fun discovering the secrets the doll contains, 'you'd love what's in her'.

The poem **ends on a note of hope and love**, reassuring us that despite enduring hardship and sacrifice there can be a happy ending.

Themes and imagery

Motherhood, family and fertility are all strong themes in the poem and are central to what the matryoshka dolls represent in Russian culture. Also called nesting dolls, they symbolise these three central pillars of Russian family life where the **babushka** (strong female matriarch) rules. The mother in this poem is similarly strong, determined and resilient, enduring great hardship and sacrifice to pass on these values to her daughter. Inside the Russian doll there lies a series of smaller and smaller identical dolls, each contained inside the last. This representation of generations of mothers and daughters in families celebrates the process of motherhood and birth. Poetry is like this too; as the reader explores a poem they can see new layers of meaning revealing themselves. On one level this is a simple poem about a mother's gift to her daughter, but **themes of loss, love, death and hope** are revealed through the language and imagery of the poem.

Poverty and hardship are also themes and Meehan often writes about the difficult lives of women, especially in her native Dublin. We see this theme in the poverty of the mother, who only has a 'fiver' to spend on dinner but is willing to sacrifice it for her daughter.

Wintry imagery represents death, hardship and loss, 'grey', 'damp', 'January', 'Bitter', 'our dead'. However, this is contrasted with the clashing bright colours of the doll which to some might seem 'gaudy' but against the gloom of winter bring hope and a sense of renewal, echoed in the primroses the writer spies in the forest.

Mythological or fairy tale imagery also adds another layer of depth and meaning to the poem. A walk into town to buy dinner becomes quest-like. The arduous trek through the woods to bring back the doll is exaggerated in a simile comparing it to the 'Holy Fire'. This simile has a mystical quality and the description of the 'fallen oak' adds to it when it is described as having a 'maw' – a word often used to describe the mouth and throat of terrifying beasts. This image is reminiscent of the monsters so common in myths and legends which often guard treasures, like the hydra in Greek mythology, which guarded the golden fleece in Jason's quest. Can you think of any other similar examples in stories or films?

Language and form

Colour, mentioned in the first line, prepares us for the contrasting moods in the poem. The bright colours of the doll and the primroses, as well as the images of fire ('Holy Fire', 'chimney'), offer hope and a promise of renewal. These are set against the dreary greys and dampness of the 'Bitter' winter, which is finally drawing to a close.

Colloquial language like 'fiver' and 'I had spent the dinner' places the poem in a domestic setting, but contrast is central to the language – we find much more exotic words like the 'carmine, turmeric, indigo, purple' colours of stanza 1 and the 'Holy Fire' of stanza 3. 'Spell' is mentioned in stanza 1, implying both a dry spell of weather but perhaps also the **magical effect the doll might have** in banishing the gloom of winter.

Contrast is also evident in the lack of a rhyming scheme while at the same time the long vowel sounds and half-rhymes add a lyrical quality. Note the long sounds in 'our dead had been too much with us' and 'through the woods'. The rhyme of 'oak' and 'smoke' in stanza 4 also has an alliterative quality. You should be able to find more examples of these sound effects as you explore the poem.

The repetition of 'seven' is interesting; it is the distance from the town to their home and also the age of the child and it is a number that features heavily in fairy tales (e.g. the seven dwarves), myths and religion (e.g. the seven deadly sins).

The poem consists of five unrhymed stanzas, each of four lines, featuring some enjambment (run-on lines) for example in stanza four 'Saw / the first primroses'.

Exam-Style Questions

Understanding the poem

1	What attracted the speaker to the doll, according to the first stanza?
2	What details in the second and third stanzas suggest that life has not been easy for the speaker in the poem?
3	Look closely at stanzas 3 and 4 and describe the journey the mother makes home with the doll, pointing out any important details you notice.
4	What was the speaker certain of, according to the final stanza?

Thinking about the poem

1	The poet uses contrast widely in the poem. Point out some examples of this in the imagery and language of the poem and comment on their meaning and effect.
2	What fairy tale elements does the poem contain? Having listed them, offer your opinion as to why the poet might have wanted to include them to tell the story of the poem.
3	Look at the use of personal pronouns in the poem (stanza 1: 'Her', 'my', 'they', 'us', etc.). Who or what does each one refer to? Trace the use of these throughout the poem.
4	Read the notes on what the 'Holy Fire' refers to. How might the doll be like a 'Holy Fire' for the speaker and her daughter?
5	What sound effects stood out most to you and why?
6	'I knew you'd love your gaudy doll, / you'd love what's in her'. What do you think the speaker means by these lines from the final stanza?
7	What is the overall theme of the poem, in your opinion?

Understanding the poem

1	Turn the poem into a fairy tale or myth adding any details you think will help create this genre effectively.
2	Write a dialogue between the mother and her daughter (or possibly another family member) when she returns with the doll but no dinner.
3	Share anecdotes about a childhood gift which meant a lot to you.
4	Create a comic strip based on the events of the poem, being mindful of the colours and images mentioned.

SNAPSHOT

- Colour
- Contrast widely used
- Mythical/fairy tale element
- Russian influence
- Themes of motherhood and birth
- Sound effects
- Light and dark
- Hope and renewal
- Symbolism of the doll

Caitríona O'Reilly

b. 1973

Interlude   557

Biography

Caitríona O'Reilly was born in Dublin in the early 1970s and was raised in County Wicklow. She studied English and Ancient History at Trinity College Dublin, later completing her PhD on the poet Sylvia Plath. She published the poetry collection *The Nowhere Birds*, from which this poem comes, in 2001.

As well as writing poetry, O'Reilly writes reviews and critical essays. She has written for BBC Radio and has also published some fiction. She held the Harper-Wood Studentship at St John's College, Cambridge and has won prizes for her work, including the Rooney Prize for Irish Literature. She divides her time between Wicklow and Hull in the UK. Sinéad Morrissey wrote of her: 'O'Reilly has what so few poets have: a language all of her own, so much so that any image or line is instantly recognisable as hers' (*The Guardian*).

Interlude

Before you read

Have you ever experienced a break or a holiday which you feel changed you somehow? Reflect on this and discuss in pairs or small groups.

With its *gelati* and bougainvillea-draped sculpture,
Italy hovered like a rumour five miles further.
Binn was worthy, litterless, Swiss;

where to breathe was like a sea-plunge, even in June.
Populated by six-foot clean-limbed blondes,   5
they bled pure gold, if they bled at all. Anaemic Knut

('like *Hamsun*') was an exception. He composed
electronically ('like *Kraftwerk*') and afterwards
dropped by for *Kräutertee*. I'd never even heard of *Hunger*.

Hector, who had a scar from nipple to navel, called me 'pure'   10
in nasty English. There was a failed seduction
by a man with a handlebar moustache and gold tooth,

a silly crush on a stout-legged father of five …
The summer dragged to an end. Where the sun once fell
tremendously there was a noise of thunder.   15

I cracked the ice on the *bier-garten* tables, folded umbrellas,
bid a farewell to the urinals. A thousand pounds
in the heel of my shoe might have bought three months

in a Berlin flat. But in the airport a kitten wailed in a basket
dementedly and a jittery pilot sweated over his charts   20
and I was back, convincing them I'd ever been elsewhere.

Glossary

Title	*Interlude*: an interval, a break between two significant periods (like the interval in a play)
1	gelati: Italian ice cream
1	*bougainvillea*: brightly coloured large-flowered plants native to hot countries
3	*Binn*: a region in Switzerland, near the Italian border
6	*Anaemic*: pale, lacking in iron
6–7	*Knut Hamsun:* a Norwegian writer; *Hunger* is his most famous work
9	Kräutertee: herbal tea
16	bier-garten: a beer garden

Guidelines

O'Reilly included this poem in her 2001 collection *The Nowhere Birds*. The speaker describes her experiences working in a Swiss beer garden near the Italian border one summer.

Commentary

Stanzas 1–3

The poem begins with a sense of 'so near and yet so far'. The glamour, beauty and glorious food of Italy is only five miles away, but its ice cream, flora and art are 'like a rumour' to the speaker, who is working in Binn, Switzerland. Here, although it is June, the air is cold, 'to breathe was like a sea-plunge'. This place is summed up in the three words 'worthy, litterless, Swiss', suggesting **a sterile and dull environment** which takes itself rather more seriously than its exotic neighbour.

The Swiss are like gods, 'six-foot clean-limbed blondes, / they bled pure gold, if they bled at all'. The poet may be comparing the Swiss to the Greek gods who had ichor (a golden substance) instead of blood, and were immortal.

> **Kraftwerk is a German band formed in Düsseldorf in 1970 by Ralf Hütter and Florian Schneider. Composers, innovators and pioneers of electronic music, they performed using synthesisers and had a robotic style of playing and singing.**

Despite this, the Swiss men who become acquaintances of the speaker are rather less than god-like! The first is Knut, who was 'Anaemic' and seemed rather full of himself, 'He composed / electronically ("like *Kraftwerk*").' He seems to make our speaker feel inadequate: 'I'd never even heard of *Hunger*'.

Stanzas 4 and 5

Another less than god-like male acquaintance is 'Hector', who 'had a scar from nipple to navel' and was scathing about the speaker's rejection of his advances, calling her '"pure" / in nasty English'; in other words, 'frigid' like the Swiss air!

Another two disastrous dalliances follow; 'a failed seduction' by a very dubious-looking man who not only had a 'handlebar moustache' but also sported a 'gold tooth'. Another man, who was a 'silly crush', was not only 'stout-legged' but had five children too. Given that she'd earlier described the Swiss as 'god-like' we might well wonder why she is connecting with such odd men.

Then we have the sense of the summer working in Binn slowly coming to a close: 'The summer dragged to an end.' There is an **atmosphere of menace** created as the weather turns stormy: 'there was a noise of thunder'.

Stanzas 6 and 7

This **sense of an ending** continues as ice gathers on the beer-garden tables and she folds the umbrellas. There's some humour as she 'bid a farewell to the urinals' and travels to the airport with 'A thousand pounds' tucked into her shoe. She knows she could go to Berlin with the money but maybe the thought of more Germanic culture is too much. She decides to go home, perhaps spurred on to this decision by such omens as a kitten wailing 'dementedly' and the nervous pilot 'jittery' and sweating 'over his charts'. It's unclear whether she is transferring her own misgivings onto the kitten and the pilot, but her decision to go home is made and when she gets there she takes pains to try to convince 'them' that she hadn't been changed by her summer in Binn, 'convincing them I'd ever been elsewhere'.

Themes and imagery

As the title suggests, the poem is based on an interval in the speaker's life; a break from the norm when she took a summer job in Switzerland. However, this is not just a 'time out'; the speaker is clearly changed by her experiences. **Change and sexual awakening** have left her unwilling to continue her travels after some less than enjoyable encounters with various strange men. Real passion and romance is embodied by Italy, 'with its *gelati* and bougainvillea-draped sculpture', merely 'five miles further' but the speaker doesn't get any closer than this. She encounters four specific odd men who make her feel

inadequate, insult her and look strange. She seems naïve and unprepared for dealing with men, reflected by what she experiences later in the airport, 'a kitten wailed in a basket / dementedly and a jittery pilot sweated'. Once home she seems to want to put on a show of not having changed, but we sense that she has, and perhaps has not enjoyed the experience.

Comparisons are used throughout the first half of the poem, 'like a rumour', 'like a sea-plunge', 'like *Hamsun*', 'like *Kraftwerk*' and reflect the speaker's discontent and **her sense of being out of her depth**. Similarly, the imagery used to describe the Swiss suggests that she feels inadequate in their presence, 'they bled pure gold'. Perhaps this is why she gravitates towards less than perfect specimens like 'Anaemic Knut'; 'Hector' with his scar; 'handlebar moustache' man; and 'a stout-legged father of five'. The 'thunder' and 'ice' mentioned in stanzas 5 and 6 imply growing unease and discontent, ending with the speaker's fraught flight home.

Form and language

The poem is arranged in **seven tercets** (three-line stanzas) of unrhymed verse; however, sound effects serve to give the poem a more lyrical quality. The staccato effect of the phrase 'six-foot clean-limbed blondes' might mirror the harsh-sounding German dialect in Binn, further developed by using German words and references such as '*Kraftwerk*', '*Kräutertee*' and '*bier-garten*'.

There is alliteration here too, in phrases like 'nipple to navel' and 'father of five', while we hear sibilance in such phrases as 'litterless, Swiss'. Again, these lift the poem from free verse to something more pleasing to the ear. Look at the poet's use of punctuation, for example parentheses (brackets) and ellipsis (...) and see what effect they have on the poem. For the English-speaking reader the fact that somewhere called 'Binn' is 'litterless' might raise a smile! Is there evidence elsewhere of **a wry sense of humour**?

The last line contains a number of 'e' sounds and is somewhat awkward to say; 'convincing them I'd ever been elsewhere'. Might this convey that the speaker feels awkward about her experiences in Switzerland and would rather not address them with her family?

Exam-Style Questions

Understanding the poem

1   What is your understanding of the title of the poem, having explored it in detail? Refer to specific details in the poem throughout your answer.

2   Would you say the experiences of the speaker were positive or negative? Explain, with reference to the poem.

3   What is the effect of the use of the German words in the poem?

4   Examine and comment on the poet's careful use of sound effects and punctuation in the poem. Look at sibilance, alliteration, enjambment, parenthesis, ellipsis and half-rhyme.

5   What does the speaker ultimately reveal about herself in the poem?

6   List and explain the similes/comparisons in the poem.

Thinking about the poem

1   Compare the description of Italy to that of Binn in stanza 1. Which place appeals to you more and why?

2   How does the speaker describe the Swiss race in stanza 2?

3   Describe the four specific men the speaker encounters while working in the 'bier-garten' (lines 6–13). What are your impressions of these men?

4   What details in the final three stanzas show that the summer in Binn is coming to an end? Does the speaker seem glad or sad about this, in your opinion?

5   Where does the speaker consider going next and why does she dismiss this idea?

6   What, do you think, does the speaker mean by 'convincing them I'd ever been elsewhere'? Why might she be anxious to hide how her experiences may have changed her?

Imagining

1   Write about a time in your life (real or imagined) which you felt changed you in a significant way.

2   Have a class discussion about national stereotypes, e.g. the Swiss are clean and dull, the Italians are passionate and food-loving. Is there, do you think, any truth in the descriptions of the national stereotypes? (Remember to be respectful of different cultures.)

3   Write a series of diary entries based on the poem.

SNAPSHOT

- Contrast
- Wry humour
- Sound effects
- Punctuation significant
- Use of German words
- Ambiguity

- Themes of change and awakening
- Tercets
- Similes
- Theme of change

Eileen Sheehan

b. 1963

Biography

Eileen Sheehan was born in Scartaglin, Co. Kerry, in 1963 and has lived most of her life in Killarney. Her work is widely published in journals and anthologies and she has read at major literary festivals in Ireland and abroad. She has won the Brendan Kennelly Poetry Award (2006) at the Listowel Writers' Week festival. Her work is marked by wit, by a sense of the surreal and by a lyric sensibility. Many of her poems, including those dealing with loss or darker themes, achieve a sense of quiet calm. She is a former poet-in-residence for Limerick County Council. She is one of the writers on Poetry Ireland's Writers in Schools scheme. Her collections include *Song of the Midnight Fox* (2004), *Down the Sunlit Hall* (2008) and *The Narrow Way of Souls* (2017).

Before you read

As a class, you might like to discuss how the presence of those who die survives in the world. Return to your discussion after you have read the poem.

Glossary

4	*resin*: sticky substance with a distinctive smell that oozes from some trees and plants. Used in making wood varnishes; fiddle players put it on the violin bow to give it extra grip on the strings
7	*foxglove*: tall plant with massive clusters of bell-shaped, purple-pink flowers that grows wild in hedgerows, ditches and woodland; also known as fairy bells
8	*buttercup*: wild plant that grows in meadows, with a bright yellow five-petalled flower
9	*corncrake*: shy, secretive bird, with a distinctive call; it visits Ireland in summer
18	*turret*: small tower

My Father, Long Dead

My father, long dead,
has become air

Become scent
of pipe smoke, of turf smoke, of resin

Become light   5
and shade on the river

Become foxglove,
buttercup, tree bark

Become corncrake
lost from the meadow   10

Become silence,
places of calm

Become badger at dusk,
deer in the thicket

Become grass   15
on the road to the castle

Become mist
on the turret

Become dark-haired hero in a story
written by a dark-haired child   20

Guidelines

'My Father, Long Dead' is from Sheehan's third collection, *The Narrow Way of Souls*, published in 2017 by Salmon Poetry. In this poem a daughter remembers her father with love and affection. Giving the background to the poem, Sheehan commented:

'When the title of the poem came to me, 'My Father, Long Dead', I thought that the poem was going to be a blackly-humorous piece ... [but] the poem had its own ideas about what it wanted to say. Image after image manifested in celebration of a landscape; in celebration of my father, the first storyteller I knew. The poem became for me an affirmation of the creative impulse ... It showed me the distinction between being from a place and being of a place. The storyteller entered the myth, became part of the story. As if the landscape, the story, the child, the father, the poem itself had always existed and I had just happened across them.'

Commentary

Lines 1–14

In these seven couplets **the speaker explains what her dead father has become for her**. She finds his presence in the air and in familiar scents. He has become light and shade on the river; flowers in the meadow; and the corncrake lost from the meadow. He has become silence and places of calm. For her, he has become the shy animals of the countryside, hidden from view.

Readers form their own impression of the father from these references. They may imagine him as someone sitting by a turf fire, smoking a pipe or playing a fiddle. They may see him as a countryman, familiar with the meadows and the river bank, and a lover of nature. They may picture, perhaps, a shy or retiring man, like the badger and the deer. They may imagine him as someone who could sit in silence and create an atmosphere of calm. They realise that – like the corncrake that used to be found throughout Ireland in summer but is now seen only in small areas of the northwest where there is little use of machines to mow fields and disturb its nests – he is lost to the meadows, although his spirit still resides there.

Lines 15–20

In the last three couplets the imagery moves from a landscape of woodlands and river and meadow to **a more mythical landscape of castle and turret and story**. The speaker tells us that her father has become 'grass / on the road to the castle' and 'mist / on the turret' and a 'dark-haired hero'. But these couplets are as much about what the speaker, the daughter, has become. **She has become the storyteller, taking over from her father. And her father has become a character in his daughter's story.** She has mythologised him and, in doing so, keeps both him and the tradition of storytelling alive. Through her, the road to the castle will have people walking on it, the turret will emerge from the mist, and the hero will be dark-haired, a mythic version of her father.

Themes and imagery

The poem is a meditation on one of the most profound of all questions, **'What survives of the individual after death?'** In exploring it, **Sheehan touches on love, loss, family, inheritance, storytelling, nature, and the relationship between the individual and the natural world**. In the poem, the speaker expresses a belief

that her dead father has not ceased to be but exists as a presence in nature and he is mythologised in the story she creates.

To the poet's mind, her father was of a place and the spirit of that place – of the riverbank, meadows and woodlands – has entered him and he has entered it. She now senses him in the air, in the birds and animals, in the flowers in the meadows. In death, her father is one with **the goodness and beauty of nature**. He is also present in her stories. He has become the storyteller and the musician who is part of the music and the stories.

The final word of the poem is 'child'. **At the heart of the poem is the daughter–father relationship and the love between them.** No matter how old the writer becomes, she will always be her father's child. The 'Long Dead' in the title suggests that this is not a poem about the overwhelming loss and grief experienced in the immediacy of death. It is a gentle poem about love and loss. In its gentleness and optimism, **it offers consolation**.

The imagery of the poem is evocative and allusive. There are images of light and air and water and earth, and images from stories. The dead father has no corporeal (bodily) existence, but his presence is everywhere. The images, auditory, visual, olfactory, have a fleeting, intangible quality. They are light and airy. They are insubstantial images of beautiful things that are glimpsed but soon gone. There are images of smoke and the play of light on the water; of meadows and flowers and the smell of trees; of a bird that is no longer found in the meadows; of shy animals; of stillness and silence; of a story that is not told and a pathway not walked upon; of a castle, like memory, shrouded in mist.

The corncrake, badger and deer are shy creatures, rarely seen, and in the case of the corncrake, lost from the meadow. The father's presence is like that now, just out of sight, at the corner of vision, an absence that is a presence, sensed in places of quiet and silence.

Form and language

The poem is written in ten unrhymed couplets. **In keeping with the theme of life after death, the poem has no full stop.** The poem has a conversational air, but it is not casual. The tone is affectionate and loving. It is also poised and dignified, and formal in an understated way. The phrasing, repetition and musical quality of the language give the poem a freshness, like that of a musical air. The poem deals with a central mystery of human existence in **language that is clear and simple and rooted in the known world**.

Although the couplets are not rhymed and are written in varying line lengths, the **repetition and parallel phrasing gives the poem its formal structure**. The verb '**become**' is central to the thematic concerns of the poem. It is also the key structural component, occurring at the head of nine of the ten couplets. In each case it is followed by a noun or a noun phrase. The phrasing and repetition create a prayer-like effect, an incantation, as if the speaker is calling forth the spirit of the father. The word 'become', with the meaning of 'has come to be', neatly encapsulates the belief that the soul or spirit of the person survives death and becomes one with nature, in its many forms. The fall-off in the sound of the word, where the stressed first syllable is followed by an unstressed one, mirrors the way the father's corporeal existence has fallen away and been replaced by something real but fleeting and less tangible.

The loving tone of the poem is reflected in the beauty and musicality of the language. The 'o' and 'u' sounds that recur through the poem create a mellow feeling, enhanced by the music of the repeated 's' and 'r' sounds. These sounds and the phrasing have a soothing effect.

SNAPSHOT

- Personal and lyrical
- Conversational and formal
- Tone is loving
- Use of repetition to add structure
- The presence of the dead
- Spirit of place
- Storytelling as memory
- Importance of father–daughter relationship
- Simple language
- Musical qualities of the language
- Images drawn from nature and the Irish landscape
- Depth in simplicity

Exam-Style Questions

Understanding the poem

1	According to the speaker in the first seven couplets, what has her father become?
2	What kind of world is evoked through the imagery of lines 1–14?
3	How does this world differ from that described in the last six lines of the poem?
4	The last word in the poem is 'child'. What, in your view, is the significance of this?
5	Based on the poem, what kind of person do you imagine the father to have been?

Thinking about the poem

1	What is your favourite image from the poem? Explain your choice.
2	'The poem is both conversational and formal.' Discuss this statement, illustrating your answer with examples from the poem.
3	'This is a poem about death that is not sad.' Comment on this view of the poem.
4	Which of the following statements is closest to your understanding of the poem? ■ It is a poem about death. ■ It is a poem about love. ■ It is a poem about place. ■ It is a poem about remembering. ■ It is a poem about stories. Give reasons for your answer.
5	'The poem is a celebration of the Irish landscape.' Discuss this statement, supporting your answer with reference to the poem.

Imagining

1	Working in pairs, experiment with two voices reading the poem.
2	Using the imagery in the poem as your guide, write a short passage describing the place where the father spent his life.
3	The scents of pipe smoke, turf smoke and resin have rich associations for the poet. Choose a scent that is evocative for you. Write a short poem capturing the associations the scent has for you.

Penelope Shuttle

b. 1947

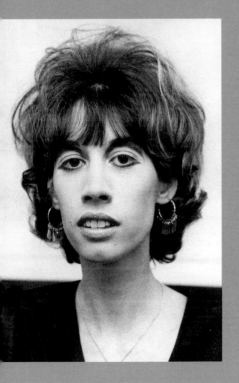

Biography

Penelope Shuttle was born in Middlesex, England in 1947. Since 1970 she has lived by the sea in Falmouth in Cornwall, in the south-west of England. The weather, the landscape and the history of Cornwall have inspired her work and, in her own words, enlarged her imagination. She was married to the poet Peter Redgrove, who died in 2003. The couple had one daughter, Zoe, who is an environmentalist.

Since 1980, Penelope Shuttle has published twelve collections of poems, all of which are highly regarded. One of her most celebrated collections is *Redgrove's Wife* (2006), a book of lament on the deaths of both her husband and her father, as well as a celebration of her husband's life and work. More recent collections are *Unsent: New and Selected Poems* (2012) and *Will You Walk a Little Faster?* (2017). She has a keen interest in yoga and has remarked on the importance of breath in determining the shape and form of a poem: 'For me it is the way the poem breathes that gives it form.' On the importance of writing in her life, Penelope Shuttle says: 'With writing (and reading) active in my life, I can concentrate on the chaos, hold experience steady. I can explore, enjoy, mourn, comprehend within my own limits, and keep pushing them as far as I can.'

Before you read

The wise owl. The treacherous snake. The brave lion. The clever fox. Humans have a long history of stereotyping different animals. What if animals were completely different from the ways we imagine them? Working in pairs, invent some new ways of describing elephants, monkeys, bears and lions. Compare your descriptions with those in the poem.

Glossary

5	*tomes*: large scholarly books	
5	*theses*: research essays	
7	*gibbering*: speaking nonsense	
	gesticulating: waving their arms, making theatrical gestures	
8	*scandalizing the punters*: shocking or horrifying the people who have paid to look at them	
10	*adopt ... stance*: the bears pose as cute teddy-like bears, disguising their real nature	
15	*rend the air*: sound piercingly with roars	
16	*sleep-lounge ... ease*: the big cats eat their food with vicious enthusiasm and then doze and lounge about	
16	*carnivorous*: meat-eating	
18	*show-business*: the animals are presented as entertainers for the public	
20	*skin after skin*: snakes regularly grow a new layer of skin and discard (shed) their old outer layer	
22	*paddock*: a small field	
22	*enclosure*: a fenced-off space	
23	*unfurred young*: human children who, unlike most of the animals on display, are not covered in fur	
31	*light fantastic*: light, nimble legs; to 'trip the light fantastic' is to dance nimbly or lightly	

Zoo Morning

Elephants prepare to look solemn and move slowly
though all night they drank and danced, partied
and gambled, didn't act their age.

Night-scholar monkeys take off their glasses,
pack away their tomes and theses,   5
sighing as they get ready for yet another long day
of gibbering and gesticulating, shocking
and scandalizing the punters.

Bears stop shouting their political slogans
and adopt their cute-but-not-really teddies' stance   10
in the concrete bear-pit.

Big cats hide their flower-presses, embroidery-frames
and watercolours;
grumbling, they try a few practice roars.
Their job is to rend the air, to devour carcasses,   15
to sleep-lounge at their vicious carnivorous ease.

What a life.
But none of them would give up show-business.

The snakes who are always changing,
skin after skin,   20
open their aged eyes and hinged jaws in welcome.

Between paddock and enclosure
we drag our unfurred young.
Our speech is over-complex, deceitful.
Our day out is not all it should be.   25
The kids howl, baffled.

All the animals are very good at being animals.
As usual, we are not up to being us.
Our human smells prison us.

In the insect house   30
the red-kneed spider dances on her eight light fantastics;
on her shelf of silence she waltzes and twirls;
joy in her hairy joints, her ruby-red eyes.

Guidelines

'Zoo Morning' is from the collection *Taxing the Rain* (1992). The poem has a **surreal quality**. It delights in challenging stereotypical representations of animals and of zoos. In comparison with the zoo animals, humans do not seem to know their role in the world. You might like to read the poem in light of Shuttle's view that the craziest dreams are often the most profound.

Commentary

As the title tells us, the scene described in the poem takes place in the morning, just before the zoo opens its doors. Like actors before a performance, the animals are preparing to put on a show for the human visitors.

Stanza 1
The elephants prepare to look solemn, though they partied all night.

Stanza 2
The monkeys put away their books and prepare to act in silly ways.

Stanza 3
The bears cease their political activities and adopt a harmless stance.

Stanza 4
The big cats put aside their genteel pastimes and get set to act the part of vicious carnivores.

Stanza 5
The narrator describes the life of the animals as show business.

Stanza 6
The snakes open their eyes and mouths for the visitors.

Stanza 7
The narrator describes the behaviour of the human visitors.

Stanza 8
The narrator suggests that animals are good at being animals, but we humans are not good at being human.

Stanza 9
In the insect house the red-kneed spider puts on a show.

Themes and imagery

The poem is **like a fable** in which animal characters are given human qualities and awareness (anthropomorphised), though they retain their animal form. Traditionally, fables were intended to reveal the weak or foolish behaviour of humans and, in doing so, encourage people to avoid repeating the mistakes made by the animal characters. In fables, animals behave like animals but speak and think like humans. The animal characters are often portrayed in stereotypical ways associated with particular species. For example, a lion is brave, but a deer is shy and timid. Because these **stereotypes** are so strong, there is scope for a writer to play with them and defeat a reader's expectations for comic or serious purposes. **Penelope Shuttle plays with our expectations in the poem.** The big cats, for example, are not aggressive and bloodthirsty; on the contrary, they are gentle, refined beings, who pursue pastimes associated with genteel women in the nineteenth century. **The reversal of the stereotype has a surreal, comic quality.**

Shuttle also plays with the familiar idea that humans are superior to animals. From medieval times, humans were regarded as existing on a higher plane than animals. Humans were spiritual beings with rational minds, though subject to animal passions. In contrast, animals lacked a spiritual side and were limited in intelligence and awareness. In 'Zoo Morning', Shuttle plays with this idea. Here **it is the humans who lack awareness, while the animals understand who they are and the roles they are expected to play** in the zoo.

The poem also confounds the stereotype of the zoo poem. In most poems about zoos, the plight of the animals is presented in such a way as to arouse the sympathy of the reader. Here it is the humans who are presented as pathetic and imprisoned by their own fears – 'Our human smells prison us' (line 29). The poem suggests that the 'authentic' experience of wild animals promised by zoos is manufactured and unreal. In Shuttle's poem, the animals conform to the ideas and stereotypes projected on them by the human visitors. They play the game. In fact, the central metaphor of the poem is that the animals are performers in a showbiz production in which **the only ones who do not understand their role are the human audience**. The metaphor turns our understanding of zoos on its head. It is the animals who are informed and in control and humans who are ignorant and patronised.

Much of the imagery and humour of the poem comes from the **central metaphor of performance**. Shuttle moves between the true nature of the different animal species and the role they play in the daytime as zoo animals. She makes the contrast as great as possible to exploit the humour of the conceit. In the poem's world, elephants are wild party animals; monkeys are earnest scholars; bears are politically engaged; big cats pursue refined and genteel pastimes. The image of the snakes changing 'skin after skin' (line 20) likens them to actors changing costumes in a play. The narrator informs us that none of the animals 'would give up show-business' (line 18). The final image of the 'red-kneed spider' dancing with joy celebrates this zoo animal, who **delights in her own nature.**

In contrast to the zoo animals, **humans are presented as a miserable species**, unable to play the roles assigned to them. Interestingly, the narrator does not take a detached view of human behaviour. Instead she speaks as a representative of her species, using the pronouns 'we' and 'us'. The tone of the two stanzas describing humans is one of disappointment. The narrator states that 'All the animals are very good at being animals.' It is an ambiguous statement given the setting of the zoo and the skill of the animals in performing their role as zoo animals. The narrator might equally have stated, 'All the animals are very good at being the animals humans expect them to be.' The judgement on humans is less ambiguous and more cutting: 'As usual, we are not up to being us.' What starts out as a poem about zoo animals turns out to be a poem about the narrator's disillusionment with her own species. In a neat reversal, it is the human visitors, rather than the zoo animals, who seem imprisoned: 'Our human smells prison us' (line 29). Is the narrator suggesting that animals can, with their heightened sense of smell, sense the fears that imprison humans? Does the line suggest that, however much humans act, their true identity is always betrayed by their smell? It is a line that can support a range of interpretations. Note the range of **negative words** used to describe humans. Children are dragged and they are 'unfurred'. They 'howl' and are 'baffled'. Human speech, considered the supreme attribute of humans, is described as 'over-complex' and 'deceitful'. This view of humans, as the species that does not understand and who cannot perform the roles assigned to them, has philosophical and environmental implications beyond the comic context of the poem.

Form and language

'Zoo Morning' is divided into nine stanzas of varying length. It is written in **free verse**; there is no rhyming scheme or regular metre and no consistency in the length of lines in each stanza. However, it is a poem that **delights in the musicality of language**. Indeed, the poet's skilful handling of the sounds and rhythms of the language adds colour and energy to each stanza and highlights the contrast between the true nature of the animals and the roles they assume. Look, for example, at the first stanza. In the first line, the monosyllabic verbs 'look' and 'move' have long vowel sounds, while the polysyllabic words, 'elephants', 'prepare', 'solemn' and 'slowly' slow the movement of the line, in keeping with the slow movement of the elephants. In comparison, lines 2 and 3 skip along, in keeping with the idea of elephants as party animals. There is a similar shift of pace and tone in the second stanza. Lines 4–6 move slowly and carefully, in keeping with the scholarly nature of the monkeys. The succession of long vowel sounds and neat, balanced phrases suggest a world of order and consideration. The final two lines of the stanza, lines 7–8, use a range of effects to suggest the wild and crazy behaviour 'the punters' expect from the monkeys: polysyllabic words, consonance, alliteration, onomatopoeia, present participles, short vowels. **The stylistic contrast between the two halves of the stanza supports the theme of the poem.** Elsewhere, the contrast between ease and menace attributed to the big cats, is encapsulated in one line, 'sleep-lounge at their vicious carnivorous ease' (line 16). The long vowels and soft sounds of 'sleep', 'lounge' and 'ease' suggest relaxation, while the spitting, hissing 'v' and 's' sounds in 'vicious carnivorous' convey menace. The halting, awkward phrasing of stanza seven (lines 22–26) reinforces the sense of humans being at odds with themselves. The music of the final stanza, with its echoing sounds and percussive effects, embodies the joy of the red-kneed spider as she loses herself in her dance.

> ## SNAPSHOT
>
> - **Humorous poem with philosophical implications**
> - **Influence of fables in presentation of animals**
> - **Imagery of performance and role play**
> - **Visitors do not see the real animals**
> - **Contrast between real animals and the roles they play**
> - **Unfavourable comparison between humans and zoo animals**
> - **Narrator disappointed with her own species**
> - **Written in free verse**
> - **Delights in sound effects and musicality of language**
> - **Joyful ending**

Exam-Style Questions

Understanding the poem

1	What is the difference between the elephants' behaviour during the night and their behaviour in the daytime?
2	How different is the night-time behaviour of the monkeys from the stereotype of the silly monkey?
3	What pastimes are attributed to the big cats? Do you find the idea of cats pursuing these pastimes an amusing one? Explain your answer.
4	In what sense is the life of the animals in the zoo a form of show business?
5	Describe the behaviour of the human visitors to the zoo.
6	Which of these words best describes the behaviour of the red-kneed spider in the final stanza? ■ Joyful ■ Embarrassing ■ Sullen Explain your choice.

Thinking about the poem

1	What, in your view, is the meaning of the line 'All the animals are very good at being animals' (line 27)?
2	Why does the poet think that we human beings 'are not up to being us' (line 28)?
3	'Our human smells prison us' (line 29). Comment on this line.
4	(a) In what way is the poem like a fable? (b) What stereotypes does the poem turn upside down?
5	'The poem challenges the assumption that humans are superior to animals.' Comment on this interpretation of the poem.
6	Trace the metaphor of performance through the poem.
7	'What the poem suggests is that zoos present a false picture of animals.' Give your response to this statement.
8	'The narrator is disillusioned with her own species.' Discuss.
9	Take a stanza of your choice and discuss the musical qualities of the language.

Imagining

1	Write a short account of a trip to the zoo that captures the performance of two or three of the animals on display.
2	Bernhardine is the matriarchal elephant in Dublin Zoo. If she could talk, what might she say about the humans she has observed in her time there?
3	Explain why you would or would not recommend the inclusion of 'Zoo Morning' in an anthology of zoo poetry.
4	'If we humans do not understand our role in relation to animals and the natural world, the earth is doomed.' Write a speech or short lyrical reflection in response to this statement.

Gary Soto

b.1952

Oranges	574

Biography

Gary Soto was born on 12 April 1952 in Fresno, California to Mexican-American parents, Manuel and Angie Soto. His father died when Soto was just five years old and the family struggled to make ends meet. He worked in the fields picking crops to supplement the family's income. Crime and poverty seemed the norm for the community where Soto grew up and he said he'd always imagined a future of poverty and hardship for himself.

Soto was at best an average student until high school, where he began to fall in love with poetry. Robert Frost, Pablo Neruda and Gabriel Garcia Marquez are all major influences.

He enrolled in college to avoid being drafted into the army and studied geography, but after reading an anthology of American poetry he was convinced that he had found his true calling. He transferred to California State University, where he achieved his MA and joined a group of poets known as the Fresno School. In 1977 he published *The Elements of San Joaquin*, which won the United States Award of the International Poetry Forum.

Soto's poetry has always focused on his own experiences. His books have sold over half a million copies and he has published almost twenty poetry collections. His eighteenth, *Meatballs for the People*, was published in 2017.

In 1999, Soto received the Hispanic Heritage Award for Literature.

He has a wife and daughter and lives between Berkeley and Fresno, California. He writes every day.

Oranges

The first time I walked
With a girl, I was twelve,
Cold, and weighted down
With two oranges in my jacket.
December. Frost cracking   5
Beneath my steps, my breath
Before me, then gone,
As I walked toward
Her house, the one whose
Porchlight burned yellow   10
Night and day, in any weather.
A dog barked at me until
She came out pulling
At her gloves, face bright
With rouge. I smiled,   15
Touched her shoulder, and led
Her down the street, across
A used car lot and a line
Of newly planted trees,
Until we were breathing   20
Before a drug store. We
Entered, the tiny bell
Bringing a saleslady
Down a narrow aisle of goods.
I turned to the candies   25
Tiered like bleachers,
And asked what she wanted—
Light in her eyes, a smile
Starting at the corners
Of her mouth. I fingered   30
A nickel in my pocket,
And when she lifted a chocolate
That cost a dime,
I didn't say anything.
I took the nickel from   35
My pocket, then an orange,
And set them quietly on
The counter. When I looked up,
The lady's eyes met mine,
And held them, knowing   40
Very well what it was all
About.

Outside,
A few cars hissing past,
Fog hanging like old   45
Coats between the trees.
I took my girl's hand
In mine for two blocks,
Then released it to let
Her unwrap the chocolate.   50
I peeled my orange
That was so bright against
The gray of December
That, from some distance,
Someone might have thought   55
I was making a fire in my hands.

Glossary

15	*rouge*: blusher – a type of make-up to add colour to the cheeks
18	*used car lot*: where second-hand cars are sold
25	*candies*: sweets and chocolate bars, confectionery
26	*Tiered*: in ascending rows
26	*bleachers*: benches, usually found in sports grounds for spectators to sit on
31	*nickel*: a five-cent coin
33	*dime*: a ten-cent coin

Guidelines

'Oranges', published in Soto's 1985 poetry collection *Black Hair*, was written in June 1983 and remains one of Soto's most famous and well-liked poems. It is a fine example of his unique style and authentic voice. **The narrator of the poem describes his first romantic encounter with a girl** when he was twelve years old. The subject matter is easy to relate to, as most people can remember the excitement and anxiety they experienced on their first date. Soto once remarked that to him 'the finest praise is when a reader says, "I can see your stories".'

Commentary

Lines 1–17

The speaker sets the scene for the reader: it is a cold, frosty December day and he is on his way to meet a girl. It is his first date: 'The first time I walked / With a girl, I was twelve'. The description of him being 'weighted down' is interesting. He may be 'weighted down' with nerves about the impending date as well as the physical weight of the oranges in his jacket. The light in her porch 'burned yellow', contrasting with the bleak winter surroundings, 'Frost cracking', and at first there is tension: 'A dog barked at me, until / She came out'. Her appearance dispels the aggression of the dog and, like her porch and the hidden oranges, she is glowing, 'face bright / With rouge'. He is glad to see her, 'I smiled', lightly touches her shoulder and they set off on their 'walk'. Despite this being his first date, he understands how to behave around girls.

Lines 18–42

A 'used car lot' may not be the most romantic setting for a first date but it indicates to the reader the type of urban environment that the speaker occupies. The mention of the 'newly planted trees' (line 19) suggests that this is an area that is making an effort to improve its surroundings.

They stop outside the drugstore. It is cold outside; their breath is visible in the air. The 'narrow' aisles overflowing with goods create a cramped and claustrophobic atmosphere. The poem reaches its climax when the speaker generously invites the girl to choose a candy. He anxiously fingers the nickel in his pocket. He sees the joy in her face as she chooses the candy, which costs more than he can afford: 'Light in her eyes, a smile / Starting at the corners / Of her mouth.' At this point it could all go terribly wrong, but his response is that of a confident young boy. To avoid her disappointment and his embarrassment, he remains silent, takes the nickel and an orange out of his pocket and catches the saleslady's eyes. Within this gaze is a tacit understanding between the saleslady and the boy. On some level she understands what is going on and sympathises with the speaker. She graciously accepts his unspoken offer. This is all conveyed with great subtlety by Soto, 'When I looked up, / The lady's eyes met mine, / And held them, knowing / Very well what it was all / About.' We don't know why she does this; perhaps she is won over by their innocence, perhaps he reminds her of her younger days, or maybe she is impressed by the speaker's ingenuity and kindness. Whatever the reason, the speaker gets away with it. He makes his girl happy and it was worth the risk.

Lines 43–56

The second section starts as the young couple go back 'Outside'. Note how Soto places the first word of the second section at the end of the last line of the first section. There is a clear division yet a connection. It marks a change of setting and mood. There is a physical closeness between the speaker and the girl that wasn't there before: they are now holding hands. The boy has a renewed sense of confidence. He calls her 'my girl'; he 'takes' her hand, and then 'releases' it to 'let' her unwrap her candy.

The dreary, cool, damp weather has no effect on the boy. It is the brightness of the orange in his hands that captures how he feels; something inside him was set alight, something 'was making a fire' (line 56).

Themes and imagery

The imagery surrounding the boy – 'cold', 'December' and 'frost cracking' – is contrasted with the warmth of the girl's rouged face and the brightness of her yellow porchlight. Throughout the poem she is associated with images of light: 'porchlight', 'light in her eyes'. This is contrasted with the gloom of the setting: 'Fog hanging' and 'gray of December'.

Contrast is used repeatedly in the poem, particularly the contrast between light and dark. Images of nature, such as the 'newly planted trees' and the 'frost cracking', are set against the urban backdrop, the 'used car lot' and the 'drug store' where the 'candies' are 'Tiered like bleachers'. This is a very original simile and adds authenticity to the American town setting of the poem, as does the couple's entrance into the drugstore, which is heralded by a little bell ringing. This **sensory detail** makes the experience very real for the reader. Another striking simile describes the pervading fog which hangs 'like old / Coats between the trees'. The fog, gloom and frost may represent the poverty of the boy and of this town, but like the 'newly planted trees' there is hope, there is an effort to be better and brighter. **New beginnings**, the growth of something natural and beautiful like their relationship may be suggested here. The boy is determined to win his girl's approval and the budding romance between them is possibly symbolised in the imagery of light which lifts the poem throughout: 'I was making a fire in my hands.' So we see the themes of love, romance, beginnings and hope communicated through the cinematic description in the poem.

Poverty is also a theme. The boy has only a nickel to spend on this date and must be resourceful because it is only half the amount required to buy the girl her preferred candy bar, 'I fingered / A nickel in my pocket … she lifted a chocolate / That cost a dime'.

It seems that love, or at least romance, is the light that will lift this twelve-year-old boy out of the 'gray of December' (which may be an image for his poverty) into a brighter world of **hope and possibility**. The passion ignited by the girl shines as sweetly and brightly as an orange on a grey December day.

Form and language

The poem is written in unrhymed short lines with two or three stresses: 'December. Frost cracking'. This gives the impression of natural speech and also helps the poet to give the story pace and atmosphere. The line length and frequent use of **enjambment** (line breaks in the middle of a sentence) create short phrases, and add a sense of breathlessness or nervousness in keeping with the situation: 'my breath / Before me, then gone' (lines 6–7). It also helps to give the poem momentum.

Soto said of his work: 'as a writer, my duty is not to make people perfect, particularly Mexican Americans. I'm not a cheerleader. I'm one who provides portraits of people in the rush of life.' Do you agree that this is a very realistic poem, or has Soto romanticised the account of this date? This might be an interesting question to discuss in groups.

Exam-Style Questions

Understanding the poem

1	What does the speaker mean when he says, 'I walked with a girl'?
2	Why is the barking dog included? Is it important that the barking stops when the girl comes out?
3	Why does the speaker describe the candies as 'tiered like bleachers'? Is this an effective simile? Find and comment on another simile in the poem.
4	Why is he 'fingering' the nickel in his pocket?
5	In your opinion, why didn't the boy say anything to the lady in the drugstore?
6	How would you describe the speaker in this poem? Is he resourceful, romantic, considerate or something else? Explain with reference to the poem.
7	Trace and explain how the connection/relationship between the boy and girl deepens as the poem progresses.
8	'The setting of the poem is vividly created and conveyed.' Discuss this statement with reference to the language and imagery in the poem.
9	Is the final line a suitable one for the poem? Explain.

Thinking about the poem

1	Compare the depiction of oranges at the beginning, the middle and the end of the poem.
2	Though there is only one point in the poem when someone speaks, there is a lot of communication between characters. Do you agree or disagree?
3	Explain the phrase 'knowing / Very well what it was all / About.'
4	Read the section on themes and choose the one you feel most closely fits what you felt was the theme of the poem.
5	What atmosphere is created by the descriptions of weather in the poem?
6	Joyce Carol Oates said: 'Gary Soto's poems are fast, funny, heartening, and achingly believable, like Polaroid love letters, or snatches of music heard out of a passing car; patches of beauty like patches of sunlight; the very pulse of a life.' Discuss this statement, giving your opinion in the context of this poem.
7	Would you like to read more poetry by this poet? Explain why or why not.
8	Write about the effect of one of the following in the poem, using quotation and reference: enjambment, imagery, contrast.
9	Trace the imagery of hands and touching in the poem. How do they add to the poem's mood and meaning?

Imagining

1	Imagine that the lady in the drugstore didn't accept the orange as payment for the candy. With the person beside you, write out the dialogue that follows.
2	Imagine you are the boy in the poem but it is fifteen years later and you are marrying the same girl. Write the part of the wedding speech where you describe the first time you went out.
3	Write one diary entry for each of the three characters on the day featured in the poem; the boy, the girl and the lady.
4	This poem has a very cinematic quality. Divide the poem into sections and in groups create a story board for your group's section. Then collate them and discuss the results.

SNAPSHOT

- Images of light and colour
- Nostalgic
- Winter
- Similes
- Short lines
- Narrative poem
- Highly visual and sensory appeal
- Rich in imagery
- Theme of youth and first love
- Accessible language
- Poverty
- Urban setting

William Stafford

1914–1993

Biography

William Edgar Stafford was born in 1914 in Hutchinson, Kansas, the eldest of four children. From his parents he gained an appreciation of books and nature. His father hunted and trapped and taught his son to respect the wilderness. The Stafford family, like millions of others, became victims of the Great Depression (1929–1939). The family travelled from place to place in search of employment. William took a variety of odd jobs, but still completed his high school education in 1933 and graduated from the University of Kansas with a BA and an MA.

Stafford was drafted into the United States Army in 1941. However, because he was a pacifist, he spent most of the Second World War in government internment camps for conscientious objectors. As an alternative to military service, he worked as a farm labourer and for the United States Forest Service. His memoir *Down by Heart* (1947) records his experiences during this period. In 1944 he married Dorothy Hope Frantz, whom he had met while working in California. The couple had four children. In 1948, after William was awarded a PhD by the University of Iowa, the family moved to Oregon, where Stafford taught at a private third-level college until his retirement in 1980.

Traveling through the Dark, Stafford's first major collection, was published in 1962. It won the 1963 National Book Award. Stafford published more than sixty-five volumes of poetry and prose and received many literary awards and prizes. He died of a heart attack in 1993, having written a poem earlier in the day containing the advice, 'just be ready for what God sends'.

Before you read

The title is suggestive.
What kind of poem do you
think will follow? Share your
thoughts with a partner.

Traveling through the Dark

Traveling through the dark I found a deer
dead on the edge of the Wilson River road.
It is usually best to roll them into the canyon:
that road is narrow; to swerve might make more dead.

By glow of the tail-light I stumbled back of the car   5
and stood by the heap, a doe, a recent killing;
She had stiffened already, almost cold.
I dragged her off, she was large in the belly.

My fingers touching her side brought me the reason—
her side was warm; her fawn lay there waiting,   10
alive, still, never to be born.
Beside that mountain road I hesitated.

The car aimed ahead its lowered parking lights;
under the hood purred the steady engine.
I stood in the glare of the warm exhaust turning red;   15
around our group I could hear the wilderness listen.

I thought hard for us all—my only swerving—,
then pushed her over the edge into the river.

Glossary

2	*Wilson River road*: a road in north-west Oregon, on the west coast of the United States. Stafford worked in the area during the Second World War
3	*canyon*: a deep gorge or valley with sheer sides, often with a river or stream at the bottom
5	*tail-light*: red light at the rear of the car
5	*back of the car*: to the back of the car
6	*doe*: female deer
10	*fawn*: young deer, in this case an unborn deer
14	*hood*: the bonnet of the car

Guidelines

'Traveling through the Dark' is the opening poem from the 1962 collection with the same title. Speaking about the origin of the poem, Stafford said: 'The poem concerns my finding a dead deer on the highway. This grew out of an actual experience of coming around a bend on the Wilson River Road near Jordan Creek in Oregon, and finding this deer, dead.' In the poem, the speaker moves to push the dead deer over the edge of the road into the river below. However, the situation changes when he discovers that the doe is carrying a still-living fawn.

Commentary

Stanza 1

The opening line of the poem suggests a happy chance: the traveller/narrator tells us that he found a deer. However, the impression of happiness is immediately nullified by the word 'dead' at the beginning of line 2. The reader quickly understands that coming across a dead deer on this road is not unusual. The narrator explains that the best course of action is to roll the dead deer into the canyon, to prevent further loss of life.

Stanza 2

In the second stanza, the narrator gives the reader more details about the dead deer. It is a doe and has recently been killed. Already the body has begun to stiffen. The narrator relates how he pulled her off the road. He states that the deer 'was large in the belly' (line 8). The language is restrained and understated.

Stanza 3

Touching the side of the deer, the speaker realises that the dead deer is carrying a still-living fawn. This makes him hesitate.

Stanza 4

Stanza 4 describes the scene as the traveller/narrator stands at the back of his car, in the dark. As he deliberates it seems as if the wilderness itself is listening.

Stanza 5

The narrator says he 'thought hard for us all' before pushing the deer over the edge of the road into the river below. The traveller makes no comment on his action, nor does he try to lessen its effect.

Themes

This short, simple poem is rich in themes.

Life and death

In the poem there is a **thin line between life and death**. The deer is a 'recent killing'. In moving the lifeless 'heap', the traveller discovers the fawn, whose situation is summarised in the brilliant line: 'alive, still, never to be born'. In finding a dead deer, the speaker also finds a new life on the verge of being born. Confronted by this reality, the traveller hesitates. He does not name the emotions he experiences in that hesitation, but the reader can guess them. Whatever his qualms, he pushes the deer 'over the edge into the river'. He does so to prevent further road accidents, with the potential loss of more lives. The fawn's life is sacrificed for the good of other human beings.

Humans and nature

In its broadest outline the poem explores **the conflict between human development and wild nature**. In discovering the dead doe, the traveller gets caught up in the drama between nature, as represented by the doe, and the human world, as represented by the motor car. The moral dilemma that arises from the clash between the human world and nature is transferred to the traveller. It is the traveller who thinks hard 'for all of us'. As he hesitates in making the decision to push the deer 'over the edge into the river', he becomes aware of the wilderness, like a sentient being, holding its breath waiting for him to decide. However, he hesitates for only a moment. He refers to this hesitation as his 'only swerving'. The choice of verb looks back to 'swerve' in line 4. The traveller suggests that he will not swerve away from his duty towards his fellow humans. It is his duty to clear the road.

Ethical life

The language and imagery of the poem suggest that our **journey through life is a journey through darkness**. In making the journey we encounter many situations where we are forced to make **moral choices**, and where there is little room to manoeuvre: 'that road is narrow' (line 4). The conflict experienced by the speaker in the poem is implied rather than stated. He recounts that he hesitated. However, he does not elaborate on the feelings or thoughts that accompanied this hesitation. We may speculate that he was caught between sympathy for the fawn and awareness of the danger posed to other drivers and their passengers by the presence of the dead deer: a dilemma between his heart and his mind; between his sympathy for the living fawn and his obligation to his fellow humans. However, we cannot be sure that this is the case. The speaker does what he thinks is the right thing to do, though the decision may not bring him happiness or satisfaction. 'I thought hard for us all' (line 17) suggests that it is not just the speaker of the poem but all humans who have to consider **what it means to act in a responsible way** for one another and for nature.

Imagery

The speaker's car is described as a living being. It is the car that 'aimed ahead' (line 13) its parking lights, as if it had the ability to act independently of the driver. The verb 'aimed' suggests a hunter aiming a rifle. It loops back to line 6, where the doe is described as 'a recent killing'. The implication is clear: the car poses a threat to wildlife. Under the bonnet, the engine purrs, like a cat. There is a striking **contrast between the inanimate car, which appears to be alive, and the animate deer, which is now dead**. In the silence, the speaker says he could hear 'the wilderness listen'. Here nature is presented as a living presence.

The imagery plays on the **contrast between cold and warmth**, the animate and the inanimate. The poet stands 'in the glare of the warm exhaust turning red'. His car did not kill the deer, but it was killed by a car. And now, as he stands over the dead deer, he draws warmth from the exhaust of a car. Does he feel complicit in the death of the deer because he, too, like the driver who killed the deer, is a driver of a car? Is that the meaning of turning red? Does he turn red not only with the heat of the exhaust but with embarrassment or shame? Does the colour red hint at the blood of the deer?

The car and the deer symbolise two themes that recur in American poetry: **freedom and the wilderness**. The car is the means by which an individual can express his or her freedom. The car provides the light by which the traveller inspects the dead deer and lights the way ahead. It also provides warmth. Its engine purrs steadily, reliable and dependable. The wilderness represents a pure form of nature, unspoilt by human contact, a form of paradise.

Form and language

The rhythms and simple language of the poem create a **conversational** feeling. Just as the approach to the subject matter is understated, so too is the skilful artifice of the poem. The opening line has ten syllables, with more than an echo of traditional iambic pentameter. This sets the pattern of the poem, with iambic phrasing (hĕr síde wăs wárm; hĕr fáwn) and ten-syllable lines threaded through the poem (lines 7, 10 and 14). The poem is divided into four stanzas of four lines each, and a concluding couplet. There is no regular rhyme but there are half-rhymes and rhyming echoes as in 'road/dead'; 'canyon/reason'; 'engine/listen'.

There are brilliant **word choices**. For example, the placing of 'dead' at the beginning of line 2, following the natural pause that occurs after line 1, is dramatic and adds weight to the word. The word 'still' (line 11) placed in a line that contains 'born', conveys at least three meanings: that the fawn is still alive; that the fawn is quiet; that the fawn will die (it is stillborn).

The use of the verb 'swerve' in lines 4 and 17 is also masterful. The first instance refers to the physical reaction of the driver taking action to avoid an obstacle; the second refers to the action of moving off a moral path, of swerving from a moral purpose.

The **tone of detachment** in the poem is achieved by the objective and documentary style in which the speaker reports what happened.

Exam-Style Questions

Understanding the poem

1	Describe as clearly as you can the place where the speaker finds the deer.
2	What, according to the speaker, might be the consequence of swerving on the Wilson River road?
3	By what light does the traveller inspect the dead deer?
4	What does the traveller discover when he goes to roll the dead deer off the road?
5	For what, in your view, is the fawn 'waiting' (line 10)?
6	In line 12, the speaker says, 'Beside that mountain road I hesitated.' Can you explain why he hesitates? Might he have more than one reason for doing so?
7	How does the traveller describe the car in the fourth stanza?
8	In line 16, the traveller refers to 'our group'. Who are the members of this group?
9	If the wilderness was listening, what outcome might the wilderness have hoped for?
10	How do you think the traveller felt when he rolled the deer over the edge of the road into the river? ■ Satisfied ■ Relieved ■ Guilty ■ Sad Explain your choice.
11	In your view, did the traveller have any realistic alternative to rolling the deer over the edge?

Thinking about the poem

1	Comment on the use of the word 'still' (line 11).
2	Choose one or more of the following words to describe the speaker of the poem: ■ Serious ■ Concerned ■ Honest ■ Foolish Explain your choice. **Or:** 'The speaker of the poem is determined and resolute. He is not paralysed by doubt or sadness.' Comment on this reading of the poem.
3	Do you sympathise with the speaker of the poem? Give reasons for your answer.
4	Which of the following is closest to your view? Explain your answer. 'In the poem, the car is presented as something steady and dependable, from which the speaker draws strength.' 'In the poem, the car is presented as a dangerous presence which threatens wildlife.'
5	One critic says that everything in the scene – the poet, the deer, the fawn, the car, the reader – is 'travelling through the dark'. Discuss this view of the poem.
6	'I thought hard for us all.' How do you interpret this line? Would you have done what the speaker did?

7	Comment on Stafford's skill in writing the poem.
8	What, in your view, is the major theme of the poem? ■ Life and death ■ Humans and nature ■ Moral choices Explain your choice.

Imagining

1	Write a poem or lyric passage inspired by the title 'Travelling through the Dark'.
2	Imagine you are the speaker of the poem. Write the short prayer that you make to the Wilderness before you push the deer over the edge of the road into the river.
3	You are the speaker of the poem. You relate the incident to your friend, who questions your decision. Write a defence of your action based on the proposition that human life is more valuable than animal life.
4	In groups of five, prepare a recital of the poem, using a combination of single, dual and choral voices. Your recital should reflect the emotional and dramatic shifts in the poem. Include any gestures or movements that you think will enhance the recital.

SNAPSHOT

- Narrative poem
- Understated approach
- Language close to everyday speech
- Poem carefully structured
- Echoes of iambic pentameter
- Half-rhymes and echoing sounds
- Brilliant choice of individual words
- Themes of life and death, humans and nature, moral choices
- A series of contrasts
- Strong presence of nature
- Quiet, matter-of-fact tone
- Abrupt ending
- Skilful writing

William Carlos Williams

1883–1963

Biography

William Carlos Williams was born in the town of Rutherford, New Jersey, 20 miles from New York City. He was the elder son of William George Williams and Raquel Helene Hoheb. His father, who had English and Danish ancestry, was a travelling salesman in the Caribbean and Latin America where he met his future wife. William and his younger brother grew up speaking both English and Spanish. William's mother passed on her love of art to her children, and their father read poetry aloud.

William began to write poetry when he was in secondary school. He studied medicine at the University of Pennsylvania in Philadelphia (1902–1906), where he met the poet Ezra Pound and was influenced by the ideas of Imagism, a movement that emphasised concentrated images presented in clear and simple language.

After graduating from medical school, Williams returned to Rutherford and began general practice. He married in 1912. He described his wife, Florence Herman, as the rock on which he built his life. Williams lived out his long life as a doctor in his home town.

Throughout the 1920s and 1930s Williams published poetry. With the publication of his long poem *Paterson*, published in five books between 1946 and 1958, his reputation began to grow in America. The first English edition of his poetry appeared after his death.

Williams believed that ordinary, everyday life should be the subject of poetry. He was open to new ideas and acted as a mentor to many young poets, including Denise Levertov. Williams published poetry, plays, novels and short stories, as well as essays, reviews and an autobiography. He died in 1963.

This is Just to Say

I have eaten
the plums
that were in
the icebox

and which   5
you were probably
saving
for breakfast

Forgive me
they were delicious   10
so sweet
and so cold

Guidelines

The poem is written in the form of a note left on the refrigerator. Writing about the way the imagination works, Williams said: 'Imagination creates an image, point by point, piece by piece, segment by segment into a whole. But each part as it plays into its neighbour, each segment into its neighbouring segment and every part into every other … exists naturally in rhythm'. 'This is Just to Say' shows the imagination at work in the way described by Williams.

Commentary

The poem is composed of twenty-eight words arranged into three stanzas of four lines, with no line having more than three words. There is **no rhyme or regular beat**.

Title
The title establishes the poem as a message or note poem.

Stanza 1
The first stanza describes what the 'I', the speaker, has done – eaten the plums.

Stanza 2
In stanza 2 the speaker shows an awareness of the probable purpose and intention of the 'you' in relation to the plums. The 'you' was saving them for breakfast. (Nevertheless, the 'I' ate them.)

Stanza 3
The third stanza invites the 'you' to forgive him, even as he tells the 'you' how delicious the plums were.

Theme

There is **no agreement or way of agreeing on the theme** of the poem. Taken at face value it is a playful 'apology' for a minor event. The speaker has indulged himself at the expense of someone else and asks forgiveness, although he does not seem ashamed of his actions. The poem may have a 'deeper' meaning of a male apologising to a female for his weakness in succumbing to temptation and for prioritising his pleasure over hers. A further version of this interpretation suggests that the male succumbs to sexual temptation, represented by the soft fruit, and asks his partner's forgiveness for his infidelity.

For some readers the poem contrasts the sensual pleasure of consuming food (eating plums) with the aesthetic pleasure of consuming art (reading a poem).

No matter which reading you choose, the speaker's reference to the pleasure he took in eating the plums seems to prioritise his experience over 'yours'. The final repetition of the intensifying word 'so' ('so sweet / and so cold') emphasises the **sensuous pleasure** that the speaker enjoyed at the expense of the 'you'. In fact, it is the man, the 'I' of the poem, who is active, who describes, eats, apologises and composes. The woman, the 'you', is entirely passive and speechless.

Tone

> The poem was written during the Great Depression (1929–1939), when fresh fruit was scarce and therefore desirable.

The **variety of interpretations** is related to the tone that emerges in an individual reading of the poem. Some readers regard the final word, 'cold', as an indication of the nature of the relationship between the 'I' and the 'you' of the poem, a relationship so cold that forgiveness must be sought for eating a few plums. An opposite view suggests that it is the 'I' who is cold, enjoying stealing the plums and feeling no remorse for doing so. In this view, the poem is more an expression of triumph than a real apology. A different interpretation suggests that the poem, and its description of eating the plums, is payment for what has been taken: the poem, offered by the 'I' to the 'you', is a fair exchange for the fruit. A further interpretation suggests that while the speaker may sound smug, the fact that the poem has been written signals a real attempt to make good the loss. He hopes that the poem/note pinned to the fridge will compensate the 'you' for the lost pleasure of eating the plums.

Real life

In describing his poetry, Williams wrote, **'No ideas but in things.'** This statement is a neat summary of his desire to write poetry that was based on real life rather than abstract ideas and this poem is based on an actual note left by Williams for his wife. The very existence of the poem has led to speculation on the nature of the relationship between the couple. In real life, the poem would have been successful if his wife had been amused and had forgiven him the 'transgression'. You might like to consider this angle in the light of the answering poem written by Florence ('Floss') to William ('Bill'), which ends with the lines:

Bill,
[...]
Plenty of bread in the bread-box
and butter and eggs—
I didn't know just what to
make for you. Several people
called up about office hours—

See you later. Love. Floss.

Please switch off the telephone.

Form and language

Williams was less interested in the traditional rhythms of poetry than in the **visual appearance** of the poem on the page. Line breaks, spacing and typography were all important to him. The twenty-eight words of the poem are arranged into three stanzas of four lines (quatrains). The lines of stanza 1 follow a three-word/two-word pattern. There is a reversal in stanza 2, with lines 5 and 6 following a two-word/three-word pattern. Lines 7 and 8 switch to a two-syllable/three-syllable pattern. The final stanza follows a two-word/three-word pattern.

In such a short poem it is notable that Williams places **words at the end of lines** that we do not normally see highlighted in poetry. These include: the preposition 'in' (line 3); the relative pronoun 'which' (line 5) and the adverb 'probably' (line 6). Interestingly, the final three lines of the poem conclude with three adjectives, 'delicious', 'sweet' and 'cold'. Some critics have pointed to the presence of the words 'just', 'saving' and 'forgive' as lending the poem an almost religious quality.

Williams's interest in the appearance of the poem on the page may explain the **absence of punctuation**. However, the arrangement of words on the page does guide our reading and encourages us to pay full attention to the sound and shape of every single word. In this way, as each word and line falls into the next, **the poem unfolds in a slow, delicious way that imitates the eating of the plums**.

Sound effects

For such a short poem, Williams achieves interesting sound effects through clever repetition. Note, for example, how the plosive 'p' and 'b' sounds repeat and echo in the first two stanzas. Note also how various forms of 's' sounds snake their way through the poem. When you combine these sounds with the long vowel sounds and the more precise 't' and 'd' sounds in the final stanza, you begin to see the **artfulness** behind the short poem. The sounds capture the physical and sensual pleasure of eating a soft fruit.

Exam-Style Questions

Understanding the poem

1	'This is Just to Say' What tone is struck by the title of the poem?
2	In the third stanza the speaker asks for forgiveness. What has he done that needs forgiveness?
3	Comment on the choice of adjectives used to describe the plums, 'delicious', 'sweet' and 'cold'.
4	Why, in your view, does the speaker describe the plums he has eaten?
5	Do you think the speaker offers a genuine apology in the poem? Explain your answer.
6	On the evidence of the poem, what is the relationship between the speaker of the poem and the 'you' to whom the poem is addressed?
7	Some readers have remarked that the words 'icebox' and 'cold' describe the emotional atmosphere of the poem. What do you think?
8	The poem has twenty-eight words. Which, if any, of the words would you replace? Explain your thinking.

9 How you would describe the speaker of the poem?
■ Apologetic   ■ Full of himself   ■ Amusing
Explain your answer.

Thinking about the poem

1 Here are two opposing views of the motives behind the writing of the poem.
■ The poem is intended to charm and disarm the 'you'.
■ Having taken her plums, the 'I' makes matter worse by describing how delicious they were.
Which of the two readings do you prefer? Explain your thinking.

2 How would you feel if you were the 'you' and found this poem on the door of your fridge?
■ Offended   ■ Amused   ■ Delighted   ■ Angry   ■ Cheated
Explain your choice.

3 Which of the following best describes the theme of the poem?
■ It is a poem about love.
■ It is a poem about guilt.
■ It is a poem about selfishness.
Explain your choice.

4 (a) Do you think a poem of small details can speak about bigger themes? Explain your thinking.
Or
(b) 'This is not a poem about eating plums. It is a poem about a marriage.' Give your response to this view of the poem.

5 'Williams is the poet of the everyday. He captures the small but important moments in life.' On the evidence of 'This is Just to Say', would you agree with this assessment of Williams? Explain your answer.

6 Do you like the poem? Give reasons for your answer.

Imagining

1 Imagine you are the 'you' of the poem. Write a poem in response to this one and suggest where you would leave it for the 'I' to find.

2 Write a poem to a friend or relative, confessing that you have borrowed and lost something of his or hers. Ask for this person's forgiveness. Imitate Williams's method of using no more than thirty words. Give consideration to the placement of each word on the page and the sound of each word.

SNAPSHOT

■ Deals with an event from real life
■ Contains only twenty-eight words
■ Carefully phrased and arranged
■ Line breaks and spacing are important
■ Sensuous language
■ No rhyme or regular beat
■ Written as a note of apology
■ Tone open to different interpretations
■ No agreement on theme
■ Nature of the relationship a source of interest
■ The 'I' prioritises his pleasure over that of the 'you'
■ Language is precise and clear

Reading Unseen Poetry

Reading the Unseen Poem

Reading a poem is **an activity in which your mind, your beliefs and your feelings are all called into play**. As you read, **you work to create the poem's meaning from the words and images offered to you by the poet**. This process takes a little time, so be patient. However, the fact that poems are generally short – much shorter than most stories, for example – allows you to read, and re-read, a poem many times over.

As you read a poem, **jot down your responses**. These notes may take the form of words or phrases from the poem that you feel are important, although you may not be able to say at first why this is so. Write questions, teasing out the literal meaning of a word or a phrase. Write notes or commentaries as you go, expressing your understanding. **Record your feelings. Record your resistance to, or your approval of, any aspect of the poem:** its statements; the choice of words; the imagery; the tone; the values it expresses.

Begin with the title. What expectations does it set up in you? What does it remind you of?

Next, read the poem and jot down **any ideas or associations brought to mind** by any element of the poem, such as a word, a phrase, an image, the rhythm or the tone.

Be alert to **combinations of words** and **patterns of repetition**. Look for those words or images that carry emotional or symbolic force. Try to understand their effect.

Note other poems that are called to mind as you read the unseen poem. In this way, you create a territory in which the poem can be read and understood.

Poems frequently work by way of **hints, suggestions or associations**. The unstated may be as important as the stated. Learn to live with ambiguity. Learn to **enjoy the uncertainty of poetry**. Don't be impatient if a poem does not 'make sense' to you. Most readers interpret and work on poems with more success than they know or admit! Learning to recognise your own competence, and trusting in it, is an important part of reading poems in a fruitful way. Remember that **reading is an active process** and that your readings are provisional and open to reconsideration.

Do not feel that you have to supply all the answers asked of you by a poem. In a class situation, **confer with your fellow students**. Words and images will resonate in different ways for different readers. Readers bring their own style, ideas and experiences to every encounter with a poem. **Sharing ideas and adopting a collaborative approach** to the reading of a new poem will open out the poem's possibilities beyond what you, or any individual, will achieve alone.

In an examination situation, of course, you will not be able to talk with your fellow students or return to the poem many times over a couple of days. **Trust yourself.**

The poem may be new to you, but you are not new to the reading of poems. **Draw on your experience of creating meaning.**

Poetry works to reveal the world in new ways. D. H. Lawrence said, 'The essential quality of poetry is that it makes a new effort of attention and "discovers" a new world within the known world.' In an examination answer, you are looking to show how a poem, and your reading of it, presents **a new view of the world**. Read the poem over, noting and jotting as you do so, and then focus on different aspects of the poem. **The questions set on the poem will help direct your attention.**

Possible Ways into a Poem

There are many ways to approach a poem; here are some suggestions.

The words of the poem

Remember that every word chosen by a poet suggests that another word was rejected. In poetry some words are so charged with meaning that everyday meaning gives way to **poetic meaning**. Often there are one or two words in a poem that carry a weight of meaning – these words can be read in a variety of ways that open up the poem for you. Think, for example, of how the words 'rusted' and 'cracked' come to signify resilience and determination in Elizabeth Bishop's poem 'The Fish'.

Here are some questions you might ask yourself:

- Are the words in the poem simple or complex, concrete or abstract?
- Are there any obvious **patterns of word usage**, for example words that refer to colours, or verbs that suggest energy and force?
- Is there a pattern in the descriptive words used by the poet?
- Are there **key words** – words that carry a symbolic or emotional force, or a clear set of associations? Does the poet play with these associations by calling them into question or subverting them?
- Do patterns of words establish any **contrasts or oppositions**; for example, night and day, winter and summer, joy and sorrow, love and death? Think of the way love and death are bound together in Keats's 'La Belle Dame Sans Merci'.

The music and movement of the poem

In relation to the sounds and rhythms of the poem, **note such characteristics as punctuation, the length of the lines, or the presence or absence of rhyme**. A short line can create a feeling of compressed energy; a long line can create an impression of unhurried thought.

Look carefully at the punctuation in a poem and the way in which it affects your reading. Think of Emily Dickinson's 'I felt a Funeral in my Brain' and the way in which the punctuation works with the line endings and the repetition to influence the flow and energy of the poem.

Consider how sound patterns add to the poem's **texture and meaning**. For example, do the sound patterns create a sense of hushed stillness, or an effect of forceful energy? In W. B. Yeats's 'The Lake Isle of Innisfree' the mixture of light, short sounds and long, easeful ones captures the peaceful life the poet imagines.

Ask yourself the following questions:

- What is the pattern of **line length** in the poem?
- What is the pattern of rhyme?
- Is there a pattern to **vowel sounds and length**? What influence might this have on the rhythm of the poem or the feelings conveyed by the poem?
- Are there patterns of consonant sounds, including **alliteration**? What is their effect?
- Are there changes in the poem's **rhythm**? Where and why do these occur?
- What part does **punctuation** play in controlling or influencing the movement of the poem?

The voice of the poem

Each poem has its own voice. When you read a poet's work, you can often recognise a distinctive, poetic voice. This may be in the poetry's rhythms or in the viewpoint the poems express. Sometimes it is most evident in the **tone** of voice.

Sometimes you are taken by the warmth of a poetic voice, or its coldness and detachment, or its tone of amused surprise.

Try to catch the distinctive characteristic of the voice of the poem, as you read. Decide if it is a man's voice or a woman's voice and what this might mean. Try to place the voice in a context; for example, is it the voice of a child or an adult? This may help you to **understand the assumptions in the poem's statements, or the emotional force of those statements**.

The imagery of the poem

Images are the descriptive words and phrases used by poets to speak to our senses. They are mostly visual in quality (word pictures) but they can also appeal to our sense of touch, smell, taste or hearing.

Images, and patterns of imagery, are key elements in the way that poems convey meanings. They **create moods, capture emotions and suggest, or provoke, feelings** in the readers.

Ask yourself these questions:

- Are there patterns of images in the poem?
- **What kind of world is suggested** by the images of the poem: familiar or strange; fertile or barren; secure or threatening; private or public; calm or stormy; generous or mean? (Images often suggest contrasts or opposites.)
- What emotions are associated with the images of the poem?
- What emotions might have inspired the choice of images?
- What emotions do the images provoke in me?
- If there are images that are particularly powerful, **why do they carry the force they do**?
- Do any of the images have the force of a **symbol**? What is the usual meaning of the symbol? What is its meaning in the poem?

The structure of the poem

There are endless possibilities for structuring a poem, for example:

- The obvious structures of a poem are the **lines and stanzas**. Short lines give a sense of tautness to a poem. Long lines can create a conversational feel, and allow for shifts and changes in rhythm.
- Rhyme and the **pattern of rhyme** influence the structure of a poem.
- The **poem is also structured by the movement of thought**. This may or may not coincide with line and stanza divisions. **Words such as 'while', 'then', 'and', 'or' and 'but' may help you to trace the line of thought**, or argument, as it develops through the poem.
- In narrative poems, a simple form of structure is provided by **the story itself** and the sequence of events it describes.
- Another simple structure is one in which the poet describes a scene, and then records his or her response to it.
- A poem may be built on a comparison or a contrast.
- A poem may be structured around a question and an answer, or a dilemma and a decision.
- The structure may also come from a series of parallel statements, or a series of linked reflections.

The structure of a poem can be quite subtle, perhaps depending on such things as word association or changes in emotions. **Be alert to a change of focus or a shift of thought or emotion in the poem.**

Quite often there is a **creative tension** between the stanza structure (the visual form of the poem) and the emotional or imaginative structure of the poem. Think, for example, of the four-line stanzas of Dickinson's 'I felt a Funeral, in my Brain', which give the impression of neat tidiness, and the alarming breakdown of consciousness described within these stanzas.

If the poem is in a conventional form such as a sonnet, consider why the poet chose that structure for the subject matter of the poem. Also note any departures from the traditional structure and consider why the poet has deviated from the convention.

On the following pages you will find some **sample unseen poems** and questions for you to try.

'Blessing' by Imtiaz Dharker

Read the following poem by Imtiaz Dharker and answer **either** Question 1 **OR** Question 2 which follow.

Blessing

The skin cracks like a pod.
There never is enough water.

Imagine the drip of it,
the small splash, echo
in a tin mug,
the voice of a kindly god.

Sometimes, the sudden rush
of fortune. The municipal pipe bursts,
silver crashes to the ground
and the flow has found
a roar of tongues. From the huts,
a congregation: every man woman
child for streets around
butts in, with pots,
brass, copper, aluminium,
plastic buckets,
frantic hands,

and naked children
screaming in the liquid sun,
their highlights polished to perfection,
flashing light,
as the blessing sings
over their small bones.

1	**(a)**	From your reading of this poem, explain your understanding of the title, 'Blessing'. (10)
	(b)	Choose one image from the poem that appealed to you. Explain your choice. (10)
	OR	
2		Write a personal response to this poem, highlighting the impact it makes on you. Your answer should make close reference to the text. (20)

'The Envoy' by Jane Hirshfield

Read the following poem by Jane Hirshfield and answer **either** Question 1 **OR** Question 2 which follow.

The Envoy

One day in that room, a small rat.
Two days later, a snake.

Who, seeing me enter,
whipped the long stripe of his
body under the bed,
then curled like a docile house-pet.

I don't know how either came or left.
Later, the flashlight found nothing.

For a year I watched
as something – terror? happiness? grief? –
entered and then left my body.

Not knowing how it came in,
Not knowing how it went out.

It hung where words could not reach it.
It slept where light could not go.
Its scent was neither snake nor rat,
neither sensualist nor ascetic.

There are openings in our lives
of which we know nothing.

Through them
the belled herds travel at will,
long-legged and thirsty, covered with foreign dust.

1	**(a)**	Based on your reading of the poem, explain what you think the poet means when she says, 'There are openings in our lives.' (10)
	(b)	Choose two images from the poem that appeal to you and explain your choice. (10)

OR

2	Discuss the effectiveness of the poet's use of language throughout this poem. Your answer should refer closely to the text. (20)

'Darling' by Jackie Kay

Read the following poem by Jackie Kay and answer **either** Question 1 **OR** Question 2 which follow.

Darling

You might forget the exact sound of her voice
or how her face looked when sleeping.
You might forget the sound of her quiet weeping
curled into the shape of a half moon,

when smaller than her self, she seemed already to be leaving
before she left, when the blossom was on the trees
and the sun was out, and all seemed good in the world.
I held her hand and sang a song from when I was a girl –

Heel y'ho boys, let her go boys –
and when I stopped singing she had slipped away,
already a slip of a girl again, skipping off,
her heart light, her face almost smiling.

And what I didn't know or couldn't say then
was that she hadn't really gone.
The dead don't go till you do, loved ones.
The dead are still here holding our hands.

1 **(a)** What do you believe is the central message of this poem? Support your answer with reference to the poem. (10)

(b) Identify two phrases or images which you find interesting in the poem. Explain your choices, supporting your answer with reference to the poem. (10)

OR

2 Based on your reading of the poem, identify the emotions expressed by the poet and explain how these emotions are conveyed in the poem. (20)

'Saint Francis and the Sow' by Galway Kinnell

Read the following poem by Galway Kinnell and answer **either** Question 1 **OR** Question 2 which follow.

Saint Francis and the Sow

The bud
stands for all things,
even for those things that don't flower,
for everything flowers, from within, of self-blessing;
though sometimes it is necessary
to reteach a thing its loveliness,
to put a hand on its brow
of the flower
and retell it in words and in touch
it is lovely
until it flowers again from within, of self-blessing;
as Saint Francis
put his hand on the creased forehead
of the sow, and told her in words and in touch
blessings of earth on the sow, and the sow
began remembering all down her thick length,
from the earthen snout all the way
through the fodder and slops to the spiritual curl of the tail,
from the hard spininess spiked out from the spine
down through the great broken heart
to the sheer blue milken dreaminess spurting and shuddering
from the fourteen teats into the fourteen mouths sucking and blowing
     beneath them:
the long, perfect loveliness of sow.

1	**(a)**	What, according to the poem, does the bud stand for? Support your answer with reference to the poem. (10)
	(b)	Identify two images that you find interesting in this poem. Explain your choices, supporting your answer with reference to the poem. (10)
		OR
2		Discuss the poet's use of language in the poem. Your answer should make close reference to the text. (20)

'For a Five-Year-Old' by Fleur Adcock

Read the following poem by Fleur Adcock and answer **either** Question 1 **OR** Question 2 which follow.

For a Five-Year-Old

A snail is climbing up the window-sill
into your room, after a night of rain.
You call me in to see, and I explain
that it would be unkind to leave it there:
it might crawl to the floor; we must take care
that no one squashes it. You understand,
and carry it outside, with careful hand,
to eat a daffodil.

I see, then, that a kind of faith prevails:
your gentleness is moulded still by words
from me, who have trapped mice and shot wild birds,
from me, who drowned your kittens, who betrayed
your closest relatives, and who purveyed
the harshest kind of truth to many another.
But that is how things are: I am your mother,
and we are kind to snails.

| 1 | **(a)** | What in your view is the dominant tone of the poem? Refer to the text in support of your answer. (10) |
| | **(b)** | Identify one interesting use of language in the poem. Explain your choice. (10) |

OR

| 2 | Write a personal response to the poem, highlighting the impact it made on you. Your answer should make close reference to the text. (20) |

Exam Advice from the Department of Education and Skills

The Department of Education and Skills published this advice to students on answering the unseen poem questions in the Leaving Certificate Examination.

> *As the Unseen Poem on the paper will more than likely be unfamiliar to you, you should read it a number of times (at least twice) before attempting your answer.*

> *You should pay careful attention to the introductory note printed above the text of the poem.*

The Department has also issued an explanation of the following phrases, which may be used in the exam questions on poetry:

'Do you agree with this statement?'

You are free to agree in full or in part with the statement offered. But you must deal with the statement in question – you cannot simply dismiss the statement and write about a different topic of your choice.

'Write a response to this statement.'

As above, your answer can show the degree to which you agree/disagree with a statement or point of view. You can also deal with the impact the text made on you as a reader.

'What does the poem say to you about …?'

What is being asked for here is your understanding/reading of the poem. It is important that you show how your understanding comes from the text of the poem, its language and imagery.

Last Word

The really essential part in reading a poem is that you **try to meet the poet halfway**.

Bring your intelligence and your emotions to the encounter with a poem and **match the openness of the poet with an equal openness of your mind and heart**. And when you write about a poem, give **your honest assessment**.

In responding to the unseen poem in the exam, **never lose sight of the question you have been asked**. Make sure that you **support every point** you make **with clear references to the poem**. Your answers do not have to be very long, but they must be **clearly structured** in a coherent way. For this reason, **write in paragraphs**. Write as **clearly and accurately** as you can.

Guidelines for Answering Questions on Poetry

Phrasing of Examination Questions

Questions may be phrased in different ways in the Leaving Certificate English examination. In the earlier years of the examination, questions were usually phrased in a general way. Some examples include:

- Poet V: a personal response.
- What impact did the poetry of Poet W have on you as a reader?
- Write an introduction to the poetry of Poet X.

However, in recent years students have been presented with more specific statements about a poet, to which they are then invited to respond. Some examples include:

- **Emily Dickinson:** "Dickinson's use of an innovative style to explore intense experiences can both intrigue and confuse." Discuss this statement, supporting your answer with reference to the poetry of Emily Dickinson on your course. (2016)
- **John Keats:** "Keats uses sensuous language and vivid imagery to express a range of profound tensions." To what extent do you agree or disagree with this statement? Support your answer with reference to the poetry of John Keats on your course. (2017)
- **Elizabeth Bishop:** From the poetry of Elizabeth Bishop that you have studied, select the poems that, in your opinion, best demonstrate her skilful use of language and imagery to confront life's harsh realities. Justify your selection by demonstrating Bishop's skilful use of language and imagery to confront life's harsh realities in the poems you have chosen. (2017)

Answering the full question

You will notice that these questions refer to more than one aspect of the poet's work. For example, the questions ask you to consider the **themes** (i.e. **the subject matter**) of the poems as well as the poet's **style**, i.e. **how he or she expresses these themes**.

Pay special attention to the guidelines that follow the opening statement. Examiners will expect discussion of all aspects of the question (e.g. observation and experience; subject matter and style; themes and language) although it is not always necessary to give exactly equal attention to both.

Do not neglect the final aspect of the questions asked: 'Support your points with suitable reference to the poems on your course.' This may take the form of **direct quotation or paraphrasing** of the appropriate lines.

Whatever way the question is phrased, you will need to **show that you have engaged fully with the work of the poet** under discussion.

Marking criteria

As in all of the questions in the examination, you will be marked using the following criteria:

- *Clarity of purpose* (30% of marks available). This is explained by the Department of Education and Skills as 'engagement with the set task' – in other words, **are you answering the question you have been asked**? Is your answer **relevant** and **focused**?
- *Coherence of delivery* (30% of marks available). Here you are assessed on your 'ability to **sustain the response over the entire answer**'. Is there **coherence** and **continuity** in the points you are making? Are the **references** you choose to illustrate your points **appropriate**?
- *Efficiency of language use* (30% of marks available). This concerns your 'management and control of language to achieve clear communication'. Aspects of your writing such as **vocabulary**, use of **phrasing** and **fluency** will be taken into account – in other words, your writing style.
- *Accuracy of mechanics* (10% of marks available). Your levels of **accuracy in spelling and grammar** are what count here. **Always leave some time available to read over your work** – you are bound to spot some errors.

Preparing for the Examination

In order to prepare well for specific questions such as those above, it is necessary to examine different aspects of the work of each poet on your course.

The poet's choice of themes

Be familiar with the issues and preoccupations of each poet on your course. In **writing about themes** in the examination, you will need to **know how the poet develops the themes, what questions are raised** in the poems and **how they may or may not be resolved**. Bear in mind that the themes may be **complex and open to more than one interpretation**.

Write about **how you responded to the poet's themes**. In forming your response, questions you should ask yourself include:

- Do the poet's themes appeal to me because they **enrich my understanding of universal human concerns** such as love or death?
- Do the themes offer me an **insight into the life of the poet**?
- Do I respond to the themes because they are **unusual or unfamiliar**?
- Do the themes appeal to me because they **reflect my personal concerns** and interests?
- Do I respond to themes that **appeal to my intellect as well as to my emotions,** for example politics, religion or history?

The poet's style or use of language

Any discussion of a poet's work will involve his or her style or use of language. In preparing for the examination you should study carefully the **individual images** or **patterns of imagery** used by each of the poets on your course.

When you write about imagery, try to analyse **how the particular poet you are discussing creates the effects he or she does** (i.e. what the poet's unique or distinctive **style** is). Ask yourself the following questions:

- Do the images appeal to my **senses** – my visual, tactile and aural senses, and my sense of taste and of smell? **How do I respond?** Do I find the images effective in conveying theme or emotion?
- Are the images **clear and vivid**, or **puzzling** in an **unusual or exciting** way?
- Are the images created by the use of **simile** and **metaphor**? Can I say why these particular **comparisons** were chosen by the poet? Do I find them surprising, precise, fresh, painterly …?
- Has the poet made use of **symbol** or **personification**? How have these devices added to the poem's **richness**?
- Does the poet **blend poetic and conversational language**? Has language been used to **denote** (to signify) and/or to **connote** (to suggest)?
- Does the poet use **simple expression** to convey his or her ideas **or complex language** to express complex ideas? An exploration of language may include **style**, **manner**, **phraseology** and **vocabulary**, as well as imagery and the techniques mentioned above.

The sounds of poetry

Many people find that it is the sound of poetry that they respond to most. It is an ancient human characteristic to respond to word patterns like **rhyme** or musical effects such as **rhythm**. This may be one of the aspects of a poet's work that makes it **unique or distinctive**.

Sound effects such as **alliteration**, **assonance**, **consonance** and **onomatopoeia** may be used for many reasons – some thematic, some for emotive effect, some merely because of the **sheer pleasure of creating pleasant musical word patterns**.

Look carefully at **how each of the poets** you have studied **makes use of sound**. Your response will be much richer if it is based on **close reading** and **attention to sound patterns and effects**.

The poet's life, personality or outlook

Since poems are often written out of **a poet's inner urgency**, they can **reveal a great deal about the personality or experience of the poet**. An examination question may ask you to discuss this aspect of a poet's work. For example, in 2016 a question on Elizabeth Bishop referred to the "unique personal experiences in her poetry."

Poems can be as revealing as an autobiography. Read the work of each of the poets carefully with this in mind. Ask yourself the following questions:

- Can I build up **a profile of the poet** from what he or she has written, from **his or her personal voice**?
- Is this voice honest, convincing, suggesting **an original or perceptive view of the world**?
- Do I find the personal issues revealed to be **moving, intense, disturbing**? What reasons can I give for my opinion?

It may also be that you like the work of a particular poet for a contrasting reason: that he or she goes beyond personal revelation to create other voices, other lives. Many poets adopt a different **persona** to explore a particular experience. Might this enrich our understanding of the world? Your response may also take this aspect into account.

Poetry and the emotions

At their best, poems celebrate **what it is to be human**, with all that being human suggests, including confronting our deepest fears and anxieties. Very often it is **the emotional intensity of a poem** that **enables us to engage with it most fully**.

Questions to consider include:

- What is the **tone** of the poem? **Tone conveys the emotions that lie behind the poems.** All of the elements in a poem may be used to convey tone and emotion. Each stylistic feature – such as the poet's choice of imagery, language and sound patterns – contributes to the tone of the poem. Look at the work of the different poets with this in mind.
- **What corresponding emotions does the work of each poet on the course create in you as a reader?** Do you feel consoled, uplifted, disturbed, perhaps even alienated?
- Does the poet succeed in conveying his or her feelings effectively, in your view?

These are issues you should consider in preparing to form your response to a specific question in the examination.

Conclusion

It is worth remembering that you will be rewarded for your attempts to come to terms with the work of the poets you have studied in **a personal and responsive way**. This may entail a heartfelt negative response, too. But even a negative response must **display close reading** and should **pay attention to specific aspects of the poems mentioned in the question**. Do not feel that you have to conform to the opinions of others – even the opinions expressed in this book!

Read the question carefully. Some questions may direct your attention to specific aspects of a poet's work – make sure you deal with these aspects in your answer.

Some questions may simply invite you to include some aspects of a poet's work in your response. **It would be unwise to ignore any hints** as to how to proceed!

You will be required to **support your answer by reference to or quotation from the poems chosen**. The Department of Education and Skills has published the following advice to students on answering the question on poetry:

> It is a matter of judgement as to which of the poems will best suit the question under discussion and candidates should not feel a necessity to refer to all of the poems they have studied.

Remember that long quotations are hardly ever necessary.

Good luck!

Glossary of Terms

allegory A story or poem in which the characters and events represent ideas about the world.

alliteration Repetition of consonants, especially at the beginning of words. The term itself means 'repeating and playing upon the same letter'. Alliteration is a common feature of poetry from every period of literary history. It is used mainly to reinforce a point or enhance the music of a poem. The alliterative phrase 'fingers fluttering' in Adrienne Rich's 'Aunt Jennifer's Tigers' captures the timid nature of the aunt.

allusion A reference to a person, place or event or to another work of art or literature. The purpose of allusion is to get the reader to share an experience that has significant meaning for the writer. The title of Elizabeth Bishop's poem 'The Prodigal' alludes to the parable of the Prodigal Son.

ambiguity Ambiguous words, phrases or sentences are capable of being understood in two or more possible senses. In many poems, ambiguity is part of the poet's method and is essential to the meaning of the poem.

assonance The repetition of identical or similar vowel sounds, especially in stressed syllables, in a sequence of words. Assonance can contribute significantly to the meaning of a poem. Keats's poetry is full of assonance, as in his description of the nightingale 'pouring forth thy soul abroad' in 'Ode to a Nightingale'.

ballad A poem or song that concentrates on telling a story. Ballads are usually composed in quatrains with the second and fourth line rhyming.

caesura The pause which occurs in most lines of poetry of any length. Sometimes, though not always, it is indicated by a punctuation mark. Possibly the most famous caesura in all literature occurs in Shakespeare's *Hamlet*: 'To be, or not to be, that is the question.' You might like to recite the line and decide how long to hold the caesura on the comma between 'be' and 'that' in the middle of the line.

colloquialism Using the language of everyday speech. The colloquial style is plain and relaxed. In much poetry of the twentieth and twenty-first centuries, there is an acceptance of colloquialism, and even slang, as a medium of poetic expression. 'Well, nearly always, anyway' is an example of everyday speech in Brendan Kennelly's 'I See You Dancing, Father'.

connotation The additional meanings that words have beyond their basic or dictionary meaning. For example, if a poet writes about a bird, as Keats writes about the nightingale, the bird may be associated in the mind of the poet and the reader with beauty, longing, escape and happiness. In this way the poem becomes not simply about a nightingale but about all the connotations or associations which the word 'nightingale' brings to mind.

consonance Repetition of consonant sounds within as well as at the beginning of words. You can hear consonance in Lawrence's poem 'The Snake', in the repeated 'l', 's', 'n' and 'd' sounds in 'trailed his yellow-brown slackness soft-bellied down'. The consonance and the long vowel sounds slow the line down.

convention Any aspect of a literary work that author and readers accept as normal and to be expected in that kind or genre of writing. For example, it is a convention that a **sonnet** has fourteen lines that rhyme in a certain pattern.

diction The vocabulary used by a writer – his or her selection of words and word combinations. Until the beginning of the nineteenth century, poets wrote in accordance with the principle that the diction of poetry had to be clearly different from the diction of current speech. There was a certain sort of 'poetic' diction, which, by avoiding commonplace words and expressions, was supposed to lend dignity to the poem and its subject. This is entirely contrary to modern practice.

elegy A poem written to commemorate someone who has died. An elegiac poem has a mournful or sad tone. Brendan Kennelly's 'I See You Dancing, Father' is an example of a modern elegy.

enjambment Also referred to as a run-on line, this is when the meaning carries over from one line of poetry into the next, almost without a pause, often creating an extra burst of energy, as in this example in Adrienne Rich's 'Aunt Jennifer's Tigers': 'The massive weight of Uncle's wedding band / Sits heavily upon Aunt Jennifer's hand'.

epigraph A quotation from another piece of literature that is placed beneath the title at the beginning of a poem. Yeats's poem 'Politics' starts with a quotation from Thomas Mann – this is an epigraph that reflects on the poem's title.

free verse Poetry that does not rhyme and does not have a regular metre. That does not mean that it lacks musical qualities, but it does not follow any conventional form. Much of D. H. Lawrence's poetry is free verse.

genre A particular literary species or form. Traditionally, the important poetic genres were epic, tragedy, comedy, elegy, satire, lyric and pastoral. Until modern times, critics tended to distinguish carefully between the various genres and writers were expected to follow the rules prescribed for each.

iamb The most common metrical 'foot' in English poetry, consisting of one unstressed syllable followed by one stressed one (˘ ´), as in the words bĕcáuse and ŭnléss. Iambic verse has a natural connection with the beat of the heart or the rhythm of walking.

iambic pentameter A line of verse consisting of five iambs (dĭ-dúm, dĭ-dúm, dĭ-dúm, dĭ-dúm, dĭ-dúm), used by Shakespeare in all his plays and sonnets, and one of the most common metres in English-language verse.

image A descriptive word or phrase used by poets to speak to our senses. The poet Cecil Day-Lewis puts the matter well when he describes an image as 'a picture made out of words'.

imagery This is a term with a very wide application. When we speak of the imagery of a poem, we refer to all its images taken collectively. Often the imagery of a poem has a certain theme or other quality in common.

lament A poem expressing deep sorrow and grief. A lament can express private grief at the death of a loved one or communal grief, such as that which follows the death of a leader. Brendan Kennelly's 'A Cry for Art O'Leary' is a lament.

lyric Any relatively short poem in which a single speaker, not necessarily representing the poet, expresses feelings and thoughts in a personal and subjective fashion. Most poems are either lyrics or feature lyrical elements.

metaphor A comparison between two elements that is implied by the words, rather than by using 'like' or 'as'. (See also **simile**.) If in a simile someone's teeth are *like* pearls, in a metaphor they *are* pearls. A metaphor is capable of a greater range of suggestiveness than a simile and its implications are wider and richer. For example, in Lawrence's 'The Humming Bird', the bird becomes a metaphor for the imagination taking flight.

metonym A word or expression that stands for something with which it is closely associated. For example, in Yeats's 'The Stare's Nest by My Window' the honey bees can be seen as a metonym for a productive society and a brighter future.

metre The rhythm or pattern of stressed and unstressed sounds in a line of poetry. Especially in traditional and rhyming forms, a line of poetry consists of a number of 'feet', and each foot is made up of two or three syllables in a specific pattern. For example, if you say 'incy wincy spider' aloud, you can hear that it has three feet of one stressed followed by one unstressed syllable (´ ˘); 'hickory dickory dock' has two feet of one stressed syllable followed by two unstressed syllables (´ ˘ ˘), and then the final word 'dock'. The different types of foot have names. The most common one is the **iamb** (˘ ´), which has its own entry above. Others are: trochee (´ ˘), anapaest (˘ ˘ ´), dactyl (´ ˘ ˘) and spondee (´ ´). The **metre** of a line of verse can be given a name according to the number and type of feet in a line. A line with four feet is called a tetrameter; a line with five feet is called a pentameter. So a line made up of five iambs would be called an **iambic pentameter**.

ode A poem written in praise of something or someone. The subject often allows the poet to express his/her emotions. Odes are written in an exalted (high-flown) style using complex stanza forms. The poem is usually addressed to the source of the poet's inspiration. The series of odes Keats wrote in 1819 is a remarkable achievement.

onomatopoeia The use of words that resemble, or enact, the very sounds they imitate. In 'Skating', Wordsworth describes how the ice 'tinkled like iron' as the children sped across it on their skates.

paradox An apparently self-contradictory statement that, on further consideration, is found to contain an essential truth. Paradox is so intrinsic to human nature that poetry rich in paradox is valued as a reflection of the central truths of human experience. John Keats's 'Ode on a Grecian Urn' explores the paradox that a world full of life and happiness can be depicted by an object that is lifeless.

pastoral To do with the countryside, particularly animals that graze in fields (pasture). In literature, it is the name given to a tradition that portrays an idealised version of country life. Yeats's 'The Lake Isle of Innisfree' draws on this pastoral tradition in its depiction of the simple rural life he imagines on the island.

persona Sometimes a poet adopts the mask or character of another person, or even an object, as the speaker in a poem.

personification The attribution of human qualities to an animal, concept or object.

quatrain A stanza form of four lines, which can be rhymed or unrhymed. The most popular rhyme schemes are *abab*, *abba* and *aabb*. Lawrence's 'Piano' is written in quatrains.

refrain A repeated line or lines (often a couplet) at the end of a series of stanzas. 'Romantic Ireland's dead and gone, / It's with O'Leary in the grave' in Yeats's 'September 1913' is an example of a refrain.

rhetoric Language which is designed to persuade or impress the reader or listener. We call such language rhetorical. Traditionally, rhetoric involved a range of techniques, but the only one commonly recognised now is the rhetorical question, which is a question that makes a point but does not expect an answer. Yeats's 'September 1913' is a highly rhetorical poem.

run-on line See **enjambment**.

sestina A poem with six stanzas of six lines each, followed by a three-line seventh stanza (known as an **envoy**). The poet uses six particular words throughout the poem as the end words of each line, but in a different order in each stanza. Elizabeth Bishop's 'Sestina' is a celebrated example.

sibilance The hissing sound associated with certain letters such as 's', 'sh'. D. H. Lawrence uses the sound to good effect in 'Humming-Bird' to suggest the lush vegetation of the primeval world: 'slow, vast succulent stems'.

simile A comparison between two things that uses a comparative word ('like' or 'as'). In Elizabeth Bishop's 'The Fish' there is a striking simile comparing the fish's skin to ancient wallpaper.

sonnet A rhymed lyric poem of fourteen lines. These fourteen lines are long enough to make possible the fairly complex development of a single theme, and short enough to test the poet's gift for concentrated expression. English poets have traditionally written one of two kinds of sonnet – the Petrarchan and the Shakespearean. The Petrarchan sonnet, named after the Italian poet who made the form popular, and favoured by Keats, falls into two divisions – the octave (eight lines rhyming *abba*, *abba*) and the sestet (six lines generally, but not always, rhyming *cde*, *cde*). The octave usually presents a problem, situation or incident; the sestet resolves the problem or comments on the situation or incident. In contrast, the Shakespearean sonnet consists of three quatrains (groups of four lines rhyming *abab*, *cdcd*, *efef*) and a rhyming couplet (*gg*). Keats's 'To one who has been long in city pent' is an example of a Petrarchan sonnet.

style A writer's manner of expression – his or her particular way of saying things. Consideration of style involves an examination of the writer's diction, use of figures of speech, order of words, tone and feeling, rhythm and movement. Traditionally, styles were classified as high (formal or learned), middle, and low (plain). Convention required that the level of style be appropriate to the speaker, the subject matter, the occasion that inspired the poem, and the literary genre.

symbol Any word or image that stands for something else. In this sense, all words are symbols. In literary symbolism, however, the objects signified by the words stand in turn for things other than themselves. Objects commonly associated with fixed ideas or qualities have come to symbolise them, for example the cross is the primary Christian symbol, and the dove is a symbol of peace. Colour symbols have no fixed meaning but derive their significance from the context: green may signify innocence or Irish patriotism or envy; red may signify anger or love or Communism. In W. B. Yeats's poem 'The Wild Swans at Coole', the swans become a symbol for passion and for the poetic imagination, which transcend time.

tercet A stanza form of three lines.

tone Every speaker must inevitably have an attitude to the person or object being addressed or talked about. The tone expresses this attitude. When one is trying to describe the tone of a poem, it is best to think of the poem as a spoken, rather than a written, exercise. A poem has at least one speaker who is addressing somebody or something. In some poems, the speaker can be thought of as meditating aloud, talking to himself or herself; we, the readers, overhear the words.

Poets Examined at Higher Level in Previous Years

2019
Brendan Kennelly
Elizabeth Bishop
W. B. Yeats
Sylvia Plath

2018
Robert Frost
Eiléan Ní Chuilleanáin
John Montague
Philip Larkin

2017
Eavan Boland
John Donne
John Keats
Elizabeth Bishop

2016
Emily Dickinson
T. S. Eliot
Elizabeth Bishop
Paul Durcan

2015
John Montague
Robert Frost
Eiléan Ní Chuilleanáin
Thomas Hardy

2014
W. B. Yeats
Emily Dickinson
Philip Larkin
Sylvia Plath

2013
Elizabeth Bishop
G. M. Hopkins
Derek Mahon
Sylvia Plath

2012
Thomas Kinsella
Adrienne Rich
Philip Larkin
Patrick Kavanagh

2011
Eavan Boland
Emily Dickinson
Robert Frost
W. B. Yeats

2010
T. S. Eliot
Patrick Kavanagh
Adrienne Rich
W. B. Yeats

2009
Derek Walcott
John Keats
John Montague
Elizabeth Bishop

2008
Philip Larkin
John Donne
Derek Mahon
Adrienne Rich

Elizabeth Bishop Revision Chart

Poem	Theme	Tone	Imagery	Language	Form	Mood	Effect
The Fish	Surviving adversity and second chances	Admiring, curious, respectful, joyful	Nature, lots of colour and unusual comparisons	Conversational; musicality brought through sound effects	Long, descriptive narrative, fable	Celebratory, elation	Allegorical – teaches a lesson; uplifting
The Bight	The creative process, how the subconscious mind works	Regretful; realistic yet hopeful	Extremely detailed; links exterior world to poet's interior thoughts	Lots of sound effects, very detailed description	Personal lyric	Regret, acceptance, optimism	Personally revealing, celebratory
At the Fishhouses	Explores the nature of knowledge and imagination	Curious, tentative; sadness, sense of loss	Symbolism, the sea a central image, similes and metaphors	Very descriptive and metaphorical; moves from external to internal	Personal lyric, meditation	Deeply analytical, philosophical	Mysterious, thought-provoking
The Prodigal	Debasement, addiction and redemption	Resigned, fretful, nervously hopeful	Religious, agricultural, light and darkness, squalor	Highlights dehumanisation of Prodigal; religious, descriptive	Double sonnet; last line doesn't fully rhyme emphasising theme	Resignation and acceptance moves to tentative optimism	Disturbing, evoking sympathy, biographical
Questions of Travel	Travel – why people do it and how it should be undertaken; home	Curious, weary, critical, admiring	Vivid descriptions of sights and sounds	Blend of poetic and conversational, use of tourist persona, questions	Long stanzas work through the questions and ideas	Wryly humorous, quirky, playful	Thought-provoking, exotic
The Armadillo	Adverse effect of mankind on natural world	Admiring, horrified, angry	Similes, animals, fire	Lots of sound effects; modern to more archaic in last stanza	Allegory	Indignant horror, sympathy	Evokes empathy for suffering animals
Sestina	Childhood loss, family, home, power of imagination	Sadness, naïvety	Personification of domestic objects, child's drawing, tears, pathetic fallacy	Childlike, repetitive	Archaic poetic seven stanza form with strict rules	Grief, incomprehension	We feel we know the poet more deeply; moving
First Death in Nova Scotia	How children try to make sense of the world and of death	Confusion, curiosity; observant	Key details anchor poem – loon, body in coffin, pictures, white and red	Childlike, repetition, mix of fantasy and domestic reality	Biographical narrative	Mixture of innocence and awareness	Moving, naïve, honest
Filling Station	Family; a mother's love	Playful: feigns confusion and disapproval	Multisensory, domestic, detailed	Conversational, descriptive, questioning	Narrative account, allegorical effect of lesson at the end	Wryly humorous, curious and enquiring	Entertaining, evokes sympathy for poet at the end
In the Waiting Room	Identity, cultural awareness, femininity	Shocked, disoriented, questioning	Descriptive, exotic, symbolism of waiting room	Moves from realistic to surrealistic description	Personal narrative	Philosophical, pondering deep questions of identity and belonging	Thought-provoking, complex, intense

Emily Dickinson Revision Chart

Poem	Theme	Tone	Imagery	Language	Form	Mood	Effect
'Hope' is the thing with feathers	Hope	Buoyant, solemn	Flight	Precise, metaphorical	Lyric, hymn-like	Optimism	Striking, vivid, immediate
There's a certain Slant of light	Despair	Oppressive, authoritative	Blurring of senses	Solemn, weighty	Lyric statement	Affliction	Sobering
I Felt a Funeral, in my Brain	Death, breakdown, limits of the imagination	Intense, disoriented	Sounds, falling	Sparse, repetitive	Intense lyric	Incomprehension	Startling
A Bird came down the Walk	Nature, harmony	Amused, whimsical, gentle	Movement, flight	Playful, gentle, metaphorical	Lyric description	Grace	Calming
I heard a Fly buzz – when I died	Death, faith	Ironic	Light, dark	Solemn, legal	Dramatic monologue	Ambiguity	Revelatory of the poet
The Soul has Bandaged moments	Elation, despair	Chilling, delirious	Freedom, entrapment	Gothic	Lyric meditation	Oppression	Chilling
I could bring You Jewels – had I a mind to	Love	Confident, playful	New World, treasures	Colourful, allusive	Love lyric	Assurance	Heartening
A narrow Fellow in the Grass	Nature	Conversational, terrified fascination	Secrecy, unpredictability	Formal, poised	Lyric description	Wariness	Quietly chilling
I taste a liquor never brewed	Joys of summer	Joyful, rapturous	Intoxication, extravagance	Playful, ornate	Lyric	Dizzy happiness	Cheering
After great pain, a formal feeling comes	Suffering	Dignified, solemn	Immobility, freezing	Formal, fragmented	Lyric meditation	Anguish	Sobering

John Keats Revision Chart

Poem	Theme	Tone	Imagery	Language	Form	Mood	Effect
To one who has been long in city pent	Natural beauty; city and country	Joyful but poignant	Nature; the angel	Descriptive; conventionally poetic	Sonnet	Pleasurable indolence	Touching
On First Looking into Chapman's Homer	Discovery; great art	Enthusiastic	Voyaging; adventure; astronomy	Poetic, metaphorical	Sonnet	Excited, awestruck	Thrilling
When I have fears that I may cease to be	Fear of premature death	Anxious, reflective	Agriculture; nature; the ocean	Rich and poetic	Sonnet	Troubled	Moving
La Belle Dame Sans Merci	Love and death	Deadpan, innocent	Nature; medieval adventure	Simple syntax; some archaic vocabulary	Literary ballad	Sombre, disillusioned	Disturbing
Ode to a Nightingale	Intense experience; beauty and transcendence	Emotional: ecstatic and grieving; celebratory	Nature; classical mythology	Descriptive, sensuous, musical	Ode	Melancholy	Thought-provoking; saddening
Ode on a Grecian Urn	Art and beauty; time and eternity	Questioning; celebratory	Classical art and life	Interrogative, analytical	Ode	Pensive, troubled	Thought-provoking; moving
To Autumn	Autumn; natural abundance	Celebratory	Nature: tactile, visual, aural	Descriptive, sensuous	Ode	Sensuous, calm	Ravishing; restful
Bright Star	Ideal love; the ideal and the real	Yearning	Distant star and human intimacy	Austere and sensuous by turns	Sonnet	Intense desire	Moving

Brendan Kennelly Revision Chart

Poem	Theme	Tone	Imagery	Language	Form	Mood	Effect
Begin	Not to give up, treat each new day as a fresh start, appreciate the world around us	Urging, encouraging, insistent	Dramatic – time and place. Mix of urban and natural images	Descriptive; sibilance	Lyric	Positive, optimistic	Uplifting
Bread	The process of creation	Cheerful, appreciative, jaunty	Religious, sexual, pregnancy and birth	'I' persona of wheat, simple and accessible	Eight tercets and a five-line stanza at the end	Grateful, animated	Affirming, ambiguous, thought-provoking
Dear Autumn Girl	Love	Admiration, love, needy?	Leaves, hair, season of autumn	Excited, enthusiastic, apologetic	Sonnet	Admiration, anxiety, apologetic	Touching
Poem from a Three Year Old	Innocence, death	Impatient, innocent	Flowers, floor, broom	Simplistic, questions, repetition	Series of questions	Curious	Thought-provoking, charming
Oliver to His Brother	Duty, death, family	Superior, sarcastic, matter-of-fact	Death, cherries	Condescending, sure	A letter; use of Cromwell's persona	Determined, critical	Interesting
I See You Dancing, Father	Filial love	Fondness, determination to remember the positive	Father dancing, eventual decline	Accessible, directed to father	Elegy	Melancholic	Nostalgic, moving
A Cry for Art O'Leary	The strength of women, mourning, Irish history, death	Grief, passionate love, anger	Blood, nature, O'Leary's horse and uniform	Impassioned, repetition, exclamations	A lament, keening – Caoineadh, lyrical	Ardent, vengeful, grateful	Moving, provokes anger and pity
Things I Might Do	Judgement, forgiveness, redemption	Wistful, confused, loving	Religious and natural	Use of questions and contrast, ambiguity	Subverted sonnet form, series of questions	Melancholy, lonely; dreamlike ending	Thought-provoking, challenging
A Great Day	Celebration, marriage, never truly knowing another	Joyful, solemnity of ceremony, intimate	Colour, the dress, trees personified	Biblical, simple, dialogue, repetition	One, two and three line stanzas	Happy	Cheery, voyeuristic
Fragments	Ageing, losing love	Lonely, regretful	Birds, old man, dying fire	Use of hanging participles	Sonnet, use of questions	Meditative, rueful	Sad
The Soul's Loneliness	The search for meaning and belief	Yearning, lonely	Everyday objects, religion and nature, domestic	Simple, direct	Five tercets, some rhyming, lack of capitalisation	Confessional, frank	Sympathy for the speaker
Saint Brigid's Prayer	Heaven's reward for a devout life	Joyful	Lake of beer and the vessels that contain beer, heaven	Both secular/pagan and religious	Prayer	Friendly, excited, inclusive, spiritual	Uplifting

D. H. Lawrence Revision Chart

Poem	Theme	Tone	Imagery	Language	Form	Mood	Effect
Baby Movements II, 'Trailing Clouds'	Mother–child relationship	Puzzlement, awe	From nature	Rich in adjectives	Free verse, with one rhyme	Weariness, sorrow	Contemplative, hypnotic
Call into Death	Grief; mystery of death	Intimate	The heavens; flight; sky and air	Simple, conversational	Quatrain with irregular rhyme	Weariness, yearning	Dreamlike, consoling
Piano	Nostalgia; the power of memory	Conflicted: sentimental but distrusting it	Piano and singing; journey in time	Descriptive, precise	Rhymed quatrains; anapaestic rhythm	Nostalgic	Moving
The Mosquito	Understanding the mosquito	Wry, combative	Magic and trickery; the mosquito	Conversational but inventive	Free verse	Fascination; frustration	Thought-provoking, amusing
Humming-Bird	Imagination; the individual soul; humming-birds	Fascinated, awe-struck	Humming-bird and primeval matter	Conversational, with repetition and rich sound patterns	Free verse	Excited; playful	Thought-provoking
Snake	Man and snake; dark gods	Spellbound, questioning, remorseful	Snake; underworld	Rich in adjectives; descriptive	Free verse	Fascination; heat and stillness	Hypnotic, unsettling
Intimates	Battle of the sexes; self-absorption	Mocking	Mirror	Plain; mock-formal	Free verse, with some rhyme	Bitter; combative	Amusing, thought-provoking
Delight of Being Alone	Being alone	Relishing, intense	Moon, ash tree	Plain	Free verse	Delighted; peaceful	Exhilarating
Absolute Reverence	Reverence; a sense of the divine	Brusque, assertive	None	Precise, definite	Free verse, with hints of rhyme	Brisk, matter-of-fact	Thought-provoking
What Have They Done to You?	Industrialisation and its effects	Angry; sometimes contemptuous	Beast of industry; the masses	Rhetorical	Free verse	Anguished	Challenging
Bavarian Gentians	Death and dying; journey to the underworld	Contemplative, then intense and ecstatic	Gentians, darkness, Pluto and Persephone	Rich in images and word music	Free verse	Sensual; dark; mystical	Awe-inspiring, invigorating

Adrienne Rich Revision Chart

Poem	Theme	Tone	Imagery	Language	Form	Mood	Effect
Aunt Jennifer's Tigers	Subjugation of women; permanence of art	Admiring, pitying	Tigers, wedding band	Accessible, rhyme	Formal stanzas and rhyming scheme	Contrast between confidence and fear	Arouses sympathy
The Uncle Speaks in the Drawing Room	Preserving the past; class division	Authoritative, dismissive, nostalgic	Fragile heirlooms, storm, angry mob	Sound effects, rhetoric	Formal stanzas and rhyming scheme	Impending violence	May be ironic
Storm Warnings	Surviving difficulty	Calm (speaker), violent (storm)	Stormy weather, domestic	Metaphorical	Dramatic lyric	Impending threat	Empathy
Living in Sin	Reality of relationships	Disenchanted	Domestic	Detailed description	Dramatic lyric	Detached observation	Realistic
The Roofwalker	Freedom, oppression	Regretful	Builders on roof, speaker beneath	Repetitive, use of questions	Dramatic lyric	Powerlessness	Thought-provoking
Our Whole Life	Communication	Frustrated	Knots, burning, pain	Economical	Free verse	Agonised	Arresting
Trying to Talk with a Man	Communication, relationships	Frustrated	Desert, atomic bomb	Terse	Dramatic lyric	Evasive	Striking
Diving Into the Wreck	Societal change, exploration	Fascinated, fearful	Diving, shipwreck	Highly evocative	Dramatic lyric	Determined	Thought-provoking
From a Survivor	Survival, marriage, divorce	Regretful, happy	The body	Direct, repetitive	Stream of consciousness; dramatic lyric	Optimistic	Autobiographical
Power	What hurts us can also give us power	Sympathetic, admiring	Radiation, sickness	Controlled, descriptive	Dramatic lyric	Serious	Thought-provoking

William Wordsworth Revision Chart

Poem	Theme	Tone	Imagery	Language	Form	Mood	Effect
To My Sister	Blessings of nature; universal love	Joyful	Landscape, weather	Sweet-sounding, plain, persuasive	Lyric address	Bright, optimistic	Uplifting
She Dwelt among the Untrodden Ways	Hidden lives, death, grief	Sad, undramatic, loving	Landscape	Spare, musical	Lyric meditation; ballad-like features	Elegiac	Touching
A Slumber did my Spirit Seal	Human fears; cycle of life; nature as impersonal force	Outwardly calm, underlying unease	Landscape, physics	Simple, ambiguous	Lyric meditation	Quiet, dark	Tense, unsettling
Composed upon Westminster Bridge	Beauty of the morning; city made beautiful; positive effects of beauty on the human soul	Admiring, quietly emotional	Light, stillness, silence, personifies the city	Flowing, descriptive, formal, harmonious	Sonnet, dramatic monologue	Positive, filled with wonder	Calming
It is a beauteous evening, calm and free	Beauty of the sunset; divine presence; child's closeness to God	Quiet, devotional	Stillness, quiet, sunset, religious	Quiet; descriptive octet; philosophical sestet; meaning not always clear	Sonnet, dramatic monologue	Religious	Revealing of the poet
The Solitary Reaper	Soothing effect of music	Spellbound	Landscape, exotic locations, solitariness	Descriptive, musical, harmonious	Lyric ballad	Thoughtful, grateful, appreciative	Uplifting
from The Prelude: Skating	Memory, pleasure of skating, freedom, visionary experience	Thrilling, joyful, nostalgic	Landscape, emphasis on sights, sounds and motion	Rhythmic, energetic, richly descriptive, full-sounding, conversational	Autobiographical narrative, dramatic monologue, reflective lyric	Joyful, excited, visionary	Joyous, uplifting, energising
from The Prelude: The Stolen Boat	Memory; power of nature; imagination; growing up	Haunted, troubled	Landscape, fairytale, mysterious, flight and pursuit	Simple, descriptive, dramatic, vague, allusive	Autobiographical narrative, dramatic monologue, reflective lyric	Troubled, confused, confessional	Intriguing
Lines Composed a few miles above Tintern Abbey	Memory; relationship with nature; nature as benign force; nature as divine presence and energy	Honest, personal, philosophical	Nature, landscape of the mind	Clear, elevated, beautiful, harmonious	Dramatic lyric, dramatic address	Joyous, anxious, urgent, optimistic	Admiration for the poet

W. B. Yeats Revision Chart

Poem	Theme	Tone	Imagery	Language	Form	Mood	Effect
The Lake Isle of Innisfree	Desire to escape to rural solitude	Yearning	Impressionistic; sights and sounds of nature	Descriptive; rich in word music	Lyric	Peaceful	Inspiring
September 1913	Betrayal of a noble ideal; Irish identity	Ironical, mocking	Petty thrift and heroic sacrifice	Energetic, rhetorical	Rhymed eight-line stanzas; iambic tetrameter	Resentful, bitter	Disturbing, questioning
The Wild Swans at Coole	Time, death, immortality	Regretful, then resigned	Autumn; swans	Musical, harmonious	Lyrical meditation	Reflective, wistful	Exhilarating
Easter 1916	Transformation of ordinary people into heroes	Detached, questioning	Theatre; drawn from nature (stone in stream)	Descriptive, controlled, incantatory	Meditation; rhymed trimeters	Solemn but celebratory	Inspiring
An Irish Airman Foresees His Death	One man's attitude to war, life and death; nationality and identity	Detached	Very little	Unadorned; carefully balanced	Reflective lyric	Resigned, at peace	Exhilarating
The Second Coming	End of order, coming of anarchy	Authoritative, dramatic	Horrific; from the Bible and mythology	Dramatic, intense	Unrhymed iambic pentameter	Fearful	Deeply troubling
Sailing to Byzantium	Art and life; time and eternity; old age	Passionate	Sensual nature and immortal art	Forceful, energetic	Lyric; tight stanza form	Frustration to exhilaration	Fascinating
The Stare's Nest by My Window	Damaging effect of civil war	Disillusioned; yearning	Honey bees set against brutality	Colloquial, blunt	Meditative lyric	Bitter, but clinging to hope	Troubling, chastening
In Memory of Eva Gore-Booth and Con Markiewicz	Time and loss; Anglo-Irish heritage	Nostalgic, bitter	Civilised beauty and setting fire to it	Descriptive, plain; subtle use of tenses	Meditative lyric; rhymed tetrameters	Bitter, regretful	Disturbing
Swift's Epitaph	Swift as champion of liberty	Solemn, scornful	Journey into death	Dignified, haughty	Epitaph	Celebratory	Challenging
An Acre of Grass	Limits imposed by old age	Determined, imploring	Great artists of the past; quiet house	Plain words, strong verbs	Meditative lyric	Frustration, aspiration	Inspiring
Politics	Politics and personal life	Frustrated, exasperated	A young woman; abstract ideas of politics	Colloquial	Lyric	Regretful	Amusing, thought-provoking
from Under Ben Bulben: V and VI	Heritage: Irish poetry and the poet himself	Authoritative, celebratory	Drawn from everyday life	Statement and instruction; strong and direct	Valediction (farewell poem)	Robust, unsentimental	Stimulating

NOTES

NOTES